THE TWENTIETH CENTURY

AN ALMANAC

THE TWENTIETH CENTURY

AN ALMANAC

INTRODUCTION BY
W. AVERELL HARRIMAN

General Editor, Robert H Ferrell
Executive Editor, John S Bowman

WORLD ALMANAC PUBLICATIONS
NEW YORK, NEW YORK

 A Bison Book

Distributed in the United States by Ballantine
Books, a division of Random House, Inc., and in
Canada by Random House of Canada Ltd.

Library of Congress Catalog Card Number
83-051725

Newspaper Enterprise Association
ISBN 0-911818-63-4
Ballantine Books ISBN 0-345-31708-4

Printed in the United States of America

World Almanac Publications
A Division of Newspaper Enterprise Association,
Inc.
A Scripps-Howard Company
200 Park Avenue
New York, NY 10166

Page 2: *The atomic bombing of Nagasaki, Japan,*
9 August 1945.
This page: *The Great Depression's Hunger March on*
Washington, DC, December 1931.
Following pages: *Building the Panama Canal, 'the*
path between the seas,' 1907.

CONTENTS

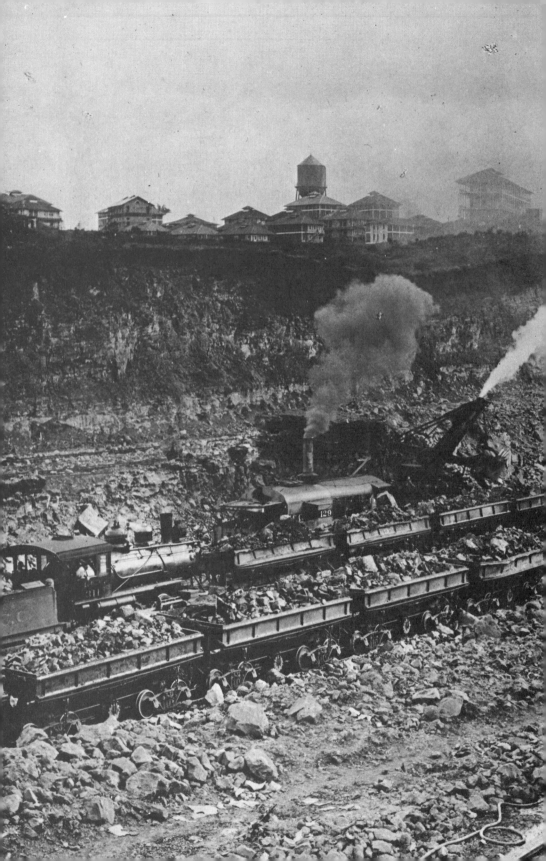

INTRODUCTION

W Averell Harriman

INTRODUCTION

Ours is the most hopeful and most fearful of centuries. Individual determination took explorers to the North and South Poles in the first decade; collective ingenuity took Americans to the moon before the seventh ended. But in between those great moments of daring and faith, political savagery brought the deaths of millions upon millions of soldiers in two world wars and millions upon millions more civilians in Hitler's camps and Stalin's, in Guernica and Coventry, in Dresden and Hiroshima, in Ottoman Turkey, Indonesia, Burundi, Biafra, Cambodia. Medicine conquered the worst diseases —measles, smallpox, malaria, polio, tuberculosis— that had ravaged earlier generations, but man remained seemingly unable to control the most ferocious killer of all, man himself.

The twentieth century began with the death of Queen Victoria and the birth of Freudian psychoanalysis. Both events marked the end of an old social order. The optimistic certainties about human progress and perfectibility, the foundation and cement of Western development and democracy through the 1800s, began to erode. Agnosticism, religious and scientific, generated extraordinary experiments, but it also bred a vast unease and a disruption of the traditions which had previously channeled our energies as much as they limited our ambitions. We have still not come to terms with the disappearance of the old boundaries of human and political behavior. In the midst of spreading disorder, wrote William Butler Yeats shortly after World War I:

Things fall apart; the center cannot hold;
Mere anarchy is loosed upon the world,
The blood-dimmed tide is loosed, and
  everywhere
The ceremony of innocence is drowned;
The best lack all conviction, while the worst
Are full of passionate intensity.

The history presented in the pages that follow can best be understood by examining the events it records in terms of modern man's search for a new 'center' that will 'hold.' It has been a frustrating search, full of astonishing discoveries but marked, as well, by dispiriting failures and dead ends. In art, for example, the colossal voyages of Pablo Picasso and Henry Moore in search of the abstraction at the center of reality turned full circle with the appearance of Andy Warhol's sterile icons and a vogue of realism whose exponents have much of the proficiency but none of the warmth of the Flemish masters three centuries earlier. In architecture, the innovative simplicity of Wright, Le Corbusier, van der Rohe became the sterility of the modern high-rise city center—row upon row of towering upended ice trays that diminished their inhabitants and denied their eyes the relief of ornament. The genius that revolutionized the speed at which information and culture traveled gave us, indiscriminately, the profundities of Chaplin and the banalities of 'I Love Lucy,' the beauty of great music and the ranting of Father Coughlin. The supplanting of linear expression, of print, by radio and then television, brought the world into our kitchens but destroyed the disciplined patterns which enabled us to weigh men and events for their meaning and value.

Most ambitious and disappointing of all has been the quest for a new, stable, and just ordering of man's relations with his fellow men. In the Century of the Common Man, as the world's population tripled in 80 years from the 1.5-billion level of 1900, and was slated to double again in less than 30 years, extraordinary leaders tried and failed to ensure a better and a secure life for their followers. Dictators and Democrats—Lenin and Lloyd George, Sun Yat-sen and Woodrow Wilson, Stalin and Hitler, Churchill and the Roosevelts, Gandhi, Sukarno, Nasser, de Gaulle and Mao—inspired or enslaved. In the midst of devastation, the great statesmen of our century nevertheless continued to build new institutions on a foundation of stubborn hope. Each effort was imperfect, but each was an advance.

Out of such crises have come remarkable achievements, whether the salvaging of capitalism in the Depression-ridden United States or the post-colonial construction of independent nations throughout Asia and Africa. But change has come violently and, in many instances, faster than we could move to shape it. Ours has been an era of unparalleled accomplishment. Nevertheless, it is rightly perceived as an age of anxiety.

After the first explosion of the atomic bomb in July 1945, Robert Oppenheimer quoted to himself from the *Bhagavad Gita* Vishnu's words: 'I am become death, the destroyer of worlds.' But neither he nor the men who used his weapon, and then built more and more of them, ever gave way completely to despair in the face of the catastrophic power they held. In such resilience it is possible to find the thread of hope that also runs through our modern history, the faith that persistence and improvisation and innovation will bring us eventually to a durable center once again.

Perhaps the greatest revolution of our time is not in the technology which can demolish or dehumanize us, but in the awakening of political consciousness among billions of men and women on all the continents whom illiteracy, disease, hunger, and hopelessness had once doomed to apathy and irrelevance. Now they too are participants in the global search for dignity, for justice, and for a secure new order. It is a stumbling search, but it goes on and may yet produce marvels. What animates it is not collective madness but individual aspiration. In the absence of a solid center, we still retain innate decency. Or, as W H Auden, another great British poet, wrote on the eve of World War II:

Defenceless under the night
Our world in stupor lies;
Yet dotted everywhere,
Ironic points of light
Flash out wherever the just
Exchange their messages;

W AVERELL HARRIMAN

May I, composed like them
Of Eros and of dust,
Beleaguered by the same
Negation and despair,
Show an affirming flame.

That 'affirming flame' continues to burn in hearts around the world. It is the energy which lights the way ahead.

p. Averell Harriman

Allied troops on the Western Front, 1916.

FOREWORD
Robert H Ferrell, General Editor

FOREWORD

As the century in which we live was about to open, its very name—'twentieth century'—sounded strange, almost too strange for people to accept; perhaps for this reason a controversy arose over the precise date on which it was to begin. At issue was whether the century would commence on 1 January 1900 or 1 January 1901. The Pope's assistance was solicited, and Leo XIII chose in favor of 1900. Protestants dismissed the opinion as a personal judgment. The contention passed into history, and the twentieth century, however calculated, began.

And what a century it has proved thus far! Because it is our own time, we may exaggerate its importance, but beyond self-consciousness the century has surely been the most progressive, the richest in the paraphernalia of human existence, and yet the most terrible in terms of lives tragically lost, of all the eras since time immemorial.

If the reader should look hastily at the twentieth century, it appears as a seamless web, a welter of uninterrupted events meaningless or profound or pedestrian, of movement and happenstance that has taken the human race from there, the century's beginning, to here, the 1980s of our time. If one looks more carefully and seeks not the political moments—which are often sensational—but rather economics, society, intellect, the century does seem to have points of movement and slowing down, marking off 'periods' or 'eras': it is these that deserve attention, that force the mind to observe change amid apparent chaos.

The century's first great period or era, as the Western world has discerned it, opened with an almost universal prospect of peace—not merely for a few years, but far into the future. Everything observable confirmed the beliefs of such leaders of industry in the United States as Andrew Carnegie, who had emigrated to the New World from the poverty of his native Scotland in the 1840s, worked as a bobbin boy at $1.20 a week, then risen to great wealth through determination and intellect, like his fictional contemporary Horatio Alger. In 1901 when Carnegie's massive steel company, the dominant firm in the United States, merged with a group put together by the financier J P Morgan, Sr as the United States Steel Corporation, Carnegie retired as the world's richest man, in possession of $480 million. He devoted his remaining years (until 1919) to attempting to give his money away—an impossible task, but he tried, as in everything he undertook. All the while he continued to believe that the world was moving toward everlasting peace. In 1910 he established a foundation for that purpose, the Carnegie Endowment for International Peace, to which he awarded $10 million, five-percent, first-mortgage bonds of the US Steel Corporation. He instructed his trustees to work for peace 'here upon this erth'—the apparent misspelling was an expression of another of his philanthropies: simplified spelling. His basic list included twelve words—program, catalog, decalog, prolog, demogog, pedagog, tho, altho, thoro, thorofare, thru, and thruout. A few of his words managed to work their way into the language, but with those exceptions his smaller hope was never fulfilled. For the larger one he remained confident, instructing his endowment's trustees that when they had achieved peace they were to award the remaining money to other projects that might ensure the perfection of man 'here upon this erth.'

Carnegie's dream partook of the latter nineteenth century, when Queen Victoria ruled Great Britain, Ireland, and India: leaders of opinion had come to believe that war between great nations brutalized the participants; only small wars, especially conflicts pitting great Western nations against primitive countries, were permissible means of changing inconvenient political arrangements. After the wars of the French Revolution and Napoleon, Western Europeans had lived uncertainly for two generations into the mid-nineteenth century, fearing recurrence of the huge conflicts that had accompanied the changeover from absolute monarchy to republicanism in France. By mid-century the uncertainty disappeared, as peace seemed ever more assured. In the latter nineteenth century conflicts between nations were, for the most part, resolved peacefully. The new century began with a similar prospect, in which Western statesmen instituted a series of peace congresses. The first met at The Hague in 1899, a second met in 1907, a third was planned for 1914.

Then Carnegie's dream of peace was shattered by the First World War—the Great War, as it became known, which opened in August 1914 and lasted until November 1918. If one includes the Paris Peace Conference of 1919, we can see now that this calamity ignominiously closed the century's initial period or era from 1900 to 1919.

The American president of that time, Woodrow Wilson, a former professor and president of Princeton University, with a bare two years of political experience as governor of New Jersey (1911–13) before he reached the presidency, watched Europe's entry into war in 1914 with a feeling akin to horror. Immediately Wilson had announced American neutrality and referred to a natural raking-out of European jealousies. With the obscure causes of the war, he said, the United States was not concerned: peace depended upon the neutrality of the people of America, who understood all peoples because they comprised all peoples. Similarly, the war's early course and consequences appalled him. Three days after the Germans sank the liner *Lusitania* in May 1915, with loss of nearly 1200 lives, including 128 Americans, he spoke to several thousand newly enfranchised American citizens in Philadelphia and told them that Americans must have a consciousness different from that of every other nation: 'I am not saying this with even the slightest thought of criticism of other nations. . . . The example of America must be the example not merely of peace because it will not fight, but of peace because peace is the healing and elevating influence of the world and strife is not. There is such a thing as a man being too proud to fight.'

ROBERT H FERRELL

After the most strenuous efforts by the President to mediate between the two sets of belligerents, the Allies and the Central Powers, the United States was itself drawn into the war in 1917 when the German Government decided to pursue a new military course that promised victory: Germany's submarines, of which there were only 133 on 1 January 1917, would blockade the British Isles and starve their people by preventing provisioning via grain ships from Argentina and Australia. It was also necessary to prevent shipment of grain from America—hence the blockade's absolute nature. Berlin knew that its decision in favor of unrestricted submarine warfare would bring the United States into the war on the Allied side. It did not seem that American entrance would make any difference, for the US Navy, large as it was, would only add to the already overwhelming preponderance of the British Navy, and the US Army was smaller than that of Portugal. Germany's leaders calculated that the United States could not raise and train any sizable body of troops for at least a year and a half; then it would not have the ships to carry them to Europe, and if it did find them, German submarines would sink them. Long before that time Germany would have won the war.

It is not too much to say that the most important decision by any government in the first two decades of the present century was that of Berlin to challenge the American principle of freedom of the seas. From that decision came Germany's defeat in 1918. Germany's unrestricted submarine warfare, as it was called (sinking of ships on sight without investigating the nature of the cargo and without provision for the safety of passengers, if any, and crew), failed when the Allies convoyed ships rather than allowing them to sail alone. The United States then raised a huge army of 4 million men, mostly draftees, trained it, and sent half of it to France. The American Expeditionary Force commanded by General John J Pershing was too large for the German Army to hold back. Early in November 1918, American divisions on the Meuse-Argonne Front broke through German lines to the outskirts of Sedan, where their artillery began shelling the four-track railroad that supplied German troops all the way from Switzerland to the Channel. The travail of more than four years of war—the Battles of the Marne, Somme, Verdun, with losses into the millions—came now to an end. The Americans did not themselves win the Great War: such an assertion would be boastfulness. But 2 million American troops made the crucial difference, for Germany could not stand against them.

There followed the Paris Peace Conference in which the victors concluded treaties with Germany, Austria, Hungary, Bulgaria, and Turkey. The treaties were vindictive instruments, as one might have expected, but they were endurable. They did not easily calculate the economics of peace, notably in requirement from Germany of what was then a gigantic sum of reparations—$33 billion—stretched out for collection until the year 1984. They did provide for a new world government, the League of Nations, which offered hope of peaceful adjustment of international disputes.

The next great period or era of twentieth-century history was marked by the following quarter-century, from 1920 to the year marking the end of World War II, 1945. Its origins, course, and consequences came in fair part out of World War I, the principal determining factor of the twentieth century. Were it not for the war of 1914–18, our world would be a far more peaceful place. The Great War opened the floodgates not merely to war but to revolution and, after 1945, to the invention of weapons that in the latter half of the century have threatened to pass beyond human control.

The Second World War derived from the First. At the outset of the years 1920–45 trouble was not much in evidence, certainly not in the United States where people sought to forget participation in the war in 1917–18 and return if not to the nineteenth century, which was impossible, then to largely personal pursuits. In the year 1931, Frederick Lewis Allen, long-time editor of *Harper's* magazine, published a portrait of the 1920s entitled *Only Yesterday* in which he showed the frivolities of the time and emphasized the life of his own social set, centered in New York City, but in many ways reflecting the feelings of the era: the lack of interest in politics, especially in international affairs, the concentration on private life. It was the last peaceful time in our century. If across the US, in the city and on the farm, it was a markedly stolid time, in no sense a decade of frivolity, much less of licentiousness, it was also an era when young men and women looked forward like their forebears to peaceful lives of threescore and ten years without intervention of such calamities as wars and revolutions.

In Europe in the 1920s the scene was not quite as tranquil, and in economics less flourishing. In Germany the first half of the decade saw an inflation that took the value of paper currency into the stratosphere, to a ridiculous height that involved housewives trundling wheelbarrows full of marks to the store or bank to make minor purchases or deposits; German industry prospered only later in the decade. In England these years were marked by widespread grinding poverty in city and countryside, with resort to the Labour Party for a short-lived but precedent-breaking (it was the first Labour Government) interlude in mid-decade; Labour returned to power in 1929. France's politics reflected the shifting ambitions of leaders who sensed that politics were changing, that economic issues were becoming a factor. A sign of the times in Western Europe was the coming to power in Italy of Benito Mussolini, who announced a state-sponsored co-operation of labor and industry (although this was all subterfuge for his own ambitions). During the 1920s his regime confined itself to minor changes in Italian life—'making the trains run on time.' His dictatorship's excesses came later, with the invasion of primitive Ethiopia in the mid-1930s, and in 1940 and after when Italy went to war in support of Germany.

13

FOREWORD

The hopes and weaknesses of the golden twenties were perhaps epitomized in the actions—and in-actions—of France's foreign minister in the latter half of the decade, Aristide Briand. Frequently head of French cabinets, he achieved the greatest satisfaction of his political career at this time, quite late in his life, when he conducted French foreign policy from the Quai d'Orsay. His name appeared daily on the pages of Europe's newspapers from 1925 onward —a time of peace symbolized by the Locarno Pact of that year among Belgium, France, Britain, Italy, and Germany, in which the German Government pledged not to disturb its border with Belgium and France and the other powers guaranteed the border. Germany at the same time concluded arbitration treaties with its two large eastern neighbors, Poland and Czechoslovakia, agreeing to settle all differences. Locarno, as it was known, was drawn up in the little Swiss city along the glimmering lake. The pact and its place of signature harkened back to the distant past, to the smallness and orderliness of the nineteenth century when major-power statesmen guaranteed Europe's peace in what was known as the Concert of Europe. In the twentieth century, it seemed, even after the Great War, statesmen were arranging peace again, and Briand was presiding over the new arrangement.

Briand was no theoretical student of Europe and the world, having learned politics in the nineteenth- and twentieth-century French experience; it was a pity that he accomplished so little in the latter twenties. He concerned himself with the security of France, a worthy if difficult cause, and sought sensibly to ensure it in part through maintenance of a large French Army—in the twenties the strongest force in Europe. He was also leader of an anti-German coalition in the League of Nations; in his labors in this regard he achieved a large reputation as an orator at the League Assembly in Geneva. All the while he sought to increase French security by arranging alliances, and in 1927 proposed to the United States what was in essence a negative military alliance, a promise by the two countries never to go to war with each other and to settle all disputes by peaceful means. The US Secretary of State, Frank B Kellogg, was unwilling to sign an alliance with France and proposed to Briand that the French and American Governments enlarge it to include all nations, hoping thereby to make it worthless. Briand accepted unreality and signed anyway. Kellogg received the Nobel Peace Prize for the Kellogg-Briand Pact of 1928 (Briand having received it for the Locarno Pact). The new pact pledged almost all nations of that time, including Germany and the Soviet Union, never to go to war and—almost needless to say—had a negligible effect upon future foreign relations. Briand proved to be an ephemeral architect of both world peace and French security.

Then the Great Depression began in the United States with the stock market crash of 1929 and spread to all the industrial nations; this cataclysmic downturn in economic life brought a much more forceful personality to power in Western Europe. Adolf Hitler soon undid all the work of Briand.

It seems almost unbelievable that one man could have destroyed the Concert of Europe of the latter twenties, fragile though it was. It is likewise difficult to believe that one man could have had such an impact on the affairs of Europe and the world. In the primitive times of European politics, the Renaissance and Reformation that saw the birth of nation states in the fourteenth and fifteenth centuries, individuals often controlled national destinies. In that sense Hitler was a throwback to earlier times. But in the days of Italian city states and princes whose names are now forgotten, governments were small, ill organized, often with little effect upon peoples they represented. Hitler came into control of a nation of 65 million people, the largest industrial base in Europe, and a tradition of efficiency in modern war. The German people placed their destiny in his hands in 1933; only later did they come to understand how he could destroy everything that had made Europe the political, economic, social, and intellectual center of the world.

The Great Destroyer first changed the military balance of Europe in his favor when German troops occupied the Rhineland—an area demilitarized by the Treaty of Versailles—in 1936. At that time governments elsewhere had turned their attention to Italy's conquest of Ethiopia. Occupation of the Rhineland allowed Germany not merely to fortify a line against France, but to prevent the French Army from going to the assistance of any country in Eastern Europe. Thus Germany could threaten all Eastern Europe, the area that French diplomacy under Briand had sought to attach to the Versailles arrangement of boundaries and peoples. The hammer blows of Hitler's plan of European domination then began in 1938 with occupation of Austria and partition of Czechoslovakia; early in 1939 the Germans took the remainder of Czechoslovakia after Hitler had told Prime Minister Neville Chamberlain of Great Britain at Munich that he had satisfied his 'last demand.' The British and French Governments thereupon offered alliances to any East European country that considered itself threatened by Germany. The Poles accepted such an alliance, the Soviet Union auctioned its support between the Anglo-French and the Germans, and Germany won in the Molotov-Ribbentrop Agreement of late August 1939. A few days later (1 September), assured of Russian neutrality, the German Army attacked Poland.

The new agony, another World War, passed through three stages before it came to an end almost six years later with Germany's surrender on 8 May 1945. In the first stage, until Pearl Harbor, 1941, Germany took Poland, holding the line in the Rhineland; in 1940 it turned on the Anglo-French and defeated them, forcing France out of the war. The Germans attacked the Russians in June 1941 and nearly overwhelmed them by the end of that year. At this point the Japanese, without informing

Berlin, attacked the American Pacific Fleet and rushed into a war that they believed was in its climactic moment of Axis triumph.

During the war's second stage, from Pearl Harbor until June 1944 and the invasion of France by the Western Allies, the three great powers in alignment against Germany—the United States, Britain, and the Soviet Union—held their own, and the Soviets began to turn back the Germans.

Beginning with the third stage, the Normandy invasion, the handwriting of German defeat was on the wall, but Germany held out almost a full year. Meanwhile the Americans had held the Japanese largely by themselves; gradually they went on the offensive. The Japanese lost all hope of victory after the summer of 1942 and their defeat by the US Navy at the Battle of Midway, but Japanese forces refused to give up until after two atomic bombings (6 and 9 August 1945) and Russia's entrance into the Far Eastern war (8 August). They surrendered 14 August 1945, more than three months after Germany's surrender.

Unlike the end of the First World War, the end of the Second saw no peace conference, only a series of discussions in 1946 by which the victors made treaties of peace with the lesser former Axis powers—Italy, Hungary, Bulgaria, and Finland. In 1945 the victors had occupied Germany and Austria. The latter regained its sovereignty ten years later. Germany has remained divided, but an agreement by the Western Allies and the Soviet Union in 1971 effectively internationalized Berlin, removing the former German capital from cold-war contentions; shortly afterward West and East Germany concluded treaties by which they recognized each other's boundaries. In the Far East the United States sponsored a peace treaty with Japan in 1951, signed by all participants in the wartime Allied coalition except the Soviet Union and the People's Republic of China, which made later arrangements with the independent Japanese Government. Korea remains divided to the present day.

The cold war of our time has constituted the third major period or era of the twentieth century: it has lasted far longer than the other two and gives evidence of lasting until the century's end. Its principal characteristic has been the rivalry between the superpowers—the United States and the Soviet Union.

At the outset of the postwar era, the Soviets seemed to hesitate before entering the cold war: they appear to have counted on Western economic collapse. A little patience on their part would cause the ripe capitalist pear to fall into their hands. In 1945–46 they apparently even suffered from the quaint delusion that the US would have to extend a large loan to the USSR and export manufactures and food there, if only to prevent its basically weak capitalist economy from collapsing immediately through inability to obtain foreign markets for unconsumable domestic surpluses. After such a frantic initial largesse, so communist doctrine appears to have

calculated, Western capitalist regimes led by the United States might succumb to economic depression of the kind that has followed every major war in modern history—but this time of a magnitude that could force a capitalist collapse.

When the hope of catastrophic depression did not immediately come true, the USSR appears to have taken up traditional diplomacy, assisted by subversion of countries in Eastern Europe and attempted subversion of those in Western Europe; in the instance of the Korean War in Asia, there was an outright resort to military force, albeit through an intermediary, a satellite.

The basic cause of the cold war remains obscure. Its roots could have reached back a generation, to the years 1918–20, when the United States participated in the Allied occupation of Murmansk, Archangel, and Vladivostok and refused to recognize the new Soviet Government, which took power in November 1917, until 1933. But these commissions or omissions seem unconvincing explanations for the cold war. Many observers have doubted that even the awkwardnesses of Soviet wartime co-operation with the United States (1941–45) could have caused the postwar dissension and rivalry. The Soviets later claimed that the long delay of the Western Allies in opening a second front in France masked a hope that the Germans and Russians would fight each other to a standstill, after which, if the Soviets won, they would be so weakened they could not cause trouble in Europe or elsewhere. Even that supposed Anglo-American delinquency (if indeed it existed) cannot explain the cold war. It is possible that during the last years of the dictator Josef V Stalin, from 1945 until his death in 1953, failing health caused by hypertension, together with his lifelong penchant for intrigue, caused him to imagine ever more reasons for enmity with the West. Russian leaders in the Stalin period may have believed that they could maintain control of the USSR only if they possessed an external enemy, the United States. Perhaps, more simply, they saw a danger to their closed system from the freedom and openness of the West, symbolized by American democracy and economic prosperity.

The first postwar American President was an unlikely opponent of the cold war, or for that matter an unlikely exponent of any course in international affairs. Until his sudden elevation from the vice-presidency in April 1945, Harry S Truman had pursued an almost entirely domestic-oriented career in American politics; he knew very little about foreign affairs. By the time of his presidency Truman had spent twenty years in American politics, a decade in Kansas City where he was a county official, another ten years as Senator from Missouri. Once he became President he had little time to study the international alternatives of his country and the world at the end of the greatest war in history. For a year and a half he held back, uncertain of what the Soviet Union desired, unsure also of how the American economy was going to turn after demobili-

FOREWORD

zation and reconversion. Only early in 1947 did he come to believe that he must take a stand.

With the Truman Doctrine, Marshall Plan, and NATO (1947–49) President Truman changed the foreign policy of the United States, from isolation with an occasional intervention to an incessant participation in world affairs. Once he sensed that the time was right, he acted characteristically for an individual brought up in the small town of Independence, Missouri. He made the United States position vis-à-vis the USSR known to the world—first in the 1947 declaration of principle known as the Truman Doctrine (that the United States would assist nations anywhere threatened by communism), then in the far-ranging economic program of 1947–48, the Marshall Plan, followed by the unprecedented NATO military alliance of 1949. Opposition of his administration to Russian pressure upon West Berlin during the Berlin blockade of 1948–49, and to Chinese and Russian pressure upon South Korea, via the government of North Korea in the Korean War of 1950–53, demonstrated future American policy in a world of two superpowers.

The countries of Western Europe watched this change with unease, if with essential appreciation, and the British Government often feared that the Americans possessed more enthusiasm for change than understanding of the slow-grinding mills of history. Britons frequently sought to play Greece to America's Rome. The French Government showed little vigor of policy until General Charles de Gaulle returned to power in the 1960s and undertook to revive the glories of an earlier France—with some success due to France's rapid economic growth during the de Gaulle era and later. West Germany, the economic miracle of the postwar era, whose economy 'took off' with the Allied currency devaluation of 1948 and thenceforth appeared a model of productivity, managed an unobtrusive politics that endeared itself to Paris and London and produced real co-operation, of the kind that Briand in the far-distant 1920s might only have dreamed. The Germans proved more friendly to American demarches against the Soviet Union than did the French and British, but muted their support enough to avoid antagonism with the new European allies. Withal the Italian Government in the postwar period basked in increasing prosperity and supported the other NATO allies.

As the new postwar American course produced some confusion among America's allies, so other events in this era proved disconcerting. The Vietnam War of the 1960s and early '70s enjoyed ever-less support within the United States, and little elsewhere. The worldwide inflation that began with Vietnam's effect upon the American dollar, and increased with the oil price rise instituted by the Organization of Petroleum Exporting Countries in 1973 and the Iranian revolution of 1978–79, was even more disheartening. Inflation afflicted everyone. Overenthusiasm of American and West European bankers for high-interest loans to Poland and Rumania, Mexico, Brazil, and Argentina, required awkward transfers of public money to debtor countries to cover the loans. The world's economy seemed to be stagnant but the 1980s brought signs of recovery.

Society in the West during the twentieth century changed markedly as the growth of cities continued, made possible by increasing industrialization and productivity of farm land the world over because of better seeds, fertilizers, and machinery. The world's population rose from 2.4 billion in 1945 toward double that number in the mid-1980s, a quantum leap that seemed supportable by industry and agriculture but raised questions about the future.

During the cold-war era the life of the intellect flourished, with production of books and scientific papers—those two visible signs of intellectual progress—rising each year, supported by higher national standards of education and the leisure that attended increasing economic productivity.

The single most disturbing development in the cold-war period was the apparent inability of the superpowers and the other members of the nuclear club—Britain, France, the People's Republic of China, India—to control nuclear weapons and carriers. The appetite of the family of nations for weapons appeared insatiable. The United States usually came out first with new weapons—nuclear bombs, hydrogen bombs, intercontinental ballistic missiles, Mirvs (multiple, independently-targeted re-entry vehicles), terrain-guided robot jets carrying nuclear or conventional bombs. The Soviet Union followed the United States with the same weapons in from four to six years, and the other nuclear powers followed the USSR.

Perhaps a proposal from the distant past, reincarnated for nuclear weaponry, will resolve the arms race: if not, it is at least the only recently discussed armament proposal that seems to favor the human race. This is the negotiation for limiting nuclear weaponry symbolized by the Strategic Arms Limitation Talks of the 1960s, '70s, and '80s: the SALT-I agreements of 1972 and the abortive SALT-II agreements a few years later. In private hands the effort for limitation has become known as the nuclear-freeze movement. In the last decades of our century, we may be inviting the disillusion that came to the movement for limitation or even abolition of conventional weapons during the late nineteenth and early twentieth century, when primary armaments were of a far simpler kind—heavy artillery on land, battleships at sea. The older disarmament movement failed. Still, the dream is immensely attractive. President Truman, from his youth at the turn of the century—he graduated from Independence High School in 1901—was accustomed to carry in his wallet some verses from Tennyson, 'Locksley Hall,' that he copied over and over. At the height of the cold war, during his presidential administration, he often read them for his own inspiration: they evoked a future time in which the battleflags might be furled in the Parliament of Man.

Robert H Ferrell

Old World to New: Slavic immigrants in New York City, 1912.

US National Democratic Convention, 1900.

ASSOCIATED PRESS

PREFACE

John S Bowman, Executive Editor

PREFACE

Population Census procedures are far from thorough in most countries but the best estimates put the world's total population at about 1,587,000,000. Divided among the continents, the estimated populations are: Asia – 875,000,000; Africa – 170,000,000; Europe – 392,000,000; the Americas – 143,000,000; Australia and Pacific Islands – 7,000,000. Divided among races, the estimates are: Caucasian – 770,000,000; Mongoloid – 540,000,000; Negroid – 175,000,000; Amerindians – 22,000,000. Divided among religions, the estimates are: Christianity – 500,000,000 (of whom Roman Catholics are 240,000,000); Mohammedanism – 200,000,000; Hinduism – 200,000,000; Buddhism – 175,000,000; Confucism and Ancestor Worship – 275,000,000; Judaism – 8,000,000. China is the most populous country, with an estimated 410,000,000. The British Empire claims 390,000,000, but at least 295,000,000 belong to India and only 38,000,000 live in the United Kingdom. The USA's 45 States and territories claim 77,000,000 (up from 63,000,000 since 1890). Japan has 41,000,000. The Dominion of Canada has 5,750,000 and the Commonwealth of Australia has some 3,750,000. The five largest cities are: London–4,500,000; New York City–3,500,000; Paris – 2,670,000; Tokyo – 1,500,000; and Peking – 1,000,000. Europe has some of the most densely populated lands—Belgium has 589 people per square mile, England and Wales 558; while Japan has 317 people per square mile and China some 270; the USA has 25 people per square mile, while Canada and Australia have 1.5 per square mile. But people are on the move, particularly from Europe and Asia to the Americas and Australia. Immigrants to the USA in 1900 number 448,572; since 1820 there have been an estimated 20,000,000 immigrants to the USA (in contrast to 250,000 between 1789 and 1820).

Health, Medicine, Mortality The world is on the verge of an 'explosion' of population, but in 1900 it is still divided into a minority with access to proper nutrition, public health aids, and the new medical services, and the mass of people who go without. Average duration of life for all people is about 33 years; one-quarter die before age six, half before age 16; only a small percentage live to be 65. Many women die in childbirth and infections related to it; many children die of such diseases as diphtheria, whooping cough, scarlet fever, and measles; vast numbers of adults die of consumption (tuberculosis), typhoid fever, bronchitis, malaria, and all-but-unknown tropical diseases. (Only in 1899 had scientists confirmed Ronald Ross's claim that the *Anopheles* mosquito transmitted human malaria.)

Science-Technology The world in 1900 is on the verge of another 'explosion': that of scientific discoveries and their wide application through technology to all areas of life. The telephone is beginning to come into use: in the USA there are now about 1,336,000 telephones. The railroad has transformed mass transportation: Europe has 161,200 miles of railroad, while the Americas have 232,060; but emphasizing the split between the 'haves' and the

'have-nots' in this new century, Asia has 26,150 miles of railroad, while all of Africa has 8580. The automobile is coming into view, although steam- and electric battery-powered vehicles appear as promising as the gasoline-powered. In all the US there are an estimated 8000 automobiles in use and fewer than 150 miles of hard-surface roads. The speed limit in New York City is 8 mph, but it is reported this year that a vehicle under construction in Jersey City will be able to go 70 mph; it is being ordered by several prominent men—at a cost of $20,000. The automo-

The steel mills of Pittsburgh in 1909.

bile is regarded as an expensive luxury or as the 'devil's wagon,' and cities in many countries are passing laws that treat it as an intruder. But this year, in Detroit, the Olds Company will begin the first 'mass production' of automobiles; 400 will be produced, but the company will return a profit to investors and starts the modern automobile industry.

International Politics The world in 1900 seems stable and peaceful: the only war underway is a minor colonial conflict between the Boers and the British in South Africa. In fact, the world is perched on a powderkeg. Ever since the Congress of Vienna in 1815, the European powers have let each other alone (with such exceptions as the Franco-Prussian War) while they went about dividing much of the world among themselves. Thus by 1900 the major colonial empires—those of Great Britain, France, Russia, Germany, Austria-Hungary, Italy, Belgium, and the Netherlands—control virtually half the world's people. Beneath the surface of the present power arrangements is great dissatisfaction. As the year 1900 begins, the cracks widen and deepen.

The bombing of Shanghai by the Japanese, 1937.

CHRONOLOGY

CALM BEFORE THE STORM 1900-1913

The World in 1900

1900-1913:
CALM BEFORE THE STORM

Commander-in-Chief Kuropatkin greets his officers in Manchuria during the Russo-Japanese War.

1 JANUARY 1900

China Two days ago, an English Christian missionary was killed by members of a secret society whose name in Chinese means 'The Righteous and Harmonious Fists,' and today an Imperial Edict is issued that is ambivalent in its criticism of the incident—only one of a growing number of attacks on foreigners and Christians by secret societies. At this point, awareness of the mounting tension is limited to the international diplomatic community in Peking, but behind it lies a history of Chinese resentment that will soon explode on the world stage.

For some decades now, China has been increasingly exploited by foreigners; indeed, it has been invaded and divided up by commercial and governmental representatives of Britain, France, Germany, Italy, Russia, and Japan. Mining and railroad projects have forced large concessions from the Chinese; ports have been appropriated by foreigners for naval stations; hard-pressed for cash and credit, China has signed away much of its future income, and foreigners are gaining a stranglehold on the Chinese economy. Meanwhile, some 2000 Christian missionaries have not only gained the right to protect themselves

and their families by laws of 'extraterritoriality,' they are also trying to get special privileges for their Chinese converts.

During the 1890s, therefore, several secret societies grew up dedicated to getting rid of the foreigners, especially Europeans and Christians. The best known is The Righteous and Harmonious Fists, and because of this name and the fact that members engage in calisthenics, Westerners have taken to calling them 'The Boxers.' The Boxers are a small group, but they can mobilize (at least in northern China) large numbers of Chinese who resent the foreign presence and power. And the Manchu Dynasty—ruled by the Dowager Empress Tzu Hsi, while the Emperor Kuang Hsi is a figurehead—is itself viewed by many Chinese as a foreign element, so the Dowager Empress and her advisers are willing to exploit the resentment and let the Boxers do what the Imperial Government cannot: attack the Westerners.

On 6 September 1899, John Hay, the US Secretary of State, sent a note to the foreign governments that were dividing China and proposed that they all support an 'open door' policy, guaranteeing 'no interference with the free commerce' between China

CALM BEFORE THE STORM 1900-1913

and any foreign state. One by one, these nations agree to this policy in principle, but their verbal agreement does not change the situation.

Nigeria For decades southern Nigeria has been controlled by the British Government while northern Nigeria was left to a private British firm, the Royal Niger Company. Growing unrest and rebellion have now led the British to declare northern Nigeria a protectorate as of this day. Fighting, however, will go on for many years.

10 JANUARY 1900

South Africa: Boer War Frederick Lord Roberts, with his chief of staff General Horatio Kitchener, arrives at Capetown to take command of British forces from General Redvers Buller. Buller is in the field, where he is trying to lead his troops to relieve the British at Ladysmith, a city under siege by the Boers since early November 1899.

The war between the Boers—their Dutch word for 'farmers'—and the British had long been in the making. They had fought a brief war in 1880–81 in which the Boers won independence for their South African Republic. The first Dutch had settled in South Africa back in the 17th century, and had become increasingly resentful of the British who encroached upon their territory. By the 1890s the Boers were led by a strong figure, Paul Kruger, who was re-elected in 1898 for his second term as president of the South African Republic. Meanwhile, the British sent on as High Commissioner in South Africa Sir Alfred Milner, a proponent of aggressive imperialism. The two men distrusted each other, and when negotiations broke down over technicalities, Kruger led his Republic and the adjacent Boer Orange Free State in declaring war against the British on 12 October 1899 (although the consensus of historians is that the Boers were provoked to this by the British).

At the outset the Boers had the great advantage in manpower and arms, and quickly began to place British strongholds and cities under siege and to defeat British forces sent against them. Mafeking, Ladysmith, and Kimberley were besieged, the Boers in the British colonies were being encouraged to revolt, and British losses were mounting; then in December came the so-called Black Week, 10–15 December, when the British were soundly defeated at Stormberg, Magersfontein, and Colenso. The arrival of Roberts and Kitchener with fresh British troops signals that the war is going to be full-scale.

13 JANUARY 1900

Austro-Hungarian Empire The Empire is showing widespread strain: class conflict, religious discrimination, anti-Semitism, above all, the demands of subject nationalities increasingly restive under the Imperial Government. Today Emperor Franz Joseph informs the Czech leader, Dr Stransky, that German must remain the language of all members of the Imperial Army. Lurking behind the language question is the issue of Czech nationalism.

16 JANUARY 1900

International The US Senate consents to the Anglo-German Treaty (of 14 November 1899) by which Great Britain renounces all rights in any of the islands of Samoa in favor of the USA and Germany. The US gains control over Tutuila and several smaller islands.

16–27 JANUARY 1900

South Africa: Boer War The British forces under General Buller cross the Tugela River and move on to capture Spion Kop (23–24 January), but after suffering heavy casualties the British will evacuate Spion Kop, and on 26–27 January they retreat back across the Tugela.

21 JANUARY 1900

Canada The second contingent of Canadian troops sails from Halifax to fight in South Africa; the first had sailed on 30 October 1899. Eventually some 8000 Canadians will go off to serve Britain in its war against the Boers. Canada had come under British rule over many years and in different ways—colonization, conquest, and treaties—and instead of seeking independence, like the US, it gained status as a Dominion in 1867 by the British North America Act (making it a self-governing, autonomous community within the British Empire). Many Canadians still feel strong ties to Britain and British interests.

27 JANUARY 1900

China Harassment and outright attacks on foreigners and Chinese who cooperate with them or convert to Christianity continues. Foreign diplomats in Peking write formal notes of protest demanding that the Chinese Government stop the Boxers and other groups leading attacks on Westerners and Christians. Some governments are dispatching more guards to their legations, but troubles in China seem remote from most countries' concerns.

31 JANUARY 1900

Philippines The final report of the USA's Philippines Commission favors a territorial government for the islands, with home rule in local affairs but US assumption of ultimate responsibility for the government. Today's report seems too little, too late for the Filipinos fighting under Emilio Aguinaldo for total independence. After defeating Spain in the Spanish-American War, the US took over the Philippines under the Treaty of Paris (December 1898). But Aguinaldo, elected president of a revolutionary government by his fellow Filipinos in June 1898, insisted that the US had promised immediate independence. On 4 February 1899 Aguinaldo-led Filipinos began an open revolution against the American forces and have been waging their fight against an increasingly heavy commitment of American troops. In the US this new war is becoming divisive.

5 FEBRUARY 1900

International The USA and Great Britain sign the

The Battle of Colenso.

first Hay-Pauncefote Treaty, giving the USA the right to construct a canal across the Isthmus of Panama but not to fortify it. On 20 December 1900 the US Senate will consent to the treaty, but only with an amendment that gives the US the right to fortify the canal: Britain refuses to accept the treaty. (The second Hay-Pauncefote Treaty will be agreed to in November–December 1901.)

14 FEBRUARY 1900

Finland Czar Nicholas II of Russia issues orders enforcing control of Russia over Finland. This is his response to a petition by 800 international figures, many of eminence, asking Russia to give Finland its liberty (Finland has been ruled by Russia since 1809).

15 FEBRUARY 1900

South Africa: Boer War British troops relieve Kimberley, a city under siege by the Boers since 15 October 1899.

18–27 FEBRUARY 1900

South Africa: Boer War British forces have been pursuing a force of Boers under one of their leading commanders, Piet Cronje, and on 18 February they encircle some 10,000 at Paardeberg. Lord Roberts, British commander-in-chief, comes in person to offer protection to the Boers if they cease resistance; by 21 February Cronje has refused even the offer of safe conduct for women and children. Finally, after heavy bombardment and a particularly strong attack

by Canadian troops, Cronje and 4000 Boers surrender.

27 FEBRUARY 1900

Great Britain In London meetings between the Trades Union Congress and the Independent Labour Party (formed in 1893) result in a Labour Representative Committee. Ramsay MacDonald is elected secretary of what will become the Labour Party in

---

THE BOER WAR

When in 1838, 470 Boers defeated 12,000 black Africans at the Battle of Blood River, these self-named Afrikaners, 'men of Africa,' judged their victory a sign from God. Africa was theirs to develop; the heathen blacks would serve. This unswerving conviction would later fortify the rag-tag army fighting in guerrilla fashion for three years against the powerful British Army. Until the 1880s Britain, in control of two colonies in South Africa, had left the two Boer republics alone. Then gold was discovered in the Transvaal, and by 1899 Britain was in a war to win the mineral wealth. With victory came unification of the colonies and the settled issue of British rights to the Transvaal. The internal affairs of the new union were left to the Afrikaners and English-speaking whites, despite efforts by organized blacks and 'coloureds' to persuade the British to guarantee their voting rights. By 1960 nonwhites had no political rights. The British won the war, but the Boers had won the peace.

CALM BEFORE THE STORM 1900-1913

1906 (he will become the first Labour Prime Minister in 1924).

28 FEBRUARY 1900
South Africa: Boer War General Buller's army, having recrossed the Tugela, relieves the city of Ladysmith, under siege by the Boers since 2 November 1899. The British now claim that the Boers in this area have been defeated.

MARCH–MAY 1900
Algeria The French carry on military operations in southern Algeria as part of their effort to put down Algerian resistance to French rule. Although Algeria was not annexed as a colony until 1842, the French have been ruling it since the 1830s.

6 MARCH 1900
USA Meeting in Indianapolis, a group forms the Social Democratic Party and nominates Eugene Debs as its candidate for President in the forthcoming election. (The party will change its name to Socialist Party in 1901.)

10 MARCH 1900
Uganda Regents for the King of Uganda and leading chiefs sign a treaty with Great Britain agreeing to organization of the government, taxation, courts, military, and other functions of their country, which is under British protection.

11 MARCH 1900
South Africa: Boer War British Prime Minister Lord Salisbury rejects peace overtures from the Boer leader Paul Kruger (on 5 March) as demanding too-favorable terms.

13 MARCH 1900
South Africa: Boer War Lord Roberts leads British troops into Bloemfontein, capital of the Orange Free State.

14 MARCH 1900
USA The US Congress passes the Currency Act, establishing the gold dollar of 25.8 grains, nine-tenths fine, as the standard of value, and placing all US money on a parity with gold. The act establishes a gold reserve of $150 million. This move to the gold standard represents a defeat for the populist-agrarian pro-silver movement led by William Jennings Bryan.

16 MARCH 1900
Canada 'Strathcona's Horse,' a cavalry unit equipped at the expense of Lord Strathcona, a wealthy Canadian, sails for duty in the Boer War in South Africa.

18 MARCH 1900
Korea The Japanese use their influence over the government of Korea to deny Russia's effort to obtain a concession for a naval station at the Korean port of Masampo. This is a step in the process that will lead Russia and Japan to war and result in Japan's annexation of Korea.

20 MARCH 1900
International US Secretary of State John Hay announces that all nations to whom he sent notes calling for an 'open door' policy in China have essentially accepted his stand, and that he considers their agreement 'final and definitive.' It comes too late to have much effect on Chinese relations with these foreign powers.

27 MARCH 1900
Great Britain Recognizing that the war in South Africa is going to take a major commitment, Parliament passes the War Loan Act, calling for £35 million to support the fight against the Boers.

APRIL–MAY 1900
Ashanti (Gold Coast) The British have been trying to exert control over Ashanti since the early 19th century, but have encountered resistance from many tribes and chiefs. On 25 March the British Governor Hodgson at Coomassie, a fort, had demanded that the Ashantis turn over their 'Golden Stool,' symbol of royalty and sovereignty. Instead, the Ashantis besiege Fort Coomassie on 6 April; continual battles ensue, with losses on both sides.

12 APRIL 1900
USA Congress passes the Foraker Act, establishing Puerto Rico as an unincorporated territory (effective 1 May). Puerto Rico has been under control of the US military since the island was ceded to the USA by the Treaty of Paris (December 1898) concluding the Spanish-American War.

30 APRIL 1900
Life/Customs In Vaughan, Mississippi, Casey Jones is bringing the *Cannonball Express* into the station when he sees the track blocked; instead of jumping out, Jones holds onto the brake and so minimizes the impact that no passengers are killed—but he himself is crushed to death. A black railroad worker, Wallace Saunders, will write a ballad about this episode that eventually becomes the basis for folk songs that make Casey Jones a legend in the USA and other parts of the world.

17 MAY 1900
China Disorder has been spreading throughout northern China as resentment against foreigners, fanned by the Boxers, aggravates the age-old problems of flooding, plague, famine, and unemployment. On this day, three villages within 100 miles of Peking are burned by Boxers and 60 Chinese Christians killed. Christians begin to take refuge in Peking, Tientsin, and other treaty ports (among them a young American mining engineer, Herbert Hoover, and the son of an American missionary, Henry Luce). Most foreign powers still do not regard this as a serious situation.

17–18 MAY 1900

South Africa: Boer War British troops relieve Mafeking, besieged by the Boers since 13 October 1899. (The British at Mafeking have been led by Major-General Robert Baden-Powell, who in 1908 will found the Boy Scouts.)

28 MAY 1900

China Attacks on and killings of foreigners and Chinese Christians have continued as the Boxers become more confident that the Imperial Court is tacitly approving. Today rioters provoked by Boxers burn the Fengtai Railway Station, junction of the Peking-Tientsin line; besiege the staff, many Belgians, in the compound; and cut the telegraph lines. The government will respond next day only by issuing another of its ambivalent edicts.

South Africa: Boer War Paul Kruger, President of the Boer Republic of South Africa, flees its capital, Pretoria, and goes to Watervalboven to evade the advancing British.

31 MAY–4 JUNE 1900

China A contingent of what will eventually number 426 foreign officers and men has been moved from their nations' ships (US, British, German, Austrian, Japanese, Italian, Russian, and French) off Tientsin and been assigned to guard the legations in Peking. Reports of attacks on foreign missionaries and engineers continue.

South Africa: Boer War The British flag is raised over Johannesburg, the major Boer city in the Republic of South Africa.

JUNE 1900

China The governor of China's province of Manchuria, which borders on Russia and has long been coveted by her, declares war on Russia as part of the Chinese uprising against foreigners. Attacks on Russians across the Amur River will lead to retaliation and invasion by the Russians.

5 JUNE 1900

South Africa: Boer War Pretoria, capital of the Boer Republic of South Africa, falls to the British led by General Buller.

6 JUNE 1900

China Boxers cut off all railroad links between Peking and Tientsin, main port city for Peking.

USA Congress passes an act authorizing a civil code and government for the territory of Alaska in an attempt to stem the lawlessness and violence attendant on the great gold discoveries that have recently brought disorderly people to the region.

9 JUNE 1900

China Boxers destroy the race course in Peking, a few miles from the legations and the center and symbol of diplomatic social life and Western privilege. Legation leaders refuse to evacuate women and

Marines in a relief party—the Boxer Rebellion.

CALM BEFORE THE STORM 1900-1913

children, but they have asked Admiral Edward Seymour of Great Britain, ranking officer of the foreign presence at Tientsin, to bring more troops to guard foreigners in Peking.

10 JUNE 1900
China A relief column of some 2000 men—largely naval personnel from the several nations' ships and led by Admiral Seymour—sets out from Tientsin to relieve foreigners trapped in Peking. During the next two weeks, this international force will defeat Chinese insurgents at several points.

12 JUNE 1900
Germany The Reichstag passes the second Navy Bill, which calls for doubling the German Navy within 20 years (to include 38 battleships). This law results from a campaign by Admiral Alfred von Tirpitz, head of the Admiralty, but it expresses a desire by Germans to challenge Britain's dominance of the seas: 'The trident belongs in our hands,' the Kaiser has declared.

13 JUNE 1900
China Baron von Ketteler, the German minister to China, beats two young Boxers with his walking stick; when word of this circulates, rioting and arson spread through Peking during the night. The Manchu Court has been wavering about how to deal with the Boxers, but the Empress decides to support them and their attacks on foreigners by issuing an edict that refers to Boxers as 'people's soldiers.'

14 JUNE 1900
Hawaii Having been annexed to the USA on 12 August 1898, Hawaii is constituted an organized territory (as called for by an act of Congress of 30 April). Sanford Dole—Hawaiian-born son of American missionaries—was appointed first governor of Hawaii on 14 May.

16–17 JUNE 1900
China Foreign legations in Peking are now all but isolated by violence rampant in the streets. Legations send out patrols of guards who seek to confront the Boxers. On the 16th, a terrible fire set by the Boxers virtually destroys the Western Quarter, then spreads to engulf many Chinese landmarks. Meanwhile, the Taku forts guarding the port of Tientsin bombard foreign ships offshore, but the forts are captured by foreign forces.

19 JUNE 1900
China After deliberations in the Imperial Palace, notes are delivered to the 11 major legations: since foreign troops are firing on Chinese, 'We break off all relations with your government.' Each legation is asked to leave for Tientsin with all its personnel, escorted by Imperial troops. A majority of foreigners wish to accept this offer, but are soon persuaded that this will mean abandoning Chinese servants and staffs to almost certain slaughter.

USA The Republican Party, convening in Philadelphia, nominates President William McKinley for re-election but chooses a new candidate for Vice-President: Theodore Roosevelt.

20 JUNE 1900
China Most foreigners in the Peking legations now accept that they are under siege. But Baron von Ketteler, the German minister, decides he will go to Chinese authorities and demand more guards for those who wish to go to Tientsin. He is killed by Boxers en route, and by afternoon it is clear that no foreigners are going to get away.

21 JUNE 1900
Philippines General Arthur MacArthur, US military governor of the Philippines, issues an amnesty proclamation to those Filipinos who will renounce the insurgent movement and accept US sovereignty. There will be little response, and fighting continues.

22 JUNE 1900
China Practically the whole foreign community in Peking, including many Chinese Christians, retreats to the British compound. In the afternoon, in an attempt to drive them out, Boxers set fire to the nearby Hanlin Yuan, the greatest library of Chinese scholarship; the flames serve only to destroy much of the library. At Tientsin the foreign community is now besieged and isolated.

23 JUNE 1900
Ashanti (Gold Coast) British Governor Hodgson and some of his British supporters flee Fort Coomassie, where they have been under siege since 6 April. They will make their way to the coast.
Turkey The Young Turks, a group that includes many students, exiles in Western Europe, and members of the Turkish military who are determined to get rid of the ineffectual Sultan Abdel Hamid, present a manifesto to the major foreign embassies in Constantinople demanding that these foreign powers end the Ottoman Sultan's rule. The Ottoman Empire has been coming apart since the early 19th century, as subject peoples began to demand freedom, such minorities as the Kurds and Armenians demanded at least tolerance, and foreign powers tried to gain territory or access at the expense of the Empire. It will take a world war to demolish the Ottoman Empire, after which the Young Turks will bring Turkey into the concert of modern nations.

25 JUNE 1900
Russia Russia mobilizes its army in eastern Siberia preparatory to acting against the Chinese; the excuse is Boxer-instigated attacks on Russian territory across from Manchuria, but Russia has been seeking control of that province for some time so as to crowd out the Japanese on the Asian mainland.

26 JUNE 1900
Japan Japan mobilizes 20,000 troops to help put

down the Boxer uprising—but also to advance its long-term interest in gaining land and power in mainland Asia.

Finland The Russian Czar orders that Russian must be the official language of Finland, despite growing unrest within Finland and increasing international concern over Russia's behavior there.

29 JUNE 1900

China The Imperial Court issues what is essentially a declaration of war against the foreigners in China and blames hostilities on them. This will become a license for the Boxers and their supporters to turn against foreigners and their Chinese converts with even greater ferocity. Most actions occur in northern China, particularly in Shantung Province, under the Manchu governor Yu Hsien, and in Manchuria, where the Roman Catholic bishop and others are burned alive after taking refuge in the cathedral in Mukden.

3 JULY 1900

Russia Trying to stem growing popular resentment, Czar Nicholas issues a decree that abolishes the banishment of dissidents and troublemakers to Siberia.

4 JULY 1900

South Africa: Boer War The two major British armies—one under Roberts, the other under Buller—join forces at Vlakfontein. The British now seem to have eliminated the Boers' capacity to mount organized military operations, as most Boer cities have been taken, units dispersed, and leaders put on the run. In fact, the Boers will turn to guerrilla tactics —and the war will drag on for almost two years.

USA At its convention in Kansas City, the Democratic Party nominates William Jennings Bryan as its presidential candidate and Adlai E Stevenson for Vice-President. (Bryan is also endorsed by the fusion Populist Party.) The Democrats adopt a platform calling for free coinage of silver (opposing the Currency Act of 14 March 1900), but their main theme will be an attack on the 'imperialism' of which they accuse the Republicans.

6–14 JULY 1900

China International forces in and around Tientsin —now about 14,000—launch an assault on this key port. After taking at least 800 casualties, the allies control the forts and the city by the 14th; the foreign troops proceed to loot the city, stealing or destroying millions of dollars worth of goods.

9 JULY 1900

Australia The Commonwealth of Australia is established by the British House of Commons, which passes the act uniting six former colonies (but not New Zealand) into a federal state. The movement to form such a federation has been underway since 1890, and by the end of July all of Australia's states will have adopted the bill.

16 JULY 1900

International A report appears in London, and spreads throughout the world, that all foreigners in Peking have been massacred. Although it is soon exposed as false, the story helps mobilize governmental support for relief of the foreigners under siege.

16–19 JULY 1900

China In response to Chinese bombardment of Russians across the Amur River, the Russians have launched an offensive against the Chinese in Manchuria. On the 19th, the Russians rout the Chinese along the Amur.

19–21 JULY 1900

China The Emperor appeals to France, Germany, Japan, and the USA to help 'mediate' the Boxer uprising. Foreign powers believe the Chinese should stop these attacks, which continue in parts of China.

23 JULY 1900

Canada The government prohibits criminals and paupers from landing in Canada. Increasing numbers of immigrants of all kinds are forcing Canada to review its immigration policy.

29 JULY 1900

Italy King Umberto (Humbert) I is assassinated by Gaetano Bresci, an anarchist, at Monza in northern Italy. He is succeeded by his son, Victor Emmanuel III (who will rule until 1946). During the next few days, the Italian Government will round up many anarchists (50 in Rome alone on 7 August).

30 JULY 1900

Great Britain Parliament passes several progressive social acts: a Mines Act (prohibiting young children from working underground), a Workmen's Compensation Act (covering accidents and illnesses), and a Railway Act (to prevent accidents). These acts are typical of legislation that advanced countries are coming to accept.

4 AUGUST 1900

China The allied expeditionary force sets off from Tientsin for Peking, comprised of some 10,000 Japanese, 5000 Russian, 3000 British, 2000 American, and 800 French (the Germans have not yet arrived).

5 AUGUST 1900

Russia There are anti-Jewish riots in Odessa and other parts of Russia. Such anti-Semitic activity— officially condoned or privately perpetrated—is not uncommon in European countries.

14 AUGUST 1900

China Several foreign units in the relief force have agreed to coordinate their movements into Peking, but at the last minute the Russian forces begin to move ahead, so all units race to be the first to relieve

CALM BEFORE THE STORM 1900-1913

foreigners. (The British troops are first into the compound.) Before the afternoon is over, all legations are relieved, including at least 400 officers and enlisted men who had been serving as guards, many civilians, and many Chinese who had taken refuge. (In the weeks under siege, 67 were killed, 120 wounded, and five died from other causes.) In Manchuria, Russia declares it has annexed the right bank of the Amur River and is moving to seize the city of Harbin and the port of Newchang.

15 AUGUST 1900
China The Empress and some of her family, the court, and retainers flee (after executing some retainers considered disloyal, while others commit suicide) and make their way slowly to Sian, 700 miles southeast of Peking and capital of Shensi Province. (They will arrive on 26 October.) In Peking foreign troops begin to move through the city, not only inflicting losses on the Boxers, but destroying and pillaging the property of innocent Chinese. In subsequent weeks foreign civilians (including diplomats) join the troops in what becomes one of the most shameful lootings on record: the famed Peking Observatory is virtually dismembered, and many artistic and cultural valuables stolen. By 28 August, the allies have taken over the Imperial City, but have been ordered to stay out of the innermost Forbidden City; now the allied leaders call on the Imperial Court to return. Elsewhere in China, Boxers continue their attacks on missionaries and their converts. The Russians advance in Manchuria.

27 AUGUST 1900
South Africa: Boer War Buller leads his British forces at Bergendal, in the northern Transvaal, where they defeat the Boers under Louis Botha; the next day Botha is forced to retreat into the hills.

29 AUGUST 1900
Italy Bresci, the assassin of King Umberto I, is tried and sentenced to life imprisonment; he will commit suicide in jail on 22 May 1901. One unexpected outcome of the incident is that Padre Volponi, a Catholic priest, is given eight months in jail for stating that regicide is sometimes justifiable.

31 AUGUST 1900
South Africa: Boer War Lord Roberts and his forces occupy Johannesburg.

2 SEPTEMBER 1900
Ireland In a large demonstration in Dublin's Phoenix Park, the Nationalists take the lead in demanding that Ireland be free of British rule. Such a demand goes back several centuries, but this time it will not be stilled until Ireland gains its sovereignty in 1937; the controversy over Northern Ireland will continue long afterward.

3 SEPTEMBER 1900
South Africa: Boer War With a proclamation by

General Lord Roberts, Britain annexes the Boer Republic of South Africa. Boer resistance has been collapsing, with thousands surrendering and many others fleeing to adjacent African lands. The Boer leader, Paul Kruger, is in flight to the Portuguese colony of Mozambique. Lord Roberts and many Britons are convinced the war is over, but soon Boers will begin to attack British railroads and cut communication lines in South Africa, and a guerrilla war will drag on.

China The Russians have had their eye on Manchuria since the 16th century, and the Boxer Rebellion has given them the desired excuse to invade and conquer it. The Russians now control both sides of the Amur River, the Russo-Manchurian boundary, and at Blagovestchensk, a Russian town with a sizable Chinese population, Russian Cossack troops drive some 5000 Chinese residents into the Amur, where they are clubbed, stabbed, and drowned. Similar incidents are reported elsewhere along the Amur, and travelers on the river report that it is virtually blood-red and clogged with bodies.

8 SEPTEMBER 1900
Environment A hurricane with winds up to 120 mph and a tidal wave sweep in from the Gulf of Mexico and devastate Galveston, Texas; some 6000 people die (most by drowning) and property damage is estimated at $20 million. Several looters are found with ring fingers cut from the dead. There are two secondary results of this disaster: one of the first motion pictures of such an event is made (and shown as *Galveston Cyclone*), and the commission form of government, set up to deal with the emergency, is permanently adopted the following year.

11 SEPTEMBER 1900
South Africa: Boer War President Paul Kruger and others in his party arrive in Lourenço Marques, Mozambique; Kruger will depart on a Dutch ship on 20 October and arrive in Marseilles on 22 November, whence he will set out to try to gain support from European powers.

13 SEPTEMBER 1900
Austro-Hungarian Empire Among restive subjects of the Empire are the Poles; attending maneuvers of the Imperial Army in Galicia, a Polish province, Emperor Franz Joseph receives a deputation from the Polish 'parliament,' but leaves them in no doubt that they will lose even nominal autonomy if they continue to make demands.

14 SEPTEMBER 1900
China There are now 62,000 foreign troops in Peking and nearby cities; they are still defeating the Boxers in confrontations, but attacks on isolated Chinese Christians continue, providing foreign troops with the excuse to continue attacks on Chinese.

15 SEPTEMBER 1900
International A Boer delegation issues an appeal at

5 NOVEMBER 1900

The Hague, Netherlands, that the major powers intervene in the war in South Africa. This Boer peace delegation has been traveling through Europe—and even to Washington, DC—since April; its members choose The Hague because there is to be an International Court of Arbitration here, as established by the First Hague Conference (1899).

17 SEPTEMBER 1900
Australia The Commonwealth of Australia is proclaimed (but will not take force until 1 January 1901) by the British Government. This culminates a growing movement toward independence from Britain and a unified central government in Australia; a convention had drawn up a constitution for a federal union of the six colonies which was approved by the Australians in 1898–99 voting.
USA Anthracite coal miners go out on strike for better wages; management will refuse concessions at first, and the strike will drag on till 25 October, by which time the owners will have been persuaded that their stand is harming President McKinley's campaign.

OCTOBER 1900
International Crete, the large island south of Greece, is one of several troubled dependents of the Ottoman Turkish Empire. Under Turkish rule since 1669, the Cretans fought a series of revolts throughout the 19th century, the last (1898) resulting in the Great Powers' (Britain, France, Italy, Russia) forcing Turkey to give Crete autonomy under a High Commissioner they would appoint. Since 26 November 1898, this has been Prince George, younger brother of the King of Greece, and during this month he will be traveling in Western Europe to visit heads of state and enlist support for a union of Crete with Greece. (It will not be achieved until 1913.)
Turkey Still another troubled people of the Turkish realm are the Armenians, an ethnic-religious (Christian) minority long persecuted and even massacred. During this month, more persecutions flare; Russia intervenes and provides relief, but it is merely a temporary measure for the Armenians.
China During this month German troops sent to participate in the relief of Peking arrive, led by Count von Waldersee, who assumes the role of commander of the International Relief Force. Having come too late to take part in the true relief, the Germans send out 'punitive expeditions' against the Boxers and are soon engaged in looting the Chinese populace.

4 OCTOBER 1900
Ashanti (Gold Coast) In a final confrontation, some 4000 rebellious Ashantis are defeated by the British. Survivors flee, but by 14 November the leader of the rebellion will be captured and the British will regain control over this colony.

10 OCTOBER 1900
China Foreign ministers in Peking begin their first serious negotiations over what conditions their nations will impose on the Chinese. Some nations demand more severe penalties than do others, but they will agree on a compromise proposal fostered by the French Government: punishment (including death for some) of those responsible for the Boxer uprising; indemnities for governments, organizations, and individuals; dismantling of forts, including the Taku forts at Tientsin; and other terms that will force the Chinese to accept occupation in some areas. In Manchuria, meanwhile, the Russians capture the major city of Mukden on this day, part of their own plan to take over the whole province.

16 OCTOBER 1900
International Great Britain and Germany sign the Anglo-German Treaty, in which they agree to maintain the territorial integrity of China and support the 'open door' policy called for by US Secretary of State Hay. This is not quite as disinterested or magnanimous as it might first appear: both Britain and Germany are determined to retain access to China in the face of growing Russian and Japanese influence.

18 OCTOBER 1900
Germany Count Bernhard von Bülow, member of a distinguished German family, becomes Chancellor (succeeding Prince Hohenlohe, who resigned on 16 October). Bülow is regarded as an elegant lightweight, not dedicated to any particular cause except to please the Kaiser and promote the role of Germany: it is von Bülow who first refers to Germany's need for 'a place in the sun,' and although he is forced to resign in 1909, this will characterize Germany's ambition for the next 40 years.

25 OCTOBER 1900
South Africa: Boer War Great Britain annexes the former Boer South African Republic, renaming it the Transvaal Colony.

NOVEMBER 1900
China Allied military units continue to fight Boxer-led resistance in cities and outposts, while anti-Christian outbreaks continue.
Belgian Congo Since 1885 King Leopold of Belgium has been king of the so-called Independent State of the Congo, a vast African territory that he has taken over as his personal estate (although in 1889 he wrote in his will that he was making Belgium the 'heir' to his 'real estate'). As Belgians have been trying to control the Congo territory, there have been attacks and killings by both sides. During this month the Belgians wage an especially harsh campaign to punish Africans who are refusing to work the rubber trees (one of the main sources of wealth). Villages are burned and Africans massacred. Reports of incidents and atrocities begin to reach the world.

5 NOVEMBER 1900
Cuba Under US military control since the end of the Spanish-American War in 1898, Cuba now calls

CALM BEFORE THE STORM 1900-1913

its own constitutional convention. It will meet for several months, but participants will learn that any constitution must incorporate conditions before the US withdraws. The conditions become known as the Platt Amendment, passed by the US Congress on 2 March 1901, and Cuba will be forced to accept it.

6 NOVEMBER 1900
USA In the national elections, President McKinley and his Vice-President, Theodore Roosevelt, defeat the Democrats' William Jennings Bryan: the popular vote is 7,219,530 to 6,358,071; the electoral college vote is 292 to 155.

7 NOVEMBER 1900
Canada In Dominion elections, the Liberal Government led by Wilfrid Laurier retains its majority.

9 NOVEMBER 1900
International China has resumed nominal control of Manchuria, but in a secret agreement the Chinese governor of Manchuria grants the Russians such rights as keeping troops along the railroad lines and controlling the civil administration. This agreement will be disavowed by the governments of both countries, but Russia will continue to exert its influence in Manchuria, ostensibly to protect its Trans-Siberian Railway.

22–30 NOVEMBER 1900
France Paul Kruger, exiled President of the Boer Republic of South Africa, is given a popular welcome when he lands at Marseilles. The President of the French Republic, Loubet, will receive him on 24 November, and the Chamber of Deputies and Senate will pass resolutions of sympathy for his cause on the 29th and 30th. All this pro-Boer sentiment is little more than anti-British sentiment, and sympathy is almost all the French offer Kruger and his Boers.

29 NOVEMBER 1900
South Africa: Boer War General Horatio Kitchener assumes command of the British forces in South Africa from General Lord Roberts, who will return to Britain convinced the war is over.

30 NOVEMBER 1900
International The First Isthmian Canal Commission, appointed by the US President, having examined possible routes for a canal, issues its report favoring that through Nicaragua over the Panama route. The French had begun a canal through Panama in 1880, but the company went bankrupt and work stopped. Some influential forces want this Panama Canal to be continued by the USA.

1 DECEMBER 1900
Germany The Kaiser declines to meet with Paul Kruger, the exiled Boer leader; on 10 December Chancellor von Bülow will announce that Germany cannot intervene in any way in the conflict in South

William Jennings Bryan.

Africa. As with so many of the major powers, this decision is based on Germany's determination to preserve its options over its own colonies.

Mexico Porfirio Díaz is inaugurated for his sixth consecutive term as President of Mexico.

14 DECEMBER 1900
International France and Italy sign a secret agreement by which Italy recognizes France's right to exploit Morocco in return for France's conceding her the same right in Tripoli.

16 DECEMBER 1900
USA To deal with destructive confrontations between labor and management, a National Civic Federation is formed for arbitration of labor disputes. The president is Mark Hanna, the Ohio capitalist, and vice-president is Samuel Gompers, respected labor leader; their essentially meliorative approach will not go far in resolving differences.

17 DECEMBER 1900
The Vatican Pope Leo XIII closes the 'Holy Door' of St Peter's in Rome, ending the Jubilee Year of 1900.

19–20 DECEMBER 1900
South Africa: Boer War Kitchener offers protection to all Boers who will surrender and asks the Dutch community of Pretoria to convey this offer, but leaders in the field refuse to surrender; although organized military operations are largely over as the year ends, the guerrilla war continues.

19–24 DECEMBER 1900
France The Chamber of Deputies (19 December) and Senate (24 December) pass a bill calling for an end to agitation or prosecutions against those involved in the Dreyfus affair, which has divided

France since 1894, when Captain Alfred Dreyfus was convicted of treason—primarily because he was a Jew. This latest bill, however, is designed not so much to exonerate Dreyfus as to protect those who have hounded him. It is recognized as such by Emile Zola, the French novelist who has championed Dreyfus, and on 22 December he writes a letter (in the newspaper *Aurore*) to President Loubet protesting this latest amnesty bill.

23 DECEMBER 1900

Philippines As American forces defeat the Filipino insurgents and impose civil authority, some Filipinos form a Federal Party with a platform recognizing US sovereignty.

24 DECEMBER 1900

China The ministers accredited to Peking have been conferring since October and have now reached agreement, adopting terms proposed by the French. Today they meet for the first time with the Chinese representatives of the Empress and present their list of 'irrevocable conditions' before their nations will withdraw troops. The Chinese, knowing the situation in Peking and elsewhere, realize they must agree to these terms and submit them to the Empress, now in Sian. (But it will be 7 September 1901 before the final agreement is signed.)

OTHER EVENTS OF 1900

Science Max Planck, German physicist, proposes the quantum theory: namely, energy is transmitted in tiny bundles (quanta), not in continuous emissions. Three investigators, working independently, come upon the work of the Austrian monk Gregor Mendel —published in 1866 but ignored—in which his experiments with controlled pollination provide the basis for modern genetics and support for the theory of evolution. Karl Landsteiner, an Austrian pathologist, discovers the first system of blood types (A, B, and O), crucially important in blood transfusions.

Medicine/Health During the summer, Major Walter Reed and other Americans conduct experiments in Havana, Cuba, to prove that yellow fever is transmitted by the *Aëdes aegypti* mosquito when carrying an infective virus; Jesse Lazear, one of the doctors, dies from the bite of an infected mosquito.

Technology At Cob Point, Maryland, Reginald Fessenden, a Canadian electrical scientist, demonstrates the first radio-telephone to relay recognizable speech through the air regardless of barriers between transmitter and receiver. Ferdinand von Zeppelin, a German, conducts the first trial flight of the gas-filled lighter-than-air vehicle that will come to be named for him. The Boer War in South Africa scores several 'firsts' in technology and warfare: the first motorcycle in warfare; the first motor truck; the first use of radio in naval war; and the first time battle scenes are filmed on moving pictures.

Social Sciences On Crete a British archaeologist, Arthur Evans, begins excavations at Knossos that reveal a sophisticated palace and culture that he names 'Minoan.' Off the Greek island of Antikythera, a sponge diver finds the wreck of an ancient ship and brings up a bronze instrument that will be identified (in 1959) as a kind of computer for calculating positions of the sun and moon and employing a differential gear, one of the major mechanical inventions of all time. Wilhelm Wundt, a German who will become known as the 'Father of Modern Psychology,' publishes his seminal work *Comparative Psychology*, while the Austrian psychoanalyst Sigmund Freud, whose work is to have such an effect in later years, publishes his *Interpretation of Dreams*.

Literature Published this year are: Joseph Conrad's *Lord Jim*; Theodore Dreiser's *Sister Carrie* (which is attacked as obscene and soon removed from sale by the publisher); Colette's *Claudine à l'école* (first of her semi-autobiographical Claudine books); L Frank Baum's *The Wonderful Wizard of Oz*; and Beatrix Potter's *The Tale of Peter Rabbit*. In France the Académie de Goncourt is established; it will award a prestigious annual Prix Goncourt for the best French fiction.

The Arts Among the important works are: Picasso's *Le Moulin de la Galette*, Cezanne's *Still Life with Onions*, and Sargent's *The Sitwell Family*.

Music Puccini's *Tosca* premieres in Rome, and Sibelius's *Finlandia* is performed in Helsinki. The first 'jazz band' is claimed to have originated in New Orleans by Buddy Bolden, a black musician.

Sports/Leisure W G Grace, the Englishman most responsible for the style and method of modern cricket, retires after scoring 54,000 runs. Dwight Davis, an American, presents a silver bowl for an annual competition in lawn tennis between Britain and the USA; by 1904 the competition will be open to all nations, and the Davis Cup will help convert tennis from an elite to a popular game. In the US, a new baseball association, the American League, is formed; it will be 1903 before the National League (founded 1876) recognizes its teams as 'major league' and plays a World Series. In the second modern Olympics, held in Paris, the American track-and-field athlete Raymond Ewry wins three gold medals, the first of ten he will win over the years, still a record for individual gold medals.

Life/Customs The 'cake walk' becomes an international dance fad. The first known sex education course is introduced into a school, when Dr Martin Cholzen, in Breslau, Prussia, lectures on aspects of human sexuality and 'the importance of cultivating self-control.'

Miscellaneous A major World Exhibition is held in Paris. The International Ladies Garment Workers Union is founded in New York City, which starts to construct its first subway system. This spring, in Kansas, Mrs Carrie Amelia Nation begins her crusade against alcoholic drinks by leading groups of women to attack and sometimes destroy saloons with stones, tools, and even hatchets. Motivated by Christian zeal and an almost mystical sense of mis-

CALM BEFORE THE STORM 1900-1913

sion (including a belief that her name, 'Carry A Nation,' was preordained), plus bitterness over her first marriage to a drunkard, she will influence leading Americans to adopt Prohibition. (Her second husband will divorce her in 1901—for desertion).

1 JANUARY 1901
Australia The Commonwealth of Australia is founded; the British monarch will remain as head of state and be represented in Australia by a Governor-General—the first being Lord Hopetoun. Caretaker Prime Minister, until elections, is Edmund Barton, who had worked for the new federation from his colony of New South Wales. The Parliament is bicameral, with a House of Representatives elected by constituencies of roughly the same size, and a Senate formed with the same number from each of the six states; the Prime Minister and cabinet are members of the House and its leading party. A High Court is to function as a supreme court of appeals and arbitration. The Parliament will meet in Melbourne until the new capital is ready at Canberra (in 1927).

4–10 JANUARY 1901
China The Dowager Empress and advisers, exiled at Sian, receive the note with the conditions from the foreign nations for withdrawing troops. At first the Empress will try to modify some of the more stringent terms, but when persuaded that the foreigners will not negotiate any further, she issues the acceptance order to her representative in Peking.

10 JANUARY 1901
Life/Customs Oil is discovered in the Spindletop Field, near Beaumont, Texas; this is the first of the great oil-fields that will so change the life of the ensuing decades.

22 JANUARY 1901
Britain Queen Victoria, aged 82, dies on the Isle of Wight; since succeeding to the throne in 1837, she has given her name, image, and values to most of the past century. She is succeeded by her 59-year-old son, Edward VII, as the royalty of Europe—many her descendants—prepare to pay their final respects.

31 JANUARY 1901
Austro-Hungarian Empire The Reichsrath—dissolved on 7 September 1900 by Emperor Franz Joseph—reopens after the recent elections have defeated extremists.

FEBRUARY 1901
China As negotiations proceed over final details of terms demanded by the foreigners, leaders of the Boxer uprising are named by the diplomats as 'deserving death'; many will be killed, others allowed to commit suicide, some banished, and some will flee.
Russia The crops begin to fail this year, leading to famine throughout much of Russia; the government will try to organize relief, but many Russians are increasingly impatient with its role. Students in St Petersburg and other major cities begin riots and disturbances that will result by the end of March in hundreds of arrests. Strikers add their support. The leading writer, Leo Tolstoy, sends an open letter of protest to the Czar; Tolstoy will be excommunicated for 'radicalism,' but by June the Czar will be forced to pardon the students. Russia remains restless.
South Africa: Boer War Despite appeals from the Burghers of Pretoria, the Boers have continued their guerrilla war against the British. Kitchener has begun to try new tactics: he is building a network of 'blockhouses,' small forts, and forcing Boers off farms into detention camps. Both sides are suffering heavy casualties.

2 FEBRUARY 1901
Mexico The government has been trying to put down an insurrection by Yaqui Indians in Sonora Province since 1896; today, government troops are ambushed and defeated badly, with 100 killed.
USA Congress passes the Army Reorganization Act, placing the minimum number of men under arms at 58,000.

4 FEBRUARY 1901
Austro-Hungarian Empire Emperor Franz Joseph delivers a speech from his throne to smooth over the problems threatening the Empire. He condemns the demands of national groups and calls for economic and social reform, but this will not satisfy the fundamental aspirations of many of his subjects.

11 FEBRUARY 1901
Serbia Former King Milan IV, who led Serbia in its fight for independence from Turkey, dies in Vienna where he has been living in exile since 1890. Milan had been unable to calm the turbulence afflicting Serbia's internal and external affairs—he had been shot on a visit to Belgrade in July 1899—and now his son Alexander I is having little more success.

21 FEBRUARY 1901
Cuba The constitutional delegates adopt a constitution much like that of the USA, but the US will insist that it incorporate certain provisions to be spelled out in the Platt Amendment (accepted by Cuba on 12 June).

25 FEBRUARY 1901
USA The United States Steel Corporation is organized by combining several smaller companies (including Carnegie's steel company, for Andrew Carnegie wishes to retire and devote his wealth and time to philanthropy). J P Morgan is the leading spirit of the merger, the first billion-dollar corporation in US history.

26–28 FEBRUARY 1901
South Africa: Boer War General Kitchener confers

Andrew Carnegie.

with Boer general Louis Botha at Middleburg about peace conditions; Botha has recently failed in a raid on Natal, and the Boer cause looks hopeless, but negotiations break down over the question of amnesty for some of the Boers.

27 FEBRUARY 1901
Great Britain A General Committee of National Liberal Federation meets and adopts a resolution deploring the continuation of the war in South Africa and condemning the British Government's insistence on unconditional surrender by the Boers.
Russia Revolutionaries assasinate the minister of propaganda to avenge repression of students.

2 MARCH 1901
USA Congress passes the Army Appropriations Act, with two important amendments. The Spooner Amendment authorizes the President to establish a temporary civil government for the Philippine Islands. The Platt Amendment sets forth the conditions under which the US will withdraw its forces and allow Cuba to govern itself under its new constitution. Conditions include a prohibition on Cuba's making any treaty with a foreign power, and authorization for the US to intervene to preserve law and order or Cuban independence. Cuba is to be a protectorate of the USA and is forced to accept these terms (until the US abrogates the amendment on 29 May 1934).

4 MARCH 1901
USA William McKinley is inaugurated president for a second term; Theodore Roosevelt is Vice-President.

15 MARCH 1901
International Germany's Chancellor von Bülow declares that the agreement Germany signed with England in October 1900, to restrain foreign aggression and maintain open trade, does not apply to Manchuria; this leads to an immediate end of Britain's attempt to form an Anglo-German-Japanese bloc to stop Russia's actions there.

23 MARCH 1901
Philippines American Army General Frederick Funston and a group of officers pretend to be prisoners of Filipino scouts and are led into the camp of Emilio Aguinaldo, leader of the insurgents; Aguinaldo is captured, and as most of the other rebel leaders have been captured previously, the insurgent movement will soon collapse.

29–30 MARCH 1901
Australia Australians hold the first elections for their new Parliament; no party gets a majority, but protectionists are in control and Edmund Barton becomes the first Prime Minister.

5 APRIL 1901
Bulgaria Under threats from the Ottoman Turkish Government, Bulgaria is forced to arrest the leaders of the Macedonian Committee; Macedonians have long been agitating for independence from Turkey, and although peoples in the region support their cause, no country dares confront Turkey.

15 APRIL 1901
Papacy Pope Leo XIII issues an allocution deploring hostile actions against the Roman Catholic Church throughout Europe; he condemns the French Government for recent laws requiring the registration and control of religious associations and the closing of Roman Catholic schools.

19 APRIL 1901
Philippines Recently captured insurgent leader Aguinaldo issues a proclamation advising his countrymen to end their rebellion and use peaceful means to work with the US toward independence. Although fighting goes on for another year, the rebellion ends; prisoners who take an oath of allegiance are released, and the American military is in control.

8 MAY 1901
India A severe drought since 1899 has led to widespread famine, and although international relief efforts have provided funds, a report by a British-appointed commission estimates today that some 1,250,000 Indians have died. The commission claims that India's growing population is placing too-heavy demands on the country's agriculture.

9 MAY 1901
Australia The first Australian Parliament opens in Melbourne, although the first working session will not be until 21 May.

CALM BEFORE THE STORM 1900-1913

USA A financial panic begins to follow the struggle between two groups to control the railroads between the Great Lakes and the Pacific. The winner, the Northern Securities Company, will be the initial target of Theodore Roosevelt when he begins his fight against 'Big Business' in 1902.

27 MAY 1901
USA The Supreme Court hands down the first of three decisions this year in the so-called Insular Cases; although this first case, *De Lima v Bidwell*, seems to decide simply that customs duties can no longer be levied on goods sent to the USA from Puerto Rico, since it is no longer a foreign country, the effect of this and the subsequent decisions is to establish the principle that although some US laws will apply to such territories as Puerto Rico and the Philippines, full privileges of citizenship must be conferred specifically by Congress.

31 MAY 1901
Greece At the opening of the Greek National Assembly, Prince George, High Commissioner of Crete, asks it to endorse the union of Crete with Greece; delegates pass such a resolution, but on 18 June the Four Powers, which control Crete, reject this move.

12 JUNE 1901
Cuba The constitutional convention—knowing that the USA will not withdraw its troops until it does so—adopts the Platt Amendment as part of its constitution.

1 JULY 1901
France The climax of recent years' efforts by the French Government to restrict the role of the Catholic Church and clergy, the Association Law, is promulgated; it calls for strict regulation of religious communities and associations in France, but is clearly aimed at Roman Catholic groups, many of which—including the Jesuits and the Benedictines—will leave France rather than comply.

4 JULY 1901
Philippines William Howard Taft, a former Federal judge, is installed as first governor-general of the Philippines; Taft declares amnesty for all who take an oath of allegiance. On 16 July Miguel Malvas, successor to Aguinaldo as leader of the insurgents, will call for continuation of the fight, but he will surrender on 16 April 1902.

12 JULY 1901
Canada Striking Canadian salmon fishermen on the Pacific coast, resentful of the nonunion Japanese who continue to fish, maroon and imprison 47.

Germany A debate has emerged in Germany over the tradition of dueling—revived in recent decades as part of the Prussian image of aristocratic-warrior elitism—and today a group of 104 German aristocrats presents a declaration against dueling. It will not gain much support, the Reichstag will fail to pass any laws against dueling, and the tradition will go on.

20 JULY 1901
Morocco For decades Morocco has been threatened by Spain, France, and Britain, each wanting to take part of the country. Today Morocco signs an agreement with France fixing Morocco's frontier with Algeria (itself a French colony), giving France control over Morocco's frontier police, and regulating trade and police functions: all of this is a step toward France's taking over Morocco as a colony.

22 JULY 1901
Great Britain The House of Lords, sitting as the nation's highest court, hands down its decision in the Taff Vale Case: the Taff Vale Railway Company had sued a striking union, which claimed that it couldn't be sued because it was neither a corporation nor an individual. The Lords rule that a trade union can be sued for actions of members. This will have the immediate effect of consolidating British labor, leading many to join the new Labour Party.

AUGUST–DECEMBER 1901
Russia Due to poor harvests and famine, oppressive taxation, student riots, and strikes over working conditions, Russia is becoming increasingly unsettled, with several cities in a virtual state of siege.

15 AUGUST 1901
South Africa: Boer War Great Britain issues a proclamation calling on the Boers to surrender by 15 September or face banishment and confiscation of their property. There are engagements almost daily, with heavy losses on both sides, but this proclamation will not stop the conflict.

17 AUGUST 1901
Great Britain The Royal Titles Act adds the words 'and of the British Dominions beyond the Seas' to the monarch's style: the imperial flourish comes with the century that will see Britain lose most of its 'Dominions beyond the Seas.'

2 SEPTEMBER 1901
USA Vice-President Theodore Roosevelt, speaking at the Minnesota State Fair, quotes an adage which he had claimed as an African proverb in a personal letter of the previous year: 'Speak softly and carry a big stick; you will go far.' This is picked up by the press and incorporated into Roosevelt's personal and public image.

6 SEPTEMBER 1901
USA President McKinley, visiting the Pan-American Exposition in Buffalo, New York, is shot by Leon Czolgosz, regarded as a half-crazed anarchist. McKinley's wounds seem to be healing, but gangrene sets in: he will die on 14 September.

31 DECEMBER 1901

7 SEPTEMBER 1901
China Representatives of 11 foreign nations and of China sign what is variously known as the Peace of Peking or the Boxer Protocol. It establishes that China is to pay $333 million in indemnities (with the USA to get $25 million); permits the stationing of foreign troops in Peking; and leaves Russian troops in Manchuria. China remains hostage to foreign powers. (It is estimated that about 250 foreign missionaries, including 50 children, were killed by the Boxers; 32,000 Chinese converts to Christianity were also killed.)

14 SEPTEMBER 1901
USA President McKinley dies of his wounds at 2:15 AM. Theodore Roosevelt arrives at the same house in Buffalo and is sworn in as President at 3:00 PM. At 42 he is the youngest man to serve as President of the United States.

26 SEPTEMBER 1901
Ashanti (Gold Coast) The Ashanti Kingdom is annexed by Great Britain and placed under the governor of the Gold Coast.

16 OCTOBER 1901
International Baron Hayashi of Japan begins negotiations in London to make an alliance with the British and strengthen Japan's position against the Russians.

22 OCTOBER 1901–31 JANUARY 1902
International At the Second Pan-American Congress, held in Mexico City, the participating American states agree to adhere to the Hague Convention of 1899 and settle disputes by peaceful means.

25 OCTOBER 1901
Great Britain Joseph Chamberlain, Colonial Affairs Secretary, makes an anti-German speech at Edinburgh; when word reaches Germany, it leads to widespread agitation against the British and eventual breakdown (on 27 December) of negotiations for an Anglo-German alliance.

30 OCTOBER–1 NOVEMBER 1901
South Africa: Boer War In one of the bloodiest of the on-going engagements between the British and the Boers, Louis Botha's force charges a British column at Brakenlaagte; the British lose their commander and 60 others, with 165 wounded; the Boers count 44 dead and many wounded.

7 NOVEMBER 1901
Turkey A French fleet seizes the customs house on the Turkish-ruled island of Mytilene, because the Turks have refused to settle France's indemnity claims for losses suffered by French subjects in 1896. The Porte, as the Ottoman Turkish Government is known, quickly concedes: the Sultan signs the agreement, and by 11 November relations between the two countries are restored.

18 NOVEMBER 1901
International The USA and Great Britain sign the Second Hay-Pauncefote Treaty, or Interoceanic Ship Canal Treaty, abrogating the Clayton-Bulwer Treaty of 1850. Britain has now accepted the conditions that she had rejected in the First Hay-Pauncefote Treaty: namely, that the US will be allowed to fortify and defend any canal it builds across the isthmus of Central America. The US Senate will consent to this treaty on 16 December.

18 NOVEMBER 1901
Austro-Hungarian Empire The German-speaking and German-oriented members of the Reichsrath issue a manifesto warning the non-German nationalists within the Empire to cease their 'obstructionist' demands.

25 NOVEMBER–7 DECEMBER 1901
International Prince Ito of Japan comes to St Petersburg hoping to get the Russians to grant Japan concessions in Korea, but drops this goal and decides to make an alliance with Britain.

26 NOVEMBER 1901
International Italy and Britain sign an agreement fixing the frontier between their colonies of Eritrea and Sudan in East Africa. Italy had once tried to control a vast part of this region, but the Ethiopians, or Abyssinians, had defeated them at Adowa in 1896, so Italy had to restrict its colonial aspirations to Eritrea.

DECEMBER 1901
Ireland There is mounting protest against British rule, and during this month many Irish begin a campaign for nonpayment of rent to absentee English landlords; by the end of December, many who agitated for this—including four members of Parliament—will be sentenced to prison.

25 DECEMBER 1901
South Africa: Boer War At Tweefontein, a British force is camped on a hill slope; at 2:00 AM it is attacked by Boers coming down from the other side. The British lose 57, with 80 wounded; the Boers lose 30, with 50 wounded.

31 DECEMBER 1901
Cuba In the first election under their new constitution, Cubans elect a Congress and their first President, Tomas Estrada Palma.

OTHER EVENTS OF 1901
Medicine/Health Gerrit Grijins, a Dutch physiologist who has been working with Christian Eijkman in the Netherlands East Indies, proposes that the causative factor in the disease of beriberi is not a bacterium or toxin (as Eijkman believed) but what Grijins calls a deficiency of a 'protective substance' in the polished rice. Eijkman had established that those who ate whole (unhulled) rice did not contract

39

CALM BEFORE THE STORM 1900-1913

beriberi, but it is Grijins's concept that becomes the basis of modern theory on vitamins. American Army Major William Gorgas wipes out yellow fever in Havana by applying the discoveries made by Walter Reed and others the previous summer.

Technology On 11 December, Guglielmo Marconi, the Italian electrical inventor, sends the first transatlantic radio signal (the Morse Code for *S*) from a station at Cornwall, England, to St John's, Newfoundland. (In the spring of 1902, Canada's Parliament will vote $80,000 for Marconi to construct a wireless station in Nova Scotia.) In Brooklyn, New York, A C Bostwick drives the first auto known to exceed the speed of a mile a minute (but his record will be surpassed by two others at the same event).

Ideas/Beliefs Rudolf Steiner, a German philosopher, breaks away from the Theosophists to found anthroposophy, which attempts to explain the world in terms of a spiritual nature.

Literature Rudyard Kipling's *Kim*; Thomas Mann's *Buddenbrooks*; Frank Norris's *The Octopus*; Maurice Maeterlinck's *The Life of the Bee*; and Booker T Washington's *Up From Slavery*.

Drama Anton Chekhov's *The Three Sisters*.

The Arts Edvard Munch's *Girls on the Bridge* and *White Night*; Picasso's *The Old Woman*; and Maillol's sculpture *Seated Woman (La Méditerranée)*.

Music Richard Strauss's opera *Feuersnot* premieres in Dresden and Dvorak's opera *Rusalka* in Prague; Rachmaninoff's Piano Concerto No 2; the first of Edward Elgar's five Pomp and Circumstance Marches (*Land of Hope and Glory*); Ravel's *Jeux d'eau*. Scott Joplin's *The Easy Winners* is published as he and others make 'rags' a popular musical form.

Sports/Leisure England recognizes boxing as a legal sport under the Queensberry Rules (but in many US states and other countries boxing is still illegal).

Life/Customs The December issue of the *Ladies Home Journal* has the first advertisement for Christmas-tree lights, a nine-socket string set made by the Edison General Electric Company.

Miscellaneous In Russia the Socialist Revolutionary Party is founded as an alternative to Marxist Socialism; it stresses socialization of land and agriculture and a federal government, but the party will be pushed aside by the Bolsheviks. The Trans-Siberian Railroad reaches Port Arthur (Lu-shun) in China. In Detroit the first mass-produced gasoline-driven car, an Olds, appears in April; 433 are made by the end of 1901; 2500 in 1902; 5508 in 1904. The first models are sold at $650, making it the cheapest car at this time.

4 JANUARY 1902
International The French Panama Canal Company offers to sell its rights to build a canal to the US for $40 million; this will tip the balance away from those favoring a canal through Nicaragua.

8 JANUARY 1902
Ireland The United Irish League holds its convention in Dublin. There are now 1200 branches of this leading force for unification of all Ireland and its independence from Britain. The United Irish League will become increasingly active this year, particularly in calling for boycotts of those Irish who do not support its goals—for some Irish want either to remain linked to Britain or simply to be left alone.

10 JANUARY 1902
Germany Although it has professed neutrality in the Boer War, Germany is becoming annoyed at Britain's actions, especially Chamberlain's speech (of 25 October 1901), which Germans see as challenging their worldwide interests. In the Reichstag today, Chancellor von Bülow joins others in attacking British actions in South Africa.

18 JANUARY 1902
USA After three reports in recent years have favored the route through Nicaragua for a canal, the Isthmian Canal Commission concedes to pressures and issues a 'supplementary report' that recommends the route through Panama.

24 JANUARY 1902
International Denmark and the USA sign a treaty under which Denmark will sell the Danish West Indies to the USA for $5 million (these are the Virgin Islands—St Croix, St Thomas, and St John.) The US Senate will approve this, but the Danish assembly will reject the treaty on 16 May; the sale will be postponed till 1917.

30 JANUARY 1902
International Britain and Japan sign a treaty that they have been negotiating for many months. It commits each country to supporting an independent China and Korea, although it acknowledges Japan's 'special interest' in Korea. Each country is to consult the other before entering into agreements with other powers. Each will aid the other if attacked by two or more powers. Clearly it is a very delicate alliance, and its 'secret agenda' warns other powers not to interfere with British or Japanese imperial ambitions.

1 FEBRUARY 1902
International Secretary of State Hay protests granting Russia exclusive privileges in China, on ground that it runs contrary to the 'open door' policy granting all nations equal rights there.

FEBRUARY–MARCH 1902
Russia Student riots spread and are worst in St Petersburg. Police and troops suppress them, and on 25 March 567 students tried for rioting and 'political disaffection' will be judged guilty; most will be sentenced to short prison terms, but 95 will be banished to Siberia.

17–20 FEBRUARY 1902
Spain A general strike in Barcelona and nearby

towns leads to government-troop reprisals that leave 40 dead. Martial law is imposed in some areas, and the Spanish Senate suspends constitutional guarantees.

18 MARCH 1902
Turkey Turkey grants a German syndicate the first concession to construct a railroad through Turkish territory to Baghdad, to be linked to Berlin.

20 MARCH 1902
International France and Russia issue a joint declaration that approves of the Anglo-Japanese Alliance (of 30 January) but stipulates that they have the right to protect their interests in China and Korea.

8 APRIL 1902
International Russia and China sign the Convention of Evacuation, under which Russia agrees to evacuate Manchuria within 18 months. In fact, as the months pass, Russia presents new demands and within a year will have moved to consolidate its occupation of Mukden Province, in southern Manchuria. Japan is concerned with Russia's actions in this area.

8–18 APRIL 1902
Belgium There has been increasing unrest in Belgian society, as people demand better education, better work and living conditions, the right to strike, and universal male suffrage. The Socialists organize demonstrations on 8 April, especially in Brussels and Liège, and a general strike takes hold in several cities. In the rioting that ensues, many Belgians are killed, but the government does pass certain electoral reforms.

15 APRIL 1902
Russia Rioting and arson continue, and peasants are plundering estates to find food. Today the Russian minister of interior, Sipyengin, head of the secret police, is assassinated by the 'Terror Brigade' of the Socialist Revolutionaries. He is succeeded by Viacheslav Plehve, who will quickly become the most dreaded man in the government. Plehve moves quickly to put down the peasants, then tries to suppress every group that might have differences with the Czar's government.

29 APRIL 1902
USA Congress extends the Chinese Exclusion Act (of 1882), prohibiting immigration of Chinese laborers from territories to the mainland. It is clearly aimed at the Chinese presently in the Philippines.

10 MAY 1902
Portugal Portugal is bankrupt, but its parliament passes a bill converting its external debt. Contributing to Portugal's troubles is a recent revolt in its colony of Angola; it will not be put down until 6 September.

12 MAY 1902
USA Some 140,000 miners of anthracite coal (mostly in Pennsylvania) go out on a strike called by the United Mine Workers after the owners have refused even to recognize the UMW, let alone to negotiate or submit to arbitration. The strike will drag on through the summer, as the price of coal rises, until President Roosevelt threatens to have the army run the mines and the strike ends on 21 October.

20 MAY 1902
Cuba The United States withdraws its troops from Cuba as the first president, Tomas Estrada Palma, is installed.

22 MAY 1902
International President Roosevelt signs a treaty with Mexico under which both countries agree to submit a long-standing dispute over interest payments (the so-called Pious Fund) to the Court of Arbitration at The Hague. Roosevelt does this to show and encourage support for the Hague Tribunal. The decision in this first case will be handed down on 14 October, when the court decides in favor of the USA, calling for Mexico to pay her $1,420,682.

30 MAY 1902
Spain King Alfonso XII—who was installed as a constitutional monarch only on 17 May—suspends the Cortes, Spain's parliament; tomorrow, labor troubles and riots lead the king to impose martial law. Many Spaniards do not want hereditary rule.

31 MAY 1902
South Africa: Boer War The war is ended by the Treaty of Vereeniging. The Boers have surrendered unconditionally and must accept British sovereignty. The British have agreed to amnesty for the Boers, will pay £3 million to restock farms and offer loans for repatriation, will allow Boer representation in the government and use of their language in courts. British casualties include 5774 killed in action and some 16,000 dead from disease, with £223 million in costs. The Boers lost at least 4400 in action, plus 70,000 wounded. On 2 June General Kitchener will congratulate the Boers on their 'good fight' and welcome them as citizens of the British Empire.

JUNE–NOVEMBER 1902
Australia During its first session, Australia's new Parliament passes three acts that establish the 'White Australia' policy—that Australia would keep out (or at least keep down) non-European immigration. The most far-reaching, the Immigration Restriction Act, authorizes immigration officers to give written tests in English or any European language, an obvious ploy that gives the officers discretion to keep out almost all nonwhites. But this same Parliament will extend the right to vote in federal elections to adult women (at least native-born or British naturalized).

CALM BEFORE THE STORM 1900-1913

5 JUNE 1902
Germany Kaiser Wilhelm II responds to growing demands from Polish and other Slavic peoples living within German territory by calling for more 'Germanization' of the Slavs.

17 JUNE 1902
USA Congress passes the Newlands Reclamation Act, which establishes a fund from sale of public lands to build irrigation dams for arid Western lands. Behind it lies President Roosevelt's plan to retain vast tracts of public land, the basis of the federal park system.

28 JUNE 1902
International Germany, Italy, and the Austro-Hungarian Empire renew their Triple Alliance for six more years.
USA Congress passes the Spooner, or Isthmian Canal, Act, which authorizes the President to purchase the rights and property of the French Panama Canal Company and to enter into a treaty with Colombia, owner of the Panama territory. But Colombia resents the role of the French, and Roosevelt will become impatient with the negotiations with Colombia.

JULY–AUGUST 1902
France Much of France is in an uproar over the closing of 2500 Catholic schools, run by nuns and priests, for noncompliance with the Religious Associations Act (in effect since 1 July 1901). The Premier is forced to defend the government's actions against attacks by some of his own deputies as well as by the Roman Catholic hierarchy, and demonstrations are leading to arrests. On 9 August Lt Colonel de Saint Rémy will be arrested for refusing to help close a convent school because this conflicts with his own religious beliefs; he will be courtmartialed, sentenced to one day's imprisonment, and forced to retire.

1 JULY 1902
USA Congress passes the Philippine Government Act, providing that the Philippines be governed by a commission appointed by the President, with consent of the Senate. The inhabitants of the Philippines are to be treated as citizens of their land, not of the USA.

4 JULY 1902
Philippines Civil government is established by a proclamation from President Roosevelt, who offers a general amnesty to insurgents.

12 JULY 1902
Great Britain Arthur Balfour succeeds Lord Salisbury, who retired as Prime Minister on 11 July. Balfour is Salisbury's nephew and will prove an able public official.

17 JULY 1902
Australia Lord Tennyson, son of the poet, is named to succeed Lord Hopetoun, first governor-general of Australia.

24 JULY 1902
Turkey The Sultan Abdal-Hamid, under pressure from within the Ottoman Empire, appoints a commission to consider reforms that might pacify Macedonian revolutionaries. Many of the indigenous peoples in the large territory known as Macedonia will refuse to accept cosmetic reforms, and violence, assassinations, and kidnappings will continue.

9 AUGUST 1902
Great Britain The coronation of King Edward VII and Queen Alexandra takes place at Westminster Abbey.

SEPTEMBER 1902
Finland There has been unrest in Finland under Russian rule, especially since April, when Russian Cossacks brutally put down disturbances protesting the forced levy of Finnish youth for the army. By the end of this month, the Finnish Senate is under a Russian governor-general and restrictive laws are imposed. Many Finns begin to emigrate.

SEPTEMBER–DECEMBER 1902
Russia Hoping to stem the rising tide of unrest, the Czar pardons 120 dissidents sent to Siberia. This does not stop the labor protests, riots, clashes with troops, arrests, and deaths that are now part of daily life in Russia.

7 SEPTEMBER 1902
Australia The whole nation observes a 'day of humiliation' and prays for rain, as a terrible drought kills livestock and threatens crops. Rain begins to appear on 10 September.

17 SEPTEMBER 1902
International The US Government sends a note to Rumania protesting that country's harassment and persecution of Jews. Anti-Semitism is rife throughout Europe, and many Jews are emigrating to the New World.

10 OCTOBER 1902
Ireland Irish landowners—principally English aristocrats—meet in Dublin and consider a motion to sponsor a conference between their representatives and those of their Irish tenants, but this is rejected (77–14). Since the no-rent campaign began in 1901, incidents and evictions have increased.

13 OCTOBER 1902
USA President Roosevelt threatens to start using army troops to work coal mines struck since 12 May; this brings the owners to agree to abide by a Commission of Arbitration.

20 OCTOBER 1902
France The Chamber of Deputies appoints a com-

mittee to consider questions on the separation of Church and State in France. This is in response to continuing unrest over the Association Law, but in general the deputies support government policies in closing Catholic schools.

21 OCTOBER 1902
USA President Roosevelt declares that the coal miners' strike that began 12 May is over. The Commission appointed by the President on 16 October will release findings on 22 March 1903.

NOVEMBER 1902
Ireland The United Irish League's tactics are not supported by all Irish, however much they may wish for independence from the English; this month Ireland's Roman Catholic hierarchy breaks with League leaders: not unexpectedly, it prefers less violent confrontations.

1 NOVEMBER 1902
International France and Italy sign an Entente, under which Italy agrees to remain neutral if France is attacked. This is France's attempt to neutralize the Triple Entente.

8–20 NOVEMBER 1902
International Kaiser Wilhelm II of Germany visits England in an effort to improve relations between the countries (King Edward VII is his uncle). Like many Germans, the Kaiser both respects and resents Britain, and his visit does little to stop the rivalry that will eventually bring war.

18 NOVEMBER 1902
Life/Customs In the *Washington Evening Star*, a cartoon by Clifford Berryman shows President Theodore Roosevelt refusing to shoot a captive bear cub (allegedly inspired by a real incident.) A Brooklyn toymaker, Morris Mitchom, will claim that he was so taken by the cartoon that he made a bear of brown plush and displayed it with the cartoon as 'Teddy's Bear.' The German Steiff Company exports a similar toy to the US this year which is also said to be popularly known as a 'Teddy Bear.' (The name is not found in print until 1906.)

21 NOVEMBER 1902
Canada The government appoints a commission to consider revising, classifying, and consolidating the many public statutes passed in Canada over the years.

7–20 DECEMBER 1902
Venezuela Britain and Germany issue an ultimatum (7th) to Venezuela demanding that President Cipriano Castro pay claims for damages caused during his takeover of the government in 1899; when he fails to act, they isolate the Venezuelan fleet at Caracas (9th) and blockade the coast (10th); by the 13th, British and German ships begin to bombard the Venezuelan forts at Puerto Bello, so Castro asks

Sir Wilfred Laurier—Canadian Prime Minister.

President Roosevelt to arbitrate; by the 17th, Britain will agree to arbitration except over 'first rank' claims; by the 20th, Italy has joined Britain and Germany in the blockade, and Roosevelt is asked by all parties to arbitrate.

11 DECEMBER 1902
International The US signs a treaty with Cuba allowing for a 20 percent reduction on tariff rates on imported Cuban products. The Senate will consent on 19 March 1903, but the treaty will not be proclaimed until 17 December 1903.

18 DECEMBER 1902
Great Britain Parliament passes the Education Act, which will come to be regarded as the most important legislation of Balfour's government. It reforms the school systems of England and Wales, bringing secondary schools under committees of local authorities (broadened in their membership) and bringing church schools into the state's system. The Royal Commission on the South African War begins meetings in London; it has been established because of widespread charges of disorganization and inefficiency within the British military, particularly the army, which many people feel contributed to heavy British casualties during the Boer War. The findings of this commission will lead to the so-called Esher Committee (7 November 1903), which considers broad reorganization of Britain's War Office.

25 DECEMBER 1902
Papacy Pope Leo XIII, at his annual Christmas reception, endorses the Christian Democratic movement now emerging in Europe as an attempt to offer

CALM BEFORE THE STORM 1900-1913

an alternative to the Socialists, Communists, and other more radical groups that appeal to the many who have no share in the promises and potentials of modern society.

31 DECEMBER 1902
Austro-Hungarian Empire The *Ausgleich*, or Compromise, of 1867 is renewed in modified terms: this agreement gave the Magyars, or indigenous Hungarians, at least nominal power in a Kingdom of Hungary that was supposedly equal to Austria. In fact, Emperor Franz Joseph of Austria usually insists on imposing his will on the empire.

OTHER EVENTS OF 1902
Science Working at McGill University in Montreal, Ernest Rutherford and Frederick Soddy announce their theory of radioactivity (a process in which electrically charged particles, known as alpha and beta rays, break away from an element and leave atoms of a different element) and the 'half-life' rate of decay of radioactive elements. In Paris, Pierre and Marie Curie have now isolated a decigram of pure radium and determine its atomic weight and other properties. Oliver Heaviside, an English physicist, announces the existence of a layer in the upper atmosphere that asists the conduction of radio waves over long distances. Josiah Gibbs publishes his *Elementary Principles in Statistical Mechanics*, one of the works that makes his reputation as the father of modern physical chemistry.
Technology Huburt C Booth, an English engineer, issues a prospectus for the first true vacuum cleaner (which he was led to invent after observing cleaners in British railway coaches simply blowing the dirt around). And Willis Carrier, an American, invents the first scientific system for cooling and cleaning circulating air. Simon Lake, an American, invents a periscope for submarines. Canada begins to exchange wireless telegraph messages with England in December, the same month she is linked by cable to Australia and New Zealand.
Environment On 7 May Soufrière Volcano on St Vincent Island, British West Indies, erupts, killing over 1000 people, covering more than one-third of the island, and dispersing heavy ash on nearby Barbados. On 8 May Mt Pelée, on Martinique, French West Indies, erupts so suddenly that it destroys the city of Saint-Pierre and kills 38,000 people. (Among the few survivors is a prisoner buried in the local jail.) Captain Robert Scott's expedition in Antarctica fails to reach the South Pole; his ship gets locked into ice and it is 1904 before his party is rescued. In the Arctic, Lt Robert Peary also fails to reach the North Pole.
Ideas/Beliefs William James publishes *The Varieties of Religious Experience*.
Literature Henry James's *The Wings of the Dove*; Joseph Conrad's *The Heart of Darkness*; André Gide's *The Immoralist*; Rudyard Kipling's *Just-So Stories*; A Conan Doyle's *The Hound of the Baskervilles*; Owen Wister's *The Virginian*; and the Brazi-

Marie Curie.

lian classic by Euclydes da Cunha, *Revolt in the Backlands (Os Sertoes)*.
Drama/Entertainment Maxim Gorki's *The Lower Depths*, August Strindberg's *The Dream Play*, and J M Barrie's *The Admirable Crichton*. George Méliès directs his science-fantasy film *A Trip to the Moon*. In New York City, Alfred Stieglitz and other photographers found the Photo-Secession to promote photography as an art form.
The Arts Monet's *Waterloo Bridge*, Gaugin's *Riders by the Sea*, and Rodin's sculpture *Romeo and Juliet*.
Architecture In New York City, the Flatiron Building—an unusually shaped 20-story steel skyscraper designed by Daniel Burnham—is completed. And in Illinois, Frank Lloyd Wright finishes his first 'prairie-style' home, the Ward Willets house.
Music Debussy completes his opera *Pelléas and Melisande*; Mahler's Fourth Symphony; Sibelius's Symphony No 2; Schoenberg completes his *Gurrelieder* and Charles Ives his second symphony (which will not be performed till 1951).
Sports/Leisure The first US post-season college football game, the Tournament of Roses, is played in Pasadena, California; Michigan defeats Stanford, 49–0. President Theodore Roosevelt publishes his *Outdoor Pastimes of an American Hunter*, which will spark national interest in outdoor activities.
Miscellaneous Lev Bronstein, a radical Russian imprisoned in Siberia since 1898, escapes with a forged passport bearing the name of Trotsky; he will adopt this name and make his way to London to join a group of Russians working with Vladimir Ulyanov on a revolutionary newspaper; Ulyanov adopts the name of Lenin. In Washington, DC, the Carnegie Institution is founded with a $10 million gift from Andrew Carnegie; its goal is to study and

work for international peace. The will of Cecil Rhodes (died 26 March) establishes scholarships in his name at Oxford University, England, for young men from North America, Australia, and Germany.

1–9 JANUARY 1903
India At Delhi a great *durbar*, or formal reception, marks the coronation of King Edward VII as Emperor of India. Hundreds of Indian princes and notables attend, and the British release some 16,000 prisoners in honor of the occasion. Despite these outward displays of good feeling, Indians on the frontiers are in open revolt against the British, while many others question their right to rule the great subcontinent.

22 JANUARY 1903
International The Hay-Herran Treaty concerning the USA's rights to the Panama Canal is signed by the Colombian chargé d'affaires in Washington, DC. Provisions include a 100-year lease on a 10-mile-wide strip in Colombia's province of Panama; the price is $10 million and an annual rental of $250,000. The US Senate will consent to the treaty on 17 March, but it will be rejected by the Colombian Senate on 12 August: Colombians do not want to cede sovereignty over the proposed Canal Zone to the US.

11 FEBRUARY 1903
USA Congress adopts the Expedition Act, which authorizes the Attorney General to 'expedite' anti-trust cases through the courts; this reflects growing popular support for President Roosevelt's 'trust-busting' campaign.

13 FEBRUARY 1903
International In response to the blockade of its ports since December 1902, Venezuela signs a protocol of agreement with Great Britain, Germany, and Italy; President Roosevelt has assisted in the mediation and persuaded all parties to refer their claims to the Court of Arbitration at The Hague.

23 FEBRUARY 1903
International The US and Cuba sign an agreement by which Cuba releases Guantanamo and Bahia Honda to the US for naval stations. (Many decades later, these naval stations would figure in the conflict between the US and Cuban revolutionary Fidel Castro.)
Turkey The Sultan agrees to an Austro-Russian plan to reform the government of Macedonia in yet another effort to stifle the rising disorder among the rival Bulgarian, Serbian, and Greek populations there. The new plan calls for a reorganization of Macedonia's finance system and the formation of a gendarmerie to be composed of Moslems and Christians proportionate to the population at large.

5 MARCH 1903
International The Germans and the Turks agree on a revised Baghdad Railway Convention (superseding that of March 1902); construction of the Turkish link is due to begin in July.

15 MARCH 1903
Nigeria After years of fighting between the British and the rebellious Africans, the British claim supremacy over 500,000 square miles, thus controlling all northern Nigeria.

18 MARCH 1903
France Following through on its attacks on Roman Catholic institutions, the French Government dissolves the Catholic religious orders.

22 MARCH 1903
USA The Anthracite Coal Commission, set up by President Roosevelt on 16 October 1902, submits its recommendations for shorter hours, a 10-percent wage increase, and an 'open shop.' Considering that mine owners have refused even to recognize the United Mine Workers as representing the workers, this at least constitutes a step forward for the union.

APRIL 1903
International Germany, having obtained the concession to build the railroad to Baghdad, has been trying to get Britain and France to cooperate in financing this project, but a press campaign in those countries culminates this month in their governments' refusal to support the Germans.

6–13 APRIL 1903
Holland Railroad and dock workers go out on strike, but the government passes anti-strike bills, calls out the troops, and promptly ends the strikes. This will incite union and socialist movements among Dutch workers.

1–4 MAY 1903
International King Edward VII of Great Britain visits Paris, where he is feted in a first step toward improving Anglo-French relations—and worsening Anglo-German relations. The culmination will come with the signing of the *Entente Cordiale* (8 April 1904).

15 MAY 1903
International In what is clearly a warning to Russia, Lord Lansdowne, the Conservative foreign secretary, states that Britain would 'regard the establishment of a naval base or fortified port in the Persian Gulf as a very grave menace . . . and would resist it by all means at her disposal.'

20 MAY 1903
International Britain's House of Commons begins a debate on the charges of poor administration and ill treatment of natives in Belgium's colony in the Congo Free State; Britain has become involved because of a report by her consul, Roger Casement, charging atrocities, and because Britain wants to

CALM BEFORE THE STORM 1900-1913

appear as standing for 'civilized' treatment of colonial peoples. On 19 August Britain will send a note to Belgium protesting conditions in the Congo; on 19 September King Leopold will deny charges of cruelty to the natives and reject interference by foreign powers, but in February 1905 he will have been pressured to send a commission of inquiry to the Congo.

10–11 JUNE 1903
Yugoslavia In Belgrade, a military coup d'etat—led by the Queen's brother-in-law and other officers—kills King Alexander I of Serbia, Queen Draga, and many officers.

15 JUNE 1903
Yugoslavia The Serbian Assembly meets and elects Prince Peter Karageorgevitch king. He asserts that he 'will be faithful to the traditions of his ancestors and that all that has passed will be buried in oblivion.' On 17 June the more liberal constitution of 1889 will be restored, and on 25 June Peter will take the oath as king under this constitution and move to establish the new policies.

6–9 JULY 1903
International President Emile Loubet of France and Minister of Foreign Affairs Theophile Delcassé visit London, furthering the cause of the *Entente Cordiale* between Britain and France.

20 JULY 1903
Papacy Giuseppe Sarto is elected Pope Pius X. Known as the 'pope of the poor and humble,' Pius X is opposed to modernists in the Church who would reform dogmas and policies.

17 JULY–23 AUGUST 1903
Russia The Social Democratic Workers Party meets, first in Brussels and then in London because its leaders have been forced into exile by the Russian government. Founded in 1898 by Marxists, this party will develop into the Communist Party of the Soviet Union; but already, at this 1903 meeting, it is splitting into factions: the Mensheviks, led by Plekhanov, advocate a gradualist revolution, while the Bolsheviks, led by Lenin, advocate a thorough and immediate revolution. After the Bolshevik Revolution of October 1917, the Mensheviks will be suppressed.

12 AUGUST 1903
International The Japanese Minister to Russia, under instructions from his government, presents a note to the Russian Government protesting its failure to evacuate Manchuria (as Russia had agreed to do) but suggesting that Japan will allow Russia some role in Manchuria if she will give Japan a free hand in Korea.

29 AUGUST 1903
Russia The Finance Minister, Count Witte, is dismissed in what is seen as a victory for those in Russia who want their country to expand into Manchuria and Korea in defiance of the Japanese.

16 SEPTEMBER 1903
Austro-Hungarian Empire The dispute between the Magyars of Hungary and Emperor Franz Joseph has long been smoldering, one point of friction being the Emperor's insistence that Hungarians serve in the Imperial Army and speak German. Today the Emperor declares that this policy of a 'unified' Imperial Army will be maintained; despite his proclaimed 'conciliation,' the Hungarian Magyars remain bitterly opposed.

18 SEPTEMBER 1903
Great Britain Joseph Chamberlain, Secretary for Colonial Affairs in Balfour's Cabinet, has openly sided with the Tariff Reform League in calling for major tariff changes to give Britain advantages in trading with her colonies and with foreign nations. Prime Minister Balfour rejects this, so Chamberlain resigns today from the Cabinet.

24 SEPTEMBER 1903
Australia Following the resignation of Edmund Barton to become a justice of the High Court, Alfred Deakin becomes the second Prime Minister of Australia. Like Barton, Deakin is a liberal protectionist, and he will remain Prime Minister for most of the next seven years.

1–3 OCTOBER 1903
Turkey A new program for reforms in Macedonia—to replace those of 23 February—is approved at Muerzstag, Austria, by the Austrians, Russians, and other powers interested in the question. This new agreement forces Turkey to allow foreigners to supervise Macedonia's government, to accept a foreign general as head of the gendarmerie, and to give Christians more power. The Porte, the Ottoman Turkish Government, will reject this program at first, but by 25 November it will have been pressured into accepting it.

3 OCTOBER 1903
International Responding to Japanese proposals of 12 August, the Russian Government submits counterproposals; this instigates weeks of negotiations that will go on into January 1904. The sticking point is Russia's insistence on a free hand in Manchuria, and this will end negotiations—and cause war.

20 OCTOBER 1903
International The Joint Commission set up on 24 January by Great Britain and the United States to arbitrate the disputed Alaskan boundary rules in favor of the US; the deciding vote is Britain's, which embitters Canada. The US gains ports on the Panhandle coast of Alaska.

30 OCTOBER 1903
International In violation of their promise to

evacuate Manchuria, the Russians reoccupy Mukden and reinforce their troops in Manchuria. Besides offending the Chinese, this convinces the Japanese that the Russians threaten their interests in Korea.

2 NOVEMBER 1903
International President Roosevelt orders three ships of the US Navy, which he has sent into the sea off the Isthmus of Panama, to maintain 'free and uninterrupted transit' across the Isthmus: in fact, he is ordering the US Navy to prevent Colombia from landing troops on its own province of Panama to put down the imminent uprising instigated by a triumvirate of Panamanian businessmen and French agents of the Panama Canal Company.

3 NOVEMBER 1903
International The expected uprising of the Panamanians occurs about six o'clock in the evening, without bloodshed; the new government organizes itself during the night, with the local fire department becoming the army. The lobbyist for the French canal company, Philippe Buneau-Varilla, is made Panamanian minister to Washington. Presence of the USS *Nashville* prevents Colombians from reaching Panama City.

Italy Giovanni Giolitti becomes Premier of Italy; a progressive liberal, he will hold this post through most of the next decade and introduce social, agrarian, and labor reforms.

4 NOVEMBER 1903
International Panama and Colombia wake up to news that insurrectionists have declared an independent Republic of Panama.

6 NOVEMBER 1903
International At 11:35 AM, President Roosevelt is notified by the US consul in Panama that the independent Republic exists; by 12:51 that afternoon, Secretary of State Hay instructs the consul to declare *de facto* recognition—the quickest recognition ever granted to a new government by the USA.

7 NOVEMBER 1903
Great Britain As a result of strong criticisms made by the Royal Commission on the British Army's conduct of the Boer War, a three-man committee headed by Lord Esher is charged with reorganization of the War Office and British forces.

17 NOVEMBER 1903
International In the Treaty of Petropolis, Bolivia cedes the territory of Arce to Brazil; Bolivia gains rail and water outlets to the east.

18 NOVEMBER 1903
International The United States and the new Republic of Panama sign the Hay-Buneau-Varilla Treaty—over the protests of Colombia—giving the US permanent rights to a 10-mile strip in return for $10,000,000 and an annual fee of $250,000 after nine years. The

THE IRISH PROBLEM

Some problems seem to be resolved in the course of a century or two, while others, like the Irish Problem, go on and on. The struggle between England and Ireland really began in the 12th century, but its contemporary outbreak started in the late 19th century—when William Gladstone, British Prime Minister, introduced bills (1886 and 1893) to give Home Rule to Ireland. This served only to define the true obstacle to an independent Ireland: the six counties in the north, or Ulster, whose inhabitants were largely Protestant and of Scottish or English descent. These Ulster 'Orangemen' were not about to give up their ties to Britain and be overruled by the Catholic majority of a united Ireland. A Home Rule Bill was, in fact, passed by Parliament in 1914, but World War I became an excuse for suspending it; efforts to enforce it would probably have brought on outright civil war in any case. Instead, the violence that followed the Easter Rebellion of 1916 and the guerrilla warfare that ensued led only to a compromise that seemed to settle the issue: there would be a Catholic Irish Free State, but there would also be a Protestant Northern Ireland. The compromise seemed to work until the late 1960s, when the Catholic minority in Northern Ireland began to protest against second-class status. Those with a knowledge of history experienced a sense of *déja vu*: the names had changed, but the characters and conflicts, the false hopes and irresolvable dilemmas, the bitter prejudices and passions—all remain to this day.

A British Army patrol near Armagh, Northern Ireland.

independence of Panama is also guaranteed, and the US will be allowed to occupy and control the strip as well as construct a canal there.

17 DECEMBER 1903
Technology Near Kitty Hawk, North Carolina, Orville and Wilbur Wright from Ohio make the first

CALM BEFORE THE STORM 1900-1913

four sustained flights in powered heavier-than-air planes. Orville makes the first, flying 120 feet in 12 seconds; Wilbur flies the longest, 852 feet in 59 seconds. The plane weighs 745 lb; its 179-lb 4-cylinder engine develops 12 horsepower.

29 DECEMBER 1903
French Equatorial Africa   The French have acquired a vast territory since 1840; today, by decree, they divide their French Congo into four autonomous districts: Gabon, Chad, Ubangi-Shari, and Middle Congo.

OTHER EVENTS OF 1903
Science   Ivan Pavlov, a Russian physiologist investigating digestive glands and salivary secretions, makes his first statement about 'conditional reflexes': adaptive physical actions that can be stimulated by conditioning or controlled by learning. His experiments with dogs that salivate at the sound of a bell will go on over several years and provide the objective basis for research as well as explanations for behavior. Walter Sutton, an American researcher, publishes proof that chromosomes carry genes of heredity.

Medicine/Health   Willem Einthoven, a Dutch physiologist, develops the electrocardiograph, an instrument for measuring the heart's electrical activity; it will be 1930 before modern methods of electrocardiography are developed, primarily by Frank Wilson, an American physician.

Technology   Poulsen, a Danish electrical engineer, invents a device to generate continuous radio waves, crucial for radio communication. A cable is completed between San Francisco and Manila, and President Theodore Roosevelt sends the first message.

Social Sciences   Frederick W Taylor publishes an article titled 'Shop Management' and founds modern scientific management (called for some time 'Taylorization').

Ideas/Beliefs   George Moore publishes his *Principia Ethica* and Henri Poincaré publishes his *Science and Hypothesis*. Two other influential books of this year are W E B DuBois's *The Souls of Black Folk* and Helen Keller's *The Story of My Life*.

Literature   Samuel Butler's *The Way of All Flesh* (posthumous); Joseph Conrad's *Typhoon*; Frank Norris's *The Pit*; Henry James's *The Ambassadors*; Jack London's *The Call of the Wild*.

Drama/Entertainment   George Bernard Shaw's *Man and Superman* and Hugo von Hofmannsthal's *Electra*. The first 'long' motion picture with an original story is produced by the Edison Company in New Jersey: *The Great Train Robbery*. (Previous films were even shorter, often depicting single situations.) Max Aronson (Anderson) plays the lead. He will make more movies than any other actor and become the world's first male 'movie star.' And the first theater devoted exclusively to motion pictures opens in Tokyo.

The Arts   Käthe Kollwitz, a German artist, begins *The Peasant War*, a series of revolutionary etchings.

And Picasso paints *The Old Guitarist*, one of his celebrated 'Blue Period' works.

Architecture   Construction of Giles Gilbert Scott's Liverpool Cathedral begins.

Music   Bruckner's Symphony No 9, premiered posthumously in Vienna; Eugene D'Albert's opera *Tiefland*; Frederick Delius's *Sea Drift*. The first complete opera is recorded on phonograph discs in Milan (by Gramaphone Company of London): Leoncavallo's *Pagliacci*. And Enrico Caruso, who began recording in 1902, records *Vesti la giubba*, the first serious record to sell over 1,000,000 copies.

Sports/Leisure   The first Tour de France bicycle race is held; it will remain the premier long-distance race. In the USA, the National, American, and several minor leagues join to form 'Organized Baseball' and set up a ruling body; the first post-season series is then played, with the American League's Boston Red Sox defeating the Pittsburgh Pirates five games to three.

Miscellaneous   British suffragist Emmeline Pankhurst founds the Women's Social and Political Union to advance the rights of women. Henry Ford founds the Ford Motor Company with $100,000, while the Krupp Works are founded in Essen, Germany. In Boston, King C Gillette begins manufacturing the first safety razor with disposable blades. In Chicago, on 30 December, the Iroquois Theatre burns (during a show by Eddie Foy, a popular comedian) and 602 people lose their lives (the third most costly fire in US history in terms of human life): this will lead to stricter codes for theater safety.

4 JANUARY 1904
USA   In *Gonzales v Williams*, the Supreme Court rules that Puerto Ricans are not aliens and may not be refused admission into the continental US. Not until 1917 will citizenship privileges be extended.

11 JANUARY 1904
Southwest Africa   The Herrero people begin an uprising against the Germans who control their land; it will spread, and in October 1904 the Hottentots will also join in. Before the uprising is suppressed in 1908, thousands of African and German lives will be lost.

29 JANUARY 1904
Great Britain   The three-man Esher Committee (appointed 7 November 1903), which has considered ways to improve the British military, submits its preliminary plan. Among recommendations is an Army Council to supervise reorganization of the entire army and a Defence Committee, under chairmanship of the prime minister, to supervise broader policies of the military. (This latter will become known as the Committee of Imperial Defence.)

6 FEBRUARY 1904
International   Japan notifies the Russians that in view of Russia's delaying tactics and provocative military activities, Japan is ending negotiations and recalling its minister from Moscow.

8 FEBRUARY 1904

Russo-Japanese War Without warning, Japanese torpedo boats make a night attack on Russian ships near the naval base at Port Arthur, Manchuria. Russian losses are light, but confusion reigns because there has been no declaration of war.

9 FEBRUARY 1904

Russo-Japanese War   Japanese land troops at Chemulpo (Inchon), near Seoul, Korea; within the next three weeks they will have advanced to the Yalu River, the border of Manchuria.

10 FEBRUARY 1904

Russo-Japanese War   Japan and Russia declare war.

22 FEBRUARY 1904

International   The Hague Tribunal gives its decision in claims against Venezuela (referred to it on 13 February 1903): it sets the sums to be paid by Venezuela and gives preferential treatment to the three powers that initiated the blockade—Britain, Germany, and Italy.

23 FEBRUARY 1904

International   Having occupied Korea, Japan signs a treaty with Korea under which it becomes a Japanese protectorate in return for Japan's help in safeguarding it against other powers. Korea is forced to annul recent concessions to Russia.

29 FEBRUARY 1904

International   President Roosevelt appoints a seven-man Panama Canal Commission to proceed with completing a canal at the Isthmus.

6 MARCH 1904

Russo-Japanese War   The Japanese fleet bombards Vladivostok, the major Russian port on the Pacific.

14 MARCH 1904

USA   In a landmark case, *Northern Securities Company v United States*, the Supreme Court finds that the company has violated the Sherman Anti-Trust Act. This is the first case that Roosevelt has undertaken in his campaign to bring Big Business within the restraint of law, and it will enhance his image as a 'trustbuster.'

28 MARCH 1904

Russo-Japanese War   Japanese troops advance in Korea, defeat the Russians at Chengju, and capture the town.

8 APRIL 1904

International   Great Britain and France establish their *Entente Cordiale*, toward which they have been working since July 1903. In the most literal sense, it is a technical treaty settling long-standing disagreements over Morocco, Egypt, Africa, and the Pacific; beyond that, France recognizes Britain's priorities in Egypt in return for Britain's guaranteeing free access to the Suez Canal—while secret articles allow for the end of Moroccan independence and its division between France and Spain. Perhaps the most significant aspect of this *entente* is that Britain and France,

Defending Port Arthur from a Japanese attack during the Russo-Japanese War.

CALM BEFORE THE STORM 1900-1913

traditional enemies, are moving together—and away from Germany.

13 APRIL 1904
Russo-Japanese War A squadron of the Russian fleet is decoyed out of Port Arthur by Japanese maneuvers; when they realize they are sailing into a trap, the Russians turn back, but their battleship *Petropavlovsk* hits a mine and sinks, with a loss of 700 men, including the Russian Admiral Makarov.

24–30 APRIL 1904
International President Loubet of France visits King Victor Emmanuel III of Italy and pointedly ignores the Pope, exacerbating relations between the French government and the Roman Catholic Church.

26 APRIL 1904
Australia John C Watson leads the first Labour government of Australia, when Alfred Deakin resigns, but Watson himself will resign in August.

26 APRIL–1 MAY 1904
Russo-Japanese War General Kuroki leads the Japanese Army against a large Russian force at the Yalu River, pursues them along the river, and surrounds the Russians, who suffer heavy losses (1370 killed).

MAY 1904
Russo-Japanese War This month, the Japanese land troops along the south coast of Manchuria; by the 30th they have captured the city of Dairen.

18 MAY 1904
International In Morocco, a brigand, Raizuli, kidnaps Ion H Perdicaris, an American citizen; attempts to free him fail until late June when, at the Republican Party's Convention, US Secretary of State John Hay announces the dispatch of a cable to Morocco: WE WANT PERDICARIS ALIVE OR RAIZULI DEAD. Perdicaris is freed—enhancing the Republicans' image and approach to foreign affairs.

21 MAY 1904
International In yet another of the incidents driving France and the Catholic Church apart, France recalls its ambassador to the Vatican—this to protest the Pope's attempt to discipline two French bishops.

25–26 MAY 1904
Russo-Japanese War In two days of bitter fighting, the Japanese Army soundly defeats the Russians at Kinchan and captures the forts at Nanshan. The Japanese suffer heavy casualties, but they have now cut off Port Arthur from the land. General Nogi stays with the Third Army to place the port under siege, while the main Japanese forces proceed northward against Russian forces led by General Kuropatkin.

14–15 JUNE 1904
Russo-Japanese War At the battle of Telissu (or

Adjutant General Alexei Kuropatkin.

Wafangkau), the Japanese rout the Russians and inflict heavy casualties.

21 JUNE 1904
USA The Republican Party, in its convention at Chicago, nominates Theodore Roosevelt for President, but not without opposition from those he calls 'malefactors of great wealth.'

6 JULY 1904
Russo-Japanese War Two Russian cruisers move into the Red Sea and begin to stop ships of Britain, Germany, and other nations they believe friendly to Japan; this will be protested by the British Government, and on 3 September the Czar will order Russian ships to desist.
USA The Democratic Party, meeting in St Louis, nominates the little-known New York judge Alton B Parker for President—virtually assuring the election of Roosevelt.

28 JULY 1904
Colombia After losing Panama, Rafael Reyes becomes dictator; his first actions try to put the country's finances in order.
Russia Interior Minister Viacheslav Plehve is assassinated; as leader of the most reactionary elements of the government, he has been hated for his repressive policies. Other assassinations have accompanied the crop failures and industrial depression that are plaguing Russia.

11 AUGUST 1904
Russo-Japanese War The Russian fleet in the harbor at Port Arthur is now exposed to Japanese guns on the hills above the harbor; Russian ships try to escape, several get out to sea, but most are forced back into harbor by the Japanese.

17 AUGUST 1904
Australia George H Reid succeeds John Watson as Prime Minister; holding office less than a year, and regarded by many as an opportunist, Reid and his government still manage to pass an important piece of legislation, the Conciliation and Arbitration Bill, establishing a court with powers to deal with interstate industrial disputes.

24 AUGUST–4 SEPTEMBER 1904
Russo-Japanese War In a series of engagements over several days, in what is known as the Battle of Liaoyang (from the town at the center of the action), 200,000 Japanese troops wear down 150,000 Russian troops; although the Japanese suffer heavier casualties (18,000 men to the Russians' 16,000), the Russians are forced to retreat to Mukden.

7 SEPTEMBER 1904
International A British expedition, led by Sir Francis Younghusband, had set out from India for Tibet in July 1903; after defeating Tibetan forces in several engagements, they have made their way to the sacred capital, Lhasa, by August 1904. Today, the British force the Dalai Lhama to sign a treaty that grants Britain trading posts in Tibet and guarantees that Tibet will not concede territory to foreign powers. This is Britain's way of taking advantage of Russia's preoccupation with the war against Japan, for Russia is known to have had ambitions in Tibet.

21 SEPTEMBER 1904
Italy A general strike, called by the Socialist Party and supported by dissatisfied elements, has spread throughout Italy; there have been incidents of violence, especially in Milan, and three miners were killed by troops. A reaction has set in because of the violence, and by today the strike ends.

26 SEPTEMBER 1904
Canada Earl Grey is appointed Governor-General (he will serve till 1911).

2–15 OCTOBER 1904
Russo-Japanese War The battle of Shaho is fought about 15 miles south of Mukden, and after initial success the Russians are driven back; both sides suffer casualties, the Japanese admitting to 16,000 and the Russians' estimated as high as 60,000.

OCTOBER 1904
Russo-Japanese War The Russian Baltic Squadron, led by Admiral Rozhdestvensky, leaves Russia, having been delayed for eight months to wait for four new battleships. Before arriving off Korea in May

1905, this fleet will have made an epic voyage, for many crewmen are untrained and the ships have to be coaled every 10 days.

3 OCTOBER 1904
International The French and the Spanish sign a treaty that ostensibly guarantees the independence of Morocco, but secret clauses anticipate Morocco's division between these powers.

20 OCTOBER 1904
International Bolivia and Chile sign a treaty ending the War of the Pacific; it recognizes Chile's possession of the coast, but provides for construction of a railway to link La Paz, Bolivia, to Arica on the coast.

21–28 OCTOBER 1904
International The Russian Baltic Squadron, en route to the Pacific, fires on British fishing trawlers at Dogger Bank, in the North Sea; the British are outraged but the government urges calm; by the 28th Czar Nicholas II agrees to refer the question of compensation to the Hague Tribunal. (It will find Russia guilty on 25 February 1905 and order her to compensate the British.) As it happens, on the 21st President Roosevelt also called for a second peace conference at The Hague in hope of ending the Russo-Japanese War.

25 OCTOBER 1904
Russo-Japanese War The Japanese begin a heavy bombardment of the Russian-held forts at Port Arthur, under siege since June.

27 OCTOBER–23 NOVEMBER 1904
International The Germans and the Russians engage in negotiations over a mutual defense treaty, both nations seeking to exploit their tensions with Britain; when Russia insists on consulting France, negotiations end.

8 NOVEMBER 1904
USA Theodore Roosevelt and his running mate Charles W Fairbanks defeat the Democrats by 2,500,000 votes (the electoral college vote is 336 to 140). On election night, Roosevelt declares: 'Under no circumstances . . . will I be a candidate for President in 1908.' He will come to regret this remark, for it weakens his control over Congress during his next term.

NOVEMBER 1904
Russia Representatives of 32 of the country's 34 *zemstvos*, or community councils, hold a congress in St Petersburg and demand a republican-style constitution and civil liberties. The Czar will respond on 26 December with a decree favoring mild reforms, but he rejects the idea of a constitutional assembly. The road to revolution has opened.

6 DECEMBER 1904
USA In his annual message to Congress, President

CALM BEFORE THE STORM 1900-1913

THEODORE ROOSEVELT, 1858–1919

The 26th president of the United States, Theodore Roosevelt, was born to a prominent family in New York City and studied at Harvard University. In 1884 he headed the New York legislature and the following year became president of the New York police board. He resigned as assistant secretary of the navy to lead Roosevelt's Roughriders in the Spanish-American War (1898) and returned to the governorship of New York State (1898–1901). Nominated by the Republicans for vice-president in 1900, he assumed the presidency the next year when William McKinley was assassinated. Elected in his own right in 1904, he worked for a strong navy, civil service reform, conservation and regulation of trusts. In the 1912 elections the Republican Party split, Roosevelt supporters forming the Progressive Party, which lost to Woodrow Wilson. In 1913 Roosevelt published his *Autobiography*, embodying his love of the outdoors, an early awareness of conservation needs, and his commitment to traditional American ideals. He worked vigorously for US entry into World War I and died soon after hostilities ended.

Roosevelt articulates what comes to be known as 'the Roosevelt Corollary' (to the Monroe Doctrine of 1823). Roosevelt asserts that because the USA, under the Monroe Doctrine, has forbidden foreign interference in the Western Hemisphere, the USA has responsibility to insist on redress for wrongs inflicted upon a foreign state by any country within the Western Hemisphere. Roosevelt is saying that the US reserves the right to intervene in Latin American nations when it decides to. The 'Corollary' will be invoked within a few weeks (in the matter of the Dominican Republic's debts).

OTHER EVENTS OF 1904

Medicine/Health Colonel William Gorgas goes to the Isthmus of Panama to work against yellow fever so that work on the canal can proceed. In New York City, the Rockefeller Institute for Medical Research opens.

Technology Mt Wilson Observatory, near Pasadena, California, is founded by George E Hale.

Social Sciences Sigmund Freud publishes *The Psychopathology of Everyday Life* and Max Weber publishes *The Protestant Ethic and the Spirit of Capitalism.*

Literature Joseph Conrad's *Nostromo*; W H Hudson's *Green Mansions*; the first volume of Romain Rolland's *Jean-Christophe* (the tenth will appear in 1912); Henry James's *The Golden Bowl*; Hermann Hesse's *Peter Camenzind*; Jack London's *Sea-Wolf.*

Drama/Entertainment Chekhov's *The Cherry Orchard*; J M Synge's *Riders to the Sea*; Frank Wedekind's *Pandora's Box*; J M Barrie's *Peter Pan*; W B Yeats's *On Baile's Strand.* In Dublin, the Abbey Theatre is first used by the Irish National Theatre Society. In New York, George M Cohan's musical *Little Johnny Jones* has two hit songs, 'Give My Regards to Broadway' and 'The Yankee Doodle Boy.'

The Arts Picasso's *The Two Sisters*, Henri Rousseau's *The Wedding*, and Cezanne's *Mont Sainte Victoire.* Max Beerbohm publishes *The Poet's Corner*, drawings of English authors.

Architecture In Chicago, Louis Sullivan completes the Schlesinger & Mayer Department Store (later better known as the Carson, Pirie, Scott Building).

Music Puccini's *Madame Butterfly* premieres in Milan; Leon Janacek's opera *Jenufa* premieres in Brno; Mahler's Fifth Symphony.

Sports/Leisure The first Olympic games are held in the USA—at St Louis, as part of the Exposition. Cy Young of the Boston Red Sox pitches the first 'perfect game' in modern baseball, never allowing a Philadelphia player to reach first.

Life/Customs France establishes the 10-hour work day and a Conference on White Slave Trade is held in Paris—both signs of a growing social conscience. A New York City policeman arrests a woman for smoking a cigarette in public. Helen Keller graduates from Radcliffe College with honors despite her multiple handicaps. And the first true daily comic strip appears in the *Chicago American*: 'A Piker Clerk,' by Clare Briggs; it deals with betting on sports, and because William Randolph Hearst considers it vulgar it is dropped after two weeks. But on 15 November 1907, 'Mr A Mutt' by Bud Fisher appears on the sports page of the *San Francisco Chronicle*; he will be joined by Jeff on 29 March 1908, and they are still going strong.

Miscellaneous Baltimore experiences a terrible fire, the second worst in the US (in terms of property damage) after Chicago's. The *Norge* is wrecked on

Rockall Reef off Scotland and 651 lives lost. The worst ship disaster in US history occurs on 15 June on the Hudson River, where the SS *General Slocum*, returning from a day excursion, catches fire; 1030 lives are lost, including many women and children. The Rolls-Royce Company is founded in England.

2 JANUARY 1905
Russo-Japanese War Port Arthur has been cut off by sea since 8 February 1904 and by land since early June 1904; today Russian forces surrender to the Japanese commanded by General Nogi, who receives the forts, ships, arms, and other property. Russian officers are allowed to leave for Russia but soldiers are taken prisoner. Although the Russians had blown up the forts and many of their ships, it is still a major loss: when word reaches the Russian people, it will have a devastating effect on national morale.

20 JANUARY 1905
International The so-called Roosevelt Corollary (to the Monroe Doctrine) is tested when the United States begins supervision of the Dominican Republic's national and international debts. Although the US Senate withholds approval, Roosevelt makes an agreement with the Dominican Government.

22 JANUARY 1905
Russia In St Petersburg, a large demonstration of workers, led by Father Gapon, marches to the Winter Palace with the intention of presenting a petition to the Czar. As they approach the palace, troops fire on them and Cossacks charge; 70 are killed and 240 wounded in what comes to be known as 'Bloody Sunday.' As reports of this event spread to other parts of Russia, there are new demonstrations and strikes, but the government's troops suppress them ruthlessly.

29 JANUARY 1905
Russia Czar Nicholas II, unsettled by the rising violence, sanctions several proposals for reforming the criminal code, establishing workingmen's insurance, and improving conditions of workers. These minor changes will do little to stop disorders throughout Russia during ensuing months.

1 FEBRUARY 1905
Austro-Hungarian Empire Count Stephan Tisza, Prime Minister of Hungary since October 1903, resigns following results of elections at the end of January. Tisza and his Liberal Party had tried to take a more conciliatory course with Emperor Franz Joseph; the new coalition government, headed by Francis Kossuth, son of the Hungarian patriot Louis Kossuth, will now try to force the Austrians to agree to accept Hungarian as the language of the Hungarian branch of the Imperial Army, precipitating a crisis within the Empire.

21 FEBRUARY–10 MARCH 1905
Russo-Japanese War The Japanese defeat the Rus-

sians in a long battle at Mukden, the large Manchurian city that is Russia's last major outpost. The Japanese have now extended their land forces to the limit, and the Russians might have been able to turn the tide with large reserves except for unrest at home.

3 MARCH 1905
Russia Czar Nicholas II agrees to convoke a 'consultative assembly' and concedes other points including an edict of religious toleration, relief for the Jews, the right to speak Polish in Polish schools, and cancellation of certain debts.

12 MARCH 1905
Italy The continuing strikes and disorders that unsettle Italy force out Premier Giovanni Giolitti. (He has held his post since 3 November 1903 and will return on 29 May 1906.)

24 MARCH 1904
Crete A group of Cretans dedicated to Crete's union with Greece, led by Eleutherios Venizelos. meet at the village of Therisso and proclaim a union in defiance of the Great Powers (who want Crete to remain quiescent within the Ottoman Empire). During the ensuing weeks, several hundred supporters of Venizelos will create disturbances on Crete but the mass of islanders will not join any uprising.

31 MARCH 1905
International Kaiser Wilhelm II of Germany visits Tangier, Morocco, and proclaims Germany's support of Moroccan independence and equal opportunity for all powers to trade there. This is a challenge to France, whose emissary St Rene Taillander has sought to convince the Sultan of Morocco to countenance 'reforms' that would make Morocco a virtual protectorate of France. The Kaiser has been encouraged to make this speech by Chancellor von Bülow; it is only one of several German moves to challenge France, Britain, and other powers in an effort to gain a 'place in the sun.'

6 APRIL 1905
International The Germans' scheme has worked, and today they accept an invitation from the Sultan of Morocco to an international conference to discuss matters relating to Morocco. This will inflame the French, who feel that Morocco is their preserve.

21 APRIL 1905
Crete The elective assembly of Crete proclaims union with Greece, following the lead of the Venizelos forces. There are clashes between active insurrectionists and forces of the Great Powers, resulting even in several deaths, but Prince George, the High Commissioner, and the consuls of the Great Powers will work to keep the insurrection from taking hold among the mass of Cretans.

25 APRIL 1905
South Africa The former Boer colony of the Trans-

CALM BEFORE THE STORM 1900-1913

vaal is granted a new constitution by the British, but Boers condemn it as not giving them enough say in their government. Among those leading the resistance is the Het Volk Party, organized in January by the former Boer War commander Louis Botha.

1–5 MAY 1905
International Trying to placate the Germans in the crisis over Morocco, Prime Minister Rouvier of France says that the Germans would have their own port there. The Germans insist on going ahead with the conference suggested by the Sultan.

8 MAY 1905
Russia The Union of Unions organizes under the chairmanship of Paul Miliukov. This joins liberal groups who demand parliamentary government and universal suffrage.

27–28 MAY 1905
Russo-Japanese War The Russians' Baltic Squadron, underway since October 1904, has arrived too late to help the Russian fleet in Port Arthur, so it is ordered north to Vladivostok. As the Russians (including eight battleships, eight cruisers, and four coast-defense ships) move into Tsushima Strait between Japan and Korea, the Japanese fleet draws up in a line—four battleships and eight armored cruisers. Admiral Togo commands the Japanese, Admiral Rozhdestvensky the Russians. In the initial exchange of fire, many Russian shells do not explode, and the Japanese gain the initiative. During the day, fog sets in, but the Russians plow northward; in each encounter they lose more ships. During the night, the Japanese send in torpedo boats to finish the job. By morning, Russia has lost six battleships, including its flagship, four cruisers and several other vessels. Admiral Nebogatov, second in command, surrenders: only three small ships get to Vladivostok. It is a crushing defeat and will serve to awaken the world to the strength of Japan.

JUNE–AUGUST 1904
Russia There is virtual chaos in Russia during these summer weeks—strikes among workers, unrest among farmers, uprisings among the national groups in the border provinces, mutinies within the military.

6 JUNE 1905
France Théophile Delcassé, foreign minister since 1898, has been trying to convince his fellow cabinet members to ally with Britain to frighten off the Germans in Morocco. Prime Minister Rouvier and others fear that this would lead to war, so today Delcassé is forced to resign.

7 JUNE 1905
Norway Sweden acquired Norway from Denmark in 1814, and their union was affirmed by an act of 1815; although Norway was supposedly an independent kingdom, it was ruled by the Swedish king. During the 19th century, the movement for an inde-

pendent Norway had spread. Today, Norway's Storting, or parliament, declares that the union with Sweden is dissolved; this will be ratified by a plebiscite on 13 August.

8 JUNE 1905
International President Roosevelt, sensing a desire for peace among all powers and peoples involved, sends identical notes to Japan and Russia urging them to negotiate an end to their conflict and offering his personal services.

27 JUNE 1905
Russia The battleship *Potemkin* had left Sevastopol on 25 June for firing practice; when some of the crew reject the meat served, as spoiled, an officer shoots a crewman; enraged sailors fire on their officers, killing the captain and all but five others. A committee of 20 sailors takes charge of the ship, which sails for Odessa.

28 JUNE 1905
Russia The *Potemkin* arrives at Odessa, where sailors take the body of the dead crewman ashore amid an outpouring of popular sympathy; many sailors now begin to join civilians in revolutionary actions that include burning granaries, quays, and ships in harbor. In the ensuing confrontation with government troops, hundreds are killed.

30 JUNE 1905
Russia The crew of the battleship *Georgei Pobiedonosets* mutinies in support of the *Potemkin*; then the whole Black Sea Fleet is effectively out of operation, as crews sabotage engines, and officers are forced to send sailors ashore to avoid worse problems. (The *Pobiedonosets* crew will surrender to Russian authorities on 3 July.)

30 JUNE 1905
Australia George H Reid, conservative Prime Min-

54

1 SEPTEMBER 1905

The naval battle of the Sea of Japan.

ister since 17 August 1904, is forced to resign. Alfred Deakin returns to power on 5 July.

8 JULY 1905
France Feeling assured now of US support, France agrees to a conference with Germany over the Moroccan crisis.

Russia The *Potemkin* surrenders to Rumanian authorities at Constanta: the Rumanians will turn the ship over to the Russian authorities on 9 July. The *Potemkin* incident will long serve as a symbol of revolutionary possibilities.

24 JULY 1905
International Czar Nicholas II and Kaiser Wilhelm II, visiting each other's yachts, sign the Björkö Treaty, a return to the proposals rejected in October-November 1904, whereby each country agrees to come to the other's defense if attacked by European powers. Nothing will come of this treaty, as France threatens to refuse to honor its treaty obligations with Russia if the Czar's government supports the German treaty.

29 JULY 1905
International In negotiations promoted by President Roosevelt to end the Russo-Japanese War, the US Secretary of State, William Howard Taft, makes a secret agreement with Japan's Prime Minister Katsura: the US agrees to let Japan have free rein in Korea in return for Japan's non-interference with the US in the Philippines.

5 AUGUST 1905
International The first meeting of the Russian and Japanese peace commissioners takes place at President Roosevelt's home at Oyster Bay, New York. The formal Peace Conference opens at the US Naval Base at Portsmouth, New Hampshire.

12 AUGUST 1905
International The British and Japanese renew their alliance (of January 1902) for 10 more years; they now agree to provide for mutual support even if attacked by one other power.

19 AUGUST 1905
Russia The Czar issues a manifesto in which he grants a constitution: its principal concession is a Duma, or state council, to be elected by a limited franchise; the Duma is to be limited to studying legislation, with the Czar retaining a veto over all proposals.

20 AUGUST 1905
China Sun Yat-sen is a young Chinese revolutionary determined to bring down the Manchu regime; forced into exile in 1895, he has traveled throughout the world—including the US and Hawaii —trying to organize overseas Chinese to support his goals. Today, in Tokyo, he forms the first chapter of the T'ung Meng Hui, a union of all secret societies dedicated to bringing down the Manchus.

1 SEPTEMBER 1905
Canada Alberta and Saskatchewan are established

CALM BEFORE THE STORM 1900-1913

as provinces (from part of the former Hudson's Bay Company Territory).

5 SEPTEMBER 1905
International The Treaty of Portsmouth is signed (at the US Naval Base at Portsmouth, New Hampshire), concluding the Russo-Japanese War. Russia will pay no indemnity to Japan but will cede the southern part of Sakhalin Island to her, promise to recognize Japan's interests in Korea, and transfer the southern part of the Liaotung Peninsula to Japan. Manchuria is returned to Chinese administration, and Russia receives payment for its loss of land. President Roosevelt will receive the Nobel Peace Prize for his role as mediator.

Australia About 50 prominent men meet in Sydney's Australia Hotel to found the National Defence League to work for compulsory military training for all Australian males; their ever-present apprehension about Asians has been stimulated by Japan's recent victory over Russia.

28 SEPTEMBER 1905
International France and Germany reach agreement on the agenda for the conference on Moroccan matters (to meet in January 1906).

20–30 OCTOBER 1905
Russia Starting with a strike of railway workers, a general strike spreads through much of Russia until a million workers are out. Transportation, communications, gas and light stop; there are no newspapers; several large cities are in darkness; disorders and plundering occur.

26 OCTOBER 1905
Norway Norway signs the Treaty of Separation with Sweden (whose Riksdag, or parliament, had acquiesced on 24 September). The Norwegians have selected as their king Prince Charles of Denmark, who ascends the throne as King Haakon VII.

Russia Workers of St Petersburg form the first *soviet*, or council, to direct strikers. This soviet is a moderate socialist, not a radical communist, group.

30 OCTOBER 1905
Russia With Russia virtually paralyzed by the strike, the Czar has vacillated between a punitive or a conciliatory line. Finally he issues a manifesto granting a constitution: the new Duma will have true legislative powers, the franchise is greatly extended, and civil liberties are guaranteed. Count Witte, a moderate, is named Prime Minister.

31 OCTOBER 1905
Russia The Czar's manifesto becomes known. Moderates generally support it, and will thus become known as 'Octobrists', with the more progressive taking the name of the Constitutional Democratic Party. The Social Democrats reject it. Meanwhile, the St Petersburg workers' soviet, now with branches elsewhere, will try to organize strikes.

NOVEMBER–DECEMBER 1905
International The Porte, or Ottoman Turkish Government, has been arguing with the Great Powers over the conditions set forth for Macedonia—the number of officers, control of finances, and other factors. The Great Powers move ships toward Turkey to threaten the Sultan.

11 NOVEMBER 1905
Crete High Commissioner Prince George declares amnesty for all leaders of the insurrection that has been disturbing Crete during recent months—but which never gained mass support.

22 NOVEMBER 1905
International Fleets of the Great Powers land forces on the Turkish island of Mytiline (Lesvos) and occupy the customs house, threatening the Sultan to force acceptance of their plan to reform conditions in Macedonia and the Ottoman Empire.

28 NOVEMBER 1905
Ireland The *Sinn Fein* (Irish for 'We, Ourselves') organizes as a political party dedicated to an independent Ireland. (Sinn Fein traces back to 1899, when Arthur Griffith founded it as a cultural-nationalist movement.)

4 DECEMBER 1905
Great Britain Arthur Balfour and his government resign under fire for several policies, in particular because many Britons dislike the Education Act of 1902, which allows denominational schools to continue with state support. Balfour expects to be recalled; instead, he is replaced on 5 December by Sir Henry Campbell-Bannerman, leader of the Liberals (who remains Prime Minister till 5 April 1908).

9 DECEMBER 1905
France The Act for Separation of Church and State is promulgated today, abrogating the Concordat of 1801 and related acts. The new act guarantees freedom of conscience, but puts all religious groups on their own, no longer giving support to religion.

16 DECEMBER 1905
International The Ottoman Turkish government accepts the international controls plan of the Great Powers, so troops and fleets at Mytiline are withdrawn.

Russia Prime Minister Witte feels that his position is strong enough to assert control over what he perceives as disruptive elements. He has members of the St Petersburg soviet arrested because of their efforts to stir up a general strike.

22 DECEMBER 1905–1 JANUARY 1906
Russia The arrest of St Petersburg Soviet members leads to an uprising of Moscow workers; there is fighting in the streets and bloodshed, but troops remain loyal to the government and by the New Year the uprising is put down.

10 FEBRUARY 1906

OTHER EVENTS OF 1905

Science In what will become one of the 'hinge years' of science, an obscure German patents clerk in Zurich, Switzerland, Albert Einstein, publishes five seminal articles in the *Annalen der Physik*: (1) 'A New Determination of Molecular Dimensions,' his doctoral thesis; (2) a paper on the motion of small particles suspended in a stationary fluid, (providing a theoretical explanation of Brownian motion); (3) a paper postulating that light is composed of individual quanta (later called 'photons') having the properties of particles and waves (accounting for, among other phenomena, the photoelectric effect); (4) a theory of relativity, treating motion as relative between two systems of reference and space-time as a four-dimensional continuum; (5) a final paper establishing the equivalence of mass and energy, expressed as $E = mc^2$. John S Haldane and J G Priestley, British physiologists, publish a paper showing that breathing is regulated by the effect of carbon dioxide (CO_2) on the brain.

Technology Rayon yarn is first commercially produced in Coventry, England; rayon is the first synthetic textile yarn capable of being woven and dyed. The New York Central Railroad's 'Twentieth Century Limited' now goes between New York City and Chicago in 18 hours; the first motor bus service is begun in London; and there are now some 78,000 automobiles registered in the USA (compared to only 300 ten years before).

Social Sciences Having been asked about 1900 to develop a set of tests to identify mentally deficient children in Paris, Alfred Binet and Theodore Simon, French psychologists, publish results of their initial tests and rating children by 'intelligence quotient' (IQ). The Binet-Simon tests will be adopted and modified by others in later years. Sigmund Freud publishes *Three Contributions to the Theory of Sex*.

Ideas/Beliefs George Santayana publishes the first of his five-volume work The Life of Reason.

Literature Oscar Wilde's *De Profundis* (posthumous); E M Forster's *Where Angels Fear to Tread*; Heinrich Mann's *Professor Unrat* (later the basis of the film *Blue Angel*); Christian Morgenstern's *Galgenlieder*. A Conan Doyle yields to his public and publishes *The Return of Sherlock Holmes*, and Natsume Soseki publishes his Japanese classic *I Am a Cat*.

Drama/Entertainment Shaw's *Major Barbara* (his *Mrs Warren's Profession* is closed in New York by the police, who arrest its producer). Michel Fokine choreographs *The Dying Swan* for Anna Pavlova. In Pittsburgh, a 'nickelodeon' is the first regular theater devoted to moving pictures in the USA.

The Arts Matisse's *Luxe, calme et volupté*; Rousseau's *Jungle with a Lion*; Cezanne's *Les Grandes Baigneuses*. Picasso, settled in Paris, begins his 'Pink Period.' In Dresden a group of German artists found *Die Brücke* (The Bridge) to revive graphic arts. And in Paris a group of young artists exhibiting in the annual Salon d'Automne employ such bold colors and violent distortions that they are dubbed 'Les *Fauves*' ('The Wild Beasts'); they include Matisse, Rouault, and Derain. In New York City, Alfred Stieglitz opens a gallery, '291' (from its location on Fifth Avenue), to exhibit photography as a fine art.

Music Strauss's opera *Salome*; Debussy's *La Mer* and *Suite Bergamasque* (including 'Clair de lune'); Franz Lehar's operetta *The Merry Widow*; and Mahler's *Kindertotenlieder*. Albert Schweitzer, a German musician, publishes his seminal work *J S Bach, the Musician Poet*.

Sports/Leisure World boxing champion James Jeffries of the USA retires undefeated.

Miscellaneous The union Industrial Workers of the World (IWW)—soon to be dubbed 'The Wobblies'—is founded in Chicago by Eugene Debs and William Haywood. The Rotary Club is founded in Chicago. In the Bloomsbury section of London, a group of intellectuals and artists begins to meet at the homes of Virginia, Vanessa, and Adrian Stephens; they come to be known as 'The Bloomsbury Group,' and will include E M Forster, Clive Bell, Roger Fry, Lytton Strachey, and John Maynard Keynes.

1 JANUARY 1906

Russia The uprising of Moscow workers that began on 22 December 1905 is quelled; government troops turn against the people and reimpose order in brutal punitive raids known as 'the Black Hundreds'. Prime Minister Witte secretly arranges for loans from France and Britain with the idea of bypassing the Duma's control of finances.

10 JANUARY 1906

International The British and the French begin consultations on military and naval issues. The Liberal Foreign Secretary Edward Grey refuses to make a public promise to support France in the event of an attack, but secretly agrees to the 'moral obligation' of Britain.

12 JANUARY 1906

Great Britain The Liberals win an overwhelming majority in Parliament and Henry Campbell-Bannerman remains as Prime Minister. Liberals push to pass reform bills, including revisions to the Education Act of 1902 to satisfy the nonreligious.

16 JANUARY–7 APRIL 1906

International The international conference on the Moroccan problem meets at Algeciras, Morocco. France's position is generally supported by all except Germany and Austria, and until the dismissal of Germany's delegate Baron Holstein (on 5 April) for his unseemly belligerence, the threat of war hangs over the conference.

10 FEBRUARY 1906

Great Britain Britain launches the HMS *Dreadnought*, a battleship with 10 12-inch guns, capable of speeds up to 21 knots. This all-big-gun ship will symbolize the arms race that culminates in World War I.

CALM BEFORE THE STORM 1900-1913

17 FEBRUARY 1906
France Clément Armand Fallières is elected President of France, but power lies with Georges Clemenceau. After the tensions of the Dreyfus Affair and the Moroccan Crisis, France opts for a revival of nationalism and royalism, but an epidemic of strikes by workers and protests by those involved in the nation's wine industry will lead to violence in the coming months.

24 FEBRUARY 1906
Cuba Tomas Estrada Palma defeats José Gomez in the election for president, but Gomez and followers refuse to accept the results and sponsor an uprising. Among other charges, Gomez labels Estrada Palma a tool of 'Yankee imperialism,' and soon Palma is calling for US troops to help put down the uprising.

7 APRIL 1906
International Parties involved sign the Algeciras Act, reaffirming the independence and integrity of Morocco and guaranteeing economic freedom to all who deal with her. France and Spain retain their agreed-upon priority in Moroccan affairs.

8 APRIL 1906
Austro-Hungarian Empire After the King of Hungary has threatened to impose a universal suffrage act—confronting the Magyar-Hungarians with the prospect of being outvoted—the Independents and their coalition collapse; all parties agree to elections this month, with the new parliament to meet in May. The Hungarian nationalist movement, which focuses on the use of Hungarian in the Imperial Army, temporarily recedes.

14 APRIL 1906
USA President Theodore Roosevelt, in a speech at the cornerstone-laying of the new House Office Building, compares those writers who are exposing corruption in America to 'men with a muckrake' (an allusion to Bunyan's *Pilgrim's Progress*). This soon becomes 'muckrakers,' and although Roosevelt was critical of their ways, the term applies favorably to crusading writers.

18–19 APRIL 1906
USA A terrible earthquake, followed by fires, reduces much of San Francisco to ruin: damage is estimated at $375 million, and 500 people die.

2 MAY 1906
Russia The Czar dismisses his moderate Prime Minister Witte and appoints Ivan Goremykin, a conservative bureaucrat.

6 MAY 1906
Russia The government promulgates the Fundamental Laws on the eve of the meeting of the First Duma. The Czar proclaims his intention to retain absolute control over the government; the Duma's budgetary powers are to be restricted, and the Czar

Clemenceau visiting a French aviation camp.

GEORGES EUGENE BENJAMIN CLEMENCEAU, 1841–1929

Physician, author, statesman, and warrior, during the desperate days of World War I Premier Georges Clemenceau, 'The Tiger,' displayed the will-power, idealistic republicanism, and stark perception of reality which made him justly famous. Imprisoned for radicalism as a student, Clemenceau later fought chauvinistic nationalism, clericalism, and anti-Semitism in the Dreyfus affair and concentrated his journalistic efforts on preparedness against Germany. As chairman of the Paris Peace Conference after World War I, however, 'Father Victory' was unable to achieve his harsh objectives against Germany. One of the shapers of modern France, Clemenceau spent the last years of his life writing, lecturing, and traveling, widely esteemed both at home and abroad.

claims the right to legislate by decree when the Duma is not in session.

10 MAY–21 JULY 1906
Russia The First Duma meets, having been elected by broad suffrage—but in an election boycotted by radicals. The Constitutional Democratic Party forms the largest group (known as the 'Cadets,' from the acronym CD) and is willing to make such demands on the government as general amnesty, responsible ministers, and expropriation of land for peasants. The more moderate 'Octobrists' resist such demands and the assembly will end in deadlock.

14 MAY 1906
International There has been a mounting dispute between Great Britain and the Ottoman Empire about whether the Sinai Peninsula belongs to Palestine or Egypt. After Britain's ultimatum (of 3 May), the Sultan today gives the Sinai to Egypt.

19 MAY 1906

Portugal The Portuguese have become increasingly discontented with their extravagant and licentious King Carlos I (in power since 1889); to deal with revolts and strikes, he today appoints João Franco as Prime Minister with dictatorial powers; parliamentary government is suspended, the press gagged, and opposition suppressed.

21 MAY 1906

International The USA and Mexico sign an agreement over distribution of the waters of the Rio Grande, increasingly diverted to the US for irrigation.

22 MAY 1906

Canada A British garrison leaves Esquimalt, on the Pacific coast, after a military occupation that began in 1858: these were the last British soldiers stationed in Canada.

31 MAY 1906

Spain Alfonso XIII, King of Spain, marries Princess Eugenia of Battenburg (granddaughter of Queen Victoria); a failed attempt on the king's life will gain the army support for a law to prosecute offenses 'against the fatherland and army' by court-martial.

5 JUNE 1906

Germany The Reichstag passes new navy legislation, increasing the total tonnage in Germany's fleet and calling for widening of the Kiel Canal to allow passage of the largest battleships. Germans are now determined at least to keep pace with Britain as a major naval power.

29 JUNE 1906

USA Congress passes one of the more progressive pieces of legislation called for by Roosevelt, the Hepburn Act, which permits regulation of rates charged by railroads, pipelines, and terminals engaged in interstate commerce.

30 JUNE 1906

USA Congress passes two more pieces of progressive social legislation, the Meat Inspection Act and the Pure Food and Drug Act. These laws owe much to the 'muckrakers' whom Roosevelt criticized; Upton Sinclair's novel *The Jungle* (1906) had caused an uproar over conditions in the meat-packing industry.

4 JULY 1906

International In a Tripartite Pact, Great Britain, France, and Italy declare they will guarantee the independence and integrity of Ethiopia (Abyssinia)—but they also lay claim to their own 'spheres of influence' in that land.

12 JULY 1906

France The Court of Appeals reverses the decision of the court-martial that found Captain Alfred Dreyfus guilty of treason; exonerated, Dreyfus will be restored to his position in the army (by a bill passed in the Chamber of Deputies on 13 July), where he is promoted to Major and awarded the Legion of Honor. The Dreyfus Affair had always been about much more than Captain Dreyfus—simply stated, it was a case of Reactionaries versus Progressives—and many of the real issues remain unresolved.

21 JULY 1906

Russia Czar Nicholas II dissolves the First Duma. The Cadet leaders adjourn to Viborg, Finland, where on 23 July they issue the so-called Viborg Manifesto, calling on the Russian people to resist paying taxes. They gain little support.

23 JULY 1906

International The Third International American Conference convenes in Rio de Janeiro, Brazil. On the 27th, US Secretary of State Elihu Root will assure member states that the USA wishes 'for no territory except our own.'

15 AUGUST 1906

International King Edward VII of Britain visits Kaiser Wilhelm at Cronberg, Germany, to discuss the escalating rivalry between their nations' naval forces, but they cannot agree on solutions.

1 SEPTEMBER 1906

Australia By proclamation of the Governor General of Australia, British New Guinea (the western half of New Guinea) is declared a federal possession of Australia and renamed Papua. Australians view this as territory that might prove vital for their defense and feel the British have done little to enforce their interests there.

24 SEPTEMBER 1906

Crete Prince George of Greece, convinced that he can no longer serve the cause of Crete, resigns as High Commissioner. Alexander Zaimis succeeds him.

29 SEPTEMBER 1906

Cuba The US military, whose aid has been requested by the beleaguered President Estrada Palma, assumes control of the island under the Platt Amendment. William Howard Taft is named provisional governor, but he will be succeeded by Charles Magoon on 3 October; American control will remain until 1 February 1909.

7 OCTOBER 1906

Persia Elected delegates meet in Tehran, the capital, and proceed to draw up a constitution; on 30 December, the Shah will sign it, but he dies several days later and is succeeded by his son, Mohammed Ali Shah, who is hostile to the constitutional movement. There will be few gains for popular government.

11 OCTOBER 1906

USA The San Francisco Board of Education

CALM BEFORE THE STORM 1900-1913

orders segregation in separate schools of Japanese, Chinese, and Korean children. President Roosevelt is outraged, for he is aware of the delicate balance in international relations that can be upset by this action. The Japanese ambassador protests on 25 October, and Roosevelt persuades the mayor of San Francisco to get the order rescinded (on 13 March 1907). Behind all this lies many Americans' fear of Japanese immigration, which Roosevelt will work to limit by a 'gentlemen's agreement' with the Japanese Government.

20 OCTOBER 1906
International The Anglo-French Convention on the New Hebrides confirms and elaborates on the 1887 agreement for joint control of these Pacific islands. This will satisfy Australians' fear that the British would let the French take control of the islands.

6 NOVEMBER 1906
China Government ministries are reorganized as part of the movement toward constitutional government; but in fact the Manchu princes retain control and there is little gain for the Chinese people.

9 NOVEMBER 1906
USA President Roosevelt sets off for a 17-day trip to Puerto Rico and Panama on the battleship *Louisiana*; he is the first American President in office to travel outside the country.

22 NOVEMBER 1906
Russia Peter Stolypin, Prime Minister since June, introduces agrarian reforms, including remitting unpaid dues to the communes and allowing peasants to withdraw from the communes and take their share of land for private ownership. Although Stolypin is a well-intentioned conservative who hopes to win support for the present constitutional government, his reforms are another instance of too little too late.

28 NOVEMBER–13 DECEMBER 1906
Germany A parliamentary crisis arises as the Center Party, which has held the balance between Conservatives and Socialists since 1890, abandons the Conservatives and refuses to vote for funds to support the military operation against Africans revolting in Southwest Africa. Attacks on the government in the Reichstag become so extreme that Bülow dissolves that body on 13 December and calls for new elections.

6 DECEMBER 1906
South Africa The British grant Transvaal self-government.

18 DECEMBER 1906
Australia In their national elections, the Protectionists lose seats, but Alfred Deakin retains office as Prime Minister.

21 DECEMBER 1906
Great Britain Parliament passes two important pieces of social legislation. The Trade Disputes Bill legalizes peaceful picketing and exempts unions from liability for damages resulting from any illegal acts by its members. (This reverses the Taff Vale judgment of the House of Lords on 22 July 1901, and is a response to the growing union movement.) The Workingmen's Compensation Act develops principles laid down in acts going back to 1880 and broadens employers' liability for accidents.

OTHER EVENTS OF 1906
Science Walter H Nernst, a German physical chemist, publishes his theory on behavior of matter at temperatures approaching absolute zero; this becomes known as the 'third law of thermodynamics.'
Medicine/Health August von Wassermann, a German bacteriologist, introduces a blood test for syphilis. (Wassermann will develop inoculations for cholera, typhoid, and tetanus.) In England, Frederick G Hopkins, having experimented with foods to determine their effect on growth and development in rats, publishes some of his findings and concludes that 'accessory food factors' (beyond, that is, such basics as proteins, carbohydrates, fats, minerals, water) are necessary for growth; it will be 1912 before these are called 'vitamines.' Jules Bordet, a French scientist, discovers the bacterium that causes whooping cough.
Technology At Brant Rock, Massachusetts, Reginald Fessenden, the Canadian experimental physicist, broadcasts the first radio program: on Christmas Eve he plays 'O Holy Night' on the violin and reads from the Gospel of St Luke, with poetry and other songs. The program is picked up by ships' radio operators within five miles, and a subsequent broadcast on New Year's Eve is picked up in the West Indies. Lee De Forest, American inventor, announces he has made the first three-element vacuum tube, which will advance radio's development. Thomas Edison invents a 'cameraphone' that synchronizes projector and phonograph; in London, the French-born Eugene Lauste patents a sound-on-film process

Immigrants arriving in New York Harbor.

22 MARCH 1907

Edison and his talking machine.

appointed to her husband's post after he dies in a traffic accident—the first woman professor at the Sorbonne.

26 JANUARY 1907
Austria Universal and direct suffrage—limited to males over 24—is introduced, a reform long demanded by the socialists and others. But the effect is to release class and nationalistic conflicts within the country.

7 FEBRUARY 1907
Germany Results of the national elections held within the last two weeks reveal that Bülow's scheme has worked: he has rallied conservatives against the threat of a socialist government, and the conservative coalition takes over the Reichstag.

FEBRUARY–DECEMBER 1907
Honduras-Nicaragua The two countries drift into war, largely because of expansionist ambitions of Nicaragua's President José Zelaya. The Hondurans are defeated and their capital occupied; Zelaya places a president of his choice over Honduras and then indicates he is ready to invade El Salvador. With the threat of a general war hanging over all of Central America, the US and Mexico intervene and call for a Conference of Central American States.

26 FEBRUARY 1907
South Africa Louis Botha's Het Volk Party wins a majority in the elections in Transvaal; Botha takes over as Premier on 4 March, and the Boers gain at least some of the power they had failed to win in war.

5 MARCH–16 JUNE 1907
Russia The Second Duma meets, and because more progressive parties have participated in elections, this is a more radical body than the first. The Cadets now find themselves in a position analogous to that of the Octobrists before them—trying to save the constitutional system and avoid giving the Czar any pretext for intervening. But the radicals persist, and by 16 June the Czar dissolves the Duma.

14 MARCH 1907
USA By Presidential order, the US excludes Japanese laborers from entering the country. There is a genuine fear among many Americans about the flood of unskilled immigrants; on 26 February 1907, Congress set up a commission to study this problem. There is undeniable prejudice against Oriental immigrants, and Roosevelt attempts to calm these feelings.

22 MARCH 1907
South Africa The new Boer government of Transvaal passes an Asiatic Registration Bill that restricts immigration from India. The Indian community in South Africa will begin a long resistance, led by a young Indian lawyer, Mohandas Gandhi, who this year organizes his first *satyagraha* ('holding to the

(but it will be 1910 before he can demonstrate it).

Environment Captain Roald Amundsen, the Norwegian explorer, arrives in the Bering Strait after voyaging since 1903 on the first ship known to have passed from sea to sea through the Northwest Passage. Although the San Francisco earthquake receives more publicity, an earthquake in Valparaiso, Chile, leaves 20,000 dead, and a typhoon at Hong Kong kills 10,000. President Roosevelt signs a bill establishing the first US National Monument, Devil's Tower, in Wyoming.

Literature John Galsworthy's *The Man of Property* (the first in a long series of novels, The Forsyte Saga, the last published in 1935); Upton Sinclair's *The Jungle*; Paul Valéry's *Monsieur Teste*; O Henry's *The Four Million* (includes 'The Gift of the Magi'); and three Japanese classics, Natsume Soseki's *Young Master* and *Pillow of Grass* and Toson's *Broken Commandment*.

Drama/Entertainment Paul Claudel's *Partage du Midi* and Gerhart Hauptmann's *Und Pippi tanzt*. Ruth St Denis begins her modern dance. Vitagraph (USA) releases the first animated cartoon; by James S Blackton, it has 8000 drawings of a man rolling his eyes and blowing smoke, a dog jumping through a hoop, and similar repetitious activities. Australia releases its own first full-length (over an hour) film, *The Story of the Kelly Gang*.

The Arts Picasso's *Portrait of Gertrude Stein*; Matisse completes *The Joy of Life*; Monet begins *Les Nymphéas*; Rouault's *Before a Mirror*.

Architecture Frank Lloyd Wright completes the Unity Temple in Oak Park, Illinois, the first public building to display its concrete construction.

Music Ralph Vaughan Williams completes the first of his *Norfolk Rhapsodies*; Charles Ives's *The Unanswered Question*.

Miscellaneous The Dutch begin work on the Zuider Zee drainage project, and the Simplon Tunnel opens, $12\frac{1}{2}$ miles under the Alps between Italy and Switzerland. Night shift work for women is forbidden internationally. The British Patents Act provides protection for inventors. Albert I, Prince of Monaco, founds the Oceanographic Institute. Marie Curie is

CALM BEFORE THE STORM 1900-1913

truth'), a campaign of civil disobedience through nonviolent resistance to unjust laws.

12 APRIL 1907
Switzerland The parliament passes a new army bill reorganizing the nation's forces into a standing militia, with training required for all males.

MAY–JULY 1907
France Demonstrations by the grape growers in southern France lead to winemaking legislation.

14 MAY 1907
Sweden Sweden adopts almost universal suffrage for elections to its lower house and proportional representation for both houses.

16 MAY 1907
International In the Pact of Cartagena, Great Britain, France and Spain agree to maintain the status quo in the Mediterranean and along the Atlantic coast of Europe and Africa.

10 JUNE 1907
International France and Japan sign an agreement to maintain the independence and integrity of China, equality for all nations in trading with China, and the status quo in the Far East. As with all treaties of this kind, each country agrees to recognize the other's 'spheres of influence' in the region.

14 JUNE 1907
South Africa The Transvaal Government decides to repatriate Chinese laborers brought in since 1903; there are some 50,000, who have been the center of strife in many areas.

15 JUNE–18 OCTOBER 1907
International The Second Peace Conference meets at The Hague; it had been called originally, at the suggestion of Theodore Roosevelt, for October 1904, but postponed by the Russo-Japanese War. Some of the 46 participating nations try to get general agreement to stop the arms race, but Germany resists. Participants do agree to forbid war as an instrument for collecting debts and formulate rules of war and the rights of neutrals.

16 JUNE 1907
Russia The Czar dissolves the Second Duma and issues an edict that will increase representation of propertied classes while reducing that of peasants, workers, and national minorities.

1 JULY 1907
South Africa The Orange River Colony, known as the Orange Free State, is granted self-government by the British.

19–20 JULY 1907
Korea Under pressure from the Japanese, the Emperor of Korea abdicates in favor of his son, a figurehead.

25 JULY 1907
Korea Japan obtains a protectorate over Korea from the new emperor. One of Japan's first acts is to dismiss the Korean Army, which will lead to an unsuccessful uprising.

30 JULY 1907
International Russia and Japan sign an agreement similar to that Japan signed with France (10 June 1907), guaranteeing the freedom of China while recognizing each other's special interests.
Philippines The Filipinos elect their first legislature; it will meet on 16 October.

30 JULY–5 AUGUST 1907
Morocco Due to attacks on foreigners in Casablanca, the French bombard that city and land troops to occupy the Atlantic-coast region of Morocco.

3–5 AUGUST 1907
International Kaiser Wilhelm and Czar Nicholas meet at Swinemünde, mainly to discuss Germany's plan to build the railroad to Baghdad. The Czar is anxious to assure the Kaiser that any agreements of Russia with Great Britain are not aimed at Germany. Before the month is out, Russia will sign an agreement with Britain that aligns Russia against the Triple Alliance powers.

16 AUGUST 1907
Morocco Mulay Hafid, brother of the Sultan of Morocco, is proclaimed Sultan by supporters at Marrakesh, instigating what will become a civil war. Mulay will be supported by Germany while France supports the Sultan.

A PLACE IN THE SUN

By the beginning of the 20th century, Europe's major powers had extended their influence around the world by colonial acquisition. The most ambitious of these imperialistic quests was that of Great Britain. With land holdings in Africa, Asia, and the Pacific, it was said that 'The sun never sets on the British Empire.' But another prominent European force, Germany, was determined to have its 'place in the sun' and a claim to international superiority. Of the many conflicts between the two nations, competition for control of the seas was the most obvious. England feared that Germany's ship-building campaign was an attempt to challenge the power of the British Empire. Rivalry intensified as the two nations reached an impasse in naval-issue negotiations and continued to expand their fleets. Great Britain stayed ahead in the race and in 1906 launched the *Dreadnought*, the first all-big-gun battleship. As a result, Germany proceeded full speed ahead with its own navy. 'A place in the sun' would be sought on the world's sea roads and battlefields.

16 DECEMBER 1907

31 AUGUST 1907
International The Anglo-Russian Entente, or Convention, is concluded after lengthy negotiations. Both nations agree to recognize China's control of Tibet; Russia agrees not to interfere in Afghanistan, where Britain feels it has a role; and they agree to divide Persia into spheres of influence. Although nothing in this agreement is explicitly hostile to Germany, it appears to place Russia on the side of Britain and France as opposed to Germany.

5 SEPTEMBER 1907
International King Edward of Great Britain meets Russia's Foreign Minister Alexander Izvolski at Marienbad as part of Izvolski's campaign to strengthen Russia's relations with Britain; Izvolski rushes about Europe assuring each country of Russia's good intentions.

6 SEPTEMBER 1907
Papacy Pope Pius X issues the encyclical *Pascendi dominici gregis*, in which he condemns the 'modernist' movement and establishes councils to combat 'modern errors'—an attempt to censor new ideas.

26 SEPTEMBER 1907
New Zealand New Zealand gains the status of a Dominion within the British Empire.

1 OCTOBER 1907
USA A downturn in the stock market leads to a run on banks starting today; Roosevelt will be forced to call on the financier J P Morgan to help manage the financial crisis: the depression that results will last a year.

27 OCTOBER 1907
Germany The first trial in the so-called Eulenberg Affair, which will rock the highest circles of Germany, ends today. Prince Philip Eulenberg is a cultivated aristocrat and former diplomat; an old friend of the Kaiser's, he enjoyed an intimacy that aroused jealousy in men like Bülow and Count Holstein (the diplomat whom the Kaiser had 'fired' from the Algeciras Conference for belligerency). Holstein found a supporter in Maximilian Harden, editor of the magazine *Die Zukunft*, who for his own reasons began to print a series of articles in the fall of 1906 alleging that Eulenberg and other highly placed men were homosexuals. At first the Kaiser simply ignored the stories and implications, but when public opinion began to turn against the court and government, he supported legal action against Harden. This first trial finds in favor of Harden, but subsequent trials reveal scandals that tarnish everyone.

8 NOVEMBER 1907
Australia In a landmark decision for Australia, Justice Henry B Higgins of the Court of Conciliation and Arbitration rules that the Sunshine Harvester Works must pay 'fair and reasonable wages,' which he then defines as 'to meet normal needs of the average employee regarded as a human being living in a civilized community.' As vague as this may sound, the 'Harvester Judgment' becomes the touchstone for establishing wages for all Australian laborers.

13 NOVEMBER–20 DECEMBER 1907
International The Conference of Central American States—convoked in response to the war between Honduras and Nicaragua—meets in Washington, DC: it tries to settle disputes among these states and even to promote unification among them; it creates a Central American Court of Justice to decide disputes, but although the court is set up in 1908 it is not influential.

14 NOVEMBER 1907
Russia The Third Duma meets; with elections held under the Czar's edict limiting the franchise, a conservative majority holds sway and suppresses the radical-revolutionary elements. Prime Minister Stolypin manages to reform parts of the government (police, banks, education) and the relative order of these years allows economic growth.

7 DECEMBER 1907
Egypt The First Nationalist Congress meets under leadership of Mustapha Kemal; its program is liberal rather than revolutionary, and stresses cultural affairs as much as political. When its leader, Kemal, dies on 10 February 1908, the nationalist movement collapses.

15 DECEMBER 1907
Persia The Shah leads a coup d'etat against the liberal Prime Minister Nasir ul-Mulk and imprisons him, but a popular uprising forces the Shah to restore Nasir ul-Mulk.

16 DECEMBER 1907
USA In a grandiose gesture, President Roosevelt sends the Battle Fleet on a round-the-world cruise. It consists of 16 battleships and will return on 22 February 1909; meanwhile, it becomes known as 'The Great White Fleet.' It is generally received with enthusiasm in ports of call, and it announces America's presence as a world power. The US Navy learns that it is heavily dependent on foreigners for fuel and supplies—that world-power status will require a greatly expanded support system.

OTHER EVENTS OF 1907
Science Near Heidelberg, Germany, a fossil human ancestor belonging to an extinct species known as *Homo erectus* is found. This species lived from one to three million years ago, and includes such fossil specimens as the Java Man (discovered 1891) and the Peking Man (to be discovered in 1927).
Technology Lee De Forest, pioneer American radio developer, begins what might be regarded as the first broadcasts from a studio, on the top floor of the Parker Building in New York City. Although at first experimental and always limited to a small audience,

CALM BEFORE THE STORM 1900-1913

these broadcasts continued intermittently over four years; De Forest started with phonograph records, recitals, and talks in his studio, but in 1910 will broadcast Caruso and others 'live' from the Metropolitan Opera House.

Social Sciences Maria Montessori, an Italian physician and educator, takes charge of nursery schools in a slum neighborhood of Rome and begins to apply teaching techniques and materials that will become 'the Montessori Method' and spread to other countries. And Carl Gustav Jung, a young Swiss psychiatrist, meets Sigmund Freud; they become friends and Jung at first espouses Freud's ideas; gradually they diverge (in part because Jung rejects Freud's emphasis on sexual instincts), and by 1913 Jung will make a clear break. Jung goes on to establish himself as one of the major thinkers and psychotherapists of the century (based on such concepts as 'archetypes of the collective unconscious'). Alfred Adler, another psychotherapist, publishes his *Study of Organ Inferiority and Its Psychical Compensation*.

Ideas/Beliefs William James publishes *Pragmatism* and Henri Bergson publishes *Creative Evolution*.

Literature Joseph Conrad's *Secret Agent*, Maxim Gorki's *Mother*, Jack London's *White Fang*, Robert Service's *Songs of a Sourdough*, and Selma Lagerlöf's *The Wonderful Adventures of Nils*.

Drama/Entertainment Shaw's *Major Barbara*, J M Synge's *Playboy of the Western World*, and Strindberg's *The Ghost Sonata*.

The Arts Picasso's major work, *Les Demoiselles d'Avignon*, and Rousseau's *The Snake Charmer*. The first Cubist paintings are exhibited in Paris, as this movement is launched by Picasso and Braque.

Music Rachmaninoff's *The Isles of the Dead* and Delius's opera *A Village Romeo and Juliet*.

Joseph Conrad.

Life/Customs In the beginning of the Boy Scout movement, 20 British boys participate in a camp in Dorset, England, led by Lt-General Sir Robert Baden-Powell, a hero of the Boer War. The camp stresses such activities as woodcraft, knot-tying, cooking, boat and fire drill and has a distinctly military atmosphere, including a bullet-riddled Union Jack that had flown over Mafeking, which Baden-Powell had defended during a seven-months' siege. The first official Boy Scout Troop will be formed in Glasgow, Scotland, on 26 January 1908.

4 JANUARY 1908

Morocco At Fez, one of Morocco's major cities, the rebel leader Mulay Hafid, brother of the present Sultan, or leader of Morocco, is proclaimed Sultan. The former Sultan, Abdul Aziz, has lost support through a mixture of personal foibles (he seems more interested in model trains than in his country's problems) and political powerlessness in the face of such countries as France and Spain. His brother, more austere and conservative, has been gathering support for his revolt for a year now. The Germans have backed Mulay Hafid through determination to counter French power in North Africa. By August, Mulay Hafid will be Sultan.

27 JANUARY 1908

International The Austrian Government, through its foreign minister Count Alois Aehrenthal, announces it will build a railroad through territory later to be called Yugoslavia all the way to Salonika. Behind this seemingly minor and helpful plan lies Austria's intention to curb rising anti-Austrian agitation among the Serbians and Montenegrins in this region. The Russians see it as a violation of agreements with Austria, while the British view it as an attempt by the Ottoman Turks to bribe Austria to oppose reforms in Macedonia. By now, hardly a step can be taken anywhere without one or another of the Great Powers feeling it is being threatened.

1 FEBRUARY 1908

Portugal King Carlos I and the Crown Prince are assassinated in Lisbon. Carlos has become unpopular because of his personal extravagances as well as for having appointed João Franco, now running the government. Manuel II, the younger son, becomes king and dismisses Franco; he restores constitutional government, but his personal extravagance soon forfeits the respect of his people.

3 FEBRUARY 1908

USA The Supreme Court rules in *Loewe v Lawlor* (better known as the Danbury Hatters' Case) that a secondary union boycott is a restraint of trade and that the Sherman Anti-trust Act applies to combinations of labor as well as of capital. This will brake the growing power of unions.

18 FEBRUARY 1908

USA The American ambassador to Japan is given

a note by the Japanese in which they agree to restrict Japanese emigration to the US and to accept President Roosevelt's order of 14 March 1907. This becomes known as the 'Gentlemen's Agreement.'

24 FEBRUARY 1908
USA In a swing to the more liberal side, the Supreme Court in *Muller v Oregon* favors an Oregon law limiting maximum hours a woman may work and denies that it curtails liberty of contract guaranteed by the 14th Amendment.

8 APRIL 1908
Great Britain Herbert Asquith, formerly chancellor of the exchequer, becomes Prime Minister after Henry Campbell-Bannerman resigns (5 April) because of poor health. David Lloyd George replaces Asquith as chancellor of the exchequer.

11 APRIL 1908
International The US and Canada sign conventions regarding the protection of food fishes in contiguous boundary waters, said boundaries being defined in these agreements.

23 APRIL 1908
International Germany, Sweden, Denmark, and Russia sign the Baltic Conventions, while Germany, Great Britain, Denmark, Sweden, Netherlands, and France sign the North Sea Conventions; under both, all signatory powers agree to maintain the status quo on the shores of the respective seas and to consult signatories whenever this status quo might be threatened.

7 MAY 1908
Austria-Hungary Emperor Franz-Joseph celebrates his golden jubilee with festivities throughout the empire.

13–15 MAY 1908
USA President Roosevelt convenes the White House Conservation Conference; its limited goal is to discuss the report of the Inland Waterways Commission on interdependence of the nation's natural resources, but it will have repercussions throughout the nation and the world. On 8 June Roosevelt will appoint Gifford Pinchot to head the National Conservation Commission, the beginning of government involvement in the nation's environment.

25 MAY 1908
International The Central American Court of Justice (resulting from the Washington Conference of 14 November 1907) is inaugurated at Cartago, Chile.
China-USA The US Congress votes to remit half of the imdemnity awarded to the USA after the Boxer Rebellion; China will set aside this half ($12,220,350) to establish a Tsung Hua College (in 1911) and to send hundreds of Chinese students to US colleges between 1911–27. (In 1924, the USA will cancel the outstanding sum from the other half.)

King Edward VII of England.

30 MAY 1908
USA Congress passes the Aldrich-Vreeland Act, which frees banks to issue notes backed by commercial paper and bonds of state and local governments; considered an emergency measure, it has no safeguards for the credit supply. The same bill establishes a National Monetary Commission to investigate and report on banking systems of European countries as compared to that of the US.

9–10 JUNE 1908
International King Edward VII of Great Britain visits Czar Nicholas II at Reval, Russia, for what is designated an 'interview.' In addition to discussing the growing power of Germany, the two leaders seem to agree on recent British plans for reforms in Macedonia. Some of the Young Turks will interpret this agreement as a threat to Turkish territory.

10 JUNE 1908
Australia The Parliament passes the Invalid and Old Age Pensions Act; by providing for pensions for British subjects (excluding the aborigines) at age 65, this marks the beginning of government-sponsored social security in Australia.

14 JUNE 1908
Germany The Reichstag passes the Fourth Navy Bill, calling for more shipbuilding.

16–20 JUNE 1908
USA The Republican Party convenes in Chicago. Theodore Roosevelt had promised in 1904 not to seek another term; he picks his successor, William Howard Taft.

CALM BEFORE THE STORM 1900-1913

23 JUNE 1908
International The USA suspends diplomatic relations with Venezuela because of the refusal of Cipriano Castro's government to compensate Americans for injuries suffered in the uprising of 1899.
Persia Shah Mohammed Ali leads a successful counterrevolution (aided by the Russian legation and a Cossack brigade); the Shah shuts down the assembly, dispenses with the liberal constitution granted on 30 December 1906, executes liberal leaders, and imposes martial law. Some Persians, particularly at Tabriz, revolt against the Shah's moves, but government troops suppress these uprisings.

5 JULY 1908
Turkey Niazi Bey, a chief organizer of the revolutionary movement in Turkey, raises the standard of revolt at Resna, Macedonia: the Sultan arrests several officers known to support the movement, but other officers desert and revolution spreads.

7–10 JULY 1908
USA The Democratic Party meets in Denver and nominates William Jennings Bryan on the first ballot.

8–13 JULY 1908
Turkey The uprising is spreading: Enver Bey joins in on 8 July and by the 13th the Committee of Union and Progress—generally known as the 'Young Turks'—supports the insurgents.

24 JULY 1908
Turkey After days of discussion with his ministers, Sultan Abdul Hamid announces he is restoring the liberal constitution of 1876 and will become more responsive to demands of dissidents. The Young Turks consider this a victory and call an end to the uprising. In fact, this apparent unity is based largely on widespread Turkish resentment of the Reval interview (9–10 June) between Britain and Russia.

11 AUGUST 1908
International King Edward VII of Britain meets with Kaiser Wilhelm at Friedrichshof, Germany. The main point of contention is the increasing size of Germany's navy.

13 AUGUST 1908
International King Edward VII meets with Emperor Franz Joseph of Austria at Ischl; there the king tries to persuade the Emperor to counsel Germany against aggressive policies—which is to say anti-British policies.

16 AUGUST 1908
Turkey The Committee of Union and Progress, 'The Young Turks,' announces a program for reforms and respect for the rights of all within the Ottoman Empire, regardless of race or religion.

20 AUGUST 1908
USA-Australia America's Great White Fleet arrives in Sydney, Australia, to be greeted with a tremendous welcome; a week later the fleet will proceed to Melbourne; before it leaves for Japan, 221 American sailors desert to remain in Australia.

23 AUGUST 1908
Morocco The last forces supporting Sultan Abdul Aziz are defeated at Marrakesh by supporters of his brother, Mulay Hafid, who proclaims himself Sultan of all Morocco. Mulay Hafid has come to power by promising to restore order by putting down factions and restore honor by eliminating foreign influence: before long he will be asking for French help against internal dissidents.

12 SEPTEMBER 1908
Canada Canada appoints a Civil Service Commission, initiating a more equitable system for selecting civil servants.

16 SEPTEMBER 1908
International Austria's foreign minister, Count Aehrenthal, meets Russia's foreign minister Izvolski at Buchlau, and they reach an informal agreement: Austria will be allowed to annex Bosnia and Herzegovina, in return for which the Austrians will allow Russian warships to pass through the straits connecting the Black Sea to the Mediterranean. They also agree to allow Prince Ferdinand of Bulgaria to declare Bulgaria an independent republic. Having 'settled' such matters, Izvolski will now tour Europe to gain more support for breaking up the now-weakened Ottoman Empire.

25 SEPTEMBER 1908
International The so-called Casablanca Affair develops when German deserters from the French Foreign Legion, given refuge and safe conduct by a German consular official in Casablanca, are taken by French authorities. This exacerbates tension between France and Germany in Morocco and elsewhere. By November 10 the two countries agree to submit this affair to arbitration.

5 OCTOBER 1908
Bulgaria Prince Ferdinand (a German prince from Saxe-Coburg) declares the independence of Bulgaria from the Ottoman Empire and assumes the title of Tsar. This is part of the plan conceived by Izvolski and Aehrenthal.

6 OCTOBER 1908
International Austria-Hungary proclaims annexation of the provinces of Bosnia and Herzegovina, presently part of the Ottoman Turkish Empire. The Turks are outraged and make military preparations. The Russian Government, unaware that its foreign minister, Izvolski, has worked to support this move, instructs him to oppose it and embrace the cause of the Serbians, the Slavic people in the region. Izvolski will claim that the Austrians had deceived him. The Germans essentially support the Austrians, while the

French and British do little more than call for an international conference.

7 OCTOBER 1908

Crete Taking advantage of the crisis within the Ottoman Empire, Cretans again proclaim union with Greece. Lacking the support of the Great Powers, the Greek government will reject this gesture.

9–14 OCTOBER 1908

International Russian foreign minister Izvolski is in London to salvage what he can of his grand scheme, specifically to get Britain to support Russia's desire to open the Black Sea straits to Russian warships. Britain has no desire to complicate its own relations with Turkey, so Izvolski's plans collapse. The only result of the Buchlau meeting (of September 16) is that Austria has gained Bosnia-Herzegovina and Bulgaria is independent. Izvolski will spend the autumn traveling through Europe to patch up his master plan, to little avail.

12 OCTOBER 1908–3 FEBRUARY 1909

South Africa A constitutional convention meets, first at Durban and then at Capetown, to discuss relations among the colonies. Sentiment for a true union is now strong, and delegates agree on recognition of the king of England, to be represented by a governor-general, with a two-chamber parliament to legislate internal affairs.

18 OCTOBER 1908

Belgium By act of parliament, the Congo Free State is annexed to Belgium as the Belgian Congo. It has been King Leopold III's private possession since 1885, but under pressure at home and abroad, he 'gave' it to his country on 20 August 1908. The Belgian Government will attempt to deal with abuses that accumulated under the king's rule.

28 OCTOBER 1908

International The English newspaper the *Daily Telegraph* prints an interview with Germany's Kaiser Wilhelm, who characterizes himself as personally friendly to Britain but suggests that the German people are hostile. There is an immediate uproar in both countries, especially Germany, and the kaiser will come under attack in the Reichstag. Chancellor Bülow, who should have at least tried to prevent publication of such indiscreet remarks, will attempt to defend the kaiser. Both the kaiser and Bülow emerge from this crisis weakened in reputation and influence.

3 NOVEMBER 1908

USA The Republican candidate, William Howard Taft, wins the presidential election with an electoral vote of 321 compared to 162 for Bryan; the popular vote is 7,679,006 to 6,409,106.

7 NOVEMBER 1908

International The Netherlands blockade the Venezuela coast in retaliation for Venezuela's dismissal (on 22 July) of the Dutch minister on charges that the Netherlands' offshore colony of Curaçao is harboring political refugees from Venezuela.

10–11 NOVEMBER 1908

Germany The Reichstag holds a heated debate over Kaiser Wilhelm's interview in the *Daily Telegraph*; little direct action can result, but the kaiser and Chancellor Bülow are clearly damaged by the debate.

12 NOVEMBER 1908

Australia Andrew Fisher assumes the position of prime minister for what turns out to be a short-lived second Labour government. (Alfred Deakin will be back as prime minister on 2 June 1909.)

14 NOVEMBER 1908

China The Dowager Empress Tsu Hsi, effective ruler of China since 1898, dies. As successor, she appoints Pu Yi, a remote claimant who is still a child: power is with the reactionary Prince Ch'un, the regent. Although the Empress Tsu Hsi could claim some achievements, most of her actions turned Chinese reformers against the Ch'ing Dynasty.

Cuba Liberal candidate José Miguel Gomez wins national elections for president; the American occupation troops will soon leave (1 February 1909), but the Liberal party is so split and the country becomes so unstable that there will be threat of another occupation.

30 NOVEMBER 1908

International The US Secretary of State, Elihu Root, and Japan's ambassador to the USA, Baron Takahira, exchange notes in what becomes known as the Root-Takahira Agreement; they affirm support for an independent China with an 'open door' policy and for the status quo in the Pacific. This implies America's acceptance of Japanese control in Korea and Manchuria.

4 DECEMBER 1908–26 FEBRUARY 1909

International The world's ten leading maritime nations attend a Naval Conference in London. They agree on rules for blockade, convoys, and seizure of contraband, but the convention will not be ratified by all the nations.

9 DECEMBER 1908

Germany The Reichstag adopts a progressive social law restricting hours of factory work by young people and women: no child under 13 is to be employed, while children 13–14 can work only six hours a day.

17 DECEMBER 1908

Turkey The new parliament convenes, with Young Turks the majority. A new conflict threatens the Turkish Empire, as subject nationalities resist centralized government, no matter how liberal, and resent Turkish as the official language.

CALM BEFORE THE STORM 1900-1913

25 DECEMBER 1908
International Russia's Foreign Minister Izvolski delivers a Christmas message to Europeans that attempts to undo problems of his own making: he calls for a league of the Balkan States with Turkey—unrealistic in view of the many competing claims within the region.

OTHER EVENTS OF 1908
Science Godfrey Hardy, an English mathematician, and W Weinberg, a German physician, discover independently an algebraic equation that describes the genetic equilibrium within a population—resolving the controversy over the proportions of dominant and recessive genetic traits within a large mixed population: their equation becomes known as 'The Hardy-Weinberg Law.' Ernest Rutherford establishes that the alpha particle is a helium atom. Hermann Minkowski, a Russian mathematician, develops four-dimensional geometry, which will play an important role in the theory of relativity.
Environment On 30 June, at 7:14 AM, a colossal explosion occurs in a remote region of Siberia; although local people are soon aware of its effects, it will be 19 years before scientists can investigate, to find that all trees had blown down within a radius of some 30–40 km and surface material was charred within a radius of 20 km. The earth's magnetic field was disturbed at the time, skies in northwest Europe were brighter than usual, and barometric pressure changed. The cause of the explosion is still not agreed upon: suggestions include a comet, meteor shower, 'natural' nuclear explosion, 'anti-rock,' or a spaceship. It is regarded as the largest such explosion in recorded history. On 28 December, eastern Sicily and southern Italy are hit by a powerful earthquake accompanied by a massive *tsunami*, or tidal wave, which rushes ashore at Messina, Sicily, destroying about 90 percent of its buildings: 150,000 die.
Literature Anatole France's *Penguin Island*; E M Forster's *A Room with a View*; Arnold Bennett's *The Old Wives' Tale*; Kenneth Grahame's *The Wind in the Willows*.
Drama/Entertainment Isadora Duncan, the American dancer, achieves her first triumphs in London and New York City.
The Arts Matisse's *Red Room* (or *Harmony in Red*); Monet's *The Ducal Palace, Venice*; Brancusi's sculpture *The Kiss*. In New York, the 'Ashcan School'—so called because of its then novel focus on realistic urban life—begins to emerge; its members will include Robert Henri, John Sloan, George Luks, George Bellows, William Glackens, and Everett Shinn; their preferred name was 'The Eight,' for they included other artists and saw themselves as concerned with far more than promoting ashcans as subject matter.
Music Ravel's *Rhapsodie Espagnole* and *Gaspard de la Nuit*; Debussy's *The Children's Corner*; Mahler's Seventh Symphony; Bartok's String Quartet No 1; Oscar Straus's operetta *The Chocolate Soldier* (based on Shaw's *Arms and the Man*).

Sports/Leisure The first major heavyweight fight between a black and a white boxer takes place in Sydney, Australia, on 26 December when Jack Johnson of Texas meets Tommy Burns of Canada: each boasted records of 57–3 against men of their own color; Johnson is declared the winner in the 14th round and will claim the world's heavyweight championship; although challenged by James Jeffries, 'The Great White Hope,' in 1910, Johnson will hold the crown till 1915.
Life/Customs The first Bibles are placed in hotel rooms (in Superior Hotel, Iron Mountain, Montana) by the Gideons. The first Girl Scouts meet in Glasgow, Scotland; they will form an organization separate from the Boy Scouts in 1909.
Miscellaneous Henry Ford introduces his Model T; it sells for $850, expensive at the time, and is mass-produced; as sales increase, its price goes down—to $310 by 1926. It will change the face and habits of a nation.

1 JANUARY 1909
Great Britain After 30 years of promotion, the Old Age Pension Law is finally instituted. This early example of social legislation provides a pension for every British subject over 70 with low income.

2 JANUARY 1909
China The government comes into Manchu hands with dismissal of the adviser to the former dowager empress, Yuan Shih-kai, and the 4 October death of her other counselor, Chang Chih-tung.

1 FEBRUARY 1909
Cuba US forces withdraw from the island after liberal José Miguel Gomez becomes president. Ensuing political instability will bring a threat of US intervention in 1912.

8 FEBRUARY 1909
Morocco France and Germany achieve a pact on Morocco that reaffirms the independence and integrity of the country. Germany accedes to France's special political interests in the region, while France recognizes German economic interests there.

13 FEBRUARY 1909
Turkey Grand Vizir Kiamil Pasha, a liberal and reformer, is forced to resign by the Committee of Union and Progress in parliament. The committee is dominated by Turkish nationalists who appoint Hilmi Pasha in his place.

26 FEBRUARY 1909
International Austria and Turkey conclude an agreement in which Turkey recognizes Austria's 1908 annexation of Bosnia and Herzegovina and is to receive compensation.

2 MARCH 1909
International European powers intervene to prevent war between Austria and Serbia over Austrian an-

nexation of Bosnia and Herzegovina, on which Serbia also had designs. Serbia ignores advice from the powers to accede to the annexation.

10 MARCH 1909

Malaya In a treaty with Siam, Great Britain gains suzerainty and protection over Kelantan, Trengganu, Kedah, and Perlis. Together with Johore, they will comprise the Unfederated Malay States, under British control.

12 MARCH 1909

Great Britain Alarmed over increasing German naval strength, Parliament passes a new naval appropriations bill.

18 MARCH 1909

International Russia and Bulgaria reach an agreement in which late-19th-century Russian financial claims are cancelled to meet compensation due to Turkey from Bulgaria.

21 MARCH 1909

International Germany sends Russia a diplomatic note requesting recognition of the Austrian annexation of Bosnia and Herzegovina and cessation of support to Serbia in the controversy. Anxious to avoid war, Russian Foreign Minister Alexander Izvolski yields, placing Great Britain in an awkward position.

26 MARCH 1909

Persia In support of Mohammed Ali Shah's coup d'etat against the constitutional government, a Russian military force invades northern Persia to relieve the siege of Tabriz. The Russians use harsh means to ensure occupation of the city. The Shah will be deposed on 12 July by tribal leader Ali Kuli Khan. Twelve-year-old Sultan Ahmad Shah, his son, will be installed, although a regent supported by radicals will rule.

31 MARCH 1909

International In a diplomatic note to Austria, Serbia recognizes the Bosnian annexation and promises to maintain friendly relations with Austria.

APRIL 1909

Armenia At Aradna and elsewhere in the Armenian region of Turkey, Moslem Turks massacre thousands of Armenians because of agitation against Turkish rule. The Turks have been trying for some time to eradicate this ethnic group—between 1894–97 alone, they killed some 200,000.

APRIL–MAY 1909

France Labor troubles since 1906 climax in a strike by Paris postal workers who call for the right to form unions and to affiliate with the Confédération Général du Travail. The first demand is granted and the second denied by the Clemenceau government, which treats the workers harshly. Over 200 workers

are dismissed and civil servants banned from striking. Labor agitation will continue into 1911, with a railroad strike in October 1910 and a vineyard workers' strike in Champagne the following year.

9 APRIL 1909

USA Congress passes the Payne-Aldrich bill—another high tariff act that brings no economic relief. President Taft signs it with no sign of disapproval, and although he will sponsor much progressive legislation, his lack of political acumen loses him liberal support.

13 APRIL 1909

Turkey In Constantinople, the primarily Albanian First Army Corps seizes the parliament building and telegraph offices, forcing Hilmi Pasha to resign. Violent attacks by conservatives and the Mohammedan Union on the committee government have motivated the revolt, which will be suppressed on 24 April by Mahmud Shevket Pasha's liberation army. After execution of the mutiny's leaders, committee rule is re-established. This will open the way to revival of German influence.

19 APRIL 1909

Bulgaria A convention with Turkey recognizes Bulgarian independence. A further pact with Russia will denote responsibility for financial settlement. Despite a November draft treaty of alliance with Russia, Bulgarian ruler Ferdinand will try to maintain a balance between Austria and Russia, to further his Macedonian aspirations.

26 APRIL 1909

Turkey Sultan Abdul Hamid is deposed by unanimous vote of parliament for his support of the recent

---

PROGRESSIVE SOCIAL LEGISLATION

'Our democratic friends will pipe in vain when the people see princes concerned with their well-being.' Thus Otto von Bismarck, Germany's conservative chancellor, summed up a struggle for political control that began in the 1880s. As the work force grew in the increasingly industrialized nations of Europe, socialist sympathies grew with it. Protective social legislation became Bismarck's method of 'stealing the socialists' thunder.' By the 1890s Germany had developed a system that provided all workers with sickness and accident insurance and guaranteed retirement income. By 1916, in Great Britain, the Liberal government had guaranteed workers the same, along with a minimum wage and progressive taxation. World War I brought France the provinces of Alsace and Lorraine along with their German social programs. Not until the Great Depression would the United States join these industrial nations with similar laws; although Roosevelt would not have used those words, he was in fact following Bismarck's prescription for 'stealing the socialists' thunder.'

CALM BEFORE THE STORM 1900-1913

counterrevolution. He is succeeded by Sultan Mohammed V.

1 JUNE 1909
USA Harvard-educated W E B DuBois helps to found the National Negro Committee, which will become the National Association for the Advancement of Colored People (May 1910), in order to promote equality and equal opportunity for blacks, intellectually and economically.

JULY 1909
Crete The European powers accede to Crete's assertion of independence from the weakened Ottoman Empire; they will withdraw the international peace-keeping force by the end of the month. Cretans who raise the Greek flag are persuaded to take it down. But Cretan-Greek leader Eleutherios Venizelos is in control and eager to effect a union with Greece.
Spain Extremists protest inequality of military service vis-à-vis the Moroccan crisis, which draws from the poorer classes. In Barcelona revolutionaries burn convents and massacre priests. Repressing the revolt, the monarchy will execute anti-clericalist Francisco Ferrer on 13 October.

14 JULY 1909
Germany Chancellor Bernhard von Bülow, who has come increasingly into disfavor—the climax being his handling of the kaiser's interview with the British *Daily Telegraph*—resigns. Dr Theobald von Bethmann-Hollweg, a conciliator who seeks closer ties with Britain, succeeds him and will remain in office until 1917.

20 SEPTEMBER 1909
South Africa The British Parliament passes the South Africa Act, effective 31 May 1910. It approves the constitution drafted by a convention meeting from October 1908 to February 1909. The constitution calls for union of Cape Colony, Natal, Orange River Colony, and Transvaal, and delineates the political and judicial structure of the new self-governing union. Both English and Dutch are established as official languages.

27 SEPTEMBER 1909
USA President Taft sets aside some 3 million acres of oil-rich public land (including Teapot Dome, Wyoming) for conservation purposes.

24 OCTOBER 1909
International Italy and Russia sign the Racconigi Pact in which both nations promise to support the status quo in the Balkans. Italy also agrees to support Russian goals in the Dardanelles, while Russia promises not to interfere with Italian aspirations in Tripoli.

30 NOVEMBER 1909
Great Britain The House of Lords rejects the

'People's Budget' prepared by Chancellor of the Exchequer David Lloyd George and passed by the Commons on 5 November. This budget tries to shift the tax burden to the wealthy through income and inheritance taxes and other devices. The Lords insist the budget should be put to the test of an election. Although denouncing this action as unconstitutional, Prime Minister Asquith calls for an election.

16 DECEMBER 1909
Nicaragua A conservative revolution, coupled with US pressure, forces President José Santos Zelaya from office. The US has opposed his interference in other Central American states and his belligerent policies.

17 DECEMBER 1909
Belgium King Leopold II dies in Brussels. His reign (since 1865) has been marked by ambitious African colonialism. He is succeeded by his nephew Albert I, who will be a much more popular monarch.

OTHER EVENTS OF 1909
Medicine/Health Paul Ehrlich, a German bacteriologist, and Sahachiro Hata, a Japanese researcher working with him, discover salvarsan (arsphenamine), a chemical compound that works to treat syphilis. Since it is the 606th compound tried, it is sometimes known as '606' as well as 'the magic bullet,' and Ehrlich is regarded as one of the founders of modern chemotherapy.
Technology On 25 July Louis Blériot, a Frenchman, flies a monoplane across the English Channel; his flight from Calais to Dover takes $36\frac{1}{2}$ minutes and

Gustav Mahler.

27 APRIL 1910

his plane will be featured at the first Paris Air Show, which will become a biennial event. The first airplane flight in Canada, by J McCurdy under supervision of Alexander Graham Bell, takes place at Baddeck, Nova Scotia. In San Jose, California, Charles D Herrold begins broadcasting from his School of Radio; with records, vocalists, and news, he has what is perhaps the first station with scheduled service by 1911; he is assigned the call letters SJN in 1912 (KCBS since 1949).

Environment On 6 April Robert E Peary, his black assistant, Matthew Henson, and four Eskimos reach the North Pole; this is conceded to be the first expedition to reach this pole, but another American, Dr Frederick A Cook, claimed to have reached it on 20 April 1908. On 16 January members of a British expedition in the Antarctic, headed by Ernest Shackleton, reach and plant a flag on the South Magnetic Pole; on 9 January other members of the expedition had come within 97 miles of the geographic South Pole, but were forced to turn back because of food shortages.

Social Sciences Sigmund Freud comes to the US for lectures at Clark University in Worcester, Massachusetts.

Literature André Gide's *Strait Is the Gate*; Gertrude Stein's *Three Lives*; H G Wells's *Tono-Bungay*; and Nagai Kafu's *The River Sumida*. Filippo Marinetti, an Italian poet, publishes in France's *Le Figaro* a 'manifesto' that launches the Futurist movement in literature and art. Ezra Pound publishes his first books of poetry, *Personae* and *Exultations*, in London; in Paris Andre Gide and others found the *Nouvelle revue française*, soon to become an influential literary journal.

Drama/Entertainment Maurice Maeterlinck's *The Blue Bird*; J M Synge's *Deirdre of the Sorrows*. Sergei Diaghilev, a Russian impresario, brings his Ballet Russe to Paris. The German actress Henny Porten, who has appeared in films by the German director Oskar Messter since 1907, emerges as the first film 'star.'

The Arts Matisse's *The Dance*; Picasso's *Harlequin*; Bonnard's *Standing Nude*. Matisse completes the first of *The Backs*, massive sculptured reliefs in progress till 1930.

Architecture Frank Lloyd Wright completes the Robie House in Chicago, demonstrating his innovative horizontal design.

Music Strauss's opera *Elektra* opens in Dresden; Schoenberg's *Erwartung*; Rimsky-Korsakov's *The Golden Cockerel*; Ralph Vaughan Williams's *Fantasia on a Theme by Tallis*; Wolf-Ferrari's opera *The Secret of Susanna* opens in Munich; Franz Lehar's *The Count of Luxemburg*; Mahler's *Symphony No. 9*. W C Handy composes a campaign song that will become known as *Memphis Blues*, the first 'blues' to be written down.

JANUARY 1910
Great Britain A general election is fought over veto power of the House of Lords and related issues. Irish

President William Howard Taft.

Nationalists support the Liberals on condition that the Lords be reduced in number so they cannot defeat home rule for Ireland. Liberals lose many seats, but retain a majority in Parliament.

20 FEBRUARY 1910
Egypt Christian Copt Premier Butros Ghali, in power since November 1908, is assassinated by a nationalist fanatic, bringing the violent Islamic agitation to a crisis. In 1911 the new British Consul-General, Lord Kitchener, will begin granting liberal concessions.

26 MARCH 1910
USA An amendment to the 1907 Immigration Act bans admission of criminals, paupers, anarchists, and diseased persons to the US. Some countries have been scouring their jails and asylums to send inmates to America.

APRIL–JUNE 1910
Albania The Turkish Army violently suppresses an insurrection calling for Albanian autonomy. Protests against Turkish rule continue in Arabia. Albanians, joined by dissatisfied officers at Monastir, will attempt a second insurrection on 25 June.

13 APRIL 1910
Australia In national elections, the Labour Party wins a clear majority in the House of Representatives. Andrew Fisher forms his second government, which will last until 1913. The program of social reforms continues, and subsidies to desirable white immigrants are resumed.

27 APRIL 1910
South Africa Louis Botha and James Hertzog establish the moderate nationalist South African Party, which promotes equality of Britons and Boers as well as independent status for South Africa in the

71

CALM BEFORE THE STORM 1900-1913

Empire. In the first elections on 15 September, the party wins a decisive victory against the British-imperialist Union Party led by Dr Leander Starr Jameson.

6 MAY 1910
Great Britain   King Edward VII dies after occupying the throne for nine years. This genial man loved sports and good living and gave his name to an idyllic age—the calm before the storm. He is succeeded by his second son, George V.

10 MAY 1910
Great Britain   The House of Commons passes three resolutions on political reform: (1) The House of Lords cannot veto a money bill; (2) Maximum life of Parliament should be five years, not seven; and (3) If three successive sessions of the Commons pass a bill, it will become law even if the Lords vetos it.

18 JUNE 1910
USA   Congress passes the Mann-Elkins Act—legislation for railroad reform. Interlocking railroad directorates, overtly involved in political corruption, are brought under the Interstate Commerce Commission.

4 JULY 1910
Japan   In a mutual defense agreement with Russia, the two nations delineate their spheres of interest in Manchuria, undermining a plan of 1909 by US Secretary of State Philander C Knox to 'neutralize' Manchurian railroads, and hence spheres of influence, through internationalizing their ownership.

22 AUGUST 1910
Korea   Japan annexes Korea and renames it Chosen, then begins a program of assimilation and economic development.

28 AUGUST 1910
Montenegro   Nicholas I, who first assumed power in 1860 and had his reign interrupted by Turkish rule, again proclaims himself king.

31 AUGUST 1910
USA   While on a tour of 16 states, Theodore Roosevelt makes a speech in Kansas advocating 'a square deal': property shall be 'the servant and not the master of the commonwealth.' These words will prove a rallying cry for the Progressive Movement, and preface Roosevelt's entry into the 1912 presidential race.

7 SEPTEMBER 1910
Newfoundland   In The Hague, the International Court arbitrates a fishing-rights dispute between Newfoundland (still separate from Canada) and the US.

15 SEPTEMBER 1910
South Africa   Louis Botha, a leader in the Boer War against the British, becomes premier of the Union when his South African Party wins an overwhelming victory at the polls.

5 OCTOBER 1910
Portugal   A Lisbon insurrection forces the extravagant new monarch, Manoel II, to escape to Britain. The Republic of Portugal is proclaimed, with a provisional government under Dr Theodor Braga. This government is opposed to the Catholic Church, which supports the monarchy. On 20 April 1911 separation of church and state will be instituted.

18 OCTOBER 1910
Greece   Eleutherios Venizelos, the Cretan Greek who has led the effort to unite Crete with Greece and force reforms on the Greek Government, becomes prime minister as a result of August elections demanded by the Military League, a group of army officers who want a restricted role for the monarchy. Heading a minority government, Venizelos will ask for elections in December, from which he will emerge with a majority that permits him to distance himself from the military and effect major reforms.

4–5 NOVEMBER 1910
International   Russian Czar Nicholas II pays a visit to German Emperor Wilhelm II at Potsdam. They forge tentative agreements on spheres of influence in the Middle East—the Russians are to have a free hand in northern Persia and promise to support the Baghdad Railway. This independent diplomatic action of Russia's is greatly resented by the British.

8 NOVEMBER 1910
USA   For the first time since 1894, the nation elects a Democratic Congress, including the first socialist ever to sit in Congress, Victor L Berger of Milwaukee. In Dutchess County, New York, young Franklin Delano Roosevelt is elected to the state senate.

ENTENTE AND OTHER FACADES

The threat of continental war had haunted Europe for 40 years before the coming of World War I. Preceding this global conflict, diplomatic tensions and insecurities had led the European states to create self-protective networks that appeared to guarantee peace. In reality, these alignments indicated where each nation would stand when World War I erupted. The opposing blocs in the prewar years consisted of the Triple Alliance of Germany, Italy, and Austria-Hungary, and the Triple Entente of Great Britain, France, and Russia. But this balance of power did little to mitigate the discordant tenor of Europe. Germany's aggressive quest for international dominance created a coalition of European countries fearful of German imperialism and military power. Entente failed for many reasons, including mutual antagonisms and mistrust.

20 NOVEMBER 1910

Mexico A revolution erupts against long-time dictator Porfirio Díaz.

Russia At remote Astapovo Railway Station, Count Leo Tolstoy dies of pneumonia after fleeing his estate to seek a more ascetic refuge. His funeral will be marked by nationwide strikes and street demonstrations—signaling revival of the revolutionary movement. Although Tolstoy had shared the goal of the revolutionaries—a classless society—the means he proposed were different: moral perfection of the individual, observance of the Christian law of love, and repudiation of violence.

28 NOVEMBER 1910

Great Britain Parliament is dissolved with a second general election scheduled for early December. The Liberals will gain only two seats.

OTHER EVENTS OF 1910

Science American biologist Thomas H Morgan discovers that genes are located on cell structures called chromosomes and that genes on one chromosome are linked and inherited. Halley's Comet passes across the earth's sky, not to appear again until 1987.

Medicine/Health The Carnegie Foundation for the Advancement of Teaching issues a report titled *Medical Education in the United States and Canada* prepared by Abraham Flexner, an American educator: it concludes that only one of the 155 medical schools in North America (Johns Hopkins) provides acceptable medical education. This is a potent source of reform to medical education and thus medical care.

Technology Hydrogenation of coal to produce liquid fuel is achieved.

Environment Robert Scott and his English expedition sail from New Zealand on their ill-fated attempt to reach the South Pole.

Ideas/Beliefs Bertrand Russell and A W Whitehead publish the first of their three-volume (third in 1913) *Principia Mathematica*, a seminal work in logic.

Literature E M Forster's *Howard's End*; Rainer M Rilke's *Notebooks of Malte Laurids Brigge*; Paul Claudel's *Cinq grandes odes*; Karl May's *Winnetou*.

Drama/Entertainment Hauptmann's *The Rats*; Galsworthy's *Justice*. The first giant movie theater opens, the 5000-seat Gaumont Palace (formerly the Hippodrome Theater) in Paris.

The Arts Henri Rousseau's *The Dream*; Modigliani's *The Cellist*; Picasso's *Nude Woman*. In Munich, the Russian artist Wassily Kandinsky abandons representation and starts a nonobjective style utilizing bright colors and abstract forms. In London, Roger Fry organizes a Post-Impressionist Exhibition introducing the work of Cezanne, Van Gogh, and Matisse.

Architecture In Barcelona, Antoni Gaudi completes his Casa Mila, an apartment house in an idiosyncratic art-nouveau style. In Glasgow, Charles R Mackintosh finishes his Glasgow School of Art building, anticipating modern architectural features.

Music Stravinsky's *Firebird* premieres in Paris with the Diaghilev Ballet Russe; Mahler's *Eighth Symphony*; Elgar's *Violin Concerto in B Minor*; Busoni's *Fantasia Contrapuntistica*; Arturo Toscanni conducts the American premiere of Puccini's *Girl of the Golden West* at the Metropolitan Opera in New York.

Sports/Leisure Jack Johnson, black American boxer, defeats Jim Jeffries, who has emerged from retirement as 'The Great White Hope.'

Miscellaneous The first policewoman, Mrs Alice Stebbins Wells, is appointed by the Los Angeles Police Department. A former social worker, she promotes the cause of policewomen (by 1916 the US has 17 cities employing them).

22 FEBRUARY 1911

Canada Parliament resolves to maintain union with the British Empire, while controlling domestic fiscal affairs.

24 FEBRUARY 1911

International Japan and the US conclude a treaty that continues restrictions on Japanese laborers.

7 MARCH 1911

Mexico US President Taft orders 20,000 troops to the Mexican border in support of beleaguered dictator Díaz and to protect American capital of over $2 billion invested in Mexico.

13 APRIL 1911

USA The House of Representatives votes to institute direct election of senators to Congress, a step toward direct democracy.

12 MAY 1911

Persia American economic expert W Morgan Schuster arrives by invitation of the Majlis to assume almost dictatorial power over Persia's finances. Russia resents this and will try to frustrate his reforms.

15 MAY 1911

USA The Supreme Court finds Standard Oil Company guilty of 'unreasonable' restraint of trade—articulating a new judicial principle, 'the rule of reason.' This case is a precedent for future regulation of big business.

Great Britain The House of Commons passes the Parliament Bill again to limit the power of the House of Lords. The Lords will pass the bill on 20 July with amendments unacceptable to Prime Minister Asquith. When he threatens to create enough peers to pass the original bill, the Lords relent and pass the legislation as drafted, on 10 August.

21 MAY 1911

Morocco Despite German warnings, the French enter Fez ostensibly to quell anti-European agitation. This advance, and German dissatisfaction with the 8 February 1909 agreement, will lead to the second Moroccan crisis (June–November).

CALM BEFORE THE STORM 1900-1913

25 MAY 1911
Mexico The reactionary dictatorship of Díaz, in power since 1876, is overthrown by revolutionaries active since 1910. The moderate liberal Francisco Madero will become president on 6 November, initiating an era of economic and social revolution.

26 MAY 1911
Germany Legislation is passed organizing Alsace and Lorraine as an autonomous state with a legislature.

6 JUNE 1911
Nicaragua The US and Nicaragua sign a treaty granting an American loan secured by customs duties collected by a US-approved collector-general. The pact fails to win consent of the US Senate.

11 JUNE 1911
Greece The national assembly, now dominated by Premier Venizelos and supporters, adopts a more liberal constitution—one of the reforms Venizelos effects during June.

1 JULY 1911
Morocco The German gunboat *Panther* arrives off Agadir, an Atlantic coast port, allegedly to protect German interests and nationals in Morocco. This is Germany's attempt to signal opposition to France's takeover of Morocco, and to indicate to the world that Germany will assert herself on the international stage. The French dispatch their own warship; the powers choose sides, with Russia and Britain supporting France; stock exchanges register the threat of war. Negotiations gradually defuse the crisis, with a November agreement between France and Germany.

13 JULY 1911
International Great Britain and Japan renew their alliance of 1902 for another four years. This pact will become the reason for Japan's entry into World War I on the Allied side.

1 AUGUST 1911
Great Britain Transportation workers begin a major strike. Labor unrest will continue through 1912 with railwaymen's and coal miners' strikes, resulting in the 29 March 1912 minimum wage law.

10 AUGUST 1911
Great Britain For the first time the House of Commons votes a salary—of £400 annually—for its members.

24 AUGUST 1911
Portugal Dr Manoel de Arriaga is elected president of the Republic of Portugal after the constituent assembly adopts a liberal constitution (20 August).

14 SEPTEMBER 1911
Russia In Kiev Prime Minister Peter Stolypin is assassinated. His regime has been characterized by harsh measures to control dissidents. Vladimir Kokotsev succeeds him.

28 SEPTEMBER 1911
Tripolitan War Hostilities break out between Italy and Turkey over Italian territorial aspirations in North Africa. On 5 October the Italians will occupy Tripoli and subsequently other coastal towns. On 5 November Italy will proclaim annexation of Tripoli, despite resistance by a small Turkish force under Enver Bey with Arab support.

10 OCTOBER 1911
China Revolution begins with a bomb explosion and the discovery of revolutionary headquarters in Hankow. The movement will spread rapidly through west and south China, forcing abdication of the last Ch'ing emperor, six-year-old Henry Pu-Yi. By 26 October the Chinese Republic will be proclaimed, and on 4 December Premier Yuan Shih-k'ai will sign a truce with rebel general Li Yuan-hung.

4 NOVEMBER 1911
Morocco France and Germany conclude an agreement ending the Agadir crisis. Germany agrees to allow the French a free hand in Morocco, even to establishing a protectorate, while France cedes part of the French Congo along with two strips of territory connecting the area to the German Cameroons. This settlement avoids basic issues—the rights of colonial peoples whose lands are used as pawns, and underlying conflicts between major powers.

11 NOVEMBER 1911
Persia The Russians issue an ultimatum to Persia and follow it with invasion of northern Persia to impose political control over the Russian sphere of interest. The Russians ignore British protests.

20 NOVEMBER 1911
France Lenin—who spends the 10 years following 1907 in exile in Paris, Switzerland, and Cracow—attends the Paris funeral of Paul and Laura Lafargue. The two socialists had died in a suicide pact in the belief that their political usefulness was at an end: Laura was the daughter of Karl Marx. In his eulogy, Lenin warns that 'world bourgeois parliamentarism is coming to a close.'

DECEMBER 1911
Great Britain Parliament passes the National Insurance Act that provides insurance for both loss of health and prevention and care of sickness, as well as for unemployment. Employer, employee, and the state will contribute to the fund.

12 DECEMBER 1911
India During his coronation celebration at Delhi, the King-Emperor George V proclaims transfer of the Indian capital from Calcutta to Delhi and reversal of the partition of Bengal.

SUN YAT-SEN, 1866–1925

Sun Yat-sen, one of the century's extraordinary revolutionaries, grew up in a Christian family and became a doctor of medicine, but long felt he was destined to lead the revolution that would overthrow the Manchu Dynasty. His first attempt, in 1895, failed, but he left China, traveled around the world raising funds and support for his cause, and finally saw the revolution succeed in 1911–12. He was elected the first president of the new Chinese Republic, but was forced to flee to Japan when a powerful warlord, Yuan Shih-kai, attempted to enthrone himself. Sun Yat-sen returned after Yuan's death and re-established himself. He rejected the communist dogma of class war and admired Western industrialism even as he opposed Western imperialism. Sun's idealistic *Three Principles of the People*—nationalism, democracy, and socialism—became the guidelines of his revolution. He died in 1925, and was succeeded by his disciple, General Chiang Kai-shek.

30 DECEMBER 1911

China A Nanking revolutionary provisional assembly elects Sun Yat-sen, recently back from Europe, president of the United Provinces of China. Sun will resign this office to ensure national unity when Yuan Shih-k'ai is elected provisional president of the Chinese Republic by the national assembly on 15 February 1912.

OTHER EVENTS OF 1911

Science Ernest Rutherford announces his theory of the nucleus of the atom, rejecting the previous notion of atoms as 'building blocks' to see them as miniature solar systems, with a central nucleus and particles of negative electricity—electrons—spinning around it. This model, modified by Niels Bohr in 1913, will be accepted in essence by modern physics.

Technology Charles Kettering, American engineer, develops the first practical electric self-starter for automobiles.

Environment On 3 November Scott and his team set off for the South Pole. On December 15 Roald Amundsen, the Norwegian explorer, raises his flag at the South Pole after a dog-sledge journey that began on 19 October.

Social Sciences Hiram Bingham, an American archaeologist, discovers the ruins of the Inca capital Vilcabamba below the peak known as Machu Picchu, 8000 feet above sea level; this Peruvian site will remain one of the most impressive archaeological discoveries of all time. Franz Boas, German-born but resident in America since 1889, at Columbia University since 1896, publishes *The Mind of Primitive Man*; Boas is training a generation of anthropologists who will have a crucial role in the discipline. Swiss psychiatrist Herman Rorschach develops an ink-blot test by which a subject describes what he or she perceives for interpretation by a trained psychologist who can thus deduce certain tendencies in the

Literature Edith Wharton's *Ethan Frome*; Joseph Conrad's *Under Western Eyes*; Katherine Mansfield's *In a German Pension*; Max Beerbohm's *Zuleika Dobson*; Pio Baroja's *The Tree of Knowledge*; Stephen B Leacock's *Literary Lapses*.

The Arts Chagall's *I and My Village*; Braque's *Man with a Guitar*. In Munich, Kandinsky and Franz Marc form *Der Blaue Reiter* ('The Blue Rider'), a group of artists dedicated to a particular aesthetic, whose name derives from a Kandinsky painting.)

Music Stravinsky's *Petrouchka*; Strauss's opera *Der Rosenkavalier*; Ravel's *Valses Nobles et Sentimentales*; Mahler's *Snng of the L;rth*; Charles Ives's *Symphony No 3* (virtually unknown until it wins a Pulitzer Prize in 1947).

Miscellaneous In New York City a fire at the Triangle Shirtwaist Company kills 145, almost all of them women trapped in the unsafe building; the tragedy will lead to demands for reform of working conditions among New York's garment workers. Near Perth, Australia, the University of Western Australia is founded with a bequest from Sir Winthrop Hackett, a newspaper baron.

JANUARY 1912

Germany In Reichstag elections, Socialists win 110 seats to become the strongest party. They will cooperate with Progressives to achieve their goals of social reform.

Russia In a Prague Bolshevik Conference called by Lenin, 14 hand-picked voting delegates (including two czarist secret-police agents) elect a Bolshevik central committee, breaking with the more conserva-

Marc Chagall.

CALM BEFORE THE STORM 1900-1913

tive Mensheviks. Through this maneuver, Lenin seizes control of the Social Democratic Party and co-opts the absent Stalin as a member of the committee.

JANUARY–FEBRUARY 1912
Tripolitan War Italian naval vessels bombard Syrian coastal towns in the continuing conflict with Turkey. Austria puts pressure on Italy to enforce the Triple Alliance, which forbids Italians from warlike maneuvers along the Aegean and Balkan coasts.

9 JANUARY 1912
Honduras The US lands Marines in Honduras to protect American property and investment in the Central American state.

12 JANUARY 1912
USA Labor agitation increases when workers strike against sweatshop conditions in the textile mills of Lawrence, Massachusetts. They are protesting a wage cut under a new law that limits working hours. The strike will last two months, and the militant Industrial Workers of the World will use the struggle as an excuse to move into the Northeast.

8 FEBRUARY 1912
International British emissary Lord Haldane journeys to Berlin to suggest that Britain might support German colonial aspirations in Africa if Germany

agrees to hold to her current naval strength. Reluctant to make concessions, Germany will publish a new bill on 8 March, calling for a sizable naval increase. This will bring an abrupt end to discussions with the British.

13 MARCH 1912
International Bulgaria and Serbia conclude an alliance pact ostensibly against Austria, but it secretly provides for a possible war against Turkey, spelling out territorial division of lands currently under Turkish control, including Macedonia. A 12 May military convention will supplement this treaty.

30 MARCH 1912
Morocco In the Treaty of Fez, the Sultan Mulay Hafid is forced to allow a French protectorate. On 24 May French General Louis Lyautey is named resident-general of Morocco in a program to restore order quickly to the region. On 11 August Mulay Hafid will abdicate rather than rule as a French puppet. He is succeeded by Mulay Yusuf.

11 APRIL 1912
Ireland In the British Parliament, a bill for Irish home rule is introduced. It proposes that Ireland be granted its own bicameral parliament and be required to send representatives to the British House of Commons. Protestants of Ulster denounce the bill at once, seeing no protection for themselves in a Catho-

The 1912 strike in Lawrence, Massachusetts.

THE MEXICAN REVOLUTION

In the years following the 1910 revolution in Mexico, successive presidents rose and fell from power: when calm at last prevailed, millions of Mexicans had lost their lives by violence. Long after the revolutionary upheaval, the transformation of Mexican society continued. Most significant was the commitment to extensive land reform. Both accomplishments and problems remain as legacies of the revolution. Once-landless peasants now communally operate their *ejidos*, but many still wait for land, cannot obtain credit, or lack access to irrigation facilities. There has been massive industrial development since 1940, a rising per-capita income from 1940–70, and improvement in education and health. Nevertheless, income distribution remains unequal; unemployment is high; inflation threatens to impoverish the middle classes. Since 1929 the Party of Revolutionary Institutions has held power, balancing the competing interests of its constituencies, keeping economic and social difficulties under control. With the collapse of Mexico's oil strategy beginning in 1978, the party's ability to hold the coalition together and to meet unfulfilled expectations is called into question.

lic Ireland. In Belfast on 28 September they will sign a covenant pledging resistance to home rule.

18 APRIL 1912
Tripolitan War In continuing hostilities, Turkey closes the Dardanelles Straits until 4 May after an Italian naval bombardment of the coastline. Russia's commerce suffers greatly.

4–16 MAY 1912
Tripolitan War Italian forces occupy Rhodes and other Dodecanese Islands, establishing a foothold in the eastern Mediterranean and threatening French and British interests. Peace negotiations between Turkey and Italy will begin in July.

JUNE 1912
Liberia An international loan is arranged for the bankrupt African republic. A US commission has supported the government since 1909 with financial aid and military protection against internal insurrection.

5 JUNE 1912
Cuba The US lands Marines to protect American interests during an uprising by black Cubans. This is in opposition to President Taft's new policy of 'dollar diplomacy' toward Latin American nations, in which American capital is to reform corrupt governments. All too often, the result of this policy will be to stabilize harsh administrations, creating long-lasting animosity toward the US.

18 JUNE 1912
USA At the Chicago national Republican Conven-

A Women's Suffrage demonstration—New York, 1912.

CALM BEFORE THE STORM 1900-1913

tion, the party is split between President Taft, supported by the Conservatives, and Theodore Roosevelt, who heads the Progressives. When Taft is nominated for a second term, Roosevelt and his followers form the Bull Moose Party, draining liberal elements from the Republican Party. On 2 July the Democratic convention chooses Woodrow Wilson as its presidential candidate. On 5 August the Bull Moose Party will nominate Roosevelt.

JULY 1912
Nicaragua Civil war breaks out, and the US intervenes to protect the conservative government (and American interests). In November an election will be held, under supervision of American military forces, that chooses conservative Adolfo Díaz as president. The US will establish a legation guard of Marines at Managua.

22 JULY 1912
Great Britain In the face of ever-increasing German naval power, the Admiralty decides to recall British warships from the Mediterranean and base them in the North Sea.

14 OCTOBER 1912
Greece Cretan representatives are admitted to the Greek assembly. In so doing the Greek Government challenges the Turkish Government.

18 OCTOBER 1912
Tripolitan War The Treaty of Lausanne ends the Tripolitan War between Turkey and Italy. The Turks agree to cede Tripoli, and the Italians to restore the Dodecanese Islands to Turkish sovereignty. During 1913 the Italians will pacify the interior of Tripoli.
First Balkan War The First Balkan War breaks out, with Bulgaria, Serbia, and Greece opposed to Turkey.

28 OCTOBER–3 NOVEMBER 1912
First Balkan War Hostilities continue as the Bulgarians achieve a victory against the Turks at Lulé Burgus, from whence they will advance to the Chatalja Lines, last bulwark before Constantinople. Russians warn Bulgarians against occupying Constantinople, enforcing their warning by threatening use of their fleet. But the 17–18 November Bulgarian attack on the Chatalja Lines will fail.

5 NOVEMBER 1912
USA In the presidential election, Democrat Woodrow Wilson wins by a landslide 435 electoral votes to Theodore Roosevelt's 88 and President Taft's 8. Popular vote is 6,293,454 for Wilson, 4,119,538 for Roosevelt, 3,484,980 for Taft, demonstrating that the Republicans might have won had their party not split.

24 NOVEMBER 1912
First Balkan War Conflict grows into an acute international crisis, as Austria proclaims opposition

to territorial access to the Adriatic Sea for Serbia and support for an independent Albania. The Serbs are supported by Russia and France, and Austria by Italy and Germany. Britain is sympathetic to Austria. Austria and Russia begin to mobilize, but Russia is unwilling to risk war and abandons Serbia.

27 NOVEMBER 1912
Morocco A treaty between Spain and France delineates spheres of interest in Morocco.

28 NOVEMBER 1912
Albania An assembly at Valona declares Albania independent of the Ottoman Empire, rejecting the grant of autonomy made by the Turkish Government on 20 November.

5 DECEMBER 1912
International The Triple Alliance among Italy, Austria, and Germany (originally signed in 1882) is renewed for six years, beginning July 1914. This diplomatic move is inspired by instability resulting from the Balkan War.

23 DECEMBER 1912
India Terrorist agitation continues as British Viceroy Lord Hardinge is wounded by a bomb explosion in Delhi. He will recover and continue as viceroy until 1916.

OTHER EVENTS OF 1912
Science Victor Hess, an Austrian physicist, makes a balloon ascent with an instrument that measures radioactivity; he discovers that radioactivity increases with altitude and concludes that there must be some source in space; later this will be confirmed and named 'cosmic rays.' Frederick Soddy, an English physicist, demonstrates the existence of isotopes—atoms of the same element that differ in atomic weight. Alfred Wegener, German meteorologist, proposes a theory of 'continental drift,' whereby a 'supercontinent' (which he calls Pangaea) began to break up about 200 million years ago, eventually forming continents of today. Wegener could not explain how these great masses moved, and his theory was rejected and largely forgotten until the 1950s when the new science of paleomagnetism began to confirm it. Only in the 1960s did geologists begin to adopt Wegener's hypothesis as part of the theory of plate tectonics.
Medicine/Health Polish biochemist Casimir Funk proposes that the substance in rice hulls that prevents beriberi (discovered in 1901 by Grijins) belongs to a group of chemical compounds Funk calls 'vitamines' ('amines essential to life').
Environment Robert Scott and four companions reach the South Pole on 18 January, only to discover that Amundsen had been there a month earlier; Scott and his companions are so exhausted by their return journey that they all die by 29 March; their bodies are found the following spring.
Social Science Alfred Adler, an Austrian psycho-

logist originally identified with Freud's circle, has been drawing away to found his own group; this year he publishes *The Neurotic Constitution*, setting forth concepts of his school, known generally as 'individual psychology.' Emile Durkheim, influential French sociologist, publishes *The Elementary Forms of Religious Life*.

Literature Thomas Mann's *Death in Venice*; Anatole France's *The Gods Are Athirst*; Rabindranath Tagore's *Gitanjali*; Stephen B Leacock's *Sketches of a Little Town*.

Drama/Entertainment Shaw's *Pygmalion*; Paul Claudel's *Tidings Brought to Mary*.

The Arts Franz Marc's *Tower of Blue Horses*; Picasso's *The Violin*; Marcel Duchamp, a French artist, paints *Nude Descending a Staircase, No 2*, an extraordinary rendering of motion in a modernist style; it will be the sensation of the New York Armory Show in 1913, and Duchamp will continue to astonish with such departures as his Mona Lisa with a moustache.

Music Strauss's opera *Ariadne auf Naxos*; Schoenberg's *Pierrot Lunaire*; Ravel's *Daphnis and Chloé*; Mahler's *Ninth Symphony*. Al Jolson records 'Ragging the Baby to Sleep,' which becomes an immediate hit and will sell a million copies within the first two years (a record prior to World War I).

Miscellaneous On the night of April 14–15, the British liner *Titanic*, touted as 'unsinkable,' hits an iceberg in the North Atlantic on its maiden crossing and goes down with loss of 1500 lives; it will remain the most notorious disaster of the century, and have the effect of improving safety conditions on ocean liners. Over Jefferson Barracks, Missouri, Albert Berry makes the first parachute descent from an airplane; he pretends to be delivering a message to the US Army to demonstrate the efficacy of parachuting in warfare.

6 JANUARY 1913

First Balkan War Attempting to end hostilities, the London Peace Conference, in session since 17 December 1912, breaks down because Turkey refuses to cede Adrianople, the Aegean islands, and Crete. On 22 January the European powers will persuade Turkey to give up Adrianople, and the London Peace Conference will resume on 20 May.

12 JANUARY 1913

Russia After using other pseudonyms over the years, Josef Dzhugashvili signs himself Stalin ('man of steel') in a letter to the *Social Democrat*. During the past year he has been in Vienna editing the revolutionary organ *Pravda*.

16 JANUARY 1913

Ireland The British House of Commons passes the Irish Home Rule Bill, but the Lords will reject it on 30 January. The Commons will pass the bill again on 7 July, and Lords reject it on 15 July. Each time, opposition of the Ulster Protestants to the bill will intensify.

23 JANUARY 1913

Turkey The Young Turks, including Enver Bey, lead a coup d'état against the Turkish Government, which was about to cede Adrianople to the Balkan States as a condition of settling the First Balkan War. Mahmud Shevket Pasha is installed as grand vizir.

18 FEBRUARY 1913

Mexico President Francisco Madero is overthrown by the ruthless General Victoriano Huerta, friend of the landowners. Huerta's coup d'état has been countenanced by American diplomat Henry Lane Wilson. Four days later Madero is executed 'while attempting to escape' as the US masses troops on the Mexican border. The US refuses to recognize Huerta, who is opposed by a revolutionary movement led by Venustiano Carranza. On 16 February President Taft had promised nonintervention in Mexican internal affairs.

25 FEBRUARY 1913

USA The 16th Amendment to the Constitution becomes law, providing the legal basis for the institution of a graduated income tax.

4 MARCH 1913

USA In his inaugural speech, Woodrow Wilson decries the human cost of the nation's remarkable industrial achievement. With a solid Democratic House behind him, Wilson will attempt to reform the hitherto intractable tariff and banking systems, with little success.

18 MARCH 1913

Greece King George I is assassinated. He will be succeeded by Constantine I.

3 APRIL 1913

Great Britain Suffragist Emmeline Pankhurst is sentenced in the Old Bailey to three years' imprisonment for incitement to violence, after she accepts responsibility for the placement of a bomb in Lloyd George's new house, then under construction. The new Cat and Mouse Act will prevent suspension of her sentence after a hunger strike in prison, as in the past; she will be liable to rearrest each time she regains her strength. Over the next year she will be rearrested 12 times, but serve a total of only 10 days, because she adds to her hunger strike a refusal to drink or sleep, causing more rapid weakness and a quicker release from jail. When World War I begins, she will turn to helping the war effort.

8 APRIL 1913

China The elected bicameral parliament convenes, as mandated by the 10 March 1912 Nanking Provisional Constitution. President Yuan Shih-k'ai, attempting to increase his own powers, will purge parliament of its Kuomintang or Nationalist members, led by Sun Yat-sen, on 4 November. Two months later Yuan, who has monarchist aspirations, will dissolve parliament.

CALM BEFORE THE STORM 1900-1913

WOODROW WILSON, 1856–1924

The 28th president of the United States, Woodrow Wilson, was born in Staunton, Virginia, and studied at Princeton and Johns Hopkins. He practiced law in Atlanta, taught at Bryn Mawr and Wesleyan, and became president of Princeton in 1902. His reforms as governor of New Jersey (1911–13) brought prominence in Democratic politics and the presidential nomination (1912). His two terms as president saw passage of the prohibition and women's suffrage amendments to the Constitution, discord with Mexico, and America's participation in World War I. His 'fourteen points' for a just and lasting peace (1918) were widely admired, but the Paris Peace Conference fell far short of what he had envisioned (he attended as head of the US delegation, an unprecedented event in American statesmanship). Isolationists attacked the concept of a League of Nations, and the Senate rejected the Treaty of Versailles. Wilson's health broke down near the end of his second term after a strenuous national speaking tour (1919) to elicit popular support for the League. He died five years later, leaving a distinguished body of work on history and jurisprudence that is still esteemed even by his critics.

10 APRIL 1913
Montenegro During the Montenegrin siege of Scutari, the Montenegrin coastline is blockaded. Nicholas I will capture Scutari on 22 April, but Austrian pressure will force him to depart on 5 May.

14–24 APRIL 1913
Belgium A general strike is called to protest the electoral system. It ends when the government promises reform, which will be delayed by the war until 6 May 1919.

16 APRIL 1913
First Balkan War The Bulgarians and the Turks agree to an armistice that will be accepted by the other nations involved.

7 MAY 1913
First Balkan War An ambassadorial conference in St Petersburg, Russia, awards the town of Silistria to Rumania in compensation for Bulgaria's other territorial gains in the First Balkan War. Dissatisfied, the Rumanian Government demands more.

30 MAY 1913
First Balkan War The Treaty of London ends the First Balkan War. Turkey cedes all territory west of a line from Enos to Midia, gives up claims on Crete, and leaves disposition of Albania and the Aegean islands to the European powers.

31 MAY 1913
USA The 17th Amendment establishes popular election of senators, who had been chosen by state legislatures and were often unresponsive to the electorate.

1 JUNE 1913
Serbia The government concludes a ten-year treaty with Greece against Bulgaria. Serbia wishes to pursue Macedonian aspirations with Greece's help.

11 JUNE 1913
Turkey Grand Vizir Mahmud Shevket Pasha is assassinated, resulting in continuing Young Turk terrorism until World War I. The triumvirate of Enver Bey, Mehmet Talaat Pasha, and Jemal Pasha will rule in what is left of the Ottoman Empire.

14 JUNE 1913
South Africa The government passes the Immigration Act, which restricts entry and free movement of Asians. It leads to widespread agitation and rioting by resident Indians, led by Gandhi.

16 JUNE 1913
South Africa The government passes the segregationist Natives Land Act, which restricts purchase or lease of land by native Africans. The act sets aside certain land areas as reserves.

29 JUNE 1913
Second Balkan War The attack by Bulgarian General Michael Savov on Greek and Serbian positions leads to the Second Balkan War. On 10 July Rumania will declare war on Bulgaria. Serbians and Greeks use the situation to carry out their planned attack on Bulgaria. Turkey will enter the war against Bulgaria, defeated on 30 July.

30 JUNE 1913
Germany To increase the peacetime strength of the German Army, the Reichstag easily passes the Army and Finance Bills, which provide for 4000 officers,

15,000 noncommissioned officers, and 117,000 men. The Socialists oppose the measure. This defense buildup will be financed by a national defense tax imposed only once on real and personal property. As a concession to the Socialists, the financial burden will not be borne by the lower classes.

12 JULY 1913

Ireland At Craigavon, 150,000 Ulstermen gather and resolve to resist Irish Home Rule by force of arms. By December 100,000 Ulstermen have volunteered; since the British Liberals have promised the Irish nationalists Home Rule, civil war appears imminent.

20 JULY 1913

Second Balkan War In continuing hostilities, the Turks take back Adrianople, which they will keep by the 29 September Treaty of Constantinople.

21 JULY 1913

Egypt The government announces a new constitutional system and electoral law.

10 AUGUST 1913

Second Balkan War After the Bulgarian defeat in the war, the Treaty of Bucharest gives Rumania the northern Dobrudja, and Serbia and Greece areas of Macedonia they have occupied. Bulgaria loses Monastir and Ochrid to Serbia and Salonika and Kavalla to Greece, as well as a sizable area of its Aegean coast.

29 SEPTEMBER 1913

Second Balkan War The Treaty of Constantinople between Turkey and Bulgaria restores peace. The Turks recover Adrianople and the Maritza River line.

3 OCTOBER 1913

USA Under President Wilson's urging, Congress enacts the Underwood-Simmons Tariff—the first tariff reform since the Civil War. Duties are reduced on 958 items, including foodstuff, clothing, and raw materials, with textile rates cut 50 percent. Loss of revenue will be made up by the graduated income tax.

18 OCTOBER 1913

International Austria demands that within eight days Serbia leave Albanian soil, occupied since 23 September. Serbia yields to Austrian pressure. On 30 October an Austro-Italian note will demand that Greece evacuate southern Albania by 31 December.

1 NOVEMBER 1913

Mexico Less than a week after a US nonintervention promise, President Woodrow Wilson demands that Mexican dictator Huerta resign.

13 DECEMBER 1913

International British Foreign Minister Sir Edward Grey proposes that southern Albania be divided between Greece and Albania, with compensation to Greece in the Aegean islands. This plan will be accepted, but the Greeks will not evacuate southern Albania until 27 April 1914.

14 DECEMBER 1913

Greece King Constantine I declares the union of Crete with Greece, the first time these two regions have been united.

OTHER EVENTS OF 1913

Science Niels Bohr, the Danish physicist, refines Rutherford's 1911 description of the atom; Bohr says electrons travel in successively larger orbits, outer orbits hold more electrons, and those in the outermost orbit determine chemical properties of the atom. Harlow Shapley, American astronomer, develops an improved method for measuring the distance of stars by spectroscopic observations.

Technology The first electrically-powered refrigerator for home use, a Domelre, is made in Chicago. Gideon Sundback of Hoboken, New Jersey, obtains a patent for a 'separable fastener,' the first to work with meshed teeth on parallel tapes; Sundback's device is soon manufactured by the Talon Slide Fastener Company—in 1922 the B F Goodrich Company will coin the word 'zipper' for such slide fasteners used on rubber boots.

Environment Canadian-born Vilhjalmar Stefansson, of Icelandic parentage, begins a five-year period of residency and exploration in the Arctic Circle after several Arctic expeditions; he will return with discoveries about the environment and the Eskimos.

Social Science John B Watson, American psychologist, introduces his concept of 'behaviorism,' claiming that only study of observable behavior in humans and animals reveals their nature. Watson will publish his first statement in 1919, *Psychology from the Standpoint of a Behaviorist*, and his ideas will influence child care and education for years.

Ideas/Beliefs Henry Adams's *Mont-Saint-Michel and Chartres* is published (privately printed in 1904).

Literature D H Lawrence's *Sons and Lovers*; Alain-Fournier's *Le Grand Meaulnes*; Guillaume Apollinaire's *Alcoöls*; Shiga Naoya's *Han's Crime*; Marcel Proust publishes, at his own expense, *Swann's Way*, first part of *À la recherche du temps perdu (Remembrance of Things Past)*, its last part to come posthumously in 1928.

The Arts Wilhelm Lehmbruck's *Standing Youth* and Umberto Boccioni's *Unique Forms of Continuity in Space* are masterworks of modern sculpture. In New York City, the Armory Show introduces many works of modern art to Americans.

Music On 29 May the Parisian premier of Stravinsky's *Le sacre du printemps (The Rite of Spring)* provokes violent protest by many in the audience. Anton von Webern's *Five Pieces for Orchestra*; and Rachmaninoff's *The Bells* make their debuts.

Life/Customs In the *New York World* the first crossword puzzle appears; it is compiled by the English-born Arthur Wynne, who based it on a childhood game, 'Magic Square,' and has only 32 words with basic definitions.

THE SENSELESS WAR 1914-1918

1914-1918:
THE SENSELESS WAR

Men of the Canadian Corps going over the top at the Battle of the Somme—September 1916.

5 JANUARY 1914
USA Henry Ford, whose automobile manufacturing plant is revolutionizing what had been a luxury product, extends his reforms to workers by announcing a minimum wage of $5 a day, an 8-hour workday, and profit-sharing.

10 JANUARY 1914
China Yuan Shih-kai, president of the new republic, dissolves parliament and appoints a special group to prepare a constitution of his own design: he will set himself up as dictator, preparatory to an attempt to make himself emperor.

21 FEBRUARY 1914
Russia In a secret meeting in St Petersburg of civil and military leaders, Foreign Minister Sazonov convinces them to support a plan for seizing the straits, controlled by Turkey, that block Russia's access to the Mediterranean. This is one of several such secret decisions by European powers that indicate readiness to resort to force to achieve national goals. Other foreign ministers are engaged in alliances and plans that will bring the major nations into World War I.

9–11 APRIL 1914
Mexico-USA President Wilson has refused to recognize Huerta as President of Mexico on the ground that he has not been elected by the people. When sailors from an American ship, *Dolphin*, go ashore at Tampico, Mexico, for supplies, they are arrested (on 9 April) and then released. Admiral Henry Mayo demands an apology and 'salute to the American flag.' Huerta refuses the latter and on 11 April breaks off diplomatic relations.

20 APRIL 1914
Mexico-USA President Wilson, having dispatched more naval ships to Mexico, asks a joint session of Congress to approve armed force if necessary to make Huerta agree to America's terms. Congress votes approval.

21 APRIL 1914
Mexico-USA US Marines and sailors take Veracruz, a major Mexican port. Nineteen Americans and 200 Mexicans are killed. US forces will hold Veracruz until 23 November.

THE SENSELESS WAR 1914-1918

25 APRIL 1914
Mexico-USA   President Wilson is persuaded by the ABC Powers—Argentina, Brazil, and Chile—to accept mediation in the conflict with Mexico. Stopping shipment of supplies for Huerta will be a factor in pressuring him to resign in May.

15 MAY 1914
International   Colonel Edward House, President Wilson's adviser, sails for Europe to persuade major powers to reduce armies and navies and use their resources to develop waste areas of the world. From Germany, House will report that 'Everybody's nerves are tense; it only needs a spark to set the whole thing off.' Before he returns on 29 July, the 'spark' will have been supplied.

20 MAY–30 JUNE 1914
Mexico-USA   Representatives of the US and Mexico meet at Niagara Falls with representatives of Argentina, Brazil, and Chile to resolve differences. Huerta resigns, replaced by General Carranza (whom the US has been backing) as 'provisional' president. Its goal achieved, the US signs an agreement with Mexico on 24 June.

25 MAY 1914
Ireland   Britain's House of Commons passes a compromise Home Rule Bill: the nine Ulster—Northern Ireland—counties will be allowed to vote on whether to remain in a united Ireland for six more years—in effect, postponing the problem. World War I will put off any change in Northern Ireland's status.

13 JUNE 1914
International   Greece and Turkey have been heading toward conflict for months over claims to Aegean islands; Venizelos announces today that Greece intends to annex Chios and Mytilene (Lesbos), two large islands off the Turkish coast. Because each nation has been trying to gain support from other powers, any war threatens to spread.

28 JUNE 1914
WW I: Prelude   At Sarajevo, capital of Bosnia, Archduke Francis Ferdinand, heir to the Austro-Hungarian throne, and his wife are assassinated by a young Bosnian, Gabriel Princip. Although Princip and two other Bosnians planned the assassination, high Serbian officials not only knew of the plot but provided support. In Sarajevo there will be anti-Serbian riots, and Austrian officials and private citizens are quick to blame the Serbians.

5 JULY 1914
WW I: Prelude   Kaiser Wilhelm privately assures Austria-Hungary of German support against Russia if the latter decides to aid Serbia. Behind this readiness lies the Kaiser's long-standing desire to punish the 'Slavs'; Austria-Hungary has been looking for an excuse to repress its Slavic subjects permanently.

US Marines at Vera Cruz, 1914.

20–27 JULY 1914

WW I: Prelude European diplomats are trying to avert the collision their policies have made all but inevitable. French President Poincaré goes to Russia to reaffirm France's support; Britain's foreign secretary, Edward Grey, proposes that major powers mediate the crisis, but his own secret agreements with Russia and France have encouraged resort to arms.

23 JULY 1914

WW I: Prelude Austria-Hungary has been preparing an ultimatum to the Serbian Government for two weeks: this afternoon it is presented. Although the terms are not stringent—suppressing the Serbians and their anti-Austrian elements—the fact that Austria-Hungary demands acceptance within 48 hours makes peacekeeping difficult.

25 JULY 1914

WW I: Prelude Serbia meets the deadline and gives an apparently conciliatory reply to the ultimatum. As instructed, the Austrian ambassador in Belgrade breaks off diplomatic relations. But Serbia had begun to mobilize even before presenting its reply.

26–28 JULY 1914

WW I: Prelude The foreign ministries and leaders of major states work feverishly to avert war. Edward Grey's proposal that France, Germany, Italy, and Britain work out a solution seems to elicit support, and various tactics are considered. One is that Austria-Hungary occupy Belgrade temporarily as a pledge that Serbia will satisfy its demands.

28 JULY 1914

WW I The Austro-Hungarian Government decides against mediation and declares war on Serbia.

29 JULY 1914

WW I The Austrians bombard Belgrade. Russian diplomats and generals are urging general mobilization, but the Czar calls for partial mobilization.

30 JULY 1914

WW I The Czar is persuaded to general mobilization. 'Think of the responsibility you are advising me to take,' he protests: 'Think of the thousands and thousands of men who will be sent to their death!'

31 JULY 1914

WW I Germany sends messages to Russia and France that refer to the 'threatening danger of war' and demand that Russia cease mobilizing and that France announce neutrality. The London and New York Stock Exchanges close to avoid panic trading.

1 AUGUST 1914

WW I Germany declares war on Russia and mobilizes. France mobilizes. Germany signs a secret treaty in Constantinople calling for Turkey's entry on the side of the Central Powers.

THE JULY 1914 CRISIS

It began on 28 June 1914 with the assassination of the Archduke Francis Ferdinand, heir to the Austro-Hungarian Throne, shot by a Bosnian revolutionary in Sarajevo. Political assassinations were not uncommon; neither was trouble between Austria-Hungary and the Serbians, whom they blamed for allowing, if not instigating, the assassination. The assassin was caught, and for several days little came of the event. But Leopold von Berchtold, the Austro-Hungarian foreign minister, would not be appeased: he obtained a promise from the Germans to support him in actions agsinst Serbia; induced Emperor Franz Joseph to countenance severe retaliation; then issued an ultimatum to Serbia with conditions to which he knew it could not agree. Serbia was conciliatory and offered to submit the dispute to international arbitration, and Germany showed little enthusiasm for drastic action. But once Austria-Hungary declared war on Serbia, Germany knew that Russia would take Serbia's part. So it was that 'the guns of August' began to fire. The resultant world war had less to do with an assassination in June than with the breakdown of the balance of power.

Archduke Francis Ferdinand.

2 AUGUST 1914

WW I Germany quickly occupies Luxembourg and sends an ultimatum to Belgium, demanding that the German Army be allowed passage to attack the French.

3 AUGUST 1914

WW I Germany declares war on France.

THE SENSELESS WAR 1914-1918

A Russian unit heading for the front lines.

4 AUGUST 1914
WW I German troops enter Belgium early in the morning. Great Britain sends an ultimatum demanding that Germany respect Belgian territory and neutrality. Britain declares war on Germany at midnight.
USA The US proclaims neutrality in the war between Austria and Germany, on the one side, and Serbia, Russia, France and Britain on the other. On 5 August the US will offer to mediate.

5 AUGUST 1914
WW I Austria-Hungary declares war on Russia (but not, for the moment, on France and Britain). Britain begins to mobilize. German troops are passing through Belgium and meeting resistance.

6 AUGUST 1914
WW I Serbia and Montenegro declare war on Germany. The British cruiser HMS *Amphion* is sunk by a German mine in the North Sea.
USA The US cruiser *Tennessee* sails from New York with $5 million in gold to aid Americans stranded in Europe by the war.

7 AUGUST 1914
WW I The Germans bombard forts protecting the Belgian city of Liège. The French invade their former province of Alsace, possessed by Germany since 1871. Russians invade East Prussia, and troops of the British Expeditionary Force (BEF) begin to land in France.

7–27 AUGUST 1914
WW I: Africa British and French forces invade the German colony of Togoland in East Africa; they will capture it by the 27th.

10 AUGUST 1914
WW I The Germans occupy Liège and the French fall back in Alsace.

12 AUGUST 1914
WW I France and Britain declare war on Austria-Hungary.

15 AUGUST 1914
South Africa The first large public gathering of Boers who do not want to support Britain in a war against Germany is reported; British authorities will try to suppress this movement, but discontent spreads.
USA Secretary of State William Jennings Bryan, in a letter to J P Morgan, declares that loans to any of the belligerents go against US neutrality.

19 AUGUST 1914
USA In a message to the Senate, President Wilson urges the American people to be 'neutral in fact as well as in name.' But many young Americans will join British forces, form the Lafayette Escadrille in France, or serve as ambulance drivers. Isolationists and pacifists endorse neutrality, as do those who favor Germany.

Kaiser Wilhelm II before the outbreak of World War I.

THE SENSELESS WAR 1914-1918

20 AUGUST 1914
WW I The Germans occupy Brussels, capital of Belgium. In East Prussia the Russians defeat the Germans at the Battle of Gumbinnen.

21–22 AUGUST 1914
WW I The French Fifth Army is badly beaten by the Germans at Charleroi, on the Meuse River in Belgium. The French fall back.

23 AUGUST 1914
WW I: Western Front The Belgian city of Namur falls to the Germans, and the battle of Mons begins; next day, British forces at Mons fall back, and by the 25th the Allies will be in retreat south of the Meuse River.
Eastern Front The Germans are beaten by the Russians at the Battle of Frankenau, but two German generals, Paul von Hindenburg and Erich Ludendorff, are assigned to command in East Prussia.
Asia Japan declares war on Germany and begins to bombard the Chinese port of Tsingtao, where the Germans have a concession. Japan appears to be honoring its alliance with Britain (signed in 1902) but has its own goal of gaining control of China's Shantung Province and the port of Tsingtao.

26–29 AUGUST 1914
WW I: Eastern Front At the Battle of Tannenberg, the Russian Second Army is surrounded and captured by the Germans; so severe is the defeat that the Russian commander, Samsonov, shoots himself.

31 AUGUST 1914
WW I: Western Front The Germans have taken Amiens, France, on the Somme River to the west, and the Allies have drawn back to a line southeastward to Verdun. The Germans are on the offensive.

2 SEPTEMBER 1914
USA The Treasury Department establishes the Bureau of War Risk Insurance to provide up to $5 million worth of insurance for merchant ships and their crews.

3 SEPTEMBER 1914
WW I: Western Front With Germans at the Marne River, north of Paris, the French move government offices to Bordeaux.
Eastern Front Lemburg, capital of Galicia, is taken after a three-day battle in which the Russians rout the Austrians.

4 SEPTEMBER 1914
WW I: Diplomatic France, Russia, and Britain agree in a Pact of London that none will make a separate peace.

5 SEPTEMBER 1914
USA President Wilson, believing America can remain aloof, orders the US Navy to make its wireless stations accessible for any transatlantic communications—even to German diplomats sending coded messages. One such message, the Zimmermann telegram, intercepted by the British and turned over to Wilson on 24 February 1917, will help bring America into the war.

5–14 SEPTEMBER 1914
WW I: Western Front The French and the British launch an offensive to drive the Germans back across the Marne; the French military governor of Paris commandeers 1200 taxicabs to carry reinforcements to the front. By 9 September the British are crossing the Marne and the Germans are halting their offensive.

10–12 SEPTEMBER 1914
WW I: Eastern Front In a three-day battle at the Masurian Lakes in East Prussia, Germans defeat the Russians.

14–18 SEPTEMBER 1914
WW I: Western Front After retreating in the Battle of the Marne, the Germans have dug in along the Aisne River. They withstand an Allied assault on their lines, and by the 18th both sides begin a series of attempted flanking movements to the northwest that will become known as 'The Race to the Sea.' Both Germans and Allies try to get to the coast, strategic for controlling supplies.

18 SEPTEMBER 1914
Great Britain The Irish Home Rule Bill becomes law by receiving royal assent, but it is amended so as not to take effect until the war ends. The Welsh Disestablishment Bill is also approved but similarly suspended (there has been a movement in Wales since 1894 to 'disestablish' the Anglican Church from control of the Archbishop of Canterbury, and this bill passed the Commons on 19 May).

22 SEPTEMBER 1914
South Africa Louis Botha, premier of the Union of South Africa, assumes command of the armed forces, having dismissed General Beyers because of his resistance to aiding the British in the war against Germany.

26–28 SEPTEMBER 1914
WW I: Eastern Front On the East Prussian frontier, the Germans try to cross the Nieman River. The German Ninth Army arrives in Galicia to support the Austrians. On the 28th the Russians cross the Carpathians and enter Hungary.

1 OCTOBER 1914
Arabia The Prince of Asir, the southern region of Arabia, rises in revolt against the Turks; this action will inspire other Arab leaders to revolt.
Canada The first division of Canadian troops, 33,000, sails for Britain. Most of the Canadians are volunteers, anxious to prove their loyalty to the Commonwealth.

German infantry troops in their trenches.

6 OCTOBER 1914
WW I: Eastern Front   The Russians are falling back along the front in Poland and Galicia.

13 OCTOBER 1914
South Africa   In response to martial law imposed by the British yesterday, some Boers begin to rise in revolt. On the 24th they will be joined by former General Beyers and another prominent Boer, Christian de Wet. Although the Boer revolt will never attain any great following, it will be 8 January 1915 before the last group is captured.

15 OCTOBER 1914
USA   Congress passes the Clayton Anti-Trust Act, which the labor leader Samuel Gompers calls 'labor's charter of freedom.' It exempts unions from antitrust laws; strikes, picketing, and boycotting become legal; interlocking directorates become illegal for corporations, as does setting prices that would effect a monopoly.

The government announces it will not forbid extension of credits or shipment of gold to belligerents; this repudiates Secretary of State Bryan's declaration of 15 August.

15–20 OCTOBER 1914
WW I: Eastern Front   The Germans threaten to take Warsaw, but after several days are forced to retreat.

16 OCTOBER–7 NOVEMBER 1914
WW I: Asia   Tsingtao, the finest natural port in the Far East, is taken by the Japanese. The Germans have lost their foothold in China, and the Japanese gained access to Shantung Province.

19 OCTOBER–11 NOVEMBER 1914
WW I: Western Front   The 'race to the sea' has ended close to the Channel, near the Belgian city of Ypres and the Yser River. The Germans have been trying to cut off Allied access to the sea (in what is known as the Battle of the Yser, 16–19 October); now the Allies take the offensive in the First Battle of Ypres. They take terrible losses until the Germans resume the offensive on 29 October; by 11 November rains and mud finally defeat both sides, which settle down for the beginning of the stabilized front that will characterize the war in the west until late in 1918.

29 OCTOBER 1914
WW I: Turkey   Primarily because of the pro-Ger-

THE SENSELESS WAR 1914-1918

Soldiers of the Czarist Army on their way to the front—1914.

man sympathies of Enver Pasha, the minister of war, Turkey enters the war on the side of Germany by having its warships bombard several Russian cities on the coast of the Black Sea. (Russia will declare war against Turkey on 2 November.)

1 NOVEMBER 1914
WW I: Naval   Off Coronel, Chile, a small British squadron (two armored cruisers plus two lighter cruisers) under Admiral Craddock attacks a German squadron (two armored cruisers plus three lighter ones) under Admiral Graf von Spee; within two hours, the British armored cruisers are sunk and the other two flee. The First Lord of the Admiralty, Winston Churchill, bears much of the responsibility for this disaster, but his reputation and the British Navy's will be restored on 8 December when the same German squadron is defeated off the Falkland Islands.

2 NOVEMBER 1914
WW I: Diplomatic   Great Britain declares the entire North Sea a military area: neutral ships will transit it at their own risk. Since hostilities began, British ships have been stopping vessels from neutral countries suspected of carrying cargoes considered contraband, but Britain pays for such goods when seized. German submarines are trying to limit attacks to warships, in part because Germany still hopes to keep America out of the war, mainly because the submarine is a new instrument of war—the Germans possess few of them and are uncertain how to use them.

5 NOVEMBER 1914
Great Britain   Britain declares war on Turkey and annexes Cyprus, occupied since 1878; the immediate reason is to keep it from being taken by Turkey.

6 NOVEMBER 1914
WW I: Middle East   The British land troops (mostly from the Indian Army) at the head of the Persian Gulf in Mesopotamia, and will begin to move westward in an attempt to draw Turkish troops from other fronts.

9 NOVEMBER 1914
WW I: Naval   Off Cocos Island, near Sumatra, the Australian cruiser *Sydney* sinks the German cruiser *Emden*, which has been attacking British shipping in the Pacific.

11 NOVEMBER–31 DECEMBER 1914
WW I: Eastern Front   The Germans mount a major attack against the Russians in Poland. For the first two weeks they push the Russians back and move toward the city of Lodz, but by 24 November Russian reinforcements arrive and the Germans are almost trapped at Lodz; they escape and fighting continues until the end of the year, when the Germans abandon their attempt to capture Warsaw.

22 NOVEMBER 1914
WW I: Middle East   Indian troops take Basra in Mesopotamia.

Joffre and Foch in 1914.

THE SENSELESS WAR 1914-1918

23 NOVEMBER 1914
Mexico-USA American troops leave Veracruz, Mexico, where they have been since 21 April.

DECEMBER 1914–JANUARY 1915
Mexico With Mexico embroiled in civil war, President Carranza and supporters leave Mexico City, and two of his rivals for leadership of the revolution, Francisco 'Pancho' Villa and Emiliano Zapata, move in with their supporters. During January they leave the city to continue the struggle in the countryside, and by the end of 1915 Carranza will have gained control over much of Mexico.

2 DECEMBER 1914
WW I: Southern Front The Austrians take Belgrade, capital of Serbia, but by 13 December will have been defeated. On the 14th the Serbians will reoccupy Belgrade.

6 DECEMBER 1914
WW I: Eastern Front The Germans take Lodz, Poland, and prepare for an assault on Warsaw.

8 DECEMBER 1914
WW I: Naval Off the Falkland Islands in the South Atlantic, the German squadron under Spee that defeated the British off Coronel, Chile, on 1 November is confronted by two British battlecruisers commanded by Admiral Sturdee, as well as the two ships that fled from Coronel. By evening, four out of five of the German ships are sunk. This Battle of the Falklands boosts prestige and morale in the British Navy.
South Africa Boers rebelling against the British have recently suffered several defeats; when one of their leaders, General Beyers, accidentally drowns today, the rebellion will all but collapse, although it will be 8 January 1915 before the last rebels are captured.

17 DECEMBER 1914
Egypt Great Britain proclaims Egypt a protectorate and appoints Prince Hussein Kamel as Sultan; as with Cyprus, the reason is to prevent Egypt—particularly the Suez Canal—from falling into the hands of Germany or Turkey.

26 DECEMBER 1914
WW I: Diplomatic The US Government protests British interference with American merchant ships at sea, but this same day the Germans announce they will treat food as contraband, subject to seizure; this will weaken America's protest to Britain.

28 DECEMBER 1914–4 JANUARY 1915
WW I: Eastern Front The Turks have been fighting the Russians in Armenia for weeks; they are repulsed by the Russians on 28 December. In heavy fighting during the following week, the Turks are forced to retreat.

31 DECEMBER 1914
WW I As the year ends, the world finds itself engulfed in a war that would have seemed like an unimaginable nightmare only six months before. From the Franco-Belgian coast down across France's borders with Germany; in Poland, Turkey, and Serbia; in Egypt and Mesopotamia; in East Africa and across the Pacific, and on the seas around the earth, hundreds of thousands of men are under arms and killing one another. Until almost four years later, still more men will join the shooting and millions will have died.

OTHER EVENTS OF 1914
Medicine/Health Edward C Kendall, American biochemist, isolates thyroxine, used for treatment of endocrine deficiencies. Dr Alexis Carrel, French-American surgeon, performs the first successful heart surgery on a dog; the techniques in this and other operations will provide the basis for much modern surgery on the heart and other organs.
Technology As World War I begins, new technology contributes to its ferocity: the first bombing raid from a German Zeppelin occurs and both sides begin to battle-test the new developments in aviation.
Literature James Joyce's *Dubliners*; Henry James's *The Golden Bowl*; André Bely's *St Petersburg*; Natsume Soseki's *The Heart*; Amy Lowell's *Sword Blade and Poppy Seeds*.
Drama/Entertainment The first full-length feature film in color, *The World, The Flesh and the Devil*, is produced and shown in London.
The Arts De Chirico's *Mystery and Melancholy in a Street*; Braque's *The Guitarist*; Raymond Duchamp Villon's sculpture *The Great Horse*.
Architecture In Cologne, Germany, an exhibition by an arts and crafts group, *Werkbund*, serves as a showcase for a new generation of German architects.
Music Ralph Vaughan Williams's *London Symphony*; Prokofiev's *Scythian Suite*.
Miscellaneous The *Empress of Ireland* goes down with 1029 lost and the *Storstad* sinks with 1023.

1–17 JANUARY 1915
WW I: Eastern Front The Russians launch a campaign into Bukovina (the western Ukraine across northeastern Rumania) and occupy most of it.

8–15 JANUARY 1915
WW I: Western Front The French launch a drive on the Germans in the area of Soissons, north of Paris, but are repulsed.

18 JANUARY 1915
WW I: Diplomatic Japan submits a secret ultimatum to Yuan Shih-kai, now ruling China; known as the Twenty-One Demands, it lists requirements in Shantung, leases in Manchuria, and other privileges that would make China a virtual Japanese dependency. Yuan will manage to get slight modifications, but on 25 May he is forced to accede to most of Japan's demands.

Georges Braque in 1922.

24 JANUARY 1915
WW I: Naval In the Battle of Dogger Bank, in the North Sea, the British sink the German cruiser *Blücher*, but several of their own ships are severely damaged.

28 JANUARY 1915
USA President Wilson vetoes a bill that would require immigrants to pass a literacy test. Congress passes legislation authorizing the United States Coast Guard.

30 JANUARY 1915
WW I: Diplomatic President Wilson's confidant Colonel Edward M House sails for Europe on the *Lusitania* to mediate a peace settlement. But parties believe they can get what they want by force and are in no mood for negotiations.

31 JANUARY 1915
WW I: Eastern Front Germans attack the Russians at Bolimov and allegedly use tear gas for the first time in the war.

3 FEBRUARY 1915
WW I: Egypt Turks attempt to cross the Suez Canal with the aim of capturing it, but they are repulsed and are soon in full retreat east of the canal.

4 FEBRUARY 1915
WW I: Diplomatic The British Foreign Office warns neutrals that ships carrying grain to Germany will be seized; Germany retaliates by proclaiming that the entire sea around the British Isles will be treated as a war zone.

7–27 FEBRUARY 1915
WW I: Eastern Front In fighting around Masuria, East Prussia, the Germans encircle the Russians near the Nieman River, take 100,000 prisoners, and push the Russians eastward.

10 FEBRUARY 1915
WW I: Diplomatic President Wilson warns Germany that the US will hold it 'to a strict accountability' for 'property endangered or lives lost.' Wilson protests to Britain on use of the US flag on British merchant ships to deceive the Germans.

13–28 FEBRUARY 1915
WW I: Western Front The French try to move the Germans back in the Champagne region: by the end of the month, they will have gained a few hundred yards—at a cost of 50,000 French casualties.

19 FEBRUARY–18 MARCH 1915
WW I: Turkey The British Navy has been bombarding the outer Dardanelles forts since November 1914, but now they and the French try to force the straits: they are forced to pull back.

10–12 MARCH 1915
WW I: Western Front The British attack at Neuve Chapelle; because they cannot make a preliminary bombardment, they catch the Germans by surprise, but after a breakthrough they are unable to advance.

11 MARCH 1915
WW I: Naval The British declare a blockade of all German ports: they intend to stop ships before they enter the North Sea or the English Channel. On 30 March the US will protest this blockade as interference with legitimate trade.

4 APRIL 1915
WW I: Diplomatic Germany protests vigorously to the US, claiming it must insist that Britain lift its blockade and assert American neutrality.

20 APRIL–19 MAY 1915
Armenians The Armenians have been persecuted by the Turks in recent decades; with the excuse that the Armenians are aiding the invading Russians, the Turks begin a massacre of this Christian minority. On 20 April the Armenians rise and seize the town of Van, which they are able to hold until the Russians relieve them on 19 May. But many thousands of Armenians are killed during this period.

22 APRIL–25 MAY 1915
WW I: Western Front The Second Battle of Ypres is fought, with futile and costly attacks by both sides. The Germans began their assault with a first-time use of poison gas on the Western Front.

THE SENSELESS WAR 1914-1918

A poster showing the Lusitania.

25 APRIL 1915
WW I: Turkey   The British have decided to try to capture Constantinople and force Turkey out of the war by a landing on the Gallipoli Peninsula (one of the chief proponents of this plan is Winston Churchill). On this day, 75,000 troops (30,000 Australians and New Zealanders; 17,000 French; the rest English) are put ashore at six points, mostly at the tip, Cape Helles, others at what becomes known as Anzac Cove (an acronym for Australia-New Zealand Army Corps). Landings are easy, but the British will fail to exploit them.

26 APRIL 1915
WW I: Diplomatic   In London, Italy signs a secret treaty with Britain, France, and Russia in which it agrees to enter the war on the Allies' side in return for territory in Austria-Hungary.

1 MAY 1915
WW I: Naval   Without warning, the American tanker *Gulflight* is sunk by a German submarine. Germany offers reparation, and promises not to attack again without warning. On this same day, the German Embassy publishes in New York newspapers a warning that anyone sailing into the war zone on a British ship will do so at his own risk. This day, the British liner *Lusitania* sails, with many Americans aboard.

2–4 MAY 1915
WW I: Eastern Front   Field Marshal von Mackenser and his German troops, reassigned from the Western Front, have been in the Carpathian region for about a week: the plan is to aid the Austrians, long threatened by the Russians. Launching a joint attack on 2 May, Austro-German forces push the Russians back by 4 May; soon the Russians are giving up thousands of prisoners and retreating.

6 MAY–13 JULY 1915
WW I: Turkey   The Allies on Cape Helles launch three attacks to enlarge their beachheads; after terrible losses, they advance about three miles.

7 MAY 1915
WW I: Naval   The large British liner *Lusitania* is sunk without warning off the Irish coast; 1198 die, including 128 Americans. Germans claim the vessel was carrying munitions—which the British deny— and that in any case they had warned Americans (as recently as 1 May) not to travel under the British flag.

9 MAY–18 JUNE 1915
WW I: Western Front   In the Second Battle of Artois, the French achieve some gains, but only with harrowing casualties.

13 MAY 1915
WW I: Diplomatic   Secretary of State Bryan sends a note to Germany demanding that Germany disavow the attack on the *Lusitania* and make immediate reparations. (The German ambassador, Count von Bernstorff, had offered condolences for the loss of American lives on 10 May.) Bryan, however, tells the Austrian ambassador that he wrote the note only 'to pacify excited public opinion,' and that Germany 'need only make suitable concessions . . . to put an end to the dispute.' Germany's Foreign Secretary Zimmermann shows this message to the US ambassador in Germany. Bryan is forced to resign on 8 June (Bryan's stated reason is that he is a pacifist and cannot sign the second and stronger *Lusitania* note).

23 MAY 1915
WW I: Diplomatic   Italy declares war against Austria-Hungary, hoping to gain the South Tyrol and Trieste, largely Italian-speaking areas under Austrian control. (Italy will not declare war against Germany until 27 August 1916.)

26 MAY 1915
Great Britain   Herbert Asquith, Liberal Prime Minister, forms a coalition government with the Conservatives, restive with the progress of the war. Among those forced out is Winston Churchill, First Lord of the Admiralty, whose Gallipoli campaign is beginning to shape up as a disaster.

3 JUNE 1915
WW I: Eastern Front   Austro-German forces recapture Przemysl, a crucial city in southeastern Poland, and the entire Russian front begins to collapse.

9 JUNE 1915
WW I: Diplomatic   President Wilson sends the second *Lusitania* note to Germany, demanding reparations and prevention of 'recurrence of anything so obviously subversive of the principles of warfare.' Wilson refuses to recognize the 'war zone' that Germany has proclaimed around the British Isles.

10 AUGUST 1915

Admiral von Tirpitz.

17 JUNE 1915
USA The League to Enforce Peace is organized at Independence Hall in Philadelphia, with William Howard Taft as president. Members hope to get Europeans and other peoples to form a union of states like the one begun at Independence Hall; its program looks toward the future League of Nations.

20 JUNE–14 JULY 1915
WW I: Western Front The Germans launch an offensive in the Argonne but fail to break French lines.

23 JUNE–7 JULY 1915
WW I: Southern Front Italians launch the first of what will become 11 battles to dislodge the Austrians from the Isonzo River, which keeps the Italians from Trieste. During the first ten engagements, the Italians will suffer over 500,000 casualties and gain little ground. Not until 18 August 1917, with the Eleventh Battle of the Isonzo, will the Italians make headway.

2–3 JULY 1915
USA Erich Muenter, an instructor in German at Cornell University, explodes a bomb in the US Senate reception room; he is not caught, and next day he shoots J P Morgan, Jr for representing the British government in war contract negotiations. Muenter is caught, but he commits suicide in jail three days later.

8 JULY 1915
WW I: Diplomatic The Germans reply to Wilson's second *Lusitania* note by saying that Americans may sail on clearly marked neutral ships, but Germany does not deal with Wilson's other demands.

9 JULY 1915
WW I: Africa Germans in Southwest Africa are now isolated by troops from South Africa under Premier Louis Botha, to whom they surrender this day.

15 JULY 1915
USA The head of German propaganda in the US, Dr Heinrich Albert, loses his briefcase on a subway in New York City; examination of its contents reveals an extensive network of German espionage and subversion across the US. Secretary of the Treasury William G McAdoo releases this information to the *New York World*, which begins publishing details on 15 August, to the dismay of Americans professing neutrality.

15 JULY–5 AUGUST 1915
WW I: Eastern Front The Austro-German forces launch an offensive along the Eastern Front; gradually the Russians are pushed back, and by 5 August the Germans are in Warsaw.

21 JULY 1915
WW I: Diplomatic Wilson sends the third *Lusitania* note, warning Germany that future infringement of American rights will be deemed 'deliberately unfriendly.'

28 JULY 1915
Haiti Because of virtual anarchy, US Marines go ashore in Haiti on orders from President Wilson. (A small force has been ashore since 1 July.) This will lead to an occupation that goes on till 1934.

5 AUGUST 1915
International The Latin-American Conference convenes in Washington, with representatives from leading South American nations joining the US to discuss conditions in Mexico, where such rebels as Pancho Villa are causing havoc.
WW I: Eastern Front With the Germans now in Warsaw, the Russians prepare to evacuate cities to the east, including Riga.

6 AUGUST–20 DECEMBER 1915
WW I: Turkey The British land more troops at Suvla Bay on the northern shore of Gallipoli in an effort to break the stalemate on the peninsula. The British command is unable to exploit the situation, and a series of costly attacks fails to dislodge the Turks. As weeks pass, the British face the inevitable—and evacuate Gallipoli.

10 AUGUST 1915
USA General Leonard Wood sets up a training

THE SENSELESS WAR 1914-1918

MOHANDAS K GANDHI, 1869–1948

Known in India as *Mahatma* ('great soul') or simply *Bapu* ('father'), Mohandas K Gandhi is unquestionably one of the key figures of the 20th century. Deeply religious, garbed in the handmade loincloth of the Indian laborer, and identifying with the disadvantaged, he had a rare sense of humor and at the end of his life feared the formation of a cult in his name. Born into a shopkeeping caste and educated in England, he left India in 1893 to practice law in South Africa. During 21 years in Johannesburg he championed the Indian community's struggle against discrimination and perfected the philosophy and technique of *satyagraha* ('soul-force'), a program of nonviolent civil disobedience that expanded throughout his lifetime to include constructive domestic programs. On his return to India he made himself the leader in the struggle for independence from British rule, and gained international fame through his fasting and nonviolent techniques. Fighting always for truth and human dignity, this great liberator was assassinated in 1948 by a Brahmin who feared Gandhi's advocacy of Hindu-Muslim tolerance. Gandhi wrote copiously, and his nonviolent techniques have been adopted around the world, notably in America by Martin Luther King, Jr.

camp in Plattsburg, New York, the first of many such 'Plattsburgs' that will train volunteer civilians. Wilson will not endorse the idea until 4 November.

19 AUGUST 1915
WW I: Naval The British liner *Arabic* is sunk without warning as it leaves Liverpool for New York: two Americans are among the dead. On 1 September the German ambassador to the US pledges again that German submarines will no longer sink liners without warning and providing for safety of passengers and crew.

5 SEPTEMBER 1915
WW I: Eastern Front Czar Nicholas II, distressed by increasing Russian losses, assumes personal command of his nation's military forces. It is clearly a symbolic act.

16 SEPTEMBER 1915
Haiti The US signs a treaty with Haiti that makes Haiti a protectorate: the US Senate will consent to this on 28 February 1916.

22 SEPTEMBER–6 NOVEMBER 1915
WW I: Western Front The Allies launch an offensive that centers on Loos and Champagne; they make some gains, but after weeks of heavy fighting have little to show except casualties.

28 SEPTEMBER 1915
WW I: Middle East The British take the Mesopotamian city of Kut al-Amara, and prepare to capture Baghdad.

5 OCTOBER 1915
WW I: Southern Front Allies land troops at the northern Greek city of Salonika; Greece is nominally neutral, but allows this landing.

11 OCTOBER 1915
WW I: Diplomatic Despite international protest, Edith Cavell, an English nurse in Belgium, is executed by the Germans for aiding the escape of Allied prisoners.

15 OCTOBER 1915
WW I: Diplomatic US bankers arrange a $500 million loan to the British and French.

19 OCTOBER 1915
International Through the efforts of the Latin-American Conference, President Wilson agrees to recognize Venustiano Carranza as president of Mexico.

21 OCTOBER 1915
WW I: Diplomatic William Jennings Bryan's successor as US Secretary of State, Robert Lansing, sends a note to Britain protesting interference with US shipping.

Czar Nicholas at the front.

27 OCTOBER 1915
Australia Andrew Fisher is replaced as Labour Prime Minister by William 'Billy' Hughes, who will advocate a more active role for Australians in the war.

7 NOVEMBER 1915
WW I: Naval An Austrian submarine sinks the Italian liner *Ancona* without warning; 27 Americans are among the 272 who lose their lives.

22–24 NOVEMBER 1915
WW I: Middle East General Townshend has led his victorious British troops to within 24 miles of Baghdad, capital of Mesopotamia, but he is now overextended and the Turks can call up reinforcements; after taking the first Turkish line of defense, Townshend is forced to retreat. This becomes a near rout, and the British are saved only by going back to Kut al-Amara, where from 3 December until 29 April 1916 they remain besieged.

1 DECEMBER 1915
WW I: Diplomatic The US requests that Germany withdraw its military and naval attachés from the Embassy in Washington.

3 DECEMBER 1915
WW I: Western Front General Joseph Joffre becomes Commander-in-Chief of the French Armies. On 16 December General Douglas Haig will become the new commander of the British forces in France and Flanders.

4 DECEMBER 1915
USA Henry Ford's peace ship, *Oscar II*, sails for Europe 'to get the boys out of the trenches by Christmas.'

10 DECEMBER 1915–9 JANUARY 1916
WW I: Turkey Allied forces have had to recognize that they can make no headway on Gallipoli. By a clever stratagem of withholding fire for increasingly long periods, they accustom the Turks to silent periods, during which they then evacuate all their troops without loss of life. Gallipoli will go down as an ill-conceived military adventure (and it will be some time before his countrymen will cease to hold it against Winston Churchill).

27 DECEMBER 1915–13 JANUARY 1916
USA The Iron and Steel Workers strike in East Youngstown, Ohio, demanding an eight-hour-day, an increase in wages, and other concessions; the strike will end in their favor, as the US needs steel for armaments.

28 DECEMBER 1915
WW I: Great Britain Today the British Cabinet recognizes the true nature of the war by deciding to institute compulsory military service, with single men to be conscripted before married ones. (Already the British casualties—killed, wounded, and missing —total 550,000.) Although no one in authority will admit it, both Allied and Central Powers now feel they are going to win by sheer numbers of troops committed and, if necessary, sacrificed.

THE SENSELESS WAR 1914-1918

The Russian Duma—1915.

OTHER EVENTS OF 1915

Science Albert Einstein announces his general theory of relativity, an attempt to express the basic laws of physics by covariant equations; it postulates gravity as a curved field in the space-time continuum created by the presence of mass.

Medicine/Health The British chemist James Kendall isolates the bacillus that causes dysentery. And although aspirin powder has been available by prescription since about 1897, the first aspirin tablets are sold to the public by Germany's Bayer pharmaceutical firm.

Technology The first transcontinental phone call is made between Alexander Graham Bell in New York City and his longtime assistant, Thomas Watson, in San Francisco. This year also sees the beginning of a wireless service between the US and Japan. Henry Ford's company produces its millionth car.

Environment A great earthquake centered at Avezzano, Italy, leaves 30,000 dead.

Literature D H Lawrence's *The Rainbow*; Conrad's *Victory*; Kafka's 'The Metamorphosis'; Ford Madox Ford's *The Good Soldier*; Vladimir Mayakovsky's *The Cloud in Trousers*; Akutagawa Ryunosuke's *Rashomon*; Gabriela Mistral's *Sonnets of Death*; W S Maugham's *Of Human Bondage*.

Drama/Entertainment D W Griffith's *Birth of a Nation* is released, the first of the epic films and, despite its controversial subject, crudely treated, it has an important influence on filmmaking.

The Arts Picasso's *Harlequin*; Juan Gris's *Still Life and Landscape*; Archipenko's *Woman Combing Her Hair*.

Music Ravel's *Ma Mère l'Oye (Mother Goose)*; Manuel de Falla's opera *El Amor Brujo (Love the Sorcerer)*; Charles Ives completes *Piano Sonata No 2*.

Life/Customs For all the grimness of the war on the front lines, it inspires such popular songs as 'Keep the Home Fires Burning' and 'Pack Up Your Troubles in Your Old Kit Bag.'

7 JANUARY 1916

WW I: Diplomatic In response to pressure from President Wilson, Germany notifies the State Department that it will abide by strict international rules of maritime warfare.

9 JANUARY 1916

WW I: Turkey Last troops of the expeditionary force on Gallipoli leave the lines during the night under cover of rounds fired off to deceive the Turks. The British have suffered 214,000 casualties in what is regarded as one of the worst-conducted campaigns of the war.

10 JANUARY 1916
Mexico In retaliation for President Wilson's recognition of the Carranza government, members of Pancho Villa's revolutionary army take 17 American mining engineers from a train and shoot 16 of them in cold blood.

10 JANUARY–16 FEBRUARY 1916
WW I: Eastern Front The Russians launch an offensive in Armenia, and by 16 February have captured the Turkish city of Erzerum.

24 JANUARY 1916
Great Britain The Military Service Bill, calling for conscription of men for war service, passes the House of Commons; it goes into force on 9 February (even though the British Labour Party Conference votes against compulsory service on 27 January).
USA The Supreme Court rules that a federal income tax is constitutional.

11 FEBRUARY 1916
WW I: Diplomatic Germany and Austria-Hungary notify the US that they will sink any armed merchant ships starting on 1 March.

16 FEBRUARY 1916
WW I: Diplomatic The US rejects the right of Germany and Austria-Hungary to sink armed merchant ships. On this same day the German ambassador in Washington announces that Germany will pay an indemnity for American lives lost on the *Lusitania*.

18 FEBRUARY 1916
WW I: Africa The last German garrison in the German colony of Cameroons surrenders.

21 FEBRUARY–18 DECEMBER 1916
WW I: Western Front The Germans launch an attack to take one of France's strongest fortress-cities, Verdun, on the Meuse River northeast of Paris. The French fall back, and by 25 February the Germans have taken the outer fort at Douaumont; by 6 June they have taken another fort at Vaux. But by this time, the French—under General Henri Pétain—have been able to bring up reinforcements and supplies, and the Germans never do get to Verdun. Both sides suffer terrific casualties before the battle exhausts itself in December.

22 FEBRUARY 1916
WW I: Diplomatic Colonel House, Wilson's emissary, is in London and with British Foreign Secretary Edward Grey drafts the House-Grey Memorandum: 'Should the Allies accept [the American idea of a conference to end the war] and should Germany refuse it, the United States would "probably" enter the war against Germany.'

5 MARCH 1916–25 NOVEMBER 1917
WW I: Africa In a concerted effort to capture the Germans in their colony of East Africa, British troops, South Africans (led by General Jan Smuts), Belgians, and Portuguese invade East Africa; by 3 September the British will take the key port of Dar es Salaam, but the Allies are unable to trap the small force led by German General Paul von Lettow-Vorbeck. By the end of 1916, most of the South African troops under Smuts will leave after suffering heavy losses to disease. Fighting resumes in July 1917 after the rainy season, but it is not until 25 November 1917 that Lettow-Vorbeck is forced to lead his force into Portuguese East Africa.

9 MARCH 1916
Mexico-USA Pancho Villa leads 1500 men on a raid to Columbus, New Mexico, and kills 17 Americans. Americans are outraged and President Wilson will immediately order an expedition 'to capture Villa dead or alive.'

15 MARCH 1916
Mexico-USA General John J Pershing crosses into Mexico with 6000 soldiers to capture Villa. President Carranza has grudgingly allowed this; although he has opposed Villa, he recognizes that Villa is something of a Robin Hood figure and that Mexicans in any case resent this 'invasion' by the Yankees. The Americans will pursue Villa until February 1917, unable to capture him.

24 MARCH 1916
WW I: Naval German submarines torpedo the French Channel packet *Sussex*, which is unarmed. No Americans are killed, but several are aboard and endangered. On 18 April Secretary of State Lansing warns Germany that the USA may break diplomatic relations unless such attacks are stopped. American relations with Germany are becoming very strained, and the public is supporting Wilson's position against so-called 'unrestricted' submarine warfare, that is, sinking ships without warning, without first examining the nature of the cargo and, if necessary (in event the ship is carrying contraband and subject to destruction) providing for the safety of passengers and crew.

21 APRIL 1916
Ireland Sir Roger Casement, an Ulster Protestant who has become an ardent Irish nationalist, lands on the Irish coast from a German submarine; he is attempting to get German aid for an uprising. He will be arrested on 24 April and executed by the British on 3 August. (Casement had been knighted by the British for exposing the atrocious treatment of natives in the Belgian Congo and South America earlier in the century.)

24 APRIL–1 MAY 1916
Ireland The Irish Republican Brotherhood, a branch of the Sinn Fein led by Patrick Pearse, revolts against the British in Dublin on the Monday after Easter (the Easter Uprising). The revolt is largely confined

THE SENSELESS WAR 1914-1918

General John J 'Black Jack' Pershing in Mexico.

to Dublin, and within a week the British have suppressed it. They proceed to execute 15 leaders, which has the effect of making the Easter Uprising a rallying point for many Irish who had not previously supported violent means to independence.

29 APRIL 1916
WW I: Middle East British troops besieged in Kut el-Amara since 3 December 1915 surrender to the Turks. Since January the British have been trying to relieve the siege; on one occasion they sent a mission that included T E Lawrence, then with British intelligence in Cairo, in an effort to bribe the Turks to let the British 'escape'; the Turkish general proudly boasted that English gold could not win back what English arms had lost, and Lawrence's mission failed.

MAY 1916
International Britain's Foreign Office sends Sir Mark Sykes on a secret mission to Paris where he reaches an agreement with a French official, Picot: under the Sykes-Picot Agreement, England and France decide in essence to divide up the vast Middle East now under the Ottoman Turks, with certain Arab states assigned to each other's 'sphere of in-

fluence' and other lands and cities taken outright. Russia receives the Turkish provinces in northeastern Asia Minor. When the Italians learn of this agreement, they demand a share as well: on 19 April 1917 diplomats of the respective powers agree to give Italy Smyrna and the Turkish province of Adalia. Aside from being a secret agreement that will complicate postwar settlements, it violates an agreement the British made in 1915, to recognize the independence of Syria, Arabia, and Mesopotamia.

15 MAY 1916
Santo Domingo-USA Claiming that the US must act to quell dangerous disorder, the government orders US Marines to land in Santo Domingo. The American occupation will continue until 1924.

15 MAY–17 JUNE 1916
WW I: Southern Front The Austrians launch a major offensive in the Trentino, the Austro-Hungarian province bordering northeastern Italy; by 31 May the Austrians have pushed back the Italians and occupy the Italian city of Asiago. But this will be the farthest point reached by the Austro-Hungarians, who must send troops to deal with the Russian offensive under Brusilov.

VIVA LA REVOLUCION

EMILIANO ZAPATA

A Mexican revolutionary poster showing Emiliano Zapata.

THE SENSELESS WAR 1914-1918

Irish prisoners being marched along a Dublin quay under British guard—1916.

27 MAY 1916
USA President Wilson addresses the League to Enforce Peace, founded in 1915, and gives public support to the idea of a league of nations.

31 MAY–1 JUNE 1916
WW I: Naval In the major naval battle of the war, the British Grand Fleet encounters the main German fleet off the island of Jutland. Scouting groups join battle in the late afternoon, and the British lose two battlecruisers. By six that evening, Britain's Admiral John Jellicoe has brought the main fleet—including 24 dreadnoughts—into line against the smaller German fleet, but after 20 minutes the Germans escape behind a smoke screen. Shortly after seven o'clock the British make another attack, but German destroyers counter with torpedoes and the British are repulsed. During the night Jellicoe tries to interpose his fleet between the Germans and their base, but a failure of communications allows the Germans to get away. The British have lost more ships, but have driven the Germans back into port.

4 JUNE 1916
WW I: Eastern Front General Aleksei Brusilov begins a massive Russian offensive along a line from the Pripet Marshes in Poland south to Rumania; the Austrians are dislodged from their positions during

the early weeks, and Russians capture such cities as Lutsk, Czernowitz, and Brody. By the end of September this offensive runs out of manpower and Brusilov must pull his forces back to their original line. Although the offensive aided the Allies' cause in general, the almost 1 million casualties the Russians suffer will engender support for internal revolution.

5 JUNE 1916
WW I: Middle East The Sherif Hussein—descended from Mohammed and guardian of the holy cities of Medina and Mecca—proclaims a revolt of the Arabs in the province of Hejaz. Because of his position within the Moslem world, his action will undermine the Turkish Empire. Four of his sons will lead Arab armies against the Turks: one, Feisal, will be the Arab chosen by T E Lawrence as prime beneficiary of British support.

6 JUNE 1916
China Yuan Shih-kai, who has ruled much of China since 1912, dies. The central government virtually collapses in the face of warlords who assert themselves in some regions, and such revolutionaries as Sun Yat-sen, determined to make a new nation.

7 JUNE 1916
USA Theodore Roosevelt declines nomination of

The British battleship Superb *opening fire at the Battle of Jutland—31 May 1916.*

The Invincible *at Jutland.*

THE SENSELESS WAR 1914-1918

Rear Admiral Hood—lost with the Invincible.

the Progressive Party and throws his support to Charles Evans Hughes, who will receive the Republican nomination on 10 June. This spells the end of the Progressive Party.

14–16 JUNE 1916
USA As the Democratic Convention convenes in St Louis, President Wilson leads a 'Preparedness Parade' in Washington; then, on the slogan 'He kept us out of the war,' Wilson obtains his party's nomination on 16 June.

14–21 JUNE 1916
WW I: Diplomatic Representatives of eight Allied nations hold an economic conference in Paris at which they discuss ways to cripple their enemies' economic power during and after the war.

21 JUNE 1916
Mexico-USA President Carranza orders his troops to oppose American soldiers at Carrizal, Mexico; 18 Americans are killed or wounded. The Mexicans warn that there will be a repetition unless Americans leave Mexican soil, but Americans refuse to go until order is restored along the border. In July the two nations agree to arbitration.

1–14 JULY 1916
WW I: Western Front The first phase of the Battle

of the Somme sees the French and the British launch a major offensive along the Somme River northwest of Paris. The British suffer horrendous casualties on the first day's attack across no man's land (20,000 killed, 40,000 wounded), but after two weeks the Allies have made a few gains. The two sides settle down to a battle of attrition.

26 JULY 1916
WW I: Diplomatic The US protests the 'Blacklist' issued by the British (on 18 July) forbidding trade with some 30 US firms.

4 AUGUST 1916
USA The US signs a treaty with Denmark under which the latter sells its West Indies, or Virgin Islands. The Senate will consent on 7 September, and the islands become US territory on 1 January 1917.

4 AUGUST–30 DECEMBER 1916
WW I: Egypt The Turks attack the British line at Romani in the northern Sinai, but a counterattack by the Egyptian Expeditionary Force throws the Turks back—by 5 August they are retreating eastward. The British arrive at the border of Palestine on 30 December.

29 AUGUST 1916
USA The US Congress passes the Jones Act, which promises Philippine independence when the islanders have demonstrated an ability to govern themselves.
This same day, Congress passes the Naval Appropriation Act (with $313 million for building the navy) and the Army Appropriation Act ($267 million for strengthening the army); the latter act creates a Council of National Defense, to 'coordinate industries and resources for national security and welfare.'

30 AUGUST 1916
Greece Much of Greece is torn between factions that want to enter the war on the side of the Allies—a

---

DAVID LLOYD GEORGE, 1863–1945

One of the great leaders to emerge in Britain during World War I, as prime minister during the last half of the war, David Lloyd George played a key role in producing the victory that finally ended that conflict. Considered a radical in his earlier years as a Liberal Party leader, Lloyd George gained recognition through his bitter opposition to England's policy during the Boer War. At home his own war on poverty did much to strengthen morale. His budget, which included increased taxes on income, land, and luxuries, as well as his Unemployment Insurance Act, survived numerous Conservative attacks and are credited with pulling England through its postwar depression. Foreign policy failures eventually crippled this distinguished statesman and returned power to the Conservatives. A year prior to his death Lloyd George became First Earl of Dwyfor.

7 DECEMBER 1916

position espoused by Venizelos—or join the Central Powers, a position taken by King Constantine. Meanwhile, with French encouragement, a group of Venizelist supporters declares a 'revolution' in Salonika, the second-largest Greek city. In the next few days the Allies will use this movement as an excuse to make demands on King Constantine and the government and back up the demands by stationing a fleet off the harbor of Piraeus.

1–8 SEPTEMBER 1916
USA Despite the war, President Wilson is able to get Congress to pass progressive legislation. On 1 September the Keating-Owen Act bars from interstate commerce any item made by children. (On 3 June 1918 the Supreme Court will rule this act unconstitutional—as encroaching on state laws.) On 3 September Wilson signs the Adamson Bill providing an 8-hour day on interstate railroads (it prevents a national railroad strike). On 7 September the Workmen's Compensation Act brings 500,000 federal employees under its protection. On 8 September the Emergency Revenue Act doubles the rate of income tax and adds inheritance and munitions profits taxes.

11–18 SEPTEMBER 1916
Greece The Germans enter the northern Greek city of Kavalla and a week later force Greek Army units to surrender; the 25,000 men are sent to Germany as 'guests.' The Greek Government demands their return.

15 SEPTEMBER 1916
WW I: Western Front At the battle of Flers Courcelette in the ongoing Somme campaign, the British introduce tanks, which make a deep penetration, but are too few and slow to exploit it.

30 SEPTEMBER 1916
Greece Venizelos has gone to Crete, the base of his support, where he announces that he is forming a Provisional Government as an alternative to the one in Athens. He is determined to bring Greece into the war on the side of the Allies.

7–9 OCTOBER 1916
WW I: Naval The German submarine *U-53* arrives off Newport, Rhode Island, and sinks nine British merchant ships in international waters.

16 OCTOBER 1916
WW I: Middle East T E Lawrence, the British scholar and archaeologist assigned to Intelligence at Cairo, arrives at Jedda, Arabia, to investigate the Arab revolt against the Turks. The revolt has bogged down—the Arabs are unable to wrest Medina from the Turks. On this visit Lawrence meets Feisal, son of Sherif Hussein, and decides he is the man to back. Lawrence will return to Cairo and convince the British of his views; they announce recognition of Hussein as King of the Hejaz on 16 December.

Greece The Allies send troops to Athens to maintain order and take possession of three Greek warships at Piraeus.

19 OCTOBER 1916
Greece The French and British, meeting at Boulogne, France, extend formal recognition to the National Provisional Government proclaimed by Eleutherios Venizelos and his supporters.

26 OCTOBER 1916
USA Addressing the Chamber of Commerce in Cincinnati, President Wilson declares that 'The business of neutrality is over. The nature of modern war leaves no state untouched.'

28 OCTOBER 1916
Australia The government of William Hughes holds a national referendum seeking support for its proposal of compulsory conscription. It is rejected, and some in the Labour Party move for a vote of no confidence, but Hughes continues as Prime Minister and forms his own National Party.

7 NOVEMBER 1916
USA Woodrow Wilson is re-elected President by a popular vote of 9,129,606 to the Republican Hughes's vote of 8,538,221; the electoral vote of 277 to 254 reveals how close a contest it is, but the Democrats retain control of both Houses of Congress. Jeannette Rankin of Montana is the first woman elected to the House of Representatives.

13–18 NOVEMBER 1916
WW I: Western Front At the Battle of Ancre, the final phase of the Battle of the Somme (underway since 1 July), the British seem to win, but the rains and mud make it impossible for either side to exploit any victories. As the battle winds down, the Allies accept 600,000 casualties and the Germans 650,000—all to enable the British to advance seven miles.

24 NOVEMBER 1916
Mexico-USA Representatives of the two countries sign a protocol at Atlantic City, under which Pershing's troops will withdraw and each nation's army guard the borders. President Carranza of Mexico will refuse to accept it on 18 December.

1 DECEMBER 1916
Greece There is virtual civil war in Athens, as royalists fight Venizelists, and the Allies determine on a Venizelist victory. Claiming that their own nationals are endangered, the British, French, and Italians send some 3000 marines from Piraeus to Athens. They exchange fire with troops loyal to King Constantine, but an armistice is reached and the Allies withdraw. They continue to keep Greece under a virtual blockade.

7 DECEMBER 1916
Great Britain David Lloyd George, who had re-

THE SENSELESS WAR 1914-1918

A gas attack in France—late World War I.

signed from the government of Asquith on 5 December because he believed the war was not being pursued properly, becomes prime minister of a coalition government.

12 DECEMBER 1916

WW I: Diplomatic Germany issues a note saying the Central Powers are willing to enter peace negotiations. It will be rejected by the Allies on 30 December —in part because President Wilson had responded with his own note on 18 December asking that all warring powers state the 'terms upon which the war might be concluded.' The Allies choose to see this as favoring the Central Powers, for Germany had accepted Wilson's request on 26 December.

15–18 DECEMBER 1916

WW I: Western Front The French launch one last major assault at Verdun and achieve some gains, but the campaign ends in a stalemate. The French count 360,000 casualties and the Germans 450,000.

29 DECEMBER 1916

Russia The monk Rasputin, who has exercised growing influence over the Czar's family and even over government appointments, is murdered by several highly placed Russians who decide he is an evil genius. Their action comes too late to save the Czar or his government.

OTHER EVENTS OF 1916

Science Karl Schwarzschild, a German astronomer who is on his deathbed, communicates to Einstein his concept of a gravitational radius—essentially a precursor of the concept of a 'black hole.' It will be 1939 before J Robert Oppenheimer (with George Volkoff and Hartland Snyder) describes this concept in full. Not until the 1970s will astronomers begin to observe phenomena in space that appear to confirm the existence of black holes: invisible objects with such strong gravitational forces that nothing—not even light—can escape them (thus the apellation 'black holes,' which pull everything into themselves).

Medicine/Health The first special ward for plastic surgery is established at Cambridge Military Hospital, Aldershot, England, to deal with increasing numbers of seriously wounded soldiers; this is the beginning of modern plastic surgery.

Technology The first tank is used in warfare, the 'Little Willie' of the British Army.

Literature Joyce's *Portrait of the Artist as a Young Man.*

Drama/Entertainment Eugene O'Neill's first play, *Bound East for Cardiff*; Leonid Andreyev's *He Who Gets Slapped.*

The Arts Claude Monet works on the large murals entitled *Water Lilies* for the Musée d'Orangerie in Paris. In Zurich Tristan Tzara, Hans Arp, and Hugo Bak start the Dada movement in art and literature

Colonel T E Lawrence, the mystery man of the desert.

THE SENSELESS WAR 1914-1918

(its name, meaning 'hobbyhorse,' said to have been chosen at random from a French dictionary). Playful, experimental, deliberately shocking, this 'anti-art' movement will fade by 1922.

Music Gustav Holst completes *The Planets*. Enrique Granados's opera *Goyescas* (based on piano pieces of the same name) opens in New York.

1 JANUARY 1917
WW I: Middle East T E Lawrence has returned to Arabia in December as military adviser to Feisal, the son of the Sherif Hussein whom the British have decided to support with arms, supplies, and money; on this day he joins Feisal's forces and begins the adventures that will lead to Damascus in October 1918—and to his own legend as 'Lawrence of Arabia.'

10 JANUARY 1917
WW I: Diplomatic The Allied governments respond to Wilson's note (of 18 December 1916) and give their terms for ending the war, most of which are unacceptable to the Central Powers.

16 JANUARY 1917
Greece The Greek Government accepts an ultimatum by the Allies (principally France and Britain) on 31 December 1916 and agrees to reparations for Allied losses sustained in recent actions in Greece and to other terms that make Greece subject to Allied control.

31 JANUARY 1917
WW I: Naval Germany declares that as of 1 February it will wage unrestricted submarine warfare against all ships it decides are aiding its enemies in any way.

Mexico President Carranza announces a new constitution with many liberal elements, most of which his regime will not implement.

3 FEBRUARY 1917
WW I: Diplomatic Citing Germany's announcement of renewed submarine warfare as reason enough, Wilson breaks off diplomatic relations with Germany, stating that 'this government has no alternative consistent with the dignity and honor of the United States.' This day, a German submarine sinks the USS *Housatonic* without warning.

5 FEBRUARY 1917
Mexico-USA The last of the American troops commanded by General John Pershing leave Mexico. They have not caught Pancho Villa, but they have put him on the run. Both he and Carranza will be assassinated within the next year.

17 FEBRUARY 1917
Australia A newly formed Nationalist Party takes over a coalition government: it is essentially the creation of William Hughes, whose own Labour Party had voted no confidence in him (14 November

1916). Remaining as Prime Minister, he will lead the Nationalists to victory in a general election he calls on 5 May 1917.

23 FEBRUARY–5 APRIL 1917
WW I: Western Front The Allies have built their forces and are preparing an offensive, but the Germans withdraw to an elaborately prepared defensive position, the Hindenburg Line. (The Germans call it their Siegfried Line.)

28 FEBRUARY 1917
USA Wilson's request for permission to arm merchant ships is introduced into Congress, but Senator Robert LaFollette leads a filibuster against the legislation. 'A little group of willful men have rendered the great government of the United States helpless and contemptible,' Wilson charges. His Attorney General finds that the requested powers are inherent in the presidency, and on 9 March Wilson issues the necessary directive.

1 MARCH 1917
WW I: Diplomatic Wilson has permitted Germany to use the American wireless transmission system, and Germany has taken advantage to send coded diplomatic notes. British Intelligence has been intercepting them and on 16 January decoded a message from Germany's Foreign Minister Zimmermann to the German ambassador in Mexico. In this soon-to-be notorious 'Zimmermann Telegram,' he instructed the ambassador to ask for Mexico's entry into the war on the side of the Central Powers—in return for receiving New Mexico, Texas, and Arizona! The British have held this message until they could steal a copy from the German embassy in Mexico City—so as to give the impression that the loss came from insecurity in the embassy, rather than systematic interception and decoding by British Intelligence. On 26 February they give it to the American ambassador in London. At first Wilson can scarcely believe it is authentic. Persuaded that it is, he allows the State Department to publish it this day, and it unleashes a storm of outrage—even among that declining group composed of neutrals and pro-Germans.

3 MARCH 1917
Mexico-USA The two nations renew diplomatic relations.

5 MARCH 1917
USA President Woodrow Wilson is inaugurated for a second term. This same day he receives a cable from the American ambassador in London that 'France and England must have a large enough credit in the United States to prevent a collapse of world trade.'

8–16 MARCH 1917
Russia Strikes and riots in Petrograd—protesting shortages of food and coal, continuation of the war, autocratic government—become so serious that

Street marchers in Russia during the 1917 Revolution.

Czar Nicholas dispatches troops to restore order; instead, many troops begin to support the strikers. On 11 March the Czar—who is away on the front lines trying to bolster the fighting spirit of his army—tries to dissolve the Duma. Events have moved too far, and some of the more liberal members of the Duma, headed by Alexander Kerensky, work out a compromise with the radical socialists who comprise the Petrograd Soviet. On 14 March a provisional Duma ministry is formed to run the government. On 15 March Czar Nicholas II abdicates. (He and his family will be held prisoners until their execution in July 1918.) The provisional government assumes power, with a liberal nobleman, Prince George Lvov, as premier and Kerensky as minister of justice. The 'February Revolution' is concluded (so called because it is February in the Orthodox Old Style calendar, not replaced until 1918). This provisional government, which Kerensky actually heads, will offer a few reforms but not the fundamental changes that radical socialists and Bolsheviks feel are necessary.

11 MARCH 1917
WW I: Middle East The Turks having evacuated Baghdad, capital of Mesopotamia, the British forces now move in to occupy it.

12 MARCH 1917
WW I: Naval A German submarine sinks an unarmed US merchant ship, the *Algonquin*. This same day President Wilson has given an executive order to arm US merchant ships.

20 MARCH 1917
USA With the sinking of three more American merchant ships by German submarines in recent days, Wilson's cabinet meets and agrees informally that war is inevitable. Tomorrow Wilson will call for a special session of Congress for 2 April, to receive a message about 'grave questions of national policy.'

22 MARCH 1917
USA-Russia The United States is the first government to recognize the new government of Russia.

26 MARCH 1917
WW I: Middle East The British win a battle at Gaza against the Turks, but on 18–19 April the

THE SENSELESS WAR 1914-1918

Rioters fleeing in the streets of Petrograd.

Turks, with German aid, will defeat the British at Gaza, slowing the British advance on Jerusalem.

31 MARCH 1917
USA The Virgin Islands (St Croix, St John, and St Thomas) are taken over by the United States. They had been sold to the US in 1902, but the Danish Parliament rejected the terms: now Denmark has sold the islands for $25 million by a treaty signed 4 August 1916.

2–6 APRIL 1917
USA President Wilson addresses a special session of Congress and asks for a declaration of war against Germany: 'The world,' he says in a famous phrase, 'must be made safe for democracy.' By 6 April both Houses have concurred, and shortly after one that afternoon Wilson signs the proclamation declaring 'a state of war.'

9–16 APRIL 1917
Russia A group of Bolshevik revolutionaries en route to Russia, led by Vladimir Ilyich Lenin, are allowed by German authorities to travel from Switzerland across Germany in a 'sealed train.' Lenin has been in exile in Switzerland since 1914, attempting through writings and personal authority to direct the Bolsheviks, the most radical of Russian Communist groups, who probably number barely 50,000 throughout Russia. With the revolution that has seen the Czar abdicate and Kerensky rise to power, Lenin is determined to get back to Russia.

The Germans agree to let him pass because it is in their own interest to keep Russia unsettled; they know that Lenin and the Bolsheviks are against Russia's continuing the war. Traveling through Germany, then Sweden and Finland, Lenin and his group arrive in the evening at Petrograd's Finland Station, to be received as returning heroes. Lenin will set about organizing the revolution that he has worked for since his youth.

9 APRIL–3 MAY 1917
WW I: Western Front In the hard-fought Battle of Arras along a 12-mile front, Canadian troops distinguish themselves by taking Vimy Ridge.

16 APRIL–9 MAY 1917
WW I: Western Front In the Second Battle of the Aisne, French troops are ordered to assault impregnable German defenses and suffer such withering fire that some of them mutiny.

24 APRIL 1917
USA Congress passes the 'Liberty Loan Act,' authorizing the Treasury to issue a public subscription for $2 billion in bonds for the war. Offered to the public on 2 May, it will be oversubscribed by half by 15 June. On 25 April the first loan to Britain, $200 million, is made under this act.

18 MAY 1917
USA Having declared war, the US has taken steps to prepare for combat. On 4 May a flotilla of destroy-

ers has arrived at Queenstown, Ireland to aid in convoying ships to England; on 15 May the first officers' training camps opened; this day, Congress passes the Selective Service Act, calling for enrollment of all men between 21 and 30, who will then be drafted by lot into the army. The first units of the American Expeditionary Force, to be commanded by General John J Pershing, are ordered to France.

7–14 JUNE 1917
WW I: Western Front The British detonate mines beneath the German-held Messines Ridge, high ground dominating the Ypres salient, and capture the ridge after a sharp attack, part of the British plan for an offensive in the Ypres area.

11 JUNE 1917
Greece King Constantine, faced with either a civil war or foreign occupation, steps aside in favor of his second son, Alexander; Constantine does not abdicate but leaves the country (on 13 June), opening the way for Venizelos and supporters.

15 JUNE 1917
Ireland The British grant amnesty to the prisoners taken in the rebellion of 1916 in an effort to calm their troubled relations with the Irish.

16 JUNE 1917
Russia The first all-Russian Congress of Soviets ('councils') meets in what will become the final phase of a communist takeover of the government.

19 JUNE 1917
Great Britain The British royal family—which has had strong German ties since George I—renounces its German names and titles and adopts the name of Windsor.

26 JUNE 1917
WW I: USA The first American combat troops begin to disembark in France (Pershing and some of his staff having been in Paris since 13 June). On 4 July, as Pershing lays a wreath at the tomb of the Marquis de Lafayette, a member of his staff, Captain Charles Stanton, will declare: 'Lafayette, we are here.'

27 JUNE 1917
Greece Venizelos takes over as prime minister and promptly severs relations with the Central Powers, bringing Greece into the war on the side of the Allies.

1–24 JULY 1917
WW I: Eastern Front The Russian Army has

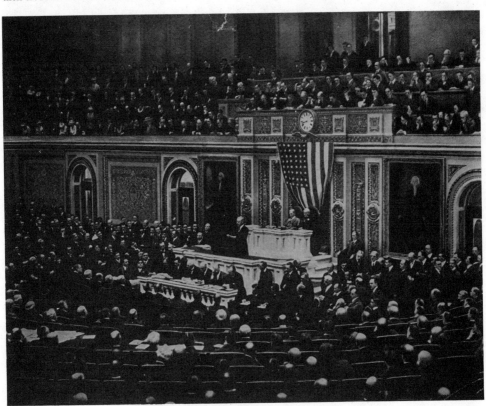

President Wilson asking for a declaration of war—2 April 1917.

General John J Pershing landing in France.

THE SENSELESS WAR 1914-1918

become demoralized and ineffective as a result of revolution. The Bolsheviks and their soviets want to end the war, which they see as benefiting the imperialist and capitalist nations at the expense of the masses. The Kerensky Government decides to continue the war, and General Brusilov is ordered to mount a new offensive in the Galicia region of Austria-Hungary. He will have some success in the first three weeks, but a German-Austrian counterattack will then turn back the Russians.

16–22 JULY 1917
Russia Urged on by Bolsheviks of the Petrograd Soviet—now the most influential such council in Russia—armed workers and soldiers try to seize power from the Kerensky Government. Lenin's role is ambiguous, as he appears not to be in command nor in favor, but he comes to Petrograd to take control. When the uprising fails, he flees to Finland (where he will remain in exile again until 21 October).

19 JULY 1917
Germany A majority in the German Reichstag passes a resolution that Germany does not desire to take territory and wants peace; the chancellor, George Michaelis, successor to Bethmann-Hollweg, chooses to interpret it in a way that leads to inaction. Meanwhile, mutinies occur within the German fleet during the next two weeks.

20 JULY 1917
WW I: USA The first numbers are drawn for the draft under the Selective Service Act.

22 JULY 1917
Russia Alexander Kerensky, the socialist who has been the leading member of the government headed by Prince Lvov since 16 March, succeeds Lvov; it is

an attempt to deter radical elements who demand drastic solutions to Russia's problems.

31 JULY–6 NOVEMBER 1917
WW I: Western Front Field Marshal Haig begins what he hopes will be the turning point of the war, the Third Battle of Ypres. As weeks pass, the British make gains, but the battle will drag on into November with heavy casualties on both sides.

5 AUGUST 1917
WW I: USA The entire National Guard is taken into national service, subject to presidential rather than state control.

9 AUGUST 1917
WW I: Canada Parliament passes the Compulsory Military Act, although many French-Canadians from Quebec Province oppose it.

13 AUGUST 1917
Spain There is a revolt in Catalonia, the northeastern province that has long seen itself as independent from Spain and will continue to try to assert independence in the ensuing decades.

18 AUGUST–12 SEPTEMBER 1917
WW I: Southern Front Having launched 10 previous assaults (since 23 June 1915) on the Austrians along the Isonzo River west of Trieste, the Italians mount the Eleventh Battle of the Isonzo and succeed in driving the Austrians back five miles. The Austrians now appeal to the Germans for aid.

31 AUGUST 1917
China In Canton Sun Yat-sen and his supporters—disenchanted with the government in Peking, essentially a creature of the warlords—have been active since July in trying to organize a rival regime. Today their 'rump' parliament establishes a military government and elects Sun Yat-sen commander-in-chief; this will have little effect beyond a further division of northern and southern China, and Sun Yat-sen will leave this government in May 1918.

7–15 SEPTEMBER 1917
Russia The former commander-in-chief of the Russian Army, Lavr Kornilov, marches on Petrograd at the head of a counterrevolutionary force, but the revolt collapses, Kornilov is arrested, and on the 15th Kerensky feels strong enough to declare Russia a republic.

12 OCTOBER 1917
Canada Liberal and Conservative Parties form a union government led by Robert Borden with the goal of full support to the war. On 19 December the new government will get support in a nationwide election.

14 OCTOBER 1917
WW I: Espionage Mata Hari, a dancer in Paris, is

Czar Nicholas with the Czarina Alexandra and the Crown Prince.

THE SENSELESS WAR 1914-1918

executed by the French after being convicted of passing military secrets to the Germans. Actually a Dutchwoman whose real name is Margaretha Zelle, Mata Hari had scandalized and entertained Paris for some years with her exotic dances in scanty costumes. Intelligent and facile in languages (she had lived in Java), she came to know many highly placed men and appears to have passed information to the Germans. Arrested on 13 February 1917 and tried, she claimed it was all a ruse to aid the Allied cause: evidence against her is ambiguous, but the French are suffering terrible battle losses. Mata Hari is shot.

21 OCTOBER 1917
WW I: USA The first US troops enter front lines at Sommervillier; they are under French command.

24 OCTOBER–12 NOVEMBER 1917
WW I: Southern Front The Germans have reinforced the Austrians opposing the Italians. Using poison gas, they capture key Italian positions around Caporetto; Austro-German forces drive the Italians back to the Piave River, 15 miles north of Venice at its closest point. In the rout the Italians suffer 320,000 casualties, and the Battle of Caporetto becomes the worst disaster in Italian military history.

25 OCTOBER 1917
USA Women have been demanding the right to vote for years, and many feel that they are close to achieving it. President Wilson has not shown much commitment, but endorses equal suffrage today in addressing a group of women from New York State. On 27 October 20,000 women will march in a suffrage parade in New York, and on 6 November New York State will adopt a constitutional amendment giving women the right to vote in state elections. As the largest state and the first on the eastern seaboard to do so, New York will have an important effect on the burgeoning movement to grant the vote to all women in all elections.

NOVEMBER 1917
Russia With their homeland in turmoil due to the revolution, many Russian troops will desert the front lines during November and make their way back home.

2 NOVEMBER 1917
International Arthur Balfour, foreign secretary in David Lloyd George's government, issues the 'Balfour Declaration' that will become significant—and troublesome—in later years in the Middle East: 'His Majesty's Government view with favor the establishment in Palestine of a national home for the Jewish people, and will use their best endeavours to facilitate the achievement of that object, it being clearly understood that nothing shall be done which may prejudice the civil and religious rights of existing non-Jewish communities in Palestine or the rights and political status enjoyed by Jews in any other country.' In its implicit recognition of Zionist goals,

and anticipation of the State of Israel, this declaration contains the seeds of the strife in Palestine.

6 NOVEMBER 1917
WW I: Western Front In the final attack in the Third Battle of Ypres (underway since 31 July), Canadian troops capture the village of Passchendaele. Little else results from this battle except 250,000 casualties on both sides, and the offensive comes to an end as winter weather moves in.

7 NOVEMBER 1917
Russia Lenin has been back in Petrograd since 21 October, and he and his Bolsheviks have been awaiting the moment to make their revolutionary bid. Today armed workers begin to take over points in Petrograd; by evening, workers, soldiers, and sailors are attacking the Winter Palace, seat of Kerensky's government. The Bolshevik Revolution has survived its first day. (It will be known to Russians as 'The October Revolution' because it occurs on 26 October in the Old-Style calendar still in use.) Delegates from soviets throughout Russia select a Council of Commissars to direct affairs; Lenin is chosen as its head, with Leon Trotsky as minister of foreign affairs. Supported by their soviets throughout Russia and the Red Guard, or Bolshevik, Army, Lenin and Trotsky and their circle try to extend their revolution, not without great opposition. Kerensky himself will attempt a counterrevolution on 10–12 November, but it fails and he flees to Paris. Elsewhere, many military officers, aristocrats, middle-class Russians, and members of ethnic and frontier groups will immediately begin to oppose the Reds—as the Communists are known from their flag. This opposition will become known as the Whites. The Bolsheviks, meanwhile, make contact with the Germans and indicate desire to end Russia's participation in the war.

20 NOVEMBER–7 DECEMBER 1917
WW I: Western Front In the Battle of Cambrai, the British use tanks in a way that shows their potential in warfare; although the British break the German line and take many villages and prisoners, they fail to consolidate their position, and in the final week a German counterattack forces them to withdraw.

26 NOVEMBER 1917
WW I: Diplomatic The new government of Russia offers an armistice to Germany and Austria-Hungary.

29 NOVEMBER–3 DECEMBER 1917
WW I: Diplomatic A Supreme Allied War Council meets at Versailles to define war aims but cannot reach agreement.

5 DECEMBER 1917
WW I: Diplomatic At Brest-Litovsk (then in Poland, now within the USSR), Russian and German delegates sign an armistice. Negotiation over

---

RUSSIA LEAVES THE WAR

Russia's liberal-democratic revolution of March 1917 was short-lived. The following month, Nikolai Lenin, leader of the Bolshevik faction of the Russian Social Democratic Party, would be on his way back from exile in Switzerland in a sealed train, allowed passage by the Germans in the hope that he would undermine the provisional government and take Russia out of the war. They gambled successfully. The war-weary Russians had sacrificed millions in battle for the czar; now their liberal leaders were resolved to continue the conflict. When the Bolsheviks promised 'peace, bread and land,' the people were listening. Soldiers threw down weapons; peasants seized lands; workers' councils took over major cities. On 7 November 1917 the new government of the first successful communist revolution took power. Five months later, it fulfilled its promise of peace in the Treaty of Brest-Litovsk with Germany. World War I had brought Russia to revolution; the new regime took Russia out of the war.

---

details of the peace will begin in this city on 21 December (with a treaty signed here on 3 March 1918).

5–24 DECEMBER 1917
WW I: Southern Front Austro-German forces launch an offensive against the Italians on the western end of their line, around Asiago.

6 DECEMBER 1917
Finland Taking advantage of the temporary relaxation of authority in Russia, Finland declares itself a republic (just as the Ukrainians had done on 20 November).

7 DECEMBER 1917
WW I: USA The 42nd Division, nicknamed the Rainbow Division because it is composed of units from the National Guards of many of the states, arrives in France. Americans who will later achieve fame serve in this division, including its chief of staff, Colonel Douglas MacArthur.

9 DECEMBER 1917
WW I: Middle East British forces under General Allenby capture Jerusalem; although it has little strategic value, this is an important psychological blow to the Ottoman Turks.

18 DECEMBER 1917
USA The 18th Amendment, authorizing prohibition of alcohol, is approved by Congress and sent to the states for ratification. The movement to prohibit sale and consumption of alcohol has received a tremendous boost from the war, for it has been promoted as a patriotic duty while soldiers are dying on the battlefields. King George V of Britain had announced in April 1915 that he would abstain for the duration. Australia held a plebiscite on 6 June

1916 and a majority voted for six-o'clock closing of bars. The American military has imposed limits on the sale of alcohol. Canada will adopt Prohibition on 31 December 1917. It appears to be a 'noble experiment' whose time has come.

20 DECEMBER 1917
Australia A second nationwide referendum on military conscription is rejected by Australians. Yet some 400,000 Australians will serve voluntarily during the war, with 60,000 deaths and 165,000 wounded—a sacrifice far out of proportion to their country's population.

OTHER EVENTS OF 1917
Social Sciences Freud's *Introductory Lectures on Psychoanalysis*.
Literature T S Eliot's *Prufrock and Other Observations*; Knut Hamsun's *Growth of the Soil*; Norman Douglas's *South Wind*; Juan Ramon Jiminez's *Platero and I*.
Drama/Entertainment Pirandello's *Right You Are If You Think You Are*.
The Arts Joseph Stella's *Brooklyn Bridge*; Jacques Lipchitz's *Man With Mandolin*; Modigliani's *Crouching Female Nude*. In Holland Piet Mondrian starts a magazine, *de Stijl* ('the style'), that gives its name to a school known as the International Style, involving such artists and architects as Gropius, Mies van der Rohe, and Le Corbusier. And Picasso's sets and costumes for the ballet *Parade* allegedly inspire the first use of the term 'surrealist' by Apollinaire.
Music Prokofiev's *Classical Symphony*; Respighi's *Fountains of Rome*; Ravel's *Le tombeau de Couperin*; Manuel de Falla's *Three-Cornered Hat*; Hans Pfitzner's opera *Palestrina*; Arnold Bax's *Tintagel*.
Miscellaneous In one of the worst marine disasters of all time, the munitions ship *Mont Blanc* collides with another vessel in the harbor of Halifax, Nova Scotia, on 6 December: the resultant blast and spreading fires kill some 2000 people, injure thousands more, and destroy much of the adjacent section of Halifax.

8 JANUARY 1918
International In a speech before Congress, President Wilson sets out his 'Fourteen Points' for world peace. Most of them are specific to borders, national sovereignty, reparations, and war-related issues, but the final point will cause ripples in international relations for many years. It asks for 'a general association of nations . . . under specific covenants for the purpose of affording mutual guarantees of political independence and territorial integrity to great and small states alike.' Although he has not originated this concept, Wilson will provide the impetus for the League of Nations and its successor, the United Nations, but not all countries will see this as a workable idea. Clemenceau, the French premier with whom Wilson will soon be negotiating peace, will exclaim: 'President Wilson and his Fourteen Points bore me. Even God Almighty had only ten!'

THE SENSELESS WAR 1914-1918

But Allied planes will drop copies of Wilson's Fourteen Points over enemy countries, giving encouragement to their governments to end the war.

16 JANUARY–3 FEBRUARY 1918
WW I: Diplomatic   Austria and then Germany are disrupted by strikes, especially in Vienna and Berlin: people in every land are becoming impatient with leaders who continue the war. Yet on 24 January, Germany and Austria reject the peace proposals offered by the US and Britain.

10–18 FEBRUARY 1918
WW I: Diplomatic   Trotsky feels that German terms offered in the negotiations at Brest-Litovsk are unfair, so he declares that Russia is leaving the war. But on the 18th, Germany renews its offensive against the Russians and makes dramatic gains against the disorganized and dispirited Russian troops.
Finland   With Bolsheviks now trying to assert power throughout all of Russia and its dependent lands, General Carl G von Mannerheim gathers an army known as the 'White Guard' (in contrast to the Bolsheviks' Red Guard) that will mount a counter-revolution. Germany will send troops to aid the White Guard.

11 FEBRUARY 1918
WW I: Diplomatic   President Wilson makes another speech before Congress and announces the 'Four Principles' (freedom of navigation, an end to secret diplomacy, and similar items) that supplement his Fourteen Points.

MARCH 1918
Russia   Lenin and his Bolshevik Government transfer their operations from Petrograd to Moscow, which becomes the de facto capital of Russia (as it had been until Peter the Great moved it to his creation, St Petersburg, in 1712). Not until 30 December 1922, however, will Moscow become the official capital.

3 MARCH 1918
WW I: Diplomatic   The Bolsheviks are under such pressure from internal counterrevolutionary forces, and the Germans have made such rapid incursions—having taken Kiev on 1 March—that they sign a peace treaty at Brest-Litovsk, accepting virtually all terms offered by the Central Powers. The Russians give up Finland, much of Poland, the Baltic States, and the Ukraine. Freed from the Eastern Front, the German Army determines to make a final assault on the Allies on the Western Front before American reinforcements can become overwhelming, ensuring an Allied victory.

21 MARCH–4 APRIL 1918
WW I: Western Front   With 207 divisions against the Allies' 173, the Germans launch their major offensive in an attempt to split the French and British forces along the Western Front. (To the Germans this offensive is known as the *Kaiserschlacht*, or Emperor's Battle; to the Allies it is the Second Battle of the Somme). By 23 March the Germans have advanced 14 miles to the Somme River—an enormous gain in comparison to the years of fighting along this front for small bits of territory. But by 4 April the German offensive runs out of troops and supplies and bogs down in a salient reaching to nine miles east of Amiens. On 23 March, however, the Germans had begun to shell Paris, 75 miles away, with their 'Big Bertha' long-range guns (so named after Bertha von Krupp, proprietress of the Krupp Munition Works).

28 MARCH 1918
WW I: Western Front   General Ferdinand Foch of France was appointed on 26 March to be grand coordinator of the Allied armies (whose generals often disagree on strategy); today General Pershing, commander of the American forces, who has insisted from the beginning that his troops fight as independent units, offers to let General Foch assign American troops wherever they are needed in the crisis. Pershing and Foch make a plea to Wilson to get more troops over quickly, as the situation on the Western Front is desperate. Pershing's magnanimous gesture, however, has little effect, for shortly after he makes it the battle lines straighten out and the need for immediate American reinforcements lessens. American troops do not become engaged in large numbers until early summer 1918—at which point they are coming across from the New World by the tens of thousands daily, hundreds of thousands monthly, until by November 1918 Pershing's command comprises more than 2 million American soldiers.

16–20 APRIL 1918
Great Britain   The House of Commons passes a new Military Service Bill that is far more drastic (possibly taking males up to 55 years of age) and that may extend to Ireland. Irish Nationalist MPs, however, supported by Irish bishops, decide unanimously to oppose conscription of Irish males.

MAY 1918
Russia   During this month, the Bolsheviks and their supporters find themselves besieged on all sides, and it appears that Russia is about to be dismembered. German troops take over the Ukraine, set up a puppet government, and aid the Finns in fighting off the Red Guards. The Cossacks—semi-autonomous forces who had long enjoyed privileges under the Czars for serving as repressive police—have turned against the Bolshevik Government; one of their leaders, Colonel Semenov, begins an outright war against Red Guards in Siberia and enjoys considerable success in early stages. Georgians in the Caucasus proclaim independence (23 May). The Poles see a chance to get free of the Russians and seek protection of the Central Powers. Czechoslovaks

German troops advancing on the Western Front.

also see their chance, and in return for promises of support from the Allies, a large force of Czechoslovak troops fights its way across Russia to Vladivostok, against the Red Guards. Meanwhile, the Allies have turned openly against the Bolsheviks. They feel betrayed by Bolshevik withdrawal from the war and point out that they gave quantities of arms and other supplies to the Czar's government, which they do not want used by the Bolsheviks. The Allies will also justify their anti-Bolshevik policy on the ground that the Bolsheviks are not only repudiating debts assumed by the former government, but revealing secret agreements made by the Allies with previous Russian Governments. Behind all this lie the Allies' hatred and fear of the Bolshevik movement, which has claimed its goal as the overthrow of all established 'bourgeois' states. Before the summer is over, the Allies will land thousands of troops on Russian soil, ostensibly to protect supplies they have sent to Czarist forces. Purposes of the Allies vary, with the French and British ready to depose the Bolsheviks, the Japanese more concerned with getting Russian territory in Siberia, and the Americans caught between these conflicting desires and hoping only to show solidarity with Allied policies in Western Europe (and trusting that even a minor American military presence—about 7000 troops—in the Far

East would prevent the Japanese from despoiling Russia in Siberia).

24 MAY 1918

Russia General Poole, a British officer, lands at Murmansk, the Russian port on the Barents Sea. His announced mission is to head a contingent of 520 British Royal Marines sent here in April and May to prevent German and Finnish forces from taking Murmansk—in other words, they are helping their recent ally in its war against the Germans. Soon this North Russia Expeditionary Force will be augmented by French, Italian, and Serbian troops to the number of 18,000, and they will find themselves fighting the Bolsheviks.

27 MAY–25 JUNE 1918

WW I: Western Front The Germans mount their third offensive designed to overwhelm the Allies, this time attacking French forces along the Aisne River northeast of Paris. Within two days the Germans take Soissons and Rheims; by 31 May they have pushed the French across the Marne River; by 3 June the Germans reach Château-Thierry. On 4 June the French—with the aid of US troops—stop the Germans at Château-Thierry as they attempt to cross the Marne; the Americans counterattack at

THE SENSELESS WAR 1914-1918

Field Marshal von Hindenburg (left) with Quartermaster General Ludendorff.

Marshal Foch and General Pershing—June 1918.

Belleau Wood and help to hold the Germans. After weeks of intense fighting, US forces take Belleau Wood, but at the cost of 9500 casualties.

JUNE 1918

WW I: Naval Under a plan promoted in part by Assistant Secretary of the Navy Franklin D Roosevelt, US ships begin laying mines between the Orkney Islands, off Britain, and the coast of Norway, with the idea of isolating German submarines.

Russia The Czech troops that had fought with Russia against the Germans have now turned against the Bolsheviks and seized Omsk, a Siberian city, and control part of the Siberian railroad. They will soon move into other Siberian cities, and their commander, General Horvath, will proclaim a new government for Siberia, opposed to the Bolsheviks.

15–24 JUNE 1918

WW I: Southern Front The Austrians launch an attack across the Piave River, but with the aid of British and French troops, the Italians are able to beat them back.

29 JUNE 1918

Russia A provisional government opposed to the Bolsheviks establishes itself at Vladivostok, the Russian port on the Sea of Japan.

30 JUNE 1918

USA Eugene Debs, prominent Socialist and pacifist, is arrested on charges of denouncing the government, a violation of the Espionage Act of 1917: on 14 September Debs will be sentenced to 10 years in prison (but will be released by President Warren G Harding in 1921).

15 JULY–6 AUGUST 1918

WW I: Western Front In the Second Battle of the Marne, the Germans make what is their final drive of consequence. They almost take Rheims, but by 18 July General Foch orders the Allies to counterattack. Later the German Chancellor would write: 'On the 18th even the most optimistic among us knew that all was lost. The history of the world was played out in three days.' From this point on the German forces will be essentially on the defensive, if not on the run.

16 JULY 1918

Russia Czar Nicholas and his family have been held prisoner since March 1917; they have recently been moved to Ekaterinaburg in the Urals. Fearing that advancing counterrevolutionary White Russians may be able to free the Czar, the local communist council meets during this day and decides to do away with the imperial family. In the evening the Czar, his wife, their five children (including the hemophiliac heir, Alexis), and four servants are taken to a cellar and shot or bayoneted to death; their bodies are destroyed by fire and acid. (In the years that follow, there will be claims that one child, Anastasia,

escaped, but this possibility has never been accepted.) Although Lenin and other Bolshevik leaders have not been involved in the decision to execute the Czar, it is clearly an act that makes their way easier.

18 JULY 1918

WW I: Western Front The Allies' counterattack begins. Next day the Germans are retreating across the Marne; by 2 August the French have retaken Soissons; by 6 August the Germans' salient at the Marne has been eliminated.

3 AUGUST 1918

Russia The first Allied troops land at Archangel, the Russian port on the White Sea, following landings at Murmansk, to the north, during July. On the same day the first British forces land at Vladivostok, on Russia's Far Eastern coast; the British have been assured by the Japanese and the Americans that they will also send troops here. The Japanese land on 11 August, Americans on 17 August. Eventually some 10,000 US troops will serve in Vladivostok (and the last will not leave until January 1920). Allied troops will see little action in Siberia; their most important role is unintended—preventing the Japanese from seizing more territory on the Asian mainland. Some 5000 US troops will eventually serve in the Murmansk-Archangel area too, remaining there until 1919.

8–12 AUGUST 1918

WW I: Western Front The Allies launch their final offensive with what the British know as the Battle of Amiens and the French as the Battle of Montdidier. On the first day 554 British tanks plus superior numbers, including many Australian and Canadian troops, overwhelm the Germans: their commander, General Ludendorff, will call this 'the black day of the German Army.' By the second day about 400 tanks are out of action and the Germans move in reserves; but the offensive routs the Germans, who never recover from this body blow.

15 AUGUST 1918

USA-Russia The US and the Bolshevik Government break diplomatic relations.

12–14 SEPTEMBER 1918

WW I: Western Front The Germans are retreating all along the Western Front, pulling back to their Hindenburg (Siegfried) Line. The American First Army forces the Germans back from the St Mihiel salient.

14 SEPTEMBER 1918

WW I: Diplomatic Austria-Hungary sends a note to the Allies requesting peace discussions, but the Allies will reject the overture on the ground that there is little to discuss.

26 SEPTEMBER–11 NOVEMBER 1918

WW I: Western Front Americans attack in the

THE SENSELESS WAR 1914-1918

US troops going into action in the Argonne Forest.

London Irish Rifles firing at a hidden enemy during daylight patrol 'Albert,' 6 August 1918.

Soldiers at the front hurling grenades from their trenches—16 September 1918.

Open warfare on the Somme—August 1918.

THE SENSELESS WAR 1914-1918

Soldiers of Company A, 126th Infantry Division in a front-line trench, 1918.

General Pershing decorating Brigadier General Douglas MacArthur—7 September 1918.

Meuse-Argonne on the 26th and the British and Belgians attack in the Armentières region on the 28th. Fighting will continue right up to the signing of an armistice, and there will be terrible casualties on all sides.

1 OCTOBER 1918

WW I: Middle East Arabs and British units take Damascus, Syria, from the Turks.

3 OCTOBER 1918

Germany Germany forms a new government with Prince Maximilian of Baden as Chancellor.

4–23 OCTOBER 1918

WW I: Diplomatic Germany and Austria send requests for an armistice to President Wilson (who will not receive them until 7 October). Wilson then asks for clarifications, as the Germans send more notes. Finally, on 23 October, Wilson feels satisfied that the Germans are accepting his terms and agrees to transmit their request to the Allies. The Germans have agreed to suspend submarine warfare, to cease such inhumane practices as the use of poison gas, and to withdraw troops back into Germany.

24 OCTOBER–3 NOVEMBER 1918

WW I: Southern Front Italian forces have been greatly strengthened under their commander, General Diaz; supported by some British and French troops, they begin to push the Austrians back along the entire line from the Gulf of Venice across into Trentino. In what is known as the Battle of Vittorio Veneto, the Austrians are routed, saved only by an armistice on 4 November.

26 OCTOBER 1918

WW I: Diplomatic Germany's supreme commander, General Erich Ludendorff, resigns, protesting the terms to which the German Government has agreed in negotiating an armistice. This will set the stage for his later support of Hitler and the Nazis, who claim that Germany did not lose the war on the battlefield but were 'stabbed in the back' by politicians.

30 OCTOBER 1918

WW I: Diplomatic Turkey signs an armistice with the Allies, agreeing to end hostilities at noon on 31 October.

31 OCTOBER 1918

Disease In the worst global epidemic, or pandemic, of the century, influenza—the acute, contagious, respiratory viral infection—has been spreading around the world since May. During October it

THE SENSELESS WAR 1914-1918

American Infantry in Vladivostok.

begins to ravage both civilians and military in Europe and the United States (some 2200 deaths a week will be recorded in London during October). Before it runs its course during 1919, the influenza will kill 20 million people—perhaps twice as many as World War I.

1–3 NOVEMBER 1918
WW I: Diplomatic As hostilities on battlefields are winding down, conflict shifts to the political sphere. Vienna is in a state of virtual revolution, as the Austro-Hungarian Empire is coming apart. A Czech National Council in Prague has declared itself the government on 28 October. The Serbs re-enter Belgrade this day and declare a Serbian National Council at Sarajevo. In Budapest rioting soldiers seize the government and Count Tisza, who has long championed Hungarian unity with Austria, is assassinated on 31 October; Count Michael Karolyi immediately becomes prime minister and begins a series of reforms. Meanwhile, the Kaiser has been stripped of all power (as of 28 October) and Germany is now ruled by its Reichstag. Thousands of German sailors with the fleet at Kiel will mutiny on 3 November; they seize the city, set up councils of workers and sailors, fly the red flag of the communists, and persuade other important North German cities to join in revolution.

4 NOVEMBER 1918
WW I: Diplomatic The Allies' armistice with Austria-Hungary, signed 3 November, goes into effect.

At Versailles a conference of Allied representatives agrees on peace terms to be offered to Germany.

6 NOVEMBER 1918
WW I: Western Front The Germans are now in general retreat as French and American forces cross the Meuse and move to take Sedan.
WW I: Diplomatic At Cracow, Poland, a Polish Republic is proclaimed. German delegates leave Berlin to meet General Foch and discuss armistice terms.

7 NOVEMBER 1918
WW I: USA A 'false armistice' is celebrated by Americans due to premature reports of Germany's acceptance of terms.

8 NOVEMBER 1918
WW I: Diplomatic General Foch receives the German delegates in his railroad car and forces them to ask for an armistice.

9 NOVEMBER 1918
Germany Kaiser Wilhelm is forced to abdicate. Berlin is overrun by strikers, and Prince Max is forced to resign as chancellor: a German Republic is proclaimed by the Social Democrats and less radical socialists. The more radical Sparticists, Karl Liebknecht and Rosa Luxemburg, will refuse to join the government headed by Friedrich Ebert. The king of Bavaria has abdicated (7 November), and a Bavarian Republic is declared at Munich.

1 DECEMBER 1918

10 NOVEMBER 1918
Germany Kaiser Wilhelm and his son enter Holland.

11 NOVEMBER 1918
WW I: Diplomatic The armistice is signed at five in the morning in a railroad car in the forest of Compiègne, north of Paris. Hostilities formally end at eleven this morning. When all costs are totaled they will come to 10 million dead and 20 million wounded in battle, with at least another 5 million civilians lost to starvation and disease; at least $337 billion has been directly expended on the war, with untold billions attributable to indirect costs.
Poland Josef Pilsudski, pro-German leader of the Polish struggle for freedom from Russia, returns to Warsaw and declares an independent Polish Republic, which he will head.

12 NOVEMBER 1918
Austria-Hungary Emperor Charles I abdicates the throne of Austria (and on the 13th will abdicate the throne of Hungary). Although he will attempt to regain the Hungarian throne in 1921, it is the end of the House of Habsburg.

13 NOVEMBER 1918
WW I: Diplomatic With Germany defeated, the Soviet Government of Russia feels secure enough to announce annulment of the treaty of Brest-Litovsk, signed 3 March, which was so unfavorable to Russia.

14 NOVEMBER 1918
Czechoslovakia The independent Republic of Czechoslovakia is proclaimed, with Thomas Masaryk as its first president. Masaryk, himself a Slovak, will be revered by Czechs and Slovaks and recognized as the father of modern Czechoslovakia.

18 NOVEMBER 1918
Belgium Belgian troops re-enter Brussels, lost to the German invaders on 20 August 1914.
Latvia Latvia declares itself an independent republic, but it will be 1920 before both Russia and Germany recognize its independence.

26 NOVEMBER–13 DECEMBER 1918
WW I: Aftermath With crossing of the German frontier by the French on 26 November, the Allies' occupation of the Rhineland will commence; British and American troops will cross into Germany on 1 December. Americans will occupy Coblenz on the Rhine by 11 December, and the British will cross the Rhine on the 12th to occupy the Cologne bridgehead.

1 DECEMBER 1918
Iceland Iceland becomes a sovereign state but remains in union with Denmark.

US troops on Armistice Day, 1918.

THE SENSELESS WAR 1914-1918

TOMAS MASARYK, 1850–1937, and
JAN MASARYK, 1886–1948

The lives of this father and son span and embody the fate of Czechoslovakia in the 20th century. Tomas Masaryk was the son of a coachman to the Austro-Hungarian Emperor Franz Joseph; he obtained a good education and upon entering the Austro-Hungarian Parliament in 1891 proceeded to fight for the rights of the Slavic minorities within the empire. When Austria-Hungary went to war in 1914, he fled and came eventually to the US, where he tried to enlist the support of immigrant Czechs and Slovaks and of President Wilson for an independent Czechoslovakia. He had his way at the Paris Peace Conference, and was elected the first president of the new republic. Although he could not always satisfy the disparate groups in the new nation, he left it relatively strong when he retired in 1935. In October 1938, the Germans moved in and took over the Sudetenland, Russia helped itself to another section, and Masaryk's Czechoslovakia was dismembered. His son Jan had been serving in the Czech foreign service, and in 1940, when the Czech government in exile settled in London, he became its foreign minister. He retained this post when the government returned to Prague after the war, but in 1948 his body was found in a courtyard three stories below his apartment. It could never be proven whether he was pushed or had committed suicide to protest the communist seizure of the nation his father had founded.

President Tomas Masaryk.

USA First US troops arrive back from Europe in New York City.

4 DECEMBER 1918
WW I: Diplomatic With a large contingent of historians, geographers, political scientists and economists, President Wilson sails for Europe as head of the American delegation to the Peace Conference. He does not include anyone from Congress, where Republicans will soon hold a majority in the Senate, and will pay dearly for this error in the years that follow.
Yugoslavia The Kingdom of the Serbs, Croats, and Slovenes is proclaimed; it will not change its name to Yugoslavia ('southern Slavs') until 1929.

14 DECEMBER 1918
Great Britain In the general election, the coalition government of David Lloyd George wins a clear majority. Sinn Fein candidates from Ireland—profiting from resentment at British actions after the Easter Uprising and attempts to conscript Irish males—win 73 of 105 Irish seats. These Sinn Fein members refuse to take their seats in Westminster, London; instead, they will meet in Dublin as the Dail Eireann (House of Deputies) on 21 January 1919, and declare the Irish Republic.

16–18 DECEMBER 1918
WW I: Aftermath As Germany finds itself powerless, its troops evacuate Finland, give over Kiev in the Ukraine to revolutionary forces, and pull back from Estonia as Bolshevik forces move in. In Berlin a conference of workers' and soldiers' councils from all over Germany takes effective control of the government, delegating temporary authority to the Ebert Government until the elections of 19 January 1919 can select a new national assembly.

20–31 DECEMBER 1918
WW I: Aftermath The Allies are not willing to stand by and watch the Bolsheviks extend their power. Not only are they supporting forces in the Murmansk-Archangel and Vladivostok regions, they are now landing troops at Odessa in the Crimea and at Riga, Latvia.

25 DECEMBER 1918
WW I: Diplomatic After spending Christmas Day with the American troops in France, Wilson will go on to London (26 December) for preliminary discussions about the forthcoming peace conference at Versailles. Although some regard him as idealistic, he speaks for the hopes of many and is greeted in public appearances with enthusiasm and called 'Wilson the Just.'

OTHER EVENTS OF 1918
Science Harlow Shapley, the American astronomer, discovers the dimensions of the Milky Way.
Technology At the Mount Wilson Observatory, near Pasadena, California, the 100-inch reflecting

President Wilson reading the Armistice terms to the US Congress—11 November 1918.

telescope goes into use; it will remain the world's largest telescope until the advent of the 200-inch telescope on Mount Palomar.

Social Science Leonard Woolley and H R H Hall begin important excavations on the site of ancient Babylonia.

Literature Gerard Manley Hopkins's *Poems* are published posthumously: Hopkins, an English Jesuit, had died in 1889, but only now will his work be allowed to have a wide effect on modern poetry. Alexander Blok's *The Twelve* is an epic poem celebrating the Russian Revolution. Rupert Brooke's *Collected Poems* are published after his death on a troopship. Lytton Strachey's *Eminent Victorians* and Apollinaire's *Calligrames* come off the press.

Music Stravinsky's *Histoire du Soldat*; Puccini's opera *Gianni Schicchi*; Elgar's *Cello Concerto*.

Miscellaneous Russia adopts the metric system and the Gregorian Calendar. At Cloquet, Minnesota, and environs a fire leaves some 560 dead.

US Peace Conference officials—House, Lansing, Wilson, White, Bliss.

1919-1932:
A BORROWED PEACE

Peasants revolt in the streets of Canton, China—1927.

3 JANUARY 1919
International Herbert Hoover, who has been the efficient head of the US Food Administration and the Interallied Food Council during the war, is put in charge of war relief in Europe. Hoover had been instrumental in getting a clause into the Armistice agreeing to supply food to defeated nations, although in the case of Germany this clause would not be immediately respected. Hoover will also be named head of the Supreme Economic Council, which will have great influence on European economic affairs during the chaotic armistice period. His handling of the situation brings praise and will help to lead him to the US Presidency.

5 JANUARY 1919
Germany The left-wing Spartacus organization instigates a revolt in Berlin in an attempt to prevent elections of a National Constituent Assembly and a constitution for postwar Germany. Terrified at the spread of Bolshevism into Germany, the army, in concert with the free-wheeling Freikorps—bands of armed men recently returned from the front—ruthlessly suppresses the rebellion. Within a ten-day period, some 1000 Spartacus members are killed,

including the leaders Karl Liebknecht and Rosa Luxemburg.

19 JANUARY 1919
International The Paris Peace Conference begins in the Palace of Versailles outside Paris. Consideration of the German treaty will take until June. Thirty-two powers participate. The purpose is to reshape the world and create an organization to prevent future war. It begins with a serious error of judgment: Germany is not represented. The Big Four who will dominate the proceedings are British Prime Minister David Lloyd George, French Premier Georges Clemenceau, Vittorio Orlando of Italy, and Woodrow Wilson of the United States. Baron Makino represents Japan. For the first time in an international meeting, British Dominions are recognized as full members.

Germany National elections take place on schedule, as agreed to by the November 1918 conference of representatives of newly formed German governments. There is universal male suffrage over the age of 20. The Socialists win 163 seats, independents 22, and the remaining 236 seats are divided among parties across the political spectrum. The purpose of the elections is to form a National Constituent Assembly to draft a Constitution.

21 JANUARY 1919
Ireland The militant nationalist Sinn Fein organization has won three-fourths of the Irish seats in the British Parliament, but instead of going to Westminster the members hold a Congress in Dublin today and declare Ireland independent of Great Britain. Eamon De Valera will be proclaimed president and Arthur Griffith vice-president. The British and Northern Irish are not prepared to accept this step and violence ensues. This Anglo-Irish War lasts until 1921 and ends by setting up the Irish Free State, consisting of 26 of the 32 counties of Ireland. The other six coalesce as Northern Ireland, remaining part of Great Britain.

3 FEBRUARY 1919
USSR The Bolshevik Army is defeated in a series of encounters with White Russians in the Caucasus. Throughout the year White Russians will continue to fight to recapture the government from the Bolsheviks. They are led by General Anton Denikin, Admiral A V Kolchak, and others and get considerable international support. At Omsk, Kolchak heads the government of Western Siberia. He has 190,000 foreign troops including Japanese, British, and Americans, plus 300,000 Russians. The anti-Bolsheviks are initially successful, capturing the Crimean Peninsula, taking much of Siberia with the help of the Japanese, and making inroads into the north. However, Lenin's great organizer, Leon Trotsky, Commissar of War, manages to rally the peasants and workers to defeat attempts to overthrow the new soviets, and by April 1920 the last foreign anti-Bolshevik 'guerrillas' will have left Russian soil.

6 FEBRUARY 1919
Germany The short-lived and much-vilified Weimar Republic begins its existence as the National Assembly convenes in Weimar, a small city southwest of Berlin. Friedrich Ebert is elected President and asks Philipp Scheidemann to form a government. Since this government will support the Versailles Treaty (the peace treaty for Germany) it will not receive proper allegiance from the German nation, which feels badly betrayed.

23 FEBRUARY 1919
Italy Benito Mussolini forms the *Fasci del Combattimento*. His followers adopt black shirts as their uniform and form into military-style units called *squadristi*. We are 'the gypsies of Italian politics,' explains Mussolini.

MARCH 1919
Russia Lenin founds the Third International, the purpose of which is to bring about revolution in all countries. Revolutionary cells must take their directives from the central organization in Moscow. Cells may not ally themselves with other organizations, except to support the Socialists—but, as the International adds, only in the way that 'the hangman's rope supports the convict.' Lenin's call for world revolution instills fear in middle and upper classes around the world, lending strength and purpose to right-wing dictatorial groups otherwise without lofty aims. The communist revolutionaries will also infiltrate nationalist and independence movements, as well as workers' groups, adulterating legitimate popular aspirations for better conditions in the industrial world.

1 MARCH 1919
Korea A coalition of Christian, Buddhist, and Chondo-kyo leaders declares Korea independent of an astonished Japan. What starts as a dignified declaration ends with hundreds dead, thousands tortured and wounded, as the Japanese conquerors suppress the nationalist movement. Reforms will be instituted on 19 August, and it will become easier for Koreans to live and advance within their own society.

25 MARCH 1919
International Woodrow Wilson's dream of a League of Nations becomes a reality when the League Covenant is adopted at the Paris Peace Conference. It will become part of the final Treaty of Versailles and other peace treaties signed in the environs of Paris: with Austria (Treaty of Saint-Germain), Hungary (Trianon), Bulgaria (Neuilly), and Turkey (Sèvres). The main objectives of the League are to prevent war, oversee peace, organize for international co-operation, and discharge obligations involved in the treaties of 1919–20. Its organization consists of a legislative, an executive, and a judicial branch separate from member governments. Its organizational weakness is that it represents nations, not people, so that it soon becomes a place for diplomats to argue in a world forum rather than a source of action for troubled areas.

5 APRIL 1919
Ireland Eamon de Valera is elected president of the Sinn Fein Dail, the executive body of the organization for Irish unity and independence.

10 APRIL 1919
Mexico Emiliano Zapata, the revolutionary, is assassinated by an agent of President Carranza. An illiterate, Zapata had fought primarily with the goal of agrarian reform and will become a hero to Mexico's peasants.

14 APRIL 1919
India Since returning from South Africa, Mohandas K Gandhi has begun his passive resistance movement, which the British see as leading to rebellion, but which Gandhi sees as leading to a unified, independent India. He calls his nonaggressive methods *satyagraha*, or 'soul force.' Nervous British rulers have decreed harsh measures. At Amritsar this day,

A BORROWED PEACE 1919-1932

inspired by Gandhi's program of 'nonviolent non-support,' an unarmed crowd of thousands of Moslems and Hindus has gathered to protest the government's methods. The British shoot into the throng, killing 400 and wounding perhaps 1000. The episode does much to convince Indians that co-operation with the British will not work.

20 APRIL 1919
Montenegro King Nicholas abdicates under duress. The country votes to join in the nation made up of Serbs, Croats, and Slovenes. In 1929 this kingdom will adopt the name of Yugoslavia.

30 APRIL 1919
International In Paris German rights to China's Shantung Province are transferred to Japan against the will of China, which withdraws from the conference. China will be the only League member to participate in the conference without signing the Versailles Treaty. The decision on Shantung will lead to a militant student movement in China aimed at a unified nation. This will become the goal of the Kuomintang, or Nationalist, movement.

3 MAY 1919
Afghanistan Afghan forces begin fighting British and Indian troops in the Punjab. Fighting is instigated by the Amir Amanullah of Afghanistan. It includes bombing from airplanes. A peace will be signed by all parties on 8 August.

4 MAY 1919
China In reaction to news from the Paris Peace Conference that the Allies intend to turn over Shantung to Japan, there are widespread demonstra-

tions, organized by students. This provides the name, the May Fourth Movement, that will inspire Mao Tse-tung and others to work for a Marxist-Communist Revolution to redress wrongs perpetrated in and against China.

6 MAY 1919
International General Jan Smuts has devised a new and useful formula for Big Four redistribution of conquered territories and colonies. It is the mandate. Under this formula German East Africa is given to Britain and German South West Africa to South Africa (some of this territory is later transferred to Belgium). German-held islands in the Pacific north of the equator (except for Yap with its important cable station) are handed over to Japan.

7 MAY 1919
International A draft of the Versailles Treaty is shown to the Germans. The terms do not always follow Wilson's Fourteen Points, the condition for Germany's surrender. Full responsibility for World War I is laid upon Germany, which is prevented from rearming and must pay $5 billion immediately, plus an indemnity of an indeterminate amount. Danzig is declared a free city. Alsace-Lorraine will be handed over to France. The left bank of the Rhine is to be occupied by Allied troops for up to 15 years, and the Saar Basin administered by the League of Nations. Germany will not be allowed to enter the League. Germany loses about 7 million people and 87,000 square miles of territory.

26 MAY 1919
WW I: Aftermath The Supreme Council of Allies, meeting at Versailles, decides to recognize two White Russian leaders, Admiral Kolchak and General

PRE-1914 BOUNDARIES
BOUNDARIES AFTER TREATY OF VERSAILLES, 1919
TERRITORIES LOST BY GERMANY
UNDER LEAGUE OF NATIONS CONTROL
DEMILITARISED ZONE

Denikin, and support them against the Bolsheviks, even to the extent of sending troops.

JUNE–JULY 1919
WW I: Aftermath The Poles are determined to hold back the Russians and gain territory; having occupied part of Lithuania in April, they occupy eastern Galicia, then move into Ruthenia and the Western Ukraine. They will meet little opposition until December 1919. It will be February 1920 before the Russians are in a position to launch a counter-attack.

4 JUNE 1919
United States The proposal to adopt the 19th Amendment to the Constitution, which will enfranchise American women, goes to the States for ratification.

19 JUNE 1919
Turkey Objecting to dismemberment of his country by the Allies, Mustafa Kemal declares his Turkish Nationalist Congress, headquartered in Ankara, independent of Constantinople.

20 JUNE 1919
Germany Philipp Scheidemann resigns as chancellor of the new German Republic which he has done so much to set up, refusing to sign the peace treaty. Gustav Bauer, a Socialist, is asked to form a Cabinet.

21 JUNE 1919
International The German Navy, feeling betrayed by the terms of the peace treaty, scuttles most of its ships interned at Great Britain's Scapa Flow naval base, south of the Orkney Islands.

28 JUNE 1919
International In the Galèrie des Glâces, in the Palace of Versailles near Paris, delegates authorized by the German Republic sign the Versailles Treaty, in the same room in which half a century earlier (1871) the King of Prussia had accepted the Imperial office, bringing about the German Empire.

Wilson has set his hope for peace on the League of Nations, where international disputes can be heard to avoid war. He hopes problems arising from the peace treaty will be solved through the League. Wilson will fail to convince the United States to ratify the treaty, and neither Germany nor the USSR is invited at the outset to be a member.

31 JULY 1919
Germany The Weimar Constitution establishing the German Republic is adopted. It is on a federal basis, allowing for formation of new German states.

A BORROWED PEACE 1919-1932

Germany adopts a parliamentary system. Every German male over 20 years of age receives the vote, although electoral lists must go through party organizations, diminishing the power of individual voters. Two houses of government are formed: one, the Reichstag, is based on proportional representation of one member for each 60,000 votes; the upper house, known as the Reichsrat, is made up of representatives from the 17 states. The executive consists of a cabinet headed by a chancellor, responsible to the Reichstag. The president is head of state for a period of seven years and can appoint and dismiss the chancellor. During the next two years, democratic governments are established in Austria and Czechoslovakia (1920), Poland, Turkey (Asia Minor), Estonia, and Yugoslavia (1921).

4 AUGUST 1919
Hungary The Communist Bela Kun has come to power in Hungary. With Socialist support, he sets up a Soviet Republic. His violent 'dictatorship of the proletariat' (and reign of terror) is short-lived as Rumanians enter Budapest. Kun escapes to Austria and subsequently to Russia. Rumanians occupy the country until November, when they leave under Allied pressure, taking much Hungarian machinery and rolling stock. The new Hungarian Government will negotiate the Treaty of Trianon next year.

3 SEPTEMBER 1919
USA Instead of negotiating reservations to the Versailles Treaty with the Senate, Wilson sets out on a tour of the country to rouse public opinion. Many leaders of American opinion endorse the League, particularly William H Taft and Elihu Root, who have been sponsoring their 'League to Enforce Peace.' At this juncture Massachusetts Senator Henry Cabot Lodge backs the Covenant, as do labor unions and financial and industrial leaders. But Wilson does not attempt to rally support, in fact, his rigidity soon alienates many. Ultimately, the Senate, led by Lodge, brings the noble dream to an end by entangling the treaty in reservations, knowing that Wilson will not compromise.

10 SEPTEMBER 1919
International The Allies sign a peace treaty with Austria. China will sign the Austrian treaty, and by this indirect route become a member of the League of Nations.

12 SEPTEMBER 1919
International The poet Gabriele D'Annunzio organizes a militant nationalist group and takes Fiume (Rijeka) for Italy. His men adopt blue shirts as their uniform. Fiume will declare independence from the Italians on 15 December, although the area will continue under dispute.

Germany Adolf Hitler joins the obscure German Workers' Party as its seventh member. In a beerhall in Munich, he meets the founder, Anton Drexler. Hitler is not concerned with workers' rights, but

finds agreement for his fanatical German nationalism and anti-Semitism, his opposition to the Berlin government which unforgivably made peace with the Allies, and his respect for the Army. Hitler sympathizes with the activities of anti-left-wing paramilitary organizations now congregating in the anti-republican atmosphere of Bavaria.

25 SEPTEMBER 1919
USA Showing signs of exhaustion, Wilson suffers a breakdown in Colorado, followed by a massive stroke on his return to Washington (2 October). For five weeks the President is between life and death. Outside his family and doctor, few see him. By 1 November he is able to work for short periods, but never recovers his health.

27 SEPTEMBER 1919
International British troops which have been forced to winter over while fighting the Soviets leave the North Russian city of Archangel. White Russians, Czechoslovakians, Americans, Japanese, and motley groups of other nationals are still trying to undo the Bolshevik takeover of Russia. Today the last 5000 of 17,000 troops and supporters evacuates Archangel. On 13 December White Russian troops under Anton Denikin surrender Kharkov to the Bolsheviks.

19 NOVEMBER 1919
USA The Senate refuses to consent to the Versailles Treaty, 55 to 39.

28 NOVEMBER 1919
Great Britain In a by-election in Plymouth, Lady Nancy Astor, wife of Viscount Waldorf Astor, is the first woman elected to the House of Commons. Nancy Langhorne Astor was born in Virginia. Respected by women's groups across the nation, she is popular in her constituency, which will return her to parliament until 1945.

OTHER EVENTS OF 1919
Science On 29 May an expedition sponsored by the Royal Society of London observes a total eclipse of the sun in the Gulf of Guinea, off Africa. This confirms predictions incorporated in Einstein's theory of relativity. Ernest Rutherford changes nitrogen into oxygen by sending rays from radium through the nitrogen—the first time one chemical element is artificially transmuted into another.

Technology The first nonstop flight across the Atlantic is made by a Vickers Vimy bomber piloted by Captain John Alcock of the RAF and navigated by Lieutenant Arthur Brown of the Royal Flying Corps; they left from St John's, Newfoundland on 14 June and covered the approximately 1960 miles in 16 hours, 12 minutes. The first airship also crosses the Atlantic, a British dirigible R34 flying from Scotland to Roosevelt Field, New York, in 108 hours, 12 minutes on 2–6 July. And the first operational airline service is inaugurated between Berlin and Weimar. The Deutsche Luft-Reederei carries mail, papers, and passengers (in open cockpits); it adopts as its emblem a crane rising in flight, which will be the emblem of the later Lufthansa.

Social Sciences J B Huizinga's *The Waning of the Middle Ages.*

Literature Sherwood Anderson's *Winesburg, Ohio*; James B Cabell's *Jurgen*; Maugham's *The Moon and Sixpence*; Blasco Ibáñez's *Four Horsemen of the Apocalypse*; Yeats's *Wild Swans of Coole*; and the Japanese Toson's *A New Life.*

Drama/Entertainment Shaw's *Heartbreak House.*

The Arts Käthe Kollwitz's *Memorial to Karl Liebknecht*; Brancusi's *Bird in Space*; Picasso's *Pierrot and Harlequin.*

Architecture Walter Gropius assumes a position as school administrator in Weimar, renaming the school *Das Staatliche Bauhaus* and setting forth innovative curricula; the school will close in 1925, but Gropius will reopen it in Dessau, where he begins to design buildings in the 'Bauhaus style.' When the Nazis come to power in 1932, the Bauhaus will relocate in Berlin, then close for good in 1933, many participants emigrating to the US, where the Bauhaus style continues to be significant.

Music Strauss's opera *Die Frau Ohne Schatten*; Bartok's *The Miraculous Mandarin*; Janacek's *Diary of One Who Vanished.*

1 JANUARY 1920

USA Responding to worldwide fear caused by the Russian Revolution, the nation is caught up in a Red hunt. Attorney General A Mitchell Palmer has authorized raids on private houses and labor headquarters without warrants. In one night his deputies in 33 separate cities arrest 4000 people. Many are Russians, some Communists, but most are victims of headline hunting. 'Do not let the country see Red,' pleads the sick Wilson. When 300 innocent people are arrested in Detroit, they are held for a week, one day without food. In New England hundreds are arrested.

10 JANUARY 1920

International Inauguration of the League of Nations. The first meeting of the Council will be in Paris on 16 January. On 19 March the US Senate will vote again not to join.

16 JANUARY 1920

USA The 18th Amendment is ratified. It prohibits sale of alcoholic beverages. The Amendment will be repealed in 1933, the only Constitutional Amendment discarded.

FEBRUARY–MAY 1920

WW I: Aftermath The Russians launch a counterattack against the Poles, who have been trying to extend their nation eastward.

2 FEBRUARY 1920

Estonia Estonia declares independence, and signs a peace treaty with its neighbor, the USSR.

7 FEBRUARY 1920

Russia Admiral Kolchak surrenders to Bolshevik troops. He is executed, bringing to an end resistance supported by foreigners, and the Bolsheviks capture Odessa the next day.

6 FEBRUARY 1920

International The Saar region of Germany is turned over to the League, with France to have economic control.

29 FEBRUARY 1920

Czechoslovakia Trying to maintain independence from Germany and the USSR, Czechoslovakia adopts a constitution.

1 MARCH 1920

Hungary Nikolaus Horthy is elected Regent of Hungary, which has adopted a constitution on 28 February.

10 MARCH 1920

Ireland The Home Rule Act is passed by the British Parliament. It divides Ireland into two parts: 26 counties in the south loyal to the Sinn Fein independence movement, and six loyalist counties in the north shaped from the Ulster area. The Ulster counties accept the terms of Home Rule, which create a semi-independent state, leaving taxing power in Westminster but providing for a 13-member representation in the British Parliament. Home Rule is rejected by the southern counties, where the Anglo-Irish War continues for another year.

11 MARCH 1920

Syria The country has fought off French domination and now proclaims Emir Feisal king; on 25 April both Syria and Lebanon will be handed over to France as mandates.

13 MARCH 1920

Germany When the government is forced to cut back the army to 100,000 men, military groups begin to plot revolt. The signal comes when Captain Hermann Ehrhardt is ordered to demobilize his brigade; instead the commandant of Berlin orders Ehrhardt to take the Capital. He is joined there by World War hero General Erich Ludendorff (later a supporter of Hitler) and an East Prussian politician named Wolfgang Kapp, from whom the unsuccessful Putsch gets its name. The army turns a blind eye to the insurgents. Says Chief of Staff Hans von Seeckt, 'troops do not fire on troops.' The revolt is ended by a general strike called by the Socialists. The army is not reprimanded; instead the workers' strike adds to right-wing fears of a Bolshevik takeover as Communists take advantage of the disorder. Seeckt is put in charge of quelling the 'Red Army' operating in the Ruhr, an area under League jurisdiction.

28 MARCH 1920

USSR Anton Denikin's White Russian troops are

A BORROWED PEACE 1919-1932

defeated at Novorossijsk on the Black Sea. The British help Denikin to escape.

31 MARCH 1920
China Determined to have control of the Chinese Eastern Railway, the Japanese co-operate with Western forces and then back Semenov's cruel dictatorship in Siberia. They declare inability to withdraw troops, but deny territorial designs. American and Allied troops withdraw from Siberia next day. The Japanese troops are the only foreign force left on Russian soil, and will remain until October 1922.

6 APRIL 1920
International To force German evacuation of the Ruhr area, the French occupy Frankfurt, Darmstadt, and Hanau. They will stay until 17 May. This same day the Moscow government approves an 'independent-democratic' transition government in Siberia to be called the Far Eastern Republic.

25 APRIL 1920
International Mesopotamia and Palestine are put under British mandate by the Supreme Allied Council. Syria and Lebanon pass under French rule. King Feisal of Syria will not recognize the French mandate until late in August. On 25 August the French proceed into Damascus.
Poland Nervously watching a Soviet buildup of 20 divisions along the Russo-Polish border, Poles decide on an attack in the Ukraine. Josef Pilsudski leads the troops in a fight that proceeds until early June, when a Soviet cavalry officer, Budenny, rallies a counterattack.

30 APRIL 1920
Great Britain Tired of fighting, and fearful of being drawn into the bickering over borders that continues on the Continent, the British end conscription.

5 MAY 1920
USA Nicola Sacco and Bartolomeo Vanzetti are arrested on charges of robbery and murder of a paymaster at a shoe factory in Braintree, Massachusetts. On tenuous evidence, the two men will be convicted in 1921 and held until 23 August 1927, when they will be executed.

11 MAY 1920
International Although Japan persists in seeing Manchuria, Mongolia, and the Maritime Province of Siberia as of 'special interest,' it reluctantly agrees to join with Britain and the United States in strengthening China to take a more active part against incursions from Russia. This move weakens Japanese influence on the mainland.

20 MAY 1920
Mexico President Venustiano Carranza, under attack by American petroleum companies for nationalization of subsoil rights, faces armed rebellion by the right-wing Sonora triumvirate (Adolfo de la Huerta,

Alvaro Obregon, and Plutarco Calles). Fleeing Mexico City, Carranza is assassinated. He is succeeded by Huerta, who will turn over the administration to Obregon on 1 December.

JUNE 1920
WW I: Aftermath The Poles now advance on Kiev in the Russian Ukraine, thus provoking the Russians to embark on a full-scale counteroffensive.

4 JUNE 1920
Hungary The Treaty of Trianon (so named from the palace at Versailles where the Allies signed their agreement) is accepted by Hungary, which becomes a landlocked domain, shrinking from 125,000 square miles to 36,000, and from a population of 22 million to 8 million.

1 JULY 1920
Palestine Under the League, Britain has a mandate over Palestine. Sir Herbert Samuel takes over as high commissioner. The Arabs continue resistance, instigating riots and terrorism. The Arabs are afraid of losing their identity and territory to 60,000 Jews in Palestine.

4 JULY 1920
International The provisional government of Siberia's Maritime Province agrees to hand over parts of the strategic oil- and coal-rich Sakhalin Islands to Japan. Japan has already increased its power in the Maritime Province by an agreement signed 29 April.
Poland The Polish defense line, thinly extended over an 800-mile front, buckles under the onslaught of Soviet troops. By the end of July the invaders are before Warsaw. This European bastion against communism seems about to crumble.

11 JULY 1920
Germany East and West Prussia vote in a plebiscite to become part of Germany. Nonetheless, a slice of West Prussia 50 miles wide and 100 miles long will be handed over to Poland to provide a 'Polish Corridor' to the sea.

12 JULY 1920
International Lithuania and Soviet Russia, which have been battling over borders, agree to a peace treaty leaving Lithuania independent.

21 JULY 1920
Ireland The nationalist Sinn Feiners, aiming for independence, and the Unionist groups, willing to settle for limited British rule, engage in street fighting. Unionists have been reinforced by 1500 British Auxiliaries and some 5800 British troops.

10 AUGUST 1920
Turkey The Treaty of Sèvres, signed by Sultan Mohammed VI, is ratified by the government but will later be repudiated by Mustafa Kemal and the

under direction of General Maxime Weygand, the Poles, led by Generals Sikorski and Pilsudski, defeat the Soviets in the Battle of the Vistula at the gates of Warsaw. Within the week Polish troops will take 70,000 prisoners, while 100,000 Soviet troops flee to East Prussia. The victory will lead to favorable peace terms for Poland when a treaty with Soviet Russia is signed at Riga on 18 March 1921. Four million Ukrainians and Byelorussians come under Polish rule.

24 AUGUST 1920
International With British approval, Greece is encouraged to take the offensive against Turkish nationalists in Asia Minor. Also this month, Greece gets the Dodecanese Islands from Italy.

26 AUGUST 1920
United States The 19th Amendment to the Constitution is ratified. It gives women the right to vote.

23 SEPTEMBER 1920
International Despite Japanese protest China withdraws recognition of czarist representatives in China. Extraterritorial status is thereby lost to resident Russians, causing hardship.

2 OCTOBER 1920
International The Chinese Eastern Railway, important to Russia and China, has been a point of contention since 1896. In 1919 the railway was put under Allied control, and now the Chinese sign an agreement with the Russo-Asiatic Bank, largely French and Russian, which will oversee the railway but give local supervision to China.

2 NOVEMBER 1920
USA Warren G Harding wins the presidential election by 404 electoral votes to James Cox's 127; Harding's popular vote is 16,152,200 to the Democrats' 9,147,353.

12 NOVEMBER 1920
International By the terms of a treaty signed at Rapallo, Italy, the Dalmatian coast between Italy and Yugoslavia is ceded to Yugoslavia but Italy gets Istria, the peninsula between Trieste and Fiume, and Fiume, or Rijeka, is to become a free state. This will prove to be only a temporary solution.

14 NOVEMBER 1920
International The Bolshevik army occupies Sebastopol, ending anticommunist attempts to regain the government of Russia.

OTHER EVENTS OF 1920
Science Albert A Michelson, American astronomer, provides the first accurate measurement of a star's diameter, that of Betelgeuse.
Environment In one of the worst earthquakes recorded, some 180,000 are killed in Kansu Province, China.
Social Sciences H G Wells's *Outline of History*.

VLADIMIR ILYICH LENIN, 1870–1924

Principal leader and legend of the Soviet Union, Vladimir Ulianov (Nikolai) Lenin was the founder of the Russian Communist Party and the world's first Communist Party dictatorship. He was intelligent, dynamic, implacable, opportunistic, coldly impersonal in his economic reasoning and political hatreds, living only for the furtherance of Marxism. For three years after seizing power in 1917 he grappled with war and anarchy, employing force and terror to achieve the destruction of free enterprise and the creation of a classless society, determined that Soviets (councils of workers, soldiers, and peasants) should be the instruments of total, global revolution. Experience led him to modify the cold fervor of his methods, but few men have fought so hard to change the shape of human civilization or worked with such a sense of destiny. His body, embalmed for veneration, is on perpetual display in a crystal casket in a mausoleum in Moscow's Red Square.

Turkish National Assembly. Turkey retains Constantinople but the Dardanelles and Bosphorus come under international supervision. Smyrna, Adrianople, and Gallipoli will go to Greece.

11 AUGUST 1920
International Latvia and Soviet Russia sign a peace treaty after a three-week campaign in which Red troops are driven from Lettgalen, leaving Latvia independent.

15 AUGUST 1920
International With strategic help of the French

A BORROWED PEACE 1919-1932

Literature D H Lawrence's *Women in Love*; Sinclair Lewis's *Main Street*; Valéry's *Le Cimetière marin*; Colette's *Chéri*; Kafka's 'In the Penal Colony'; Pound's *Hugh Selwyn Mauberley*.

Drama/Entertainment O'Neill's *Beyond the Horizon* and *Emperor Jones*; two important films, *The Cabinet of Dr Caligari* and Charlie Chaplin's *The Kid*.

The Arts Modigliani's *Reclining Nude*; Matisse's *Odalisque*.

Music Stravinsky's *Pulcinella*; Ravel's *La Valse*; Milhaud's *Le Boeuf sur le toit*.

Life/Customs The USSR becomes the first country to legalize abortion. The decree will be replaced in 1936 by a more restrictive law.

Miscellaneous In February at Writtle, England, Marconi inaugurates the first public broadcasting station. But the station that comes to be recognized as the first to broadcast daily programs is Station 8MK (later WW) in Detroit, Michigan, which begins on 20 August with a program called 'Tonight's Dinner.' The first station organized as a commercial venture (for Detroit's was still experimental) is KDKA in Pittsburgh, Pennsylvania; it began irregular broadcasts on 29 September and regular semi-weekly broadcasting on 2 November after being licensed.

9 FEBRUARY 1921
International Poland and the USSR sign the peace

treaty of Riga, bringing an end to overt Russian military incursions into the heart of Europe. Poland gives up claims to the Ukraine.

India The first Indian Central Legislature is opened in New Delhi by the Duke of Connaught. It is still responsible to Britain through the governor-general. Gandhi, leader of the National Congress Party, voices the demand for a unified India, independent of Britain but with full dominion status within the Commonwealth. The British will continue to work toward dominion status for India, but fail to invite Indian participation. The British do not wish to involve the hereditary princedoms in discussions, nor do they see how to deal with religious antagonism between Moslems and Hindus.

12 FEBRUARY 1921
Great Britain Winston Churchill is appointed colonial secretary.

21 FEBRUARY 1921
International The London Conference on the Near East begins. The issue is the Allies' 1920 Treaty of Sèvres, which had given part of Turkish Asia Minor to Greece.

25 FEBRUARY 1921
Mongolia The Living Buddha, Hutuktu, is crowned king as the country declares independence from China.

26 FEBRUARY 1921
International The USSR signs treaties respecting the integrity of Persia and of Afghanistan.

27 FEBRUARY 1921
Italy The Fascists incite riots in Florence.

5 MARCH 1921
International The US warns Costa Rica and Panama to settle disputes peacefully.

16 MARCH 1921
International Britain signs a trade agreement with the USSR, also sending a trade mission to Moscow. This same month the Americans refuse to make trade agreements with the Soviets. Meanwhile, the Bolsheviks sign a treaty with the Kemal faction in Turkey.

20 MARCH 1921
Germany Upper Silesia votes for amalgamation with Germany in a plebiscite that is 63 percent in favor of the move. Unhappy, the Allied Supreme Council will refer the problem to the League of Nations, which will recommend partition. On 26 October both Poland and an unhappy Germany will accept League boundaries.

23 MARCH 1921
Germany With the stark announcement that it will be unable to meet its reparations payments on 1

20 OCTOBER 1921

May, Germany causes consternation in financial capitals of Europe and the US. Britain has imposed 50 percent duties on German goods; in America, tariffs make German goods all but prohibitive. Germany asks the US to mediate, but the Americans refuse. The decline of the German mark is another reason why reparations are hard to meet.

7 APRIL 1921
China The revolutionary leader Sun Yat-sen is elected President of China at Canton. But China is divided into north and south and subject to rivalries of warlords. Extraterritorial rights weaken Chinese authority.

24 APRIL 1921
Germany Held under Allied auspices, a plebiscite in the Tyrol favors merging with Germany. Unhappy with the outcome, the Allies give the area to Italy. Salzburg will vote to merge with Germany by the end of May. In many cases the self-determination clause of the Versailles Treaty is carried out; nonetheless, millions of Germans will be separated from their country.

11 MAY 1921
Germany The Allied Supreme Council has warned Germany to pay reparations or the entire Ruhr Valley will be occupied by 12 May. On this last day, Germany agrees.

14 MAY 1921
Italy The Fascists gain 29 seats in parliament.

21 JUNE 1921
Commonwealth The United Kingdom, the Dominions, and India, meeting at the Imperial Conference in London, become the British Commonwealth of Nations. Large questions as to political composition and constitutional contradictions remain.

16 JULY 1921
International Encouraged by the British, King Constantine of Greece launches a drive to take Asia Minor from nationalist forces under Kemal. Initially the Greeks defeat the Turks; the Turks then rally and prevent Greek troops from capturing Ankara. By August Constantine will have returned to Athens, leaving his troops to fight on until defeated at Smyrna in 1922.

21 JULY 1921
USA To prove his contention that air power is superior to sea power, Colonel William Mitchell demonstrates how bombs from planes can sink the captured German battleship *Ostfriesland*.

29 JULY 1921
Germany Hitler is made president of the new National Socialist (Nazi) Party over strong objection from those who foresee a turn into extremist

nationalism. The following month he sets up the Gymnastic and Sports Division, which will become the *Sturmabteilung* or SA, the Stormtroopers. Hitler sees the SA as 'an offensive force at the disposal of the movement,' against democratic and socialist movements. He does not wish it to confront the police or the army. His dream is 'revolution by permission.' In Bavaria especially, but also throughout Germany, the army and the police remain permissive of right-wing violence.

16 AUGUST 1921
Ireland Members of the Dáil swear allegiance to the Irish Republic at their first meeting, held at Dublin House. Seven days later the British declare a truce with Sinn Fein.

23 AUGUST 1921
International Austria and the US formally end war. Two days later the US signs treaties ending the war with Germany, and with Hungary on the 29th.

26 AUGUST 1921
Germany Matthias Erzberger is murdered. He had signed the armistice, and was hated by the military and paramilitary nationalist movements. Other factions in Germany resented his policy of national taxation, Catholicism, and centralist programs. His murder is carried out by the Organization Consul, composed of ex-Freikorps men.

9 SEPTEMBER 1921
International Guatemala, Honduras, and San Salvador agree to a Central American Union.

22 SEPTEMBER 1921
International The League of Nations accepts memberships of independent Estonia, Latvia, and Lithuania.

18 OCTOBER 1921
USSR Biding its time, Soviet Russia agrees to independence for the Crimea.

19 OCTOBER 1921
Portugal To stamp out republican sympathy, the military has allowed cruel retaliation against President Paes's supporters. The opposition assassinates the new prime minister, Antonio Granjo, and others held responsible for atrocities. For the next two years there will be a series of governments, many of which last two to three weeks. Not until 1925 will the country achieve some stability.

20 OCTOBER 1921
International The Germans and the Allies come to agreement over reparations. At a meeting in Wiesbaden it is understood that they will be made in cash and in kind, but not to the fixed amount of 269 billion gold marks ($33 billion), which the Germans insist is impossible.

On this same day, the French and Mustafa Kemal

A BORROWED PEACE 1919-1932

nationalists sign a treaty at Ankara fixing the Turko-Syrian border. The French, with Italian help, have been arming the Kemal faction, creating dissension among the Allies and trouble in the Aegean. The Bolsheviks have recognized Kemal's government.

21 OCTOBER 1921
Hungary The former King Karl has staged one unsuccessful *coup d'etat* against Nikolaus Horthy's interim government. Now he leads a second effort to regain the throne. He is arrested by Horthy's soldiers and expelled from the country. On 7 November Hungary will pass a law invalidating the Habsburg line of succession to the throne.

5 NOVEMBER 1921
International Soviet Russia signs a treaty with Mongolia, temporarily supporting the new government against Chinese and Japanese incursions.

12 NOVEMBER 1921
International The United States opens the Washington Disarmament Conference. The primary object is limitation of naval armaments and agreement on the position of all powers in the Pacific and Far East. Great Britain, France, Italy, China, Japan, Portugal, Holland, and Belgium attend; Russia is not invited. It is agreed that Britain, the US, Japan, France, and Italy will limit battleships and aircraft carriers on a ratio (representing hundreds of thousands of battleship tonnage) of 5-5-3-1.67-1.67.

A Four-Power Treaty signed 13 December 1921 pledges Britain, the US, Japan, and France to consult in event of a threat to peace in the Pacific region—replacing the Anglo-Japanese Alliance of 1902. The Nine-Power Treaty, signed by the conference nations, recognizes the principle of the open door in Eastern Asia.

6 DECEMBER 1921
Canada Mackenzie King, leader of the Labor Party and architect of a liberal coalition, becomes prime minister.

16 DECEMBER 1921
Ireland The Anglo-Irish Treaty, agreed to by the British Parliament and Sinn Fein, is ratified by Parliament. The treaty recognizes the Irish Free State, giving it dominion status within the British Commonwealth. The Ulster Government has the option to leave the new state, which it chooses to do, maintaining arrangements agreed to under the Home Rule Act of 1920. The Parliament of Southern Ireland will accept the treaty in January 1922.

OTHER EVENTS OF 1921
Science In Zambia, Africa, a fossil of an early form of *Homo sapiens* is found; known as Rhodesian Man, he lived perhaps 200,000 years ago.
Medicine/Health Working during the summer at the University of Toronto Medical School, Frederick Banting, a Canadian, and Charles Best, his American

WILLIAM LYON MACKENZIE KING,
1874–1950

Canada's Mackenzie King was prime minister longer than any other leader in the history of parliamentary government. Short, stocky, a lifelong bachelor with a reputation for being stuffy and old-fahioned, King had none of the charisma associated with great statesmen. Although a devout Presbyterian, he believed in spiritualism and sought to communicate with deceased associates. Gaining early expertise as a labor relations advisor, Mackenzie King's concern for working conditions led to his appointment as first Canadian minister of labor. As prime minister (and secretary of state for external affairs for all but two of his 21 years in office) he promoted unity between French-speaking and English-speaking Canadians and guided Canada to independence from English foreign policy. World War II dominated his last twelve years in office, during which he often served as a conciliatory link between Roosevelt and Churchill. The war also saw him reverse himself on the stand against conscription that had led him to power as Liberal leader, occasioning his famous pronouncement, 'Not necessarily conscription, but conscription if necessary.'

assistant, isolate insulin (on 27 July). Because their work was based on the hypothesis that such a hormone existed in the pancreas and was necessary to use sugar, they then administered the insulin to a dog that had had its pancreas removed to prove that it was indeed the hypothetical hormone. The first human subject to benefit from insulin will be 14-year-old Leonard Thompson, a diabetic who will be treated with insulin on 14 January 1922; with the aid of subsequent injections, he will lead a normal life. Insulin will be synthesized in 1964.
Social Sciences At the Jean Jacques Rousseau Institute in Geneva, Switzerland, a Swiss psychologist, Jean Piaget, begins researches in child psychology: over the next decades he will produce seminal findings about children's development, learning, and thought.

Ideas/Beliefs Ludwig Wittgenstein, Austrian philosopher, publishes his influential *Tractatus Logico-Philosophicus*.

Literature Dos Passos's *Three Soldiers*; Huxley's *Chrome Yellow*; Garcia Lorca's *Book of Poems*.

Drama/Entertainment Shaw's *Back to Methuselah*; O'Neill's *Anna Christie*; Pirandello's *Six Characters in Search of an Author*; Karel Capek's *Insect Play*. A sensation of the Paris season is the ballet *Les Mariés de la Tour Eiffel*, a composite work by *Les Six* (Poulenc, Milhaud, Auric, Honegger, Tailleferre, and Durey) with a scenario by Jean Cocteau.

The Arts Picasso's *Three Musicians*; Klee's *The Fish*.

Music Prokofiev's opera *Love for Three Oranges*; Janacek's opera *Katia Kabanova*; Honegger's opera *King David* (later revised as an oratorio).

Miscellaneous In the USA the first World Series broadcast is made by WJZ of Newark, New Jersey, which broadcasts a play-by-play account of the New York Giants versus the New York Yankees. The plays are telephoned from the stadium to Newark and beamed from there.

15 JANUARY 1922

Ireland Arthur Griffith is elected president of the Irish Free State after Eamon de Valera resigns, expressing opposition to the Anglo-Irish Treaty of London agreed to on 6 December 1921 and adopted by the Dáil in a 64 to 57 vote. De Valera will lead the militant opposition groups who seek a unified Ireland with a republican government independent of Great Britain.

22 JANUARY 1922

Papacy Pope Benedict XV dies. His successor, Cardinal Achille Ratti, will be elected on 6 February and will be known as Pius XI.

4 FEBRUARY 1922

International After boycotts and international pressures, Japan agrees to return Shantung Province to China.

9 FEBRUARY 1922

International The World War Foreign Debt Commission is established by Congress to settle the problem of Allied war and postwar loans. Great Britain owes $4 billion, France $3 billion, and Italy $1,600,000,000. Other countries are indebted to the United States. None save Finland will be able to pay in full. Wilson had insisted on repayment: later the commission will settle for $11,500,000,000 with interest of just over 2 percent payable over 62 years. The arrangement is based on Germany's meeting its reparation obligations. Since Germany is unable to pay agreed-upon amounts, the money is unavailable. For the second time, Britain offers to remit debts and reparations due it on condition that the United States not hold London to repayment. Wilson refuses. A great deal of anti-American feeling is generated, since Europeans feel that America has profited from the war through contracts for war supplies and postwar relief. For many Americans, default reinforces their suspicion of foreigners. Harding and Coolidge will both stand against canceling. By 1925 deep cuts will have to be made, Mussolini's Italy being the first to receive relief, with 80 percent cancelled, followed next year by France with 60 percent. Meanwhile, Germany is unable to pay either interest or debt, and in 1923 France will enter the Ruhr Valley in an effort to force payment. American loans to Germany will finally be subscribed—mostly by private investors—but too late to undo the damage.

18 FEBRUARY 1922

USA The Capper-Volstead Act allows farmers to buy and sell co-operatively without the risk of prosecution under antitrust laws.

21 FEBRUARY 1922

Egypt Great Britain ends its protectorate over Egypt. Egypt and Great Britain will jointly oversee the Sudan.

Ireland De Valera calls a convention of the Sinn Fein, declaring the Republican Government the only legitimate one in all Ireland.

15 MARCH 1922

International Facing realities, France, which up until now has insisted on currency for all reparations from Germany, agrees to accept raw materials as part payment.

18 MARCH 1922

India The British sentence Mohandas K Gandhi,

A woman with her flask during Prohibition.

A BORROWED PEACE 1919-1932

Members of the Russian Army on guard.

THE BOLSHEVIK REVOLUTION

Churchill called it an effort 'to strangle the infant Bolshevism in its crib.' Armies from the West and Japan fought alongside Russian counterrevolutionaries to defeat the Bolsheviks during the Civil War (1918–21), but the Bolsheviks prevailed. They established the Communist International (Comintern) to indoctrinate foreign communists and return them to their countries to promote revolutionary activity. Between 1919 and 1939, the noncommunist world responded to the Red Menace with repression. The frightening specter of communism became a useful tool for demagogues: part of Europe fell under dictatorship. The United States was spared so extreme a response, but the Palmer Raids (when 3000 allegedly subversive aliens were arrested and threatened with deportation) showed the impact on America. The very word 'Bolshevik' became synonymous with the most radical kind of revolutionary. In fact, the word in Russian means merely 'majority'— and that is what those who opposed them were determined to keep the Bolsheviks from becoming.

beloved leader of the disenfranchised, to six years' imprisonment for his part in the mounting civil disobedience campaign. He will be released in January 1924.

7 APRIL 1922

USA The Teapot Dome oil-deal scandal begins when Interior Secretary Albert B Fall leases part of the naval oil field to the Mammoth Oil Company, owned by Harry Sinclair. A subsequent lease of a second naval oil reserve in Elk Hills, California, goes to Edward L Doheny. On 15 April Senator John

B Kendrick of Wyoming, on a tip from a constituent, asks in the Senate for Fall to explain the arrangement. A Congressional investigation follows that will take two years before Fall, Sinclair, Doheny, and others are convicted of bribery and conspiracy. Six years later, in 1931, Fall is sent to prison for a year.

16 APRIL 1922

International To the consternation of diplomatic circles, German Foreign Minister Walther Rathenau signs the Treaty of Rapallo with Soviet Russia. Germany had been asked by Prime Minister David Lloyd George to participate in the 'Checkers Scheme,' a possible structure for a 'United States of Europe,' but Rathenau saw British and French diplomats dealing separately with the Soviets. Fearing exclusion, he re-establishes diplomatic and trade relations without consulting the Allies.

15 MAY 1922

International Germany turns over the Upper Silesia region to Poland under Allied pressure and despite a plebiscite in favor of merging with Germany.

1 JUNE 1922

Italy Over 50,000 Fascists gather for a meeting in Bologna. Mussolini warns that he will lead a full-scale revolt against a government favoring 'anti-Fascist reaction,' but the government already gives the Fascists a free hand against left-wingers.

5 JUNE 1922

International Succumbing to politics rather than

1 NOVEMBER 1922

economic realities, a bankers' committee of the Reparations Commission refuses an international loan to Germany.

16 JUNE 1922
Ireland The intransigent Republicans are beaten in a national election in which splinter parties participate. The vote is in favor of the Treaty of London, which leaves the Irish Free State as a dominion within the British Commonwealth.

24 JUNE 1922
Germany Foreign Minister Walther Rathenau is assassinated by Nationalists inflamed by Hitler's speeches. A Jew, Rathenau had wished to bridge the gulf between middle and laboring classes. He was the advocate of 'Fulfillment' (repayment of reparations, some of which he had managed to decrease). Hitler, forced today to begin a month-long prison sentence for paramilitary operations, rails against a 'Jewish sell-out' of Germany to the Bolsheviks. One of the tenets of Hitler's organization is that Jews shall not have citizenship nor hold office; another is that the Treaty of Versailles must be repudiated.

26 JUNE 1922
Germany The emergency decree under Article 48 of the Weimar Constitution is invoked by the government to deal with deteriorating economic conditions. The German mark has been falling. Bavaria, with its many paramilitary groups acting under the local police and army, is a threat to national unity. In the north, the German Racial Freedom Party, another right-wing nationalist group, is formed.

29 JULY 1922
International Greek troops have routed Turkish forces and are on their way to Constantinople, but the Allied Powers forbid their taking the city. With French and Italian help, the nationalist Turks in Asia Minor will rally.

President Warren G Harding.

1 AUGUST 1922
Italy The socialist *Alianza del Lavoro* declares a national strike. It collapses, but not before the Fascists have destroyed union and socialist headquarters in Livorno, Genoa, and other cities, and deposed the socialist government in Milan.

12 AUGUST 1922
Ireland President Arthur Griffith dies. Ten days later Commander-in-Chief Michael Collins is murdered in an ambush by independent republicans. Civil war ensues.

9 SEPTEMBER 1922
International Turks invade Smyrna, raze the city, and end the Greek presence in Asia Minor. Greece's King Constantine will abdicate later in the month. Some million and a half refugees will have to be admitted to Greece. This is accomplished with help of the League of Nation's Refugee Settlement Commission. On 30 January 1923 Moslems are exchanged for Greek-Orthodox minorities in Turkey. Bulgaria and Greece had exchanged populations in 1919.

22 SEPTEMBER 1922
USA Congress passes the Cable Act. An American woman who marries an alien will not lose citizenship; neither will a woman marrying an American automatically become an American citizen.

29 SEPTEMBER 1922
Italy Mussolini lines up support from the Vatican and the monarchy.

3 OCTOBER 1922
USA Rebecca L Felton, 97 years old, is sworn in as the first woman Senator in American history, to be replaced the next day by the newly elected Senator from Georgia. Mrs Felton had long been prominent in Georgia politics, and was appointed by the governor as a gesture to fill out the term of a deceased Senator.

27 OCTOBER 1922
Italy Liberal Luigi Facta's cabinet resigns in the face of threats from Mussolini that 'either the Government will be given to us or we will seize it by marching on Rome.' Mussolini calls for a general mobilization of Fascists. Victor Emmanuel III refuses to sign a declaration of martial law.

30 OCTOBER 1922
Italy Staying close to the Swiss border just in case, Mussolini sends his Black Shirts into Rome. The Fascist takeover is almost without bloodshed. Next day Mussolini arrives in Rome in morning coat to present his cabinet to the king. The Fascist *Squadre* are demobilized as Mussolini is made prime minister. 'What a character!' exclaims his wife.

1 NOVEMBER 1922
Turkey Mustapha Kemal takes Constantinople

A BORROWED PEACE 1919-1932

A 1922 Ford showroom.

from Mohammed VI and brings the Ottoman Empire to an end. He proclaims the Republic of Turkey and proceeds to renegotiate the Treaty of Sèvres.

2 NOVEMBER 1922
International A Berlin Conference of financial experts is called to discuss the German currency crisis.

4 DECEMBER 1922
International The Second Central American Conference meets in Washington. Nicaragua and Honduras need help in resolving differences. The result is a treaty of neutrality and reinstitution of a Central American Court of Justice. The US retains a right under the Roosevelt Corollary to intercede in Latin American affairs.

OTHER EVENTS OF 1922
Social Sciences In the Valley of the Kings, Luxor, Egypt, Howard Carter and Lord Carnarvon, both Britons, discover the relatively untouched tomb of a young king, Tutankhamen, one of the most spectacular finds in the history of archaeology. The world will look on as the incredibly rich find is revealed; it will not only lead to an interest in archaeology and Egyptology, but give rise to claims that a curse falls on those who participate in uncovering the tomb. And in India (later to be part of Pakistan), excavations begin at the ancient city of Mohenjo-daro, complementing those at another nearby ancient city, Harappa, as sites of the early Indus Valley civilization of India.
Ideas/Beliefs Oswald Spengler, a German historian and philosopher, publishes the second volume of his influential work *The Decline of the West*.
Literature James Joyce's *Ulysses* is published in Paris; T S Eliot's *The Waste Land*, perhaps the most influential poem of the century; Sinclair Lewis's *Babbitt*; Pasternak's *My Sister's Life*; Hermann Hesse's *Siddhartha*; Sigrid Undset completes *Kristin Lavransdatter*; Galsworthy completes the first trilogy of The Forsyte Saga; e e cummings's *The Enormous*

Room; Roger Martin du Gard begins his 10-volume *Les Thibaults*; Katherine Mansfield's *The Garden Party*.
Drama/Entertainment Pirandello's *Henry IV*. In Berlin, the first sound-on-film productions are shown; the evening includes a cinematic story with dialogue recorded on the film, *Der Brandstifter (The Arsonist)*.
The Arts Klee's *Twittering Machine*; Miro's *The Farm*.
Architecture Frank Lloyd Wright's Imperial Hotel is completed in Tokyo; it will survive the earthquake of 1923.

T S Eliot.

James Joyce with Sylvia Beach.

ST 1923
a simple ceremony at 2:30 AM conducted by
, a justice of the peace, Calvin Coolidge is
is thirtieth President of the United States.

ST 1923
Gustav Stresemann is named chancellor
gn minister during riots and strikes.

JST 1923
ie United States Steel Corporation, under
over a year, relents and institutes the
r day, a milestone for labor. Steelworkers
tomed to work from 12 to 14 hours, seven
ek. Other industries will follow US Steel.

JST 1923
nal Mussolini orders the Greek Govern-
pologize for the deaths of an Italian general
taff on the Greco-Albanian border. When
ks refuse, the Duce orders bombardment
pation of the island of Corfu.

KEMAL ATATURK, 1881–1938

emergence of Turkey as a modern nation in
ntury was due largely to the implacable energy
sion of one man, born Mustafa Kemal, who
ler of his country took the not unwarranted
Atatürk, 'Father of the Turks.' He was instru-
l in the liberal Young Turk revolution of 1908,
deposed the sultan. Despite quarrels with the
overnment about its German allegiance, he
irkish forces to victory over the Allies at
oli during World War I. When the Allies
ted the sultanate after the war, Kemal
ed a resistance movement that expelled the
invasion in 1920 and abolished the sultanate
n 1922. Becoming president of the new Turkish
lic in 1923, Kemal changed Turkey into a
n secular country in the Western mold by
s force of will. As violent and vindictive as his
s often were—particularly those directed at
–his nation mourned his passing in 1938.

President Calvin Coolidge.

1 SEPTEMBER 1923
Japan In a catastrophic earthquake that strikes the
centers of Tokyo and Yokohama, 140,000 people are
killed and fires cause extensive damage.

14 SEPTEMBER 1923
Spain Miguel Primo de Rivera becomes dictator in
a military coup secretly agreed to by King Alfonso,
who remains on the throne. Rivera declares martial
law. He will govern for seven years.

15 SEPTEMBER 1923
USA Oklahoma Governor J C Walton places the
State under martial law to quell the Ku Klux Klan.

26 SEPTEMBER 1923
International The Commonwealth Conference is
held in London. Britain recognizes the right of the
Dominions to make treaties with foreign powers.

25 OCTOBER 1923
USA The Teapot Dome scandal comes to public
attention as Senator Thomas J Walsh of Montana,
chairman of a subcommittee, reveals findings of the
past 18 months. His case will result in conviction of
Harry F Sinclair of Mammoth Oil, and later in conviction of Secretary of the Interior Albert B Fall, the
first Cabinet member in American history to go to
jail.

8 NOVEMBER 1923
Germany In a beer hall in Munich, Adolf Hitler,
with the backing of General Erich Ludendorff
attempts a Putsch against the government. The coup

10 JANUARY 1923
International The last American troops in Germany are withdrawn.

11 JANUARY 1923
International Taking advantage of a delay in arrival of timber shipments, the French (with co-operation from Belgium) claim default in reparation payments and occupy the industrial heart of Germany, the Ruhr. German workers refuse to work; mine owners refuse to deliver coal. The government will subsidize this passive resistance to the amount of 320,000 gold marks a week until late September. This will ruin the German mark, which begins its last plunge. There are 75 quadrillion paper marks in circulation backed by 722 million gold marks. German exchange, which was 4.2 marks to the dollar before the war, is now 160,000 to the dollar, down from 110,000 two weeks earlier. August will see the mark fall to 1 million to the US dollar, and by November it will be at an astronomical 130 billion. The mark can drop by half during the time it takes a laborer to stand in line for a loaf of bread.

13 JANUARY 1923
Germany Taking advantage of chaotic conditions, Hitler stages a demonstration of 5000 Stormtroopers and denounces the 'November crime,' the setting up of the German Republic in November 1918. During 1923, with help from Ernst Röhm, Hitler joins with other nationalistic and extremist organizations, while maintaining his leadership of the National Socialist (Nazi) Party.

3 MARCH 1923
International Not wanting to involve itself in foreign issues the US refuses to become a member of the International Court of Justice (the World Court).

14 MARCH 1923
International The Allies give Vilna and East Galicia to Poland.

15 MARCH 1923
USA Charles F Cramer, assistant to Charles R Forbes, head of the Veteran's Bureau, commits suicide. He is a member of Harding's inner circle, the so-called Ohio Gang. His death bodes ill for the president. Jesse Smith, friend to Attorney General Daugherty, has already committed suicide after being told to leave Washington by Harding. Forbes will soon resign as director of the Veteran's Bureau.

9 APRIL 1923
USA In *Adkins v Children's Hospital* the Supreme Court finds that the minimum wage law for women and children, adopted in the District of Columbia, is unconstitutional. Organized labor is being weakened.

26 APRIL 1923
Great Britain The Duke of York marries Lady

Elizabeth Bowes-Lyon. It is
are to be the future king and

1 MAY 1923
Germany In an unabashe
and Ernst Röhm undertak
May Day demonstrations, ir
away as Nuremberg to take
army and the police refu:
bluffs his way into army barr
ammunition. He is reprim
Lossow; Hitler gives back tl
Putsch.

4 MAY 1923
USA New York State disr
ings and repeals its Prohil
Bootlegging has become bi
forcement act is circumvent
easies,' 'moonshiners,' 'run
and 'medicinal purposes' ar(
that alcohol gets to 'dry' (
indifferent to the safety of c
their liquor, or unskillfully
to be sold under false label:
at home, as is home-brewed
Prohibition decade over 300
convicted under the Volste:
enforce Prohibition at the fe(

6 JULY 1923
USSR The Central Execu
the Treaty of Union, signed
1922, and the Russian Empil
Soviet Socialist Republics.
White Russia (comprising 9
the Ukraine (with 2 percei
which is itself a federation of
Azerbaijan. The following
Uzbek will join, and in 1929,
arrangement is an apparent (
soviets replacing parliament:
the Communist Party, and
ment is a sham.

10 JULY 1923
Italy Mussolini dissolves al

24 JULY 1923
International The Treaty o
Turkey and the Allies. It rei
Sèvres, in Turkey's favor, est
Anatolia, Cilicia, Adalia, S
and Constantinople. At Tui
gives the Dodecanese Islan
Straits are demilitarized and

2 AUGUST 1923
USA President Harding su
ptomaine poisoning and de
seems to be recovering when
or what is then called apople

3 AU
USA
his fat
sworn

6 AU
Germ:
and fc

13 AL
USA
pressu
eight-1
are ac
days a

31 AL
Intern:
ment 1
and hi
the G
and oc

T
this
and
as l(
nan
mer
whi(
new
led
Gal
rein
mo
Gre
agai
Rep
moc
ruth
refo
Isla:

146

10 JANUARY 1923
International The last American troops in Germany are withdrawn.

11 JANUARY 1923
International Taking advantage of a delay in arrival of timber shipments, the French (with co-operation from Belgium) claim default in reparation payments and occupy the industrial heart of Germany, the Ruhr. German workers refuse to work; mine owners refuse to deliver coal. The government will subsidize this passive resistance to the amount of 320,000 gold marks a week until late September. This will ruin the German mark, which begins its last plunge. There are 75 quadrillion paper marks in circulation backed by 722 million gold marks. German exchange, which was 4.2 marks to the dollar before the war, is now 160,000 to the dollar, down from 110,000 two weeks earlier. August will see the mark fall to 1 million to the US dollar, and by November it will be at an astronomical 130 billion. The mark can drop by half during the time it takes a laborer to stand in line for a loaf of bread.

13 JANUARY 1923
Germany Taking advantage of chaotic conditions, Hitler stages a demonstration of 5000 Stormtroopers and denounces the 'November crime,' the setting up of the German Republic in November 1918. During 1923, with help from Ernst Röhm, Hitler joins with other nationalistic and extremist organizations, while maintaining his leadership of the National Socialist (Nazi) Party.

3 MARCH 1923
International Not wanting to involve itself in foreign issues the US refuses to become a member of the International Court of Justice (the World Court).

14 MARCH 1923
International The Allies give Vilna and East Galicia to Poland.

15 MARCH 1923
USA Charles F Cramer, assistant to Charles R Forbes, head of the Veteran's Bureau, commits suicide. He is a member of Harding's inner circle, the so-called Ohio Gang. His death bodes ill for the president. Jesse Smith, friend to Attorney General Daugherty, has already committed suicide after being told to leave Washington by Harding. Forbes will soon resign as director of the Veteran's Bureau.

9 APRIL 1923
USA In *Adkins v Children's Hospital* the Supreme Court finds that the minimum wage law for women and children, adopted in the District of Columbia, is unconstitutional. Organized labor is being weakened.

26 APRIL 1923
Great Britain The Duke of York marries Lady Elizabeth Bowes-Lyon. It is little thought that they are to be the future king and queen of England.

1 MAY 1923
Germany In an unabashed bid for power, Hitler and Ernst Röhm undertake to break up socialist May Day demonstrations, inviting Nazis from as far away as Nuremberg to take part in the violence. The army and the police refuse to intervene. Röhm bluffs his way into army barracks and takes arms and ammunition. He is reprimanded by General von Lossow; Hitler gives back the arms and calls off the Putsch.

4 MAY 1923
USA New York State disregards Harding's warnings and repeals its Prohibition enforcement act. Bootlegging has become big business, and the enforcement act is circumvented on all sides: 'speakeasies,' 'moonshiners,' 'rumrunners,' 'highjacking' and 'medicinal purposes' are only a few of the ways that alcohol gets to 'dry' destinations. Gangsters, indifferent to the safety of customers, regularly 'cut' their liquor, or unskillfully 'convert' wood alcohol to be sold under false labels. 'Bathtub' gin is made at home, as is home-brewed ale and wine. During the Prohibition decade over 300,000 lawbreakers will be convicted under the Volstead Act, which seeks to enforce Prohibition at the federal level.

6 JULY 1923
USSR The Central Executive Committee accepts the Treaty of Union, signed in Moscow in December 1922, and the Russian Empire becomes the Union of Soviet Socialist Republics. It is a confederation of White Russia (comprising 92 percent of the area), the Ukraine (with 2 percent), and Transcaucasia, which is itself a federation of Georgia, Armenia, and Azerbaijan. The following year Turkestan and Uzbek will join, and in 1929, Tajikistan. The political arrangement is an apparent democracy, with elected soviets replacing parliaments. Real power rests with the Communist Party, and representative government is a sham.

10 JULY 1923
Italy Mussolini dissolves all non-Fascist parties.

24 JULY 1923
International The Treaty of Lausanne is signed by Turkey and the Allies. It renegotiates the Treaty of Sèvres, in Turkey's favor, establishing her rights over Anatolia, Cilicia, Adalia, Smyrna, eastern Thrace, and Constantinople. At Turkey's insistence Greece gives the Dodecanese Islands back to Italy. The Straits are demilitarized and internationalized.

2 AUGUST 1923
USA President Harding suffers from an attack of ptomaine poisoning and develops pneumonia. He seems to be recovering when he dies of an embolism, or what is then called apoplexy.

A BORROWED PEACE 1919-1932

3 AUGUST 1923
USA In a simple ceremony at 2:30 AM conducted by his father, a justice of the peace, Calvin Coolidge is sworn in as thirtieth President of the United States.

6 AUGUST 1923
Germany Gustav Stresemann is named chancellor and foreign minister during riots and strikes.

13 AUGUST 1923
USA The United States Steel Corporation, under pressure over a year, relents and institutes the eight-hour day, a milestone for labor. Steelworkers are accustomed to work from 12 to 14 hours, seven days a week. Other industries will follow US Steel.

31 AUGUST 1923
International Mussolini orders the Greek Government to apologize for the deaths of an Italian general and his staff on the Greco-Albanian border. When the Greeks refuse, the Duce orders bombardment and occupation of the island of Corfu.

President Calvin Coolidge.

KEMAL ATATURK, 1881–1938

The emergence of Turkey as a modern nation in this century was due largely to the implacable energy and vision of one man, born Mustafa Kemal, who as leader of his country took the not unwarranted name Atatürk, 'Father of the Turks.' He was instrumental in the liberal Young Turk revolution of 1908, which deposed the sultan. Despite quarrels with the new government about its German allegiance, he led Turkish forces to victory over the Allies at Gallipoli during World War I. When the Allies reinstated the sultanate after the war, Kemal mounted a resistance movement that expelled the Greek invasion in 1920 and abolished the sultanate again in 1922. Becoming president of the new Turkish Republic in 1923, Kemal changed Turkey into a modern secular country in the Western mold by ruthless force of will. As violent and vindictive as his reforms often were—particularly those directed at Islam—his nation mourned his passing in 1938.

1 SEPTEMBER 1923
Japan In a catastrophic earthquake that strikes the centers of Tokyo and Yokohama, 140,000 people are killed and fires cause extensive damage.

14 SEPTEMBER 1923
Spain Miguel Primo de Rivera becomes dictator in a military coup secretly agreed to by King Alfonso, who remains on the throne. Rivera declares martial law. He will govern for seven years.

15 SEPTEMBER 1923
USA Oklahoma Governor J C Walton places the State under martial law to quell the Ku Klux Klan.

26 SEPTEMBER 1923
International The Commonwealth Conference is held in London. Britain recognizes the right of the Dominions to make treaties with foreign powers.

25 OCTOBER 1923
USA The Teapot Dome scandal comes to public attention as Senator Thomas J Walsh of Montana, chairman of a subcommittee, reveals findings of the past 18 months. His case will result in conviction of Harry F Sinclair of Mammoth Oil, and later in conviction of Secretary of the Interior Albert B Fall, the first Cabinet member in American history to go to jail.

8 NOVEMBER 1923
Germany In a beer hall in Munich, Adolf Hitler, with the backing of General Erich Ludendorff attempts a Putsch against the government. The coup

JOSEF STALIN, 1879–1953

Assuming control of the USSR and the Russian Communist Party in the period after Lenin's death (1924), Josef Stalin came to be revealed as one of the most tyrannical rulers of the century. The son of a shoemaker, he studied for the Orthodox priesthood, but was expelled from the seminary for his rebellious attitude and his espousal of Marxist ideas. He became a staunch communist in Lenin's faction, worked toward the revolution, and in 1913 was exiled to Siberia. During his years there he changed his name from Dzhugashvili to Stalin, meaning 'man of steel.' Once the Bolsheviks seized power, Stalin became one of Lenin's top aides; after Lenin's death he crowded out Trotsky and other rivals and strengthened his grip on the Communist Party, the Soviet government, and finally all of Russian society. He eliminated those he perceived as threats through executions, exile, and prison camps, while modernizing the Soviet economy and industry. He signed a nonaggression pact with Hitler, but once Russia was invaded Stalin pushed his people to heroic measures of defense and counteroffense. He drove hard bargains in his meetings with the other Allied leaders, and extended Soviet influence in postwar Eastern Europe. On his death, his body was enshrined beside Lenin's tomb, but it was removed in 1961 by order of the 22nd Communist Party Congress, after which his reputation declined in the USSR.

27 DECEMBER 1924
International The United States signs a treaty with the Dominican Republic, which supersedes that of 1907. In July the US had withdrawn its Marines and ended its occupation.

31 DECEMBER 1924
Italy Following harassment of liberals and moderates, Mussolini orders suppression of opposition newspapers.

OTHER EVENTS OF 1924
Science Louis de Broglie, a French physicist, hypothesizes that energy particles should exhibit wavelike properties, a prediction that modifies the quantum theory and leads to the development of wave mechanics. At Taung, South Africa, Raymond Dart, an Australian anthropologist, finds the fossil of a primitive humanlike creature that he and others will call *Australopithecus*, 'southern ape,' established to have lived a million years ago.
Technology The first circumnavigation of the globe by airplane is accomplished by four US Army planes in a flight of 175 days.
Social Sciences At its Hawthorne Plant, near Chicago, Illinois, Western Electric Company begins to study the effect of improved lighting on employees; the investigation will go on for 20 years and become a landmark in social psychology, revealing that no matter how physical conditions change—even when lighting is reduced—productivity and morale seem to increase. Investigators come to realize that this is tied to the development of a cohesive social group that 'relates' to its supervisors: it is the psychological, not physical, conditions that are enhancing productivity.
Literature Mann's *Magic Mountain*; E M Forster's *A Passage to India*; St John Perse's *Anabasis*; Neruda's *One Desperate Song*; André Breton, a French poet, publishes a 'Manifesto of Surrealism' that founds a movement growing out of Dadaism; surrealism will have a considerable following among writers and painters.
Drama/Entertainment Sean O'Casey's *Juno and the Paycock*; O'Neill's *Desire Under the Elms*; Noel Coward's *The Vortex*.
The Arts Picasso's *Still Life with Biscuits and Green Tablecloth*.
Architecture In Utrecht, Holland, Gerrit Rietveld builds his Schroeder House, one of the first works in the International Style.
Music George Gershwin's *Rhapsody in Blue*; Respighi's *Pines of Rome*; Schoenberg's 12-tone technique is used for his first complete work, the *Suite for Piano*.
Sports/Leisure The first Olympic Winter Games are held at Chamonix, France, from 25 January to 4 February.

6 JANUARY 1925
Italy Mussolini forms a cabinet composed entirely of Fascists.

A BORROWED PEACE 1919-1932

10 JANUARY 1925
International Allies refuse to evacuate the Cologne area as agreed. The British will begin to pull out in December.

16 JANUARY 1925
USSR In the aftermath of Lenin's death, Josef Stalin, Secretary of the Central Committee, and Leon Trotsky, Commissar of War, have battled for leadership; Trotsky now resigns as chairman of the Russian Revolutionary Military Council.

20 JANUARY 1925
International The Soviets and Japan sign a convention resuming relations. Russia agrees for the first time to limit revolutionary activity of the Third Communist International so as to allay Japanese fears of world revolution. Japan agrees to leave the northern Sakhalin, but retains rights to half the oilfields there, plus coal and timber concessions.

2 FEBRUARY 1925
USA The country waits in suspense as men in relays of dog teams attempt to reach Alaska with an antidiphtheria serum. During the worst part of winter, the country's northernmost territory has been swept by a deadly epidemic of diphtheria. Blinded by cold, Gunnar Kasson, in a superhuman final push, delivers the serum to Nome.

27 FEBRUARY 1925
Germany Backed by 4000 followers, Hitler makes a speech after leaving prison and overcoming party opposition to his rule. His plan now is to reach power using the legal means of a democracy but not refusing intimidation to get votes.

28 FEBRUARY 1925
Germany President Friedrich Ebert dies, a socialist and voice of moderation in the storm of German politics.

4 MARCH 1925
USA Calvin Coolidge is inaugurated President.

12 MARCH 1925
China Sun Yat-sen dies in Peking. He had been both a nationalist and a communist, but his successor Chiang Kai-shek will use communist help only to further unification of China; then he will expel the Russian military advisors led by Michael Borodin and crack down on internal communist movements.

3 APRIL 1925
Great Britain The economy is returned to the gold standard at pre-1914 rates.

23 APRIL 1925
International Having badly defeated Spain and driven her out of Spanish Morocco, the native Riffi, led by Abd-el-Krim, turn on the French in French Morocco. Fighting will continue for almost two

years before Abd-el-Krim is forced to surrender. The Spaniards will help the French.

25 APRIL 1925
Germany The 77-year-old Field Marshal Paul von Hindenburg is elected President. Hindenburg is an ultraconservative, but his election serves at first to strengthen the republic.

4 MAY 1925
International The Geneva Conference takes up the question of outlawing poison gas. (The international agreement against it is one of the few that will be honored.)

5 MAY 1925
USA John T Scopes, a teacher in the schools of Dayton, Tennessee, is arrested for teaching Darwin's theory of evolution. He will be brought to trial in July. Speaking for the prosecution will be William Jennings Bryan. The defense will be conducted by Clarence Darrow. The country is variously amused, excited, or outraged by the clash between Science and Religion. Scopes loses and is fined $100.

PAUL VON HINDENBURG, 1847–1934

President, soldier, and national hero, General Hindenburg was recalled from retirement in 1914 to command the German Eighth Army. He distinguished himself on the Eastern Front and was appointed chief of staff, becoming military leader of Germany during World War I and one of the most powerful men in Europe. He was unable to repeat his victories in the West, and with the breaking of the Siegfried or Hindenburg line brought home 2 million troops from various fronts. During the 1918 revolution he supported the German Republic, and in 1925 was elected president, helping free the Rhineland from French occupation five years in advance of treaty stipulations. In 1931 he was re-elected president but was unable to form a stable regime, and invited Hitler to form a cabinet. Such was Hindenburg's prestige that Hitler waited until his death to abolish the presidency and subvert constitutional government.

10 MAY 1925
China To control demonstrations against foreigners, British troops in Shanghai fire into a crowd. A boycott ensues against British goods.

16 JULY 1925
Iraq The first parliament is opened by King Feisal in Baghdad.

5 OCTOBER 1925
International The Locarno Conference meets, and under the able direction of Germany's foreign minister Stresemann, the Germans agree to recognize their frontiers with France, and Belgium. Germany will apply for membership in the League of Nations.

12 OCTOBER 1925
International Germany and the USSR sign trade agreements. The Soviet military high command has been secretly training German military elements. The Germans are trying to circumvent the Versailles Treaty ban on use of planes and tanks.

31 OCTOBER 1925
Persia Reza Khan, an army officer who set up a dictatorship in 1921, becomes Shah, ending the Kajar Dynasty that has ruled Persia since 1794, and beginning the Pahlevi Dynasty which will rule until overthrown in 1979.

OTHER EVENTS OF 1925
Science Robert A Millikan, an American physicist, proposes the name 'cosmic rays' for the radiation from space that Victor Hess discovered in 1912.

Technology Although two Englishmen (Lionel Guest and H O Merriman) had recorded a service in Westminster Abbey with an electrical process as early as 1920, the first commercial phonograph records—developed in the Bell Telephone Laboratories and released by Victor Records—are sold in April. And in October the first television transmission of a moving image—with gradations of light and shade and permitting recognition of a face—are sent in an attic workroom by one of the pioneers of television, the Englishman John L Baird. Although Baird did not succeed in producing a high-definition system for commercial service, his work qualifies him for the title 'inventor' of television; in 1928 he will be the first to transmit television in color and to send a television image across the Atlantic.

Social Sciences Near Folsom, New Mexico, archaeologists discover fine flint tools that, based on geological deposits, date back 10,000 years—the first evidence that human beings lived in the New World so early.

Ideas/Beliefs Alfred North Whitehead's *Science and the Modern World*.

Literature F Scott Fitzgerald's *The Great Gatsby*; Kafka's *The Trial*; Virginia Woolf's *Mrs Dalloway*; Dreiser's *An American Tragedy*; Dos Passos's *Manhattan Transfer*; Yeats's *A Vision*; Andre Gide's *The Counterfeiters*; Sinclair Lewis's *Arrowsmith*; Ezra Pound begins to publish his *Cantos*, an epic series that will continue till 1960.

Drama/Entertainment Chaplin's *Gold Rush*; Eisenstein's *Battleship Potemkin*.

The Arts Picasso's *Three Dancers*; Derain's *Landscape*; Matisse's *Still Life with Pineapple*.

Music Alban Berg's opera *Wozzeck* premieres in Berlin; Shostakovich's *First Symphony*; Aaron Cop-

The Chinese students march—2 June 1925.

A BORROWED PEACE 1919-1932

land's *Symphony for Organ and Orchestra* is introduced in the US.

Miscellaneous *The New Yorker* begins to publish and will quickly establish itself as a magazine influential in shaping American taste, humor, and writing. Clarence Birdseye, an American, markets quick-frozen fish (having observed in Labrador by 1915 that such fish were palatable when thawed). Charles K Ogden, an English linguist and psychologist, begins to develop 'Basic English,' reducing English to 850 words that could be an international language.

3 JANUARY 1926
Greece Theodore Pangalos, having taken over as prime minister in a bloodless coup in June 1925, makes himself dictator. Opposition leaders are exiled to Santorini Island. On 22 August, he will be deposed and imprisoned in Crete.

8 JANUARY 1926
Saudi Arabia In a coup against King Hussein, Ibn Saud becomes King of Hejaz. Saud changes the name of the country to Saudi Arabia and founds a dynasty.

27 JANUARY 1926
International The US Senate adopts a resolution suggesting that the United States join the Permanent Court of International Justice (World Court). The Court is to have jurisdiction over international problems brought by member nations. The resolution contains five reservations, four of which are accepted without question, but the fifth—refusing the court's right to give advisory opinions on a dispute in which the United States is involved—is rejected by other members.

31 JANUARY 1926
International The last British troops withdraw from Cologne, Germany, as agreed.

10 MAY 1926
International US Marines land in Nicaragua to quell a revolt and shore up the government of Adolfo Diaz; the US military presence will remain until 1933.

12 MAY 1926
Poland Josef Pilsudski stages a coup in a dispute over command of the army. He marches into Warsaw and with the help of a railway strike takes over the government. He will strengthen the executive against the legislative branch.

18 MAY 1926
International The Preparatory Commission for a World Disarmament Conference holds its first meeting. The US, Great Britain, and Japan participate, but the USSR does not.

20 MAY 1926
USA Expanding Federal powers, Congress enacts

Marshal Josef Pilsudski.

the Air Commerce Act. Up until this year the government has kept hands off civil aviation, except to subsidize air mail; this act will allow licensing of aircraft and pilots.

23 MAY 1926
International Abd-el-Krim surrenders to French forces, bringing an end to the Riff war in Morocco. Spain and France will reassert their control over their respective areas.

22 JUNE 1926
Canada The government declares that any treaty that requires Canadian military or economic participation must be ratified by the Canadian Parliament. This is another step toward complete independence within the British Commonwealth.

28 JUNE 1926
Canada Prime Minister MacKenzie King resigns because of Governor-General Lord Byng's refusal to grant a second dissolution of government within one year.

28 JULY 1926
International Panama and the US sign a pact protecting the Canal in case of war.

6 SEPTEMBER 1926
China Chiang Kai-shek and his Kuomintang (Nationalist) troops, allied with the communists, reach Hankow.

25 DECEMBER 1926

BENITO MUSSOLINI, 1883–1945

It is tempting to say that Mussolini was a man who showed great promise as a youth but got mixed up with the wrong crowd. Unfortunately, his record as leader of Italy allows no such oversimplification. The son of a blacksmith (like Tito) and a schoolmistress, he was a rebellious youth who became a teacher and then a journalist. He adopted the socialist cause, but was expelled from the Socialist Party in 1914 because he wanted Italy to enter the war against Germany. After serving in the war, he rejected both socialism and communism and adopted an aggressive nationalism that appealed to Italians by promising a revival of the glories of ancient Rome. The Fascist Party adopted black shirts and terrorism but promised law and order, and its 'march on Rome' (October 1922) pressured the king to make Mussolini head of the government. He introduced some reforms that improved order and reduced unemployment, but the price for 'making the trains run on time' was total control of the government and society, suppression of any opposition, press censorship, prison camps, and secret police. 'Il Duce,' as he liked to be called, often resembled a comic-opera dictator, but it was not comic for those locked up, exiled, or murdered. In search of a larger stage, he invaded and conquered Ethiopia in 1935–36, but when he joined Hitler he was in over his head. In July 1943 his fellow Fascists disowned him, and although German paratroopers rescued him two months later and set him up again in northern Italy, he was a puppet. His final act—hanged upside down with his mistress in Milan—was a fiasco, but by that time the audience had left.

8 SEPTEMBER 1926
International   Thanks to Stresemann's diplomacy, Germany is admitted to the League of Nations with a permanent seat on the Council.

4 OCTOBER 1926
USSR   Trotsky and Grigori Zinoviev, founders of the Communist Party, are expelled from the Politburo. Josef Stalin is consolidating his power.

19 OCTOBER 1926
British Commonwealth   The Imperial Conference in London accepts equal status for Dominions as autonomous communities. A public statement attempts to define the commonwealth: Britain and the Dominions 'are autonomous communities within the British Empire, equal in status, in no way subordinate one to another in any aspect of their domestic or external affairs, though united by a common allegiance to the Crown, and freely associated as members of the British Commonwealth of Nations.'

25 DECEMBER 1926
Japan   Hirohito succeeds to the imperial throne upon the death of his father, Yoshihito.

OTHER EVENTS OF 1926
Technology   On 16 March in Auburn, Massachusetts, Robert H Goddard demonstrates the first liquid-fuel rocket flight (although he had already shown in 1920 the lifting force of rockets using liquid oxygen and ether); his rocket traverses 184 feet in 2.5 seconds (about 60 mph). But his work will go unrecognized until after World War II, when German rocket experts pay tribute to Goddard's efforts. Lt Commander Richard E Byrd and Floyd Bennett, flying from Spitzbergen, a Norwegian island, accomplish the first flight over the North Pole, making the round trip in 15 hours. Roald Amundsen, the Norwegian first to the South Pole, and Umberto Nobile, an Italian airman-explorer, fly over the North Pole and other regions of the Arctic.
Social Sciences   R H Tawney's *Religion and the Rise of Capitalism.*
Literature   Hemingway's *The Sun Also Rises*; Kafka's *The Castle*; Isaak Babel's *Red Cavalry*; Faulkner's *Soldiers' Pay*; D H Lawrence's *Plumed Serpent*; A A Milne's *Winnie-the-Pooh*; T E Lawrence's autobiographical *Seven Pillars of Wisdom* (republished as *Revolt in the Desert* in 1927).
Drama/Entertainment   O'Casey's *The Plough and the Stars*; the first film version of *Ben Hur*, with Ramon Navarro. An invitational performance at the Warner Theater in New York City on 5 August includes a film in which personalities talk or perform music and then a feature picture, *Don Juan* (with John Barrymore and Mary Astor), but the sound is synchronized with phonograph records, so it is not regarded as a true 'talkie.'
The Arts   Chagall's *Lovers' Bouquet*; Picasso's *Still Life with Foliage*; Henry Moore's *Draped Reclining Figure.*

A BORROWED PEACE 1919-1932

Music Puccini's unfinished opera *Turandot* is performed in Milan posthumously.

1 JANUARY 1927
China Chiang Kai-shek's Kuomintang troops reach Hankow. He will negotiate to end extraterritorial concessions to Britain in cities within his jurisdiction.

18 FEBRUARY 1927
International The United States and Canada establish diplomatic relations. The first Canadian minister to present his credentials is Charles Vincent Massey. William Phillips will be the first minister to Canada from the United States. On 2 August, in ceremonies drawing the two countries closer, the Prince of Wales and Vice-President Dawes open the International Peace Bridge which links the US with Canada at Buffalo, New York.

21 MARCH 1927
China Almost without a struggle, Kuomintang forces take the economic capital of China, Shanghai. Nanking falls three days later to one of Chiang's most brutal generals, Cheng Chien; scenes of barbarity follow, as the conquerors set upon foreigners, murdering, mutilating, raping, pillaging. American and British destroyers shell the city and rescue their nationals. The Chinese are repulsed by atrocities inflicted on foreigners, weakening popular backing for the Kuomintang. The Kuomintang declares that all territory south of the Great River is under its control; because much of the North is sympathetic to its cause, only Shantung, Honan, and Manchuria now remain outside the jurisdiction of the Kuomintang and its allies. Chiang's dream of a unified China is within reach.

24 MARCH 1927
China Aims of the radical, international (and Russian) communists diverge from Chiang Kai-shek's national goals, opening a rift in the Nationalist movement. Chiang Kai-shek has been dropped from the Central Executive Committee.

4 MAY 1927
International The US undertakes to supervise elections in Nicaragua.

9 MAY 1927
Australia Parliament House is opened in Canberra, marking formal transfer of the government to the new city.

21 MAY 1927
USA Charles A Lindbergh flies his monoplane, the *Spirit of St Louis*, from New York to Paris, the first

Charles A Lindbergh and The Spirit of St Louis.

solo Atlantic crossing. Lindbergh covers the 3600 miles in $33\frac{1}{2}$ hours. His flight is tracked by millions, and when he lands at Orly Airport, 100,000 people are on hand to greet him.

15 JULY 1927
Austria   Riots and strikes engulf Vienna when Nazis accused of murdering a small boy and an old man go free. In the ensuing disorders 89 people are killed. The riots are quelled, but the Socialists then call a general strike.

AUGUST 1927
China   Mao Tse-tung, a young Chinese Communist, feels that the future depends upon millions of peasants, not on the urban proletarians, and leads several hundred peasants to a base in the Ching-Kang Mountains. This marks the beginning of Mao Tse-tung's 22 years 'in the wilderness,' during which he will develop the ideas and tactics of guerrilla warfare that will succeed in conquering China.

2 AUGUST 1927
USA   Coolidge scotches any moves to induce him to run for what might be construed as a third term as President. He says no more than 'I do not choose to run in 1928.'

2 SEPTEMBER 1927
Turkey   The People's Party leader, Mustapha Kemal, receives the right to nominate all candidates to government.

6 NOVEMBER 1927
International   On the 19th Chiang Kai-shek supports the move to abrogate China's extraterritorial treaty with Belgium, adding that China will not 'at any time recognize any treaties or agreements which were made with other nations by any government in China previous to that of the Nationalist forces.'

15 NOVEMBER 1927
International   The League Council admits Canada as an elected member.

18 DECEMBER 1927
International   The USSR breaks off diplomatic relations with China because of anticommunist measures by Chiang Kai-shek.

25 DECEMBER 1927
International   The Mexican Congress reverses its Constitution of 1917 and grants unlimited concessions to foreigners for lands on which 'positive' acts have been performed before 1 May 1917. The effect is to nullify one of the Constitution's social and political reforms, enacted to curb the drain on Mexican natural resources.

27 DECEMBER 1927
USSR   Stalin overcomes his enemies at the All-Union Congress. Trotsky is expelled from the Com-

LEON TROTSKY, 1879–1940

The most powerful man in Russia under Lenin, Leon Trotsky (born Lev Bronstein) was a revolutionary writer and editor in Western Europe and an efficient organizer of the triumphant Red Army. It was widely assumed that he would become the head of the Soviet Government after Lenin's death. He was outmaneuvered by Stalin, expelled from the Communist Party in 1927, and exiled to Soviet Central Asia, from which he left Russia never to return. Trotsky waged a bitter fight against Stalin from abroad. Refused admission by most countries, he eventually found asylum in Mexico, where he was murdered by a Soviet agent.

munist Party as a deviationist. In January 1928 he is banished to Turkestan.

28 DECEMBER 1927
USA   US Secretary of State Frank B Kellogg proposes a pact for the renunciation of war as an instrument of national policy.

OTHER EVENTS OF 1927
Science   Werner Heisenberg, a German physicist, proposes the 'uncertainty principle' to explain the phenomena reported increasingly by the new physics on subatomic particles—in effect, that all laws of physics are statements about probabilities, not certainties. American geneticist Hermann J Muller discovers that treating an organism with X-rays will create artificial mutations of the genes. Georges Lemaître, a Belgian astronomer, publishes in an obscure journal his theory that the expanding universe was the result of a catastrophic explosion of a primordial atom that contained all the matter of the universe. It will be 1930, however, before he sends a

A BORROWED PEACE 1919-1932

reprint of this work to Arthur Eddington, the noted British astronomer, an initiator of the theory of an expanding universe; not until the 1940s will this concept of 'the big bang' origin of the universe receive real consideration among astronomers. By that time, many scientists will have contributed to the theory, including the Russian mathematician Alexander Friedmann; Willem de Sitter, a Dutch astronomer; and George Gamow, a Russian-American astrophysicist. Before the 1970s this would become the prevailing theory among cosmologists: namely, that the universe was 'born' in a primordial explosion about 13 billion years ago.

Environment In one of the worst floods in the US to this time, the Mississippi destroys $285 million worth of property.

Social Sciences At Choukoutien, near Peking, China, Davidson Black, a Canadian anthropologist, finds fossil remains of people who lived 400,000 years ago; they will become known as Peking Man, belonging to the species *Homo erectus*.In ensuing years partial remains of at least 30 individuals are found, along with animal bones and stone tools; in 1941, however, with war about to close off China, the fossil remains are lost in shipment; although casts had been made, the originals have yet to be located. On the site of the ancient Sumerian city of Ur, in Iraq, where excavations have been underway since 1922, Leonard Woolley and his staff begin to reveal the extensive royal cemetery, a rich find, with its evidence of mass burials.

Ideas/Beliefs Heidegger's *Being and Time*.

Literature Woolf's *To the Lighthouse*; Thornton Wilder's *Bridge of San Luis Rey*; Hermann Hesse's *Steppenwolf*; Arnold Zweig's *The Case of Sergeant Grischa*; Mazo de la Roche's *Jalna* (the first of the 16-volume Whiteoaks of Jalna series).

Drama/Entertainment The first widely seen talking feature film, *The Jazz Singer*, opens in New York City on 6 October; made by Warner Brothers and starring Al Jolson, the sound was on a special disc, with dialogue and singing limited to sequences; this picture's success led to the rapid development of 'talkies.'

The Arts Jacob Epstein's sculpture *Madonna and Child*; Dufy's *Casino de Nice*; Matisse's *Figures with Ornamental Background*.

Architecture Buckminster Fuller, an American designer, designs an all-metal prefabricated house suspended around a mast so that it can be lifted off; called the 'Dymaxion House,' it is one of Fuller's most innovative ideas, the best known being his geodesic dome.

Music Stravinsky's *Oedipus Rex*; Bartok's *Mikrokosmos*; Ernst Krenek's *Johnny Strikes Up*; Kurt Weill's first version of *Rise and Fall of the City of Mahagonny*; Jaromir Weinberger's *Schwanda the Bagpiper*; George Antheil's *Ballet Mecanique*.

Sports/Leisure The American baseball star Babe Ruth hits 60 home runs during this season (a record that will stand until Roger Maris hits 61 in the extended season of 1961).

16 JANUARY 1928
International The Sixth International Conference of American States opens in Havana. President Coolidge presides at the opening.

20 FEBRUARY 1928
International A measure of independence for Transjordan is granted by Britain. The nomadic population of 300,000 Arabs is led by Emir Abdullah, brother of King Feisal of Iraq. A Council and an elective Assembly are authorized, but the British reserve the right to send in troops, and a resident agent for the British High Commissioner of Palestine is authorized to overrule the wishes of the Emir. Transjordan is primarily a buffer between Palestine and the marauding Arabs of the desert.

9 APRIL 1928
Turkey The government renounces Islam as a state religion.

19 APRIL 1928
International Some 5000 Japanese troops occupy Shantung along the Kiaochow-Tsinan Railroad in defiance of the Nationalists. By 11 May Japan will be in control of the area, and a Chinese request for League mediation is ignored. By then 25,000 Japanese are in Shantung. China retaliates with a highly effective economic boycott.

7 MAY 1928
Great Britain Expanding woman's suffrage, the age limit is reduced from 30 to 21, bringing it into line with the male voting age.

31 MAY 1928
Greece Following resignation of the government, Eleutherios Venizelos again forms a Liberal government. Elections on 19 August will give the Liberal Party a majority.

8 JUNE 1928
China Nationalist troops enter Peking. China is almost under Chiang Kai-shek's control. The hitherto independent Chang Hsueh-liang will declare the allegiance of Manchuria to Chiang Kai-shek's Kuomintang on 31 December, at which point, with the support of Warlords Feng Yu-hsiang, Yen Hsishan and Chang, Chiang Kai-shek will have won dictatorial control of a unified China.

15 JUNE 1928
USA The Republican Party meets in Kansas City, Missouri, to nominate Herbert Hoover of California for President and Charles Curtis of Kansas for Vice-President. Hoover declares: 'We in America today are nearer the final triumph over poverty than ever before in the history of the land.'

19 JULY 1928
Egypt King Fuad stages a coup against the government and dissolves parliament.

Herbert Hoover on his campaign train.

25 JULY 1928
International China is given tariff autonomy in a treaty signed at Peiping between the USA and China. (Following establishment of the national government in Nanking on 8 June, the name Peking, meaning 'Northern Capital,' has been changed to Peiping, meaning 'Northern Peace.')

27 AUGUST 1928
International The Pact of Paris, also known as the Kellogg-Briand Pact after its two formulators, is signed by the United States and 14 other nations. In March of the previous year Aristide Briand, the French Foreign Minister, had a conversation with Professor James T Shotwell of Columbia University, which led Briand to propose publicly the 'outlawry of war.' In June of the same year, Secretary of State Frank B Kellogg acknowledged the proposal. Briand proceeded to draft a bilateral treaty; as enthusiasm mounted for the idea, Kellogg submitted a multinational agreement for discussion. On 13 April other nations were consulted. It was easy to subscribe to the proposal, which committed neither men, money, nor machines. The idea was to outlaw war as an instrument of national policy in favor of world opinion and diplomatic skills. The pact will be signed by 62 nations, just ten years prior to the outbreak of the most desolating war in history. Kellogg will be awarded the Nobel Prize for Peace in 1929.

30 AUGUST 1928
India The British Cabinet has sent out Sir John Simon with a special commission to look into Indian demands for independence; these include Indian participation in drafting a new constitution and the same Dominion status accorded Canada. These demands will be reiterated in the Nehru Commission's Report made public this day. Gandhi's powerful All-India Congress Party, which has returned to the Legislative Assembly with an overwhelming majority, boycotts the commission. One of Gandhi's tenets is that the prince-ruled Native States must not be separate from the rest of India. Gandhi thus raises the opposition of the hereditary rulers to his vision of an all-India independent democracy. The Moslem minority, too, fears a state in which it does not have protection from the Hindu majority.

6 OCTOBER 1928
China Chiang Kai-shek is made President of a nominally united country and repudiates communist support.

7 NOVEMBER 1928
USA Republican Herbert Hoover wins the election by 444 electoral votes to 87 for Alfred Smith. Popular vote shows 21,392,000 votes for Hoover to 15,016,000 for Smith. Democrat Franklin Delano Roosevelt is elected governor of New York State.

19 NOVEMBER 1928
International Herbert Hoover leaves for an extended goodwill tour of South America.

A BORROWED PEACE 1919-1932

PROHIBITION AND THE JAZZ AGE

Perhaps it is 'only in America' that a combination of morality, idealism, and the law could result in an attempt to prohibit the consumption of alcohol. Other countries had individuals and groups who were dismayed at the toll taken by excessive drinking. But it was in the US that the 'temperance movement' made the most headway: by World War I more than half the States were already 'dry,' and during the war sales to servicemen were forbidden, while some restrictions were placed on making alcohol (under the claim it diverted resources from the war effort). On the morning of 16 January 1920, the nation woke up to find itself officially and permanently sober via the 18th Amendment. Ironically, if not predictably, the effect of Prohibition on American society was almost the opposite of what had been intended. Drinking, alcohol abuse, and lawlessness probably increased during the 1920s, which became not the Temperate Age, but the heyday of the flapper, speakeasies, bootlegging and bathtub gin. In the arts, though, it was a decade of liberation and experiment. Jazz came into its own. Harlem saw a veritable 'renaissance' of creativity. By the time the 21st Amendment repealed the 18th in December 1933, a social experiment had failed but a social revolution—not all to the bad—had occurred.

A captured rum-runner's stash.

26 NOVEMBER 1928

USA Although the mood of the country is isolationist, at the diplomatic level the US is still extending its participation in international affairs. Today the United States is represented at the International Conference on Economic Statistics of the League of Nations; on 10 December the Pan-American Conference on Conciliation and Arbitration convenes in Washington at Coolidge's invitation; on 12 December the International Civil Aeronautics Conference opens in Washington with delegates from many countries including the United States.

21 DECEMBER 1928

USA The Federal Government enters the field of hydroelectric power, hitherto deemed the sector of private business. The Federal Government has undertaken ever-larger projects for its citizens, projects larger than any one state can shoulder. On 15 May Congress has passed the Flood Control Act, which provides $325,000,000 for control of flooding on the Mississippi. The project will take ten years. On 22 May the Jones-White Merchant Marine Act was passed, providing subsidies to private shipping companies, and blurring the edge between private enterprise and government. On 25 May Congress passed the Muscle Shoals Act for government ownership of a hydroelectric plant at Muscle Shoals, Tennessee.

OTHER EVENTS OF 1928

Science Paul Dirac, an English physicist predicts that there is an antiparticle to the electron, the positron—to be confirmed in 1932. John von Neumann, Hungarian-American mathematician, states his 'minimax theorem,' the cornerstone of modern games theory.

Medicine/Health During his summer holidays, Alexander Fleming, a Scottish bacteriologist, had left some culture plates in his laboratory at St Mary's Hospital, London; on return, he is about to clean them when he notices the absence of expected staphylococcus colonies in the vicinity of a mold. He studies this phenomenon, and on 13 March 1929 he will read to the Medical Research Club a paper entitled 'Cultures of a Penicillium,' having made his first clinical tests on 9 January; no one present asks any questions, nor is there discussion of the fact that the group has just been the first to hear about the first antibiotic developed by man. It will be 11 years before the first purified penicillin is prepared, to be applied clinically on 12 February 1941, but as there is not enough available, the patient dies on 15 March. However, the next patient is successfully treated, and production begins on a larger scale. The first commercial penicillin is made at Bromley-by-Bow, England, and delivered 11 September 1942.

Technology On 25 May Amelia Earhart, American aviatrix, becomes the first woman to pilot a plane across the Atlantic. The German dirigible *Graf Zeppelin* completes the first commercial flight of an airship on 15 October, covering the 6630 miles from Germany to New Jersey in $4\frac{1}{2}$ days.

Environment Roald Amundsen is lost in the Barents Sea in his effort to rescue the Italian explorer Umberto Nobile, who had crashed in his airship *Italia* after a flight to the North Pole. A hurricane in Florida leaves over 1800 dead.

Social Sciences Margaret Mead, an American anthropologist, publishes *Coming of Age in Samoa*: based on experiences among the Samoans in 1925–26, it will be a seminal work in cultural anthropology.

Literature D H Lawrence's *Lady Chatterley's Lover*; Aldous Huxley's *Point Counter Point*; Virginia Woolf's *Orlando*; Evelyn Waugh's *Decline and Fall*; Ford Madox Ford, with *The Last Parade*, completes his tetralogy Parade's End (begun in 1924 with *Some*

Do Not); William Butler Yeats's *The Tower*; Garcia Lorca's *Gypsy Ballads*; Tanizaki Junichiro's *Some Prefer Nettles*; Morley Callaghan's *Strange Fugitive*; Wyndham Lewis's *The Childermass*.

Drama/Entertainment Jean Giraudoux's *Siegfried*; O'Neill's *Strange Interlude*; Marcel Pagnol's *Topaze*. On 21 July *The Lights of New York* is released, the first all-talking picture with over 6000 feet of film and with sound on the film. Walt Disney releases *Steamboat Willie*, his first animated cartoon starring Mickey Mouse; Disney used his own voice for Mickey.

The Arts Utrillo's *Square St Pierre and Sacré Coeur*; Max Beckmann's *Black Lilies*; Charles Demuth's *I Saw the Figure 5 in Gold* prefigures Pop art of the 1960s.

Music Ravel's *Bolero*; Gershwin's *An American in Paris*; Brecht-Weill's *Threepenny Opera*.

Miscellaneous On 11 May in Schenectady, New York, Station WGY, operated by the General Electric Company, becomes the first to broadcast scheduled television service, three transmissions a week, totaling one and one-half hours. On 11 September WGY transmits the first TV play, *The Queen's Messenger* by Hartley Manners; it lasts 40 minutes, and there are reports of reception all the way to the West Coast.

3 JANUARY 1929
International Bolivia and Paraguay submit their dispute to the Pan-American Union.

5 JANUARY 1929
Yugoslavia In what is still being called the Serbo-Croat-Slovene Kingdom, King Alexander I takes dictatorial powers and abolishes the constitution. Opposition parties are forbidden.

14 JANUARY 1929
Afghanistan Civil war begins as Habibullah forces King Amanullah to abdicate.

31 JANUARY 1929
USSR Leon Trotsky is exiled from the Soviet Union. His supporters are hunted by the secret police.

1 FEBRUARY 1929
China China announces a new tariff schedule. Most powers have agreed to respect China's integrity and will begin dismantling their extraterritorial privileges next year.

9 FEBRUARY 1929
International Taking a leaf from the book of Western diplomacy, the USSR, Poland, Estonia, Latvia, and Rumania sign the Litvinov Protocol renouncing war. Turkey will sign on the 27th.

11 FEBRUARY 1929
Papacy Mussolini signs the Lateran Treaty with the Vatican. It establishes the Vatican as a City State with the Pope as temporal ruler. The state comprises the Vatican buildings, St Peter's, and approximately 100 acres. Italy agrees to pay compensation of $100 million for Church lands seized by the government. Italy will oversee appointments of bishops and pay salaries of bishops and priests, all of whom must swear allegiance to the state, king, and government.

13 FEBRUARY 1929
USA Congress passes the Cruiser Act, authorizing 15 new cruisers and one aircraft carrier.

14 FEBRUARY 1929
USA In Chicago six gangsters are lined up against a garage wall and shot by a rival gang; this will become known as 'The St Valentine's Day Massacre.'

24 FEBRUARY 1929
Austria A three-way battle occurs among the private armed forces of the Socialists, the unofficial squads of the Nazis, and the local defense forces (*Heimwehr*). In Vienna this day, 6000 Fascists and 18,000 Socialists march through the city, but serious clashes are avoided.

17 MARCH 1929
Spain Student riots bring reprisals as Rivera's government closes Madrid University. Rivera's dictatorship is becoming unpopular.

3 APRIL 1929
Persia The government agrees to sign the Litvinov Protocol.

25 APRIL 1929
USSR The first Five-Year Plan establishing extraordinarily high production goals is set by Stalin. Industrial production is to be increased up to 400 percent. In agriculture it means an increase of 150 percent and collectivization of the peasants and their farms. The brutal means toward achieving this goal result in the deaths by famine and disease of an estimated five million people. The industrialization of the Soviet Union is to be paid for by agriculturists—their production will now be forced from them by close state supervision; hence the collectivization, which is not done for the sake of efficiency in agriculture but to force produce from the peasants.

20 MAY 1929
International Succumbing to boycotts and international pressures, Japanese troops begin to evacuate Shantung.

27 MAY 1929
USA The Supreme Court, in *United States v Schwimmer*, upholds a lower court's denial of citizenship to Rosika Schwimmer, a Hungarian immigrant who is an avowed pacifist. Justice Oliver Wendell Holmes, in one of his dissents, argues that freedom to hold unpopular ideas is perhaps the most funda-

A BORROWED PEACE 1919-1932

mental principle of the US Constitution. On this day the Supreme Court also rules that the use of the 'pocket veto' by a President is constitutional.

3 JUNE 1929
International   The Arica treaty is signed by Bolivia, Chile and Peru. Arica is given to Chile, Tacna to Peru, and Bolivia settles for railway rights. In September Bolivia and Paraguay will settle their dispute by treaty.

7 JUNE 1929
International   Financial experts in Paris announce their agreement on the Young Plan—named after Owen Young, the American lawyer who advances it—that sets up a reduced reparations schedule for Germany to replace the Dawes Plan. The resulting Young Plan proposes a reduction in payments from $32 billion to $8 billion over 58 years and without foreign supervision.

1 JULY 1929
USA   The Immigration Act of 1924 goes into effect (delayed from the original date called for, 1 July 1927); figures for US population in 1920 will be used as the base on which to figure national quotas; it is an attempt to keep the country's ethnic 'composition' what it has been—predominantly Northern European.

10 JULY 1929
International   The Chinese seize the Chinese Eastern Railway in Manchuria.

24 JULY 1929
International   Hoover proclaims that the Kellogg-Briand Pact is in effect.

AUGUST–SEPTEMBER 1929
USA   Stock market prices rise; in September the common stock price index reaches 216, the peak of a three-year bull market.

24 AUGUST 1929
Palestine   Incensed by Jewish use of the Wailing Wall at the ancient Temple of Jerusalem for religious purposes, Arabs incite attacks on non-Zionist Jews. Arabs are trying to get the British to renounce the Balfour Declaration of 1917, which favors Jewish settlement of the region side-by-side with the Palestinians.

5 SEPTEMBER 1929
France   Aristide Briand proposes a European federal union.

3 OCTOBER 1929
Germany   Gustav Stresemann, a voice for moderation in international affairs, dies. Nazi power is growing daily.
Yugoslavia   The Serbo-Croat-Slovene Kingdom changes its name to Yugoslavia.

4 OCTOBER 1929
International   Prime Minister Ramsay MacDonald of Great Britain comes to Washington, DC, to discuss naval parity with President Hoover. On 7 October Britain invites the US and three other naval powers (France, Italy, Japan) to a disarmament conference in London in January 1930.

23 OCTOBER 1929
USA   In the second greatest trading day in the market's history, stocks on the New York Exchange fall dramatically. Over 6 million shares are sold.

24 OCTOBER 1929
USA   On what will be known as 'Black Thursday,' the first day of the final stock market debacle, 13 million shares are traded. The ticker is still recording transactions at 7:00 PM, although trading ended at 3:00 PM.

29 OCTOBER 1929
USA   On 'Black Tuesday,' 16 million shares are sold, at declining prices. This is the most catastrophic day in market history, the herald of the Great Depression. By mid-November $30 billion of the $80 billion worth of stocks listed in September will have been wiped out.

17 NOVEMBER 1929
USSR   Continuing his purge of rivals, Stalin forces the expulsion of Nikolai Bukharin and other ranking members from the Communist Party.

18 NOVEMBER 1929
International   Russia sends troops into Manchuria. In the ensuing fighting, over 2000 Chinese are killed.

30 NOVEMBER 1929
International   The second Allied Occupation Zone of the Rhineland is evacuated, according to the Young Plan.

6 DECEMBER 1929
India   Hoping to avert rebellion, the Viceroy and Indian leaders discuss Dominion status for the sub-continent. Fighting between Moslems and Hindus is becoming increasingly violent.
Turkey   The Turkish Government gives women the vote.

19 DECEMBER 1929
Great Britain   The Coal Mines Bill is passed by Parliament. It allocates quotas and provides for a $7\frac{1}{2}$ hour day.

22 DECEMBER 1929
International   China and the USSR come to terms over joint management and use of the Chinese Eastern Railway.

28 DECEMBER 1929
China   With Japanese troops gone, and Russian

28 DECEMBER 1929

REPARATIONS LEAD TO DEPRESSION AND WAR

After the Treaty of Versailles, whereby Germany acknowledged her 'war guilt,' France and England assessed reparations in 132 billion gold Marks ($33 billion). It was the way to clear their war debts to the United States, but Germany refused to pay. Beginning in 1924, a large US loan followed by investments began a continuous flow of American money into the German market. The circle now closed, production seemed to recover throughout the industrial world as money moved from America to Germany, thence to France and Britain, then back to America. But in 1929 the American stock market crashed, bringing down with it the flimsy European credit markets. The international banking system collapsed and, inevitably, reparation payments ceased. By 1932 there was an official count of 30 million unemployed in the industrialized world. The response—a rise of extreme economic nationalism—would set the stage for a second and larger world war. There would be some reparations after World War II, but the Western powers had learned that it was counterproductive to try to extract reparations from the losers.

Rear Admiral Richard E Byrd.

influence diminished, Chiang Kai-shek proudly proclaims the end of extraterritoriality in China.

OTHER EVENTS OF 1929

Science Edwin Hubble, an American astronomer, proposes a new law derived from observations at the Mt Wilson Observatory and confirming current theory of the expanding universe: Hubble's Law, as it becomes known, states that the distances between galaxies are continuously increasing at a rate that increases with the distance between the galaxies. Hubble has observed that shifts in the colors emitted by the stars in galaxies alters toward the longer wavelengths, the so-called red shift. Andrew Douglass, an American astronomer, has been seeking tree specimens in the Southwest since 1901 to discover the effect of sunspots on the earth's climate and vegetation; only this year, after correlating tree rings of progressively older specimens, does he realize that he can establish a tree-ring record that provides absolute dates that will help archaeologists date human artifacts. This begins the science of dendrochronology.

Technology On 24 September Lieutenant James H Doolittle makes the first 'all-blind' flight in an airplane at Mitchell Field, New York, using only the instrument panel—although there was another pilot on board in case of emergency. On 28–29 November, Lieutenant Commander Richard E Byrd of the US Navy, the Norwegian-American Bernt Balchen, and two crewmen make the first airplane flight over the South Pole; they travel from and to their base at Little America, and with one stop for fuel fly 1700 miles in 19 hours.

Social Sciences Richard and Harriet Lynd's *Middletown*.

Ideas/Beliefs Ortega y Gasset's *The Revolt of the Masses*.

Literature Faulkner's *The Sound and the Fury*; Hemingway's *A Farewell to Arms*; Thomas Wolfe's *Look Homeward, Angel*; Virginia Woolf's *A Room of One's Own*; Evelyn Waugh's *Decline and Fall*; Robert Graves's *Goodbye to All That*; Alfred Döblin's *Berlin Alexanderplatz*; Erich Maria Remarque's *All Quiet on the Western Front*.

Drama/Entertainment Cocteau's *Les enfants terribles*; Jean Giraudoux's *Amphitryon 38*; R C Sherriff's *Journey's End*; Elmer Rice's *Street Scene*. Martha Graham, an American dancer who had

Ernest Hemingway.

A BORROWED PEACE 1919-1932

Margaret Sanger with geneticist Leon Cole.

appeared with the Denishawn Company, forms her own group. On 16 May the Academy of Motion Picture Arts and Sciences makes its first awards in Hollywood, California: the best picture is *Wings*, Janet Gaynor is best actress, and Emil Jannings best actor. The awards will not become known as 'Oscars' until 1931 (after, allegedly, a secretary of the Academy remarks that the statuette 'looks like my uncle Oscar').

The Arts The Museum of Modern Art opens in New York City. The Spanish painter Salvador Dali becomes the most prominent Surrealist. Picasso's *Woman in Armchair*; Grant Wood's *Woman with Plants*.

Architecture Mies van der Rohe's German Pavilion at the Barcelona International Exhibition is a seminal work; it will be taken down, but reconstructed in the 1980s.

Miscellaneous A patent is issued for a coin-operated vending machine that cannot be defrauded. In New York City Margaret Sanger's birth-control clinic is raided by the police (after complaints by the Daughters of the American Revolution). France begins the Maginot Line to protect itself from invasion.

2 JANUARY 1930
USA With prices falling, national income collapsing, and unemployment approaching 4 million, President Hoover meets with Congressional leaders to discuss a public works program. On 31 March Congress will authorize $230 million for erecting public buildings and on 4 April, $300 million for federal aid to states for roads.

21 JANUARY 1930
International An international Naval Conference

meets in London to continue work begun at the Washington Conference of 1921–22. The US, Great Britain, and Japan agree on ratios, sizes, and schedules for their fleets, but France and Italy reject them. The US Senate will consent to this treaty on 21 July 1930.

23 JANUARY 1930
Germany Wilhelm Frick becomes the first Nazi to take office when he is made Minister of the Interior for Thuringia. Hitler is gathering German businessmen and money is pouring into Nazi coffers, since the Nazi Party does not promise support for the working class. Hitler continues his theme of a strong Germany including annexation of German populations and lands lost through the Versailles Treaty.

28 JANUARY 1930
Spain King Alfonso asks the dictator Primo de Rivera to resign. De Rivera leaves for France, where he dies a month and a half later.

6 FEBRUARY 1930
Haiti A US commission recommends reforms for the island and suggests Stenio Vincent as president.

12 MARCH 1930
India Mohandas K Gandhi begins an active civil disobedience campaign. He leads his followers to Dandi and breaks the government Salt Laws by manufacturing a token amount of salt from sea water.

28 MARCH 1930
Turkey The new Nationalists change the name of Constantinople, with its hated connotations of Greek pretensions, to Istanbul.

30 MARCH 1930
Germany Heinrich Brüning replaces Hermann Muller's Socialist cabinet with a coalition of the right.

2 MAY 1930
Canada The government imposes high tariffs that affect trade with the US, while maintaining preferential treatment for Great Britain. Neither policy helps alleviate the Depression, as it spreads around the world.

5 MAY 1930
India Gandhi is arrested for civil disobedience in the march to Dandi to manufacture salt in an attempt to break up the government's salt monopoly. By the end of the year 54,000 Indians will have been convicted, 23,000 will still be in prison.

6 MAY 1930
International Japan reluctantly consents to China's tariff autonomy, but negotiates a three-year agreement that protects Japan's primary exports.

14 MAY 1930
USA The Hawley-Smoot Tariff Bill is moving

11 DECEMBER 1930

DISARMAMENT

International efforts toward disarmament did not really begin until the 1920s. During the 19th century the issue came up at several peace conferences, including that at The Hague in 1899. Then came the Treaty of Versailles after World War I, under which Germany was forced to disarm and limit the size of its army. This was in the age-old tradition of crippling the loser in a war; the difference was that the other nations involved agreed to work toward general disarmament and incorporated this goal in the Covenant of the League of Nations. The first attempt came with the Washington Naval Conference of 1921–22, when the major powers agreed to limit the total tonnage of battleships and aircraft carriers. The London Naval Conference of 1930 continued these efforts by limiting the great powers' cruisers and destroyers. Meanwhile, in 1925 the League of Nations set up a commission to explore general disarmament. It took years just to agree on an agenda, but in 1932 the conference convened in Geneva. It made little progress, as France remained distrustful of Germany, while Germany claimed it had the right to military equality with other major states. The deadlocked conference recessed; when it reconvened, Hitler had come to power. In October 1934 he withdrew Germany from the conference. This League-sponsored disarmament conference collapsed that same year. Before the decade was out Hitler was rearming Germany at an accelerated pace, and other nations were rejoining the race. It took World War II to convince the 20th century of the need to return to the search for disarmament.

---

toward Congressional acceptance; this bill will raise duties, and many see it as a potential threat to international trade. Today a petition signed by some 1028 economists is made public; they protest such a law because of its appalling national and international repercussions. The economists urge Hoover to veto the bill.

17 JUNE 1930
USA Hoover signs the Hawley-Smoot Tariff, raising duties on many items—in some cases so high that they are prohibitive.

30 JUNE 1930
Iraq Great Britain agrees to recognize the independence of Iraq upon its admission to the League, which will be in 1932.

1 JULY 1930
Germany The last Allied troops withdraw from the Rhineland.

16 JULY 1930
Germany President von Hindenburg decrees passage of the budget when the Reichstag fails to enact it. This is the first sign that the hitherto moderate but essentially autocratic Hindenburg, elected to a second seven-year term, is drifting into right-wing politics.

7 AUGUST 1930
Canada Conservatives, led by R B Bennett, win the government from the Liberals. Next day Bennett will call a special session to deal with problems stemming from the deepening Depression.

9 SEPTEMBER 1930
USA The State Department issues an order prohibiting immigration of virtually all foreign laborers because of mounting unemployment.

14 SEPTEMBER 1930
Germany Chancellor Brüning has resigned and called for national elections, despite warnings from moderates that the conditions caused by the Depression might spell disaster for the moderate center parties. In today's elections the Nazis gain 107 seats in the Reichstag, mainly from moderates. With 6,400,000 votes, the Nazis become the second-largest party in the government. They profit from unemployment caused by the spreading Depression. Some 3 million are now out of work. Hitler's success is welcomed in many parts of the world by people ready for any defense against Bolshevism.

OCTOBER 1930
USA Unemployment is now estimated to have reached at least 4,500,000, but Hoover persists in his determination 'to preserve individual and local responsibility.' This month he appoints a Committee on Unemployment Relief, but it calls only for federal leadership of programs run by state and local agencies, not for direct financial aid.

30 OCTOBER 1930
International Turkey and Greece sign a treaty of friendship at Ankara.

2 NOVEMBER 1930
Ethiopia Ras Tafari, who has shared power with the Empress Zauditu until her death in April, now proclaims himself Emperor and changes his name to Haile Selassie. He will maintain absolute control until 1974.

4 NOVEMBER 1930
USA Hoover asks Congress to appropriate up to $150 million for additional public works; Congress authorizes $116 million on 20 December.

14 NOVEMBER 1930
Commonwealth The annual Imperial Conference comes to a close in London. To Canada's disappointment, Britain has rejected a request for preferential tariff treatment to aid Dominion wheat.

11 DECEMBER 1930
USA The Bank of the US, a major private New York bank with 400,000 depositors, closes. There have now been 1300 bank closures since the autumn of 1929.

A BORROWED PEACE 1919-1932

The Chrysler Building in New York City—the ultimate in art deco architecture.

14 APRIL 1931

12 DECEMBER 1930
Germany The last Allied troops withdraw from the Saar.
Spain Strikes and unrest bring increasing disorder.

OTHER EVENTS OF 1930
Science Clyde Tombaugh, an American astronomer working at Lowell Observatory, Flagstaff, Arizona, discovers on 18 February the planet that Percival Lowell had posited on the basis of his mathematical calculations. Tombaugh waits until Lowell's birthday, 13 March, to announce this and names the planet Pluto (in part because the astronomical abbreviation PL forms Lowell's initials).
Technology Ernest O Lawrence and his staff at the University of California, Berkeley, invent the cyclotron, a spiral atom-smasher that will prove essential to studying the nuclear structure of atoms. Frank Whittle, an English aeronautical engineer, files a patent for a jet-propelled aircraft; this will become the basis for modern jet engines, although Whittle's first successful test flight will not occur until May 1941. Otis Barton, an American inventor, and William Beebe, an American naturalist, make the first successful deep-sea dive in the bathysphere, an enclosed pressurized vehicle Barton has designed. This will lead to other, more sophisticated vehicles that allow humans to explore the ocean depths. The first known detection of airplanes by radio waves is observed by Albert H Taylor and Leo C Young, of the Naval Aircraft Radio Laboratory of Anacostia, District of Columbia. This will be only one step toward what will eventually be called 'radar.'
Social Sciences John Maynard Keynes's *Treatise on Money*.
Ideas/Beliefs Freud's *Civilization and Its Discontents*.
Literature T S Eliot's *Ash Wednesday*; Evelyn Waugh's *Vile Bodies*; Dos Passos's *42nd Parallel*; Hesse's *Narcissus and Goldmund*; Mann's 'Mario and the Magician'; Faulkner's *As I Lay Dying*.
Drama/Entertainment Noel Coward's *Private Lives*.
The Arts Grant Wood's *American Gothic*; Matisse's *Odalisque*; Picasso's *The Acrobat*; Edward Hopper's *Early Sunday Morning*.
Architecture Le Corbusier completes his Savoye House, which fulfills his goal of 'a machine to be lived in.'
Music Stravinsky's *Symphony of Psalms*; Shostakovich's ballet *The Golden Age* and his opera *The Nose*; Milhaud's opera (to Claudel's text) *Christophe Colombe*.
Life/Customs A copy of James Joyce's novel *Ulysses*, sent from its Paris publisher to a New York publisher, is seized by the US Bureau of Customs on the ground that it is obscene.
Miscellaneous The Nobel Prize for Literature is awarded for the first time to an American, Sinclair Lewis. In Princeton, New Jersey, the Institute for Advanced Study is established with an endowment from Louis Bamberger and his sister, Mrs Felix Fuld; it is designed to give leading scholars—at first in the sciences, but eventually in other disciplines—the chance to pursue their work. Albert Einstein, in exile from the Nazis, will become head of the Institute in 1933.

7 JANUARY 1931
USA A report from the President's Emergency Committee for Unemployment Relief claims there are now between four and five million unemployed; furthermore, the Depression is deepening daily and spreading throughout the world.

26 JANUARY 1931
India So that he may participate in discussions with the government, Gandhi is released from prison at the insistence of Lord Irwin, the British Viceroy of India.

FEBRUARY 1931
Great Britain Leaving the Labour Party, Sir Oswald Moseley organizes the fascist New Party, which will prove unacceptable to British voters in the October general elections. The following year Moseley will organize the British Union of Fascists.

4 MARCH 1931
India Discussions between Gandhi and the government result in the Delhi Pact. In this agreement, Gandhi promises to cease civil disobedience, the Congress agrees to recognize the London round-table conferences, and Lord Irwin agrees to free all political prisoners who committed no violence.

8 MARCH 1931
International Turkey and the USSR conclude a naval agreement which stipulates that neither nation will increase its fleet in the Black Sea without six months' notice.

21 MARCH 1931
International A plan is issued for a German-Austrian customs union. The proposal elicits an outcry from France, Italy, and Czechoslovakia that the union constitutes an infringement of Austrian sovereignty. In the face of these international objections, Germany and Austria withdraw the plan on 3 September, just before it receives a negative judgment from the World Court.

25 MARCH 1931
USA Nine young black boys are arrested in Scottsboro, Alabama, and charged with raping a white woman. In the course of three trials, they will be found guilty, but the Supreme Court will overturn their conviction on 1 April 1935. The Scottsboro Case will become a *cause célèbre* for all determined to obtain justice for Black Americans.

14 APRIL 1931
Spain After the elections of 12 April decisively affirm the Republican cause, and Republican leader Niceto Alcalá Zamora demands the king's abdica-

165

A BORROWED PEACE 1919-1932

tion, King Alfonso XIII leaves Spain without abdicating. Alcalá Zamora organizes a provisional government with himself as leader. On 28 June the Constituent Assembly elections result in an overwhelming majority for the Republican-Socialist coalition. The assembly finds King Alfonso guilty of treason on 12 November and confiscates royal property. On 9 December a new constitution providing for universal suffrage and religious freedom is adopted. The following day, Alcalá Zamora is elected first president.

22 APRIL 1931
International Egypt and Persia conclude a treaty of friendship, the first alliance between Egypt and another Moslem state.

5 MAY 1931
China In Nanking a People's National Convention adopts a provisional constitution that guarantees personal freedom and education.

11 MAY 1931
Austria The Credit-Anstalt collapses despite government efforts to shore up this key financial institution. The bankruptcy results partially from French withdrawal of short credits in order to force abandonment of the proposed German-Austrian customs union. The Credit-Anstalt bankruptcy will lead to the economic collapse of the rest of Central Europe.

16 JUNE 1931
Austria Despite the uncertain economic climate within Great Britain, the Bank of England offers 150,000,000 schillings to shore up the Austrian national bank. Meanwhile, guided by politics, the French refuse financial help to Austria.

20 JUNE 1931
USA President Hoover proposes that all nations declare a one-year moratorium on intergovernmental debts and reparation payments. The recent Austrian bank failure is beginning to have repercussions in international finance. Hoover's proposal will soon be accepted by all major nations, and by July the moratorium is in effect. At first it has the effect of helping the world's stock markets and financial communities, but initial confidence soon wanes.

21 JUNE 1931
Austria To ward off total financial collapse, Christian Socialist Karl Buresch forms a new coalition government of Christian Socialists and Agrarians. The Buresch Government will last just under a year.

13 JULY 1931
Germany The Danatbank declares bankruptcy, leading to the closing of all banks until 5 August. This financial collapse leads to a Depression in which more than 6 million people are without work by the end of the year. Economic crisis creates social conditions for the growth of Communism and National Socialism.

1 AUGUST 1931
Great Britain After the May Committee prediction of a staggering £100,000 governmental financial deficit for the fiscal year and its recommendation of severe economies, the US and France extend credits to the Bank of England of £25 million each. But this proves to be only a stop-gap.

19 AUGUST 1931
Germany In Basel, Switzerland, an international committee of bankers issues the Layton-Wiggin report calling for a six-month extension of credit to Germany. Despite this measure, Germany remains insolvent.

24 AUGUST 1931
Great Britain As a result of the financial crisis, the Ramsay MacDonald cabinet resigns, and MacDonald forms a coalition government of Conservatives, Liberals, and Labour. In opposition to this move, the Labour Party expels its leaders MacDonald, Philip Snowden, and J P Thomas.

7 SEPTEMBER 1931
India In London Gandhi is the only representative of the Congress at the second round-table conference. The talks break up on 1 December, when no agreement is reached on representation of religious and social minorities in the proposed Indian Government.

10 SEPTEMBER 1931
Great Britain The severe economic measures instituted by the government lead to street riots in London and Glasgow. On the 15th there is a naval mutiny in Invergordon over pay reductions.

13 SEPTEMBER 1931
Austria An attempted *coup d'état* by the *Heimwehr*, the fascist private army organized in 1927 by the Christian Socialists and led by Walter Pfrimer, fails.

18 SEPTEMBER 1931
China Japanese troops in a railway zone in Manchuria move out of the zone to attack Chinese troops whom they accuse of blowing up a piece of track on the Japanese-owned South Manchuria Railway. This military action is in violation of the Kellogg-Briand Pact of 1928, to which Japan was a party. The subsequent occupation of all Manchuria launches Japan on a course that will lead to its participation in World War II.

21 SEPTEMBER 1931
International Great Britain goes off the gold standard. This leads to a further erosion of confidence in the banks, and in the USA many citizens begin to withdraw money from banks and hoard gold. In

September and October 827 more American banks will close.

11 OCTOBER 1931

Germany Adolf Hitler wins the support of wealthy publisher Alfred Hugenberg. In addition to providing funds for the National Socialist Party, Hugenberg gives Hitler's speeches wide coverage. Ruhr industrialists Emil Kirdorf and Fritz Thyssen will also lend support to the Nazi movement, which now numbers some 800,000 members.

16 OCTOBER 1931

International The League of Nations Council asks the USA to send a representative to attend discussion of the crisis caused by Japanese actions in Manchuria; two days later the US Consul General in Geneva is delegated. In the end the League's efforts to oppose the Japanese aggression will prove futile.

25 OCTOBER 1931

International After joint discussions in Washington, DC, President Hoover and Premier Pierre Laval of France publicly declare that both countries will adhere to the gold standard. They also agree that when the moratorium ends, new terms for international debts will probably have to be negotiated.

NOVEMBER 1931

China Mao Tse-tung, the young Communist leader who had fled to the countryside after Chiang Kaishek's crackdown on Communism, establishes the first Chinese Soviet Republic, with himself as chairman, in a remote region of Kiangsi Province. From this bastion, Mao's—and the Communists'—power will spread to all China.

7 DECEMBER 1931

USA Hundreds of American 'hunger marchers' have descended on Washington, DC, but are turned away from the White House when they try to give President Hoover their petition seeking employment at a minimum wage.

11 DECEMBER 1931

Great Britain After a series of revisions, Parliament passes the Statute of Westminster, drawn up by the 1930 Imperial Conference to embody the principles of the Balfour Declaration. The statute enumerates terms of autonomy possessed by the Dominions of the British Commonwealth. Dominions are allowed to have their own foreign policies and the option of exempting themselves from British law: in effect, virtual sovereignty. This statute applies to the United Kingdom, Canada, Australia, New Zealand, South Africa, Ireland, and Newfoundland.

19 DECEMBER 1931

Australia Widespread dissatisfaction leads to the fall of the Scullin Labour government. Joseph A Lyons, leader of the United Australia Party, forms a new government that remains in power until 1939.

The conservative approach of Lyons provides stability during the Depression. Although at its worst 25 percent of the labor force is unemployed, Australia recovers fairly quickly because of the worldwide rise in gold and wool prices.

OTHER EVENTS OF 1931

Science In a German scientific periodical, Kurt Goedel, a Czech-American mathematician, first publishes what will become known as 'Goedel's Proof,' a landmark in modern mathematical logic: within any rigidly logical-mathematical system, there are propositions (or questions) that cannot be proved or disproved on the basis of the axioms within that system (and therefore, among other things, it is uncertain that the basic axioms of arithmetic will not give rise to contradictions). At Columbia University, Harold Urey and his colleagues discover 'heavy hydrogen,' an isotope of hydrogen that is named 'deuterium.' And American experimenter Karl G Jansky discovers radio waves emanating from space; he will report his findings in 1932, thus effectively launching the modern discipline of radio astronomy (although it will be the late 1930s before the first true radio telescopes are constructed).

Technology Professor Auguste Piccard, a Swiss physicist, ascends to 52,000 feet in a balloon, the first venture by humans into the stratosphere. Wiley Post and Harold Gatty circle the globe in 8 days and 15 hours (elapsed flight time), a record for the time.

Environment After severe monsoon rains, huge flood waves sweep down China's Yangtze River, destroying dikes and dams and inundating over 35,000 square miles in one of the worst floods in recorded history; some 40,000,000 Chinese are left homeless or otherwise deprived, while some cities remain flooded for four months.

Literature Pearl Buck's *The Good Earth*; Woolf's *The Waves*; Faulkner's *Sanctuary*; Saint-Exupéry's *Night Flight*; Pablo Neruda's *Residence on Earth*; George Seferis's *Strophé*; Hermann Broch's *The Sleepwalkers*.

Drama/Entertainment O'Neill's *Mourning Becomes Electra*; Chaplin's *City Lights*; Martha Graham premieres her modern-dance classic *Primi-Mysteries*.

The Arts Salvador Dali's *The Persistence of Memory*, the archetypal Surrealist painting (with its drooping watch); Epstein's sculpture *Genesis*; Bonnard's *The Breakfast Room*.

Architecture The Empire State Building, under construction since 17 March 1930, formally opens on 1 May. It has 102 stories and is 1250 feet (381 m) high; in 1950 a TV tower will bring its height to 1472 feet; it will remain as the world's tallest structure until 1972, when New York City's World Trade Center will overtake it (to be surpassed in turn by Chicago's Sears Tower in 1974).

Music Walton's *Belshazzar's Feast*; Ravel's *Concerto for the Left Hand*; Sergei Rachmaninoff's music is banned in his native Russia as 'decadent . . . bourgeois.'

Miscellaneous In Detroit, Michigan, Elijah Muham-

A BORROWED PEACE 1919-1932

mad, an American black (born Elijah Poole), founds the Black Muslims.

4 JANUARY 1932
India The new British viceroy, the Earl of Willington, proclaims the Congress illegal and arrests Gandhi once more. Willington's inflexibility has inspired Gandhi's renewal of civil disobedience following his 28 December return from the London Conference. The nonviolent demonstrations in response to Gandhi's arrest are countered by new British repressive measures. But from May 1933 to May 1934, Gandhi will increasingly turn from the civil disobedience movement to improving the status of India's depressed classes, whom he renames the *Harijans*, or children of God.

7 JANUARY 1932
USA Prompted by Japan's attacks upon Chinese forces in Manchuria, Secretary of State Stimson sends diplomatic notes to Japan and China saying the US will not recognize any territory taken contrary to the 1928 Kellogg-Briand Pact.

22 JANUARY 1932
USA President Hoover signs the bill establishing a Reconstruction Finance Corporation. The agency will start operations on 2 February with $5 million in funds, and authorization to borrow up to $2 billion through tax-exempt bonds. It is to lend money to such institutions as banks, insurance companies, building and loan societies, agricultural credit corporations, farm mortgage associations, and railroads so that these bodies can stimulate the economy. This is President Hoover's belated recognition that the US economy and work force need government aid to get out of the Depression.
USSR The Soviet Government begins its second Five Year Plan to develop heavy industries primarily to produce defense goods. This year a devastating famine, resulting in part from ill-judged governmental agricultural policies, ravages the Ukraine and the northern Caucasus. The government tries to keep news of the famine from reaching the world.

28 JANUARY 1932
China Some 70,000 Japanese troops land at Shanghai and drive out the Chinese 19th Route Army over the next month. On 5 May an agreement between combatants sets a demilitarized zone and ends the boycott against Japanese goods.

2 FEBRUARY 1932
International Sixty nations, among them the USSR and the USA, meet in Geneva for a disarmament conference. Although the session lasts until July, it achieves little, primarily because of inflexibility of the French, who propose a system of international police so that security can precede disarmament. German representatives demand equality for their nation. The disarmament conference will reconvene on the same date the following year.

16 FEBRUARY 1932
Ireland After years of Republican agitation and terrorist activity, the elections result in a Republican victory, with support of Labour deputies.

18 FEBRUARY 1932
China In Manchuria, an independent country of Manchukuo, comprised of the three eastern provinces, is declared. The Japanese control it from behind the scenes, and on 9 March install former Chinese emperor Henry Pu-yi as regent. On 15 September the Japanese will issue a protocol proclaiming Manchukuo as a protectorate.

27 FEBRUARY 1932
USA Congress passes the Glass-Steagall Act authorizing the Federal Reserve Bank to expand credit and release government gold to business interests. There has been hoarding of both gold and currency as well as foreign withdrawals. This new act is an attempt to get money circulating.

29 FEBRUARY 1932
Finland General Kurt Wallenius leads his fascist Lapua organization in a second unsuccessful coup d'état. The arrest and conviction of Wallenius and 50 of his followers leads to the demise of the organization.
Great Britain In Parliament, there is opposition against the Protective Tariffs Acts which end free trade. But the acts survive the heated debate, and British farmers and manufacturers are guaranteed protection against foreign imports, helping restore the national economic stability.

9 MARCH 1932
Ireland Eamon de Valera is elected president, with the intention of abolishing the loyalty oath to the British Monarch. Over the summer protracted trade negotiations will dissolve into a tariff war with Great Britain.

13 MARCH 1932
Germany In the national presidential elections, Field Marshal Paul von Hindenburg wins with 18 million votes, but falls short of the required majority over his opponents Adolf Hitler (with 11 million) and Communist candidate Ernst Thälmann (with 5 million). A new election is scheduled for April.

16 MAY 1932
Japan Premier Ki Inukai is assassinated by military reactionaries, ending party government in Japan. A new nonpartisan government will be organized under Viscount Makoto Saitō.

29 MAY 1932
USA Veterans begin to arrive in Washington, DC, where 17,000 set up camp to press their demand that they be allowed to cash in their bonus certificates from World War I. They become known as the Bonus Army.

2 OCTOBER 1932

31 MAY 1932
Germany After resignation of Chancellor Heinrich Brüning, inspired by Hindenburg's refusal to allow division of bankrupt East Prussian estate lands for use by small farmers, Franz von Papen organizes a 'ministry of barons,' excluding the National Socialists.

16 JUNE 1932
International At the Lausanne Conference, representatives of Great Britain, France, Germany, Italy, Belgium, and Japan meet to renegotiate World War I reparations payments. In the three-week session, an agreement is reached to replace the German foreign debt with 5 percent bonds for Reichsmarks (3 billion). Failure of the US Congress to approve the measure in December renders it invalid. Thus the 1929 Young Plan continues in effect. In the end, only Finland will repay its debt to the US in full. Germany will discontinue all payments, as the National Socialists label reparations 'interest slavery.'
Germany The Papen Government drops the ban on Nazi storm troops which former Chancellor Brüning had imposed 13 April. This grants apparent sanction to the National Socialist movement, which flourishes anew. One result is the increase in street violence between opposing political factions.

17 JUNE 1932
USA The Senate rejects the Patman Bonus Bill demanded by the Bonus Army of World War I veterans. Many of those camped decide to leave, especially since the government offers funds to pay for their return home. But about 2000 will remain until the end of July.

5 JULY 1932
Portugal Antonio de Oliviera Salazar, minister of finance, becomes premier with virtual dictatorial powers. His strict regime will be marked by opposition to totalitarian government, leading to sporadic defiance and attempts on Salazar's life, but Salazar will remain as dictator until 1968.

20 JULY 1932
Germany Chancellor von Papen deposes the socialist prime minister and other officials in Prussia. Martial law is imposed on Berlin and Brandenburg, ostensibly because of the civil disorders resulting from Nazi storm-troop activity.

21 JULY 1932
International To find ways to improve their economies, representatives of Great Britain, Australia, New Zealand, South Africa, Rhodesia, Ireland, and Canada meet for the month-long Imperial Economic Conference in Ottawa, Canada. New trade tariffs are negotiated, giving preferential status to dominion exports of raw materials and to British manufactured imports. This principle of imperial preference will lead to the resignation of free-trade advocates from the British cabinet.

25 JULY 1932
USSR The USSR concludes nonaggression pacts with Poland, Estonia, Latvia, and Finland, and negotiates a similar treaty with France on 29 November. This Soviet strategy of stabilization with its Western neighbors derives from expansionist activity of the Japanese along Russia's Far Eastern border with Manchuria.

28–29 JULY 1932
USA After an unsuccessful police attempt to remove the last 2000 members of the Bonus Army from Washington, President Hoover calls in the military to evict the veterans. The troops are led by the Army Chief of Staff General Douglas MacArthur; his aide is a young major, Dwight D Eisenhower.

31 JULY 1932
Germany In the Reichstag elections, the National Socialists gain 230 seats, Socialists 133, Center 97, and the Communists 89. No majority results, as the Nazis and the Communists refuse to participate in a coalition government.

10 AUGUST 1932
Spain General José Sanjurjo, opposing the radical socialist programs of the Alcalá Zamora regime, seizes Seville in an attempted revolution. This conservative movement is suppressed by troops loyal to the government.

13 AUGUST 1932
Germany Offered by Hindenburg the position of vice-chancellor under Papen, Hitler refuses. He announces that he is prepared to hold out for 'all or nothing.' The lack of a decisive majority will lead to the 12 September dissolution of the Reichstag following a Communist motion of no confidence in the Papen ministry.

16 AUGUST 1932
India To resolve the matter of minority representation, British Prime Minister MacDonald extends the principle of separate communal electorates to the Untouchables. This 'communal award' is unacceptable to Gandhi, who begins a 'fast unto death.' He ends the fast when he and Untouchable leader B R Ambedkar agree on the Poona Pact, which increases the representatives to be chosen by the Untouchables in a primary election. In November the Third India Conference in London will produce few results.

25 SEPTEMBER 1932
Spain The Republican government of Alcalá Zamora grants the Catalan request for autonomy. Catalonia is to have its own president, government, flag, powers of taxation, and Catalan as its official language. This precedent will lead to similar demands by the Basques and other regional groups.

2 OCTOBER 1932
China A League of Nations commission of inquiry

A BORROWED PEACE 1919-1932

John Maynard Keynes.

led by the Earl of Lytton issues a report denouncing the Japanese seizure of Manchuria, and recommending an independent government in Manchukuo under Chinese sovereignty with international advisers and police.

4 OCTOBER 1932

Hungary After the resignation of Count Stephan Bethlen, because of the nation's financial chaos, nationalist and anti-Semite Julius Gömbös assumes power. He opposes return of the Habsburg Monarchy and allies himself with Fascist Italy to further Hungary's territorial aspirations.

8 NOVEMBER 1932

USA Franklin Delano Roosevelt and the Democrats win the election by a landslide. Roosevelt receives 22,809,638 votes to Hoover's 15,758,901, and the Democrats gain control of both houses of Congress. In the electoral college vote, Roosevelt's lead is even more impressive—472 to 59. The election campaign had not presented a clear choice, but the

KEYNESIAN ECONOMICS

It is generally conceded that the most influential economist of the 20th century—on both theoretical economists and practical politicians—has been Englishman John Maynard Keynes (1883–1946). Roosevelt's New Deal of the 1930s is usually cited as the prime instance of the application of Keynesian ideas, including the claim that a government willing to engage in deficit spending can increase employment and income. It is true that the New Deal did practice some deficit spending in its first years, and it helped to reduce unemployment on an interim basis. But Roosevelt soon decided to balance the budget again, and by 1937 the US was sliding back into a sharp recession. As deficit spending went down, unemployment rose from 14 percent to 19 percent by 1938. It would fall slowly to 14 percent in 1940, but the real cure then was the government spending necessary to undertake the US role in World War II. If any country practiced Keynesian economics in the 1930s, it was Hitler's Germany, where large-scale expenditures helped to pull the economy from depression. The famed autobahns are only one testimony to the public-works programs that re-employed the Germans; rearmament was more important. Keynes bears no responsibility for Hitler's Germany, but neither should he be credited—or blamed—for Roosevelt's economic policies. Over the decades Keynesian economics has been applied in many nations: like all economic theories, sometimes it works, sometimes it doesn't.

American people were desperate for some alternative to Hoover, and Roosevelt exuded confidence. As further evidence that Americans wanted reasonably traditional solutions, they gave Socialist Norman Thomas only 882,000 votes, and Communist William Foster 103,000.

17 NOVEMBER 1932

Germany Chancellor von Papen resigns after the increasingly tenuous political situation fails to achieve stability through new elections. The 6 November elections had continued the deadlock, with Communists gaining votes from the Nazis.

24 NOVEMBER 1932

Germany President von Hindenburg offers a limited chancellorship to Hitler, who refuses. Hitler demands full political powers—a position unacceptable to Hindenburg.

29 NOVEMBER 1932

Persia The government cancels the concessions of the Anglo-Persian Oil Company, of which the British Government is the largest shareholder. A renegotiation of the contract results in the new concession of 29 May 1933, which restricts the area of oil exploration and increases taxes and royalties owed by the oil company.

27 DECEMBER 1932

South Africa In an attempt to deal with its severe economic problems, the Union of South Africa goes off the gold standard.

OTHER EVENTS OF 1932

Science James Chadwick, British physicist, discovers the neutron, an uncharged subatomic particle that is part of the nucleus. John Cockcroft and Ernest T S Walton, British physicists, artificially accelerate atomic particles and for the first time transmute atomic nuclei. Carl D Anderson, American physicist, discovers the positron, a positively charged electron, the first known antiparticle.

Technology Edwin Land, American inventor, makes the first polaroid glass, which organizes all rays of light in such a way as to cut down on glare; it will have many applications in the years ahead and will allow Land to develop his Polaroid camera. August Piccard, the Belgian physicist, betters his previous year's ascent by going to some 55,000 feet in the airtight gondola attached to a helium-filled balloon. Piccard, his brother Jean, and his son Jacques will achieve other 'firsts' in ascending into the stratosphere and descending into the ocean depths in the bathyscaphe they develop. Amelia Earhart becomes the first woman to make a solo flight across the Atlantic (between Newfoundland and Northern Ireland).

Environment A terrible earthquake in Kansu Province, China, leaves 70,000 dead.

Literature Huxley's *Brave New World*; Faulkner's *Light in August*; Valentin Kataev's *Time, Forward!*

Drama/Entertainment Hauptmann's *Before Sunset*; Cocteau's film *The Blood of a Poet*; Johnny Weissmuller stars in the first Tarzan film, *Tarzan, The Ape Man*, and Shirley Temple makes her first film, *Red-Haired Alibi*. Kurt Jooss premieres his expressionist ballet *The Green Table*.

The Arts Picasso's *Girl Before a Mirror*; Alexander Calder, American sculptor, exhibits his first 'mobiles,' hanging constructions moved by the air.

Architecture The Philadelphia Savings Fund Society Building, designed by George Howe and William Lescaze, is completed: it is considered one of the first international-style skyscrapers.

Music Duke Ellington's *Creole Rhapsody*, a jazz work for orchestra, begins to gain him a reputation as a serious Afro-American composer.

Miscellaneous The first major part of Holland's Zuider Zee reclamation project is completed (begun in 1919). The Shakespeare Memorial Theatre opens at Stratford-on-Avon. Charles A Lindbergh, Jr, the 19-month-old son of Charles and Anne Morrow Lindbergh, is kidnapped from their house in Hopewell, New Jersey. A note demanding a ransom of $50,000 is received, the sum is paid as directed, but the child is not returned; he is found dead on 12 May. Bruno Hauptmann is discovered with some of the ransom money in September; he is convicted of murder and electrocuted in 1936, although he protests innocence to the end. The Lindbergh case will lead to Congress's adopting the death penalty in kidnapping cases that involve crossing state lines.

1933-1939:
THE ROAD TO WAR

The advance on Madrid.

8 JANUARY 1933
Spain From Barcelona, a radical uprising led by anarchists and syndicalists spreads to other cities. Although government forces check the revolt, lower-class dissatisfaction with socialist programs persists. A second such uprising will occur in Barcelona in December, with ten days of street fighting.

13 JANUARY 1933
Philippines The US Congress passes the Howes-Cutting Bill over the veto of President Hoover. This legislation presents an independence plan for the Philippines that still mandates the US right to military and naval bases, review of Philippine judicial decisions by the US Supreme Court, and a schedule of tariffs on Philippine exports to the US. The Philippine legislature rejects the plan in October because of its trade and immigration restrictions.

30 JANUARY 1933
Germany Adolf Hitler becomes chancellor on the invitation of President von Hindenburg, who now regards Hitler as the best alternative to the chaos currently threatening Germany. Hitler's appeal to the German populace is multifold. He receives strong support for his denunciation of the Versailles Treaty, and for his promise to make the nation strong and respected again. The middle classes, suffering from the economic Depression, are attracted by his proposed elimination of Jewish commercial and professional competition. Hitler's unrelenting opposition to communism is also a telling point in his favor.

12 FEBRUARY 1933
Great Britain Before the Oxford Union, the university's debating society, there is a debate on the proposition 'That this House will in no circumstances fight for its King and Country.' This pacifist position —appealing to British youth, who are only too aware of the terrible waste of World War I—wins 275 to 153. (On 9 February 1983, the same debate will be held, but this time the pacifists lose, 416 to 187.)

16 FEBRUARY 1933
International In a Geneva conference, the Little Entente (Czechoslovakia, Rumania, Yugoslavia) is reorganized, with the original treaties converted to indefinite duration and with a permanent governing body. This move toward greater solidarity is a result of the rise of the Nazis to power in Germany.

172

25 FEBRUARY 1933

Palestine British High Commissioner Sir Arthur Wauchope rejects an Arab demand for making the sale of Arab lands illegal and calling for restricted immigration. This denial leads to an Arab policy of noncooperation with the British and to an economic boycott of British goods. In December Palestinian Jews will conduct a series of protests calling for more liberal immigration policies. Their riots are motivated by the persecution of Jews in Germany.

27 FEBRUARY 1933

Germany During the agitated campaign preceding the Reichstag elections, a fire, probably set by the Nazis, destroys the Reichstag building. Hitler blames the fire on the Communists, and President von Hindenburg uses it as an excuse to issue emergency decrees that suspend constitutional liberties of speech and press, among other rights. This move gives unrestricted freedom to terrorist tactics of the Nazi storm troops.

4 MARCH 1933

Austria Engelbert Dollfuss dissolves the parliamentary government and bans parades and gatherings in response to the agitation following the Nazi takeover in Germany. On 8 March he suspends freedom of the press. The Austrian Nazis defy Dollfuss by staging a widespread riot in Vienna on 29 March.

USA Franklin Delano Roosevelt is installed as the 32nd president. Declaring in his inaugural speech that 'The only thing we have to fear is fear itself,' Roosevelt sets out to restore the confidence of the Depression-scarred nation. Between March and June, in what becomes known as the 'First Hundred Days,' he persuades a willing Congress to create a series of New Deal agencies to provide for the people's welfare. Among them are the Civilian Conservation Corps, Federal Emergency Relief Administration, Agricultural Adjustment Administration, Tennessee Valley Authority, Farm Security Administration, and National Recovery Administration.

5 MARCH 1933

Germany The elections fall short of their aim to secure a clear Reichstag majority. Together, the Nazis and their Nationalist allies—a party of big business and old aristocracy—gain slightly more than half the seats. Although the Nazis are still a minority, their political opponents—the Center Party, the Socialists, the Communists, and others—are disorganized and confused.

16 MARCH 1933

International At the Geneva disarmament conference, in session since 2 February, British Prime Minister Ramsay MacDonald proposes that the European armies be reduced by half a million, and that France and Germany be given equality. The Germans object, maintaining that the Nazi storm troops should not be included in the totals. The conference will finally end inconclusively in October, as the Germans insist they be allowed 'defensive weapons' immediately.

23 MARCH 1933

Germany Hitler is granted his demand for the right to rule by decree for four years. In the Reichstag and Reichsrat vote, only the Social-Democrats—still the second-largest party—oppose this Enabling Law. The Catholic Center helps to provide the votes needed for passage. Hitler immediately uses these dictatorial powers (to be in effect until April 1937) to consolidate his position. The independent trade unions, other political parties, separate German states, and the Jews become his first victims.

27 MARCH 1933

Japan After the League of Nations adopts the Lytton Report condemning Japanese military actions in Manchuria (25 February), the Japanese representative announces that Japan will withdraw from the League in two years. This incident marks the first step toward the demise of the League. Japan's actions will prove an example for aggressors elsewhere in the world.

1 APRIL 1933

Germany Hitler strikes quickly at the Jews, with a national boycott of Jewish businesses and professionals. In the months following, many Jewish businesses are eliminated, and Jewish doctors and lawyers forbidden to practice. With the 7 April Civil Service Law, Jews are eliminated from government service posts. Also included under this law are teachers, notaries, and other semi-public servants.

FRANKLIN DELANO ROOSEVELT, 1884–1945

The 32nd president of the United States, Franklin D Roosevelt was a distant cousin of Theodore Roosevelt. Born at Hyde Park, New York, educated at Harvard and Columbia Law School, he made a career in New York State politics as an independent Democrat and Wilson supporter. In 1913 he became assistant secretary of the navy and in 1920 ran unsuccessfully for vice-president. He returned to New York as a governor (1929–33) after a long fight against infantile paralysis, which had struck him in 1921. He defeated Herbert Hoover for the presidency as the Democratic candidate in 1932, with repeal of Prohibition and economic recovery from the Great Depression as strategic issues. His 'New Deal' won popular support, and he was re-elected in 1936 and 1940. Dissatisfied with American neutrality in World War II, Roosevelt bolstered the Allied cause with such programs as Lend-Lease until the Japanese attack on Pearl Harbor brought America into the war in 1941. In 1944 he was elected to an unprecedented fourth term. His Atlantic Charter conference with Churchill and wartime meetings with Churchill and Stalin at Tehran and Yalta had profound implications for the postwar world. Roosevelt died at Warm Springs, Georgia, three weeks before the Nazi surrender.

THE ROAD TO WAR 1933-1939

President Franklin D Roosevelt and his dog, Fala.

8 APRIL 1933
Australia Continuing economic difficulties lead the state of West Australia to vote 2 to 1 to secede from the British Commonwealth. A March 1934 petition to the king will be rejected by Parliament, which requires the approval of the Australian nation.

2 MAY 1933
Germany After the traditional May Day celebration honoring labor, Hitler's police seize the headquarters of all the independent trade unions and place their leaders under arrest. The independent unions are replaced by a new Nazi-dominated labor front. On 17 May strikes and lockouts are banned. The Nazi Government will soon be able to eliminate unemployment, through labor camps for young people, public works programs, and increased industrial production to achieve rearmament. The Nazis win much of the labor force to their cause by organization of *Kraft Durch Freude* ('Strength through Joy'), which offers workers low-cost vacations, inexpensive entertainment, and other benefits.

3 MAY 1933
Ireland The Dail, or legislature, under De Valera,

abolishes the loyalty oath to the British Crown and subsequently votes to eliminate the political powers of the British governor-general. It declares appeals to the British Privy Council illegal.

10 MAY 1933
Germany Around midnight thousands of Berlin students, urged on by Nazi Propaganda Minister Joseph Goebbels, stage a book burning—destroying some 20,000 books that the Nazis consider decadent, subversive, or 'un-German.' Included are books by Germans—Thomas Mann, Albert Einstein, Stefan Zweig, Erich Maria Remarque—and by foreigners (Jack London, Helen Keller, H G Wells, Sigmund Freud, Marcel Proust). Other burnings will follow.

17 MAY 1933
Spain In its continuing program of social reform, the government issues the Associations Law regulating the religious establishment. Church schools are banned and Church property nationalized. These actions evoke protests from the Vatican.

26 MAY 1933
Antarctica The Australian Government lays claim

President Eamon De Valera at an election rally in Dublin—9 January 1933.

THE ROAD TO WAR 1933-1939

to one-third of the continent, a geographical area equivalent to that of Australia itself. The 1930s are an especially active period of exploration of this southernmost land mass. American Commander Richard E Byrd conducts three air and land expeditions, while Norwegian Captain Hjalmar Riiser-Larsen leads two. And in 1934–37 Australian John Rymill leads the British Graham Land Expedition, while American Lincoln Ellsworth completes a transcontinental flight (1935–36) and leads a second expedition in 1938–39, claiming 430,000 square miles for the USA. On 14 January 1939 Norway will claim one million square miles—one-fifth of Antarctica.

28 MAY 1933
International In elections held in the free city of Danzig, the National Socialists led by Albert Forester win a victory. Thus the resident Nazis will take over the city government on 20 June and begin to cooperate with Nazi Germany. But during the following years, the League of Nations commissioner and Polish Government will help to protect rights of Poles in Danzig and maintain independence of the city.

12 JUNE 1933
International The World Economic Conference meets in London to seek a pact on international currency stabilization. The desired results are not obtained, and Great Britain will pursue a policy of neo-mercantilism and promote a campaign to 'buy British.'

14 JUNE 1933
Austria Relations between Austria and Germany disintegrate as the government expels Hitler's 'inspector for Austria,' Theodor Habicht. In retaliation, the Germans commit a series of terrorist acts. On 19 June Austria dissolves its Nazi Party, but Nazi agitation and violence will continue, with a 3 October attempt on Dollfuss's life.

14 JULY 1933
Germany The National Socialist Party is proclaimed the only legal party in the nation. This action culminates the systematic destruction of all the other political factions since the 27 March Reichstag fire. At that time the Communist Party was banned and its leaders arrested. On 10 May the Socialist parties had been outlawed and their assets seized. Under strong government pressures, the Nationalist Party had dissolved itself on 27 June, and the Catholic parties had done the same on 5 July.

15 JULY 1933
International Italy, Great Britain, France, and Germany sign the Four-Power Pact. This pact, which is to prove of little importance, was an obsession with Mussolini, who sought to replace the influence of the smaller nations in the League of Nations by that of a major power bloc.

5 AUGUST 1933
Poland Poland concludes an agreement with the city government of Danzig, which has recently come under National Socialist control. The pact guarantees the Polish inhabitants of Danzig fair treatment and assures Danzig a share of the Polish sea trade.

4 OCTOBER 1933
Czechoslovakia The day before a government ban, the Sudeten National Socialist Party voluntarily disbands. This government action follows Nazi disruption among the over three million Germans who inhabit the Czech border region. But this ban does not mark the end of National Socialism in the nation. Under the leadership of Konrad Henlein, the Nazis soon resurface in the guise of the *Sudetendeutsche Partei*.

10 OCTOBER 1933
International At Rio de Janeiro, nations of the Western Hemisphere sign a nonaggression and conciliation treaty. President Roosevelt adopts a 'good neighbor' policy toward Latin America and announces through Secretary of State Henry Stimson a policy of nonintervention in Latin American affairs at the 3 December 7th International American Conference at Montevideo, Uruguay.

14 OCTOBER 1933
International The Geneva disarmament conference breaks up as Germany proclaims withdrawal from the disarmament initiative, as well as from the League of Nations effective 23 October. With this action, Germany adopts a policy of independent action in foreign affairs.

17 OCTOBER 1933
USA Indicative of the rising tide of anti-Semitism and anti-intellectualism in Hitler's Germany, Albert Einstein arrives to make his new home in Princeton, New Jersey. During the coming years, the cream of Germany's artistic and intellectual elite will move to America. Among the more notable emigrés are Thomas Mann, Bertolt Brecht, Kurt Weill, Fritz Lang, and Erich von Stroheim.

12 NOVEMBER 1933
Germany With National Socialists now the sole legal political party, a new Reichstag is chosen. Ninety-two percent of the voters choose Nazi candidates (there are no opposition candidates), and 93 percent of the voters approve Germany's withdrawal from the League of Nations. Despite Nazi threats, 3 million Germans opposed to the Nazis cast invalid ballots as signs of their disapproval. However, under the provisions of the Enabling Act, the Reichstag has become all but obsolete. Occasionally this group of Nazi leaders is called together to hear Hitler's orations.

16 NOVEMBER 1933
International After conferring at the White House

with Soviet Commissar for Foreign Affairs Maxim Litvinov, President Roosevelt announces that the US will resume diplomatic relations with the USSR, suspended since 1919. Trade relations are restored and the USSR agrees to refrain from communist propaganda in the US.

19 NOVEMBER 1933

Spain The first official elections for the *Cortes*, or Parliament, result in the parties of the Right—comprised of Conservative Republicans, Clericals, and Monarchists—gaining 44 percent of the vote, while the Left wins only 21 percent. Lack of a decisive majority leads to a new series of unstable and unpopular coalition governments.

28 NOVEMBER 1933

North Africa The Moroccan-Tunisian Railway is opened, connecting the French colonial possessions. This route will prove especially useful in military situations, allowing France to complete pacification of Morocco in 1934 with final domination of the Atlas region. But the Moroccan nationalist movement, inspired by the Egyptian prototype, will begin in November 1934 when a group of European-educated young Moroccans presents a *Plan of Moroccan Reforms*.

5 DECEMBER 1933

USA The 21st Amendment, repealing Prohibition, goes into effect when Utah becomes the 36th state to ratify, ending the 'noble experiment.'

21 DECEMBER 1933

Newfoundland The large island off the east coast of Canada loses its status as a British Dominion and reverts to a Crown Colony. This action is taken because of corrupt and incompetent management of Newfoundland's economic affairs.

OTHER EVENTS OF 1933

Technology Wiley Post, an American aviator who is blind in one eye, completes the first solo airplane flight around the world between 15–22 July. He covers some 15,600 miles from Floyd Bennett Field, New York, via Germany, Moscow, Alaska, and back in 7 days, 18 hours, 49 minutes.

Social Sciences The first rock paintings of prehistoric inhabitants of the Sahara Desert region are found at Tassili. Leonard Bloomfield, American linguist, publishes *Language*, a seminal work in the field.

Ideas/Beliefs In a major decision for free speech and the creative arts, Federal Judge John Woolsey in New York City lifts the US ban on the importation and sale of James Joyce's *Ulysses*; Woolsey calls it 'a sincere and honest book. . . . I do not detect anywhere the leer of a sensualist.'

Literature Malraux's *Man's Fate*; Ignazio Silone's *Fontamara*; Gertrude Stein's *The Autobiography of Alice B Toklas*; Vera Brittain's *Testament of Youth*; Pearl Buck's translation of the Chinese classic *All Men Are Brothers*; James Thurber's *My Life and Hard Times*; James Hilton's *Lost Horizon*.

Drama/Entertainment O'Neill's *Ah, Wilderness!*; Garcia-Lorca's *Blood Wedding*; the original film version of *King Kong*. George Balanchine, a Russian choreographer, moves to the USA; in 1934, with Lincoln Kirstein, he will start the School of American Ballet; in the years that follow, Balanchine, through his ballets and teaching, will become the major influence on modern ballet and one of the great creative geniuses of the century.

The Arts Giacometti's sculpture *The Palace at 4 AM*; Epstein's sculpture *Ecce Homo*.

Music Shostakovich's *Piano Concerto*; Strauss's opera *Arabella*.

Miscellaneous Albert Einstein, having been informed by the Nazis now ruling Germany that he has been deprived of his citizenship, positions, and property, settles in the USA at the Institute for Advanced Studies in Princeton, New Jersey, where he will remain until his death in 1955. In England, the Oxford Union Society, the university's debating club, approves the motion that those attending will refuse to fight for King and Country.

14 JANUARY 1934

Spain In the Catalan elections, parties of the moderate Left are victorious. This result marks a protest against the increasing conservatism in the nation. Luis Companys becomes president of Catalonia.

26 JANUARY 1934

Poland Germany and Poland conclude a ten-year nonaggression pact which offers Poland guarantees that the Nazis will refrain from trying to seize the Polish Corridor by force of arms. This treaty marks the first break in the French alliance system.

2 FEBRUARY 1934

USA President Roosevelt establishes the Export-Import Bank of Washington to encourage commerce between the USA and foreign nations, by such means as short-term credits for exporting agricultural products, long-term credits for exporting industrial products, and loans to American exporters when the foreign buyers cannot obtain enough exchange to pay in dollars. This first bank will concentrate on encouraging trade with the USSR. In March a second bank will aid in trade with Cuba. By 1936 these operations will be consolidated in order to concentrate on trade with Latin American nations.

6 FEBRUARY 1934

France Royalist and fascist agitation against the Republican government culminates in violent street riots in Paris and other cities. Political unrest derives from the December 1933 Stavisky case involving a fraudulent bond issue that appeared to implicate prominent government officials. To avert civil war, a coalition cabinet of leaders from all parties except the Royalist, Socialists, and Communists is estab-

THE ROAD TO WAR 1933-1939

lished on 8 February. Agitation will continue with a general strike on 12–13 February.

9 FEBRUARY 1934

International Representatives of Greece, Rumania, Yugoslavia, and Turkey forge the Balkan Pact. Intended to prevent the advance of any other hostile nations, this treaty is a counterpart to the Little Entente. Failure of Bulgaria to participate in this diplomatic initiative marks fatal weakness in the agreement.

11–15 FEBRUARY 1934

Austria After a government decree banning all political parties except Dollfuss's Fatherland Front, an uprising occurs when government forces and the *Heimwehr* raid Socialist headquarters. Socialist leaders who avoid capture flee the country. By this misjudged action, Dollfuss and the Christian Socialists win the enmity of Vienna's working classes. At the same time, they have eliminated their best allies against the Nazis.

17 MARCH 1934

International The Rome Protocols are signed by Austria, Hungary, and Italy, a close alliance. In the face of increasing German hostility, the Austrians lean toward Italy for support. In Rome, Austria's Dollfuss and Hungary's Gömbös work out trade and policy agreements. The Rome Protocols represent a fascist counterpart of a Danube bloc to oppose the French-supported Little Entente.

24 MARCH 1934

Philippines The US Congress passes the Tydings-McDuffie Act, which guarantees Philippine independence in ten years after Philippine legislative approval. (Independence comes on 4 July 1946.)

7 APRIL 1934

Spain In Barcelona the socialists conduct a widespread strike, which government troops are able to quell only with difficulty.

12 APRIL 1934

USA The Senate establishes a committee to investigate manufacture and sale of munitions, specifically the extent to which this trade influenced and profited from the role taken by the USA in World War I. Hearings will go on into 1936 and findings will encourage the isolationist-neutralist elements, who feel confirmed in their view that wars are fought to profit a minority.

30 APRIL 1934

Austria The national assembly endorses a new constitution that establishes a virtual dictatorship under Dollfuss. On 10 July Dollfuss will reorganize his cabinet along fascist lines.

3 MAY 1934

Germany In the process of Hitler's reorganization of the nation's judicial system, the People's Court is instituted to try cases of treason—a widely applied concept. This judicial reform places Nazi goals and the welfare of the state as overriding legal principles. All traditional legal protections are abandoned. The treason cases tried in the People's Court are secret proceedings, and appeals can be made only to Hitler. Concentration camps have already existed since 1933, and thousands of opponents to the Nazi regime are held without trial.

5 MAY 1934

USSR The nonaggression pacts between the USSR and Poland and the Baltic States of 25 July 1932 are extended into ten-year agreements. In early June the USSR will cement relations with Czechoslovakia and Rumania by concluding similar pacts with these nations. These Soviet diplomatic initiatives are promoted by the Nazi rise to power. Russia's political security is threatened by open hostility of the Nazis toward communism. Despite these irreconcilable political differences, trade continues and even increases between the USSR and Germany during the next few years.

10–11 MAY 1934

USA A severe dust storm lifts an estimated 300 million tons of topsoil from Texas, Oklahoma, Arkansas, Kansas, Colorado, and other states. Much of it is blown all the way to the Atlantic Ocean. This is only one of many storms that have created the Dust Bowl, due to improper plowing and farming.

29 MAY 1934

Cuba The US and Cuba sign a treaty releasing Cuba from its status as a US protectorate, in effect since the Spanish-American War. On 24 August American Secretary of State Cordell Hull will sign a reciprocal trade agreement with Cuba.

5 JUNE 1934

South Africa The South African Party led by Jan Smuts and the Nationalist Party led by Prime Minister Hertzog join to form the United South African National Party, or United Party for short. The faction of the Nationalist Party opposed to this coalition, led by Daniel F Malan, continues to promote republican and antinative policies.

14–15 JUNE 1934

International Hitler visits Mussolini in Venice to forge closer relations between the two fascist superstates. At this first meeting, the two dictators make a poor impression on each other and there are no diplomatic agreements. In actuality, this attempt at friendship is premature, as German and Italian interests collide over the attempted Nazi coup in Austria in July.

23 JUNE 1934

Albania Albanian resistance to Italy's ever-increasing meddling in the nation's affairs ends when

嬉敵砲轟擊時我士兵在蓋溝內以砲敵彈

Troops of General Sun Tien-ying's rebellion against the Nanking Government.

an Italian fleet arrives in Durazzo. The Albanian Government meekly submits to Italian domination. Italy strengthens control of the Albanian Army and is granted the right to colonize areas of Albania, with other privileges.

30 JUNE 1934

Germany A dramatic Nazi purge occurs with the summary execution of 77 persons on the pretext of participation in an alleged plot against Hitler and his regime. Many of those executed, leaders high in the Nazi hierarchy, are feared by Hitler as radical members of the social revolutionary wing of the party. The aim of this faction has been incorporation of Nazi storm troops into the army, as well as widespread property reforms. More prominent victims of the Great Blood Purge include Catholic leader Erich Klauserer, radical Nazi Gregor Strasser, practiced organizer Ernst Röhm, and General Kurt von Schleicher.

1 JULY 1934

Germany The Nazi regime stops all international German debt payments. Although in accounting terms the nation is bankrupt, Germany is able to achieve its remarkable arms buildup through barter arrangements with other countries.

25 JULY 1934

Austria A Nazi coup d'état occurs when a Nazi group captures the Vienna radio station and broadcasts Dollfuss's resignation. They follow up with assassination of Dollfuss, but *Heimwehr* troops quell the Nazis. German troops are massed on the border, but the united support of Italy and Yugoslavia prevents German action. Invaluable is the quick initiative of Mussolini, who masses a large army on the Brenner Pass as a signal to the Germans to desist. On 30 July Dollfuss's close supporter Kurt von Schuschnigg takes control of the government and renews ties with Italy and Hungary through economic pacts.

2 AUGUST 1934

Germany President von Hindenburg, aged 87, dies. This leads to a plebiscite on 19 August that endorses Hitler as president. In actuality, the law combining the presidency and the chancellorship had already been passed on 1 August. Hitler prefers to be known under the title of *Der Führer*.

12 SEPTEMBER 1934

International Representatives of the Baltic States of Latvia, Lithuania, and Estonia sign the treaties of the Baltic Pact. The pact mandates common action to defend the independence of the states, and a common foreign affairs policy, with semiannual conferences of foreign ministers. Although the Baltic States view communism as a danger, the Nazi rise to power in Germany had led to Baltic diplomatic initiatives to the USSR to prevent German intervention on behalf of German landowners in the Baltic States. The

THE ROAD TO WAR 1933-1939

Adolf Hitler in Munich—22 May 1938.

ADOLF HITLER, 1889–1945

Adolf Hitler, the instigator of World War II, was born in Austria to a lower-middle-class family and grew up with ordinary schooling. He failed to gain admission to the Austrian Academy of Painting and obtained work in an architect's office in Vienna until 1912, when he moved to Munich to become a free-lance illustrator. He enlisted in the German Army when World War I broke out and served throughout the war. Embittered by the Allied victory and the subsequent Republican revolution within Germany, Hitler formed the National Socialist (Nazi) Party in 1919. Its 'unalterable program' was a radical mixture of ardent German nationalism, Nietzsche's philosophy of the superman, and the anti-Semitic writings of Stewart Chamberlain. Hitler's rare gift for spellbinding oratory began to attract large crowds to his public tirades against the 'corrupting parliamentary system' and the 'alien' Jews within Germany. His attempted coup of 1923 was premature, but during the year he spent in prison as a result, he wrote *Mein Kampf*, a sensational account of his life and ideas that soon became a best-seller and a kind of Bible for the Nazi movement. By 1933 Hitler had built up his party enough to become chancellor and de facto dictator of Germany. The Holocaust began. Aggressions against Austria and Czechoslovakia were followed by the invasion of Poland (1939) that began World War II. Hitler committed suicide in 1945 when the Russians entered Berlin.

Baltic Pact ignores the issue of Lithuania's claim to Vilna, now under Polish sovereignty. By this time, all three Baltic nations are under dictatorship—in Lithuania under Anatanos Smetona, in Latvia under Karlis Ulmanis, and in Estonia under Konstantin Paets.

18 SEPTEMBER 1934
USSR Although it had denounced the international forum, the Soviet Union now joins the League of Nations. This move is a result of Nazi hostility toward communism. The USSR assumes an active role in the League to further European security. Meanwhile, the Soviets begin an intense armament program and in several years the Russians will possess a respectable air force; their navy's strength will be in submarines.

6 OCTOBER 1934
Spain Catalan President Companys declares Catalonia independent of Spain. Government troops move quickly to suppress this initiative. A result of the affair is that the Catalan statute is suspended in order that it may be revised. Elsewhere in Spain, government troops quell a miners' uprising in Asturia, where a communist regime has seized power.

9 OCTOBER 1934
Yugoslavia In Marseilles, a Macedonian revolutionary associated with Croat terrorists centered in Hungary assassinates both King Alexander of Yugo-

slavia and French foreign minister Louis Barthou. The two had been on a tour of European capitals in quest of an alliance system against Nazi Germany. The assassination stirs a threat of war between Yugoslavia and Hungary, but a confrontation is prevented by the League of Nations.

16 OCTOBER 1934
China Mao Tse-tung's Communist Government has spread its influence over several million Chinese since November 1931, and his Red Army has held off sporadic attacks by Nationalist troops. But recently Chiang Kai-shek has committed crack army units, so Mao decides he must abandon his base in Kiangsi Province. With his pregnant wife and about 30,000 Red Army troops, he sets out on this day for what will become the 'Long March.' For the next year Mao and his supporters will make their way across the often difficult terrain to Shensi Province in northwest China—traveling 6000 miles (9700 km). Only 7000 will complete the trip, making contact with Red forces there on 25 October 1935.

24 OCTOBER 1934
India After his suspension of nonviolent activity, Gandhi resigns from the Congress. This gives greater political freedom to the younger leaders of the Congress, although Gandhi will maintain ultimate power over its policies.

28 NOVEMBER 1934
Great Britain In yet another unpopular speech, Winston Churchill warns Parliament of the German air menace. Throughout the 1930s, drawing on his historical perspective, Churchill speaks out against Hitler. The British Government and people, desperate to avoid another war, delude themselves into seeing Hitler as a leader whose aim is peace. Churchill relies on sympathizers within the British military and industry who report to him on defense capabilities vis-à-vis Nazi Germany.

1 DECEMBER 1934
USSR Serge Kirov, a close associate of Stalin, is assassinated. The Communist Party purge of 1933 is renewed, as older party leaders and government officials are tried and convicted of treason.

5 DECEMBER 1934
Ethiopia At Ualual, on the disputed Ethiopian-Somaliland border, Italian troops clash with Ethiopian. Italy will seize this incident as an excuse to conquer Ethiopia, beginning in October 1935. This has been Italy's expansionist dream since the turn of the century, despite professed friendship for Ethiopia during the interim.

29 DECEMBER 1934
Japan Japan denounces the Washington Naval Treaty of 1922 and London Naval Treaty of 1930 and says it will withdraw from both as of December 1936.

THE ROAD TO WAR 1933-1939

OTHER EVENTS OF 1934

Science Frédéric Joliot and Irène Joliot-Curie, French physicists, discover that they can induce radioactivity by bombarding elements with alpha particles.

Technology The first practical test of a special apparatus for radar is conducted by Dr Rudolph Kuehnold, chief of the German Navy's Signal Research Department, on 20 March. With equipment devised in 1933, he reflects radio waves off ships up to 600 yards away; by October he is demonstrating echos from ships up to seven miles at sea. But radar cannot be credited to a single individual; it involves numerous ideas and techniques evolved in several countries over years of effort. In the USA, work on radar will begin this year but the first demonstration will not occur until 1936; in Great Britain, Robert Watson-Watt gives the first demonstration of a practical apparatus on 26 February 1935. The term 'radar' is not even coined until about 1940 (allegedly by Commander S M Tucker of the US Navy). The Du Pont Laboratories in the US announce success in spinning a synthetic fiber of great durability; at first it is called 'polymer 66,' but it soon becomes known as 'nylon.'

Social Sciences At Biskupin, Poland, a spectacular Iron Age site, excavations begin that will continue through 1938 and be resumed after the war. At Duke University, in North Carolina, J B Rhine, American psychologist, begins experiments using a special deck of 25 cards with five different symbols to test for powers of extrasensory perception (ESP). (While one of the subjects turns the cards and concentrates on each symbol, the other writes down what is 'seen' by ESP.) Rhine is not the first to investigate parapsychology, but he becomes an important influence in the field.

Ideas/Beliefs Lewis Mumford's *Technics and Civilization*. Arnold Toynbee publishes the first volume of *A Study of History*.

Literature Evelyn Waugh's *A Handful of Dust*; Robert Graves's *I, Claudius*; Henry Miller's *Tropic of Cancer*; John O'Hara's *Appointment in Samarra*; Fitzgerald's *Tender Is the Night*; Saroyan's *The Daring Young Man on the Flying Trapeze*; Dylan Thomas's *Eighteen Poems*.

Drama/Entertainment Garcia-Lorca's *Yerma*; Cocteau's *The Infernal Machine*. In New York City, Lincoln Kirstein and George Balanchine—a young Russian choreographer who had come to the US in 1933—start the American School of Ballet.

Music Prokofiev's *Lieutenant Kije Suite*; Rachmaninoff's *Rhapsody on a Theme of Paganini*; *Four Saints in Three Acts*, music by Virgil Thomson and words by Gertrude Stein, is premiered in Hartford, Connecticut. Shostakovich's opera *A Lady Macbeth of Mzensk* (which brings him into disfavor with the Soviet authorities; he will revise it in 1962 as *Katerina Ismailova*); Hindemith's symphony drawn from his opera *Mathis der Maler*; Roy Harris's *First Symphony*. In England, the Glyndebourne Festival is founded.

Miscellaneous On 28 May five girls are born to Ovila and Elzire Dionne, in Ontario, Canada; they are the first quintuplets known to survive more than a few hours and are adopted by the entire world. Off the coast of New Jersey, the *Morro Castle* burns, with a loss of 134 lives; in Hakodate, Japan, a fire leaves 2015 dead. The first laundromat—called a 'Washateria'—opens in Fort Worth, Texas. Dell Publishing Company of New York puts on sale for 10 cents the first comic book for the public, *Famous Funnies*; Superman will appear in a comic book in June 1938.

1 JANUARY 1935

Turkey With the enactment of a law mandating the use of family names, President Mustapha Kemal selects the name Kemal Atatürk, which translates as 'Father of the Turks.' He will be re-elected for another four-year term on 1 March.

7 JANUARY 1935

International The Marseilles Pact between France and Italy is concluded. This treaty was negotiated by French foreign minister Pierre Laval, who included French concessions to Italian territorial claims in Africa, in the hope of gaining Italian support against Germany. Favorable terms of the pact, including cession of part of French Somaliland to Italy, encourage Mussolini to press Italian claims in Ethiopia. On 23 February he dispatches Generals De Bono and Graziani, along with a sizable military force, to Eritrea.

13 JANUARY 1935

Germany In accord with the Treaty of Versailles, the League of Nations conducts an election in the Saar Basin. Given options of union with France, reunion with Germany, or extension of administration by the League, 90 percent of voters endorse reunion.

15 JANUARY 1935

USSR Continuing the Communist Party purge of December 1934, Communist leaders Grigori Zinoviev, Leo Kamenev, and others are convicted of treason and conspiracy in a series of show trials. They are sentenced to prison terms of five to ten years.

24 FEBRUARY 1935

Switzerland The populace votes to lengthen military training. This is a prelude to Swiss commitment to an ambitious armament program. Included are mechanization of the army, development of air defenses, and modernization of border defenses.

1 MARCH 1935

Germany In accord with the League-of-Nations-administered election of 13 January, the Saar Basin is returned to Germany. This increase in territory marks the first expansionist gain of the Third Reich.

9 MARCH 1935

Germany In defiance of the Treaty of Versailles,

Germany has secretly begun to rearm. This fact is casually leaked to the world in an informal public announcement that Germany has an air force. When British foreign secretary Sir John Simon visits Berlin on 25 March, he asks Hitler about the size of the air force and is informed, 'We have already reached parity with Britain.'

16 MARCH 1935
Germany In a dramatic move, Hitler denounces terms of the Treaty of Versailles that mandate German disarmament. Going further, he reinstates conscription and declares the German Army will be upgraded to 36 divisions. Hitler rationalizes these measures as provoked by failure of other powers to achieve disarmament, as outlined in the peace pact—in fact, in opposition to the Versailles timetables, the French and Soviet military forces have achieved vigorous growth. Hitler's proclamation evokes a unified protest from Great Britain and Italy under the leadership of France.

22 MARCH 1935
Persia/Iran By formal decree, Persia changes its name to Iran.

8 APRIL 1935
USA Congress adopts the Emergency Relief Appropriation Act, authorizing almost $5 billion for immediate relief; it will be used to set up programs, the most important being the Works Progress Administration.

11 APRIL 1935
International Summoned by France, the Stresa Conference meets to work out a strategy in response to Germany's announced intention to rearm. The question of protecting Austria's autonomy is discussed. Italy supports the conference, but its intentions are lost in the morass of the Ethiopian affair.

23 APRIL 1935
Poland After close to 20 years of revision and planning, Poland adopts a new constitution. The democratic, parliamentary system of government, honored too often in its breach, comes to an end despite calls from the Socialists and the Peasant Party for return to true democracy.

2 MAY 1935
International France and the USSR sign an alliance pact, as part of the French strategy of reviving ties with the Little Entente and with Poland. France has also tried to achieve an eastern pact among Germany, Poland, and the Soviet Union to ensure stability in Eastern Europe, but neither Germany nor Poland make moves in this direction. Hitler's announcement of German rearmament has led France to seek ties with the USSR.

6 MAY 1935
USA The Works Progress Administration, best

DEPRESSION WORLDWIDE

The Great Depression of 1929–39 put the world into a state of economic collapse. All the industrial nations, regardless of political system, suffered declining incomes and sharp increases in unemployment, while underdeveloped countries, because they depended for income on markets in the industrial world, suffered too. Only Russia, between two Five-year Plans, achieved significant economic growth—but at great human cost. Germany, the hardest-hit industrial nation, owed recovery to its public-works programs and to rearmament. Other attempts at recovery created brief popular-front governments in Spain and France, fascist regimes in Eastern Europe, and foreign-conquest policies in Italy and Japan to divert attention from domestic woe. In an effort to insulate themselves, nations resorted to tools of economic nationalism that made matters worse. Nationalistic xenophobia, critically exaggerated by the Depression, would help foster global conflict. Hitler's rise was facilitated by both the desperate state of economic affairs and the fear of communist hegemony. World War II may have led the world out of Depression, but the Depression had helped lead the world into war.

---

known of the New Deal programs, begins—putting millions of Americans to work at reasonable wages building roads, bridges, parks, airfields, and public buildings. The WPA will set up programs that provide employment for artists, musicians, actors, writers, and scholars. By the time the program ends in June 1943, it will have spent some $11 billion and employed some 8,500,000 Americans. The WPA will be charged with waste and inefficiency, and to critics of Roosevelt's New Deal, it stands as the symbol of his misguided efforts. But for millions of Americans it provides essential work and income.

16 MAY 1935
International The USSR and Czechoslovakia conclude a mutual assistance pact that calls for the USSR to support Czechoslovakia if invaded, provided France does likewise. This alliance is greatly resented by Germany.

19 MAY 1935
Czechoslovakia In general elections, the *Sudetendeutsche Partei* wins a decisive victory in the German-speaking regions. With 44 seats in the coalition government, the Sudeten Party, many of whose members are Nazis, now becomes the second most powerful in the nation.

7 JUNE 1935
France Pierre Laval's prestige has risen because of his diplomatic successes; when he becomes premier, his cabinet is granted quasi-dictatorial powers to end the economic Depression. But Laval's policy of deflation is to prove unpopular and ineffective.
Great Britain In the aftermath of a general election that continues the majority of the coalition govern-

THE ROAD TO WAR 1933-1939

ment, Stanley Baldwin replaces Ramsay MacDonald as prime minister. Sir Samuel Hoare is foreign secretary, and the popular Anthony Eden becomes minister for League of Nations affairs.

9 JUNE 1935
China Japanese force the Chinese to submit to the Ho-Umezu Agreement, which stipulates that any troops objected to by the Japanese must remove themselves from Hopei. Occupation of Manchukuo has proved troublesome for the Japanese, with guerrilla and bandit activity, so they try to organize a local Chinese Government that will allow them to exploit the resources and markets of North China.

18 JUNE 1935
International Great Britain and Germany conclude a naval agreement in which Germany agrees to limit her navy to not more than 35 percent (a figure suggested by Hitler) of the British Navy. By joining this pact, Hitler is able to calm the fears of British pacifists, and to disturb the unity of the French and English alliance. By signing the pact, Britain accepts de facto German rearmament. The French consider this agreement a betrayal, since they fear this British acquiescence will encourage the Germans to new treaty violations.

23 JUNE 1935
Ethiopia British minister for League of Nations affairs Anthony Eden arrives in Rome to offer concessions in the Ethiopian situation. Mussolini rejects these overtures as insufficient.

27 JUNE 1935
Great Britain Results of the so-called Peace Ballot are announced. This public opinion poll in which over 11.5 million had voted since the fall of 1934 overwhelmingly supports peace through the League of Nations, armaments reductions, and economic sanctions against aggressors. Political leaders pay close attention to these results, seeing them as support of their pacifist policies.

4 JULY 1935
Austria Despite opposition of the Little Entente and France, Schuschnigg's government repeals the antimonarchy laws and restores part of the Habsburg property. This move for return of the monarchy is instigated by Prince Rüdiger von Stahremberg, commander of the *Heimwehr*, possibly with Mussolini's support.

5 JULY 1935
USA President Roosevelt signs the National Labor Relations Act, a major piece of legislation that sets up a National Labor Relations Board empowered to supervise elections by which workers vote for their own collective bargaining units. Sections of the law support the right of employees to join labor organizations, and set forth unfair labor practices by employers.

25 JULY 1935
USSR Worldwide Communists convene for the Third International. They resolve to cease opposition to military rearmament in their own nations and support their own governments, even though they may be bourgeois. Conferees agree that the USSR will support democratic nations against their common enemies, the fascist states.

2 AUGUST 1935
India The British Parliament passes the Government of India Act: Burma and Aden are separated from India, and the political structure and processes for the new India spelled out. Goal of the act is to found an All-India Federation of both the Indian States and the provinces of British India. This aim is to be frustrated by the opposition of the Indian National Congress, as well as of the Indian States.

14 AUGUST 1935
USA President Roosevelt signs the Social Security Act—one of the most far-reaching pieces of legislation in American history. It sets up a system of guaranteed retirement pensions with contributions from both workers and employers. The act assists states in providing financial aid to dependent children, the blind, and aged who do not qualify for social security. Beyond this, the act establishes a system of unemployment insurance. Although modified over the years, and occasionally attacked, this act becomes the foundation of America's security for the aged in decades to come.

16 AUGUST 1935
Ethiopia After a Paris conference attended by Britain, France, and Italy, Italy is offered generous terms for economic development in Ethiopia, dependent on Ethiopian acquiescence. With Italy's refusal of this concession, it becomes apparent that her ultimate intention is conquest of Ethiopia.

31 AUGUST 1935
USA President Roosevelt signs the Neutrality Act, which forbids shipment of arms and munitions to belligerents once a state of war exists. The act authorizes the president to prohibit American civilians from traveling on ships of belligerents.

3 SEPTEMBER 1935
Ethiopia The arbitration tribunal of the League of Nations submits a report on claims of Italy and Ethiopia in Ualual, the disputed region of the border of Italian Somaliland. After the clash of 5 December 1934, the Italians have insisted on an apology and reparations, and the Ethiopian regime has called for an investigation of respective responsibilities. The tribunal finds neither side at fault, since each considers the area as within its realm. The matter of the rightful possession of Ualual is not considered.

15 SEPTEMBER 1935
Germany In Berlin, the government proclaims the

Nuremberg Laws (after the city where Nazi congresses are held and racial policy drawn). With these infamous laws, Germany legitimizes persecution of the Jews. Jewish Germans are deprived of all rights of citizenship, and intermarriage between Jews and Aryans is banned. Although they must give up almost all property, many Jews choose to leave Germany rather than face what may come. Many more of these anti-Semitic laws will be issued in the following years.

2 OCTOBER 1935
Ethiopia The Italian Expeditionary Army begins the invasion of Ethiopia. On 6 October the Italians capture Adua. On 7 October the League of Nations names Italy as the aggressor and considers sanctions.

10 OCTOBER 1935
Greece General George Kondylis effects a coup and influences parliament to vote for restoration of the monarchy. On 3 November an irregular election will call for return of the king.

8 NOVEMBER 1935
Ethiopia After a long march, the Italian army captures the fortress of Makallé. Marshal Pietro Badoglio assumes command of forces, who begin a march through mountainous terrain.

15 NOVEMBER 1935
Philippines Manuel Quezon y Malina, elected 17 September, is inaugurated as first president of the commonwealth. The USA retains power over the country's foreign relations, defense, and economic policies. And Philippine judicial cases may be appealed to the US Supreme Court.

MANUEL LUIS QUEZON, 1878–1944

The life of Manuel Quezon, first president of the Commonwealth of the Philippines, paralleled the history of his people. He was born when the Philippines were still under Spanish rule. While studying law, he joined the insurrection led by Emilio Aguinaldo, and after the Spanish-American War he fought against American forces until 1901. After a brief imprisonment, he was admitted to the bar, but he spent the next 30 years devoted to one goal: complete independence for the Philippines. Not only through elective offices, but more importantly through his efforts to modify the US policies, he brought about the establishment of the Commonwealth in 1935—only semi-autonomous, but promised full independence in 1946. When the Japanese invaded, Quezon was forced to flee to Corregidor (where he was sworn in for his second term) and in March 1942 he finally had to leave on a submarine. He went to the US with his government-in-exile, and died from tuberculosis on 1 August 1944, only a few months before the Philippines were liberated. He was not forgotten, however: his native province was renamed for him, as was a city (between 1948–76 it served as his nation's capital). But his true memorial is as a model for vigorous and democratic leadership.

---

18 NOVEMBER 1935
Ethiopia The League of Nations votes to apply economic sanctions against Italy, but the crucial oil sanction is not considered. Italy reacts by severing economic ties with participating nations and institutes a strict system of control on food and raw materials. Meanwhile, France and Great Britain continue to seek a compromise solution, resulting in the Hoare-Laval proposals that excite public outcry in their unjustified concessions to Italy. International tensions reach the point where England and Italy are close to war in the Mediterranean. Despite a large fleet at Alexandria, and the promised support of France, Greece, Yugoslavia, and Turkey, Great Britain remains cautious because of weakness in air power.

24 NOVEMBER 1935
Greece King George II of Greece returns from exile in Great Britain. Despite restoration of the monarchy, the political influence of General Kondylis remains unassailable. On 1 December King George will call for general amnesty.

President Emilio Aguinaldo.

THE ROAD TO WAR 1933-1939

12 DECEMBER 1935
Egypt The constitution of 1923 is restored, a move long called for by nationalists. The interim constitution had done away with many democratic processes.

18 DECEMBER 1935
Great Britain As a result of widespread indignation over the Hoare-Laval proposals, which called for cession of large areas of Ethiopia to Italy, Foreign Secretary Sir Samuel Hoare resigns in disgrace. He is replaced by Anthony Eden.

OTHER EVENTS OF 1935
Medicine/Health Gerhard Domagk, a German bacteriologist, demonstrates that prontosil, forerunner of sulfa drugs, can kill streptococcal bacteria in mice; this marks the beginning of synthetic chemical compounds that will greatly reduce disease. At the Mayo Clinic in Rochester, Minnesota, the first 'blood bank' is established; it keeps blood under refrigeration for use in transfusions. The first artificial heart—a spirally coiled glass tube and pump—is used experimentally; it has been developed by Dr Alexis Carrel and Charles Lindbergh.

Technology Although several types of helicopters have been used since 1905, the first flight of a practical helicopter—capable of full take-off and forward flight control as well as stability and reasonable speed—occurs in France on 26 June.

Environment An earthquake in India leaves 60,000 dead.

Social Sciences Konrad Lorenz, an Austrian zoologist, describes the learning behavior of ducklings and goslings and notes how the young 'imprint' on natural and foster (including human) parents; this is only one of Lorenz's contributions to the study of animal behavior, or ethology, the discipline that he founds.

Literature Steinbeck's *Tortilla Flat*; George Seferis's *Mithistorima*; Isherwood's *Mr Norris Changes Trains*; Kawabata Yasunari's *Snow Country* (first version).

Drama/Entertainment T S Eliot's *Murder in the Cathedral*; Clifford Odet's *Waiting for Lefty*; Auden and Isherwood's *The Dog Beneath the Skin*; Giraudoux's *Tiger at the Gates (The Trojan War Will Not Take Place)*.

The Arts Max Beckmann completes his triptych, *Departure*; in Paris, the Catalonian-Spanish Julio Gonzalez begins a series of wrought-iron sculptures that will have a far-reaching effect on the art.

Music George Gershwin's opera *Porgy and Bess*; Roy Harris's *Second Symphony*; Prokofiev's ballet *Romeo and Juliet*. Nazi Germany bans 'jazz' of black or Jewish origin; Benny Goodman introduces 'swing' to a broader public.

Sports/Leisure The first night game between US baseball teams is played on 24 May at Crosley Field, Cincinnati; the Reds defeat the Philadelphia Phillies 2–1, after President Roosevelt turns on the lights.

Life/Customs Penguin Books of Great Britain issues the first 10 'literary' titles in cheap paperback editions (the first is *Ariel*, a biography of Shelley by André Maurois); although by no means the first paperbound books, these mark a revolution in Anglo-American book culture. Parker Brothers, a game company in Salem, Massachusetts, introduces a board game, MONOPOLY, developed by Charles Darrow of Philadelphia in 1931–33. It was initially rejected by Parker Brothers and Darrow made it himself and sold 5000 sets during 1934 before Parker Brothers bought him out. After Christmas 1935 the game becomes a fad and ends up as the best-selling patented game of all time.

Miscellaneous On 16 April a Pan American Clipper, a 19-ton flying boat, leaves San Francisco for Hawaii: arriving in Pearl Harbor 18 hours, 39 minutes later, it is the first transpacific transport plane. A parking meter designed by an American, Carlton Magee, is set up in Oklahoma City, the first such device put to use by any city.

15 JANUARY 1936
International Japanese representatives withdraw from the Second London Naval Conference, the aim of which is to control naval expansion. Italy will do likewise, but the US, France, and Great Britain will sign an agreement on 25 March.

20 JANUARY 1936
Great Britain King George V dies, distracting the British populace from the Ethiopian imbroglio. Edward VIII succeeds to the throne.

22 JANUARY 1936
France Inept diplomatic handling of the Ethiopian crisis brings down the Laval government. Suspicions exist that Laval supports reactionary forces. A new cabinet is organized under Albert Sarraut.

16 FEBRUARY 1936
Spain In the general elections, parties of the Left resoundingly defeat those of the Right. Three days later Manuel Azaña will organize a new cabinet; among its first acts are proclamation of general amnesty and restoration of Catalan autonomy. Social reform programs, including land redistribution, are reinstated. And government opposition to the church resumes.

26 FEBRUARY 1936
Japan To establish a military dictatorship, an insurgent group of young army officers assassinates former government leader Viscount Saitō, finance minister Korekiyo Takahashi, and other prominent political figures in Tokyo. Seventeen conspirators will be condemned to death by a 7 July military tribunal. During the decade, military reactionaries have assassinated other Japanese leaders.

29 FEBRUARY 1936
USA The Second Neutrality Act extends the 1935 Act through 1 May 1937, and adds a prohibition against granting any loans or credits to belligerents.

3 MARCH 1936

Great Britain In response to increasing international tensions the defense budget rises. The new funds go primarily to augment the Fleet Air Arm, pay for 250 new aircraft designated for home defense, and add four infantry battalions.

7 MARCH 1936

Germany With denunciation of the 1925 Locarno Pacts, Germany reoccupies the Rhineland—territory that was to remain demilitarized. Hitler rationalizes this move by citing danger from the Franco-Soviet alliance, and accompanies his expansionism with vague and reassuring offers of new treaties and alliances never to be realized. The balance of power is drastically altered, jeopardizing French ability to protect Eastern allies. Hitler's bluff succeeds, as the French are anxious to avoid bloodshed. Great Britain's mood is similar—refusal to apply military pressure or economic sanctions. On 12 March Great Britain, France, Belgium, Italy, and the League of Nations will denounce this German treaty violation. Tensions are high between France and Germany, but the crisis ends.

9 MARCH 1936

Japan The new premier, Koki Hirota, organizes a cabinet dominated by military figures, among them General Juichi Terauchi. The new government institutes a program of developing heavy industry.

9–10 MARCH 1936

Czechoslovakia After Premier Milan Hodža visits Vienna, a Czech-Austrian trade treaty will be signed on 2 April. Austria is seeking support in the face of German and Italian machinations. And Czechoslovakia, with French approval, seeks closer ties with Austria, Hungary, and the Little Entente. Meanwhile, Czechoslovakia is rearming and constructing a series of fortifications along its border with Germany.

30 MARCH 1936

Great Britain In what is to be the largest naval construction project in 15 years, the government publishes its intention to build 38 warships.

31 MARCH 1936

Great Britain Opposition to policies of Prime Minister Stanley Baldwin appears when Lord Eustace Percy resigns from the cabinet. Baldwin is generally condemned for his handling of the Hoare-Laval proposals for a solution to the Ethiopian crisis.

1 APRIL 1936

Austria Schuschnigg reinstates military conscription, in violation of the 1919 Treaty of Saint Germaine, to create a more dependable army than the Heimwehr, led by Prince Stahremberg.

7 APRIL 1936

South Africa The Representation of Natives Act is passed, solidifying government policy toward the blacks. In Cape Province, blacks may register but their names will be included on an electoral roll separate from that of white voters. The blacks' electoral privilege extends to allowing them to elect three whites to represent them in the Union Parliament. They may also elect representatives to a native council with advisory powers.

10 APRIL 1936

Spain The *Cortes*, or legislative body, endorses removal of incumbent President Alcalá Zamora from office for misuse of power. On 10 May Manuel Azaña will be chosen president.

28 APRIL 1936

Egypt After the death of King Fuad, his son, the popular King Farouk, becomes monarch. His rule is to provide a new stability, as royal usurpation of power becomes a dead issue. (Farouk will reign until 1952.)

2 MAY 1936

Egypt In the first elections under King Farouk, the Nationalists make impressive advances. Nahas Pasha organizes a cabinet that negotiates a treaty of 27 August with Great Britain.

5 MAY 1936

Ethiopia Italian forces reach Addis Ababa and capture the Ethiopian capital, as resistance collapses.

9 MAY 1936

Ethiopia Italy formally annexes Ethiopia and incorporates it into Italian East Africa together with Eritrea and Italian Somaliland. From his balcony on the Palazzo Venezia, Mussolini proclaims King Victor Emmanuel the Emperor of Abyssinia. He declares that the conquest of Ethiopia is only the beginning of the great age of fascist imperialism. Italy's allies—Germany, Austria, and Hungary—immediately recognize the annexation. Great Britain and France will recognize it in 1938.

14 MAY 1936

Austria Kurt Schuschnigg forces Heimwehr commander Prince Stahremberg to give up his offices of vice chancellor and head of the Fatherland Front. Stahremberg is the only internal threat to Schuschnigg's dictatorship.

1 JUNE 1936

Italy Austrian leader Schuschnigg visits Mussolini in Rome. The Duce persuades Schuschnigg to agree to a German-Austrian pact, concluded on 11 July. Mussolini's initiative comes from desire for Germany's support in the Italian conquest of Ethiopia.

5 JUNE 1936

France The majority gained by the Popular Front in the 3 May general elections leads to organization of the first Popular Front ministry under Socialist Party head Léon Blum. The government institutes a

THE ROAD TO WAR 1933-1939

program of widespread social reform. Among its first measures are the 40-hour week, nationalization of the Bank of France, suppression of fascist groups, nationalization of the munitions industry, and compulsory arbitration in labor disputes. The working classes are delighted, while capitalists feel alienated. This legislation leads to a sharp rise in production costs and now France, which has seemed relatively immune from the worldwide Depression, faces inflation and a flight of capital. Concurrently, increased international tensions call for costly rearmament.

17 JUNE 1936
Canada The Supreme Court nullifies the majority of the 'New Deal' programs initiated by the Socialist government of Prime Minister Richard Bennett in 1935.

4 JULY 1936
Ethiopia Emperor Haile Selassie pleads in vain for League of Nations assistance in expelling Italians from his country. Following Italian annexation of Ethiopia, the League Council will vote to discontinue all sanctions against Mussolini. With this ballot, the effectiveness of the League of Nations as a force for world peace ends. In the crises that follow, the League is virtually ignored.

11 JULY 1936
International Germany and Austria conclude an agreement in which Germany promises to respect Austria's independence, while Kurt Schuschnigg promises to lead Austria in a course appropriate to a German State.

17 JULY 1936
Spain The Civil War begins as Spanish Army units in Morocco proclaim a revolution against the Madrid government, now headed by the leftist-oriented Popular Front that has been unable to

---

HAILE SELASSIE I, 1892–1975

Claiming direct descent from King Solomon and the Queen of Sheba, Haile Selassie ruled Ethiopia as emperor from 1930 to 1974. Although he abolished slavery and introduced a written constitution, he retained complete power in major policymaking, and his support of higher education is now seen primarily as an attempt to replenish the educated elite decimated during the Italian occupation of World War II. As potentate and promoter of black African unity during the 1960s, however, Ras Tafari—as he was known before his accession—became the reluctant godhead of the seminal Jamaican Rastafarians (a group he considered lunatics). His reputation became tarnished because of his slow approach to educational, political, and land reform, which led to his deposition in 1974. The 'Conquering Lion of Judah' remains a controversial figure in the story of Africa's emergence.

---

check civil violence. The following day the uprising engulfs the mainland military posts of Cadiz, Seville, Saragossa, and Burgos. But in Madrid and Barcelona, the government resists. The insurgent leaders, Generals Francisco Franco, Emilio Mola, and José Sanjurjo, are supported by all parties of the Right—Clericals, Monarchists, and Conservative Republicans. Rebel leaders have behind them most of the army and air force, and huge numbers of North African troops. The Spanish Civil War is a conflict that prefigures World War II in its opposing ideologies and use of new weapons and tactics.

19 JULY 1936
China Despite active Japanese opposition, Chiang Kai-shek wins control of Kwantung, and on 6 September, of Kwangsi. Regional Chinese leaders call for war against Japan, as do Communists. But Chiang is not yet prepared to move against the Japanese.

20 JULY 1936
International In Montreux, an international conference votes to grant Turkey permission to refortify the Straits of the Bosporus and the Dardanelles. Turkey's request to do so stems from the Ethiopian crisis.

Spain Near Lisbon, en route to assume the position of Spanish Head of State, General José Sanjurjo dies as his airplane crashes on takeoff. Of the two remaining rebel leaders, General Mola is having difficulty in the north, but Franco is in full control of Morocco and of the veteran Army of Africa.

24 JULY 1936
Spain General Mola establishes a provisional rebel government, the Junta of National Defense under General Miguel Cabanellas, in Burgos. Franco, still abroad, will become a member of the Junta in early August.

AUGUST 1936
Germany At the Berlin Summer Olympics, Hitler uses the occasion to impress the world with organizational achievements of the Third Reich. But black American Jesse Owens wins four gold medals in track and field, discrediting Nazi theories of Aryan superiority.

6 AUGUST 1936
Spain Franco flies to Seville. At his request, Hitler has supplied transport aircraft to carry 1500 men of the Army of Africa to Seville, beginning on 29 July. And Italian fighter planes have covered merchant ships ferrying 2500 men with equipment from Morocco to Spain. Foreign involvement in the Civil War is extensive. Germany and Italy send 'volunteers' and equipment to support rebel forces, and the USSR provides the Leftist Government with assistance. Numerous Western writers and intellectuals also volunteer on the government side, forming international brigades—among the more noted par-

ticipants in and observers of the conflict are Ernest Hemingway, W H Auden, and Simone Weil. But many are disabused of their romantic notions by the harsh realities of the war and by strict Communist discipline.

7 AUGUST 1936
USA The government issues a proclamation of nonintervention in the Spanish Civil War. This is yet another signal to Hitler and Mussolini that democracies are not prepared to oppose the advance of fascism.

15 AUGUST 1936
Spain Rebel forces seize Badajoz and begin to move eastward up the Tagus to capture Talavera and Toledo.

19–23 AUGUST 1936
USSR As a footnote to the 1935 purges, Communist leaders Zinoviev, Kamenev, and some of their followers are retried as Trotskyites. They 'confess' to plotting with enemy powers against the Stalin regime, and are convicted and summarily executed.

27 AUGUST 1936
Egypt Egypt concludes a favorable treaty with Great Britain which calls for withdrawal of British forces, except for 10,000 men to be restricted to Suez Canal Zone duty. The British naval base at Alexandria is to be dismantled in eight years. Egyptian troops may re-enter the Sudan, and there may be unrestricted Egyptian emigration into that region.

29 AUGUST 1936
Rumania Political members of the Right force out Foreign Minister Nicholas Titulescu, who has links with the Little Entente, France and Russia in opposition to Germany. The Right is friendly toward Germany.

SEPTEMBER–NOVEMBER 1936
USA The presidential campaign is now in full swing, with Roosevelt and his New Deal under attack. About 80 percent of newspapers endorse the Republican opposition, elements of which become vitriolic in accusing Roosevelt of attempting to impose a centralized economy. Minor parties of both the Left and the Right try to appeal to those still suffering from the Depression by offering more drastic solutions. Roosevelt inspires such strong feeling that the prominent periodical *The Literary Digest* predicts a landslide victory for Republican aspirant Alfred M Landon.

4 SEPTEMBER 1936
Spain In Madrid a new Popular Front Government is organized under Largo Caballero. Both the Basques and the Catalonians are represented. On the same day, rebel forces overwhelm Irun, and eight days later will take San Sebastian.

9 SEPTEMBER 1936
Syria France and Syria sign a treaty of friendship and alliance. This pact provides that the French mandate will end in three years and Syria will join the League of Nations. Lebanon, with whom France signs a pact on 13 November, is to keep its individuality.

10 SEPTEMBER 1936
Czechoslovakia German minister of propaganda Joseph Goebbels accuses the Czechs of allowing Soviet airports on their soil and of playing host to Soviet military aircraft. Despite the Czech denial, the Nazi campaign of denunciation continues.

27 SEPTEMBER 1936
International France, Switzerland, and the Netherlands give up the gold standard.

28 SEPTEMBER 1936
Spain In Toledo, the ancient fortress of the Alcazar, occupied by rebel forces under Colonel José Moscardó, is relieved after a two-month siege. Realizing the great propaganda value, Franco has diverted troops from Madrid to quell attacking Republicans.

1 OCTOBER 1936
China The seven secret demands presented by the Japanese to China are made public. Under threat of invasion, the Japanese demand brigading of Japanese with Chinese troops against Chinese Communists, placement of Japanese 'advisers' in all offices of government, autonomy for China's five northern provinces, and a reduction in trade tariffs to 1928 levels. The Nanking Government refuses to acquiesce despite the Japanese troops at Shanghai.

Spain After a bloodless coup d'état in Salamanca, Franco becomes Spanish Head of State in Burgos. He will be popularly known as *Caudillo*—an echo of Hitler's *Führer*—and retains personal control over the powerful Army of Africa.

2 OCTOBER 1936
France Faced with uncontrollable inflation, the Socialist Government of Léon Blum devalues the franc. Only economic co-operation by the US and Great Britain prevents chaos in world money markets.

6 OCTOBER 1936
Great Britain At a party conference Labour rejects the request of the Communist Party for affiliation. And on 12 October, fascist Oswald Moseley will lead an anti-Semitic march through London to Whitechapel, where he is driven out.

8 OCTOBER 1936
Spain The Basque Provinces win from the Popular Front Government a promise of home rule. President José Aguirre will lead the first Basque Government.

10 OCTOBER 1936
Austria Schuschnigg consolidates his power by

THE ROAD TO WAR 1933-1939

dissolving the Heimwehr, whose members are then reinstated into the Fatherland Front militia. He completes the purge by removing Heimwehr members from his cabinet. On 18 October Schuschnigg becomes Front Führer.

12 OCTOBER 1936
Palestine A general strike, called by Arab leaders to protest Jewish claims, ends. In April the Arab High Committee had been organized to unite concerned Arab groups against Jewish demands for land purchases and increased immigration. The Arab protest has resulted in riots, and Britain tries to calm the situation by bringing in troops and appointing the Reed Commission to investigate and make recommendations.

14 OCTOBER 1936
Belgium After German occupation of the Rhineland unopposed by the European powers, Belgium removes itself from military alliance with France, fearing trouble with Germany.

25 OCTOBER 1936
International The Berlin-Rome Axis is established through the new Italian foreign minister (and Mussolini's son-in-law) Count Galeazzo Ciano, who confers in Berlin until 27 October. This pact strengthens the position of Germany and Italy in opposition to Great Britain and France.

3 NOVEMBER 1936
Ireland The Dail endorses a new constitution that reinstates the Senate. This constitution omits mention of Ireland's relation to Great Britain.
USA In the presidential election, Roosevelt defeats Landon by a landslide—27,751,612 popular votes to 16,681,913, and with an even more dramatic majority in the electoral college, 523 to 8. The Democrats retain majorities in the Senate and House. Populist candidate William Lemke gets 891,858 votes, Socialist Norman Thomas gets 187,342, and Communist Earl Browder 80,181.

6 NOVEMBER 1936
Spain Rebel forces begin the siege of Madrid, forcing the government to flee to Valencia. Meanwhile, government troops endure heavy rebel air bombardment and widespread street fighting in the suburbs.

14 NOVEMBER 1936
Germany Hitler denounces the Treaty of Versailles provisions that mandate international control of German rivers. Only France, Czechoslovakia, and Yugoslavia protest.

18 NOVEMBER 1936
Spain Italy and Germany issue proclamations recognizing the government of Franco. Meanwhile, Britain and France press for nonintervention by European powers—they fear a European war.

Germany, Italy, and the USSR pay lip service to nonintervention, but continue to provide their ideological Spanish allies with assistance. Mussolini, openly supporting Franco, will send some 75,000 Italian soldiers. Hitler tries to prolong the Spanish conflict, which distracts international attention from Germany.

23 NOVEMBER 1936
Mexico Under the social and reform program of General Lazaro Cardenas, the peasants receive expropriated lands. The new Expropriation Law permits the government to seize other private property, resulting in the 1937 nationalization of the railroads and of Standard Oil and other petroleum companies.

25 NOVEMBER 1936
International The Anti-Comintern Pact is concluded by Germany and Japan. Italy joins later. Secret clauses of the pact show that the aim is to threaten the USSR from both East and West. It is not a formal alliance, as the Japanese do not want to be drawn into a European war. They hope that strengthening Germany against the Soviets, will distract Britain from Asian affairs.

1–23 DECEMBER 1936
International An Inter-American Conference for

THE NEW DEAL'S AGENCIES

'Alphabet soup' they were dubbed, usually with a derogatory tone, by critics of Roosevelt's New Deal. And there was no denying that to achieve his goals FDR extended the Federal Government's role in many areas of American life. Within the famous '100 Days' alone he got Congress to pass legislation setting up such agencies as the Agricultural Adjustment Administration (AAA), Home Owners Loan Corporation (HOLC), Public Works Administration (PWA), National Recovery Administration (NRA), and several others. But it is misleading to dismiss them as FDR's 'stacked deck.' The Tennessee Valley Authority (TVA), in some ways the most controversial—it looked like the kind of project socialists or communists wanted—was really the long-time crusade of Senator George Norris. The Civilian Conservation Corps (CCC), for all its makeshift aspects, put some 2,500,000 young Americans to work conserving forests and natural resources. The theater, arts, music, and writers' projects, all under the Works Progress (later Projects) Administration (WPA), sustained thousands of creative talents at everything from producing Shakespeare and painting murals to performing symphonies and writing guidebooks. Stopgaps some of them may have been, but imagine the US without its SSA (Social Security Administration), or the FCC (Federal Communications Commission), or the SEC (Securities and Exchange Commission). Perhaps the American addiction to acronyms turned these otherwise remote and humorless bureaucracies into something familiar and amusing.

the Maintenance of Peace meets in Buenos Aires, Argentina. It closes with an agreement by Western Hemisphere nations to consult when any faces aggression.

5 DECEMBER 1936
USSR The political structure of the Soviet Government is reorganized and a new 'democratic' constitution adopted, promising universal suffrage, secret ballot, and direct election to higher assemblies. Despite guarantee of civil liberties, the Communist Party is the only political organization allowed. This constitution, under which the USSR will govern itself in the decades that follow, is theoretically one of the most progressive and democratic ever devised; in practice, it does not lead to a democratic society.

8 DECEMBER 1936
Nicaragua Anastasio Somoza becomes president of Nicaragua in a rigged election. Head of Nicaragua's army, the National Guard, since 1933, Somoza had led what was a thinly disguised revolt by the National Guard in June, gotten himself nominated for president, and then resigned his post as chief of the army. Elected, he will reassume leadership of the army on 19 December, move quickly to consolidate his hold over the country, and rule as dictator until his assassination (1956) when his son will take over.

10 DECEMBER 1936
Great Britain King Edward VIII abdicates voluntarily to marry American-born divorcee Wallis Warfield Simpson. This move follows much gossip and refusal of the Baldwin Government to permit a morganatic marriage. Succeeded by his brother, King George VI, Edward becomes Duke of Windsor.

12–25 DECEMBER 1936
China Chiang Kai-shek is arrested by one of his generals, Chang Hseuh-liang, while visiting troops employed in blockading the Communist Shensi Province. After complicated negotiations involving the Communist leader Chou En-lai, Chiang is released, but he has been compelled to agree to take a more anti-Japanese stance. A recent defeat for the Japanese-backed warlord in Suiyuan Province has shown that the Japanese can be beaten.

OTHER EVENTS OF 1936
Medicine/Health Dr Egaz-Moniz, a Portuguese neurologist, performs the first psychosurgical operation, the beginnings of prefrontal lobotomy, or leukotomy, an operation used to alleviate uncontrollable pain or severe mental disorder.
Social Sciences John Maynard Keynes's *The General Theory of Employment, Interest, and Money* is an influential work in economics.
Ideas/Beliefs A J Ayer's *Language, Truth and Logic*.
Literature Bernanos's *Journal of a Country Priest*; Graham Greene's *This Gun for Hire*; Vladimir

The Duke and Duchess of Windsor.

Nabokov's *Despair*; Dylan Thomas's *Twenty-Five Poems*; Margaret Mitchell's *Gone With the Wind*.
Drama/Entertainment Garcia-Lorca's *House of Bernarda Alba*; Chaplin's *Modern Times*.
The Arts Mondrian's *Composition in Red and Blue*; Marino Marini's sculpture *The Horseman*.
Architecture Frank Lloyd Wright begins building a house for the Kaufmann family at Bear Run, Pennsylvania; it is known as 'Falling Water' (completed 1939).
Music Prokofiev's *Peter and the Wolf*; Bartok's *Music for Strings, Percussion and Celeste*.
Life/Customs The first popular music chart based on sales is published by *The Billboard* (4 January) in New York City; it lists the 10 best sellers, with 'Stop, Look and Listen' by Joe Venuti and his Orchestra in the top position.

2 JANUARY 1937
International The Anglo-Italian Mediterranean Agreement is signed. The pact provides for respect of rights and interests in the Mediterranean Sea, as well as independence and integrity for Spain, still in the throes of civil war.

6 JANUARY 1937
USA Congress passes a resolution that prohibits shipment of munitions to either side in the Spanish Civil War.

20 JANUARY 1937
USA In his inaugural address for his second term as president, Roosevelt hammers at the nation's economic problems, using another phrase that will often be quoted: 'I see one-third of a nation ill-housed, ill-clad, ill-nourished.'

22–30 JANUARY 1937
USSR The Communist Party purge continues with

THE ROAD TO WAR 1933-1939

WPA workers loading flood debris in Louisville, Kentucky—February 1937.

the trial and conviction of Georgei Piatakov, Karl Radek, and other leaders. Thirteen receive the death penalty. The purge goes on for the rest of the year, affecting all political levels of Soviet administration. Subsequently, the diplomatic service and even the army will be purged of Trotskyites and others objectionable to Stalin.

28 JANUARY 1937
Canada The British Privy Council's judicial committee declares unconstitutional most of the Socialist legislation of the Bennett Government, begun in 1935. This conclusion had been rendered earlier by the Canadian Supreme Court.
China The anti-Communist campaign ends as the Shensi (Communist) Government and the Nanking (Nationalist) Government agree to co-operate against their common enemy, the Japanese. For the duration of the undeclared war on Japan, all factions of the Chinese population, including Communists, will follow the orders of the central government led by Chiang Kai-shek.

8 FEBRUARY 1937
Spain Franco's rebel forces, reinforced by Italian troops, capture Malaga.

14 FEBRUARY 1937
Austria The idea of a restoration of the Habsburg Monarchy circulates when Schuschnigg insists that he has the right to decide the question. The restoration of the monarchy is vehemently opposed by Hitler and the Nazi Party, who display disapproval in a series of demonstrations.

19 FEBRUARY 1937
Ethiopia Italian control over Ethiopia remains tenuous as an assassination attempt is made on Viceroy General Rodolfo Graziani and his staff in Addis Ababa. This leads to widespread arrests and executions.

1 MARCH 1937
Poland Government supporters are unified as the Camp of National Unity by Colonel Adam Koc. This organization calls for popular support of the army, anti-Communism, support of the 1935 constitution, and land reform. Workers and peasants react by forming a Workers, Peasants, and Intellectuals Group opposed to Koc. Widespread peasant strikes will lead to sporadic violence. Hitler continues to see Poland as a buffer zone between Germany and the Soviet Union.

A scene on an abandoned farm in the Dust Bowl—Oklahoma, 1936.

5 MARCH 1937
Hungary A well-organized Nazi conspiracy is uncovered, resulting in arrest of Nazi leader Ferenc Szalasi and other plotters. The Nazis support land reform and other agrarian measures and the government is unsuccessful in quelling their activity.

14 MARCH 1937
Germany Pope Pius XI issues an encyclical titled 'On the Condition of the Catholic Church in the German Reich,' which points out the racism and paganism essential to Nazism. Despite these insights, church officials within the Reich remain silent. Hitler campaigns against the church—hounding churchmen from office either by expulsion or by commitment to concentration camps. A frequent Nazi technique is use of 'morality trials' to turn public opinion against ecclesiastics.

16 MARCH 1937
North Africa Mussolini pays a spectacular visit to Libya, ostensibly to open a new military road. Declared a Protector of Islam, he is presented with a Sword of Islam. Great Britain and France view this as a threat to their influence in the Middle East and North Africa.

25 MARCH 1937
International Italy and Yugoslavia conclude a five-year nonaggression and neutrality pact in which Yugoslavia agrees to recognize Italian sovereignty in Ethiopia. In return, Italy guarantees the existing borders and grants broad trade concessions. With this pact hostility between the two nations ends, as Yugoslav Premier Milan Stoyadinovich seeks a middle road between France and Italy.

1 APRIL 1937
India The new constitution becomes effective, but the All-India Congress Party which, as the only well-organized national political group, had won a majority in the January and February elections for the provincial assemblies, demands independence from Britain and refuses to form ministries in the provinces. After extensive negotiations, the party will begin to organize the mandated bodies in July.

2 APRIL 1937
South Africa The government bans political activity by foreigners, including nonnaturalized German residents, in Southwest Africa. Hitler's protests are ignored, and in the fall a new German Party will replace the illegal German Bund.

THE ROAD TO WAR 1933-1939

22 APRIL 1937
International Austrian leader Schuschnigg visits Mussolini in Venice. In this meeting Mussolini objects to possible restoration of the Habsburg Monarchy in Austria, opposes a proposed pact between Austria and Czechoslovakia, and warns that Italy cannot provide military protection against German aggression. Mussolini advises Schuschnigg to allow Nazis into the Austrian Government and to pursue friendly relations with Hungary. Schuschnigg ignores these suggestions and instead will try to forge alliances with Czechoslovakia, the Little Entente, and France. Within Austria, these diplomatic initiatives will dismay the Pan-Germans and the Nazis.

26 APRIL 1937
Spain In an event that excites international horror, the Basque village of Guernica is destroyed in a three-hour air raid by waves of Nazi German bombers. Of the civilian population, 1654 are killed and 889 are wounded. Franco at first denies German involvement and the extent of damage. But in 1946 Hermann Goering will admit that Guernica was a testing ground for German air strategy. The painter Picasso will decry the horrors of war and commemorate Guernica in his masterpiece of that name.

1 MAY 1937
USA President Roosevelt signs the third Neutrality Act, extending the Neutrality Acts of 1935 and 1936, due to expire at midnight. The act not only continues the ban on export of arms to belligerents and prohibits these nations from selling their securities in the US, but bans US ships from transporting arms into belligerents' zones. It requires combatant nations to pay cash for certain non-military goods purchased in the US and carry them in their own ships ('cash and carry').

17 MAY 1937
Spain The Popular Front Government of Largo Caballero is supplanted by one led by Socialist Juan Negrin. The new government resolves to win the Civil War before continuing with its program of social reform. Indalecio Prieto is named to the combined defense ministries.

28 MAY 1937
Great Britain After retirement of Stanley Baldwin, Chancellor of the Exchequer Neville Chamberlain becomes prime minister. Chamberlain designates his goal as the achievement of peace in Europe. His policy of appeasement will offer concessions to Germany and Italy.

12 JUNE 1937
USSR In the continuing purge, a secret court martial convicts and executes Marshal Michael Tukhachevsky, along with seven other ranking army generals. (Tukhachevsky had been trying to convert the army to modern lines, with emphasis on indepen-

---

THE ASCENT OF TOTALITARIANISM

The economic, political, social, and ideological crises that accumulated throughout the world in the years after World War I inevitably cast doubt on the viability of open democratic forms of government. People wanted law and order and were ready to endorse a government that promised and delivered it. So it was that Mussolini and his Fascists came to power in Italy in the 1920s and Hitler and his Nazis took over in the early 1930s. Meanwhile, the 1917 Bolshevik-Communist Revolution in Russia had consolidated its power in the person of Joseph Stalin. By the 1930s, these three leaders were running totalitarian states, differing in many of their principles and promises, but sharing such elements as appeals to nationalism, centralization of power, and control of all aspects of social life. Other leaders emulated them—for example, Franco in Spain—and groups in other countries tried to promote similar parties. (Roosevelt was challenged in the election of 1936, when both Rightists and Leftists tried to offer alternatives to the New Deal.) In their foreign policies, the totalitarian states were aggressively expansionist. Italy invaded Ethiopia—and the liberal democracies remained paralyzed. Germany began to take over territory from the Rhineland to Czechoslovakia—the democracies acquiesced. Russia consolidated its hold across Asia, then divided up Poland with Germany and helped itself to the Baltic States. Totalitarianism was in the ascendant.

---

dent tank forces.) These military leaders had been accused of conspiracy with Germany and Japan. Up to 35,000 officers will be arrested and executed or will disappear during the coming months.

18 JUNE 1937
Spain Franco's rebel forces capture Bilbao after protracted combat and numerous air attacks on the Basque stronghold. Rebels continue their push toward Santander.

8 JULY 1937
Palestine In London, the Peel Report is issued, recommending an end to the Palestine Mandate and partitioning of the area into Arab and Jewish states, with Britain retaining power over Jerusalem and Bethlehem with a corridor to the sea. Parliament is indecisive about the report, and both the Arabs and the Jews oppose its recommendations.

9 JULY 1937
International Turkey, Iraq, Iran, and Afghanistan sign a nonaggression pact. This loose alliance of Moslem states counters European imperialist plans.

19 JULY 1937
France The Léon Blum government resigns and a new government is organized under Radical Socialist Camille Chautemps, with Blum as vice-premier. This government addresses the monumental task of economic reconstruction.

Adolf Hitler and Francisco Franco.

THE ROAD TO WAR 1933-1939

Amelia Earhart inspecting her plane.

28 JULY 1937
China Japanese troops capture Peking and seize Tientsin the following day. During these early months of the war, the Chinese are at a disadvantage because of lack of equipment and organization. Meanwhile, the Japanese have been making favorable offers of settlement, but Chiang Kai-shek will decide by early August to fight.

2 AUGUST 1937
Palestine The World Zionist Congress votes to endorse the Peel Plan, after revisions favoring the Jews. Non-Zionist Jews denounce the plan as a violation of the Balfour Declaration.

11 AUGUST 1937
China At Shanghai, a large Japanese naval force is surrounded by the Chinese. After a reinforcing Japanese land army arrives, Shanghai will fall to the Japanese on 8 November.

12 AUGUST 1937
Spain The government assumes control of the Catalan Government, which had been allowed autonomy under the socialist regimes.

15 AUGUST 1937
Canada Prime Minister Mackenzie King names the Rowell Commission to revise the British North America Act. The most important task of this royal commission is to study confederate relations, especially economic and political relations between national and provincial governments.

25 AUGUST 1937
China Japan extends its naval blockade of South China to the entire coast of the country.

29 AUGUST 1937
China China and the USSR conclude a nonaggres-

sion treaty. Now the Soviets begin to sell badly-needed warplanes and munitions to China after the 5 October League of Nations condemnation of Japan. World opinion has turned against Japan due to relentless bombing of Chinese cities.

8 SEPTEMBER 1937
Palestine A Pan-Arab Conference held at Bludan, Syria, considers the Palestine question. Some 400 representatives vote against the Peel Plan. The Arab demands include an end to the British Mandate; creation of an independent unpartitioned state; cessation of Jewish immigration; and abandonment of a Jewish national homeland. The Palestinian Jews are to become a guaranteed minority within the Arab state. The conference also decides to support financially the efforts of Palestinian Arabs and boycott Jewish goods and enterprises.

5 OCTOBER 1937
USA In a major speech in Chicago, President Roosevelt attacks isolationists who are becoming vocal throughout the country. He proposes that the US lead peace-loving nations in placing aggressive nations under quarantine.

11 OCTOBER 1937
Hungary Tibor Eckhardt, leader of the Agrarian Party (the most important opposition to the Koloman Daranyi dictatorship) joins with the Legitimists. Opposition parties begin to consider restoration of the Habsburg Monarchy as the best way to subdue fascist and Nazi elements in Hungary.

13 OCTOBER 1937
Belgium In a diplomatic note to Brussels, Germany offers guarantees for the inviolability and integrity of Belgium, as long as Belgium desists from participating in military action against Germany.

16 OCTOBER 1937
Czechoslovakia At Teplitz, the Czech police quell a meeting of the Sudeten German Party. Leader Henlein decries the government's repressive measures and issues a call for autonomy of Germans within the borders of Czechoslovakia. The resulting political unrest will cause the government to postpone general elections set for November and ban protest meetings.

3 NOVEMBER 1937
International The Brussels Conference of the signatories to the 1922 Nine Powers Treaty convenes to end hostilities between China and Japan. Japan does not attend, and on 24 November the conference will fail.

17 NOVEMBER 1937
Germany British cabinet member Lord Halifax visits Hitler at Berchtesgaden to ferret out German goals and investigate ways of ensuring peace. Like many other foreign visitors, he is impressed by Nazi social and industrial successes.

'Broke, sick baby, car trouble'—California, 1937.

24 NOVEMBER 1937

Germany Financier Hjalmar Schacht is removed as minister of economics but permitted to remain as president of the Reichsbank. Although he had been successful in developing German trade through barter agreements, he is not considered radical enough by Nazi extremists. Walther Funk replaces him.

28 NOVEMBER 1937

Spain Franco declares a naval blockade of the Spanish coastline, based on the island of Majorca—this to prevent resupplying of Loyalist forces.

1–17 DECEMBER 1937

France Foreign minister Yvon Delbos attempts to resurrect the French alliance system by completing a tour of Poland, Rumania, Yugoslavia, and Czechoslovakia. He is disappointed to find little preparedness or resolution against German aggression. Both Poland and Yugoslavia prefer to act unilaterally.

5 DECEMBER 1937

Spain In the Teruel region, the Loyalists begin a counteroffensive. After Teruel is captured on 19 December, momentum of the Loyalists slows.

7 DECEMBER 1937

Turkey The government denounces its 1926 treaty of friendship with Syria. A crisis develops as the French send a military mission to Ankara, raising the threat of war.

12 DECEMBER 1937

International The US gunboat *Panay* is bombed by the Japanese and sinks in China's Yangtze River. On 14 December Japan apologizes, agrees to an indemnity, and promises to avoid such incidents.

13 DECEMBER 1937

China After heavy fighting, Nanking falls to the Japanese, as the Chinese Army withdraws. Chiang Kai-shek refuses to accept peace terms offered by the Japanese, who are growing weary of the economic burden of the war.

OTHER EVENTS OF 1937

Science Carl D Anderson and Seth Neddermeyer,

THE ROAD TO WAR 1933-1939

Generalissimo and Mme Chiang Kai-shek, 1937.

American physicists, discover particles with a greater ability than electrons to penetrate matter; years later these will be identified as mu-mesons, elementary particles predicted by the Japanese physicist Yukawa in 1935. Alan Turing, British mathematician and logician, publishes his first paper to attract attention, a seminal work on the mathematical theory behind computers; Turing will contribute many ideas to computer mathematics and programming.

Technology The first successful jet engine, based on the work of Frank Whittle, is tested in Great Britain. San Francisco's Golden Gate Bridge, begun in 1933, is completed: its span of 4200 feet (1280 meters) makes it one of the longest suspension bridges in the world. The French liner SS *Normandie* crosses the Atlantic in 3 days, 23 hours, 2 minutes and gains the symbolic Blue Ribbon. Three Russian aviators fly nonstop from Moscow to Vancouver over the North Pole (5288 miles) in June; in July three more Russians set a new nonstop distance record by flying from Moscow to Riverside, California, some 6262 miles. On 6 May the German dirigible *Hindenburg* explodes while tying up at Lakehurst, New Jersey, killing 36 people and halting commercial airship traffic and development. And on 2 July, while on a round-the-world flight, American aviator Amelia Earhart (and her copilot, Frederick Noonan) vanish over the Pacific Ocean after radio contact suddenly stops; despite endless rumors and speculation, no trace of the flier will ever be found.

Environment The Ohio and Mississippi Rivers flood their valleys, killing 135 people, leaving 1 million homeless, and destroying $400 million worth of property.

Literature Ignazio Silone's *Bread and Wine*; Ernest Hemingway's *To Have and Have Not*; John Steinbeck's *Of Mice and Men*; J R R Tolkien's *The Hobbit*; Andre Malraux's *L'Espoir (Man's Hope)*.

Drama/Entertainment Jean Renoir's classic antiwar film *Grand Illusion*; *Pins and Needles*, a musical presented by the International Ladies Garment Workers Union, opens in New York and breaks records for musicals. Walt Disney releases the first feature-length (75 minutes), all-color, animated cartoon with sound—*Snow White and the Seven Dwarfs*.

The Arts Picasso's *Guernica*; in Munich, the Nazis organize a large exhibit of what they label 'degenerate'—that is, modern—art especially that by Jewish artists.

Music Alban Berg's opera *Lulu* (only two acts of which were completed at his death in 1935) is premiered in Zurich. Shostakovich's *Fifth Symphony* restores him to favor with Communist authorities. Stravinsky's ballet *Jeu de Cartes (Card Party*, based on his favorite game of poker), premieres in New York City. The National Broadcasting Corporation forms a special symphony in New York for Arturo Toscanini, who will conduct it till 1954. Two modern classics from this year are Carl Orff's *Carmina Burana* and Aaron Copland's *El Salon Mexico*.

Sports/Leisure On 22 June Joe Louis becomes

Pablo Picasso.

world heavyweight boxing champion by knocking out James Braddock in the eighth round in Chicago; Louis is the second black to hold the title and will retain it until he retires in 1949.

4 JANUARY 1938

Palestine Britain announces postponement of partition and appointment of a new investigative commission led by Sir John Woodhead. The situation disintegrates and Sir Harold MacMichael is sent on 3 March to replace Wauchope as high commissioner. The British troop strength in Palestine increases to 30,000. Terrorist actions of both Arabs and Jews continue.

10 JANUARY 1938

China After Chinese destruction of Japanese mills, the Japanese capture Tsingtao. They move on toward the Yellow River, which they will reach in March. Although the Japanese capture large cities, the countryside remains under Chinese guerrilla control.

28 JANUARY 1938

USA President Roosevelt submits to Congress a recommendation calling for increased appropriations for building the armed forces, particularly the Navy.

THE ROAD TO WAR 1933-1939

4 FEBRUARY 1938

Germany In a major reorganization, radical Nazis replace conservative officials in key administrative posts. Hitler assumes leadership of the ministry of war, a post occupied by Werner von Blomberg. General Heinrich von Brauchitsch replaces Werner von Fritsch as commander-in-chief of the army. Foreign minister Constantin von Neurath is replaced by Joachim von Ribbentrop. This demotion for the army deprives Hitler of its expertise in strategic planning.

12 FEBRUARY 1938

Austria At a Berchtesgaden conference, Schuschnigg is bullied by Hitler into agreeing to provide amnesty for imprisoned Austrian Nazis, to include Nazis in his cabinet and to allow them greater freedom of activity. Four days later Nazi Arthur Seyss-Inquart becomes minister of the interior.

15 FEBRUARY 1938

Spain After recapture of Teruel, Franco's forces begin a dramatic drive toward the Mediterranean. On 14 April they will capture Vinaroz, cutting off Loyalists in Castile from Barcelona and Catalonia. Over the summer the two sides will confront each other across the Ebro River.

20 FEBRUARY 1938

Great Britain Foreign Secretary Anthony Eden resigns from the Chamberlain government over policy toward Italy. Lord Halifax, who had won respect as a conciliator in India, replaces him.

24 FEBRUARY 1938

Austria In response to Hitler's speech of 20 February, which guaranteed protection to German minorities in other nations, Schuschnigg guarantees protection to 10 million Germans outside the Reich, and appeals for support for Austrian independence. Nazi-provoked uprisings spread and Schuschnigg calls for a plebiscite on Austrian independence.

2-15 MARCH 1938

USSR The purge continues with trial and conviction of Nikolai Bukharin, Alexei Rykov, Genrikh Yagoda, and other Bolshevik leaders. Accused of a Trotskyite conspiracy to restore bourgeois capitalism, they are executed.

4 MARCH 1938

Czechoslovakia Premier Hodža responds to Hitler's 20 February speech by declaring that his nation intends to defend itself against any outside interference.

11 MARCH 1938

Austria Hitler issues an ultimatum calling for resignation of Schuschnigg and postponement of the plebiscite, while massing German troops on the

Hitler reviews his troops—Berlin, 30 January 1938.

border. Schuschnigg resigns and Seyss-Inquart becomes chancellor.

12 MARCH 1938
Austria Meeting no resistance, the German Army begins occupation of Austria. On 13 March Austria is proclaimed a province of the German Reich, completing the *Anschluss* (union). The international reaction is subdued, as Hitler's move was expected.

14 MARCH 1938
Austria Hitler arrives in Vienna to complete the annexation. All anti-Nazis are pursued with a vengeance—those who do not commit suicide or flee are sent to concentration camps; Schuschnigg is held in prison without trial. Persecution of Austrian Jews begins.
Czechoslovakia With the Austrian annexation, Czechoslovakia is surrounded on three sides by German-controlled territory, and Hitler reiterates his intention to improve relations between Prague and Berlin. France and the USSR announce that they will support the Czechs, per treaty agreements.

16–19 MARCH 1938
Poland While world attention focuses on Austria, the Polish Government delivers an ultimatum to Lithuania calling for an end to hostilities and restoration of relations. Lithuania submits.

18 MARCH 1938
Mexico The government expropriates the property of the American and British oil companies, valued at $450 million. Despite economic and diplomatic sanctions, Mexico stands firm. On 5 September Mexico will conclude oil barter agreements with Germany, Italy, and other nations who agree to send manufactured goods in exchange for oil.

5–6 APRIL 1938
International The foreign ministers of Denmark, Norway, Sweden, and Finland confer on developing a common defense policy for the Scandinavian States. Reluctance of Denmark to challenge the might of Germany leaves rearmament and defense policies up to the individual governments.

16 APRIL 1938
International Britain and Italy conclude a pact in which Britain promises to recognize Italian sovereignty in Ethiopia and to use influence to persuade other nations to do so. Italy is to withdraw troops from Spain at the end of the civil war, cease hostile propaganda in the Near East, and help maintain the status quo in that region. The pact will go into effect when the Spanish Civil War ends. By this agreement Britain hopes to ensure security in the Mediterranean and Italy to balance its oppressive alliance with Germany.

24 APRIL 1938
Czechoslovakia A crisis develops with Germany as Sudeten leader Henlein issues the Carlsbad Program. Among the eight proposals are demands for equality and autonomy for German-speaking regions of the state, and for revision of Czech policy toward Germany. Despite advice by France and Britain to make concessions, the Prague Government rejects Sudeten demands. In May the situation worsens rapidly as the Germans are rumored to have troops massed on the border, and the government rushes to mobilize 400,000 men. When France and Britain warn Germany, the crisis dissolves. Over the summer, Henlein and the Prague Government try to work out a compromise.

25 APRIL 1938
Ireland Britain and Ireland conclude a three-year pact that temporarily ends the trouble between them. The problem of Northern Ireland is set aside. Tariffs are dropped, and Britain hands over its Irish coastal defenses.

30 APRIL 1938
Switzerland The government asks the League of Nations for unconditional neutrality. This move derives from the increasing political instability in Central Europe, and the tenuous position of the Swiss between the League and the Rome-Berlin Axis. The League agrees, absolving Switzerland from any obligation to participate in economic sanctions against aggressors.

3–9 MAY 1938
International Hitler pays a state visit to Mussolini in Rome. The apparent purpose of the trip is to emphasize the Rome-Berlin Axis.

17 MAY 1938
USA Congress adopts the Naval Expansion Act, providing funds for a ten-year program to build a two-ocean navy.

26 MAY 1938
USA The House sets up a committee to investigate un-American activities by both Right and Left; eventually it will concentrate on activities of the Left.

11 JULY–10 AUGUST 1938
USSR A clash provoked by the Japanese occurs with Russian forces along the Manchukuo-Korean border. Fierce fighting, in which the Japanese suffer heavy losses, is followed by a truce.

19–21 JULY 1938
International To demonstrate Anglo-French solidarity, British King George VI and Queen Elizabeth pay a state visit to Paris.

31 JULY 1938
Bulgaria The government extracts an agreement from Greece, representing the Little Entente, permitting rearmament. In fact, Bulgarian rearmament is well under way with German help, even though

THE ROAD TO WAR 1933-1939

Bulgaria refuses to accede to Nazi policies. In August Bulgaria will accept a $10 million Franco-British loan for rearmament.

3 AUGUST 1938
Italy The Mussolini Government implements a racist program against the few Italian Jews—banning Jewish students and teachers from the schools, exiling Jewish immigrants who have arrived since 1919, and forbidding intermarriage of Jews and gentiles.

21–23 AUGUST 1938
International In Bled, Yugoslavia, statesmen of the Little Entente recognize Hungary's right to rearm and negotiate nonaggression pacts.

7 SEPTEMBER 1938
Czechoslovakia The second crisis with Germany begins as the Sudeten (German-speaking) faction breaks off discussions with the Prague Government. Street disturbances by extremists, once sporadic, now increase.

12 SEPTEMBER 1938
Czechoslovakia In a Nuremberg speech, Hitler demands the right of self-determination for the Sudeten Czechs. The Czech Government proclaims martial law. Sudeten leader Henlein and others escape across the border to Germany on 15 September.

15 SEPTEMBER 1938
Czechoslovakia With French support, British Prime Minister Chamberlain meets with Hitler at Berchtesgaden to defuse the Czech crisis. His plan is to cede to Germany areas where more than half the population supports *Anschluss*, but Hitler now says this is not enough. Britain and France press the Czechs to accede to German demands. During the next week both Hungary and Poland issue claims for Czech territory. On 22 September Premier Hodža resigns and a new government is formed by General Jan Sirovy.

22 SEPTEMBER 1938
China The Japanese organize a United Council for China in Peking to overthrow the Nationalist regime of Chiang Kai-shek and establish a Japanese protectorate.

22–23 SEPTEMBER 1938
Czechoslovakia Chamberlain visits Hitler a second time at Godesberg. Now Hitler demands immediate cession of the German regions of Czechoslovakia and plebiscites in areas with large German minorities. Chamberlain is willing, but the British Cabinet finds these terms unacceptable. On the 23rd Czechoslovakia calls for mobilization and the other European powers place themselves in a state of full alert. An appeal is sent to Mussolini to mediate and Hitler agrees to the Munich Conference.

29 SEPTEMBER 1938
Czechoslovakia At the Munich Conference, where the Czechs are not represented, Chamberlain, Hitler, Mussolini, French Premier Édouard Daladier, and their foreign ministers agree to Nazi demands for cession of the disputed Czech territory, as regulated by an international commission. Britain and France agree to guarantee the new Czech frontiers. Chamberlain returns home to cheers, announcing 'peace for our time.' But in a British parliamentary debate a few days later, Chamberlain is attacked and a sense of national shame arises that Britain has sacrificed a democracy to avoid war. In France the result is just as divisive—the French alliance system lies in ruins. Meanwhile, rearmament efforts start up in both nations—in Britain with an attitude of determination and unity, and in France halfheartedly and beset by political dissension.

1–10 OCTOBER 1938
Czechoslovakia As agreed at Munich, German annexation of Czech territory takes place. There is no plebiscite and the Nazis acquire 10,000 square miles inhabited by 2.8 million Germans and 700,000 Czechs.

2 OCTOBER 1938
Czechoslovakia Dismemberment of the Czech State continues. Polish forces occupy Teschen, taken by the Czechs during the 1920 Polish-Russian War. On 6 October Slovakia is granted full autonomy with Joseph Tiso as premier. On the 8th Ruthenia is granted autonomy under the name of Carpatho-Ukraine. Poland will try to arrange partition of this region among Poland, Hungary, and Rumania. On 15 March 1939 the autonomous province of Bohemia-Moravia will become a German protectorate.

20 OCTOBER 1938
Czechoslovakia In line with Nazi policy, the Com-

EDUARD BENES, 1884–1948

An impassioned nationalist in his youth, Eduard Beneš spent his life pursuing the dream of an independent Czechoslovakia, only to see that dream doomed after much struggle and many victories. During World War I Beneš formed an organization that at the end of the war became the Czechoslovak Government. Serving in various political positions (including president in 1935–38 and 1946–48) over the years, Beneš became a major peacemaker in European politics and in the League of Nations. From 1935 Beneš responded to the growing German threat as best he could, by increasing his country's ties with the Soviet Union. When Britain conceded Czechoslovak territory to the Nazis in 1938, he formed a government-in-exile, returning home in triumph upon the Allied victory. After Russian ties developed into a communist coup in 1938, the country's independence came to an end the following year. Beneš died a bitterly disappointed man a decade later.

Would Hitler have backed down if the great democracies had threatened him with war? When Hitler demanded that Czechoslovakia cede the Sudetenland with its German population, Chamberlain went to Munich and handed the area over. France had a treaty with Czechoslovakia—a democracy surrounded by dictatorships—which had mobilized and called on France to honor that treaty. Russia, fearful of Hitler's threats to destroy communism, sought common cause with both Britain and France. Did Chamberlain fear that Britain could not defeat Germany? Was his appeasement effort a fatal failure of nerve, a backing down from tyrannical threats? The West, since the Russian Revolution, had been nurturing hatred and fear of the Soviet Union. Was Britain secretly hoping to induce Hitler to go east and ultimately fight the Soviets? There is convincing evidence for each interpretation. The truth lies in the unknown motivations of a few key persons. But in the decades to come, whenever a nation faced the dilemma of meeting force with force, 'Munich' was sure to be invoked.

munist Party is outlawed and persecution of the Jews begins.

21 OCTOBER 1938
China After months of relentless bombing, the Japanese capture Canton. This victory gives control over the Canton-Hankow Railway, an essential supply line for Chinese forces. Four days later the Japanese will seize Hankow, as the Chinese Government withdraws to Chungking. The Japanese now control China's major ports, and the Chinese can get supplies only through the USSR or by the Burma Road. In November the Japanese will announce the New Order for East Asia—that Japan will be dominant, with the Western nations perhaps allowed what is left over. The USA and Britain, worried by Japan's conduct in China, now openly oppose Japanese expansionism.

8 NOVEMBER 1938
USA In the mid-term elections, Republicans make their first gains in 10 years. Democrats retain both Houses of Congress, but results are considered a rebuff to Roosevelt who had campaigned personally, endorsed his supporters, and made the election a test of his policies.

9 NOVEMBER 1938
Palestine The Woodhead Commission concludes that partition is unfeasible and calls for a conference of Jews and Arabs, both Palestinian and from neighboring countries.

9–10 NOVEMBER 1938
Germany Organized by the SS as a 'spontaneous' public demonstration against the assassination of a Paris embassy official by a Jewish refugee, the worst pogrom in the Third Reich takes place. Jewish homes,

shops, and synagogues are burned; 100 Jews are murdered, 20,000 others arrested and sent to concentration camps. The event is known as the *Kristallnacht*, from the enormous number of windows broken by Nazi thugs.

20 NOVEMBER 1938
Czechoslovakia The government agrees to German demands for rights to a highway across Moravia to Vienna, and for a canal linking the Oder and Danube Rivers. These concessions mark the state's new status as a virtual satellite of Nazi Germany.

26 NOVEMBER 1938
Poland Placed in jeopardy by the Nazi advance into Czechoslovakia, Poland renews its nonaggression pact with the USSR.

30 NOVEMBER 1938
International Tensions increase between France and Italy, as government-controlled newspapers in Italy press for Corsica and Tunisia, currently under French sovereignty.

1 DECEMBER 1938
Great Britain A voluntary national register for war service is initiated. The Czech crisis alerted Britain to her military unpreparedness. The nation proceeds with rearmament and begins to order aircraft from the USA.

6 DECEMBER 1938
International France and Germany reach a friendship pact similar to the Munich Agreement. Germany disavows interest in Alsace-Lorraine, and Hitler will cite this in the coming months as proof of his peaceful intentions.

17 DECEMBER 1938
International In a diplomatic note, Italy declares the 1935 pact with France invalid because ratifications had not been exchanged, an argument denied by France.

24 DECEMBER 1938
International Twenty-one Western Hemisphere nations adopt the Declaration of Lima at the Eighth International American Conference in Peru. Thus they reaffirm the principle of mutual consultation, but do not stress mutual defense against threats to the territorial integrity of any nation.

OTHER EVENTS OF 1938
Science Otto Hahn and Fritz Strassmann, German scientists, produce the elements barium and krypton after bombarding uranium with neutrons; they cannot explain this, but what they have discovered is nuclear fission—the splitting of the atom that will lead to the atomic bomb.
Technology The first commercially produced nylon product—toothbrush bristles—is made by E I Du Pont de Nemours in Delaware; the first patent for

THE ROAD TO WAR 1933-1939

ANTHONY EDEN, 1897–1977

The debonair Anthony Eden—who at times appeared almost like some cartoonist's image of a British statesman—proved to be made of surprisingly stern stuff. After serving two years on the Western Front in World War I, Eden graduated with honors from Oxford and was elected to Parliament in 1923. In the following years, he espoused the cause of the League of Nations but his finest moment came when he resigned as foreign secretary in 1938 because he opposed Chamberlain's appeasement of Hitler. When Churchill was called to power in 1940, Eden returned as foreign secretary and in 1955 became prime minister. His decision to join France in attempting to seize the Suez Canal in 1956 generated much criticism, and as his health began to fail he resigned in 1957. It was an unfortunate blot on the escutcheon of the Earl of Avon (1961), otherwise associated with diplomatic and peaceful solutions to international problems.

nylon was taken out on 16 February 1937; first nylon yarn for stockings will be made on 15 December 1939. Laszlo Biro, a Hungarian sculptor-journalist-hypnotist, develops the first practical ballpoint pen; Biro will flee the Nazis and move to Argentina, where he takes out his first patent in June 1943.

Environment To halt the Japanese invasion of China, the Chinese divert the Huang Ho (Yellow) River southward—flooding 20,000 square miles and killing several hundred thousand. On 21 September a tropical hurricane that has been moving up the Atlantic coast strikes New England with great force,

killing 700 people and doing millions of dollars worth of damage.

Social Science Lewis Mumford's *The Culture of Cities*; Johann Huizinga's *Homo ludens*.

Ideas/Beliefs Frank Buchman, an American evangelist, founds a movement he calls Moral Rearmament, which advocates 'world-changing through life-changing'; the movement will remain controversial because of Buchman's expressed admiration for Hitler.

Literature Nikos Kazantzakis's *Christ Recrucified (The Greek Passion)*; he also completes *The Odyssey: A Modern Sequel*, but it will not become widely known until its English translation in 1958. Sartre's *La Nausée*; Graham Greene's *Brighton Rock*; Christopher Isherwood's *Goodbye to Berlin* (to become the basis of a play, *I Am a Camera*, and a musical, *Cabaret*); Faulkner's *The Unvanquished*; Nabokov's *Invitation to a Beheading*; and a Japanese classic, Shiga Naoya's *A Dark Night's Passing*.

Drama/Entertainment Thornton Wilder's *Our Town*; Emlyn Williams's *The Corn is Green*. Shaw's *Pygmalion* is released as a movie.

The Arts Picasso's *Woman in an Armchair*; Raoul Dufy's *Regatta*.

Music Hindemith's *Nobilissima Visione*; Dimitri Kabalevsky's opera *Colas Breugnon*; Aaron Copland's ballet *Billy the Kid*.

Miscellaneous On 30 October Orson Welles broadcasts a radio play in New York, 'Invasion from Mars,' that is so realistic it causes panic in many listeners; some even take to the highways in flight.

1–6 JANUARY 1939

France In the face of Italian pressure, Premier Daladier visits Corsica and Tunisia where he is enthusiastically received. North Africans assure him they do not want to come under Italian power. The French refuse to discuss Italian cession demands, and tension between the two nations remains high.

12 JANUARY 1939

USA Roosevelt requests an additional appropriation of $525 million for defense—to upgrade air and naval forces. He will continue to submit requests for more appropriations—on 4 March and on 29 April—anticipating that the nation may become engaged in a military conflict.

17 JANUARY 1939

International Insisting on their strict neutrality, the Scandinavian states of Norway, Sweden, and Finland refuse a German bilateral nonaggression pact. But Denmark, Estonia, and Latvia enter into agreement with the Reich.

26 JANUARY 1939

Spain With Italian assistance, Franco's forces capture Barcelona, leading to the end of all Loyalist resistance. Over the next few weeks, Franco's forces will secure Catalonia, as 200,000 Loyalists flee to France.

Henry Miller.

29 JANUARY 1939
India In the Congressional elections, radical leader Subhas Chandra Bose defeats Gandhi's candidate and becomes president for a second term. Congress delegates vote against Bose's proposal of independence from Britain in six months and endorse Gandhi's nonviolence program. Because of lack of support, Bose will resign on 29 April.

27 FEBRUARY 1939
Spain Great Britain and France unconditionally recognize the Franco Government as the sole legitimate regime. This leads Spanish President Azaña, now in Paris, to resign.

6 MARCH 1939
Spain In Madrid General Segismundo Casado leads a military coup against radical Republican Premier Negrin, who flies to France. Republican General José Miaja forms a new Madrid Government that vows to seek 'peace with honor.' After defeating a small Communist uprising in Madrid, Miaja seeks a compromise with Franco.

10–16 MARCH 1939
Czechoslovakia The Prague Government deposes Premier Tiso on charges of working for the separation of Slovakia, with fascist support. Hitler promises to support Tiso, and summons President Emil Hacha and Foreign Minister Frantisek Chvalkovsky to Berlin, where he persuades them to place the fate of the Czech people 'trustingly in the hands of the

Führer.' Guaranteeing national autonomy, Hitler receives Bohemia-Moravia as a German protectorate on 15 March, and on the 16th Tiso places Slovakia under German protection. German forces overrun these areas. Hitler thus furthers his campaign for *Lebensraum* (living space) for the German people. Britain and France do nothing, saying the guarantees they gave at Munich were to the whole of Czechoslovakia and that these are rendered invalid by secession of Slovakia. But Anglo-French allies will issue a series of guarantees to other states against Germany and Italy.

15 MARCH 1939
Hungary Under the new government of Paul Teleki, Hungary invades neighboring Carpatho-Ukraine, independent from Czechoslovakia for one day. After heavy fighting, Hungary annexes the territory.

17 MARCH 1939
Palestine In London the Palestine Conference concludes without achieving a settlement. Although non-Palestinian Arabs have tried to work out a compromise, neither the Jews nor the Arabs of Palestine could come to agreement.

23 MARCH 1939
Lithuania After the 11 December 1938 elections endorsing the National Socialists, Germany annexes Memel after forcing Lithuania to agree with promises of support for Lithuanian independence.
Rumania An economic agreement is concluded with Germany that gives the Nazis access to oil at privileged terms.

28 MARCH 1939
Spain Compromise negotiations fail and the Republicans surrender unconditionally, as Madrid and Valencia are handed over to Franco. Franco institutes special tribunals to convict hundreds of Loyalists, despite the protests of France and Britain. The USA will recognize the Franco regime on 1 April. Cost of the war was heavy—700,000 died in battle, 30,000 were executed or assassinated, and 15,000 died in air raids.

31 MARCH 1939
Poland Great Britain and France offer guarantees of Polish independence formalized in a mutual assistance pact on 6 April. Similar guarantees are offered Greece, Rumania, and Turkey.

2 APRIL 1939
International Japan and the USSR conclude a year-long treaty settling a dispute over fishing rights. But in May widespread fighting erupts between the two nations on the Manchukuo-Outer Mongolia border.

7 APRIL 1939
Albania Italy conquers Albania after coastal bombardment and landing of an army that puts down

THE ROAD TO WAR 1933-1939

A Heinkle III of the Condor Legion bombing Valencia, Spain—1939.

local resistance. King Zog and his queen flee to Greece and later to Turkey. On 12 April an Albanian constituent assembly will endorse union with Italy. King Victor Emmanuel assumes the crown, and a fascist government is instituted in a 3 June constitution.

11 APRIL 1939

Hungary Hungary withdraws from the League of Nations, under influence of its recent alliance with Germany. On 3 May Hungary will institute severe anti-Semitic laws, similar to those in Germany.

14 APRIL 1939

USA President Roosevelt writes to Hitler and Mussolini, asking a 10-year guarantee of peace in Europe and the Middle East, in return for US cooperation in talks on world trade and armaments. Neither Hitler nor Mussolini show interest; indeed, Hitler revokes the German nonaggression pact with Poland and the Anglo-German naval agreement in a 28 April Reichstag speech.

27 APRIL 1939

Great Britain The government institutes conscription to augment British military forces by 300,000 men.

17 MAY 1939

Palestine The British plan mandates an independent Palestinian State within 10 years. The plan calls for an administration with powers shared by Arabs and Jews, and limits Jewish immigration, which is to cease after five years if Arabs do not agree to its continuance. Land sales and transfers are to be regulated by the government. Endorsed by the British Parliament on 23 May, the plan is opposed by Arabs and Jews. After Britain declares war on Germany, the worldwide Zionist organizations will declare solidarity with Great Britain.

22 MAY 1939

International With the Pact of Steel, Germany and Italy conclude a political and military alliance calling for military and technical co-operation.

JUNE–AUGUST 1939

International Great Britain, France, and the USSR conduct triangular negotiations to form a 'peace front' against the Nazi threat. A deadlock results from rigid Soviet demands for a full alliance and military convention, along with guarantees for the Baltic States and the Soviet right to send troops through Poland in case of Nazi advance.

7 JUNE 1939

USA King George VI and Queen Elizabeth begin the first visit of reigning British monarchs on American soil. This goodwill trip is to remind the US of its 'special relationship' with Britain, particularly in face of the increasing fascist menace in Europe.

14 JUNE 1939

China The Japanese close a blockade around the British and French concession at Tientsin after the British refuse to give up four Chinese accused of terrorism. The Japanese demand British withdrawal of support for the Chinese Nationalist Government. Fighting continues as Chinese resist, supplied by the USSR and other nations. Britain and France help with loans.

23 JUNE 1939

International France and Turkey conclude a treaty ceding the republic of Hatay to Turkey, in return for Turkey's participation in a pact of mutual aid. With this pact and the earlier one with Britain of 12 May, Turkey declares itself on the Allied side. On 30 July Britain and France will offer Greece guarantees of independence and integrity.

14 JULY 1939

USA Roosevelt asks for repeal of the arms embargo, so that the US can help such countries as Britain. On 18 July the president asks Congress to revise the Neutrality Law. And on 26 July the US will abrogate its 1911 trade treaty with Japan.

2 AUGUST 1939

USA Albert Einstein, urged by fellow scientists, writes to President Roosevelt informing him that some sort of powerful atomic bomb is feasible. This will lead to the Manhattan Project to develop the atomic bomb.

THE MOVIES: IMAGES OF THE THIRTIES AND FORTIES

The traumatic decades of the Great Depression and World War II produced few sources of pleasure —one of them was the films that came out of Hollywood. Landmark movies were made in other countries during the 1930s—France's *Grand Illusion*, Eisenstein's *Alexander Nevski*—but it was Hollywood's movies that engaged the world during the Great Depression. These were the years of defiant glamour, spectacle, sentimentality, romance and adventure; of stars like Fred Astaire, Greta Garbo, Clark Gable, Shirley Temple, Laurel and Hardy. Walt Disney's childlike images won the hearts of filmgoers of every age. Depression was not to be found at the movies. World War II inspired such European masterworks as Olivier's *Henry V* and Barrault's *Children of Paradise*, 'message' movies that never appealed to the popular imagination in the same way as Hollywood's offerings. Many of them did purport to feature wartime events— Americans had barely digested such news as the fall of Wake Island before they saw Hollywood's version of it. But whether in *Casablanca*, *Mrs Miniver*, or *Stage-Door Canteen*, Hollywood's realm was fantasy and romance. There is no real contradiction between the temper of the times and the images that flowed through contemporary films: Hollywood's 'dream factory' offered a welcome alternative to the nightmare of history.

THE ROAD TO WAR 1933-1939

Clark Gable and Vivien Leigh in Gone with the Wind.

19 AUGUST 1939

Germany Fourteen U-Boats are sent to patrol positions in the North Atlantic because of the tense international situation. The pocket battleships *Graf Spee* and *Deutschland* are deployed on 21 and 24 August, accompanied by supply ships.

20 AUGUST 1939

International In the Russo-Japanese conflict along the Manchukuo-Outer Mongolia border, the Soviets under General Gregory Zhukov win a major victory. This defeat and political developments in Europe worry the Japanese and they come to terms. This indication of the efficiency of the Red Army is little noticed in Europe.

22 AUGUST 1939

Poland Britain repeats its guarantees to Poland and pleads concurrently with Germany for a truce in Eastern Europe and for a conference on German territorial claims. Meanwhile, in late July the Poles

had given the British two Enigma coding machines, based on German versions. They give a valuable start to the code-breaking effort that will assist Allied commanders during World War II.

23 AUGUST 1939

Belgium King Leopold issues a futile call for peace on behalf of the Netherlands, Belgium, and the Scandinavian States. Belgium proclaims neutrality but mobilizes.

24 AUGUST 1939

International In a reversal of Nazi anticommunist policy, German Foreign Minister Ribbentrop signs the Soviet-German Nonaggression Pact in Moscow. Secret terms define spheres of interest—Poland is to be divided in half; Germany is to control Lithuania; the USSR is allotted Finland, Estonia, and Latvia. Later this will be revised to place Lithuania in the Soviet sphere and to give more of Poland to Germany. This treaty invalidates the Anti-Comintern Pact, and

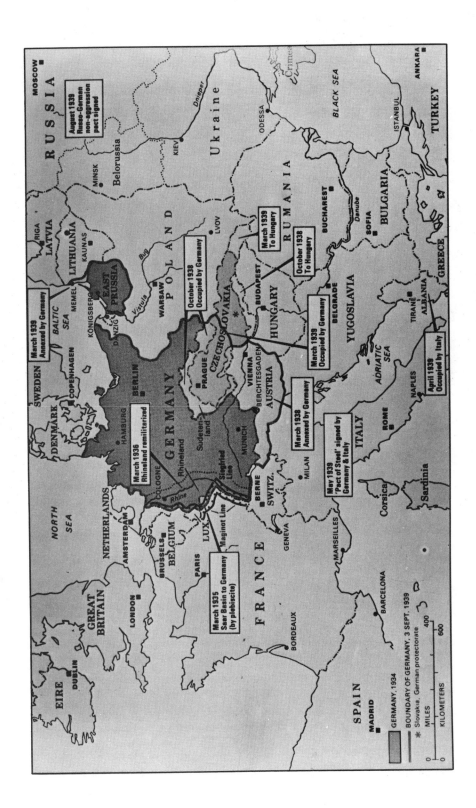

MOSCOW

RUSSIA

August 1939
Russo-German
non-aggression
pact signed

Belorussia

Ukraine

ANKARA

TURKEY

BLACK SEA

ISTANBUL

ODESSA

Crimea

Dnieper

KIEV

MINSK

RIGA

LATVIA

LITHUANIA

March 1939
Annexed by Germany

SWEDEN

KAUNAS

MEMEL

BALTIC
SEA

EAST
PRUSSIA

KÖNIGSBERG

DANZIG

Vistula

Bug

WARSAW

POLAND

LVOV

October 1938
Occupied by Germany

March 1939
To Hungary

BUCHAREST

RUMANIA

SOFIA

BULGARIA

Danube

BUDAPEST

October 1938
To Hungary

CZECHOSLOVAKIA

HUNGARY

BELGRADE

March 1939
Occupied by Germany

YUGOSLAVIA

PRAGUE

VIENNA

BERCHTESGADEN

AUSTRIA

ADRIATIC
SEA

TIRANE

ALBANIA

GREECE

April 1939
Occupied by Italy

DENMARK

COPENHAGEN

HAMBURG

BERLIN

GERMANY

March 1936
Rhineland remilitarized

Sudeten-
land

MUNICH

Rhineland

Siegfried
Line

COLOGNE

Rhine

March 1938
Annexed by Germany

MILAN

May 1939
'Pact of Steel' signed by
Germany & Italy

ITALY

ROME

NAPLES

Sardinia

Corsica

NORTH
SEA

NETHERLANDS

AMSTERDAM

BRUSSELS

BELGIUM

LUX.

Maginot Line

SWITZ.

BERNE

GENEVA

MARSEILLES

FRANCE

PARIS

March 1935
Saar Basin to Germany
(by plebiscite)

BORDEAUX

BARCELONA

GREAT
BRITAIN

LONDON

EIRE

DUBLIN

SPAIN

MADRID

GERMANY, 1934

BOUNDARY OF GERMANY, 3 SEPT. 1939

* Slovakia, German protectorate

MILES

KILOMETERS

0

0

400

600

209

THE ROAD TO WAR 1933-1939

Hitler reviews his troops—7 September 1935.

a surprised Japan resumes freedom of action. Great Britain and France see this pact as evidence of Soviet unreliability.

25 AUGUST 1939

International In a conference with the British ambassador, Hitler reiterates his demand for freedom to deal with Poland. On the 28th Britain will repeat its request for a truce, warning of British action in case of further German moves. Military preparations are stepped up in both nations as Britain withdraws shipping from the Mediterranean and Baltic Seas, and as Germany institutes rationing.

30 AUGUST 1939

Poland After intense European diplomatic activity, Poland declares partial mobilization. The following day the Germans issue a moderate 16-point proposal that never reaches Warsaw, as communications conveniently are severed. Meanwhile, German SS in Polish uniforms stage an attack on a German radio station at Gliewitz to convince the world that Poland is the aggressor.

1 SEPTEMBER 1939

Poland Without a declaration of war, German warplanes and 53 divisions invade Poland. Concurrently, Danzig's Nazi leader Forster proclaims union of Danzig with Germany. Mussolini announces neutrality. And Britain and France, while frantically

mobilizing, offer Germany the option of negotiation if forces are withdrawn from Poland. When Hitler makes no response, the Allies follow with an ultimatum. World War II is about to begin.

3 SEPTEMBER 1939

WW II: Europe The British ultimatum to Germany expires at 1100 hours, and at 1115 hours Chamberlain broadcasts the announcement that war has begun. Australia and New Zealand declare war. Chamberlain forms a war cabinet with Churchill as First Lord of the Admiralty and Eden as Secretary for the Dominions. Both have been opponents of appeasement. That afternoon the French declare war before their ultimatum expires.

4 SEPTEMBER 1939

WW II: Europe The British RAF Bomber Command carries out attacks against German warships in the Heligoland Bight. The *Admiral Scheer* is hit three times, but the bombs do not explode. Six of the 24 attack planes are lost. There is no question of attacking targets in Germany: for the next few months only leaflets are dropped. When the issue is raised in Parliament in October, the government declares that industry in the Ruhr cannot be bombed because it is private property.

5 SEPTEMBER 1939

USA The government announces neutrality. On 12

September naval patrols begin. Meanwhile, on 8 September, President Roosevelt proclaims a limited national emergency with the intention of giving himself power to act more quickly.

10 SEPTEMBER 1939

WW II: Europe The first units of the British Expeditionary Force begin to land in France. Field Marshal Lord Gort is in command. Small advance parties have been arriving since 4 September. In the first month 160,000 men, 24,000 vehicles, and 140,000 tons of supplies are sent.

16 SEPTEMBER 1939

WW II: Europe After more than two weeks of fighting throughout Poland, the Germans have Warsaw surrounded, but a surrender demand is refused. The next day, Soviet troops enter Poland in the undefended east.

17 SEPTEMBER 1939

WW II: Europe The British aircraft carrier *Courageous* is sunk by a U-Boat while on antisubmarine patrol off Ireland. The carrier *Ark Royal* had a lucky escape on 14 September while similarly misemployed.

Russian officers confer with the Japanese in 1939.

THE ROAD TO WAR 1933-1939

After these incidents, the carriers are withdrawn from such work.

25 SEPTEMBER 1939

WW II: Europe In Poland, the Germans step up bombardment of Warsaw and add heavy air attacks. Hitler wishes to complete the conquest as soon as possible: because the Polish garrison is fairly strong, it is necessary to force them to submit by terrorizing the population. The bombing continues until the surrender two days later. It is Germany's first success with the frightening new strategy of *Blitzkrieg* or lightning war.

29 SEPTEMBER 1939

WW II: Europe In a Soviet-German Treaty of Friendship, Poland is partitioned. The USSR gets slightly more land, but the Nazis now control most of the population and the industrial and mining centers. The Soviets begin to put pressure on the Baltic States. A Soviet-Estonian Mutual Assistance Pact is signed, giving the USSR bases in Estonia. Similar pacts are signed with Latvia on 5 October and with Lithuania on 10 October. Vilna is ceded to Lithuania.

2 OCTOBER 1939

International The Inter-American Conference in Panama City sets a 300-mile security zone off the coast of the Americas from which belligerents are banned. They will, of course, ignore this.

3 OCTOBER 1939

WW II: Europe The last significant units of the Polish Army surrender near Luck. The Germans have taken 700,000 prisoners and the Soviets 200,000. Polish casualties have been severe. The Germans have lost 10,000 dead and 30,000 wounded. Many Poles have escaped and will find their way to the West.

6 OCTOBER 1939

WW II: Germany In a Reichstag speech, Hitler declares that up to now he has only corrected the unjust Versailles Treaty and that he has no war aims against Britain and France. He blames warmongers like Churchill for the present state of affairs and calls for a European conference to resolve remaining differences. Both Britain and France will refuse.

9 OCTOBER 1939

WW II: Europe In his Directive Number 6, Hitler privately reveals his plan for an offensive across the Low Countries with intention of defeating strong sections of the French and British Armies when they arrive to help the Dutch and the Belgians.

19 OCTOBER 1939

WW II: Europe Hitler incorporates western Poland into the German Reich. The first Jewish ghetto is established in Lublin.

4 NOVEMBER 1939

USA Roosevelt signs the Neutrality Act of 1939,

A Nazi parade.

The Graf Spee.

repealing the embargo on arms. This act allows sale of arms to belligerents as long as they pay cash and transport them in non-American ships. Although ostensibly a neutrality plan, the act is clearly to allow the US to help Britain, France, and allies.

30 NOVEMBER 1939
Finland Since early October Finland and the USSR have been negotiating over boundary alterations. The Russo-Finnish War begins as the Soviets invade Finland and bomb Helsinki. On 2 December Finland appeals to the League of Nations for mediation. The League meets from 9 to 11 December and agrees to intervene. The Soviets refuse to recognize this offer and are expelled on 14 December. Meanwhile, Soviet forces are slowly advancing into Finland, meeting vigorous Finnish resistance.

17 DECEMBER 1939
WW II: South Atlantic In the battle of the River Plate near Montevideo, Uruguay, British cruisers trap the German cruiser *Graf Spee*, preying on Allied shipping in the Atlantic. Believing resistance is hopeless, the German commander sinks his ship.

23 DECEMBER 1939
WW II: Europe The first Canadian troops, numbering 7500 men, arrive in Britain; on 27 December the first Indian Army troops will join the British already in France.

27 DECEMBER 1939
Finland Using guerrilla-like tactics and their ability at cross-country skiing, the Finns inflict a series of defeats on the Soviets over the next ten days. Although their supply lines are cut, the Soviets receive supplies by air.

OTHER EVENTS OF 1939
Science Austrian physicist Lise Meitner, who has fled to Sweden after the *Kristallnacht* pogrom, and her nephew Otto Frisch, explain that what Hahn and Strassmann had achieved in 1938 was the first known artificially created nuclear fission, which released extra energy. (Meitner had been a coexperimenter in the Berlin project.)

Medicine/Health A Swiss scientist, Paul Muller, discovers the insecticidal properties of a compound called DDT, but it will not be until the 1940s, under the impetus of wartime conditions, that DDT will come into use.

Technology Professor Howard Aiken and his team at Harvard begin construction of the Mark I, an electromechanical computer; completed by 1944, it will soon be made obsolete by more advanced computers. Also in 1939 another American, John Atanasoff, has invented a simple electronic digital calcu-

THE ROAD TO WAR 1933-1939

A Frank Lloyd Wright-designed house, 'Falling Water,' at Bear Run, Pennsylvania.

lating machine. Much new technology is being aimed at wartime applications: radar stations are operating on the coast of Britain to give early warning of aircraft approach; balloons are up to protect against air attack; and in Germany the first jet airplane, a Heinkel, is flown.

Environment Major earthquakes in Chile and Turkey leave thousands dead.

Social Science At Sutton Hoo, in England, a superb early Anglo-Saxon burial ship is found. And at the so-called Palace of Nestor, at Pylos, Greece, Carl Blegen, an American archaeologist, uncovers tablets bearing the same Linear B script known from the Minoan palaces on Crete.

Literature James Joyce's *Finnegan's Wake* (known as *Work in Progress* since he began it in 1922) is published. Steinbeck's *Grapes of Wrath*; Henry Miller's *Tropic of Capricorn*; T S Eliot's *Old Possum's Book of Practical Cats*; Nathanael West's *The Day of the Locust*; Antoine Saint-Exupéry's *Wind, Sand and Stars*; Thomas Mann's *Lotte in Weimar*.

Drama/Entertainment T S Eliot's *Family Reunion*;

Brecht's *Mother Courage*; Saroyan's *The Time of Your Life*; Walt Disney's feature-length cartoon *Pinocchio*. On 15 December, *Gone With The Wind* premieres in Atlanta, Georgia; it will become the first movie to gross over $70 million.

The Arts Picasso's *Night Fishing at Antibes*; Graham Sutherland's *Entrance to a Lane*; Jacob Epstein's sculpture *Adam*; Henry Moore's *Reclining Figure*. Anna Mary Robertson Moses, at 79, is discovered as a 'primitive' painter and soon becomes famous as 'Grandma Moses.'

Architecture Frank Lloyd Wright completes the innovative curved administrative building for the Johnson Company in Racine, Wisconsin. (The laboratory tower will be added later.)

Music Walton's *Violin Concerto*; Prokofiev's *Alexander Nevsky Suite*; Orff's *Der Mond*.

Miscellaneous On 20 May Pan American Airways starts the first scheduled commercial transatlantic service when a Yankee Clipper, a four-engine flying boat, leaves Port Washington, Long Island; it lands at Lisbon, Portugal, 20 hours 16 minutes later.

1940-1945:
A WORLD AT WAR

TBD torpedo bombers on the deck of the USS Enterprise *during the Battle of Midway.*

3 JANUARY 1940
USA President Roosevelt submits a budget of $8.4 billion which includes some $1.8 billion for defense measures. In the coming months he will ask for and get increasingly large sums to augment military strength.

16 JANUARY 1940
WW II: Germany Hitler decides to cancel the German attack in the West, originally set for 17 January, until the spring. Reasons include continuing bad weather and capture of the German attack plans on 10 January, when two officers carrying strategic papers had been forced to land in Mechelen, Belgium.

26 JANUARY 1940
Japan The 1911 trade treaty between the US and Japan expires. American Secretary of State Cordell Hull informs Japan that the US will simply allow trade between the two nations to continue.

29 JANUARY 1940
Russo-Finnish War In diplomatic exchanges made via Sweden, it emerges that the Soviets are prepared

to negotiate with the Finnish Government in Helsinki and abandon support for their puppet Communist regime.

JANUARY–FEBRUARY 1940
WW II: Atlantic In the Battle of the Atlantic, waged largely by German U-Boats against ships of Britain and Allies, losses are mounting. In these two months the Allies lose 400,000 tons of shipping.

1 FEBRUARY 1940
Japan A record budget is presented to the Japanese Diet. Almost half is military expenditure.

1–8 FEBRUARY 1940
Russo-Finnish War The Soviets launch continuous attacks against the Mannerheim Line, and by the 8th the Finns are exhausted and short of ammunition. The Soviets will break through the line near Summa on 11 February. Meanwhile, diplomatic exchanges via Sweden achieve nothing.

5 FEBRUARY 1940
WW II: Diplomatic The British and French Supreme War Council decides to intervene in Nor-

215

A WORLD AT WAR 1940-1945

General Gamelin (left) and General Gort.

way and send help to Finland. They plan landings at Narvik and three other towns around 20 March. Compared to the meticulous German plans, these Allied preparations are irresolute. The pretext of helping Finland is unconvincing—the intention is to stop Swedish iron ore from reaching Germany.

11 FEBRUARY 1940
WW II: Diplomatic The Germans and the Soviets sign an additional trade and economic agreement. The Soviets will supply raw materials, particularly oil and food, in return for manufactured products of all kinds, including arms.

14 FEBRUARY 1940
Russo-Finnish War The British Government announces it will allow volunteers to help the Finns. This is, of course, far too late.
WW II: Atlantic The British Government announces that all British merchant ships in the North Sea will be armed. On 15 February the Germans will reply that all such ships will be treated as warships.

21 FEBRUARY 1940
WW II: Poland The Germans begin construction of a concentration camp at Auschwitz.

5–7 MARCH 1940
Russo-Finnish War Though they continue to resist valiantly, Finnish forces are outnumbered. On 5

March the Finns deduce that Franco-British promises are worthless and send a peace delegation to Moscow.

13 MARCH 1940
Russo-Finnish War In Moscow, Finland signs an armistice and treaty ending the war. Finland gives up the Karelian Isthmus, the Rybachiy Peninsula near Murmansk, and other territory, and grants a lease on the port of Hanko. Petsame is returned to the Finns. With the agreement to these moderate terms, a cease-fire begins at noon. The Finns never had more than 200,000 men in the fight and lost 20,000 dead and 45,000 wounded; the Soviets sent 1.2 million men and lost at least 48,000 dead and 158,000 wounded. The effects of Stalin's officer purges have yet to be overcome. The impression of inefficiency contributes to Hitler's decision to invade the USSR, and makes the British and the Americans hesitant to send supplies to the Soviets when the Germans do invade, since they expect that the Germans will win quickly.

18 MARCH 1940
WW II: Diplomacy Hitler and Mussolini meet at the Brenner Pass (in the Alps, connecting Austria and Italy) where Mussolini declares himself ready to join Germany and other Axis Powers in the war against Britain and France.

20 MARCH 1940
WW II: France Prime Minister Daladier is forced to resign, to be succeeded by Paul Reynaud on 21 March. Daladier has been criticized for failing to help Finland. In France this had been seen as a way for the Allies to seize the initiative in the war and to keep the fighting away from French soil, thus avoiding a repetition of the horrors of World War I.

28 MARCH 1940
WW II: Diplomatic In their Supreme War Council, the British and the French decide to agree that neither will make a separate peace.

30 MARCH 1940
China A Japanese-controlled puppet government is established in Nanking. The Japanese have persuaded Wang Ching-wei, formerly a respected Nationalist politician, to lead this body.

31 MARCH 1940
WW II: Atlantic The first German armed merchant cruiser, *Atlantis*, sails for operations against Allied shipping. Up to seven such vessels will be in service in 1940 and 1941. Better armed than their British counterparts, they cause disruption—sinking 87 ships (over 600,000 tons), or about one-fifth of British losses in this time.

7 APRIL 1940
WW II: Norway German warships begin to leave home ports for the invasion of Norway. They carry

three divisions, with three more marked for a second wave. Ships have support from 500 transport planes, over 300 bombers, and 100 fighter planes. The British observe these massive movements, as they are preparing to sail for mining of Norwegian waters, but fail to appreciate the significance of the German push.

9–27 APRIL 1940
WW II: Norway and Denmark The Germans invade Norway and Denmark. Copenhagen falls within 12 hours. The Norwegians, with help from the British and the French, put up an impressive resistance. In the 10 April First Battle of Narvik, the British and the Germans lose two destroyers each. By this time the Norwegian Government and royal family have left Oslo, and Vidkun Quisling leads a puppet government. The Germans seize most of the Norwegian stocks of arms. In the 13 April Second Battle of Narvik, a British force sinks eight German destroyers. The British and French land units, but their strategies are still irresolute. The rapid German advances lead to the British decision on the 27th to begin evacuation of forces.

29–30 APRIL 1940
WW II: Norway King Haakon and his government are evacuated from Molde on the British cruiser *Glasgow*. The Norwegian gold reserves go with them to Tromsö, where they arrive 1 May.

9 MAY 1940
WW II: Belgium The Belgian Army is placed on alert because of recent tension and signs of German troop movements. The Luftwaffe has kept Allied reconnaissance flights away from German units preparing for attack on the Western Front.

10 MAY 1940
WW II: Belgium, Luxembourg, Netherlands Germany invades the Low Countries, holding the frontier opposite the Maginot Line, while sending a secondary advance through Belgium and Holland to draw main British and French forces north in order to expose their flank. Neither Belgians nor Dutch have given the Allies any co-operation in planning joint defense, because they did not wish to compromise neutrality, or to provoke the Germans into attacking. The two sides are fairly evenly matched on the ground, but in the air the Germans are much stronger. Distribution of the Allied forces leaves much to be desired. German parachute landings inside Holland paralyze resistance there. At the end of the day, the German advance has gone almost according to plan, and it is becoming apparent that the Belgian and Dutch troops will fail to hold out long enough to receive British and French help.
WW II: Iceland British troops land on the island to set up a destroyer and scout-plane base to help in Atlantic convoy battles, and prevent German use of the island.
Great Britain Winston Churchill becomes prime minister, replacing the now discredited Neville Chamberlain. Although Churchill is far from being universally admired by his countrymen, his decisiveness, resoluteness, powers of oratory, and a soon-to-emerge charismatic appeal will not only win over most of his British critics, but play a major role in bringing the US into the war. On 15 May Churchill sends the first in a long series of telegrams to President Roosevelt, presenting a 'shopping list' of old destroyers, aircraft, and other arms. Churchill's cultivation of friendship with Roosevelt will greatly assist the Allied effort.

11 MAY 1940
WW II: Belgium, Netherlands The German offensive continues at high speed. Major parts of the Dutch Army are put out of action, and in Belgium the Germans are approaching British and French positions.
WW II: Caribbean British and French troops land on the Dutch islands of Aruba and Curaçao to protect oil installations there, as well as Venezuelan oil fields.

12 MAY 1940
WW II: Great Britain Churchill makes the first of a series of inspirational speeches in a radio broadcast. He declares, 'I have nothing to offer you but blood, toil, tears and sweat.'
WW II: Netherlands The French Seventh Army, advancing into Holland, is engaged with the German advance near Tilburg and thrown back.

14 MAY 1940
WW II: Great Britain Recruiting begins for a volunteer home defense force from men in reserved occupations, or too old or too young for military service.
WW II: Netherlands After a surrender demand has expired, the Germans heavily bomb Rotterdam. Dutch Army will capitulate the next day at 1100 hours.

15 MAY 1940
WW II: Great Britain In a vital strategy session, Air Marshal Dowding wins his argument against sending more RAF fighters to France. The decision is also made to send the first bombing raid against German industry in the Ruhr.

16 MAY 1940
WW II: Belgium Before the rapid advance of the German Panzer Corps, including Rommel's 7th Division, the British and French forces begin a retreat.
WW II: Great Britain The Admiralty decides to close the Mediterranean to British merchant shipping, adding more than 20,000 miles to the round trip from Britain to Suez and straining British resources.

17 MAY 1940
WW II: Belgium German troops enter Brussels, and the Belgian Government moves to Ostend.

A WORLD AT WAR 1940-1945

20 MAY 1940
WW II: France The Germans capture Amiens in the morning and Abbéville in the evening. The Germans have now driven a corridor at least 20 miles wide from the Ardennes to the Channel.

22 MAY 1940
Great Britain Parliament passes an Emergency Powers Act, giving the government sweeping power over persons and property of British subjects.

24 MAY 1940
WW II: France German forces are attacking Boulogne and Calais, and Royal Navy destroyers evacuate 5000 men from Boulogne. The main German armored forces make a partial halt until the 27th. Hitler may be deliberately restraining himself against the British to persuade them to come to terms.
WW II: Norway The Supreme War Council decides to end involvement in Norway, though the Norwegians are not yet informed. The Allied operation will get under way from 4–8 June, with evacuation of 24,500 men.

26 MAY–4 JUNE 1940
WW II: France Having been inexorably pushed westward by the German military, tens of thousands of British and French troops converge on the French coastal town of Dunkirk. The British Royal Navy is in charge of this Operation Dynamo. All available naval and civilian ships are dispatched to assist in removing troops, who are exposed to German bombing and shelling. By the time the Germans move onto the beach, 388,226 men have been taken off, at the cost of 80 merchant and naval vessels and many smaller craft, and 80 RAF pilots. On 4 June Churchill broadcasts his most famous speech: 'We shall fight on the beaches, we shall fight on the landing grounds, we shall fight in the fields and in the streets, we shall never surrender, and even if, which I do not for a moment believe, this island or a large part of it were subjugated and starving, then our Empire beyond the seas, armed and guarded by the British Fleet, would carry on the struggle, until, in God's good time, the New World with all its power and might, steps forth to the rescue and the liberation of the Old.'

28 MAY 1940
WW II: Belgium King Leopold agrees to surrender of the Belgian Army without consulting the Allies or his government, now in Paris.

5–22 JUNE 1940
WW II: France The Germans invade France. By 14 June Paris will fall, and by the 22nd France will capitulate. In London, on 18 June, General Charles de Gaulle pledges to carry on the fight.

7–10 JUNE 1940
WW II: Norway The British cruiser *Devonshire* carries the king of Norway and his government from Tromsö to Britain. On 9 June the king and his prime minister will order loyal Norwegian forces to cease fighting at midnight. On 10 June the Allied campaign comes to an end. The campaign has been significant for naval losses on each side—German losses have diminished the potential for invading Britain. The Germans lost 5600 men, the Allies 610.

10 JUNE 1940
WW II: Italy Eager to share the glory of victory, Mussolini issues declarations of war against Britain and France. Neither the Italian people nor their economy are prepared.

11 JUNE 1940
WW II: France Paris is declared an open city. What remains of the French forces are retreating south of the Seine and Marne. German tanks take Rheims.
WW II: Mediterranean First actions of the war in this theater are air skirmishes over Malta and in North Africa.

12 JUNE 1940
WW II: Mediterranean A British cruiser and destroyer force shells the Italian base at Tobruk. In another action off Crete, the British cruiser *Calypso* is sunk by an Italian submarine, while Turin and Genoa are bombed by the RAF.

WINSTON CHURCHILL, 1874–1965

Now generally regarded as one of the giants of contemporary history, Winston Churchill until 1940 seemed little more than a modestly successful politician and author. The son of a prominent British aristocrat and an American mother, Churchill was such a mediocre student that he was sent to military school rather than to a university. Seeking action, he volunteered for duty in British imperial campaigns in India and the Sudan (and published articles and books about his service there); resigning to run for the House of Commons, he lost. Then he went to South Africa to report on the war there, and returned a hero after he wrote of his daring escape from the Boers. His career was harmed when he sponsored the disastrous Dardanelles Campaign in World War I—as First Lord of the Admiralty—and between the wars he had little influence on Parliament. Churchill was one of the first to warn of the perils of Russia's Bolshevik Revolution and to speak out against the dangers of Nazi Germany. At the age of 66 he was asked to lead the British people through the dark days of 1940. 'I have nothing to offer but blood, toil, tears, and sweat,' he said, but he made significant contributions to the Allies' strategy and inspired them by his grand speeches and indomitable spirit (epitomized by his jaunty 'V for Victory' salute). Rejected by the British voters in 1945, he stayed on in the Commons, worked at his memoirs (he won the Nobel Prize for Literature in 1953), and returned to power in 1951 (till 1955). When he died full of honors in 1965, Winston Churchill had undeniably earned a niche in the pantheon of the 20th century's great leaders.

12–22 JUNE 1940

WW II: Baltic States On the 12th the Soviets issue an ultimatum to Lithuania demanding territory and a new government. Kaunas and Vilna are occupied by the USSR on 15 June and a new government is installed on 16 June. Similar demands are made on Estonia and Latvia. These are met on 20 and 22 June respectively. Soviet garrisons have been based in the Baltic since October 1939.

13 JUNE 1940

WW II: France West of Paris, French forces are retreating to the Loire, and the British begin evacuation of any Canadian and British forces remaining.

USA First shipment of surplus artillery weapons and rifles from government stores leaves for Britain, with a steel company as an intermediary.

17 JUNE 1940

WW II: France The Pétain cabinet takes office, announcing that they will ask Germany for terms. The British understand that these will be accepted only on condition that the French Fleet does not fall into German hands. Equally, it is German policy to prevent the French Fleet and colonies from joining Britain, and this is the reason for leniency in allowing the Vichy Government as a focus for loyalty of the French.

WW II: Great Britain Churchill broadcasts that the Battle of France is over and the Battle of Britain is about to begin, exhorting Britons to courage with the memorable words: 'Let us so bear ourselves that, if the British Empire and Commonwealth last for a thousand years, men will still say, "This was their finest hour!"'

18 JUNE 1940

WW II: Germany The RAF bombs Hamburg and Bremen.

22 JUNE 1940

WW II: France The French peace delegation signs the armistice with Germany in the Compiègne railway carriage in which the Germans had signed the surrender after World War I. The pact provides that French forces are disarmed and that three-fifths of France come under German control.

24–28 JUNE 1940

USA As its presidential candidate, the Republican Party nominates Wendell Willkie, a corporation lawyer. But since he supports Roosevelt's efforts to aid the Allies and even the New Deal, Americans are not persuaded to 'change horses in midstream.'

27 JUNE 1940

WW II: Diplomacy In a confidential meeting between British and Australian representatives and US

Winston Churchill, First Lord of the Admiralty, chatting with General Georges.

Transport moving up through a Belgian town.

The city center of Rotterdam during a Luftwaffe attack.

A WORLD AT WAR 1940-1945

Troops being evacuated at Dunkirk.

Secretary of State Cordell Hull, the British and Australians ask for help against Japan. Hull is unable to agree to economic, naval, or diplomatic measures, since the US is not prepared.

28 JUNE 1940
WW II: France   General de Gaulle is recognized by Britain as 'Leader of all Free Frenchmen.'

30 JUNE 1940
WW II: Great Britain   German forces begin to occupy the Channel Islands, the only British territory they will conquer.

JULY–OCTOBER 1940
WW II: Atlantic   This is the peak period of German U-Boat successes against Allied shipping, with U-Boats sinking ships virtually at will.

3 JULY 1940
WW II: Atlantic   To prevent the French Navy from falling into German hands, the British seize nine destroyers, two battleships, and many smaller ships after minor skirmishes at Plymouth and Portsmouth. In North Africa, the British will find it more difficult to take over French ships.

5 JULY 1940
WW II: France   Marshal Pétain's Vichy Government breaks off diplomatic relations with Britain because of the actions against the French Navy. There is an attempt to raid the British base on Gibraltar with torpedo planes, but it is unsuccessful.

5–19 JULY 1940
USA   The Chicago Democratic Convention nominates Roosevelt for President for an unprecedented third term. Henry A Wallace is his running mate.

7–8 JULY 1940
WW II: North Africa   After French battleships in Dakar and Casablanca are attacked by British units, de Gaulle criticizes the British—the first sign that he will maintain French independence and be a stormy partner.

10 JULY 1940
WW II: Great Britain   By British reckoning, this is the first day of the Battle of Britain. In addition to actions over the Channel, the Germans send 70 planes to attack dock targets in South Wales. When German air attacks and the heroic defense by the outnumbered RAF defenders cease at the end of October, Hitler's plan for invading England (Operation Sea Lion) lies in ruins along with many aircraft. The Germans will continue to 'blitz' London and other cities with bombing raids, but fail to attain control of British airspace.

15 JULY 1940
WW II: Baltic States   Plebiscites conducted in Estonia, Lithuania, and Latvia show a 'unanimous' desire for union with the USSR, and on 21 July the Soviets will annex the three states.

18 JULY 1940
Burma   In response to Japanese pressure and to

their own weakness, the British close the Burma Road to supplies going to the Chinese Nationalists. The route will reopen in October after the monsoon season.

22 JULY 1940
WW II: Great Britain The government creates the Special Operations Executive to encourage uprisings against Hitler's rule and to support clandestinely resistance movements in Occupied Europe.

30 JULY 1940
WW II: Diplomatic In Cuba, delegates of the Pan-American Union approve the Declaration of Havana, announcing that American States are prepared to ensure that no European colonies in the Western Hemisphere will be transferred to German control.

31 JULY 1940
WW II: Great Britain Air-fighter production for July is found to be 50 percent above target. Since 1 May 1200 planes have been manufactured, more than the Germans have made: the RAF is closing the gap with the Luftwaffe.

3 AUGUST 1940
WW II: East Africa The Italians invade British Somaliland. In Ethiopia the Italians have a force of 350,000 men, of whom 70 percent are natives. The British have fewer than 25,000 men, including many natives, in all of East Africa. In two weeks the British will evacuate to Aden.

6 AUGUST 1940
China The British Government announces it is abandoning the British presence in Shanghai and Tientsin Province. Forces move out later in the month.

10 AUGUST 1940
WW II: Great Britain In a major strategy move, it is decided to send a large part of the nation's tanks to the Middle East.

17 AUGUST 1940
Greece Following increased tension with Italy, the armed forces are mobilized. Among the provocations is sinking of the Greek cruiser *Helle* by an Italian submarine.

German troops parade on the Place de l'Etoile, 1940.

Hitler and staff members in Paris, June 1940.

A WORLD AT WAR 1940-1945

20 AUGUST 1940
Mexico In his heavily guarded house near Mexico City, the exiled Communist leader Leon Trotsky is mortally wounded in the head by a Stalinist agent wielding an ice axe. In May Trotsky and his wife and grandson had miraculously survived a 20-minute machine-gun barrage on the house. Trotsky is the most prominent victim of Stalin's purges.

3 SEPTEMBER 1940
USA The US agrees to send Britain 50 over-age destroyers in exchange for rights to construct bases in the British West Indies and Bermuda. This marks the beginning of the Lend-Lease agreement—an important stage in Roosevelt's efforts to accustom Americans to supporting the Allies.

11 SEPTEMBER 1940
WW II: Great Britain The Blitz continues as Germans score a direct bomb hit on Buckingham Palace, but none of the Royal Family is hurt. This boosts national morale by showing that danger is shared equally. Despite all the damage done in the Blitz, it is clear that neither casualties nor disruption of civilian life are as great as expected.

13 SEPTEMBER 1940
WW II: North Africa Italian forces begin a cautious offensive from Libya into Egypt. The Italian numerical superiority in the region has been undermined by patroling and harassing tactics by British forces. Five days later the Italian advance will come to a halt.

16 SEPTEMBER 1940
USA The Selective Service Bill becomes law, mandating compulsory registration for all males from 21 to 35. Only the day before, Canada had begun to call up men between the ages of 21–24, and the USSR had announced its intention to conscript men aged 19–20.

19 SEPTEMBER 1940
WW II: Diplomacy In Rome, Ribbentrop warns Mussolini and Ciano against attacking Greece or Yugoslavia. The Italian leaders reply dutifully that they will conquer Egypt first.

22 SEPTEMBER 1940
Japan Ending lengthy negotiations with the French Vichy Government, the Japanese enter Indochina to block aid to the Chinese Nationalists.

23–25 SEPTEMBER 1940
WW II: West Africa British and Free French forces conduct an unsuccessful operation to bring the port of Dakar under Allied control.

26 SEPTEMBER 1940
USA Roosevelt embargoes the export of scrap steel and iron outside the Western Hemisphere, except to Britain. The intention is to cut the Japanese off from vital supplies, which they will protest on 8 October—this will provide a rationalization for Japan's later attack.

27 SEPTEMBER 1940
WW II: Diplomacy In a move to deter US participation, Germany, Italy, and Japan sign the Tripartite Pact, in which they promise that each will declare war on any third party which joins the war against one of the others.

10 OCTOBER 1940
Luxembourg The Germans run a plebiscite which shows that 97 percent of the population opposes their occupation. This experiment is not repeated elsewhere.

18 OCTOBER 1940
France The Vichy Government introduces anti-Semitic laws whereby Jews are to be excluded from public service and positions of authority in industry and the media.

23 OCTOBER 1940
WW II: Diplomacy In southern France, Hitler tries to persuade Spain's Franco to join the war, offering Gibraltar and North African territory. Franco refuses to commit himself.

28 OCTOBER 1940
WW II: Greece and Albania Following an unexpired ultimatum, Italy begins its invasion, hindered by bad weather.

1 NOVEMBER 1940
WW II: Greece and Albania The Italian advance continues, as the British will decide to send half their RAF force from Egypt. The British Government believes it is necessary to fulfill guarantees to Greece to bolster neutral opinion, especially in the Balkans and Turkey. By the 14th all Greek forces are attacking the Italian invaders, and more British aid arrives. Four cruisers ferry 3400 troops and airfield staff from Alexandria to Piraeus. By 20 November another 4000 will arrive.

5 NOVEMBER 1940
USA In the presidential election, Roosevelt wins a landslide electoral-college victory over Willkie. This third-term win reflects the extent to which Roosevelt has carried the people with him in his efforts to confront domestic and international crises.

8–10 NOVEMBER 1940
WW II: Greece and Albania The Italian 3rd Alpine Division is trapped in the area of the Pindus Gorges by the Greek counterattack.

11–12 NOVEMBER 1940
WW II: Mediterranean The British conduct a brilliant attack on the Italian fleet at Taranto. The potential for such an attack on an enemy fleet in harbor is clear to the Japanese.

Cockney humor and the 'carry-on' spirit during the London blitz—September 1940.

21 NOVEMBER 1940
WW II: Greece and Albania At Koritza, Greeks capture 2000 Italian prisoners and some heavy equipment. Almost all invading forces have now been driven back to Albania.

23 NOVEMBER 1940
WW II: Diplomacy In New York, the new British Ambassador to the US, Lord Lothian, warns of the possibility of Britain running out of money and securities to pay for arms—Britain will need help in 1941.

26 NOVEMBER 1940
Poland Work begins on a Jewish ghetto in Warsaw, into which the Germans intend to herd the local Jewish population under dreadful living conditions. The Germans describe the move as a 'health measure.'

9 DECEMBER 1940
WW II: North Africa The British begin an offensive against the Italians in the western desert, with notable successes owing to their training in desert warfare. On the 13th a small British force will enter Libya.

13 DECEMBER 1940
WW II: Germany Hitler issues preparations for the German invasion of Greece, Operation Martita. On 12 November he had also issued preparations for Operation Felix, the advance through Spain to Gibraltar. And on 18 December he will issue plans for the invasion of Russia, given the code name Barbarossa.

29 DECEMBER 1940
USA In a year-end fireside chat over the radio, Roosevelt proclaims the US as the 'arsenal of democracy.' Despite a growing shift away from isolationism, 39 percent of Americans still indicate pacifist sentiments in a recent poll.

Blitzkrieg damage in Coventry, England.

A WORLD AT WAR 1940-1945

OTHER EVENTS OF 1940

Science A team at the University of California synthesizes the first transuranium element, neptunium, with the atomic number 93.

Medicine/Health Karl Landsteiner and Alexander Wiener discover a factor in the red cells of blood that can agglutinate, or clump, if these cells come into contact with an antibody: they call this the Rh factor (because they first found it in experimental rhesus monkeys), and it will become crucial in treating such conditions as congenital defects and pregnancy problems via blood transfusions. Howard Florey and Ernest Chain revive Fleming's earlier discovery of penicillin and reveal its usefulness as an antibiotic, for which the war will create a great demand.

Social Science In southwestern France, four French boys searching for a lost dog stumble into a cave near Lascaux; there they will see wall paintings, engravings, and drawings that experts will recognize as works dating to some time between 20,000–14,000 BC. Many people will visit the cave after the war, but in 1963 it will be closed to the public because of a fungus growth that threatens the paintings. William Sheldon, an American psychologist, publishes *The Varieties of Human Physique*, describing his theories about the structural elements of the human body: he will use these theories as the basis for his 'constitutional psychology,' by which he relates human personality and behavior to somatotypes, or physical types.

Ideas/Beliefs Edmund Wilson's *To the Finland Station*; A J Ayer's *The Foundations of Empirical Knowledge*.

Literature Hemingway's *For Whom the Bell Tolls*; Graham Greene's *The Power and the Glory*; Thomas Wolfe's *You Can't Go Home Again*; Arthur Koestler's *Darkness at Noon*; Dylan Thomas's *Portrait of the Artist as a Young Dog*; Mikhail Sholokov completes the fourth volume (since 1928) of *And Quiet Flows the Don*, and Mikhail Bulgakov completes his masterpiece *The Master and Margarita* (which the Soviets will not allow to be published until 1967— and its full text will appear in the West only in 1969).

Drama/Entertainment Eugene O'Neill completes *Long Day's Journey into Night*, but it will not be

German anti-aircraft artillery on the remains of a demolished bridge in Holland.

produced until 1956; Walt Disney's *Fantasia*, an innovative animated film using classical music; and Chaplin's *The Great Dictator*; Martha Graham's *Letter to the World*.

The Arts Max Beckmann's *Circus Caravan*; Picasso's *Cafe at Royan*.

Music Shostakovich's *Piano Quintet*; Anton von Webern's *Variations*; Stravinsky's *Symphony in C*.

Life/Customs The war begins to cast its shadow across the British home front, with the adoption of food rationing and the formation of the Fire Watch against enemy air attacks and the Local Defence Volunteers, or Home Guard, to defend British shores against invaders.

3–5 JANUARY 1941

WW II: North Africa British forces attack the Italians at Bardia, in Libya; Bardia is taken two days later, with 40,000 prisoners, and the Italians pull back toward Tobruk.

6 JANUARY 1941

USA In his annual state-of-the-union address, President Roosevelt asks Congress to support a lend-lease program for the Allies. He describes the 'four essential freedoms' that Americans and all like-minded peoples are dedicated to preserving—freedom of speech and worship, freedom from want and fear. These 'four freedoms' will strike a responsive chord and come to serve as a rallying cry during the war.

10 JANUARY 1941

USA The Lend-Lease Bill is introduced to Congress, not without considerable opposition by prominent Americans, including Charles A Lindbergh and former ambassador to Great Britain, Joseph P Kennedy.

WW II: Diplomatic The Russians and the Germans sign pacts on frontiers in Eastern Europe and on exchanging industrial equipment for food and raw materials.

14–15 JANUARY 1941

WW II: Diplomatic British military representatives are in Athens to discuss the Greeks' request for

A German tank in North Africa.

A WORLD AT WAR 1940-1945

British Army and RAF support against the Italians, who invaded Greece on 28 October 1940. The British can provide only small units, but promise more.

16–19 JANUARY 1941
WW II: Mediterranean Malta, Britain's island colony providing a base for Allied ships and a checkpoint for all Mediterranean shipping, comes under the first of many attacks by German and Italian planes. The Germans have been building up their air force on nearby Sicily while the British strengthened air and naval forces at Malta; in a battle off the island on 10 January, Britain's carrier *Illustrious* was damaged, but reached port for repairs. Malta will remain in a state of siege until late November 1942.

19–20 JANUARY 1941
WW II: Diplomatic Hitler and Mussolini meet, and Hitler offers to provide German forces to aid the Italians in Albania and Greece; Mussolini declines, but accepts German aid in Africa.

20 JANUARY 1941
USA Franklin D Roosevelt is inaugurated for his third term as president; his vice-president is Henry A Wallace.

22 JANUARY 1941
WW II: North Africa The Italians surrender Tobruk, a major Libyan port, to the British.

29 JANUARY 1941
Greece Prime Minister Metaxas dies and is succeeded by Alexander Korizis, who is even more willing to accept British help.

29 JANUARY–27 MARCH 1941
WW II: Diplomatic High-level military staffs of the US and Britain hold secret talks in Washington and London: they agree on a strategy—code-named ABC1—that calls for the defeat of Germany first, then Japan, should the US enter the war. Americans select sites for naval and air bases in Britain.

FEBRUARY 1941
WW II: Atlantic Although the Germans have only about 22 U-Boats operational at this time, they are sinking Allied ships at an impressive rate: 21 in January, 39 in February. German aircraft are also active—sinking 15 vessels in January and 27 in February. Most of the losses are stragglers from convoys, or independents; convoy escorts and radar are beginning to work against the Germans.

4 FEBRUARY 1941
USA The United Service Organizations, soon to become known as the USO, is formed by six national organizations to serve the social, educational, welfare, and religious needs of the growing armed forces and defense industries. The USO's best-known

activity will be the worldwide network of clubs where service personnel can relax off duty.

6 FEBRUARY 1941
WW II: North Africa Benghazi, another major Libyan port, is taken by British troops as the Italians stream westward along the coast road—thousands will soon surrender as they find themselves cut off.

9 FEBRUARY 1941
WW II: Diplomatic Churchill instructs the British commander in the Middle East and North Africa, General Archibald Wavell, that help for Greece has a higher priority than exploiting success in Africa. Churchill hopes to gain the support of everyone from Americans to Turks by this commitment to Greece, but it fails to take into account the impending commitment by the Germans to the Italians in both Greece and North Africa.

12 FEBRUARY 1941
WW II: North Africa General Erwin Rommel arrives in Tripoli, capital of Libya; on the 14th the first units of what will become the Afrika Korps begin to land at Tripoli. The Germans intend to drive the British eastward and take the Suez Canal.

17 FEBRUARY 1941
WW II: Diplomatic Under German pressure, Turkey and Bulgaria sign a friendship agreement; the Germans will be allowed passage for troops through Bulgaria, and Turkey will not construe this as an act of war. This confirms that Turkey is unlikely to join the Allied cause.

WW II: East Africa Emperor Haile Selassie, who was brought back to Ethiopia in January to help organize resistance to the Italians, joins General Orde Wingate and his 'Gideon Force' of guerrillas for what will be a nine-month campaign to drive the Italians out of Ethiopia.

19–23 FEBRUARY 1941
WW II: Greece British military leaders meet in Cairo to discuss their potential aid for Greece; Wavell agrees to send all he can from his North African forces. The British proceed to Athens and promise 100,000 troops. There is disagreement as to where the British and Greek forces should take their stand against the Germans—a serious drawback in the light of later events.

1 MARCH 1941
WW II: Balkans Prime Minister Filov brings Bulgaria into the Tripartite Pact; the next day German troops move into Bulgaria in force.

4 MARCH 1941
WW II: Norway British Commandos raid the Lofoten Islands off northern Norway; they take German prisoners, and Norwegian volunteers go back with them, but the Germans take reprisals, so many Norwegians disapprove of such raids.

WW II: Diplomatic Hitler meets Prince Paul of Yugoslavia secretly at Berchtesgaden to ask him to join the Tripartite Pact. Paul returns to Yugoslavia convinced he must decide between Britain or Germany. This same day, General Henry M Wilson, who is to command the British force being prepared for Greece, arrives in Athens to arrange final details. Wilson discovers that the Greeks refuse to bring their forces in the north back to a more defensible line.

11 MARCH 1941
USA President Roosevelt signs the Lend-Lease Act, essentially the one he requested (although Congress has limited its operation to June 1943); it empowers the President to transfer ships, arms, and other war materiel to any country vital to US interests and to defer payments. The initial appropriation (passed 27 March) is for $7 billion; by the time the Lend-Lease program ends in September 1946, over $50 billion in aid will have been extended by the US to the Allies.

13 MARCH 1941
WW II: Germany Hitler issues a secret directive for the invasion of the Soviet Union and assigns administrative control of captured territory to the SS; the ensuing atrocities will compromise potential support for the Germans from Russians hostile to Stalin's Communist government.

20–27 MARCH 1941
WW II: Diplomatic Prince Paul of Yugoslavia announces to the Royal Council that he is ready to have the nation join the Tripartite Pact. Four ministers resign, but on 25 March the prime and foreign ministers sign the pact in Vienna. Yugoslavian air force officers lead a coup that deposes Prince Paul and the council; 17-year-old King Peter takes nominal charge of the government, which is headed by General Simovic, the air force chief of staff. The change is popular among Serbian sections of Yugoslavia, less so among the Croats. In response, Hitler issues a secret directive calling for the invasion of Yugoslavia, to be co-ordinated with an invasion of Greece.

28–29 MARCH 1941
WW II: Mediterranean Off Cape Matapan, one of the southern tips of Greece's Peloponnesus, British ships engage Italian and sink three cruisers and two destroyers.

30 MARCH–25 APRIL 1941
WW II: North Africa Having recaptured El Aghelia, the Libyan port where the British had stopped their westward advance against the Italians, Rommel (ignoring instructions from the German High Command not to attack) begins to move his German and Italian troops eastward along the coast. Meeting little resistance from the British, Rommel arrives at Agedabia and on 2 April is in position to mount a full-scale offensive. By 4 April Benghazi is retaken

from the British; by 11 April, the British in Tobruk are isolated (and will not be relieved until 10 December); by 25 April Rommel's forces will be crossing into Egypt.

1–3 APRIL 1941
WW II: Middle East A nationalist politician, Rashid Ali, and a group of officers stage a coup in Iraq. They oppose the British presence in their country, and Britain will begin landing troops by 19 April to ensure access to oil.

2 APRIL 1941
WW II: Diplomatic Prime Minister Count Teleki of Hungary commits suicide rather than collaborate with Germany. The regent, Admiral Horthy, and a new prime minister continue to work with the Germans.

4 APRIL 1941
USA Roosevelt agrees to allow the British Navy to repair and refuel ships in the US.

6 APRIL 1941
WW II: Balkans German forces invade Yugoslavia and Greece. The Germans bomb Belgrade and several Greek targets (hitting a British ammunition ship in Piraeus that explodes and sinks others). Yugoslav forces are widely dispersed and unable to hold back the Germans. The Greeks have some British troops but are split along two defensive lines. **WW II: East Africa** Addis Ababa, capital of Ethiopia, is taken by British and Ethiopian troops, as the Italians begin to retreat.

9 APRIL 1941
WW II: Greece The Greek Army's defensive line in the north collapses and Thessalonika, Greece's second largest city, falls to the Germans.

11 APRIL 1941
USA Roosevelt tells Churchill that the US Navy will extend the American Defense Zone up to the line of 26 degrees west (to Iceland and the west coast of Africa). Roosevelt establishes the Office of Price Administration; under Leon Henderson, the OPA will control prices and profits and play a role in containing inflation in the US during the war.

12–16 APRIL 1941
WW II: Yugoslavia Belgrade, the capital, surrenders to the Germans on the 12th; on the 14th King Peter flies to Athens; next day the Simovic Government joins him. Exploiting this situation, the Croatians of northwestern Yugoslavia, traditional enemies of the Serbs, have declared an independent Croatian Republic; on the 16th their leader, Ante Pavelic, is sworn in as its head. In coming months, Roman Catholic Croats will kill hundreds of thousands of Yugoslavians, most of them Serbian Orthodox, some of them Jews.

A WORLD AT WAR 1940-1945

Rommel flanked by two Italian officers in a victory parade in North Africa.

13 APRIL 1941
WW II: Diplomatic The USSR and Japan sign a five-year Neutrality Agreement. For Stalin, this means the ability to transfer Russian forces from Siberia to face a possible German attack—for the Japanese, freedom to look toward the resources of the Pacific and East Indies.

14–18 APRIL 1941
WW II: Greece Greek and British forces fall back before the advancing Germans. On the 16th Wavell cancels the sailing of British reinforcements from North Africa—abandoning the Greek campaign. Greek Prime Minister Korizis commits suicide.

17 APRIL 1941
WW II: Yugoslavia A former prime minister of Yugoslavia signs an armistice with the Germans—who have lost fewer than 200 men in taking the country.

21–27 APRIL 1941
WW II: Diplomatic US military advisers meet secretly with their British and Dutch counterparts in Singapore to draw up contingency plans against Japan.

7–11 MAY 1941
WW II: Intelligence On 7 May a German weather ship is captured off Iceland, yielding secret documents on the Germans' master coding machine, Enigma. On 9 May a captured U-Boat provides both the cipher machine and code books. The Allies had known something about Enigma, but these finds will give them major help in deciphering German codes (especially since the Germans never discover their loss). It will also create occasional dilemmas—for example, deciding whether to let the Germans conduct a bombing raid on an English city rather than suspect that their code has been broken.

10–11 MAY 1941
WW II: The Blitz In their last major raid for three years, German bombers heavily damage the House of Commons.
WW II: Diplomatic Rudolf Hess, deputy leader of the Nazi Party, flies alone to Britain and parachutes into a field near Glasgow. Apprehended, he claims he is on a mission to enlist British support of Germany in a common attack on Communist Russia. He is disowned at once by German authorities and will spend over 40 years in prison.

15 MAY 1941
USA President Roosevelt, denouncing those French who are collaborating with German occupation forces, has the government take into 'protective custody' all French ships in US ports. Among them is the luxury liner the *Normandie*.

20 MAY–1 JUNE 1941
WW II: Crete After bombing Crete for five days, the Germans begin their airborne invasion of the island, starting with paratroops and gliders. There are 32,000 British troops (many of them Australians and New Zealanders) and 10,000 Greek troops aided by Cretan civilians. The Germans suffer heavy casualties during the first two days, but soon consolidate their hold on a crucial airport. King George of Greece is evacuated to Egypt on 22–23 May, and by the 27th most Allied troops are in retreat to the south coast. During the next few nights, 18,600 Allied troops are evacuated to Egypt, but thousands are left behind dead, wounded, or prisoners; the British lose three cruisers and six destroyers. The Germans admit to 7000 casualties from a force of 23,000, and Hitler decides that such large-scale airborne attacks should not be repeated. Crete will be occupied by Germans and Italians for the duration.

21–27 MAY 1941
USA On the 21st an American merchant ship, *Robin Moore*, is sunk by a German U-Boat inside the defense line (set by Roosevelt on 11 April). The American people are restless under such hostile acts: President Roosevelt on the 27th issues a proclamation declaring a state of unlimited national emergency.

23–27 MAY 1941
WW II: Atlantic British Navy ships seek out and engage the German battleship *Bismarck* and heavy cruiser *Prinz Eugen* in the Denmark Strait; the British battle cruiser *Hood* is sunk (with all but three of its 1461 men), but the German ships turn back; other British ships join in the chase, sinking the *Bismarck* on the 27th.

31 MAY 1941
WW II: Iraq Rashid Ali, leader of the Iraqi drive to expel the British, has fled to Iran, and Iraq agrees to an armistice with the British, who will set up a pro-British cabinet (on 4 June) and post troops at will.

8 JUNE 1941
WW II: Middle East British and Free French forces invade Syria, which has been occupied by Vichy-French forces who allow German aircraft to operate from Syrian bases. By 11 July the commander of the Vichy-French forces in Syria will agree to an armistice.

13 JUNE 1941
WW II: Holocaust The Vichy Government announces that 12,000 Jews have been arrested and 'interned' in camps because of a 'Jewish plot' to hinder Franco-German cooperation. The anti-Semitic laws in Vichy extend to expropriation of Jewish-owned businesses.

14–16 JUNE 1941
USA With powers derived from his declaration of emergency, Roosevelt freezes assets of Germany and Italy in the US. On the 16th he orders that all German consulates in the US be closed by 10 July.

A WORLD AT WAR 1940-1945

22 JUNE 1941
WW II: Eastern Front The Germans launch Operation Barbarossa—the invasion of the Soviet Union along a front from the Baltic to the Black Sea. To regain territory lost to the USSR in 1940, the Finns also attack across their border. The Germans deploy 3 million men, 3300 tanks, and 2770 aircraft, a tremendous logistical feat that will prove insufficient to defeat the Russians. In the early days, however, the Soviet forces are taken almost completely by surprise and the Germans advance. By noon of the first day the Soviets have lost about one-sixth of their aircraft; within the first week, German Panzer units will advance 270 miles.

22–24 JUNE 1941
WW II: Diplomatic Churchill broadcasts that Britain will send aid to the Russians; on 24 June Roosevelt follows suit at a press conference.

25 JUNE 1941
WW II: Sweden The government announces that it will allow passage of German forces up to one division strong from Norway to Finland.

23 JUNE 1941
WW II: Southeast Asia The Vichy Government yields military control of colonies in French Indochina to the Japanese.

JULY 1941
WW II: Atlantic Allied shipping losses to the U-Boats are still high (61 in June, 22 in July), and the U-Boat fleet is increasing: 63 are operational, 20 new boats will be commissioned during July, and 73 more are in training. Convoys are now given almost continuous escort; radar and radio-signal detection are improving. On 1 July the US Navy started antisubmarine patrols from bases in Newfoundland.

3 JULY 1941
WW II: USSR Stalin broadcasts for the first time since the German invasion, calling for total effort, a 'scorched earth' policy, and guerrilla warfare in the German rear. He defends his 1939 nonaggression pact with Hitler as a sign of peaceful intentions.
WW II: East Africa Italian resistance in Ethiopia ends with the surrender of several thousand troops.

7 JULY 1941
WW II: Iceland US forces land on the island to relieve the British, who have been protecting it since August 1940. The Americans are to keep the Germans from taking Iceland and to protect nearby shipping.

8 JULY 1941
WW II: Yugoslavia Germany and Italy announce their plans to dismember Yugoslavia: Croatia is to be 'independent'.

9 JULY 1941
WW II: Russia German Army Group Center,

having taken Minsk (29 June), has crossed the Dnieper and Dvina Rivers to head toward Smolensk. Some 300,000 Soviet troops have been taken prisoner.

11 JULY 1941
WW II: Syria Despite instructions from the Vichy Government, the French commander of Vichy forces in Syria accepts armistice terms from the Allies: a cease-fire goes into effect.
USA Roosevelt appoints William Donovan head of a new civilian intelligence agency; this will lead first to the Office of Strategic Services (OSS) and eventually to the CIA.

16 JULY 1941
WW II: Holocaust Hitler, Goering, Martin Bormann, and Alfred Rosenberg meet to plan for the exploitation of territory captured from the Soviets. Rosenberg takes charge of a new ministry to organize these lands for Germany's economic benefit and to eliminate Jews and Communists.

18 JULY 1941
WW II: Diplomatic Britain recognizes the Czech government-in-exile headed by Eduard Beneš. The Czechs and the Soviets sign a friendship and mutual assistance agreement in London.

19 JULY 1941
USA The US Atlantic Fleet forms TF 1 for the protection of the American forces on Iceland; the US Navy will soon commit 25 destroyers to the Iceland operation and to support ships bound there, no matter what their nationality.
WW II: Resistance The British Broadcasting Corporation (BBC) broadcasts to Europe urging creation of resistance forces, with the slogan 'V for Victory.' The BBC has been introducing programs to Europe with the Morse-code signal for V for some time. Resistance members will paint V on walls and German posters, as it becomes a symbol for Western European resistance.

24 JULY 1941
WW II: Southeast Asia The Vichy Government yields to a Japanese ultimatum by which the Japanese take military control of the French colonies of Indochina. The Japanese will begin to move in military units within four days.

26 JULY 1941
WW II: Diplomatic Japanese assets in Britain and the US are frozen—the immediate cause being the Japanese move into Indochina. Japan will retaliate on 28 July; then the Dutch freeze Japanese assets in the Dutch East Indies and cancel oil deals. Almost 75 percent of Japan's foreign trade is at a standstill, and 90 percent of its oil supplies are cut off.
Philippines Roosevelt orders that the Philippine Army be incorporated into the US Army during the tension with Japan. General Douglas MacArthur,

Left to right: *General Marshall, Roosevelt, Churchill Admiral King—10 August 1941.*

A WORLD AT WAR 1940-1945

who has been leading the Filipino forces, is assigned to command all US forces in the Far East.

30 JULY 1941
China The US gunboat *Tutuila* is damaged in an attack by Japanese bombers at Chungking; Japan apologizes for the incident, which does nothing to ease the strain between the two countries.

1 AUGUST 1941
WW II: Diplomatic Roosevelt forbids export of oil and aviation fuel from the US except to Britain, its empire, and the Western Hemisphere. Japan must either change its foreign policy or gain access to East Indies oil by force—its oil supplies are low.

5 AUGUST 1941
WW II: Russia The city of Smolensk falls to the Germans after the Russians have taken heavy casualties. Moscow is only some 200 miles away.

6 AUGUST 1941
WW II: Diplomatic The Japanese Government proposes concessions to US demands on China and Indochina in return for an end to the freeze on Japanese assets. The US rejects the proposals. The Japanese suggest that their Prime Minister Fumimaro Konoye meet with Roosevelt to discuss the issues: the US response to this will emerge from Roosevelt's meeting with Churchill (on 9–12 August).

9–12 AUGUST 1941
WW II: Diplomatic Churchill and Roosevelt hold secret meetings aboard ship in Placentia Bay, Newfoundland, and agree on joint actions should Japan attack British or Dutch possessions in the East Indies or Malaya. The meeting is best known for a statement of principles—issued 14 August—setting forth eight goals for the world, including renunciation of aggression, the right of all peoples to choose their own governments, guarantees of freedom from want and fear, and the disarmament of aggressors. By 24 September 15 anti-Axis nations, including the USSR, will endorse this Atlantic Charter, which will become the blueprint for the United Nations.

12 AUGUST 1941
WW II: France Marshal Pétain says in a broadcast that Germany is fighting 'in defense of civilization' in the war against the Soviet Union. He announces measures that will tighten the Vichy government's control over Vichy France and the appointment of Admiral Jean Louis Darlan to head the Ministry of Defense.

17 AUGUST 1941
WW II: Diplomatic The US presents a warning to the Japanese based on decisions Roosevelt took with Churchill in their meeting off Newfoundland.

25 AUGUST–9 SEPTEMBER 1941
WW II: Iran Determined to keep the Germans

from gaining access to Iran's oil supplies, Britain and the Soviet Union launch a joint invasion. There is little opposition; by 28 August a new government is giving orders to cease fire and negotiate. The final terms are agreed on by 9 September: the British and the Soviets will occupy key points excluding Teheran, the capital.

28–30 AUGUST 1941
WW II: Russia Soviet forces evacuate Tallinn, the Estonian port on the Baltic; on the 29th the Finns take Vipuri, northwest of Leningrad; on the 30th the Germans cut the last railroad link between Leningrad and the rest of the USSR.

SEPTEMBER 1941
WW II: Yugoslavia General Draza Mihajlovic has organized a resistance group, the Cetniks, against the Germans: the Allied press hails him as a hero. Meanwhile, Josip Broz (Tito), a communist, has organized his partisans to begin active operations. Mihajlovic and Tito will soon become enemies whose forces fight one another as well as the Germans.

3–6 SEPTEMBER 1941
WW II: Diplomatic The US rejects Japan's proposal that Prime Minister Konoye and Roosevelt confer. US Ambassador Grew has warned that the moderate Konoye may be replaced by a military dictatorship: on 6 September Konoye yields to military pressure and agrees to war if Japan cannot obtain oil from lands controlled by the Allies.

4–11 SEPTEMBER 1941
WW II: USA In a convoy operation, the US destroyer *Greer* is attacked by a German U-Boat and retaliates with depth charges. Roosevelt uses this incident to order, on 11 September, that US warships and planes 'shoot on sight' any Axis ship within the zone prescribed (on 11 April).

6 SEPTEMBER 1941
WW II: Holocaust By order of Reinhard Heydrich, head of the German security police, all Jews over the age of six in German-occupied lands are to wear a distinguishing Star of David. This is a harbinger of the Holocaust. Mass transportation of Jews to the concentration camps will not begin until 1942, but Auschwitz was opened in 1940 and gas chambers installed by June 1941. Experiments are underway there with such methods as Cyclon-B gas: firing squads are considered too slow for mass exterminations.

9 SEPTEMBER 1941
WW II: Russia A Spanish volunteer 'Blue Division' reports for service with the German forces on the Leningrad Front (Franco's way of repaying the Germans for their aid in the Spanish Civil War).

15 SEPTEMBER 1941
WW II: Russia The Germans capture Schlussel-

The Vichy leaders. Front row, left to right: *Marshal Pétain, Admiral Darlan, Laval.*

A WORLD AT WAR 1940-1945

burg, east of Leningrad, isolating the city from over-land contact with the rest of the Soviet Union. Some supplies can still be transported across Lake Ladoga. Before the siege is raised in early 1944, several hundred thousand Leningrad civilians will die of starvation.

16–17 SEPTEMBER 1941
WW II: Iran Contrary to their agreement of 9 September, the Allies have decided to occupy Teheran because the Shah has failed to expel all Axis nationals. The Shah abdicates in favor of the Crown Prince, Mohammad Reza Pahlavi, who will rule until overthrown in 1979. British and Soviet forces arrive in Teheran on 17 September.

19 SEPTEMBER 1941
WW II: Russia Kiev falls to the Germans. Soviet losses in over 40 days of fighting are probably over 500,000 men; the Germans have lost 100,000.

24–30 SEPTEMBER 1941
WW II: Mediterranean The British launch Operation Halberd to carry supplies to the besieged Malta. Nine transports and a fleet that includes three battle-ships and a carrier set off from Gibraltar; the Italian fleet sends both ships and planes to cut off the convoy, but sinks only one transport and damages a battleship. On the 24th the first German U-Boat gets past Gibraltar and into the Mediterranean; many will follow and do damage to Allied ships in the Mediterranean.

28 SEPTEMBER–1 OCTOBER 1941
WW II: Diplomatic A conference (proposed by Roosevelt and Churchill at their meeting off New-foundland) takes place in Moscow; W Averell Harriman represents the US, Lord Beaverbrook the British, and Vyacheslav Molotov the Soviets. On 1 October a joint declaration states that Britain and the US will provide increasing aid to the Soviet Union in its fight against the Axis.

2 OCTOBER 1941
WW II: Russia The Germans launch Operation Typhoon, a major effort to take Moscow. During the next two weeks they advance so steadily that Moscow seems doomed.

7 OCTOBER 1941
Australia The coalition government that has been running Australia has lost popular support; today a Labour Government headed by John Curtin takes over; Curtin will serve as Prime Minister until his death on 5 July 1945.

9 OCTOBER 1941
Panama A political crisis in Panama deposes Dr Anulfo Arias and installs as president Ricardo Adolfo de la Guardia, who is regarded as friendlier to the US.

12–26 OCTOBER 1941
WW II: North Africa British forces in Tobruk have been under siege since 11 April, reinforced and supplied from the sea.

15–16 OCTOBER 1941
WW II: Russia The port of Odessa on the Black Sea, surrounded by the Germans for several weeks, is evacuated by Russian troops. The 16th of October sees panic in Moscow, as the Germans are within 60 miles. The Soviet Government moves inland to Kuibyshev—although Stalin stays in Moscow—and foreign diplomats leave.

16 OCTOBER 1941
Japan Prime Minister Konoye resigns and is replaced by General Hideki Tojo. The decision to go to war has not yet been taken, but Tojo favors it and will be Japan's principal leader in the war.

17 OCTOBER 1941
WW II: Atlantic The US destroyer *Kearney* is damaged by a German U-Boat torpedo off Iceland; 11 Americans are killed.

19 OCTOBER 1941
WW II: Russia As the Germans continue to advance on Moscow, Stalin announces that the city must be defended by every means. Work is proceeding at a hectic pace on three fixed defense lines. To the south, German troops are pushing eastward to capture the Russian oil fields of the Caucasus; Kharkov will fall on 24 October.

27 OCTOBER 1941
USA In a broadcast to the nation on Navy Day, President Roosevelt flatly declares: 'America has been attacked, the shooting has started.' Realizing that many Americans are still not ready for full-scale war, he refrains from asking for such a step.

30 OCTOBER 1941
WW II: Russia German assaults on Moscow have been winding down, primarily because of the weather: mud hinders movement, and severe cold weakens the inadequately clad Germans and stalls their vehicles. Although Moscow is still threatened (the anniversary of the Russian Revolution is cele-brated in an underground station), the Germans' goal of capturing the city before the onset of the Russian winter seems to have receded.

WW II: Atlantic The US destroyer *Reuben James*, on convoy duty off Iceland, is sunk by a German U-Boat with the loss of 96 Americans.

WW II: Diplomatic President Roosevelt offers $1 billion worth of supplies to the USSR under the lend-lease program.

3 NOVEMBER 1941
WW II: Diplomatic US ambassador to Japan Joseph Grew cables a warning to Washington that the Japanese may be planning a secret attack on US

positions. Secretary of State Cordell Hull will repeat this warning to President Roosevelt and the cabinet on 7 November.

12–14 NOVEMBER 1941

WW II: Mediterranean Two British carriers, the *Argus* and *Ark Royal*, have brought fighter planes to Malta and are returning to Gibraltar on the 13th when German U-Boats attack them; the *Ark Royal* sinks 25 miles from Gibraltar.

15 NOVEMBER 1941

WW II: Russia The Germans renew their offensive against Moscow, seriously under strength from both casualties and winter weather—this winter will be the most severe ever recorded in Russia. Soviet strategy is to build reserves for a counterattack from forces now being brought over from Siberia.

17 NOVEMBER 1941

WW II: Diplomatic The Japanese ambassador to the US, Kichisaburo Nomura, and a special envoy, Saburo Kurusu, begin negotiations with the State Department in Washington. The Japanese have set themselves a deadline of the end of November to reach acceptable arrangements with the US. This same day, President Roosevelt signs a bill that amends the Neutrality Act of 1939 so as to permit US merchant ships to be armed and to call at ports of belligerents. These amendments pass Congress only by a small margin, indicating that many Americans still think they can avoid the war.

18 NOVEMBER 1941

WW II: North Africa The British launch a new offensive, Operation Crusader, sending forces across the Egyptian border and back into Libya. Their goal is to relieve Tobruk and drive the Germans and Italians as far west as possible.

19 NOVEMBER 1941

WW II: Pacific The Australian light cruiser *Sydney* is sunk by the German raider *Kormoran*, disguised as a Dutch merchant ship, with loss of the entire crew of 645. The encounter becomes known only when survivors from the sunken *Kormoran* are found.

20–26 NOVEMBER 1941

WW II: Diplomatic Japanese negotiators in Washington propose that the US remove restrictions on trade with Japan and refrain from interfering with Japan's activities in Asia and the Pacific. The US demands that the Japanese first withdraw their forces from China and Indochina.

23 NOVEMBER 1941

WW II: Russia Some German troops are now less than 35 miles from Moscow.

WW II: North Africa British and German forces clash between the Egyptian border and Tobruk; Afrika Korps losses in men and tanks are so heavy that the day becomes known to the Germans as

Totensonntag, 'the Sunday of the Dead.' In fighting around Gambut, New Zealand infantry capture the Afrika Korps headquarters and much of Rommel's communications equipment.

26 NOVEMBER 1941

WW II: Pacific A Japanese carrier force leaves its bases to move across the Pacific toward Pearl Harbor. The US will learn of the imminence of war through its ability to intercept Japanese codes; on the 27th a secret war warning goes out to overseas commanders.

Lebanon Realizing that the French cannot enforce control over their mandate (since 1920), Lebanon declares itself an independent state. It will be recognized by the Free French on 1 January 1944.

27–28 NOVEMBER 1941

WW II: Ethiopia The Allies make their final attack against the last Italian forces in Ethiopia. On the 28th, 20,000 Italians surrender, ending Mussolini's dream of an East African Roman Empire.

29 NOVEMBER–1 DECEMBER 1941

WW II: Diplomatic The Japanese Government secretly rejects the terms offered by the US, a decision confirmed on 1 December at a meeting in the presence of Emperor Hirohito. The announcement will not be conveyed to the US until 7 December. On the 29th Secretary of State Hull informs the British ambassador that negotiations between Japan and the US have broken down.

1 DECEMBER 1941

WW II: Southeast Asia British authorities in Malaya declare a state of emergency, following reports of Japanese preparations for an attack in Malaya or the East Indies.

2 DECEMBER 1941

WW II: Russia Small German forces are now in the suburbs of Moscow, within sight of the Kremlin.

WW II: Pacific A special code order, 'Climb Mount Nitaka,' is transmitted by Japan's naval headquarters to the carrier force moving toward Hawaii. This is the order to execute the attack on Pearl Harbor.

5 DECEMBER 1941

WW II: Russia Hitler agrees that the offensive against Moscow should be halted, as the increasing weakness of German forces and the ravages of winter endanger the German cause. Operation Barbarossa has failed.

6 DECEMBER 1941

WW II: Diplomatic President Roosevelt appeals to Emperor Hirohito to exercise his influence to avoid war. The US code-breaking service intercepts part of what the Japanese intend as their final message to the US Government: Roosevelt interprets it as meaning that war is imminent.

The Pearl Harbor attack. In the center the USS West Virginia *is being hit by a torpedo.*

A WORLD AT WAR 1940-1945

7 DECEMBER 1941

WW II: Pacific On Sunday morning, 7:55 Honolulu time, Japanese planes from carriers attack Pearl Harbor, Hawaii, where most of the US Pacific Fleet lies at anchor. Nineteen ships (including 8 battleships) are sunk or disabled; 188 planes are destroyed; 2403 soldiers, sailors, and civilians are killed, 1178 wounded. Japanese planes and ships also attack US bases in the Philippines, Guam, and Midway, as well as British bases in Hong Kong and the Malay Peninsula, within the next 24 hours.

Japanese envoys in Washington, DC, meanwhile, had been instructed to deliver the note rejecting the American proposal (of 26 November) by 1:00 PM Washington time—that is, shortly before Pearl Harbor is to be attacked. Delays in Washington prevent the envoys from delivering it until 2:05 PM, by which time Washington knows of the attack on Pearl Harbor. In fact, US decoders have discovered that Japan intends to break relations and presumably attack, but the authorities in Washington, both civilian and military, fail to get any clear warning through to Hawaii. Meanwhile, several clues have been picked up by the US military in the Pacific, all pointing to an imminent Japanese attack, but the US commanders at Pearl Harbor do not see this as aimed at their base. (Admiral Husband E Kimmel, Commander in Chief US Pacific Fleet, and General Walter C Short, commanding US Army forces in Hawaii, will be dismissed for their failure to take the proper steps.)

As the American people learn of the attack on Pearl Harbor—many when their favorite radio programs are interrupted this Sunday afternoon—they are shocked and outraged. 'Remember Pearl Harbor!' will become the US rallying cry until the Japanese surrender.

WW II: Diplomatic This evening in Tokyo, the American and British ambassadors will receive declarations of war from the Japanese. Not long after midnight on 8 December, the Japanese will invade the British colony of Malaya.

8 DECEMBER 1941

WW II: Diplomatic President Roosevelt appears before a special joint session of Congress, declaring 7 December 'a day that will live in infamy' and calling for a declaration of war against Japan. The Senate votes approval 82–0, the House of Representatives 388–1 (the lone dissenter being pacifist Jeannette Rankin, the first elected woman Representative, who also voted against US entry into World War I). All parties understand that this will entail war with Germany and Italy, Japan's partners in the Tripartite Pact. Great Britain declares war against Japan on this day, as do Australia, New Zealand, the Netherlands, the Free French, Yugoslavia, and several South American countries. China declares war on Germany, Italy, and Japan.

WW II: Pacific The Japanese begin their invasion of the Philippines with air raids, followed by the landing of a small force on Bataan Peninsula. They also invade Malaya and Hong Kong and occupy the whole of Shanghai, capturing the small US garrison in the international settlement.

9 DECEMBER 1941

WW II: Russia Soviet counteroffensives in both the Moscow and Leningrad sectors are making gains, but the citizens of Leningrad are starving.

10 DECEMBER 1941

WW II: North Africa Rommel has realized his Afrika Korps cannot hold out much longer against the British; since the 8th the Germans have been retreating westward. The siege of Tobruk is raised on the 10th.

WW II: Pacific The Japanese make landings and air attacks on Luzon, the principal Philippine island. They also capture the island of Guam, defended by

HIDEKI TOJO, 1884–1948

Responsible as premier for leading Japan into war with the United States, General Hideki Tojo epitomized the militarism that gained the ascendancy in Japan during the 1930s. Impressed by Hitler's power, angered by American oil embargoes that placed a strain on Japan's economy, he rushed into ill-advised war on the United States with the surprise attack on Pearl Harbor (7 December 1941). While his popularity ran high during early victories, as America gained strength he was discredited and forced to resign as premier. The son of a general, with an exclusively military background, Tojo failed at ritual suicide before being arrested as Japan's chief war criminal. He was convicted on nine counts of war crimes, condemned, and executed.

only 300 US troops. In the South China Sea, Japanese planes attack and sink British capital ships, *Prince of Wales* and *Repulse*—a military and moral blow to the Allies.

11 DECEMBER 1941

WW II: Diplomatic Germany and Italy declare war on the US, which reciprocates. Congress votes that US forces may be sent to any part of the world, and extends the term of service for those enlisted under the Selective Service Act to six months after the end of the war.

13–19 DECEMBER 1941

WW II: Mediterranean There is heavy naval activity by both sides, as the Italians try to get a convoy to Benghazi and the British try to get theirs to Malta. Both sides lose several ships; the most serious loss comes when three Italian midget submarines enter the anchorage of Alexandria and torpedo two British battleships.

16–31 DECEMBER 1941

WW II: North Africa Rommel begins to move his troops westward across northern Libya to the most defensible position, El Agheila.

18–25 DECEMBER 1941

WW II: Pacific The Japanese land on Hong Kong Island during the night of the 18th–19th; by the 25th, British forces there surrender.

19 DECEMBER 1941

WW II: Germany Hitler assumes the title of Commander in Chief of the German Army, after accepting the resignation of Field Marshal Walther von Brauchitsch, whom Hitler calls a 'vain, cowardly wretch' and holds responsible for the failure in Russia. His egocentric view of his own genius, plus his distrust of the traditional army command, will lead him to ignore wiser tactical and strategic counsel and to give increasing authority to the Waffen SS.

22–23 DECEMBER 1941

WW II: Pacific Wake Island, under air attack by the Japanese since 7 December, is invaded during the night; next day, the small US garrison surrenders.

22 DECEMBER 1941–7 JANUARY 1942

WW II: Diplomatic Winston Churchill visits Washington for a war conference with Roosevelt, then Ottawa to confer with Prime Minister William Mackenzie King. During the Washington conference, the two leaders and their military staffs agree on the general strategy of the war—concentrate first on defeating Germany, and accept further losses in the Pacific until a solid defense can be put into place. A Combined Chiefs of Staff will direct the multinational military operations.

23 DECEMBER 1941

WW II: Atlantic Free French forces occupy the French islands of St Pierre and Miquelon off the Canadian coast.

26–28 DECEMBER 1941

WW II: Arctic British commandos raid the Lofoten Islands off northern Norway and the Norwegian coast. The successful raids contribute to Hitler's fear that the British will invade the Continent via Norway, where he will continue to station considerable forces.

27 DECEMBER 1941

WW II: Pacific Manila is declared an open city by US authorities, as Japanese forces push back American and Filipino defenders on all fronts.

31 DECEMBER 1941

WW II As 1941 ends, the world is engulfed in war, most nations siding with either the Allies or the Axis. The Axis has taken the initiative. Although the German offensive in Russia has been stopped by the winter, Germany controls an area of the Soviet Union larger than Germany itself; in North Africa, the Germans will rebound for another offensive; German U-Boats (91 operational, 158 on training or trial missions) constitute a major threat, since Britain and Russia are heavily dependent on transatlantic supplies. Western Europe is under the increasingly heavy hand of the German occupation forces: during December the *Nacht und Nebel* (Night and Fog) decree allows the Gestapo to arrest anyone judged a danger to German security. In the Pacific, the Japanese appear to be all but unstoppable: the Philippines, Malaya, and soon the East Indies fall to them. It has been one of the most crucial years in history.

OTHER EVENTS OF 1941

Medicine/Health The first patient is treated with a pure form of penicillin, prepared by Howard Florey and Ernest Chain in England on the basis of work begun by Alexander Fleming in 1928. This patient dies when the supply runs out, but in May a second patient recovers. The American Red Cross Blood Donor Service is established; by the end of the war it will receive 13 million blood donations and continue its service after the war.

Technology Britain introduces its H2S radar system, allowing for identification of landmarks and urban areas by night and under poor visibility conditions. Britain's first jet fighter, the Gloster, based on the work of Frank Whittle, makes trial flights. In the United States, where the war has yet to pre-empt other activities, the first commercial television station, WNBT in New York City, begins broadcasting to about 4700 TV-set owners, including the first regular TV news with Lowell Thomas. Also in New York, CBS's station WCBW begins experimental color-television service.

Social Sciences Rebecca West's *Black Lamb and Grey Falcon*.

Literature W H Auden's *New Year Letter*; Rex

A WORLD AT WAR 1940-1945

Warner's *The Aerodrome*; Henry Miller's *The Colossus of Maroussi*; J P Marquand's *H M Pulham, Esq.*
Drama/Entertainment Orson Welles's *Citizen Kane*; John Huston's *Maltese Falcon*; Noel Coward's *Blithe Spirit.*
The Arts Picasso's *Seated Woman with a Cat*; Matisse's *Two Girl Friends*; Edward Hopper's *Nighthawks.* British artists begin to depict the war scene: Henry Moore draws refugees in air-raid shelters during the London Blitz, Felix Topolski depicts the British armed forces; other works include Stanley Spencer's *Shipbuilding on the Clyde* and Paul Nash's *Bombers Over Berlin.* In Washington, DC, the National Art Gallery is dedicated, featuring the $35 million Andrew Mellon collection.
Music Britten's *Violin Concerto*; Shostakovich's *7th (Leningrad) Symphony*, written while the city is under siege.
Life/Customs The war comes to the home front. In Britain, clothes rationing begins and 'utility' clothing and furnishings are promoted; the Civil Defence is organized to help against air raids. In the United States, colleges and universities institute military training programs, as regular enrollments decline. German and Japanese civilians are under great pressure, with Japan almost cut off from oil and other supplies and German cities constantly bombarded from the air.

1 JANUARY 1942
WW II: Diplomatic Representatives of 26 nations meet in Washington, DC, and affirm their cooperation against the Axis in the 'Declaration of the United Nations.'

2 JANUARY 1942
WW II: Pacific Manila falls to the Japanese, as US and Philippine forces pull back toward the Bataan Peninsula.

11 JANUARY 1942
WW II: Pacific Japanese forces begin their invasion of the Dutch East Indies. By 12 March the Dutch defenders will surrender.

14 JANUARY 1942
WW II: USA President Roosevelt, by proclamation, orders all aliens in the US to register with the government; the brunt of this will fall on Japanese-Americans, or *nisei*, most of them on the West Coast. Secret plans are already being made to move these *nisei* to interment camps, ostensibly because they might provide aid to the Japanese.

15–28 JANUARY 1942
WW II: Diplomatic At the Rio de Janeiro Conference, in Brazil, foreign ministers of 21 American nations resolve to break relations with the Axis. (In fact, Chile will not do so until 1943.)

20 JANUARY 1942
WW II: Holocaust At a conference in Berlin (known as the Wahnsee Conference) Heydrich presents plans to Hitler for the 'Final Solution' to the 'Jewish Problem'—transportation of Europe's Jews to extermination camps. Hitler approves, and Adolf Eichmann takes charge of the SS unit responsible for the plan.

21 JANUARY 1942
WW II: North Africa Rommel launches another offensive and begins to push the British eastward.

26 JANUARY 1942
WW II: USA The American commission investigating the disaster at Pearl Harbor releases its findings: General Short, then commander of the Army's Hawaiian department, and Admiral Kimmel, then commander of the US fleet in the Pacific, are found guilty of dereliction of duty. The debate over responsibility will continue, as some feel these two are scapegoats for malfeasance at higher levels.

29 JANUARY 1942
WW II: Diplomatic Britain and the USSR sign a treaty of alliance with Iran, guaranteeing Iranian oil supplies for the Allied cause and a route by which to supply Russia.

1 FEBRUARY 1942
WW II: Norway Vidkun Quisling is reappointed head of the Nazi puppet government.

7 FEBRUARY 1942
WW II: Germany Albert Speer is appointed minister of munitions (on the death of Todt in an air crash); only 37, an architect by training, Speer will prove a brilliant administrator and keep Germany's industry producing—despite the air raids—almost to the war's end.

8–15 FEBRUARY 1942
WW II: Pacific Since the first of the month, the British have withdrawn from the Malayan mainland to Singapore; on the 8th, the Japanese invade the island, and by the 15th, the British (including 15,000 Australian troops) are forced to surrender. The Malayan campaign has been one of the greatest disasters in British military history.

13 FEBRUARY 1942
WW II: Germany The German High Command cancels Operation Sea Lion, their plan to invade Britain. Militarily sound, the decision is a tacit recognition of Germany's limitations at sea.

16 FEBRUARY 1942
WW II: Japan General Tojo, the prime minister, outlines Japan's war aims to the Diet and refers to a 'new order of coexistence and coprosperity on ethical principles in Greater East Asia.'

19 FEBRUARY 1942
WW II: France Two former prime ministers, Rey-

Japanese being evacuated from the West Coast.

naud and Blum, are put on trial by the Vichy authorities charged with responsibility for the French defeat in 1940. They will astutely shift the blame to the French military establishment, and the trial is never concluded.

WW II: Australia In one of the few attacks on Australia itself, Japanese planes from carriers bomb Darwin in the north.

27 FEBRUARY–1 MARCH 1942
WW II: Pacific An Allied squadron of five cruisers and 11 destroyers tries to intercept the Japanese invasion force bound for Java; in a series of battles, Allied ships are almost eliminated, while the Japanese suffer slight damage to land on Java on 28 February.

MARCH 1942
WW II: USA Following through on President Roosevelt's authorization (on 20 February) to intern Japanese-Americans, thousands of these *nisei* are moved from their homes on the Pacific coast to camps in Colorado, Utah, and other inland locales. A total of 100,000 will be interned, with relatively little reaction from most Americans. Special military units of *nisei* will soon be formed and perform exemplary duty.

1 MARCH 1942
WW II: Russia The Soviet Army begins a new counteroffensive in the Crimea. The Germans estimate that by now they have lost some 1,500,000 in their Russian campaign.

7 MARCH 1942
WW II: Pacific The Japanese land their first troops on New Guinea: Australians see this as a major threat. In Burma, British troops evacuate Rangoon, the only significant port in the area; the Japanese begin to move in this same day.

9 MARCH 1942
WW II: Pacific The Dutch commander on Java surrenders 100,000 Allied troops as the Japanese take control of the island.

11 MARCH 1942
WW II: Pacific General MacArthur leaves the Philippines with his oft-quoted declaration 'I shall

A WORLD AT WAR 1940-1945

return!' He will arrive in Australia on the 17th to assume supreme command of Allied forces in the southwest Pacific. Orders from Washington leave General Jonathan Wainwright in command on the Philippines.

1 APRIL 1942
WW II: Pacific   The Japanese resume major attacks on Bataan, where the American and Filipino forces count some 24,000 men sick due to short rations and tropical diseases.

4–9 APRIL 1942
WW II: Pacific   A Japanese carrier force attacks a British force and merchant ships in the Indian Ocean, sinking 120,000 tons of merchant shipping along with one carrier, two cruisers, and four smaller Royal Navy ships.

8 APRIL 1942
WW II: Mediterranean   Malta, already desperate, suffers the worst air attack of the war. During April, the RAF will lose 126 planes on the ground and 20 in the air; by the end of April, British submarines will be forced to abandon their base at Malta, whose harbor is virtually closed to shipping. The island will continue to hold out; on 16 April King George VI will award Malta the George Cross for the collective heroism of the Maltese.

9 APRIL 1942
WW II: Pacific   Allied forces on Luzon, Philippines, surrender; 75,000 prisoners, including 12,000 Americans, are force-marched to a camp some 100 miles away, many dying of ill treatment on the way.
India   The British Government offers India autonomy after the war, but on the 16th Indian Nationalist leaders reject this, demanding immediate independence. In the ensuing disturbances, Gandhi, Nehru, and Abdul Kalam Azad are arrested, but the British release them to keep India's support in the war.

14 APRIL 1942
WW II: France   Marshal Pétain is forced by the Germans to restore Laval as prime minister of the Vichy Government. Pétain will remain as head of state, but his authority is declining; on 18 November 1942 he will empower Laval to issue decrees on his own.

18 APRIL 1942
WW II: Pacific   Sixteen US B-25 bombers, led by Major General James Doolittle, take off from the carrier *Hornet* about 650 miles off Japan and raid Tokyo and three other Japanese cities. The survivors land in China. The raid does little damage, but boosts Allied morale and diverts Japanese defense efforts.

24 APRIL 1942
WW II: Britain   Exeter is bombed by the Germans in the first of the 'Baedeker Raids,' so called because they are aimed at historical British towns selected from a Baedeker Guide.

26 APRIL 1942
WW II: Germany   Hitler addresses the Reichstag and foretells major victories in the summer ahead; he calls for a supreme effort by all Germans.

29 APRIL 1942
WW II: Pacific   The Japanese enter Lashio, Burma, cutting off the overland route to China. All supplies from the Allies must now go in by air.

4–8 MAY 1942
WW II: Pacific   In the Battle of the Coral Sea, off southern New Guinea, US Navy planes inflict heavy losses on the Japanese and prevent them from landing at Port Moresby. The US loses its carrier *Lexington*, and the *Yorktown* is damaged; the Japanese lose many valuable planes and pilots. Since all the fighting is done by planes from carriers, it is the first naval battle in history in which surface ships are not engaged.

5 MAY 1942
WW II: Pacific   British forces land on the island of Madagascar, a French possession off the east coast of Africa which will surrender to the British by 5 November.

5–7 MAY 1942
WW II: Pacific   On the 5th, the Japanese land on Corregidor, the island fortress off Bataan and the headquarters of American forces in the Philippines. On the 6th, General Wainwright must surrender some 15,000 American and Filipino troops. Next day he broadcasts an invitation to the remaining US forces on the Philippines to surrender.

15 MAY 1942
WW II: Russia   The Germans capture Kerch, main port of the Crimean Peninsula, but the Russian counteroffensive is gaining in the Kharkov region.
WW II: Pacific   The first British forces retreating from Burma reach India. The British and the Chinese have suffered terrific casualties in losing Burma to the Japanese.

26 MAY 1942
WW II: Diplomatic   Great Britain and the USSR, in London, sign a 20-year mutual aid treaty and agree to co-operate in prosecuting the war.

29 MAY 1942
WW II: Czechoslovakia   Resistance fighters attempt to kill the Nazi governor, Heydrich, in Prague; he dies of his wounds on 4 June. Between 9–11 June, the Germans obliterate the Czech village of Lidice in reprisal, killing 1000 Czechs.

31 MAY–1 JUNE 1942
WW II: Australia   Three midget Japanese sub-

A Nationalist Chinese propaganda poster in Chunking.

A WORLD AT WAR 1940-1945

Anti-aircraft crews on alert on the USS Ranger CV-4 *in North Africa, November 1942.*

marines enter Sydney Harbor and torpedo a naval depot ship, killing 19 seamen; a week later five full-sized submarines shell Newcastle and Sydney without appreciable damage.

3–7 JUNE 1942
WW II: Pacific As planes, submarines, carriers, and other US and Japanese craft engage, a great battle rages off the island of Midway. The Americans lose the carrier *Yorktown*, the Japanese four carriers and many of their best-trained pilots. The Japanese have lost the initiative in the Pacific naval war.

6–7 JUNE 1942
WW II: Pacific As a diversion from the Midway battle, the Japanese take Kiska and Attu, two of the Aleutian islands off Alaska.

10–21 JUNE 1942
WW II: North Africa Rommel's Afrika Korps launches an offensive that climaxes in the capture of Tobruk; besides 30,000 British prisoners, the Germans capture valuable rations and gasoline. Hitler promotes Rommel to Field Marshal.

18 JUNE 1942
WW II: Diplomatic Churchill arrives in Washing-

ton, DC, for another series of talks with Roosevelt and his advisers; they plan for the invasion of French North Africa and discuss the future of atomic research.

23 JUNE–1 JULY 1942
WW II: North Africa The first German troops cross the border from Libya into Egypt on 23 June; during the next week, the British pull eastward and assemble at El Alamein, where the British commander Sir Claude Auchinleck has decided to make a last stand. The Germans reach that area on 1 July.

1–2 JULY 1942
Great Britain The House of Commons debates Churchill's conduct of the war, some members claiming he has too much responsibility both at home and on the front; a motion to censure is defeated 476 to 25.

6 JULY 1942
Argentina President Castillo announces that his country will remain neutral in the war.

16 JULY 1942
WW II: Russia The Germans' summer offensive has been gaining ground as they near Rostov, move

4 OCTOBER 1942

up to the Don, and press toward the Volga. But losses have been high, Russian resistance is stiffening, and Hitler is intervening in ways that will hurt his cause.

21–22 JULY 1942
WW II: North Africa Rommel is running short of men, equipment, and supplies (which the British know through their penetration of the Ultra code). Launching a major attack, the British are unable to make a complete breakthrough.

25–28 JULY 1942
WW II: Russia Rostov falls (on the 25th) to the Germans, who now control much of the northern Caucasus. On the 28th, Stalin tries to bolster Red Army resistance with increasingly harsh discipline and more authority for officers.

29 JULY 1942
WW II: Diplomatic A combined British and American Production and Resources Board is established in London to allocate material and industrial priorities.

30 JULY 1942
Canada Parliament passes a bill requiring full conscription.

7 AUGUST 1942
WW II: Pacific American Marines land on Guadalcanal and two other small islands of the Solomons. The landings on Guadalcanal are little opposed, and by the 8th the Americans have overrun the Japanese airstrip and renamed it Henderson Field.

12–15 AUGUST 1942
WW II: Diplomatic Churchill and Harriman confer with Stalin in Moscow, explaining why the Western Allies cannot launch a 'second front' this year.

17 AUGUST 1942
WW II: Europe Rouen, France, is the target for the first all-American bombing raid over Europe. It will be 1943 before the US Eighth Air Force is ready to bomb targets in Germany.

19 AUGUST 1942
WW II: Europe Six thousand troops—mostly British and Canadian, with some Americans and Free French—make a commando raid on German installations at Dieppe, France. It is a disaster for the Allies in terms of casualties (3600) and equipment lost, but valuable lessons are learned.

22 AUGUST 1942
WW II: Diplomatic Several Brazilian ships have been sunk recently by German U-Boats; Brazil declares war on Germany and Italy.

30 AUGUST–2 SEPTEMBER 1942
WW II: North Africa Rommel launches a final

attack designed to clear Egypt of the British, but their superior artillery and air force hammer the Germans back to their starting lines (2 September).

1 SEPTEMBER 1942
WW II: Russia Fierce fighting occurs in the Stalingrad area, where some German units have reached the suburbs.

12 SEPTEMBER 1942
WW II: Atlantic A German U-Boat sinks the British liner *Laconia*, but surfaces to help survivors and radio for aid; because an American plane attacks the U-Boat, Admiral Doenitz orders an end to U-Boat rescue attempts.

23 SEPTEMBER 1942
WW II: Pacific Australians in New Guinea, having held the line against Japanese attacks, take the offensive with US air support and reinforcements.

25 SEPTEMBER 1942
WW II: USA In Washington, DC, the Maritime Commission announces construction of 488 cargo ships in the last year.

4 OCTOBER 1942
WW II: Russia General Friedrich Paulus begins his

OCCUPIED EUROPE

From their move into Czechoslovakia in October 1938 until their final surrender in May 1945, German forces occupied most of Europe. Those Europeans who survived would recall those years differently. At one extreme were the collaborators with the Germans: some, like Laval and Quisling, were overtly pro-Nazi; others were disgruntled opportunists; still others just drifted into collaboration, like the young women who became romantically involved with German soldiers. At the other extreme were those who fought against the occupying forces —the various partisan, guerrilla, underground, and resistance groups that grew up in most occupied countries. By destruction of German supplies, occasional killings, and sabotage of their own transportation and industries, they diverted German energies from the war elsewhere. They also brought death and destruction to their own countries, where the Germans retaliated by destroying entire villages and shooting innocent men, women, and children. (Another result was that in many countries resistance groups tended to split along pro- and anti-communist lines, resulting in postwar struggles for control.) For the mass of Europeans, though, occupation was another experience. Not only did food, clothing, fuel, and other necessities become scarce, occupied peoples had to resist the deadening psychological hold of an oppressive foreign regime. Many suffered from the bombs and armies engaged in the struggle to liberate them. The bell-curve of life, as usual, prevailed: at one extreme, betrayal; at the other, heroism; but at the center, survival.

A WORLD AT WAR 1940-1945

fourth series of attacks on Stalingrad; in the following days, there will be fierce fights around the city's perimeters, but the Russians hold on stubbornly.

7 OCTOBER 1942
WW II: Diplomatic Britain and the US announce that a United Nations Commission is to investigate Axis war crimes and that it will be a condition of any armistice that war criminals are to be tried.

21 OCTOBER 1942
USA Congress passes the largest tax bill in US history to date, calling for some $9 billion and including the 'Victory Tax,' a 5 percent tax on all incomes over $624, levied till the war ends.

23 OCTOBER 1942
WW II: North Africa US General Mark Clark lands in Algiers for secret talks with French leaders, from whom the US and Britain hope to enlist support for the forthcoming Operation Torch (invasion of Algeria and Morocco).

23 OCTOBER–3 NOVEMBER 1942
WW II: North Africa General Bernard Montgomery launches the attack that will become the Battle of El Alamein; by 3 November the Germans and Italians retreat westward. By 10 November the Axis powers are out of Egypt.

25–26 OCTOBER 1942
WW II: Pacific The Japanese and US Navies have fought a series of battles to supply their respective forces on Guadalcanal. On these days, in the Battle of Santa Cruz, the Japanese sink the US carrier *Hornet* and seriously damage the carrier *Enterprise*, but Japanese losses, particularly in air crews, force them to abandon their immediate plans.

3–10 NOVEMBER 1942
WW II: North Africa The Germans and the Italians are in full retreat, having lost 30,000 prisoners and 450 tanks since the British began their attack from El Alamein on 23 October.

4 NOVEMBER 1942
WW II: Diplomatic In London, the Cabinet Anti-U-Boat Warfare Committee holds its first meeting, with Churchill presiding. In its combination of highest-level political, military, and scientific personnel, such co-ordination is now typical of the Allies; the Axis will never do anything comparable.

8 NOVEMBER 1942
WW II: North Africa The Allied invasion of French North Africa begins under the supreme command of General Eisenhower. Some 107,000 American and British troops land at Casablanca, Oran, and Algiers; French resistance is inconsistent, partly because several French commanders are not opposed to an Allied victory. Admiral Darlan, Vichy France's commander in North Africa, is taken prisoner in Algiers.

10 NOVEMBER 1942
WW II: North Africa Oran falls to US troops (Casablanca will fall on the 11th). Admiral Darlan broadcasts orders to all French forces in North Africa to cease fighting.

11 NOVEMBER 1942
WW II: North Africa French authorities in North Africa sign an armistice. Suspecting that the Vichy authorities are irresolute, Hitler orders German troops into Vichy France. In Algeria, the British move eastward but are seriously hampered by German planes and troops that have been rushed into Tunisia.

13 NOVEMBER 1942
WW II: North Africa Admiral Darlan is recognized by US authorities as head of the French civil government in North Africa; this step is not well received by the British, who regard Darlan as a collaborator with the Germans.

13–15 NOVEMBER 1942
WW II: Pacific In the naval Battle of Guadalcanal, US ships inflict heavy losses on the Japanese Navy and the supply convoy it was attempting to escort. Control of the seas around Guadalcanal passes to the Americans, and the Japanese will be forced to supply their increasingly sick and hungry troops on Guadalcanal by submarine.

17–20 NOVEMBER 1942
WW II: Mediterranean A British convoy gets from Gibraltar to Malta with only one vessel hit: the period of heavy attacks on the island—which began early in 1941—is over.

19–24 NOVEMBER 1942
WW II: Russia Soviet forces begin a winter offensive along the Don, while the German troops in Stalingrad are slowly surrounded. By the 24th, some 300,000 Germans are isolated in and around Stalingrad; Goering assures Hitler they can be supplied by air, but they are doomed.

27 NOVEMBER 1942
WW II: France What remains of the French fleet has been at anchor in Toulon. As German troops move into the city, French sailors—under orders from Admiral Laborde—scuttle 3 battleships, 7 cruisers, 16 submarines, and 46 other craft.

1 DECEMBER 1942
WW II: France Admiral Darlan broadcasts from Algiers that because Marshal Pétain is a virtual German prisoner, he is assuming responsibility for the French Government.

WW II: USA Gasoline rationing, formerly limited to particular states, is extended throughout the country.

Great Britain The House of Commons receives the Report on Social Insurance prepared by the Bever-

General Montgomery, Commander of the Eighth Army, on the Western Desert, November 1942.

A WORLD AT WAR 1940-1945

idge Committee, calling for far-reaching measures designed to eliminate poverty; the laws that will emerge as a result are the foundation of Britain's postwar welfare system.

4 DECEMBER 1942
WW II: Italy   The US Air Force bombs Naples in the first such raid on mainland Italy. Churchill broadcasts a warning to the Italian people on 29 November that they must revolt against their Fascist Government or face a full-scale Allied invasion.

12–23 DECEMBER 1942
WW II: Russia   General Manstein heads an effort to relieve the Germans in Stalingrad; meanwhile, Paulus claims he lacks fuel to break out from within, and Hitler supports his decision to stay. By the 23rd, the relief troops come close enough for Paulus's army to hear the fighting, but the Russians hold the line.

24 DECEMBER 1942
WW II: North Africa   Admiral Darlan is assassinated. On 26 December General Giraud takes over as French High Commissioner for North Africa.

31 DECEMBER 1942
WW II   As 1942 ends the Allies can feel more optimistic than when the year began, but the world has little to rejoice about. In Russia, the Germans in Stalingrad are close to surrender, but others will fight tenaciously before they are driven from the country. In the Pacific, the Japanese decide today to abandon Guadalcanal—unknown to the Allies. The Japanese Navy has been crippled, but 2½ years of bitter fighting still lie ahead as the Japanese are pushed back to their home islands. The Axis is almost driven from North Africa, but this campaign is only the prelude to the move across the Mediterranean to Sicily and the Italian Peninsula. Meanwhile, millions are living—and dying—under brutal occupation troops. The Jews are being herded into extermination camps in one of the most shameful episodes in human history. Thousands of civilians will die in bombings and many more will lose their lives at sea. The war is far from over.

OTHER EVENTS OF 1942
Science   On 2 December a team of scientists directed by Enrico Fermi produces the first man-made self-sustained and controlled nuclear chain reaction; they do so in a crude atomic pile of graphite blocks and chunks of uranium metal, secreted under the stands of the University of Chicago's athletic stadium. This is the prototype of the nuclear reactors that will be developed to provide energy for peaceful applications, but its immediate effect is to be production of the atomic bomb.
Technology   Atomic research in the United States is placed under control of the top-secret Manhattan Engineer District, better known as the Manhattan Project, headed by Brig General Leslie Groves. Its

Enrico Fermi.

main task is to produce an atomic bomb. The Germans test their first V-1, a surface-to-surface guided missile, at Peenemünde, while the US Army introduces its 'Bazooka,' a small portable rocket-launcher first used in North Africa. The nylon parachute comes into use, and the Germans develop magnetic recording tape (a product they have been working on since the 1930s).
Social Sciences   Trevelyan's *English Social History*; James Burnham's *The Managerial Revolution*. The Mildenhall Hoard, an extraordinary collection of ancient Roman silver, is discovered in Suffolk, England.
Ideas/Beliefs   Erich Fromm's *Escape From Freedom*; Camus' *The Myth of Sisyphus*; C S Lewis's *The Screwtape Letters*.
Literature   T S Eliot completes *The Four Quartets* (begun in 1935); Camus' *The Stranger*; Jean Genet's *Our Lady of the Flowers*; Antoine Saint-Exupery's *The Little Prince*.
Drama/Entertainment   Thornton Wilder's *The Skin of Our Teeth*; O'Casey's *Red Roses for Me*; Eisenstein's *Ivan the Terrible*, Part I. Disney's *Bambi* and the ultimate movie, *Casablanca*, are released.
The Arts   Picasso's *Woman with an Artichoke*; Braque's *The Kitchen Table*; Matisse's *The Idol*; Piet Mondrian's *New York City*; Calder's *Horizontal Spines*.
Music   Stravinsky's *Danse concertante*; Britten's *A Ceremony of Carols*; Aram Khachaturian's *Gayane* (a ballet with the 'Saber Dance'); Roy Harris's *5th Symphony*; Strauss's *Capriccio* premieres in Munich; Copland's *Lincoln Portrait* and *Rodeo* (ballet). Irving Berlin's 'White Christmas' becomes an instant classic.

Life/Customs The US Supreme Court rules that Nevada divorces are valid throughout the US. The RCA Victor recording company presents the first 'golden disc' in recognition of sales over 1 million to Glenn Miller for his orchestra's recording of 'Chattanooga Choo Choo.' In England, Gilbert Murray, classical scholar and worker for world peace, helps found Oxfam, dedicated to eliminating starvation.

Miscellaneous In Manchuria, China, a coal mine explosion kills 1572 people. In Boston, a fire in the Coconut Grove nightclub, thronged with people celebrating a college football game, leaves 492 dead.

5 JANUARY 1943

WW II: Pacific The Japanese are beginning to execute their planned withdrawal from Guadalcanal, but the American forces do not know this, especially as the Japanese are making a stiff stand at Mount Austen.

8–10 JANUARY 1943

WW II: Russia The Russians issue a summons to surrender to the Germans commanding the trapped forces at Stalingrad, but Paulus ignores the demand. The Red Army begins an encircling offensive on the

Roosevelt and Churchill making their statements to war correspondents in North Africa, 24 January 1943.

A WORLD AT WAR 1940-1945

11th. In terms of manpower, the Germans are superior, but the Russians are well fed and clothed, with adequate fuel and ammunition. The environs of Stalingrad are littered with wrecked German transport planes.

14–24 JANUARY 1943
WW II: Diplomatic   President Roosevelt and Prime Minister Churchill meet at Casablanca, Morocco, accompanied by their Chiefs of Staff and other Allied representatives. The conference starts under a strain, as the British feel the Americans are abandoning the agreed-upon policy of defeating Germany first, while the Americans feel the British are doing too little against the Japanese. But the conference ends with general agreement on such strategies as the invasion of Sicily and Italy, continuous bombing of Germany, maintaining supplies to Russia, and the eventual invasion of France. At the closing press conference, Roosevelt announces the Allies will demand 'unconditional surrender' of Germany and Japan, which some will claim prolongs the war.

22 JANUARY 1943
WW II: North Africa   Retreating German forces pull out of Tripoli, the main port of Libya, destroying many of its installations. The British Eighth Army enters the city on the 23rd and begins using the port a week later.
WW II: Russia   The final phase of the Red Army assault on Stalingrad begins.

30 JANUARY 1943
WW II: Germany   On the 10th anniversary of Hitler's regime, Goering and Goebbels deliver speeches in Berlin: the Royal Air Force marks the occasion by a daylight bombing raid timed to coin-

cide with them. The Germans can scarcely ignore the direction of events. In Stalingrad, the Russians locate Paulus's headquarters and begin the final encirclement. Only two days before, the Nazi Government had issued a decree for mobilization of women.

31 JANUARY–2 FEBRUARY 1943
WW II: Russia   Field Marshal Paulus surrenders his units on the 31st, and within two days the remaining Germans surrender. With 150,000 Germans dead, and 50,000 Russians, Stalingrad marks an end to the Germans' Russian ambitions. When the surrender is announced to the German people, the nation observes three days of mourning.

8 FEBRUARY 1943
WW II: Pacific   British General Orde Wingate leads his 'Chindit' force—an irregular group of Britons and Indians—into Burma; Wingate and his Chindits will capture the popular imagination, but they are driven back to India in March.

9 FEBRUARY 1943
WW II: Pacific   After the last Japanese troops slip away during the night, American forces link up to recapture Guadalcanal. The Japanese have lost 10,000 killed, the Americans 1600; it is an important victory, strategically and psychologically, but Japanese resistance anticipates the long hard road to Tokyo.

14–22 FEBRUARY 1943
WW II: North Africa   Axis forces in Tunisia make a series of attacks, temporarily driving the Americans back at the Kasserine Pass, but on the 21–22 a fierce fight near Thala ends with Rommel's force exhausted. Rommel realizes Allied superiority in numbers,

Stalingrad, February 1943.

Medium guns in action during a night barrage in Southern Tunisia.

equipment, and air support; although the Germans will make some attacks in the next two weeks, they are ready to evacuate Tunisia.

22 FEBRUARY–18 MARCH 1943

WW II: Russia General Manstein begins a daring German counteroffensive when he leads an attack in the Caucasus. Outnumbered seven to one, Manstein's forces succeed in taking the city of Kharkov on 15 March. By the 18th, however, the spring thaw and lack of troops and supplies stop the Germans.

MARCH 1943

WW II: Atlantic This month will be described as the period when the Germans came closest to defeating the convoy system supplying the British and the Russians from North America. Allied shipping losses for March 1943 total 120 ships of 693,400 tons (submarines sink 627,400 tons); of these 108 ships, 72 are in North Atlantic convoys. The German U-Boat fleet loses 15 (only six in convoy battles). This proves to be the highwater mark for the U-Boats; within two months, the Allies have them on the run.

A WORLD AT WAR 1940-1945

2–4 MARCH 1943
WW II: Pacific In the Bismarck Sea, off New Guinea, US and Australian planes destroy a Japanese convoy, sinking eight transports and four destroyers, shooting down 25 Japanese planes, and killing at least 3500. This is a major setback to the Japanese plans for holding New Guinea.

5–6 MARCH 1943
WW II: Europe The British Bomber Command sends 443 aircraft to bomb Essen, Germany, the first attack in what Air Marshal Harris calls the 'Battle of the Ruhr.' By the time it ends on 12 July, there will be 43 major raids to destroy the Germans' industrial heartland; 1000 Allied aircraft are lost, and the Germans continue producing.

9 MARCH 1943
WW II: North Africa General Rommel departs for home leave. En route he meets Mussolini in Rome and Hitler in East Prussia, but fails to persuade either to withdraw troops from North Africa.

20–28 MARCH 1943
WW II: North Africa The British attack Axis forces on the Mareth Line; by the 28th Axis troops are retreating. By 11 April they will take their final defensive positions in the hills around Bizerta and Tunis.

7–11 APRIL 1943
WW II: Diplomatic Hitler and Mussolini meet at Salzburg, Austria, and discuss the lost cause in North Africa, where they decide to hold on. It is typical of the Axis' war that such decisions are made solely by Hitler, with little regard for the situation of troops in the field.

12 APRIL 1943
WW II: War Crimes The Germans announce discovery of mass graves in Russia's Katyn Forest. The bodies of 4100 Polish officers are found, apparently murdered by the Soviets in 1939. On 18 April the Russians deny the accusation. (In 1944 a Soviet investigation concludes the Germans killed the officers; a US Congressional investigation in 1952 indicts the Soviets.)

19 APRIL–16 MAY 1943
WW II: Holocaust The remaining Jews—perhaps 50,000—in the Warsaw Ghetto rise against the Germans, having seen 450,000 of their families and friends removed to labor and extermination camps. The Jews are unable to hold out, and on 16 May the Germans blow up their synagogue. At least 10,000 have died and the remainder are taken to extermination camps.

30 APRIL 1943
WW II: Sicily As part of the Allied attempt to deceive the Axis about their forthcoming invasion of Sicily (Operation Husky), a British submarine releases a corpse with false documents off the Spanish port of Huelva. The body will be identified by the Germans as that of a British major carrying letters to Allied commanders on a plan to invade Greece. This disinformation contributes to the Germans' failure to anticipate the invasion of Sicily.

MAY–JUNE 1943
WW II: Greece With British and American encouragement, Greek resistance increases, to draw German attention from Sicily. An important viaduct on the main Greek railroad route is destroyed, not only slowing German movements, but suggesting a link to a forthcoming invasion of Greece.

7–13 MAY 1943
WW II: North Africa Allied forces burst forward all along the line, capturing Tunis and Bizerta. Remaining Axis forces fall back to a peninsula for a last stand, but are so disorganized they begin to surrender. The ranking German general surrenders on the 12th, the Italian commander on the 13th. It is the end of Axis efforts to gain an African empire.

11–30 MAY 1943
WW II: Aleutians US troops land on Attu—captured by the Japanese in June 1942—and retake the island by the 30th. Six hundred Americans die and 1200 are wounded.

11–27 MAY 1943
WW II: Diplomatic Churchill and Roosevelt meet in Washington, DC, with their military planners for the Trident Conference. They agree on general strategy, including 1 May 1944 as the target day for the invasion of France.

15 MAY 1943
USSR Soviet authorities—aware that some of their allies remain suspicious of the expansionist aims of international communism—decide to dissolve the Comintern, the organization dedicated to that goal. The dissolution will be announced on 22 May.

16–17 MAY 1943
WW II: Europe A specially trained RAF squadron undertakes a precision raid on German dams that supply electricity to the Ruhr. Despite special bombs and techniques, the planes do little damage and 8 of 19 are lost.

18 MAY–3 JUNE 1943
International A United Nations Food Conference is held at Hot Springs, Virginia, producing resolutions that call for fairer distribution of resources in the postwar world.

22 MAY 1943
WW II: Atlantic Admiral Doenitz orders all U-Boats in the North Atlantic to stop operations against convoys: German losses are outweighing

Firing a heavy gun during the Battle of Kursk in the summer of 1943.

results. Allied victory in the 'Battle of the Atlantic' owes much to radar, aircraft, and code-breaking. The Allies' performance has also been well co-ordinated, with scientists designing and airmen and sailors operating the weapons produced by industry.

27 MAY 1943

WW II: Yugoslavia British officers are dropped to rendezvous with Tito's partisans, hemmed in by Axis forces. The partisans will fight their way out, and the British confirm that General Mihajlovic's forces are co-operating with the Germans while Tito's resist.

3 JUNE 1943

WW II: France Generals de Gaulle and Giraud, in exile, agree on the composition of a Committee of National Liberation under their joint presidency. De Gaulle is consolidating his position as the voice of postwar France; on 27 May his representative in Paris organized a central committee of various French resistance groups. By 1 August he will have restricted Giraud's role to that of military adviser.

10 JUNE 1943

WW II: Europe The Allies' Joint Chiefs of Staff issue the Pointblank Directive, formal instructions for priorities and goals of the bomber offensive till D-Day. British and American tactics have differed from the beginning—the British preferring night raids with heavy fighter escort and broad-area targets, the Americans daylight raids with light escort and precision targets. The Pointblank Directive is largely ignored by both sides.

5–17 JULY 1943

WW II: Russia Both Germans and Russians have assembled great forces—a total of 2 million men, 6000 tanks, 5000 aircraft—for what will be the largest tank engagement of the war, the Battle of Kursk. The Germans hope to cut off the Kursk salient in the Ukraine. The Russians are now well armed, and the Germans fail to achieve any significant gains. The Russians lose many tanks in the climactic days of the battle, but German tank losses cannot be replaced. The Soviets gain the strategic advantage in Russia.

9–10 JULY 1943

WW II: Sicily Sicily is invaded by US, British, Canadian, and French troops, with General Dwight D Eisenhower as supreme commander of forces that include 2500 ships, 3700 aircraft, and eventually 480,000 men. Opposition is light and several cities in southern Sicily are captured on the first day. The island will succumb by 17 August.

16 JULY 1943

WW II: Italy Churchill and Roosevelt issue a joint message—on millions of leaflets dropped from Allied planes over Italy—calling on the Italian people to overthrow Mussolini and surrender.

19 JULY 1943

WW II: Italy Some 500 US bombers carry out an air raid on selected targets in and around Rome. The Allies have not bombed Rome until now because of its historical, religious, and artistic significance; care is taken on this raid to avoid historic sites.

A WORLD AT WAR 1940-1945

WW II: Diplomatic Hitler and Mussolini meet in Feltre, northern Italy, where Hitler demands more effort from the Italians.

20 JULY 1943
WW II: Diplomatic President Roosevelt issues an order that the US share atomic information with the British. At a conference at Quebec in August, this will be confirmed in an agreement by which both countries also preclude release of such information to any third party.

22 JULY 1943
WW II: Sicily American troops enter Palermo, the capital; Axis troops are retreating to the northeast corner of the island as the British move up the southeastern coast.

24 JULY–2 AUGUST 1943
WW II: Europe RAF and US planes make a series of bombing raids on Hamburg, Germany, that result in some 50,000 civilian deaths and 800,000 homeless. Most of the casualties result from the fire storm created by incendiary bombs.

25 JULY 1943
WW II: Italy King Victor Emmanuel forces Mussolini to resign after 21 years as *Il Duce* of Italy. On leaving the meeting, Mussolini is arrested. Marshal Pietro Badoglio is named Prime Minister; pretending to support the Axis struggle, he will immediately look for a way to get Italy out of the war.

1 AUGUST 1943
WW II: Diplomatic Having established a puppet government in Burma, Japan announces that the country is now independent and has declared war on the US and Britain.

13–24 AUGUST 1943
WW II: Diplomatic In Quebec, Canada, Roosevelt, Churchill, and Mackenzie King meet with military planners to discuss the invasion of France and campaigns in the Pacific. It is agreed that the supreme commander of the invasion will be an American, and that continuing aid will be sent to Chiang Kai-shek in China.

16–23 AUGUST 1943
WW II: Pacific At Wewak, New Guinea, US Air Force planes destroy or disable 300 Japanese planes and kill 1500 Japanese pilots and ground crew. Wewak is an important base for Japan's Pacific operations, so this is a major loss.

17 AUGUST 1943
WW II: Sicily General George S Patton's US troops enter Messina a few hours before the British, ending the campaign in Sicily. Some 10,000 Germans have been killed and 100,000 Italians taken prisoner, but over 100,000 of their combined troops have escaped to the Italian mainland.

21 AUGUST 1943
Australia John Curtin, the recent prime minister, and his Labor Party win general elections. Curtin has organized the Australian workforce and economy for the war effort—even getting Australians to accept limited conscription—and this victory is interpreted as a vote of confidence.

26–27 AUGUST 1943
WW II: Diplomatic The US, Britain, Canada, Russia, and China give limited recognition to the French Committee of National Liberation, consolidating General de Gaulle's power.

28–29 AUGUST 1943
WW II: Denmark The Danish Government, which has tried to mitigate effects of the German Occupation while avoiding actual collaboration, refuses a German ultimatum to resign. The German commander takes over and proclaims martial law on the 29th. Fighting ensues in parts of the country, and Danes scuttle some of their navy's few ships and sail others to Sweden.

3 SEPTEMBER 1943
WW II: Italy British troops under Montgomery cross the Strait of Messina and land on mainland Italy. This same day, an Italian general representing Marshal Badoglio signs a secret armistice with the Allies, agreeing to stop Italian military resistance on 8 September.

8 SEPTEMBER 1943
WW II: Italy The Italian surrender is announced, first by Eisenhower, then by Badoglio. The main Italian fleet, as agreed, sails from Italian ports to surrender.

9 SEPTEMBER 1943
WW II: Italy Allied troops land at Salerno, south of Naples, where they encounter strong German resistance. (A small British force lands at Taranto in the 'heel' of the peninsula.)

10 SEPTEMBER 1943
WW II: Italy Germans begin to evacuate their garrison from the Italian island of Sardinia; some go on to Corsica, a French island, but starting on 14 September the French rise against them. By 4 October Free French forces will liberate Corsica.

12 SEPTEMBER 1943
WW II: Italy Mussolini is rescued—from the house where he is held by the Italian Government—by a German parachute detachment led by Otto Skorzeny. This operation in the Abruzzi Mountains is carried out with skill and daring. On 15 September Mussolini proclaims his resumption of authority, but few heed the fallen dictator.

25 SEPTEMBER 1943
WW II: Russia The Soviets take Smolensk, a major

Men of the British beach battalions hug the ground near Salerno as German bombers attack.

city west of Moscow. The Germans are retreating to the Dnieper River, where Hitler has ordered them to make a stand.

27 SEPTEMBER–1 OCTOBER 1943
WW II: Italy The people of Naples rise against the Germans and fight for three days with heavy losses. On 1 October the US 5th Army, led by General Mark Clark, takes Naples. Before evacuating the city, the Germans damage many of its cultural institutions and burn thousands of books—to punish the Italians for their 'betrayal.'

1–6 OCTOBER 1943
WW II: Russia Soviet troops cross the Dnieper River at several points: the Germans had hoped to forestall such crossings until after the winter.

12–13 OCTOBER 1943
WW II: Italy The US Fifth Army attacks German lines along the Volturno River, north of Naples in the beginning of the hard-fought battles to Rome. On

the 13th Italy declares war on Germany. As the Allied troops advance, they leave a military government in control for the duration.

19–30 OCTOBER 1943
WW II: Diplomatic In Moscow, foreign ministers of the USSR, Great Britain, and the US, with the Chinese ambassador to Russia, discuss issues of mutual interest. They sign a four-power agreement on postwar treatment of the Axis powers and on the creation of an international organization to work for peace.

1 NOVEMBER 1943
WW II: Pacific US troops begin to land on Bougainville in the Solomons. It will be 23 March 1944 before this hard-fought campaign ends with the US in control.

5 NOVEMBER 1943
USA The Senate passes the Connally Resolution calling for the US to support an international peace

A WORLD AT WAR 1940-1945

Stalin, Roosevelt and Churchill at the Teheran Conference in 1943.

organization. This complements the Fulbright Resolution passed in the House of Representatives on 21 September, and shows a trend away from post-World War I isolationism that rejected the League of Nations.

6 NOVEMBER 1943
WW II: Russia Soviet troops recapture Kiev, their third-largest city. Stalin makes a broadcast to the Russian people.

20–23 OCTOBER 1943
WW II: Pacific US troops make a costly landing on Tarawa Atoll of the Gilbert Islands—1500 of the first 5000 are killed or wounded. Tarawa is theirs by the 23rd, with 1200 additional casualties. In proportion to the forces engaged it is the costliest operation in US military history.

22–26 NOVEMBER 1943
WW II: Diplomatic Roosevelt and Churchill converge on Cairo to meet with Chiang Kai-shek, Chinese Nationalist leader. They agree that Japan must accept such terms as restoration of all Chinese territory, independence for Korea, and surrender of all Pacific islands it has seized since 1941.

28 NOVEMBER–1 DECEMBER 1943
WW II: Diplomatic Roosevelt and Churchill fly on to Teheran, Iran, to meet with Stalin (the first time these three have met). They agree on timing of the invasion of northern France and plans to invade southern France. Stalin promises to join the war against Japan when Germany is defeated.

4–6 DECEMBER 1943
WW II: International Roosevelt and Churchill return to Cairo for discussions with President Ismet Inonu of Turkey on his intentions to join the Allies.

10 DECEMBER 1943
WW II: USA President Roosevelt signs a draft bill putting those who were fathers before Pearl Harbor last on the conscription list. This is a compromise between those who argue that all men of a certain age are needed and those who resent risking fathers of young children.

12 DECEMBER 1943
WW II: Diplomatic Eduard Beneš, leader of the Czechoslovak government in exile, visits Moscow and signs a treaty for postwar co-operation with the Soviet Union.

31 DECEMBER 1943

24–29 DECEMBER 1943
WW II: Allies In a series of announcements in London and Washington, leaders of the coming Allied campaigns are named. General Eisenhower is to be Supreme Allied Commander for the invasion of Europe, with British Air Marshal Tedder as his deputy. Admiral Ramsay and Air Marshal Leigh Mallory will lead naval and air forces. General Spaatz will command US strategic bomber forces and General Montgomery the British armies.

26 DECEMBER 1943
WW II: Arctic The last operational German capital ship, the *Scharnhorst*, tries to attack an Allied convoy in the North Atlantic, but is surprised and sunk by the British battleship *Duke of York*.

31 DECEMBER 1943
WW II As 1943 ends, the Allies can foresee victory. The Russians have regained two-thirds of the territory taken by the Germans, who are pulling westward. The Italians have dropped out of the war, but Germans in Italy will fight long and hard to slow the Allied advance. The once-powerful German Navy is all but crippled (although its U-Boats will continue to take their toll). In the Pacific, the pattern has emerged: the Allies—primarily US and Australian troops—will have to fight bitterly for every stepping stone to Japan. The heartland of Europe must still be invaded. Although victory is in sight, it will cost many more lives in the months to come.

OTHER EVENTS OF 1943
Science Oswald Avery and colleagues at Rockefeller Institute demonstrate that DNA, a nucleic acid in the chromosomes of living cells, carries genetic information; they will not announce this discovery until 1944. Gerard Kuiper discovers that Titan, the largest known satellite of Saturn, has its own atmosphere.

Medicine/Health Dr Selman Waksman, the Russian-American microbiologist who coined the term 'antibiotic' in 1941, and associates at Rutgers University, isolate streptomycin. Also in the US,

large-scale production of penicillin is made possible by the discovery of a more powerful mold than that discovered in 1928 by Alexander Fleming. This year sees the publication of *Diagnosis of Uterine Cancer by the Vaginal Smear*, by Dr George Papanicalaou (with Herbert Traut), the culmination of 25 years of research during which Papanicalaou found a way of detecting cancerous cells that will lead to clinical application of the so-called Pap smear.

Technology Jacques-Ives Cousteau successfully tests an 'aqualung' he has been working on (with Emile Gagnan) since the 1930s; this self-contained underwater breathing apparatus (SCUBA) will open a new world for exploration and enjoyment: Cousteau will become a leader in oceanographic studies, underwater research, and the international movement to preserve the natural world. The 'Big-Inch' Pipeline, stretching 1300 miles from Texas to the Eastern Seaboard, goes into operation. The German Luftwaffe fires the first air-to-surface guided missile at HMS *Egret* in the Bay of Biscay.

Environment A small crack appears in a cornfield in western Mexico, the first sign of a volcanic eruption that will build a cone of 500 feet in six days; by 1952, when the main eruption ends, the cone of Paricutin will be 1345 feet (410 meters) high. Rivers feeding the Mississippi flood, covering over 12 million acres of farmland and displacing 50,000 people.

Social Sciences Harold Laski's *Reflections on the Revolution of Our Time*; Dennis Brogan's *The English People*; Walter Lippmann's *U.S. Foreign Policy*. Wendell Willkie, who lost the presidency to Roosevelt in 1940, publishes *One World* and helps convince Americans of the need to abandon isolationism.

Ideas/Beliefs Sartre's *Being and Nothingness*; Jacques Maritain's *Christianity and Democracy*; Reinhold Niebuhr completes the second volume (first in 1941) of *The Nature and Destiny of Man*.

Literature Hermann Hesse's *The Glass Bead Game*; Thomas Mann completes his tetralogy Joseph and His Brothers, 16 years in progress.

Drama/Entertainment Brecht's *Life of Galileo*; Sartre's *The Flies*; Saroyan's *The Human Comedy*. The musical *Oklahoma*, by Richard Rodgers and Oscar Hammerstein, is an immediate popular and critical hit, leading American musicals beyond show-business glitter into indigenous material.

The Arts Picasso's *The Bull's Head*, formed from a bicycle seat and handlebars cast in bronze, is one of the first *objets trouvé* ('found objects') sculptures. Mondrian's *Broadway Boogie-Woogie*; Max Beckmann's *Odysseus and Calypso*; the first one-man show by Jackson Pollock.

Music Orff's *Catulli Carmina*; Shostakovich's *8th Symphony*; Bartok's *Concerto for Orchestra*; Ralph Vaughan Williams's *5th Symphony*; William Schuman's *Secular Cantata* (which wins the first Pulitzer Prize for Music).

Life/Customs Frank Sinatra emerges as a popular singer who attracts screaming young girls to his

---

LORD BEAVERBROOK, 1879–1964

A poor Canadian boy who left school at 14, William Maxwell Aitken made a fortune in business and moved on to London to make his mark on the world. He quickly joined the inner circles of British politics as a member of Parliament, but his real power base was his newspaper empire: in both these forums, he advocated imperial strength but even fellow Conservatives found his views old-fashioned. In World War II he was invited to serve in Churchill's coalition cabinet and was notably successful in organizing Britain's industrial production. He was created a Baron in 1917, and it was fitting that this self-made Canadian of high aspirations adopted the humble name of his birthplace when he was ennobled.

A WORLD AT WAR 1940-1945

appearances, the first such 'pop idol.' The jitterbug is a fad—so is the 'zoot suit' (with its 'reet pleat').

Miscellaneous The United States introduces a 'pay-as-you-go' system by which income taxes are withheld from paychecks. There are race riots in Detroit, Mobile, and New York City as Americans begin to resist the emergence of blacks under wartime pressures. Rationing is becoming worldwide.

JANUARY–MARCH 1944
WW II: Atlantic German U-Boats are losing the battle with Allied shipping. Although they sink 54 Allied ships during these months, they lose 60. On 22 March Admiral Doenitz will order U-Boats to disperse from groups and operate singly.

4–5 JANUARY 1944
WW II: Italy Allied units attack the German Gustav Line between Naples and Rome.

19 JANUARY 1944
USA With final settlement of the wage dispute, railroads return to private ownership; the Federal Government has operated them since 27 December 1943 to avert a threatened strike.

22 JANUARY 1944
WW II: Italy Allied forces land at Anzio and Nettuno, 30 miles south of Rome, to establish a beachhead that will outflank German lines across central Italy. The Germans are caught off-guard—only 13 of 36,000 Allied soldiers ashore on the first day are killed. By the second day, some 50,000 Allied troops have landed, but American Major General Lucas fails to press the attack toward Rome.

27 JANUARY 1944
WW II: Russia The siege of Leningrad is lifted. The city has been cut off since 15 September 1941, and several hundred thousand civilians have died of malnutrition and disease.

27–31 JANUARY 1944
WW II: Diplomatic Britain, the US, and Australia protest Japanese ill treatment of prisoners of war as information comes to light; they promise trials for those responsible.

31 JANUARY–23 FEBRUARY 1944
WW II: Pacific US forces invade the Marshall Islands, where the Allies gain control within three weeks. This is the first prewar Japanese territory to be captured.

2 FEBRUARY 1944
WW II: Italy Allied attacks around Anzio are halted by large German forces now brought into position here. The Allies have temporarily lost the initiative.

3 FEBRUARY 1944
WW II: Pacific US warships shell the Kurile Islands off northern Japan, the first Allied attack on Japan's home territory.

WW II: Italy The Germans take the offensive against Allied forces at Anzio and Cassino that are trying to break the Gustav Line.

WW II: Russia Some 56,000 German troops are encircled in the 'Korsun pocket' in the Ukraine. Moscow celebrates the news, and Hitler refuses to order a retreat. It will be 17 February before the battle ends, by which time 35,000 Germans have escaped to their own lines.

15 FEBRUARY 1944
WW II: Italy The medieval monastery at the crest of Monte Cassino is heavily bombed at the request of New Zealand commanders who claim that the Germans are using it as a command post and artillery base. It will be learned that the Germans had not used the monastery until after the bombing, when the ruins and cellars provided an excellent position.

16–19 FEBRUARY 1944
WW II: Italy The Germans attack the Allies at the Anzio beachhead, but fail to make significant gains.

20–27 FEBRUARY 1944
WW II: Europe The US Air Force conducts a series of massive raids on German aircraft-industry centers in what is known as 'Big Week.' Losses are heavy (65 bombers on one raid alone), but the Germans' air capacity is seriously weakened.

2–4 MARCH 1944
WW II: Diplomatic The US Government announces on the 2nd that it is cutting off all Lend-Lease aid to Turkey because of that country's reluctance to join the war against the Axis. On the 4th, the US declares nonrecognition of Argentina, which has also failed to declare war on the Axis.

6–8 MARCH 1944
WW II: Europe With 800 fighter planes supporting them, 660 US bombers make their first raid on Berlin on the 6th; 580 bombers repeat the raid on the 8th. US losses amount to some 10 percent of their planes.

15–23 MARCH 1944
WW II: Italy After a lengthy stalemate at Cassino, a checkpoint to Allies trying to break through the Gustav Line, they launch a major bombing raid and tank assault. Losses are so high that the attack is called off on the 23rd, not to be resumed until May.

19 MARCH 1944
WW II: Hungary Germans move troops into Hungary to prevent a collapse and ensure a line of retreat for forces leaving Russia. (Admiral Horthy, the Regent, was arrested by Hitler on the 18th.) Russian gains in all sectors of the Ukraine are such that the Germans have little chance for concentrated resistance; Hitler will continue to blame his generals, but retreat is inevitable.

Allied invasion chiefs Bradley, Ramsey, Tedder, Eisenhower, Montgomery, Leigh-Mallory, Bedell-Smith.

29 MARCH 1944
WW II: Diplomatic   The US Congress approves a joint resolution authorizing up to $1,350,000,000 for the United Nations Relief and Rehabilitation Agency. This will become a massive postwar program.

2 APRIL 1944
WW II: Rumania   The first Russian troops cross into Rumania.

4 APRIL 1944
France   De Gaulle takes control of the Committee of National Liberation by becoming head of the armed forces and pushing General Giraud aside. He appoints two communists to the committee, suggesting that he is prepared to work with them in a postwar French Government.

8–10 APRIL 1944
WW II: Russia   The Russians take Odessa, the

important port on the Black Sea, and Germans fall back in the Crimea.

18 APRIL 1944
WW II: Diplomatic   The British Government bans coded radio and telegraph transmissions from the British Isles; diplomatic pouches are to be censored and diplomats forbidden to leave the country. These and similar measures are designed to maintain security for the impending Operation Overlord—the invasion of France.

22 APRIL 1944
WW II: Pacific   The Allies launch a major invasion at Hollandia, Netherlands New Guinea; the Japanese are caught off-guard and 84,000 Allied troops soon establish themselves.

8–13 MAY 1944
WW II: Russia   Hitler finally gives permission for

A WORLD AT WAR 1940-1945

full-scale withdrawal of German troops from the Crimea. Some 152,000 Germans and Rumanians are evacuated between 12 April and 13 May; 78,000 have been killed or captured.

11–18 MAY 1944
WW II: Italy   In their final attack, the Allies force the Germans from the Cassino area, including the monastery: the Gustav Line across central Italy is broken, despite opposition at other points.

18 MAY 1944
WW II: Mediterranean   The last Allied ship to be sunk by a German U-Boat in the Mediterranean goes down.

23 MAY 1944
WW II: Italy   Pinned down at Anzio since their landing on 22 January, Allied forces launch an offensive. Stiff German resistance fails to slow their progress northward: by 1 June they are ready to make the final drive on Rome.

1 JUNE 1944
WW II: Overlord   The BBC transmits the first coded message, a warning to the French Resistance that invasion is imminent. The Germans understand enough to alert some of their units.

4–5 JUNE 1944
WW II: Italy   The first American units enter Rome on the evening of the 4th, but because it is Sunday the main Allied forces are held back. The German troops have evacuated Rome, which is now an 'Open City.' On 5 June Allied forces sweep through Rome and pursue the Germans northward.
WW II: Overlord   Convoys for the invasion are already on the Channel, but because of bad weather expected on 5 June they turn back. Late in the evening of the 4th Eisenhower decides, after consultation with meteorologists, that the invasion can take place on the 6th. (If it is not carried out by the 7th, it will be July before the same ideal combination of tides and moonlight occurs.) The weather has helped put the Germans off guard—Rommel leaves for Germany to celebrate his wife's birthday and persuade Hitler to strengthen the Normandy defenses.

5 JUNE 1944
WW II: Overlord   A second message warning that invasion is imminent is sent to the French Resistance; again the Germans note its significance—but fail to alert their Seventh Army in Normandy. Just before midnight, airborne troops are en route from airfields in southern England as Allied ships approach France.

6 JUNE 1944
WW II: Overlord   D-Day begins just after midnight with the descent of two US airborne divisions, followed in the early-morning hours by 4000 invasion ships, 600 warships, 10,000 planes (only one of which is shot down), and 176,000 Allied troops. The land-ings take place along a series of beaches in Normandy between Cherbourg and Le Havre—the Americans' code-named Utah and Omaha, the Canadians' Juno, and the British Gold and Sword. The Germans have six infantry divisions near the beaches and others within range, but due to Hitler's interference and their failure to pinpoint invasion plans, they fail to stop the first troops. Despite heavy casualties in some sectors—US losses on Omaha Beach are 1000—by the day's end there are 150,000 Allied troops dug in, with thousands of vehicles and tons of materiel. It is the largest invasion in history, a day marked by both epic movements and individual heroism.

10 JUNE 1944
WW II: France   The US armies from Omaha and Utah Beaches join, and the Allies are ready to present a solid line against the Germans. From this point on—despite delays, setbacks, and reverses—the Allied forces will move inexorably eastward until Germany surrenders in May 1945.

10–18 JUNE 1944
WW II: Finland   The Russians launch an offensive against Finnish positions and break through by the 18th.

13 JUNE 1944
WW II: Weapons   The first of the German V1 flying bombs lands in England. Ten had been launched, but only four cross the Channel, one of which lands in London and kills six civilians.

15 JUNE 1944
WW II: Pacific   US Superfortresses (B-29s) based in China, bomb Yawata, the first air raid on one of Japan's main islands. In the Marianas, US forces land on Saipan; by the time it falls on 9 July, the US will have lost 3400, but the Japanese dead will number 27,000.

18–20 JUNE 1944
WW II: Pacific   In a decisive air-naval engagement, the Battle of the Philippine Sea, the Japanese lose at least 400 planes and three carriers. US losses are 50 planes in combat and another 72 that crash while trying to land on their carriers in the dark (all but 49 pilots and crew are rescued).

22 JUNE 1944
USA   President Roosevelt signs the Servicemen's Readjustment Act providing financial aid to veterans for education, housing, and other needs. This act will become widely known—and admired—as the GI Bill.

27 JUNE 1944
WW II: France   Cherbourg falls to US forces, the first major French port to come under Allied control; although its facilities are in ruins, it provides a vital foothold.

The evening of D-Day.

1–22 JULY 1944
International Delegates from 44 nations meet at a resort hotel in New Hampshire, Bretton Woods, for an economic and financial conference. They agree to set up an International Monetary Fund and an International Bank for Reconstruction and Development; many of their decisions will govern international finance for the next quarter-century.

6–11 JULY 1944
WW II: Diplomatic General de Gaulle visits Washington, DC, for talks about the postwar status of his administration and aid for Free French forces.

11 JULY 1944
USA At a press conference, President Roosevelt says he will run again if nominated: 'If the people command me to continue in office . . . I have as little right as a soldier to leave his position in the line.'

18 JULY 1944
Japan General Tojo resigns as prime minister and chief of staff; other cabinet changes manifest a growing desire among Japanese statesmen to end the war.

18–25 JULY 1944
WW II: France St Lô, a crucial link between Normandy and Brittany, falls to US forces on the 18th; by the 25th US troops will launch a 'break out,' an armored thrust to isolate the German units in

Brittany. By 10 August the US Third Army, led by Patton, will achieve this and the Allies will move eastward toward Germany.

20 JULY 1944
Germany A bomb explodes near Hitler in his headquarters in East Prussia, but he escapes serious injury. It is apparent that a group of officers and politicians has plotted to assassinate Hitler and seize power, because some of them take steps on the assumption that he is dead. Before the day is over, several leaders of the plot are executed; other active or alleged conspirators will follow them into death.

21 JULY 1944
USA Meeting in Chicago, the Democratic Party nominates Franklin D Roosevelt for an unprecedented fourth term as President. Some insiders are aware of his declining health and urge that the Vice-President be a man acceptable to a broad majority. Senator Harry S Truman from Missouri is the candidate chosen.

25 JULY 1944
Germany Goebbels is appointed Reich Plenipotentiary for Total War: new decrees cancel vacations for women involved in war work.

1 AUGUST–2 OCTOBER 1944
WW II: Poland Patriots of the Home Army (AK)

A WORLD AT WAR 1940-1945

begin open operations inside Warsaw. This army of Poles is aligned politically with the exile government in London and is generally anticommunist. The rising is timed so that when the Russians arrive in Warsaw—as they seem certain to do soon—they will find an established Polish Government. Then the Russian advance comes to a halt: the Soviets will insist that this was dictated by logistical problems, but others accuse them of giving the Germans the opportunity to wipe out anti-communist forces in Poland. Whatever their motives, the Russians refuse to co-operate with the US and British, who airlift supplies to no avail. By 2 October 200,000 Poles have reportedly been killed and central Warsaw is in ruins.

10 AUGUST 1944
WW II: Pacific   American forces retake Guam; fewer than 100 Japanese prisoners are taken from a garrison of 10,000. (One Japanese will hide in the jungle till 1972.)

12 AUGUST 1944
WW II: France   The first PLUTO (Pipe Line Under the Ocean) carries fuel from the Isle of Wight to Cherbourg. This will be one of two ambitious projects that bolster the Allied invasion, the other being the Mulberry Harbors—old ships and huge blocks of concrete and steel sunk in position off two beaches to create instant ports.

15 AUGUST 1944
WW II: Southern France   The Allies launch a new front against the Germans by invading Southern France at beachheads between Cannes and Toulon. German resistance is negligible, and the Allies start their drive up the Rhone Valley.

20 AUGUST 1944
WW II: France   The Germans arrest Pétain in Vichy for refusing to go to an area safe from the Allied advance. General de Gaulle is now in France and resistance forces claim to control eight departments.
WW II: Russia   The Soviets launch a major offensive in the Ukraine.

21 AUGUST–7 OCTOBER 1944
International   At Dumbarton Oaks, an estate in Washington, DC, representatives of the US, Britain, USSR, and China meet to discuss forming an international organization to promote peaceful solutions to international problems as soon as the war ends.

23–25 AUGUST 1944
WW II: Rumania   King Michael dismisses Marshal Antonescu and names a new prime minister, allowing Rumania to accept Russian armistice terms. On the 25th Rumania declares war against Germany.

24 AUGUST 1944
WW II: France   Resistance forces in Paris have taken most of the city within the last five days. The

German commandant, General Choltitz, disobeys Hitler's order to fight fiercely.

25 AUGUST 1944
WW II: France   General Leclerc's 4th Armored Division enters Paris, and General Choltitz surrenders.

26 AUGUST 1944
WW II: France   General de Gaulle returns to Paris

HENRI PHILIPPE PETAIN, 1856–1951

A French military hero of World War I, Pétain restored order to the ranks of the French Army after failure of the Nivelle offensive and led his forces in the heroic defense of Verdun, where he spoke the famous words 'They shall not pass.' He took supreme command of Allied forces in 1918 and ended the war as a marshal. In the 1920s he led a joint French-Spanish campaign against an insurrection in Morocco (a young Spanish officer, Francisco Franco, served under him). When Franco took over in Spain, Pétain was accused of sympathy for his Fascist Government. When France was collapsing under the German onslaught in 1940, Marshal Pétain urged an armistice; called upon to become premier, he signed one with the Germans. France was divided into a northern occupied zone and a southern unoccupied zone, with its capital at Vichy. There Pétain became nominal chief of state, collaborating with the Germans as a figurehead, with true power residing with Pierre Laval and the conquerors. The fact is that Pétain at least acceded in anti-Semitic measures, deported French workers to Germany, and urged resistance to Allied forces. When the Allies invaded southern France, he went to Germany (he later alleged as a prisoner). After the war he was tried for treason, found guilty, and condemned to death. De Gaulle reduced his sentence to life imprisonment, and he died a prisoner at the age of 95, a pathetic 'fallen hero' of the century.

to join a victory parade that ignores the few remaining German snipers.

28 AUGUST 1944
WW II: Southern France   The last German forces in Toulon and Marseilles surrender.

WW II: Hungary   A new government, led by General Lakatos, takes office and announces readiness to negotiate with the Russians.

29 AUGUST 1944
WW II: Holocaust   Russians and Polish Communists announce jointly that they have discovered evidence that the Germans have murdered 1,500,000 people in the Majdanek concentration camp. This is the first of many such harrowing discoveries.

30 AUGUST 1944
France   The provisional government of General de Gaulle is established in Paris.

SEPTEMBER 1944
WW II: Atomic Warfare   Work on the American atomic-weapons program at Los Alamos has proceeded so far that a special bomber unit is established this month. Some scientists working on the project are beginning to doubt its morality, now that the fortunes of war have turned toward the Allies. But work continues.

WW II: Allied Strategy   Allied generals disagree on how to move against the Germans. The suggested approaches are: (a) the 'broad front' advocated by Eisenhower and others—with Allied armies moving in concert and sharing supplies and support; and (b) the 'wedge-thrust,' advocated by Montgomery and others—a plan to cross Belgium, encircle the Ruhr, and cross the Rhine. The broad-front strategy will prevail.

3 SEPTEMBER 1944
WW II: Belgium   British troops enter Brussels.

WW II: Southern France   Lyons falls to French troops.

4–10 SEPTEMBER 1944
Finland   The Prime Minister has broken diplomatic relations with Germany and today asks for a cease-fire with the Russians. An armistice is signed on 10 September, providing for restoration of the 1940 frontiers and Finnish reparations. The Germans are pulling out of Finland.

5 SEPTEMBER 1944
International   The exiled governments of Belgium, the Netherlands, and Luxembourg agree to establish a customs union after the war—one of the first steps toward the European Economic Community.

8 SEPTEMBER 1942
WW II: Weapons   The first of the German V2 rockets lands in England; much faster and more powerful than the V1 bombs, these will take a heavy toll, psychological and physical, in the closing months of the war.

11–16 SEPTEMBER 1944
WW II: Diplomatic   At the second Quebec Conference (known as the Octagon Conference), Roosevelt and Churchill discuss strategies for pursuing Germans and the Japanese and their status in the postwar world.

13 SEPTEMBER 1944
WW II: Rumania   The armistice between Rumania and the Allies is signed, with terms dictated by the Russians, including reparations and cession of territory.

17–25 SEPTEMBER 1944
WW II: Netherlands   Operation Market Garden begins on the 17th. This plan, primarily Montgomery's, calls for airborne troops to seize a series of bridges over river and canal lines in Holland as an Allied route into Germany. British troops dropped near the farthest bridge, that at Arnhem, over the lower Rhine, find themselves in serious trouble with the Germans guarding the bridge. By the 25th, after several failed rescue operations, surviving troops are withdrawn from the area—with some 1100 killed and 6400 left as prisoners.

4 OCTOBER 1944
WW II: Greece   Allied forces land near Patras, on the Peloponnesus, and on some Aegean islands. Patras will be taken on the 5th.

9–20 OCTOBER 1944
WW II: Diplomatic   Churchill and Anthony Eden visit Moscow for talks with the Russians on the political future of eastern Europe. Stalin insists that Poland, Bulgaria, and Rumania are to remain in the Soviet 'sphere of influence'; Greece can come under British sway; Hungary and Yugoslavia are to come under both nations' influence. The British (and later the Americans) will go along with Stalin because they need his support against Germany and then Japan.

12–14 OCTOBER 1944
WW II: Pacific   The Allies send a series of attacks against Formosa from offshore carriers. Altogether, 71 Allied planes are lost and three ships seriously damaged.

13 OCTOBER 1944
WW II: Weapons   The Germans fire V1 and V2 rockets on Antwerp, Belgium, where their troops have been holding off the Allied troops.

14 OCTOBER 1944
Germany   Suspected of complicity in the 20th of July plot against Hitler, Field-Marshal Rommel is visited at home by two of Hitler's staff and given the choice of a public trial or suicide by poison (with a state funeral and guaranteed immunity for his wife

A WORLD AT WAR 1940-1945

and family). Rommel chooses suicide, and it is announced that he has died of wounds.

18 OCTOBER 1944
Greece The exiled Greek Government returns to Athens.

20 OCTOBER 1944
WW II: Philippines US forces land on Leyte, the Philippines.
WW II: Yugoslavia A combined attack by Tito's partisans and Russian army units completes the liberation of Belgrade.

23–26 OCTOBER 1944
WW II: Pacific The Japanese have sent a large naval force into the Leyte Gulf to disrupt the American invasion of the Philippines. Instead, in the Battle of Leyte Gulf and ensuing engagements, the Japanese suffer a major defeat, losing 24 large ships (including 4 carriers, 3 battleships, and 10 cruisers). From this point on, the depleted Japanese Navy increasingly resorts to the suicidal attacks of Kamikaze fighters, who ritually dedicate themselves to diving their planes into enemy ships.

1 NOVEMBER 1944
Yugoslavia Tito and the prime minister of the government in exile sign agreements on their country's future constitution. From this point on, Tito would impose his own version of communism in Yugoslavia while defying the authority of the Soviet Union.

5 NOVEMBER 1944
Middle East Lord Moyne, British resident minister in the Middle East, is assassinated in Cairo by two members of the Zionist Stern Gang. With the end of the war in sight, some Zionists are determined that the British will not re-establish control over Palestine.

7 NOVEMBER 1944
USA President Roosevelt wins an unprecedented fourth term, with 25,602,504 popular votes to Thomas Dewey's 22,006,285; the electoral vote is 432 to 99.

12 NOVEMBER 1944
WW II: Atlantic The German battleship *Tirpitz*, which has taken refuge in a Norwegian fjord for many months, is attacked and sunk by British bombers.

16–20 NOVEMBER 1944
WW II: Belgium Quarrels between the Belgian Government and the resistance movement are mediated by the Allies: resistance fighters agree to surrender their arms.

28 NOVEMBER 1944
WW II: Logistics The first Allied convoy reaches Antwerp, the major Belgian port.

3–29 DECEMBER 1944
Greece Police open fire on demonstrations in Athens sponsored by the communists, leading to civil war in Athens and Piraeus. British tanks and warships help put down the communists. On the 25th Churchill and Eden come to Athens for talks with Greek leaders, who announce on the 29th that a regency will be established. This is done on the 31st, and Greece is temporarily at peace.

16 DECEMBER 1944–27 JANUARY 1945
WW II: Europe The Germans mount a major offensive in the Ardennes Forest in Belgium. As the center of the Allies' line falls back, it creates a 'bulge' (leading to the name 'Battle of the Bulge'). It will be 30 December before the Allies regroup and start their counterattack; not until the end of January will the Germans be pushed back to their previous positions.

22 DECEMBER 1944
WW II: Europe While the Germans are still on the offensive in the Ardennes, the US 101st Airborne Division has become isolated in Bastogne and the Germans have demanded they surrender. The US commander, Brig Gen Anthony McAuliffe, is said to have replied today with one word—'Nuts!' The Americans in Bastogne will be relieved on 26 December and join the counteroffensive on the 30th.

JOSIP BROZ TITO, 1892–1980

Marshal Tito (Josip Broz), dictator of Yugoslavia from 1945 until his death, owed his power and reputation to his ability to hold the high ground in a field of conflicting forces. The son of a blacksmith, Tito (who adopted this name in 1934), was drafted to fight against the Russians in World War I; captured, he came out of the war a convert to communism, and returned to Yugoslavia to help organize the Yugoslav Communist Party. During the German occupation of his homeland in World War II, Tito organized and led the Partisans, which became a large and well-disciplined force that kept thousands of Axis troops tied up. As soon as Belgrade was liberated, he formed a new government, and in the elections of November 1945 (boycotted by opposition parties) his Communist Party prevailed and Tito became prime minister. So far his life had followed the pattern of many Eastern European leaders. What now distinguished Tito was the way he defied the Soviet Union while imposing his own version of communism. Stalin expelled Yugoslavia from the Cominform in 1948 but did not dare send in Russian troops. Tito emerged as leader of the nonaligned nations in the cold war and maintained the respect (and even the financial aid) of Western nations, who generally faulted him only for his suppression of free speech and press. Tito's success among the Yugoslavs came from his willingness to allow limited freedoms and traditional ways, particularly to the many small farmers. Tito was tough and autocratic, but he had to be to hold together the disparate, often hostile groups comprising Yugoslavia.

Lieutenant General Joseph W Stillwell confers with Major General Liao Yau-siang.

A WORLD AT WAR 1940-1945

The Leyte landings, 20 October 1944.

British troops moving down to the beach to board landing craft for the invasion of Holland.

31 DECEMBER 1944

WW II As the year ends, the war in Europe is clearly heading into its final phase as the Russians close in on Germany from the east and the other Allies push inexorably from the west. The failure of the recent Ardennes Offensive reveals the weakness of German forces. In the Pacific, the war's outcome seems equally clear, but the question of timing is less certain. Today the Japanese resistance on Leyte, in the Philippines, is all but over (the Japanese having lost some 70,000 to the Americans' 15,500 casualties), but many more islands bar the way to the Japanese homeland. Meanwhile, signs of strain among new governments in liberated countries are beginning to emerge. In Poland, for instance, the pro-Communist Committee of National Liberation, based in Lublin, assumes the title of Provisional Government of Poland. The government in exile and other Allies will protest to no avail. On 5 January 1945 the USSR will recognize the Lublin-based government: the 'cold war' is beginning to take shape.

OTHER EVENTS OF 1944

Science Two more laboratory-made transuranium elements are discovered—No 95, americium, and No 96, curium—by Glenn Seaborg, Ralph James, Leon Morgan, and Albert Ghiorso: the announcement will not come until 1945.

Medicine/Health The US Army uses DDT against an epidemic of typhus fever in Naples. Known as a compound since 1873, and discovered by Paul Mueller as an insecticide in 1939, this is the first successful large-scale use of DDT for health purposes. The first eye bank is established in New York City. The first total synthesis of quinine is achieved after natural quinine supplies are cut off by the Japanese.

Technology One of the first digital computers, the Mark I, (building since 1939) is completed at Harvard University; it is large (8 feet high and 51 feet long) and slow (3 seconds to multiply large numbers), but a crucial step into the computer age. The war is bringing numerous advances in aviation: the first jet

273

A WORLD AT WAR 1940-1945

Bing Crosby sings for the 381st Bomb Group in England, 2 September 1944.

plane to appear in combat is the German Messerschmitt Me-262 (flying at about 550 mph); another Messerschmitt is the first jet bomber; the first helicopter used in warfare is the Sikorsky R4. Napalm is used in warfare, and the Germans introduce their V-1 (essentially a pilotless aircraft) followed by the V-2 (a long-range rocket).

Social Sciences John von Neumann and Oskar Morgenstern's influential *Theory of Games and Economic Behavior*; Lewis Mumford's *The Condition of Man*. B F Skinner, the behaviorist psychologist, begins to raise his second child, Deborah, in an 'Air-Crib' of his own design—a controlled environment in a large plastic-enclosed criblike box that allows the baby to move around free of clothing or other constraints. The child will spend most of her first two years in this device (not to be confused with the 'Skinner box') and it will cause considerable controversy.

Ideas/Beliefs Carl Jung's *Psychology and Religion*.

Literature Jorge Luis Borges's *Fictions*; Pär Lagerkvist's *The Dwarf*; Somerset Maugham's *The Razor's Edge*; Rosamund Lehmann's *The Ballad and the Source*; Joyce Cary's *The Horse's Mouth*.

Drama/Entertainment Sartre's *No Exit*; Camus's *Caligula*; Anouilh's *Antigone*; Olivier's *Henry V* Bernstein's musical *On the Town*.

The Arts Matisse's *The White Dress*; Picasso's *Seated Woman in Blue*; Rouault's *Homo Homini Lupus*; Francis Bacon's *Three Studies for the Crucifixion*; Hans Hoffmann's *Effervescence*.

Music Shostakovich's *2nd String Quartet* and *Piano Trio*; Prokofiev's *5th Symphony*; Walter Piston's *2nd Symphony*; Roy Harris's *6th Symphony*; Bartok's *Violin Concerto*; Copland's *Appalachian Spring*; Bernstein's *Jeremiah Symphony*.

Miscellaneous At Auschwitz (*Oswiecim* in Polish), a complex of three major concentration camps and 30 forced-labor camps has been fully operational for two years: after the war it will be learned that some 4 million people—mostly Jews—have been killed here.

2–8 JANUARY 1945

WW II: Pacific The large American and Australian fleet that is to accompany the US landings on Luzon, the Philippines, comes under heavy attack by Japanese midget submarines, small surface ships, and Kamikaze planes. The cruiser *Boise*, with MacArthur aboard, narrowly escapes from a torpedo

Supplies for the US 90th Infantry Division roll through Bastogne, 27 January 1945.

A WORLD AT WAR 1940-1945

attack, and several Allied ships are damaged. The night of 7–8 January sees the last surface engagement of the Pacific campaign, with a Japanese destroyer sunk.

6 JANUARY 1945
WW II: Strategic Field Marshal Karl von Rundstedt, commanding German forces on the Western Front, asks Hitler to let him withdraw from the intense Allied counteroffensive: Hitler refuses. Meanwhile, Churchill asks Stalin if Soviet forces can go over to the offensive in Poland to take pressure off Allied armies in the Bulge: Stalin agrees.

9 JANUARY 1945
WW II: Pacific Operation Mike 1, the US landings on Luzon, begins. Japanese ground troops do not intervene in the first two days, but invading ships and troops come under heavy air attack.

12 JANUARY 1945
WW II: Eastern Front A Soviet offensive begins all along the front from the Baltic to the Carpathians. The outnumbered and underequipped German forces will soon fall back.

14 JANUARY 1945
Greece The Communists and the British agree to a cease-fire in the struggle to control Athens (and with it Greece).

17 JANUARY 1945
WW II: Poland The devastated city of Warsaw is cleared of German resistance by the Russians and a Polish unit fighting with them.

20 JANUARY 1945
USA President Roosevelt is inaugurated for his fourth term. (In 1951 the US will adopt the 22nd Amendment, limiting a president to two consecutive elected terms.)
Hungary The Hungarian Provisional Government concludes an armistice with the USSR, US, and Britain; the Hungarians agree to pay reparations and to join the war against Germany.

27 JANUARY 1945
WW II: Pacific The Ledo Road into China from Burma is finally cleared.
WW II: Western Front Troops from Patton's 3rd Army cross the Our River and take Oberhausen.

31 JANUARY 1945
WW II: Eastern Front Russian troops reach the Oder River: they are now less than 50 miles from Berlin.

4–11 FEBRUARY 1945
WW II: Diplomatic At Yalta, in the Crimea, President Roosevelt and Churchill (having spent a few days conferring on Malta) join Stalin to discuss the final phase of the war. Anxious to gain Soviet participation against Japan, Roosevelt and Churchill promise territorial concessions in the Sakhalin and Kurile Islands. The three leaders agree on the post-war borders of such Eastern European countries as Poland, in return for which Stalin concurs on fair elections within these countries. Finally, they agree to call a meeting of the United Nations in San Francisco on 25 April to establish a permanent international organization.

4 FEBRUARY–2 MARCH 1945
WW II: Pacific US troops reach the outskirts of Manila, capital of the Philippines, but 20,000 Japanese troops offer bitter resistance; it will take this month to conquer the devastated city.

13 FEBRUARY 1945
WW II: Hungary After a battle lasting almost two months, the German garrison defending Budapest surrenders. Over 100,000 Germans have been taken prisoner in this struggle.

13–15 FEBRUARY 1945
WW II: Europe A series of RAF and US raids on Dresden, Germany, leaves 70,000 dead (many of them refugees from the Eastern Front). One of the survivors is an American prisoner of war, Kurt Vonnegut, who will achieve fame as a novelist when he chronicles this experience in *Slaughterhouse-Five*. The raid will be controversial because Dresden is not an important military target, but an important cultural center.

14–15 FEBRUARY 1945
WW II: Western Front British and Canadian troops reach the Rhine River along a ten-mile front.

16–17 FEBRUARY 1945
WW II: Pacific Carrier-based planes from a large US fleet make heavy raids on Tokyo and Yokohama.

19 FEBRUARY–26 MARCH 1945
WW II: Pacific In one of the hardest-fought battles of the war, US Marines capture the Pacific island of Iwo Jima, strategically important because it is within fighter-plane range of Japan.

23 FEBRUARY 1945
WW II: Pacific US forces on Iwo Jima will take Mount Suribachi, and a photograph of their raising the American flag upon it will become a symbol of the fighting in the Far East during the war.
WW II: Atlantic German bombers sink their last Allied merchant ship.

24 FEBRUARY 1945
Egypt Ahmed Pasha, elected premier of Egypt on 8 January, is assassinated after announcing that Egypt is declaring war against Germany.

26 FEBRUARY 1945
WW II: Pacific The fighting on the fortress-island

First US Army men and equipment pour across the Remagen Bridge, 11 March 1945.

US Marines raise the flag atop Mount Suribachi on Iwo Jima, 23 February 1945.

A WORLD AT WAR 1940-1945

of Corregidor ends: thousands of Japanese fought to their deaths (only 19 are taken prisoner).

2–6 MARCH 1945
Rumania King Michael is forced by the Soviets to dismiss his government on the 2nd and on the 6th to appoint a new one dominated by Rumanian Communists. This is the first sign since Yalta that Stalin will not hold to his assurances about noninterference in other governments.

3 MARCH 1945
WW II: Pacific Japanese resistance in Manila ends after a bitter month-long fight.

7 MARCH 1945
WW II: Western Front Allied tanks reach the Rhine opposite Remagen and find the bridge there intact; troops are quickly sent across (angering Hitler, who dismisses Rundstedt). The Remagen bridge will collapse on 17 March, but by then engineers have built several others nearby.

9–10 MARCH 1945
WW II: Pacific Superfortress bombers drop tons of incendiary bombs on Tokyo; a massive fire storm is raised, thousands of homes are destroyed, and the death toll is estimated at up to 120,000. (It is probably the most deadly air raid of the war, including the atomic attacks on Hiroshima and Nagasaki.)

18–21 MARCH 1945
WW II: Pacific A large US Navy fleet attacks the Japanese home islands; Kamikaze planes attack in reply and are most effective, damaging six carriers. (The 832 dead on the USS *Franklin* make this the heaviest-ever casualty list on a US carrier.)

19 MARCH 1945
WW II: Germany Hitler orders a 'scorched earth' policy on all fronts, with industry and agriculture to be destroyed by retreating forces. But Albert Speer, his armaments minister, and many army leaders quietly refuse to carry it out.

22–25 MARCH 1945
WW II: Western Front Allied forces are now crossing the Rhine in massive numbers. By the 25th the Germans have abandoned resistance west of the Rhine and are in full retreat to the east. Some Allied units are already at the Main River.

23–31 MARCH 1945
WW II: Pacific US naval forces mount air and shelling attacks on the Ryukyu Islands in preparation for the landings on Okinawa. The Japanese reply with deadly Kamikaze attacks.

26 MARCH 1945
WW II: Pacific After a final suicidal attack, Japanese resistance on Iwo Jima is wiped out. Only about 200 of the original garrison of 20,700 remain

alive as prisoners; US casualties include 4189 dead and 15,308 wounded.

27 MARCH 1945
WW II: Weaponry The last German V2 rocket lands near London. The 1115 V2s have killed over 2700 British civilians, while another 2050 have killed thousands in Antwerp, Brussels, and Liège.

28 MARCH 1945
WW II: Diplomatic Eisenhower sends a controversial message to Stalin, informing him that the Allies intend to advance across southern Germany and Austria rather than head straight for Berlin. The British object strongly to both the warning and the strategy, arguing in favor of reaching Berlin before the Soviets. They are overruled by the Americans.

1 APRIL–22 JUNE 1945
WW II: Pacific US forces—supported by the largest naval operation yet in the Pacific—invade Okinawa. There is almost no resistance during the first few days, as the Japanese are entrenched in the south for a fierce last-ditch resistance that will go on for many weeks and take a terrible toll on both sides.

5 APRIL 1945
WW II: Diplomatic Russia's Foreign Minister Molotov informs the Japanese ambassador that the USSR will not renew the 1941 Nonaggression Pact.
Japan The government resigns, to be replaced by one with military influence; members of the new cabinet agree that no reasonable offer of peace should be turned down.

6–9 APRIL 1945
WW II: Pacific The Japanese send the battleship *Yamato* on a suicide mission to Okinawa: it has only enough fuel to reach the island, where it is to do all possible damage. Accompanied by Kamikaze fighters, the *Yamato* hits many US ships before it is sunk on the 7th.

12 APRIL 1945
USA While vacationing at Warm Springs, Georgia, President Roosevelt, aged 63, dies of a massive cerebral hemorrhage. Vice-President Harry S Truman is sworn in a few hours later to assume the monumental task of replacing a world leader in closing out the most devastating war in history.

13 APRIL 1945
WW II: Holocaust Belsen and Buchenwald, two German extermination camps, are liberated by British and American forces respectively, as the full horror of Nazi atrocities begins to emerge.

16 APRIL 1945
WW II: Eastern Front Stalin does not believe Eisenhower's message of 28 March and orders Soviet forces to make a major offensive that will beat the other Allies to Berlin. The Germans are far out-

US Marines hurdle a stone wall as they drive across Okinawa, 1 April 1945.

numbered and can do little but delay the advance.
WW II: Diplomatic The US Congress extends the Lend-Lease Act for another year, and President Truman, addressing a joint session of Congress, promises to continue Roosevelt's policies, domestic and foreign.

18 APRIL 1945
WW II: Western Front The last of 325,000 German troops taken prisoner in the Ruhr area surrender; Field Marshal Model commits suicide.

21 APRIL 1945
USSR-Poland The Soviets conclude a mutual assistance treaty with the communist-led Lublin Government, breaking Stalin's promise at Yalta to support free elections and political processes in Eastern Europe.

22–27 APRIL 1945
WW II: Diplomatic SS head Heinrich Himmler, minister of the interior, meets secretly with Count Folke Bernadotte of the Swedish Red Cross with a message to the British and Americans that Germany will surrender to them but not to the Soviets. The Allies reject this on the 27th and repeat their demands for an unconditional surrender. On the 23rd Goering

HARRY S TRUMAN, 1884–1972

Harry S Truman, 33rd president of the United States, was born to a farming family in Lamar, Missouri, and attended public schools in Independence. He served as an artillery captain in World War I, and after studying law at night in Kansas City became a county commissioner (known in Missouri as a judge). He was elected to the US Senate in 1934 and 1940. His able leadership of the committee to investigate the national defense program brought him the Democratic nomination for vice-president in 1944, and he assumed the presidency upon Franklin D Roosevelt's death in April 1945. Thrust into prominence in a crucial time, Truman confounded skeptics by his decisive handling of events. He confronted Stalin on his policy toward Poland at the Potsdam Conference and authorized use of the atomic bomb against Japan to end the Far Eastern war (1945). Changes in US foreign policy embodied in the Truman Doctrine were sustained in the Korean War. Elected in 1948 in a surprise victory over Thomas E Dewey, Truman (who called himself 'the hired hand of 150,000,000 people') continued to work toward American hegemony until 1952, when he retired to Independence and wrote his memoirs. National leaders sought him out for advice and counsel until his death nearly 20 years later.

A WORLD AT WAR 1940-1945

sends a telegram to Hitler offering to assume leadership if he is unable to continue; Hitler is so furious that he orders Goering's arrest.

25 APRIL 1945
WW II: Germany US and Soviet troops meet at Torgau on the Elbe River. The Soviets have encircled Berlin.

25 APRIL–26 JUNE 1945
International Representatives of 50 nations meet in San Francisco to draw up the constitution of the United Nations Organization. There is to be a General Assembly of all nations and a Security Council in which the US, USSR, Britain, France, and China will be permanent members while other nations sit in rotation. Perhaps the most crucial element is that each permanent member will have veto power over decisions of the Security Council; the Soviets have supported this, as they suspect they would be outvoted in many instances.

27–28 APRIL 1945
Italy Mussolini and his mistress, Clara Petacci, with other Fascist leaders, are caught by Italian partisans near Lake Como while attempting to escape to Switzerland. They are shot on the 28th and their bodies hanged upside down in the main square of Milan.

29–30 APRIL 1945
Germany Hitler marries his companion of many years, Eva Braun, and prepares his political testament in which he appoints Admiral Doenitz as his successor; he blames both Germans and Jews for failing to help him in his struggle to defeat Bolshevism. On the 30th Hitler and Eva Braun commit suicide (Hitler by shooting himself in the mouth, Eva by poison). As he had instructed, their bodies are taken outside the bunker where he has led the final stand of the Third Reich, doused in gasoline, and burned. (No traces of the bodies will be found by the Allies.)

29 APRIL 1945
WW II: Holocaust The concentration camp at Dachau is liberated by US troops; 30,000 survivors are found.
WW II: Italy The surrender of the German forces in Italy is signed at Caserta.

1 MAY 1945
Germany Admiral Doenitz broadcasts to announce that 'It is my duty to save the German people from destruction by the Bolshevists.' Goebbels and his wife commit suicide after poisoning their six children. Martin Bormann, one of Hitler's top aides, flees the bunker; despite claims that Bormann escaped to South America, there is evidence that he died nearby. Soviet troops now occupy almost all of Berlin, as American troops establish themselves along the Elbe and Mulde Rivers, where they have been ordered to remain.
WW II: Yugoslavia Tito's partisans take Trieste, possession of which will become a point of dispute between Yugoslavia and Italy after the war; in 1954 Italy will regain control there and Yugoslavia prevail in the surrounding countryside.

2 MAY 1945
WW II: Germany Soviet forces complete the capture of Berlin. Throughout Germany, Allied troops are advancing and conquering, leaving German forces little territory to defend.

3 MAY 1945
WW II: Germany The British take Hamburg.
WW II: Pacific Rangoon, Burma, falls to the British.

3–29 MAY 1945
WW II: Pacific The Japanese mount a series of Kamikaze attacks, sending some 560 planes during these days. They do considerable damage to Allied ships, including the US aircraft carrier *Bunker Hill*, which reports a death toll of 373.

4 MAY 1945
WW II: Western Front Doenitz sends envoys to Montgomery's headquarters and arranges for the surrender of German forces in Holland, Denmark, and northern Germany, effective 5 May.

5 MAY 1945
WW II: Germany Soviet units take Peenemünde, center of the Germans' rocket development; many scientists and technologists are captured by the Russians, who take them to the USSR to work on the Russian rocket program. Others, including Wernher von Braun, surrender to the Americans and will help develop the American space program.
WW II: Czechoslovakia As the Soviets are closing in on Prague, resistance forces rise against German SS units and begin a fierce battle.
USA A woman and five children are killed by a bomb falling from a Japanese balloon, near Lakeview, Oregon. Although the Japanese have been releasing these balloons for some time, this is the only one that does harm.

6 MAY 1945
WW II: Czechoslovakia US 3rd Army units under General Patton are ordered to halt their advance and allow the Soviets to occupy the rest of the country.

7 MAY 1945
WW II: Diplomatic Admiral Friedeburg and General Jodl sign the unconditional surrender of Germany at General Eisenhower's headquarters in a small schoolhouse in Reims, France. Operations are to end at 2301 on 8 May.

8 MAY 1945
Algeria Prefiguring efforts by many colonial lands to profit from the instability of their former rulers, nationalists in Algiers instigate riots.
Europe British, Americans, and other Allies celebrate VE Day. (The Soviets will observe it on 9 May, after the German surrender is ratified in Berlin.)
Spain General Francisco Franco breaks off diplomatic relations with Germany.

10 MAY 1945
Norway Quisling, the Norwegian collaborator with the Germans, is arrested with some of his supporters: he will be tried and executed.

11 MAY 1945
WW II: Europe Except for some isolated German units in Yugoslavia, the last German shots are fired.

23 MAY 1945
Great Britain Churchill resigns and forms a new caretaker government, after the Labour Party opts out of his coalition government. Elections are to be held in July.

1–13 JUNE 1945
WW II: Pacific A large US fleet completes nearly three months of operations off Okinawa; during these last days, it sustains much damage from Kamikaze attacks; on 5 June it is hit by a typhoon.

5 JUNE 1945
International The Allied Control Commission holds its first meeting in Berlin as it assumes control of the government of Germany.

11 JUNE 1945
Canada Mackenzie King and his Liberal Party are returned by general elections.

18 JUNE 1945
Great Britain William Joyce, Lord Haw Haw, goes on trial in London, charged with treason for broadcasting propaganda from Germany. He will be convicted and executed. Others, notably Ezra Pound, the American poet, and Tokyo Rose, will be similarly charged.

22 JUNE 1945
WW II: Pacific Fighting on Okinawa ends after a three-month struggle. The Americans count 11,260 dead, 33,769 wounded, 36 ships sunk, 763 planes lost; the Japanese count 120,000 troop and 42,000 civilian casualties. Many ships, including the battleship *Yamato*, and some 7800 planes have been lost.

26 JUNE 1945
International The United Nations Charter is signed in San Francisco by representatives of 50 countries.

29 JUNE 1945
WW II: Strategic President Truman sees and approves the invasion plans for Japan. They call for first landings on 1 November, with a second major invasion on 1 March 1946.

5 JULY 1945
WW II: Pacific MacArthur announces that the Philippines have been liberated (although individual Japanese will go on fighting till the end of the war).
Great Britain Voting in the general election begins, but it will be 26 July before the results are announced (because of the need to count the overseas military vote).
Australia Prime Minister John Curtin, who has led Australians through the difficult war years, dies. He will be succeeded on 13 July by Joseph Chifley.

11 JULY 1945
International The Inter-Allied Council for Berlin holds its first meeting. The Soviets agree to turn over administration of allocated sectors to the British and Americans, who themselves allocate parts of their sectors to France.

14 JULY 1945
Europe General Eisenhower announces closing of the Supreme Headquarters Allied Expeditionary Force (SHAEF).

16 JULY 1945
Atomic Technology The first nuclear explosion, of a fission bomb based on plutonium, is set off on a 100-foot tower in the desert some 120 miles southwest of Albuquerque, New Mexico, at Alamogordo

USSR troops at the Brandenburg Gate in Berlin, 2 May 1945.

A WORLD AT WAR 1940-1945

Montgomery, Eisenhower and Zhukov at Eisenhower's HQ in Frankfurt am Main, July 1945.

Air Base. (The Hiroshima bomb will use the isotope uranium 235, the Nagasaki bomb, plutonium.) This test is code-named Operation Trinity.

17 JULY–2 AUGUST 1945

International At Potsdam, near Berlin, Churchill, Truman, and Stalin meet to clarify and implement agreements reached at Yalta and other conferences vis-à-vis Germany and the former occupied countries of Europe. The British delegation leaves between 25–28 July because of the election results; on their return, Clement Attlee is the new representative. Truman, informed of the successful explosion of an atomic device, will inform Stalin on the 24th that the US has a new and powerful weapon to use against Japan; he does not identify it as an atomic weapon, but Stalin probably knows this through his espionage network. On the 26th the Allies authorize a broadcast

to Japan of what is known as the Potsdam Declaration—repeating the demand for unconditional surrender, qualified only by the assurance that there is no intention of reducing Japan to poverty in the postwar world.

26 JULY 1945

Great Britain The election results reveal an overwhelming victory for the Labour Party; Churchill and his Conservatives are out, and Clement Attlee takes over as prime minister on the 27th. The general interpretation of Churchill's defeat is that the British people see Labour as the party to lead them into the changed conditions of postwar society.

6 AUGUST 1945

WW II: Pacific A USAF plane (the *Enola Gay*, named for the mother of its pilot, Colonel Paul Tibbets) drops an atomic bomb on Hiroshima. The bomb is a uranium fission type and yields the equivalent of 20,000 tons of TNT. Sixty percent of the city is destroyed in the blast and firestorm that follows; some 80,000 Japanese are killed; many thousands more are burnt or develop radiation poisoning. The March raids on Tokyo were worse in their immediate impact, but the Hiroshima bomb will leave the world a different place.

9 AUGUST 1945

WW II: Far East The US Air Force drops it second (and last) atomic bomb—a plutonium bomb—on Nagasaki; 40,000 Japanese are killed. The Soviet Union declares war on Japan (8 August) and minutes later launches an offensive in Manchuria; the Japanese are overwhelmed by Russian manpower and equipment.

WW II: Diplomatic President Truman broadcasts after the Nagasaki bomb-drop and threatens Japan with destruction. Japan's Supreme War Council agrees late in the evening to an unconditional surrender if the Emperor is allowed some powers, a proviso that will be abandoned.

9–15 AUGUST 1945

WW II: Pacific Fighting between Allied ships and planes and Japanese planes continues along the Japanese coast after the formal end of hostilities, as not all planes are recalled in time.

13 AUGUST 1945

Palestine A World Zionist Congress in London asks the British to allow significant numbers of European Jews into Palestine.

14 AUGUST 1945

WW II: Diplomatic Japanese leaders have been holding out for Allied concessions on the emperor's power; now the emperor himself decides to end the war. He records a message to be broadcast the next day. During the night a dissident group of officers enters the Imperial Palace but fails to steal the recording. The Japanese decision is transmitted to the Allies, who announce their acceptance of unconditional surrender.

USSR-China The Nationalist Chinese sign a treaty with the Soviets agreeing to the independence of Outer Mongolia (and other concessions) in return for USSR recognition of the Nationalist regime.

15 AUGUST 1945

WW II: Pacific On this day, which the Allies observe as VJ Day, Emperor Hirohito's broadcast goes out to the Japanese; many can hardly accept the news, as tight government control has prevented most civilians from knowing the true situation of their forces.

17 AUGUST 1945

Indonesia Nationalists declare a Republic of Indonesia, independent of Dutch colonial rule. The Dutch will soon return to re-establish their authority,

and fighting goes on for four years until pressure from the United Nations forces the Dutch to accept Indonesian independence.

18 AUGUST 1945

Vietnam Taking advantage of the power vacuum in their country (as did the Indonesians the day before), a group of nationalists proclaim an independent Republic of Vietnam. One of the leaders is Ho Chi Minh, a communist revolutionary who has worked toward this goal for years. Disorders break out in which many parties are involved—the British forces who came to accept the surrender of the Japanese; the Chinese, who claim to be there for the same purpose; the French, who return to reassert control of their colony; the Americans, who at this point support Ho Chi Minh's cause; and the Japanese, who end up engaged in the fighting. Gradually, Ho Chi Minh and his supporters, the Viet Minh, are driven from the cities and towns and turn to guerrilla warfare against the French.

18–22 AUGUST 1945

Manchuria Soviet forces take over the province; by the 22nd the Japanese Army in Manchuria surrenders and Soviet troops move into Port Arthur and Dairen.

31 AUGUST 1945

USA-Palestine President Truman calls on Britain to admit immediately 100,000 Jewish displaced persons from Europe.

2 SEPTEMBER 1945

WW II: Pacific The Japanese surrender is signed on the USS *Missouri* in Tokyo Bay. General MacArthur—who on 29 August was named Supreme Commander in Japan—accepts the surrender on behalf of the Allies. (Among those present are General Wainwright, a Japanese prisoner since he surrendered at Corregidor, and General Percival, a prisoner since Singapore.) It is impossible to assign exact figures to the losses of World War II, but eventually it is estimated that civilian and military dead total 55,000,000 (of whom the USSR lost 20,000,000).

8 SEPTEMBER 1945

Korea US troops land in southern Korea to begin occupation of the country below the 28th parallel; as agreed by Allied leaders, the Russians will occupy the area north of the 38th parallel. This is intended as a temporary measure until democratic elections can be held, but both occupying countries will begin to support Koreans opposed to one another and Korea will remain divided.

12 SEPTEMBER 1945

WW II: Pacific Japanese forces in Southeast Asia surrender to Admiral Lord Mountbatten in Singapore. In the next few days, Japanese garrisons on various Pacific islands will also surrender.

The Hiroshima fire department was only 4000 feet from ground zero of the atom bomb blast.

A WORLD AT WAR 1940-1945

13 SEPTEMBER 1945
Iran With the war over, Iran requests Britain, the USSR, and the US to withdraw all troops that have occupied Iran to keep it from falling to the Axis. Iran is assured of withdrawal by early March 1946.

20–23 SEPTEMBER 1945
India Gandhi and Jawaharlal Nehru lead the All-India Congress Committee in rejecting British proposals for a government of India and calling for British withdrawal. Violence between the Moslems and Hindus is spreading, and this will prove to be the major problem.

23 SEPTEMBER 1945
Egypt Egypt demands that Britain end its military occupation, return the Sudan to Egyptian control and revise the Anglo-Egyptian treaty of 1936 giving the British privileges in Egypt.

1 OCTOBER 1945
Germany The US, Britain, and France lift most fraternization restrictions (except for marriage and living arrangements) on their occupation troops vis-à-vis the German people; Russia, taking a harder line, will not do so.

2 OCTOBER 1945
Germany General George Patton is removed from command of the US Third Army because his actions and words reveal his disagreement with the policy of uprooting all former Nazis from German society. Patton will die on 21 December 1945 from injuries in a car crash.

7–14 OCTOBER 1945
Portugal Premier Salazar loosens his grip as dictator enough to permit opposition parties and to lift censorship on the press; a week later, seeing how quick the press is to attack him, he reimposes censorship.

11 OCTOBER 1945
China Negotiations (underway since 26 August) between Chiang Kai-shek and Mao Tse-tung break down; Nationalist and Communist supporters are soon engaged in a civil war.

14–18 OCTOBER 1945
Czechoslovakia With Eduard Beneš back as president, the new National Front Government has already begun to purge, try, and execute collaborators with the Germans; now, with the backing of a provisional assembly elected on the 14th, the government embarks on nationalization of industry and reform of agriculture.

15 OCTOBER 1945
Great Britain The House of Commons votes to extend wartime emergency powers to the government for five years; in part to allow it to deal with the economic crisis precipitated by President Truman's abrupt closure of the Lend-Lease program on 1 August.

20 OCTOBER 1945
International Egypt, Syria, Iraq, and Lebanon form the Arab League to present a unified front against establishment of a Jewish state in Palestine; they warn the US that such an act would lead to war.

21 OCTOBER 1945
France Elections to the new assembly reflect the turn to the Left in many countries; the Communists hold 152 seats, the Socialists 151, and de Gaulle's Popular Republican Movement (MRP) only 138. But de Gaulle's leadership is such that on 13 November this assembly will elect him president of the provisional government; his cabinet, chosen 21 November, will include communists and socialists as evidence of his goal of uniting France.

24 OCTOBER 1945
International The United Nations comes into existence with ratification of its charter by the first 29 nations. Headquarters will be in the US.

NOVEMBER 1945
New Zealand The Labour Government—against opposition—acts to nationalize the Bank of New Zealand and to set up a government-controlled airline.

3 NOVEMBER 1945
Hungary In the first postwar national election, the anticommunist Smallholders Party wins a majority; its leader, Zoltan Tildy, forms a coalition government.

13 NOVEMBER 1945
Indonesia Achmed Sukarno becomes president of the Republic of Indonesia, still under control of the Netherlands: negotiations for more independence will soon break down.

18 NOVEMBER 1945
Bulgaria Because only one list of candidates is offered, the communist-controlled Fatherland Front wins the first postwar elections.
Iran A communist-backed group organizes a rebellion in the province of Azerbaijan; when the government tries to move against it, Soviet troops in Iran prevent them from doing so.
Portugal In the first general election in 20 years, Salazar and his party inevitably win—opposition parties have boycotted the election to protest the reimposition of censorship.

20 NOVEMBER 1945
War Crimes The trial of 21 major German war leaders begins at Nuremberg, Germany (till October 1946). This is the first such trial under international law and will be criticized by some on grounds that the crimes in question had never been defined by law.

General Douglas MacArthur (left) with Lieutenant General Robert L Eichelberger arriving in Japan.

27 NOVEMBER–15 DECEMBER 1945

Australia A strike of coalworkers in New South Wales so cripples the economy that in August 1946 Parliament will adopt the Coal Industry Bill, with a Coal Board to regulate all aspects of the industry.

29 NOVEMBER 1945

Yugoslavia The assembly elected on 11 November proclaims a Federal People's Republic of Yugoslavia, with Marshal Tito as its president.

30 NOVEMBER 1945

Italy In general elections, the Christian Democrats win; their leader, Alcide de Gasperi, forms a new government.

2 DECEMBER 1945

Albania The Communists win the general election —they are the only candidates offered—and Premier Enver Hoxha establishes long-term control over Albania.

4 DECEMBER 1945

USA The Senate consents to the treaty by which the US joins the United Nations—thus reversing a similar situation after World War I when it refused to endorse the League of Nations.

6 DECEMBER 1945

International The US extends a $3,750,000,000 loan to Great Britain (and Canada will follow soon with a $1,250,000,000 loan); this will help compensate for the termination of Lend-Lease.

13 DECEMBER 1945

Syria The French and the British promise Syria to remove all their troops (which they do by 15 April 1946).

15 DECEMBER 1945

China The US appoints General George C Marshall as special ambassador to negotiate a peaceful settlement between Chiang Kai-shek's Nationalists and Mao Tse-tung's Communists.

18–20 DECEMBER 1945

Austria The winning party in the elections (of 25 November), the People's Party, forms a coalition government with the Socialists; on the 20th Karl Renner is elected president of the Democratic Republic of Austria (re-established on 14 May).

27 DECEMBER 1945

International In Washington, DC, representatives of 24 countries that have ratified the agreement establishing the International Bank for Reconstruction and Development meet to establish it (as called for by the Bretton Woods Conference in July 1944). Known as the 'World Bank,' it will play a significant role in the postwar world by channeling funds from more developed to less developed nations.

OTHER EVENTS OF 1945

Science Melvin Calvin, an American biochemist, begins elucidating the process of photosynthesis.

Medicine/Health Purified curare (known to Europeans since Raleigh described it in 1595) is first used to produce relaxation in patients. Vitamin A is synthesized. Two American cities—Grand Rapids, Michigan and Newburgh, New York—are the first to add fluoride to their water supplies, putting to test the research carried out in the 1930s by the US Public Health Service that claims fluoride significantly reduces tooth decay without harmful side-effects. By 1950, 75 US cities will be fluoridating their water, despite continuing dispute over the practice.

Technology Canada builds the first nuclear reactor outside the US, at Chalk River, Ontario. At the University of Pennsylvania, ENIAC (Electronic Numerical Integrator and Computer) goes into its initial test runs, the first fully automatic electronic computer.

Social Studies Richard MacNeish begins years of archaeological research in Mexico that will produce many important finds about early culture in the Americas. Bossert begins to excavate at Karatepe in Anatolia and finds significant Hittite hieroglyphics.

Ideas/Beliefs Karl Popper's *The Open Society and Its Enemies*; R G Collingwood's *The Idea of Nature*.

Literature Carlo Levi's *Christ Stopped at Eboli*; Orwell's *Animal Farm*; Waugh's *Brideshead Revisited*; I B Singer's *The Family Moskat*; Hugh MacLennan's *Two Solitudes*; Henry Green's *Loving*; Cyril Connolly's *The Unquiet Grave*.

Drama/Entertainment Tennessee Williams's *Glass Menagerie*; Brecht's *Caucasian Chalk Circle*; Giraudoux's *The Madwoman of Chaillot*. The French release *Les Enfants du Paradis*, a major film made during the occupation of Paris; Rossellini's *Open City* and Hitchcock's *Spellbound*.

The Arts Rouault's *Head of a Clown*; Stanley Spencer begins his *Resurrection* series (till 1950); Calder's *Red Pyramid*; Henry Moore's *Family Group*; Epstein's *Lucifer*.

Music Britten's *Young Person's Guide to the Orchestra* and *Peter Grimes* (opera); Shostakovich's *9th Symphony*; Prokofiev's *Cinderella* (ballet); Heitor Villa-Lobos completes his ninth and final *Bachiana Brasileira* (begun in 1930); Stravinsky's *Symphony in Three Movements* and *Ebony Concerto* (written for Woody Herman, the jazz clarinetist).

Life/Leisure 'Black markets' spring up in Europe to trade in food, clothing, cigarettes, and other postwar luxuries. The world begins to learn about many of the scientific and technological breakthroughs that were kept secret during the war. France gives the vote to women. Bebop becomes a music craze in the US.

Miscellaneous The Allied Control Commission in Japan 'disestablishes' Shintoism, the traditional Japanese religion. (It is seen as a source of fanatical militarism). The first air-sea rescue by helicopter is made when the US Army recovers seamen on a wrecked barge off Long Island.

1946-1962:
IN SEARCH OF STABILITY

US tanks firing at a North Korean observation post across the Natkong River, 15 August 1950.

1 JANUARY 1946
Japan In a New Year's message, Emperor Hirohito says that he is not a living god—rather his relationship with the Japanese people is based on 'mutual trust and affection,' not 'mere legends and myths.' General Douglas MacArthur proclaims that 'The removal of this national enslavement means freedom.'

10 JANUARY 1946
International In London, at the first session of the 51-nation United Nations General Assembly, Belgian Foreign Minister Paul Spaak is elected president. In his welcoming address, British Prime Minister Attlee warns, 'The coming of the atomic bomb was only the last of a series of warnings to mankind that, unless the powers of destruction could be controlled, immense ruin' would face mankind.
China President Chiang Kai-shek announces a truce between the Nationalist government and Communists, expedited by special US envoy General George Marshall, Chiang also proclaims a series of democratic political reforms, including civil-rights provisions. But the civil war will resume on 14 April with intermittent hostilities and peace overtures. In

the earlier campaigns, the Nationalist forces are victorious.

17 JANUARY 1946
International In London, in the first meeting of the UN Security Council, Foreign Secretary Bevin announces that Britain will place under UN trusteeship its mandated territories of Tanganyika, the Cameroons and Togoland, and establish Transjordan as an independent nation.

20 JANUARY 1946
France For the third time in three months, President de Gaulle resigns, this time 'irrevocably,' in opposition to the Communist-Socialist demand for a 20-percent cut in the military budget. On 22 January Socialist Felix Gouin is elected president.

24 JANUARY 1946
International In London, the UN General Assembly votes unanimously to establish a commission on atomic energy. On 14 June the 12-member body will meet in New York for the first time to establish controls on world atomic-energy activities and to foster its beneficial uses.

IN SEARCH OF STABILITY 1946-1962

The first meeting at Yenan: Chu-Teh, Mao, Yeaton, Hurley, Chang Chih-chung, Chou En-lai.

31 JANUARY 1946
Yugoslavia The Federal People's Republic adopts a constitution resembling that of the Soviet Union.

9 FEBRUARY 1946
USSR In an election-eve speech, Stalin announces a new five-year plan mandating production increases of more than 50 percent. A 28 June purge will lead to numerous dismissals in the industrial sector for incompetence and dishonesty.

14 FEBRUARY 1946
Great Britain In its continuing program of socialization, Attlee's Labour Government nationalizes the Bank of England.
USA In response to widespread postwar labor agitation and calls for deregulation, President Truman unveils a new policy permitting restricted wage and price increases. By November he will remove all wage and price controls, except those on rents.

24 FEBRUARY 1946
Argentina Colonel Juan Domingo Perón is elected

president for a six-year term. Aided by his wife Eva, Perón will become dictator before he is ousted by a 1955 military junta.

5 MARCH 1946
International In a speech at Fulton, Missouri, former British Prime Minister Churchill declares that 'an iron curtain' has descended across Europe, with the imposition of 'police governments' in Eastern Europe.

6 MARCH 1946
Vietnam France recognizes Vietnam as an independent republic within the French Union, but this does not satisfy nationalist Communist leader Ho Chi Minh, who leads a violent campaign to expel the French and unite Indochina in one Vietnamese state.

5 APRIL 1946
Iran After a 19 March Iranian protest to the UN, the USSR agrees to withdraw its military forces from Iranian soil by 9 May. On 13 June the Communist-dominated Azerbaijan Province is returned to Iranian

The Nationalist Chinese 8th Route Army lined up to welcome General Marshall, 1946.

IN SEARCH OF STABILITY 1946-1962

control, but agitation there continues despite token reforms.

29 APRIL 1946

Palestine A British-American inquiry committee opposes the partition of Palestine and calls for an independent state with local and provincial autonomy, a solution that satisfies neither Jews nor Arabs. At a September-to-December London conference, the Arab states call for an Arab-controlled Palestine, while the Zionist Congress in Basel calls for a Jewish state. Arabs and Jews agree on only one thing—withdrawal of British forces from the Palestine Mandate.

25 MAY 1946

Transjordan The Kingdom of Transjordan, with Emir Abdullah as ruler, is proclaimed after the 22 March British recognition of independence. Close ties will continue between the two nations.

2 JUNE 1946

Italy A national referendum rejects the monarchy, even after King Victor Emmanuel's 9 May abdication in favor of his son Umberto. Italy is to become a republic, and on 13 June Umberto will leave Italy to prevent the outbreak of violence.

3 JUNE 1946

South Africa The Asiatic Land Tenure and Indian Representation Bill becomes law, restricting land ownership by Asians and granting direct representation to Indians in the Natal provincial council. The Indian Government protests by recalling its high commissioner and breaking off trade relations.

30 JUNE 1946

Poland A national referendum approves a program of governmental nationalization of industry and land reform, and establishment of a one-house parliament, as proposed by Communists.

4 JULY 1946

Philippines After 48 years of US sovereignty, the Philippines become an independent republic. In April Manuel Roxas was elected president.

22 JULY 1946

Palestine In Jerusalem, the west wing of the King David Hotel—British governmental and military headquarters—is blown up by Zionist terrorists. Some 76 persons, including British, Jews, and Arabs, perish, while 46 are injured. The British institute a city-wide curfew and arrest 376 Jews.

29 JULY 1946

International In Paris, the peace conference of the 21 nations opposing the Axis powers convenes to consider draft peace treaties with Italy, Rumania, Hungary, Bulgaria, and Finland prepared by the foreign ministers' council of Britain, the US, France and the USSR.

1 SEPTEMBER 1946

Greece In a plebiscite on restoration of the monarchy, King George II wins 70 percent of the vote. Meanwhile, accelerating Communist agitation will develop into a civil war.

30 SEPTEMBER 1946

Germany The Nuremberg international tribunal announces the verdicts in the Nazi war crimes trials. Of the 22 defendants, only Schacht, Fritzsche, and von Papen are acquitted. The rest receive sentences ranging from 10 years' imprisonment to death. Before

CLEMENT RICHARD ATTLEE, 1883–1976

Leader of the British Labour Party for twenty years, Clement Richard Attlee played a key role in Britain's transition to a socialist economy. A native and lifelong resident of London, Attlee graduated from Oxford and worked as a lawyer and a teacher, serving as an army major in World War I before entering politics. While the Labour Party was in power under Attlee's leadership (1945–51) several major industries were nationalized, a comprehensive social security system was established, and many social service acts were passed. He sought to close the gap between imports and exports and balance Britain's dollar account in the wake of World War II. Created an earl by Queen Elizabeth II in 1955, Attlee resigned as leader of the Labour Party four years after its defeat and served in the House of Lords.

his scheduled 15 October execution, Hermann Goering commits suicide.

3 NOVEMBER 1946
Japan Emperor Hirohito announces a new antiwar constitution to become effective in 6 months. It renounces the maintenance of armed forces and makes the Imperial Throne a 'national symbol.' Political power is to be wielded by the assembly.

23 NOVEMBER 1946
Vietnam French forces bomb Haiphong, killing some 6000 Vietnamese. This is the beginning of the futile French effort to hold on to colonial French Indochina.

2 DECEMBER 1946
Germany The US and Britain agree to merge their occupation zones in Germany, effective 1 January 1947. This pact aims to make the combined zones self-sustaining within 3 years at an estimated cost of $1 billion, to be split equally between Britain and the US.

11 DECEMBER 1946
Spain The UN votes to bar Spain from membership. On 4 March the US, Britain, and France had urged the Spanish people to oust the Franco dictatorship and institute democratic elections.

14 DECEMBER 1946
International The UN accepts the offer of John D Rockefeller, Jr, to buy a midtown New York City site for $8.5 million and to turn it over to the UN as its world capital. On the same day, the UN delegates unanimously approve a disarmament resolution to prohibit the atomic bomb and other weapons of mass destruction.

25 DECEMBER 1946
China The national assembly, boycotted by the Communists, unanimously adopts a new constitution that promises political equality and civil rights for all, as well as universal suffrage.

OTHER EVENTS OF 1946
Science Oceanographic researchers first observe the East Pacific Ridge, an undersea mountain range stretching diagonally from Central America southwest across the Pacific. John von Neumann, the brilliant mathematician, publishes the first of many papers that provide the theoretical basis for computer logic and design.
Technology The first radar signals are 'bounced' off the moon. The first underwater atomic bomb is exploded at Bikini lagoon in the Pacific. The electric blanket, with thermostat switch, is invented. The first jet plane takes off from an aircraft carrier (the USS *Franklin Delano Roosevelt*) and helicopters find peacetime uses.
Environment The magnetic North Pole is observed by aircraft to be 250 miles north of the charted posi-

tion. A large tsunami, produced by an earthquake centered in the Aleutians, severely damages Hilo, Hawaii.
Ideas/Beliefs Sartre's *Existentialism and Humanism*; Bertrand Russell's *History of Western Philosophy*; R G Collingwood's *The Idea of History*.
Literature Nikos Kazantzakis's *Zorba the Greek*; Miguel Angel Asturias's *Mr President*; Robert Lowell's *Lord Weary's Castle*; Robert Penn Warren's *All the King's Men*; St John Perse's *Vents*; Carl Zuckmayer's *The Devil's General*; Dylan Thomas's *Deaths and Entrances*.
Drama/Entertainment O'Neill's *The Iceman Cometh*; Sartre's *The Respectable Prostitute*; Montherlant's *The Master of Santiago*; Christopher Fry's *A Phoenix Too Frequent*; Lillian Hellman's *Another Part of the Forest*. Ballets premiered include Balanchine's *Night Shadow* and Jerome Robbins' *Interplay*.
The Arts Matisse's *1000 Nights*; Henry Moore's *Family*; Hopper's *Approaching a City*; Picasso founds his pottery at Vallauris, France; Britain establishes its Arts Council to provide government funds for the arts.
Music Britten's *The Rape of Lucretia* (opera); Menotti's *The Medium* (opera); Copland's *3rd Symphony*; Strauss's *Metamorphoses*.
Life/Leisure The first bikini bathing suit is modelled in Paris (named for 'the ultimate impact') of the atomic bomb test at Bikini. The first drive-in bank is opened by the Exchange Bank of Chicago.
Miscellaneous The United Nations Educational, Scientific and Cultural Organization (UNESCO) is founded. The BBC in Great Britain begins its Third Programme of serious cultural offerings.

10 FEBRUARY 1947
International In Paris, several peace treaties ending World War II are signed. Italy loses four border areas to France, her Adriatic islands and most of Venezia Giulia to Yugoslavia, the Dodecanese Islands to Greece, and her North African colonies; she agrees to establishment of the free territory of Trieste and payment of $360 million in reparations. Rumania loses northern territory to Russia, and Finland cedes Petsamo to the USSR and grants the Soviets a 50-year lease of the Porkhala naval base. All except Finland promptly protest the terms of the pacts. In Italy angry mobs riot, tearing down an American flag in Rome, and an Italian woman assassinates a British brigadier in protest.

20 FEBRUARY 1947
India Britain issues an ultimatum effective June 1948 for transfer of power to Indian hands, to force the Hindus and Moslems to reach agreement. At the same time, to facilitate the transition, Lord Louis Mountbatten, former Supreme Allied Commander for Southeast Asia, becomes interim viceroy.

10 MARCH–24 APRIL 1947
International In Moscow, the 5th conference of the Allied Council of Foreign Ministers meets to discuss

IN SEARCH OF STABILITY 1946-1962

drafting of the German and Austrian peace treaties, and fails to reach an accord.

12 MARCH 1947
International Before a joint session of Congress, US President Truman proposes a new foreign policy to combat communism throughout the world, and requests $400 million in aid for Greece and Turkey as a start. This anticommunist stance will become known as the Truman Doctrine.

19 MARCH 1947
China In the civil war, unabated by US mediation efforts, the Nationalists capture the Communist capital of Yenan. The Communists will rally for a series of victories that results in control over Manchuria by the end of the year.

2 APRIL 1947
Palestine After its own proposals have been rejected by Jews and Arabs, Great Britain refers the Palestine question to the UN.

31 MAY 1947
Hungary While anticommunist Premier Ferenc Nagy is out of the country, the Communists seize power by installing Lajos Dinnyes as premier and instituting a purge of other anticommunist officials. This marks the first challenge by the USSR to the Truman Doctrine.

5 JUNE 1947
International US Secretary of State George Marshall calls for a European Recovery Program that will become known as the Marshall Plan.

19 JUNE 1947
Great Britain In a parliamentary speech, Foreign Secretary Ernest Bevin, responding to Soviet opposition to the Marshall Plan, warns that British appeasement of Russia is at an end.

23 JUNE 1947
USA Congress passes the Taft-Hartley Act despite a veto by President Truman three days earlier. This landmark labor law bans closed shops, permits employer lawsuits against unions for broken contracts or damages incurred during strikes, and establishes a federal mediation and conciliation service.

6 JULY 1947
Spain A national referendum ratifies a bill of succession proposed by General Franco. This act makes Spain a monarchy again, with the choice of monarch left up to Franco, as head of state. Don Juan, the Bourbon claimant to the throne, opposes the bill.

20 JULY 1947
Indonesia Dutch forces seize government buildings and arrest hundreds of political officials after the 15 November 1946 Cheriben Agreement—calling for Dutch recognition of the Indonesian Republic—proves difficult to implement, leading to renewed fighting between Dutch and Indonesian forces.

15 AUGUST 1947
India After some 200 years of British rule, the 400 million people of the Indian subcontinent achieve independence, and are partitioned into a Hindu state (India) and a Moslem state (Pakistan). The two nations join the British Commonwealth as dominions with the right to secede after June 1948. Jawaharlal Nehru becomes the Indian prime minister, while Mohammed Ali Jinnah is sworn in as governor general of Pakistan. The independence celebrations are overshadowed by Moslem-Hindu violence in the Punjab, where in Lahore alone the death toll reaches 268 in four days.

2 SEPTEMBER 1947
International Following a foreign-policy address by US President Truman, 103 delegates of 19 Western Hemisphere nations sign the Treaty of Rio de Janeiro, the first regional defense and peace-keeping alliance under the UN charter.

23 SEPTEMBER 1947
Bulgaria The communist-dominated government has opposition leader Nikola Petkov hanged as a traitor. In November, Rumanian National Peasant Party leader Julius Maniu is sentenced to solitary confinement for life on charges of high treason.

5 OCTOBER 1947
International After a secret Polish conference, delegates from the Communist parties of nine European nations establish Cominform (The Communist Information Bureau) with headquarters in Belgrade to coordinate activities of European Communists and to oppose US 'aggression and expansion.' The delegates publish a manifesto denouncing British and French Socialists as 'traitors.'

20 OCTOBER 1947
USA The House Un-American Activities Committee opens public hearings on alleged communist infiltration in Hollywood. Among those denounced as having un-American tendencies are Dalton Trumbo, Katharine Hepburn, Ring Lardner, Jr, Clifford Odets, Irwin Shaw, Paul Robeson, Charles Chaplin, and Edward G Robinson. Among the film stars called to testify is Screen Actors Guild President Ronald Reagan, who denies that leftists ever controlled the Guild and refuses to label anyone a communist.

26 OCTOBER 1947
India The state of Kashmir enters the Indian Union. This leads to a crisis with Pakistan, since the majority of the Kashmir population is Moslem. Sporadic fighting breaks out between Indian and Moslem forces, and on 30 December the dispute is referred to the UN for mediation.

JAWAHARLAL NEHRU, 1889–1964

If Gandhi was the spiritual guide of modern India, Jawaharlal Nehru was its political mentor. First prime minister of the nation he helped to liberate, Nehru was intelligent, lucid, highly born, and an advocate of modern scientific methods. He envisioned a state-controlled economy to replace India's primitive economic structure. As an ardent democrat he rejected caste and was the first major Indian leader to view Indian difficulties as part of a world problem, taking on the responsibility of spokesman for nonaligned nations in Asia and Africa while maintaining India's neutrality. He spent a total of 18 years in prison under the British, and as prime mover of the Congress Party expended much of his family fortune to further revolutionary social and political goals. A master of English and the author of widely read books, Nehru dominated Indian affairs with a compassion, forbearance, and energy rarely seen in political leaders of any time.

29 OCTOBER 1947
International   Belgium, the Netherlands, and Luxembourg ratify a common customs union (Benelux).

11 NOVEMBER 1947
USSR   Foreign Minister Molotov announces that the atomic bomb secret has 'long ceased to exist,' leading to an American prediction that Russia will develop the bomb in the next three years. A rightist Paris newspaper prints an unconfirmed report that the USSR detonated its first atomic bomb in Siberia on 15 June.

20 NOVEMBER 1947
Great Britain   Future queen of England Princess Elizabeth marries Philip Mountbatten, Duke of Edinburgh. The Westminster Abbey ceremony is televised and broadcast worldwide.

27 NOVEMBER 1947
Australia   After one of the most violent controversies in the nation's history, the Banking Bill mandating nationalization of banks is passed by Joseph Chifley's Labour Government in an effort to alleviate inflation and depression. It will be declared unconstitutional on 11 August 1948.

29 NOVEMBER 1947
Palestine   The United Nations General Assembly adopts a resolution calling for the establishment of a Jewish state and an Arab state in Palestine, with Jerusalem to remain within an internationally administered zone; Britain abstains and the Arab states walk out of the Assembly. The decision is to take effect on 15 May 1948, when the British mandate expires.

23 DECEMBER 1947
Panama   After the national assembly votes unanimously against continued US use of military bases in Panama, Washington announces immediate American evacuation of all bases outside the Canal Zone.

24 DECEMBER 1947
Greece   In a surreptitious radio broadcast, an estimated 20,000 communists led by guerrilla general Markos Vafthiades proclaim the Free Greek Government in northern Greece. They issue a call to arms to establish the regime throughout the nation. The next day 500 Free Government sympathizers are arrested in Athens and the Communist Party is dissolved by the government. Three days later the army conducts an offensive against the guerrilla stronghold in the north.

30 DECEMBER 1947
Rumania   The last remaining monarch in the Soviet sphere of Europe, King Michael, is forced to abdicate by the communist-dominated government.

OTHER EVENTS OF 1947
Science   Willard Libby and associates at the Uni-

IN SEARCH OF STABILITY 1946-1962

versity of California (Berkeley) discover that carbon 14, a radioactive isotope of carbon, is found in all organic substances, and that after the organism dies its remains lose this radioactivity at a fixed rate over thousands of years. This rate of decay allows near-exact calculations of the organism's time of death—thus allowing archaeologists and others to place objects in an accurate time frame. The pi-meson, or pion, predicted by Hideki Yukawa in 1935, is discovered by Cecil Powell; it is an intermediary particle necessary to support the theory of strong interaction. P M S Blackett, picking up the observations of H W Babcock, an astronomer at Mt Wilson Observatory, formulates an equation based on the mass, size, rate of spin, and magnetism of spatial bodies and hypothesizes that magnetism is a property of all rotating bodies.

Medicine/Health A British research team in Nigeria finds dapsone an effective oral treatment for leprosy.

Technology At Mt Wilson Observatory, northeast of Pasadena, the 100-inch reflecting telescope goes into use, the largest telescope up to this time. The Halord Company of Rochester, New York, obtains the commercial rights to xerography ('dry writing'), a process and machine developed by Chester Carlson between 1934 and 1940. Halord becomes the Xerox Corporation and manufactures its first copier in 1950, introducing it commercially in 1959. Edwin Land gives the first public demonstration of his camera that can take, develop, and print pictures on photographic paper (in about one minute in this first model). This Polaroid Land Camera will not go on sale until 1948. On 14 October US Air Force Captain Charles 'Chuck' Yeager flies the experimental Bell X-1 through the 'sonic barrier,' attaining the speed of 967 mph at 70,140 feet altitude (Mach 1.05), faster than anyone had ever traveled.

Environment A large meteorite crashes in Sikhote-Alin, in remote Siberia, leaving a large crater. Thor Heyerdahl, a Norwegian ethnologist-explorer, sails a balsa-wood raft, *Kon-Tiki*, with five companions from Peru to eastern Polynesia to test his theory that the islands of Polynesia could have been settled by Indians from South America.

Social Studies In a cave near Jericho, above the Dead Sea, a Bedouin shepherd boy finds a group of scrolls of leather and papyrus; experts find they are versions of the Old Testament and other texts related to the Bible. Over the next few years, more such 'Dead Sea Scrolls' are found in caves; most seem to have belonged to the Essenes, a Jewish sect that flourished ca 100 BC to AD 70.

Ideas/Beliefs Simone Weil's *Gravity and Grace*; Robert Graves's *White Goddess*; *The Diary of Anne Frank*, by a young Jewish girl who hid from the Nazis for two years in Amsterdam before her capture and death at Belsen.

Literature Thomas Mann's *Doctor Faustus*; Albert Camus' *The Plague*; Malcolm Lowry's *Under the Volcano*; Vladimir Nabokov's *Bend Sinister*; Dazai Osamu's *The Setting Sun*; Auden's *The Age of Anxiety*.

Drama/Entertainment Tennessee Williams's *A Streetcar Named Desire*; Arthur Miller's *All My Sons*; Jean Genet's *The Maids*; Chaplin's *Monsieur Verdoux*.

The Arts Matisse's *The Young English Girl*; Giacometti's *Man Pointing*; Dufy's *Music*; Kokoschka's *The Matterhorn*; Moore's *Three Standing Figures*; Jackson Pollock's early action painting *Lucifer*.

Life/Customs The first tape recorder for home use is marketed (by the Brush Development Corp. of Cleveland, Ohio) and the first microwave oven for the public is sold (by Raytheon Corp). The first 'flying saucer' is reported in the US.

Miscellaneous The Greenwich Observatory, at Greenwich, outside London, the base point of the world's time and longitude, begins to move its operations to Sussex because of the bright lights of London. A ship explodes in the harbor of Texas City, Texas, killing 512.

1 JANUARY 1948
International The General Agreement on Trade and Tariffs (GATT)—negotiated at Geneva during 1947 and signed by 23 countries—comes into force. GATT is a provisional and voluntary agreement for reduction of barriers to world trade, including ongoing negotiations over specific tariff concessions and import-export quotas. In the years that follow, almost every trading nation will participate in this attempt to avoid the kind of 'trade wars' that have led to shooting wars.

4 JANUARY 1948
Burma The Union of Burma is proclaimed an independent republic, with no ties to the British Commonwealth. Sao Shwe Thaik remains as president and Thakin Nu as prime minister; the government begins nationalizing industries and resources. These changes fail to satisfy communist elements, who rebel in March.

30 JANUARY 1948
India Mahatma Gandhi is assassinated by a Hindu fanatic who resents his role in the partitioning of India. On 11 September Pakistan's Mohammed Ali Jinnah also dies. These two had done more than anyone else to liberate the Indian subcontinent from British control: their deaths will be followed by the Indian invasion of Hyderabad.

2 FEBRUARY 1948
USA President Truman presents a civil-rights package to Congress in which he calls for an end to segregated schools and employment discrimination. On 12 February a rally of Southern Democrats calls on 'all true white Jeffersonian Democrats' to unite in opposing Truman's program.

25 FEBRUARY 1948
Czechoslovakia In a bloodless coup, Soviet-supported communists seize control after infiltrating government offices and trade unions. They force

3 AUGUST 1948

President Eduard Beneš to agree to a communist government under Klement Gottwald. A widespread purge follows, transforming the nation into a Soviet satellite.

17 MARCH 1948
International Britain, France, Belgium, the Netherlands, and Luxembourg sign the Brussels Treaty, a 50-year defensive alliance providing for economic, social, and military co-operation.

29 MARCH 1948
China Despite serious Nationalist setbacks, the national assembly re-elects Chiang Kai-shek with dictatorial powers to deal with the state of emergency. Nationalist troops are losing to the Communists, and the economy suffers from inflation.

1 APRIL 1948
Germany The Soviet military government in Berlin begins a land blockade of Allied sectors of the city by refusing passage to US and British supply trains. After US and British aircraft fly 2.3 million tons of food and coal into West Berlin, the Soviet blockade and a Western counterblockade will be lifted on 30 September 1949.

1 MAY 1948
North Korea Soviet-supported communists proclaim a People's Republic in Pyongyang, claiming Korea, with Seoul as their eventual capital.

10 MAY 1948
South Korea In UN-supervised elections for a national constituent assembly, parties of the Right win a majority. Meeting on 28 May, the assembly invites delegates from North Korea, but this invitation is ignored.

14 MAY 1948
Israel The British evacuate Palestine, and the State of Israel is proclaimed in Tel Aviv. Recognition comes first from the US on 14 May, from the USSR on 17 May. Chaim Weizmann is the nation's first president. Israel is almost immediately invaded by the Arab League nations, but superior equipment and fighting enable the Jews to repulse them except in the Old City of Jerusalem. In December the Israelis finally drive the Egyptians from the Negev Desert, ignoring a UN cease-fire. They go on to invade Egypt for three days and shoot down several British planes observing the action.

26 MAY 1948
South Africa In the parliamentary election, Premier Jan Smuts's United Party is defeated by the isolationist Nationalist Party led by Dr Daniel Malan. The Nationalists pledge to uphold white supremacy.

28 JUNE 1948
Yugoslavia Cominform denounces Marshal Tito and other leaders of the Yugoslav Communist Party for 'anti-Soviet opinions incompatible with Marxism-Leninism' and for favoring Western powers. They are warned to admit their errors and return to the Moscow fold, or face expulsion from office and party. On 29 July the Yugoslav Communist Party gives Tito a vote of confidence and later expels all Comintern supporters.

5 JULY 1948
Great Britain The National Health Service Act, providing free medical care for all from 'the cradle to the grave' becomes effective. This landmark socialist legislation will cost $2 billion per year.

20 JULY 1948
USA Indictments are issued against William Z Foster, American Communist Party chairman, and 11 other leading Communists for conspiring to overthrow the US government. The rapid spread of communism in Eastern Europe and the Orient has alerted Americans to a possible danger at home. These fears result in continuing hearings of the House Un-American Activities Committee and in espionage trials.

26 JULY 1948
USA An executive order bars segregation in the armed forces and calls for an end to racial discrimination in federal employment.

30 JULY 1948
Great Britain The British Citizenship Act becomes law, giving each dominion in the commonwealth the right to decide who its citizens are, and concurrently endowing all commonwealth citizens with British citizenship. In the decades that follow, this will lead to immigration of many Asians and Africans to Britain, further straining the nation's over-extended resources.

3 AUGUST 1948
USA Alger Hiss, president of the prestigious Carnegie Endowment for International Peace and

---

ROBERT SCHUMAN, 1886–1963

A member of the French Resistance during World War II, Robert Schuman served for almost forty years in the French National Assembly, influencing the popular Republican Party with his Roman Catholic ideas on politics and striving for European unity after the war. Prime minister in 1947 and 1948, in 1950 he propounded the 'Schuman Plan' for pooling the coal and steel resources of Western Europe as a foil to Communist exploitation of economic difficulties, and in 1958 found himself president of the European Parliamentary Assembly, where his efforts to unite Europe through its finances paved the way for the Common Market. Awarded the Charlemagne Prize, he survived de Gaulle's electoral reforms and resumed his seat in the National Assembly.

IN SEARCH OF STABILITY 1946-1962

Planes of the Berlin Airlift.

former State Department official, is accused by senior editor of *Time* magazine and ex-Communist Whittaker Chambers of activity in an underground Communist cell in the 1930s. The case against Hiss is vigorously prosecuted by Representative Richard M Nixon. Hiss asserts his innocence and sues Chambers for defamation. In November new evidence discovered in a pumpkin on Chambers's farm appears to implicate Hiss as a Soviet spy. Hiss is later convicted of perjury, but will continue to protest his innocence.

15 AUGUST 1948
South Korea The Republic of South Korea is proclaimed with Syngman Rhee as president, ending US military government, but the US agrees to train South Korean military forces.

1 SEPTEMBER 1948
China The communists proclaim a North China People's Republic.

9 SEPTEMBER 1948
North Korea A Korean People's Democratic Repub-

lic is established under the presidency of Communist leader Kim Il Sung. This government, which claims authority over all Korea, is modeled on the USSR's.

17 SEPTEMBER 1948
Israel UN mediator Swedish Count Folke Bernadotte is assassinated in Jerusalem by Jewish Stern group terrorists opposed to a negotiated compromise between Arabs and Jews in Palestine. The Israeli Government orders an immediate roundup of all Stern suspects. Black American Dr Ralph Bunche takes over Bernadotte's UN mission.

2 NOVEMBER 1948
USA The presidential elections result in a surprise victory for incumbent Harry S Truman, who defeats New York Governor Thomas E Dewey by 2.2 million popular votes and 114 electoral votes. This victory is due in part to the 10,000 miles of campaigning logged on a 'Whistle Stop' tour. The Dixiecrat candidate, Strom Thurmond, receives 39 electoral votes and a little over one million popular votes. Progressive Party candidate Henry Wallace receives

no electoral college votes but some one million popular votes.

15 NOVEMBER 1948
Canada W L Mackenzie King resigns as prime minister after serving for 20 years, longer than any other prime minister in the British Commonwealth. His Secretary of External Affairs, Lester Pearson, helps Canada play an influential role in international affairs. King is succeeded by Louis St Laurent, new head of the Liberal Party.

29 NOVEMBER 1948
India Gandhi's 20-year campaign to abolish untouchability—the practice by which 40 million Hindus have been shunned by the upper castes to live in poverty and do menial labor—triumphs after his death as the constituent assembly bans the practice.

23 DECEMBER 1948
Japan Convicted as war criminals, ex-Premier Hideki Tojo and six others are hanged in Tokyo after the US Supreme Court rejects their appeal. The next day General MacArthur closes out Japan's major war-crimes cases by releasing all other suspects—an amnesty that surprises many Japanese who believe those released are as guilty as Tojo.

27 DECEMBER 1948
Hungary Jozsef Cardinal Mindszenty, an outspoken opponent of the Communist regime, is arrested on charges of spying, treason, and black-market dealings in currency. Thirteen others, including priests and monks, are also arrested. After a guilty verdict and a sentence of life imprisonment, handed down on 8 February 1949, Mindszenty will seek asylum in the American embassy in 1956.

Harry Truman glorying in the Chicago Tribune*'s classic headline mistake.*

IN SEARCH OF STABILITY 1946-1962

28 DECEMBER 1948
Egypt Premier Nokrashy Pasha is assassinated by a member of the outlawed Moslem Brotherhood because of his failure to achieve victory in the war against Israel. King Farouk names Hadi Pasha to succeed him.

OTHER EVENTS OF 1948
Science Richard Feynman, an American physicist, develops an improved theory of quantum electrodynamics—the study of electron interaction and electromagnetic radiation; Feynman's theory helps physicists predict the effect of electrically charged particles on one another in a radiation field. George Gamow and a student, Ralph Alpher, publish 'The Origin of Chemical Elements,' proposing the theory that the universe began as a highly compressed and very hot collection of neutrons from which a 'big bang' created all elements in their present quantities within minutes. The 'Big Bang' theory of creation will dominate in ensuing decades. Debating at the Lenin All-Union Academy of Agricultural Science, the president, T D Lysenko, restates his theory that characteristics of organisms can be changed by environmental influences; Lysenko has been promoting this theory for years; now he denounces those who disagree and calls for a purge of dissident scientists and books. Support for his views will erode, even in Russia. Gerard Kuiper discovers the fifth moon of Uranus and carbon dioxide in the atmosphere of Mars.
Medicine/Health Two new antibiotics, aureomycin and chloromycetin, are prepared. The World Health Organization is established and quickly begins large-scale application of DDT, particularly to control malaria.
Technology The 200-inch Hale telescope (a reflecting type) is installed at Mt Palomar Observatory in California. The first transistor demonstration is given by Bell Telephone Laboratories, where it was invented by Drs John Bardeen and Walter Brittain. Columbia Records of New York City introduces the first long-playing microgroove phonograph records to become commercially successful. (RCA Victor had introduced one in 1931, but it required an expensive phonograph and did not catch on.) The first records are made of vinylite plastic and play at $33\frac{1}{3}$ rpm; they will help revolutionize the public's musical tastes and listening habits.
Environment The largest known single stone-mass meteorite falls in Norton County, Kansas; it weighs 2360 lbs (1073 kilos).
Social Sciences Robert Braidwood, an American archaeologist, begins digging at Jarmo in the foothills of Iraq; he will reveal a site crucial to understanding the Neolithic, or agricultural, revolution. B F Skinner's *Walden Two*; Alfred Kinsey (and colleagues) publish *Sexual Behavior of the Human Male*; Norbert Wiener's *Cybernetics, or Control and Communication in the Animal and the Machine*.
Ideas/Beliefs T S Eliot's *Notes Toward a Definition of Culture*; F R Leavis's *The Great Tradition*.

Literature Mailer's *The Naked and the Dead*; Kawabata Yasunari's *Snow Country*; Patrick White's *The Aunt's Story*; Alan Paton's *Cry, the Beloved Country*; Graham Greene's *The Heart of the Matter*; Faulkner's *Intruder in the Dust*; Cesare Pavesi's *Among Women Only*; Waugh's *The Loved One*.
Drama/Entertainment Tennessee Williams's *Summer and Smoke*; Jean-Paul Sartre's *Dirty Hands*; Christopher Fry's *The Lady's Not for Burning*; Sir Laurence Olivier's *Hamlet*; John Huston's *Treasure of the Sierra Madre*. The New York City Ballet begins with George Balachine as artistic director.
The Arts George Rouault's series *Miserere*—58 aquatints and etchings done between 1916–27—is published. Braque's *The Bird*; Pollock's *Composition No 1*; Leger's *Homage to David*; Giacometti's *City Square*; Miro's *Red Sun*; Andrew Wyeth's *Christina's World*.
Architecture Pier Luigi Nervi's Exhibition Hall in Turin, an unusual single-roof structure, is completed.
Music Vaughan Williams's *6th Symphony*; Stockhausen's *Kreuzspiel*; Boulez's *Le Soleil des eaux*; Strauss's *Four Last Songs*.
Life/Customs The first electronically controlled elevators are installed in New York City. The first TV Western series—'Hopalong Cassidy,' starring William Boyd—begins on NBC.
Miscellaneous The UN adopts the Declaration of Human Rights. The World Council of Churches is inaugurated at Amsterdam, with delegates from 147 churches of 44 countries. Two major shipwrecks in the China Sea leave 1700 dead.

15 JANUARY 1949
China After a 27-hour battle, Communist forces occupy Tientsin. This major victory against the

---

GEORGE C MARSHALL, 1880–1959

George C Marshall, American soldier and statesman, was born in Uniontown, Pennsylvania, and educated at the Virginia Military Institute. Commissioned in 1901, he served in the Philippines, where his leadership qualities emerged and brought him slow but steady promotion. By 1918 he was an operations officer for army commander John J Pershing, having been made a colonel. After World War I he served in the US and China until the German invasion of Poland (1 September 1939), when he was named chief of staff, a post he held throughout World War II. Winston Churchill described him as 'the true organizer of victory' in the war. Marshall spent time in China (1945–47) as a special representative of President Truman before he became secretary of state in 1947. He originated the Marshall Plan of aid for the postwar reconstruction of Europe, which dispensed over 13 billion dollars to 16 countries in a five-year period. Marshall retired in 1949, but was called back to become secretary of defense the following year in the face of the Korean conflict. In 1953 he became the only career soldier to win the Nobel Peace Prize.

Nationalists is followed by the 21 January occupation of Peiping, where Chiang Kai-shek resigns. Vice-President Li Tsung-jen begins negotiations with the communists.

16 JANUARY 1949
Israel Israeli troops evacuate four Lebanese border towns, seized in October 1948, as Israel opens preliminary armistice talks with Lebanon and Transjordan.

25 JANUARY 1949
Israel The new nation holds its first general election, with 427,027 voters, including 30,000 Arabs, casting ballots. The Mapai, or Socialist-Labor Party, headed by Prime Minister David Ben-Gurion, polls the heaviest vote—35.8 percent—and wins 44 seats in the 120-member assembly or Knesset. The Mapam, a leftist labor party, is second, with 14.7 percent of the vote and 18 seats.

2 MARCH 1949
USA Echoing Communist leaders in Europe, national chairman of the US Communist Party William Z Foster announces that American Communists would oppose the US in a war against the Soviet Union and 'cooperate with democratic forces to defeat the predatory aims of American imperialism.' At the 20 April opening of the World Congress of Partisans of World Peace, in Paris, US delegation leader Paul Robeson declares that American blacks would never fight the Soviet Union. All this serves to fuel anticommunist activity in the US.

7 MARCH 1949
International The UN Economic and Social Coun-

Yenan—April 1946. Left to right: *Chou En-lai, Marshall, Chu-Teh, Cheng Kai-min, Mao.*

IN SEARCH OF STABILITY 1946-1962

cil votes, 14 to 3, to investigate US charges that between 8 and 14 million persons are being held in slave-labor camps in the USSR and other Eastern European countries.

8 MARCH 1949

Vietnam The French reach accord on establishing an independent Vietnam within the French commonwealth. Signing in Paris for the noncommunist Nationalists is Bao Dai, the former emperor of Annam. Under the pact, the three states of Annam, Tonking, and Cochin China may merge into either a monarchy or a republic. The French retain the right to military bases in the country. This serves to spur on the communists under Ho Chi Minh, who is further encouraged by communist victories in China.

25 MARCH 1949

China Peking (formerly Peiping) becomes capital of Communist China, as Mao Tse-tung establishes headquarters there.

31 MARCH 1949

Canada After a closely contested referendum on 22 July 1948, Newfoundland becomes the tenth province of Canada.

4 APRIL 1949

International Twelve nations sign the North Atlantic Treaty, a defense agreement that lays the foundation for the North Atlantic Treaty Organization (NATO). Under the pact's terms, the US, Canada, Britain, France, and eight other Western European nations agree that 'an armed attack against one or more of them in Europe and North America shall be considered an attack against them all.'

8 APRIL 1949

Germany In a joint communique, the US, Britain, and France announce an agreement for merging the three Western occupation zones in Germany and the early establishment of a republican government for the combined territory. Military governments are to give way to a German civilian administration, but occupation troops will remain for security reasons.

18 APRIL 1949

Ireland The independent Republic of Ireland is proclaimed, after some 780 years of British rule. Prime Minister John A Costello expresses hope that the six counties of Northern Ireland will soon unite with the Republic.

25 APRIL 1949

Germany A draft constitution for a West German Republic is signed in Frankfurt by German political leaders and representatives of the US, Britain, and France. US military governor General Lucius D Clay declares the inclusion of Germany in a Western European alliance essential to thwarting communist expansion. The Federal Republic of Germany is established on 21 May.

28 APRIL 1949

Philippines Aurora Quezon, widow of the nation's first president Manuel Quezon, her daughter, and 10 others are killed in an ambush by the Huks, a rebellious People's Liberation Army intent on seizing the government. This 20,000-man fighting force has support from farmers and the poor because of its land distribution program. Fighting between the Huks and the Philippine Army will continue for several years.

JUNE 1949

South Africa The South African Citizenship Act ends automatic citizenship for British and other Commonwealth immigrants, who must now wait 5 years to apply. The policy of *apartheid* becomes

*An Alberto Giacometti bronze sculpture—*Walking Man.

effective, banning marriages between Europeans and non-Europeans and enacting other segregation laws.

16 JUNE 1949

USA President Truman predicts that the wave of hysteria sweeping the nation as a result of the espionage and loyalty inquiries will subside. He compares this postwar phenomenon to the Alien and Sedition laws of 1798 and promises dismissal of anyone in the executive department who contributes to the alarm.

Czechoslovakia Prague police post guards at the palace of Archbishop Josef Beran after he refuses to permit Communist officials to control episcopal correspondence, telephone calls, and other business. The crisis accelerates as the government forms its own Catholic Action Committee to take over direction of church affairs from the Catholic hierarchy. On 20 June, in response, the Vatican excommunicates all active Communist supporters in the nation. On 14 October the government takes control of all church affairs, requiring all clerics to take a loyalty oath—most of the lower clergy do so.

20 JUNE 1949

International In Paris a four-week conference of the Big Four Foreign Ministers Council ends with no resolution on the unification of Germany and Berlin; it is agreed to restore Austria to her 1938 borders.

29 JUNE 1949

Korea The US removes the last of its troops from Korea, leaving a group of about 500 advisers behind.

20 JULY 1949

Israel The 19-month war between Israel and the Arab League ends when Israel and Syria sign an armistice. Similar accords have already been reached with Egypt, Lebanon, and Transjordan.

THE UNITED NATIONS EMERGES

During World War II, President Franklin D Roosevelt looked to the establishment of a peace-keeping organization of the victors in the war. He revived Woodrow Wilson's former dream, the League of Nations. The United States had never joined the League despite Wilson's advocacy, and when it proved ineffective against Japanese and Italian aggression, it was powerless to prevent World War II. Roosevelt believed that if the victors agreed among themselves, there would be hope for lasting peace. The US, the USSR, Britain, China, and France formed the Security Council, each country with veto power within the enforcement mechanism of the United Nations. This constraint of unanimous decision has severely limited its effectiveness—no UN forces or armaments control have been established because of the veto. Nevertheless, the polarized and confrontational world of post-1945 has not degenerated into world war. The United Nations, unlike the League, has nearly universal membership, and has proven an important arena for debate and diplomatic contact.

---

25 JULY 1949

International After Senatorial consent to the North Atlantic pact, President Truman asks Congress for $1.45 billion to help the European signatories, Iran, the Philippines, and Korea to arm themselves. 'So long as the danger of aggression exists,' he says, 'it is necessary to think in terms of the forces required to prevent it.'

5 AUGUST 1949

China A US State Department White Paper attributes the loss of mainland China to the Communists to the corruption and ineptitude of the Chiang Kai-shek regime.

18 AUGUST 1949

Finland The army is mobilized as communist-led unions open a strike offensive against the Socialist Government. In the north 1500 striking lumberjacks fight a pitched battle with police and troops. Government action and the support of noncommunist workers ends the agitation in September.

18 SEPTEMBER 1949

Great Britain The British pound is devalued from $4.03 to $2.80 to increase British exports and reverse the increasing dollar deficit. This results in wide-spread devaluation of other European currencies.

23 SEPTEMBER 1949

USSR US President Truman announces that the Soviet Union, which has just tested an atomic device, has nuclear capabilities.

1 OCTOBER 1949

China In Peking the Communist People's Republic of China is proclaimed, with Mao Tse-tung as chairman and Chou En-lai as premier and foreign minister. The USSR recognizes the regime immediately, followed soon by Burma, India, and Britain. The US refuses recognition.

7 OCTOBER 1949

East Germany With no elections, the German Democratic Republic is established with Wilhelm Pieck as president and Otto Grotewohl as premier of a mostly communist cabinet. The Soviet control commission ensures that the new nation is another Soviet satellite.

16 OCTOBER 1949

Greece The civil war ends after three years of fighting. American aid and the closing of the Yugoslav border by Tito have helped defeat communist rebel forces.

8 DECEMBER 1949

Taiwan (Formosa) Nationalists complete their move from mainland China to Formosa; on 1 March 1950 Chiang Kai-shek will resume the presidency of Nationalist China.

10 DECEMBER 1949
Australia In a general election a coalition of Liberal and Country Parties, opposing socialism and communism, defeats the incumbent Labour Party. Robert G Menzies forms a government on 17 December.

14 DECEMBER 1949
Israel In defiance of a UN resolution for the internationalization of Jerusalem, Israel transfers its capital there (from Tel Aviv).

16 DECEMBER 1949
China Arriving in Moscow on his first visit as head of the Chinese Communist regime, Mao Tse-tung is received at the Kremlin by Premier Stalin and other dignitaries. Mao promises full support of USSR international policies 'for the strengthening of the Communist front of peace throughout the world and the struggle against the warmongers.'

27 DECEMBER 1949
Indonesia Independence is proclaimed for the federal republic of 16 states, with Achmed Sukarno as the nation's first president. The status of Dutch New Guinea remains to be settled in future negotiations with the Netherlands.

OTHER EVENTS OF 1949
Science Macfarlane Burnet, an Australian researcher, proposes that animal tissues and organs could be successfully transplanted from one individual to another if certain conditions were met—including recognition of the factors involved in acquired immunological tolerance. This will be tested by Peter Medawar and others and become the basis of organ transplants. Gerard Kuiper discovers a second moon of Neptune and proposes a theory of planetary origin by condensation of nebular gas and dust.

Medicine/Health Cortisone (compound E) is discovered by Philip Hench to be helpful in treating arthritis. (Cortisone had first been isolated as a natural compound in 1935 and was synthesized in 1946.)

Technology The USSR tests its first atomic bomb, and the US fires a first-stage rocket at White Sands, New Mexico.

Social Sciences Claude Levi-Strauss, a French anthropologist, publishes his first crucial work, *The Elementary Structures of Kinship*. Konrad Lorenz's *King Solomon's Ring* helps popularize the discipline of ethology, the study of animal behavior. Simone de Beauvoir's *The Second Sex* anticipates many themes and goals of the women's liberation movement.

Ideas/Beliefs Erich Fromm's *Man for Himself*; Arthur Koestler's *Insight and Outlook*.

Literature George Orwell's *1984*; Yukio Mishima's *Confessions of a Mask*; Faulkner's *Knight's Gambit*; Joyce Cary's *A Fearful Joy*.

Drama/Entertainment Arthur Miller's *Death of a Salesman*; T S Eliot's *The Cocktail Party*; Carol Reed's *The Third Man*. American TV has the first situation comedy, 'The Goldbergs,' and the first thriller series, 'Suspense.'

The Arts Picasso's *Woman with a Fish Hat*; Chagall's *Red Sun*; Epstein's *Lazarus*; Kenneth Clark publishes *Landscape into Art*.

Architecture Frank Lloyd Wright completes the laboratory tower for S C Johnson & Son; Philip Johnson builds his glass house in Connecticut.

Music Hindemith's *Horn Concerto*; Bernstein's *Age of Anxiety*; Alan Rawsthorne's *Concerto for String Orchestra*.

Life/Customs UNICEF issues its first Christmas card after holding a design contest won by a seven-year-old Czech girl, Jitka Samkova; sale of Christmas cards will eventually provide 20 percent of UNICEF's budget.

14 JANUARY 1950
International A mutual aid program emphasizing economic development of South and Southeast Asia is adopted by British Commonwealth foreign ministers meeting in Colombo, Ceylon, as a basis for a Pacific pact modeled after the North Atlantic Treaty. Nations represented are Britain, Canada, Australia, New Zealand, South Africa, India, Pakistan, and Ceylon.

William Faulkner.

IN SEARCH OF STABILITY 1946-1962

A Marshall Plan shipment of wheat flour arrives in Greece, December 1949.

29 JANUARY 1950

South Africa In Johannesburg, the first of a series of riots precipitated by the government's racial policies occurs. Race riots had taken place in Durban in January 1949 between the Zulus and the Indians—with over 100 dead and 1000 injured.

31 JANUARY 1950

USA President Truman announces that he has instructed the Atomic Energy Commission to produce the hydrogen bomb—a superbomb far more destructive than that dropped on Nagasaki.

15 FEBRUARY 1950

China-USSR After two months of negotiations between Stalin and Mao, Soviet Russia and China sign a 30-year friendship and mutual defense pact in Moscow. The agreement provides that the two nations would unite in repulsing an attack by Japan or any other state, and that Outer Mongolia will be organized as an 'independent' republic.

23 FEBRUARY 1950

Great Britain In the first general election since 1945, 85 percent of the eligible voters return the Labour Government led by Prime Minister Attlee by the slim majority of six seats in the Commons—the smallest margin in more than a century. The Conservatives, under Churchill's leadership, wage their campaign on the issue of socialism vs free enterprise.

1 MARCH 1950

Great Britain In London's Old Bailey, German-born scientist Dr Klaus Fuchs, chief physicist at the British atomic research plant at Harwell, pleads guilty to violating the Official Secrets Act and is sentenced to 14 years in prison. He was arrested 3 February on information supplied by the FBI, showing that he communicated atomic information to Russian agents in Britain and in the US, where he worked on the Los Alamos Project. As a sequel in the US, the FBI makes a series of arrests, including those of Harry Gold, David Greenglass, and Julius and Ethel Rosenberg.

3 MARCH 1950

West Germany In Paris the Ministry of Foreign Affairs of the Saar Region signs an agreement with France under which the Saar is to turn over its coal mines and submit customs and economic affairs to France for 50 years. West German Chancellor Konrad Adenauer protests the pact, but the Saar will not be returned to German control until 1957.

8 APRIL 1950

India-Pakistan The Delhi Pact between India and Pakistan on treatment of minorities is signed, reducing hostilities between the two nations.

USSR-USA Over the Baltic Sea, a Soviet fighter shoots down an unarmed US Navy patrol plane, ostensibly for violating Soviet air space over Latvia. The bodies of the 10 crew members are never recovered. Similar incidents will occur throughout the decade.

27 APRIL 1950

Australia A bill is passed outlawing the Australian Communist Party.

8 MAY 1950

Vietnam In response to the communist victory in China, US Secretary of State Dean Acheson announces the decision to provide economic and military aid to the former French colony. This marks the first fateful step toward US involvement in the Vietnam War.

9 MAY 1950

West Germany The Bonn Government welcomes the Schuman Plan—which advises uniting the French and German coal industries and their iron and steel production under a single authority.

14 MAY 1950

Turkey In the first free elections in the nation's history, voters oust President Ismet Inonu's Republican People's Party, in power since the Turkish Republic was founded by Kemal Atatürk in 1923, in favor of the five-year-old Democratic Party, led by Celal Bayar. The Democrats campaigned for the return of free enterprise and against Republican economic policies which were blamed for the high cost of living.

13 JUNE 1950

South Africa The assembly supports Prime Minister Daniel Malan's segregationist Group Areas Bill, which would split the country into white and non-white zones. Those opposed point out that the whites, who are to implement the bill, number only 2.5

MAO TSE-TUNG, 1893–1976

Born into a peasant family, Mao Tse-tung was 25 when he discovered Marxist Communism. He helped found the Chinese Communist Party in 1921, and at first joined forces with the Nationalists, with whom he fell out after Sun Yat-sen's death in 1925 to begin the fierce civil war that would not end until he and his communists took control of China in October 1949. His version of communism stressed the revolutionary role of the peasants, and he was especially hard on the bourgeoisie, intellectuals, and city-dwellers. Originally an ally of Russia, he opposed the USSR over the issue of which country was the true heir of the Marxist-Leninist revolution. In the mid-1960s he unleashed a campaign against 'revisionists,' those Chinese who did not show total dedication to the revolution. Although he brought China far along the road to self-sufficiency in agriculture, he could not solve all its age-old problems. He did live to see American statesmen come to call on him after a quarter-century of enmity. Mao was the total revolutionary, and he put a quarter of the world's people on a 'long march' like his own, with many lives lost on the way.

IN SEARCH OF STABILITY 1946-1962

Chou En-lai, Mao and Chu-Teh wait for General George Marshall.

Lieutenant General Briggs (right) is greeted by General Harding in Singapore, 17 April 1950.

million, while the other races—Indians, Pakistanis, and blacks—total 10 million.

25 JUNE 1950
Korean War Equipped with Soviet-made weapons, North Korean troops cross the 38th parallel to invade South Korea. The UN Security Council calls for an immediate end to the fighting and withdrawal of invading forces.

26 JUNE 1950
Korean War President Truman authorizes the US Navy and Air Force to assist South Korean troops operating south of the 38th parallel.

27 JUNE 1950
Korean War Acting in the absence of the Soviet representative, the UN Security Council adopts a resolution on armed intervention in Korea.

28 JUNE 1950
Korean War Seoul, the capital of South Korea, is captured by invading North Korean forces.

30 JUNE 1950
Korean War US ground troops are sent to South Korea by President Truman, who signs a bill extend-

ing the military draft for another year and orders the US Navy to blockade the Korean coast.

8 JULY 1950
Korean War General Douglas MacArthur is named commander of UN troops in South Korea.

5 SEPTEMBER 1950
Korean War Invading North Koreans complete their farthest advance into the south, controlling most of the Korean Peninsula except for a UN beachhead around Pusan in the southeast.

15 SEPTEMBER 1950
Korean War UN troops in South Korea land at Inchon and press toward Seoul. This successful counteroffensive will result in the 26 September recapture of Seoul.

19 SEPTEMBER 1950
West Germany In New York, foreign ministers of Britain, France, and the US adopt an agreement to bring West Germany into the society of free nations, provide for its armed defense, and revise its military, legislative, and economic restrictions. Thus West Germany is transformed, mainly as a result of the Korean War, from a former enemy of the Western

IN SEARCH OF STABILITY 1946-1962

Chinese Communist Troops, wearing tennis sneakers and rags, surrender to US Marines south of Koto-ri.

nations to their future ally—forming a bulwark against the spread of communism.

29 SEPTEMBER 1950
Korean War   The counteroffensive continues as US and South Korean troops reach the 38th parallel. General MacArthur's call for surrender of the North Korean Army is ignored.

9 OCTOBER 1950
Korean War   Authorized by the UN General Assembly, General MacArthur orders crossing of the 38th parallel and invasion of North Korea. On 7 October the UN had established a commission for the unification and rehabilitation of Korea.
Vietnam   In Saigon, French authorities report losses estimated at 3000 to the forces of Ho Chi Minh on the Chinese border near Caobang and Thatke. French Legionnaires and Africans were outnumbered 10 to 1 by well-equipped forces instead of guerrilla units. Ho's Viet Minh cut off the water supply of Haiphong, the second largest city in Indochina.

15 OCTOBER 1950
Korean War   President Truman and General MacArthur meet on Wake Island to plan strategy.

20 OCTOBER 1950
Korean War   A two-day fight for the capital of North Korea, Pyongyang, results in the city's capture by UN troops, who advance farther north.
USSR   In a Prague conference, foreign ministers of the Soviet Union, East Germany, Poland, Bulgaria, Hungary, and Rumania denounce liberalization of West German political and military restrictions and call for German unification and a German peace treaty.

21 OCTOBER 1950
Tibet   Communist Chinese forces invade Tibet and challenge the authority of the 15-year-old Dalai Lama, hoping to replace him with the 13-year-old Panchen Lama whom they term the 'incarnate Buddha.' The communist invasion alienates India and threatens Nepal. On 10 November Tibet appeals to the UN for a peaceful settlement.

1 NOVEMBER 1950
USA   In an assassination attempt on President Truman, two Puerto Rican nationalists kill one guard and seriously injure two others. Truman is unharmed. The assassins claimed to represent the cause of Puerto Rican independence.

20 NOVEMBER 1950
Korean War   UN and South Korean troops reach the Yalu River, on the border of Manchuria.

26 NOVEMBER 1950
Korean War   Assisted by large Chinese forces, the North Koreans halt the UN counteroffensive and force its retreat.

5 DECEMBER 1950
Korean War   Pyongyang, North Korea's capital, is abandoned by UN forces. By the end of the year, the North Koreans and their Chinese allies will have driven UN and South Korean forces back to the region of the 38th parallel.

19 DECEMBER 1950
International   The North Atlantic Council names General Eisenhower supreme commander of Western European defense forces.

25 DECEMBER 1950
Great Britain   Scottish nationalists steal the Stone of Scone from the British coronation throne in Westminster Abbey. The 485-pound sandstone, on which British monarchs have been crowned for the past six centuries, is recovered in Scotland in April 1951.

27 DECEMBER 1950
Spain   The US and Spain announce that they are resuming diplomatic relations. The US will soon grant Spain a $62.5 million Marshall-Plan loan.

OTHER EVENTS OF 1950
Science   Glenn Seaborg and colleagues discover element 98, californium. A Danish deep-sea expedition in the vessel *Galathea* finds living organisms at a depth of 34,000 feet in the Pacific, far deeper than it was believed life could exist.
Medicine/Health   The first kidney transplant from

Men of the Heavy Mortar Company, 7th Infantry Regiment, cook rice in their foxhole.

IN SEARCH OF STABILITY 1946-1962

cadaver to patient is performed in Chicago.

Technology The US Atomic Energy Commission separates plutonium from pitchblende concentrate.

Environment Fred Chubb, a prospector, discovers a crater in the remote wilds of Quebec, Canada, which scientists will describe as the largest known—11,136 feet in diameter (3341 meters)—it is named the Ungava-Quebec, or New Quebec, Crater.

Social Sciences In a peat bog near Aarhus, Denmark (Tollund Fen) the well-preserved body of a man who had been hanged some 2000 years ago is excavated almost intact.

Ideas/Beliefs Pope Pius XII issues the encyclical *Humani generis*, which attacks Existentialism and other secular and scientific ideas. Arthur Koestler edits *The God That Failed*, an influential book by disillusioned Communists.

Literature Hemingway's *Across the River and into the Trees*; Ezra Pound's *Seventy Cantos*; C P Snow's *The Masters*; Anthony Powell's *A Question of Upbringing*.

Drama/Entertainment Ionesco's *The Bald Soprano*; Akira Kurosawa's *Rashomon*; Cocteau's *Orpheus*.

The Arts Willem De Kooning's *I, Woman*; Jean Dubuffet's *Nude, Olympia*; Utrillo's *Suburban Street*; Chagall's *King David*; Braque's *The Terrace*; Pollock's *One*; Dali's *The Madonna of Port Lligat*; Gabo's *Linear Construction*; Picasso's sculpture *The Goat*.

Architecture The Rome Railway Station, by Montiori and others; University City, Mexico City, by Mario Pani, Enrique de Moral, and others.

Music Bartok's *Viola Concerto*; Boulez's *Symphonie Concertante*; Hindemith's *Harmonia Mundi*; Honegger's *5th Symphony*; Menotti's *The Consul*. 'Cool' jazz begins to develop out of bebop.

Life/Customs Credit cards are introduced by the Diners Club of New York. The samba, a Latin American dance, becomes popular. China legislates away polygamy.

Miscellaneous The Schuman Plan for a European Coal and Iron Community is promulgated. A TV tower is added to the Empire State Building, raising its total height to 1472 feet.

1 JANUARY 1951

Korean War Combined North Korean and Communist Chinese forces break through the UN lines along the 38th parallel. On 4 January the South Korean capital of Seoul will be recaptured by North Korean forces.

2 MARCH 1951

Czechoslovakia Reports issuing from the country indicate that the Czech Communist Party is being purged of Titoist elements.

13 MARCH 1951

Israel The government files a claim for $1.5 billion reparations from Germany, based on the cost of rehabilitating 500,000 survivors of the Nazi holocaust now settled in Israel. The reparations may be in

---

KONRAD ADENAUER, 1876–1967

Konrad Adenauer was a man of exemplary private life whose political career did not really begin until his seventieth year. A lawyer of humble origins, he became Mayor of Cologne and played an important part in Germany's politics as a leader of the Catholic Center Party until he was dismissed from all his positions by the Hitler regime. After twelve years in political limbo, he helped draft the West German Constitution, then rose from party leader of the Christian Democratic Union to become chancellor in 1949, governing the new republic until his retirement in 1963. Domestically Adenauer championed division of powers, while his goal in foreign relations was to bind Germany firmly to the democratic West. To do so he engineered both Germany's entrance into NATO and the Franco-German Treaty of 1963 which ended many years of bitterness and contention.

---

goods. A total of $6 billion in property losses is attributed to Nazi activities. The West German Government indicates it will meet all justified claims on behalf of German Jews.

14 MARCH 1951

Korean War The UN limited offensive against communist troops forces retreat of the North Koreans and Chinese from Seoul.

29 MARCH 1951

Korean War The Chinese Communists reject General MacArthur's offer to meet with North Koreans and Chinese and seek an end to hostilities.

USA Their trial for conspiracy to commit wartime espionage and betrayal of atomic secrets to Soviet agents ends in conviction of Julius Rosenberg, Ethel Rosenberg, and Morton Sobell. On 5 April the federal court hands down the death penalty for the Rosenbergs on the basis of national jeopardy.

11 APRIL 1951

Korean War In an action both criticized and applauded by the public, President Truman removes General MacArthur from his commands in the Far East and appoints General Matthew Ridgway in his place. The dismissal results from MacArthur's public statements on policy: Truman fears that expansion of the Korean War into Chinese territory might lead to a world war, while MacArthur proposes the bombing of supply depots inside China and issues a statement threatening China with an 'expansion of our military operations.'

18 APRIL 1951

International In a move toward eventual European economic union, France, West Germany, Italy, Belgium, the Netherlands, and Luxembourg sign a Paris treaty agreeing to the Schuman Plan for a single market authority over coal and steel.

General Douglas MacArthur (right) visits the Korean front.

15 MAY 1951
Korean War North Korean and Communist Chinese forces begin their second spring offensive, but UN troops force them to withdraw a week later.

25 MAY 1951
Great Britain Foreign service officials Guy Burgess and Donald Maclean vanish mysteriously. It develops that they have defected to the Soviet Union, for which they have been spying.

27 MAY 1951
Tibet Communist China announces the 'peaceful liberation' of Tibet, whereby Tibet agrees to end resistance and become a province of the People's Republic of China. Chinese troops will be stationed in Tibet, whose troops are to merge with the Chinese Army. Tibet is to maintain 'internal autonomy,' while China will control its foreign affairs.

5 JULY 1951
Iran The International Court of Justice at The Hague rules against Iran in a dispute with Britain over nationalization of the Iranian oil industry. Britain had protested Iran's abrogation of a 1933 concession treaty. Iran refuses to recognize the court's competence to act in the dispute and on 12 September issues an ultimatum. On 4 October all British personnel of the Anglo-Iranian Oil Company are evacuated from Abadan.

IN SEARCH OF STABILITY 1946-1962

8 JULY 1951

Korean War Cease-fire negotiations begin at Kaesong—with interruptions, these talks will last some two years, with a shift of location to Panmunjom. On the battlefield, the rest of the year will be one of stalemate, although casualty figures mount.

18 JULY 1951

Spain In Madrid, General Franco and US Admiral Forrest Sherman reach agreement on American use of Spanish air and naval bases in return for US economic and military aid—ending years of Western ostracism of the Iberian nation. Britain and France disapprove. On 6 September the US will sign a pact with Portugal giving America new rights in the Azores and including these islands in the NATO defense area.

20 JULY 1951

Jordan King Abdullah Ibn Hussein is assassinated in Jerusalem by a follower of the exiled Mufti of Jerusalem, who was opposed to Jordan's annexation of Arab Palestine (completed on 24 April over the

protests of most Arab League members). Emir Talal succeeds him as monarch on 6 September.

23 JULY 1951

International Near Paris, the new NATO headquarters are opened by Supreme Commander General Dwight D Eisenhower, who says the occasion marks the intention 'to preserve peace and not to wage war, and lift from the hearts of men the fear of cell blocks and slave camps.'

16 AUGUST 1951

Egypt In the UN Security Council, the US, Britain, and France introduce a resolution calling on Egypt to lift its blockade of Suez Canal traffic bound for Israel, charging that the blockade heightens Near East tension. The Egyptian delegate counters that British troops stationed in Egypt contribute to the tensions.

1 SEPTEMBER 1951

New Zealand In general elections, Prime Minister Sidney Holland's National Party wins 50 seats to Labour's 30—a public vote of confidence for use of

US Vice-President Alben Barkley (left) visits Korea, 24 November 1951.

troops early in the year to defeat a communist-supported waterfront strike. In office since 30 November 1949, Holland has implemented a program supporting private enterprise and reversing Labour Government nationalization measures. On the same day, New Zealand, Australia, and the US sign a tripartite security pact pledging a defense buildup and mutual defense against a common agressor. New Zealand and Australia were among the early providers of troops in the Korean conflict.

8 SEPTEMBER 1951

Japan In San Francisco, 49 nations end a four-day conference by signing the peace treaty with Japan, who loses her overseas possessions but pays no reparations and retains self-defense privileges. On the same day, the US and Japan agree to a mutual security pact allowing the US to maintain troops in Japan for an indefinite period.

15–20 SEPTEMBER 1951

International Meeting in Ottawa, Canada, the NATO council agrees to invite Turkey and Greece to become members, which they will do in February 1952.

16 OCTOBER 1951

Pakistan Prime Minister Liaquat Ali Khan is assassinated by an Afghan extremist. Afghanistan has been agitating for creation of a new free state of Pushtunistan on the Afghan-Pakistani border. The moderate Liaquat Ali opposed that plan and prevented Moslem extremists from seeking war with India over Kashmir. Hopes for an early Kashmir settlement dwindle.

25 OCTOBER 1951

Great Britain In the general election, the Labour Party loses to the Conservatives, who win a majority of 16 seats. Winston Churchill becomes prime minister, with Anthony Eden as foreign secretary.

27 OCTOBER 1951

Egypt Egypt abrogates both the 1899 British-Egyptian condominium controlling the Sudan and the 1936 treaty of alliance permitting Britain to maintain troops in the Suez Canal Zone. Sudan rejects the Egyptian decision, supporting British plans for Sudanese self-determination. As Egypt threatens drastic action, the British fly reinforcements in from Cyprus and move four warships into the area. In the face of widespread anti-British riots and an 18 November clash between British forces and Egyptian police, the British stand firm.

10 NOVEMBER 1951

International Britain, France, Turkey, and the US announce plans for a Middle East defense command against outside aggression, with a statement of principles to the Arab nations and Israel asserting that the command would not interfere with local matters but would be devoted initially to advising

Middle East states. The Soviet Union warns the Arab states and Israel against joining. South Africa accepts membership on 12 November, Australia on 5 December.

29 NOVEMBER 1951

Syria A military coup deposes pro-Soviet Prime Minister Maarouf Dawalibi, who took office the day before. Army chief of staff Colonel Adib Shishakli installs Colonel Fawzi Silo as premier and defense minister.

24 DECEMBER 1951

Libya Libya becomes the first nation to achieve independence under UN auspices. The former Italian colony, now a democratic constitutional monarchy, has three provinces—Tripolitania, Cyrenaica, and the Fezzan—with Benghazi and Tripoli as cocapitals. King Idris I is the nation's monarch.

27 DECEMBER 1951

Korean War Peace efforts are blocked as a trial armistice ends with no extension proposed. Main bars to an armistice are the issues of prisoner exchange and airport construction in North Korea.

31 DECEMBER 1951

USA The Economic Cooperation Administration (ECA) of the Marshall Plan is replaced by the Mutual Security Agency, which will continue to co-ordinate economic, military, and technical foreign aid. W Averell Harriman becomes director of the MSA.

OTHER EVENTS OF 1951

Science Barbara McClintock, an American biochemist experimenting with the inherited characteristics of maize, or Indian corn, for many years, announces her discovery that the genetic center of a living cell is in constant motion, the genes breaking, moving, and recombining. Contrary to the concepts of classical genetics, this claim will long be attacked or ignored. By the 1970s other researchers are finding confirmation with the genes of other organisms; in

---

ROBERT GORDON MENZIES, 1894–1978

Destined to become the longest continuing prime minister in Australian history, Robert Menzies began his career as a successful barrister in Victoria. Leaving law for politics, he worked his way up the government ladder to become prime minister in 1939. Opposition to his mobilization for war lost him the premiership in 1941, but he regained it in 1949. A thorough conservative, Menzies strengthened ties with the US while encouraging Australia's rapid industrial growth and foreign investments during the 1950s. His anticommunism led to an unsuccessful attempt to suppress the Australian Communist Party in 1951 and to commitment of troops to Vietnam in the 1960s. He retired in 1966.

IN SEARCH OF STABILITY 1946-1962

1983 McClintock will receive the Nobel Prize for her important contribution to understanding inheritance, cell activity, and related phenomena. Niko Tinbergen, the Danish ethologist—with Konrad Lorenz, the founder of this modern discipline—publishes his most important work, *The Study of Instinct*, an attempt to synthesize current ideas about animal behavior.

Technology   The Univac I computer (on 14 June) and the Ferranti Mark I (on 9 July) are the first commercially manufactured computers in use, the former at the US Census Bureau in Philadelphia, the latter at Manchester University in England. The first electric power from nuclear energy (outside the laboratory) is employed by the US Atomic Energy Commission near Idaho Falls, Idaho; obtained from an experimental breeder, it supplies steam to a turbogenerator that produces over 100,000 watts of electrical energy. The first space flight by living creatures occurs when the US sends four monkeys 85 miles into the stratosphere in a V2 rocket from White Sands, New Mexico; this is originally concealed from the public for fear of objections.

Environment   In the Philippines, the volcano Hibokhibok emits a red-hot cloud of gas and dust that kills some 500 people.

Social Studies   Ralph Solecki, an American archaeologist, makes the first soundings in Shanidar Cave in Iraq; during the next few years he will excavate a major Paleolithic site here, inhabited from at least 100,000 BC. Henri Frankfort's *The Birth of Civilization in the Near East*; Hannah Arendt's *The Origins of Totalitarianism*; David Riesman's *The Lonely Crowd*; the first English translation of Emile Durkheim's seminal work *Suicide*.

Ideas/Beliefs   Camus' *The Rebel*; André Malraux's *The Voices of Silence*.

Literature   Kawabata Yasunari's *A Thousand Cranes*; Kazantzakis's *The Last Temptation of Christ*; Par Lagerkvist's *Barabbas*; Graham Greene's *The End of the Affair*; Morley Callaghan's *The Loved and the Lost*; J D Salinger's *The Catcher in the Rye*; Norman Mailer's *Barbary Shore*; Herman Wouk's *The Caine Mutiny*; Robert Lowell's *The Mills of the Kavanaughs*.

Eleanor Roosevelt.

Drama/Entertainment   Ionesco's *The Lesson*; Fry's *A Sleep of Prisoners*; Williams's *Rose Tattoo*; Hellman's *Autumn Garden*; Hitchcock's *Strangers on a Train*; the musical *South Pacific*.

The Arts   Hopper's *Room by the Sea*; Dali's *Christ of St John of the Cross*.

Architecture   The United Nations complex in New York City is completed, the work of Wallace Harrison and an international advisory committee including Le Corbusier and Oscar Niemeyer. Basil Spence wins the design competition for the new cathedral in Coventry, England.

Music   Stravinsky's *The Rake's Progress* (with a libretto by Auden and Kallman); Britten's *Billy Budd*; Hans Werner Henze's *Boulevard Solitude*; Arnold Schönberg completes *Moses and Aaron* (begun in 1932); Gian-Carlo Menotti's *Amahl and the Night Visitors* is televised.

Sports/Leisure   Citation becomes the first horse to win $1 million.

Life/Customs   The first live boxing match, surgical operation, and color programs are televised.

24 JANUARY 1952
Canada   Vincent Massey, a veteran dislomat, is appointed by Britain's George VI to succeed Field Marshal Viscount Alexander as governor general. Massey is the first Canadian to serve in this post.

25 JANUARY 1952
West Germany   Controversy over the Saar reaches a crisis when France decides to replace the High Commissariat there with a diplomatic mission—a move that threatens to separate the Saar from Germany

7 SEPTEMBER 1952

permanently by giving it independent status. The 30 November elections favor autonomy and alignment with France, a status rejected by the West German Government.

6 FEBRUARY 1952
Great Britain At Sandringham, King George VI dies in his sleep after undergoing surgery for lung cancer. His daughter will take the oath as Queen Elizabeth II on 8 February, but her coronation will be delayed for about a year. Winston Churchill eulogizes the king as an inspirational wartime monarch.

20 FEBRUARY 1952
International At a meeting of the NATO council in Lisbon, delegates decide to create a European army of 50 divisions provided by member nations for the defense of Western Europe. This troop strength, planned for the end of 1952, will never be achieved.

26 FEBRUARY 1952
Great Britain Prime Minister Churchill announces that the British have developed an atom bomb. The weapon will be tested on 2 October, making Britain the third nation to join the nuclear club.

4 MARCH 1952
Korean War On the propaganda front, the communists accuse UN forces of germ warfare. The UN counters that communist troops are unwell due to shortcomings in their own medical and supply services. The germ-warfare accusation will be repeated, but North Korea will not permit Red Cross investigation.

10 MARCH 1952
International The Soviet Union proposes a German peace treaty that is rejected by Britain, France, and the US because of disagreement on the unification of Germany, inability to effect free elections, and Russian insistence on using the Potsdam decisions as a basis for the pact. The Russians will reject an eight-article Austrian peace treaty proposed by the Western powers on 13 March.

15 MARCH 1952
International Under auspices of the Mutual Security Act, the US and Brazil sign a military assistance pact. The US signed similar agreements with Ecuador on 26 February, with Peru on 22 February, and with Cuba on 7 March; it will conclude such pacts with Chile on 4 April and with Colombia on 17 April. Mexico will reject the US terms for a pact.

20 MARCH 1952
South Africa The Supreme Court invalidates a law putting colored voters on separate lists. This decision is rejected by Prime Minister Malan, who sets up a Parliamentary High Court, dominated by his party, to give Parliament precedence over the Supreme Court. Malan's High Court sets aside the Supreme

Court decision but is itself declared illegal by the Appellate Court, South Africa's highest tribunal.

28 MARCH 1952
Tunisia Anti-French riots throughout the protectorate, costing some 100 lives, lead to a French crackdown. Under pressure, the Bey of Tunis removes Premier Mohammed Chenik, a supporter of Tunisian independence.

25 APRIL 1952
Korean War In a prisoner-of-war exchange, only 70,000 of 170,000 Communist prisoners (5100 of 20,000 Chinese Reds) agree to be exchanged for UN prisoners held by North Korea. Forced repatriation of prisoners remains an unresolved issue for armistice negotiators.

28 APRIL 1952
International General Dwight Eisenhower resigns as NATO Supreme Commander: General Ridgway replaces him. On 7 July Eisenhower will receive the Republican nomination for president.

26 MAY 1952
West Germany In Bonn, the US, Britain, France, and West Germany sign a pact abolishing the occupation statute and the Allied high commissions.

27 MAY 1952
International In Paris, France, West Germany, Italy, Belgium, the Netherlands and Luxembourg sign a treaty founding the European Defense Community. Reciprocal aid pacts are then signed between NATO and the EDC, and between Britain and the EDC. The aim is to establish a single unified command and to align West Germany with NATO.

25 JULY 1952
Puerto Rico Puerto Rico becomes the first commonwealth of the US, after President Truman approves its constitution on 3 July.

26 JULY 1952
Egypt King Farouk abdicates after Major General Mohammed Naguib seizes power in a coup on 23 July to press an anti-corruption plan. Farouk goes into exile and his infant son is proclaimed Fuad II, king of Egypt and the Sudan.

11 AUGUST 1952
Jordan King Talal, suffering from mental illness, is declared unfit to rule by Parliament. Seventeen-year-old Crown Prince Hussein will be installed as King Hussein I on 2 May 1953.

31 AUGUST 1952
West Germany During the past month, some 16,000 persons have escaped from East to West Berlin.

7 SEPTEMBER 1952
China The agricultural ministry reports that about

IN SEARCH OF STABILITY 1946-1962

President Truman presents the Distinguished Service Medal to General Eisenhower, 2 June 1952.

40 percent of China's farm families have been organized into cooperative 'mutual aid' groups. Starting in 1952, Chinese industry, agriculture, and social institutions are forcibly collectivized. Great numbers of people will be executed as Nationalist supporters, or as class and political enemies.

25 SEPTEMBER 1952
International The consultative assembly of the Council of Europe approves the Strasbourg Plan to develop colonies and dominions of European nations. A new trade area would include the British Commonwealth and Western Europe and its overseas possessions. The economic power of this union would match that of the US or the Soviet bloc; its organization would include a free trade concept and a system of preferential tariffs.

5 OCTOBER 1952
USSR The 19th congress of the Communist Party —the first since 1939—opens in the Kremlin, with representatives from 44 foreign states. Soviet Secretary Georgi Malenkov declares that the US is intent

on world domination and will try to achieve its aims by means of a third world war. The ten-day congress will recommend a peace drive by means of popular fronts, stressing peaceful coexistence between communist and capitalist countries, and expansion of trade with the free world to alleviate the blockade preventing strategic materials from reaching communist nations.

21 OCTOBER 1952
Kenya Great Britain declares a state of emergency in its colony of Kenya due to killings of white settlers by the Mau Mau ('Hidden Ones'), a secret group of Kikuyu tribesmen determined to gain control of their land. The British are bringing in troop reinforcements and on 22 October the authorities will arrest 110 alleged Mau Mau, including Jomo Kenyatta, the most educated, articulate spokesman for the black Kenyans' demand for independence. Kenyatta will be tried and imprisoned (even though he denies involvement with the Mau Mau and their tactics) until 1961. In December 1963 he will become the first prime minister of a newly independent Kenya.

A US Navy F4U Corsair napalms enemy positions in Korea in October 1952.

IN SEARCH OF STABILITY 1946-1962

22 OCTOBER 1952
Iran Iran breaks off diplomatic relations with Britain, after Britain's 2 October rejection of Premier Mossadegh's conditions for a settlement of the oil dispute between the two nations.

4 NOVEMBER 1952
USA Dwight D Eisenhower is elected president by the largest popular vote in US history to date (with 442 electoral votes to Adlai Stevenson's 89). Richard M Nixon is elected vice-president.

5 DECEMBER 1952
Korean War US President-elect Eisenhower visits Korea to break the stalemate in truce talks. Reviewing the front lines, he concludes there is no easy solution for the conflict.

8 DECEMBER 1952
Morocco Calling for independence from France, nationalist demonstrators riot after the assassination in Tunisia of Tunisian labor leader Ferhat Hached.

10 DECEMBER 1952
Egypt Premier Naguib announces cancellation of the 1923 constitution and formation of a committee to draw up a new and broader law. An interim constitution, giving full authority to Naguib and his Army Council for three years, is proclaimed 3 February 1953.

OTHER EVENTS OF 1952
Medicine/Health The first successful open-heart surgery is performed by F John Lewis, an American surgeon, and his team. The first artificial aortic valve (made of flexiglas) is fitted into the heart of a patient in Georgetown University Hospital, Washington, DC. The first sex-change operation is performed on George Jorgensen, an American, at Copenhagen Hospital, Denmark; he becomes an instant celebrity as Christine Jorgensen.
Technology The first test of a thermonuclear (fusion) bomb occurs when a hydrogen device is detonated on 31 October at the Eniwetok atoll in the Marshall Islands. (Russia will detonate its first fusion bomb in 1953.) Peaceful harnessing of fusion remains elusive in the decades that follow.
Environment London experiences such extreme 'smog' in December that strong measures against pollution will be instated.
Social Studies Carl Blegen and his team of archaeologists resume excavations at the Palace of Nestor, at Pylos, Greece. Other archaeologists begin work on an important pre-Greek site at Lerna. A British archaeologist, Kathleen Kenyon, begins excavating at Jericho and will turn up one of the earliest known towns. Jacques Cousteau and his colleagues find an ancient Greek ship sunk off Marseilles with 3000 amphoras, or wine urns; this marks the beginning of underwater archaeology as a specialized discipline. Grahame Clark's *Prehistoric Europe: The Economic Basis* is a seminal work for modern archaeology.

Ideas/Beliefs Simone Weil's *The Need for Roots*.
Literature Ralph Ellison's *The Invisible Man*; Ernest Hemingway's *The Old Man and the Sea*; Angus Wilson's *Hemlock and After*; Ray Bradbury's *The Illustrated Man*.
Drama/Entertainment Beckett's *Waiting for Godot*; Ionesco's *The Chairs*; Chaplin's *Limelight*; the Stravinsky-Robbins ballet *The Cage*; and the first season of the long-running Agatha Christie mystery play, *The Mousetrap*.
The Arts Picasso's *War*; Pollock's *Convergence*; Epstein's *Madonna and Child*.
Architecture Le Corbusier completes his Unité d'Habitation, an apartment house in Marseilles. Mies van der Rohe completes his pair of Lake Shore Drive Apartment Houses in Chicago, examples of his international style and personal philosophy of 'less is more.' In New York City, Lever House, the work of Gordon Bunshaft and Skidmore, Owings and Merrill, is completed. Mexico City sees completion of its University Library, by Juan O'Gorman and others.
Music Prokofiev's *7th Symphony*; Bernstein's *Trouble in Tahiti*.
Sports/Leisure At the summer Olympics, the Czech Emil Zatopek becomes the first person to win the 5000 meters, 10,000 meters, and the marathon.

9–15 JANUARY 1953
International The world's first Asian Socialist Conference meets in Rangoon, Burma. Delegates approve ties with the West's Socialist International and advocate that peasant farmers become landowners.

2 FEBRUARY 1953
Taiwan (Formosa) In a major US Far East policy

change, President Eisenhower announces that the US 7th Fleet will no longer block a Nationalist attack from Taiwan (Formosa) against the Chinese mainland.

12 FEBRUARY 1953
Egypt In Cairo, Egypt and Britain sign a pact providing for self-government in the Anglo-Egyptian Sudan and for self-determination by the Sudanese within three years, ending the 54-year old condominium. On 11 December the pro-Egyptian National Union Party wins the election for the new Sudanese Parliament.

13 FEBRUARY 1953
Guatemala Implementing a land-reform program to distribute uncultivated tracts to landless peasants, the government expropriates 234,000 acres of United Fruit Company holdings. Similar moves are made against other companies.

24 FEBRUARY 1953
South Africa To give the government dictatorial powers to repress the black and Indian movements, Parliament passes public-safety legislation. In the 15 April national election, Prime Minister Malan's party increases its majority in Parliament.

28 FEBRUARY 1953
International In Ankara, Greece, Yugoslavia and Turkey sign a five-year treaty of friendship and defense.

5 MARCH 1953
USSR In Moscow, Premier Josef Stalin dies after suffering a cerebral hemorrhage on 1 March. He is buried in the Red Square tomb beside Lenin. Georgi M Malenkov succeeds him as premier. The death of Stalin will lead to a 'thaw,' as relations with the West improve and internal repression of cultural and scientific life decreases. Many political prisoners will be freed.

VYACHESLAV MOLOTOV, 1890–1983

Although he served as premier of Russia (1930–41) it was his two long terms as foreign minister that would make Molotov a well-known figure on the international scene. One of the planners of the Bolshevik Revolution, Molotov rose to power through his close association with Stalin. In 1939 he became minister of foreign affairs, and when the war ended he began to lead Russia's campaign against the West, particularly the US and NATO. With Khrushchev solidly in power by 1957, Molotov was publicly denounced, expelled from the Communist Party's presidium, and effectively exiled as ambassador to Outer Mongolia. Although he was allowed to come back and even to hold another post, in 1962 the Supreme Soviet ordered his name removed from all towns and buildings named in his honor. It is now most associated with the firebomb known as the Molotov Cocktail.

---

16 MARCH 1953
Yugoslavia President Tito begins a five-day visit to Britain, during which Prime Minister Churchill will pledge to protect Yugoslavia, which agrees to resist aggression. Tito's strategy of increasing Western ties over the next two years is to prove successful.

7 APRIL 1953
International Swedish diplomat and economist Dag Hammarskjöld is elected by the UN General Assembly to a five-year term as secretary general. The Soviet bloc supports Hammarskjöld's candidacy.

14 APRIL 1953
Laos The Communist-led Viet Minh invade Laos with 40,000 troops, but will withdraw in May before the monsoon season begins.

25 APRIL 1953
International Ending its 11th meeting in Paris, the NATO Council adopts a long-range rearmament program for an extended emergency, discarding a 1952 premise that the threat of Russian aggression would reach its peak in 1954. The Council also cuts its goals for the armed forces, while the US pledges nuclear weapons to counter aggression.

30 APRIL 1953
International In London, a British conference with representatives from Jamaica, Trinidad, Barbados, and the Leeward and Windward Islands concludes with an agreement to establish a British Caribbean Federation.

8 MAY 1953
Vietnam President Eisenhower announces that the US is providing France with $60 million for its Indochina War. More aid will be announced in September; in 1954 three-quarters of the war costs will be met by the US.

10 MAY 1953
South Africa Unity of the ruling white majority is destroyed, as two anti-'Malanism' parties are inaugurated. Alan Paton's Liberal Party presses for full rights of citizenship for all civilized people, while the Federal Union Party calls for a federated state.

2 JUNE 1953
Great Britain In a splendid $2\frac{1}{2}$ hour ceremony, Queen Elizabeth II is crowned in Westminster Abbey. The rite is televised throughout the world.

17 JUNE 1953
East Germany In East Berlin workers protesting increased work quotas mount a demonstration that erupts into an anticommunist riot of 20,000 to 50,000 people the following day. When the demonstration becomes a general strike involving 200,000, Soviet troops quell disturbances, killing 16. After concessions and reforms are granted, the East German Government is reorganized in July.

IN SEARCH OF STABILITY 1946-1962

A street demonstration in East Berlin, 17 June 1953.

19 JUNE 1953
Egypt The military junta proclaims the nation a republic, as Major General Mohammed Naguib is named president and premier.
USA In New York's Sing Sing Prison, convicted spies Julius and Ethel Rosenberg are electrocuted. They are the first Americans executed for treason during peacetime. The Rosenberg case will remain controversial in the decades that follow, a source of both public and private debate.

10 JULY 1953
East Germany US President Eisenhower offers to send $15 million worth of food to relieve hunger in East Germany. He ignores Communist refusals, and shipments at a rate of 5000 tons a week replenish West German stocks used from 27 July to 10 October to feed East Germans, who flock to West Berlin distribution centers.
USSR First Deputy Premier Lavrenti Beria is dismissed as an 'enemy of the people.' Having confessed, he is executed on 23 December along with six

of his aides. This new purge will extend to Georgia, the Ukraine, Belorussia, and other Soviet states.

13 JULY 1953
International In Managua, Nicaragua, a meeting of the Organization of Central American States concludes with a resolution to combat communism. Guatemala alone had refused to attend the conference.

26 JULY 1953
Cuba The Batista Government quells an attack on the Moncanda Army Barracks in Santiago, led by Fidel Castro with 170 young fellow rebels against the Batista regime. Castro is captured, tried, and sentenced to prison for 15 years; he will be released by amnesty in 1955 and go into exile in Mexico. Batista imposes martial law and censorship, but Castro organizes the 26th of July Movement that will invade Cuba on 1 December 1956.

27 JULY 1953
Korean War United Nations and North Korean

Returning to Buckingham Palace after the coronation of Queen Elizabeth II.

officials sign a truce, ending the war after three years of fighting that killed 116,000 UN troops (including 54,000 Americans); 1,500,000 North Koreans and Chinese were killed or wounded. The pact provides for a cease-fire and a demilitarized buffer zone separating North and South Korea at the 38th parallel. Following a mutual aid pact with South Korea, US forces will remain there, and US military and economic aid will continue.

13–22 AUGUST 1953

Iran   The Shah issues a decree on the 13th dismissing Prime Minister Mossadegh because of the latter's increasingly radical reforms and attempts to reduce the Shah's power. A conflict between royalist supporters of the Shah and Mossadegh adherents will break out on the 16th in a civil war in principal cities. The Shah leaves the country on the 16th, and the pro-Mossadegh forces seem to be winning; on the 18th the police and army turn against them and next day regain the upper hand. Mossadegh is arrested on the 20th, and the Shah returns on the 22nd. Mossadegh will be tried by a military court in November-December and sentenced to three years in prison. (Many years later it will be revealed that the USA, through the CIA, was instrumental in creating the turmoil that brought down Mossadegh and maintained the Shah in power.)

29 AUGUST 1953

Cambodia   France and Cambodia sign an agreement giving Cambodia full control of court and police matters. On 22 October Laos receives full independence and sovereignty within the French Union.

13 SEPTEMBER 1953

USSR   Nikita S Khrushchev is elected first secretary of the Soviet Communist Party's central committee, second only to Premier Malenkov. In an agricultural policy report, Khrushchev stresses the importance of personal plots for peasants in collectives.

6 OCTOBER 1953

British Guiana   Britain sends troopships to its South American colony to quell a feared Communist attempt to establish a regime.

23 OCTOBER 1953

Rhodesia   The British colony of Southern Rhodesia is incorporated into the new Federation of Rhodesia and Nyasaland, with a population of some 4.5 million Africans and 250,000 white settlers who control political and economic affairs.

8 DECEMBER 1953

International   President Eisenhower, Prime Minis-

IN SEARCH OF STABILITY 1946-1962

A view of Operation 'Brochet' in the Red River Delta area of French Indochina, 30 September 1953.

ter Churchill, and Premier Joseph Laniel of France end a five-day conference in Bermuda. They agree on unified action to protect the West, and propose exchanging atomic energy data.

OTHER EVENTS OF 1953

Science Francis Crick, Englishman, and James Watson, American, publish their findings and theory on the 'double helix' structure of deoxyribonucleic acid (DNA), the substance that transmits hereditary characteristics. In *Nature*, the British science journal, their article opens with the words: 'We wish to suggest a structure for the salt of deoxyribose nucleic acid (D.N.A.).' In establishing the structure and function of this chemical 'code of life,' Crick and Watson opened up the new field of molecular biology. Melvin Calvin, an American biochemist, and his coworkers, begin to use radioactive carbon-14 to trace chemical reactions that occur when plants change carbon dioxide and water into sugar; these studies are crucial in understanding photosynthesis. W LeGros Clark and other British scientists prove that Piltdown Man—supposedly fossil remains of humans who lived hundreds of thousands of years ago—were a hoax, 'planted' in Piltdown, Sussex, in 1908.

Medicine/Health Dr Jonas Salk, American medical researcher, announces the success of the first clinical trials of a vaccine against polio; large-scale testing will take place in 1954 and be pronounced successful in 1955.

Environment Edmund Hillary, New Zealand, and Tenzing Norkay, Nepal, are the first to climb to the summit of Mt Everest (29,028 feet or 8848 meters), the highest point on earth.

Social Sciences Michael Ventris of England announces that he has deciphered (with the aid of John Chadwick) the Linear B script that was used on Crete and in parts of Greece between about 1450–1200 BC— this will increase understanding of the Minoans and Mycenaeans of this era. Margaret Mead edits an influential text, *Cultural Patterns and Technical Change*; B F Skinner publishes his *Science and Human Behavior*.

Literature Saul Bellow's *The Adventures of Augie March*; Alejo Carpentier's *Lost Footsteps*; James Baldwin's *Go Tell It on the Mountain*; Dylan Thomas's *Collected Poems*.

Drama/Entertainment Arthur Miller's *The Crucible*; Dylan Thomas's radio play *Under Milk Wood*; Robert Anderson's *Tea and Sympathy*; T S Eliot's *The Confidential Clerk*.

The Arts Pollock's *Blue Poles*; Francis Bacon's *Eight Studies for a Portrait*; Henry Moore's *King and Queen*; the Institute of Contemporary Art in London announces that the winner of its international competition for a sculpture of *The Unknown Political Prisoner* is Englishman Reginald Butler.

Music Shostakovich's *10th Symphony*; Britten's *Gloriana*; Stravinsky's *Canticum Sacrum*; Karl-Heinz Stockhausen's *Kontrapunkte No 1*; Vaughan Williams's *7th Symphony*; Bloch's *Concerto Grosso*.

25 JANUARY 1954

International In West Berlin, a conference of the Big Four foreign ministers (Britain, France, USA, USSR) fails to reach accord on the German and Austrian peace treaties, when the Russians insist on the 'neutralization' of the two nations.

8 FEBRUARY 1954

Malaya British officials in Kuala Lumpur announce that the Communist Party high command in Malaya has moved to Sumatra, Indonesia. This departure signifies a victory for British security forces in their six-year war against communist terrorists, but is also seen as a communist attempt to establish an Indonesian front.

25 FEBRUARY 1954

Egypt President and Premier Mohammed Naguib,

Dr Jonas Salk.

A Henry Moore bronze sculpture.

IN SEARCH OF STABILITY 1946-1962

who seized control of the government in 1952, resigns under pressure from Lt Col Gamal Abdel Nasser, vice-president and founder of the revolutionary movement. Nasser becomes premier. Dissident members of the Revolutionary Council will restore Naguib as president on 28 February and as head of the military junta, reportedly placing limitations on his governmental role. But in a reversal on 18 April, Nasser again replaces Naguib as premier. Egypt will remain under military rule until 1964.

1 MARCH 1954

USA Five members of Congress are wounded in the House of Representatives by four Puerto Ricans, one a woman, who fire pistols at random from a spectator's gallery, shouting for independence for Puerto Rico. The attackers are sentenced to prison.

24 MARCH 1954

Great Britain In London, Britain opens economic and trade discussions with Hungary—the first since 1949, when Britain broke off talks because British businessman Edgar Sanders had been imprisoned in Hungary. Similar talks with Poland are in progress and meetings with other nations are planned. On 30 April Britain will relax curbs on the export of rubber to the Soviet Union, as well as on other nonstrategic materials.

28 MARCH 1954

International In Caracas, Venezuela, the Tenth Inter-American Conference ends. Among the 120 resolutions adopted are a statement of anticommunism, a US promise to improve economic relations with Latin America, and an Argentine call for the elimination of colonies under European sovereignty.

31 MARCH 1954

USSR Soviet foreign minister Molotov proposes that the US and Western Europe enter a pact for European security sponsored by Russia; in return the Soviet Union might become a member of NATO. Calling for an end to the cold war, he says that one organization would balance the other and that Russian participation would offset the 'offensive character' of NATO. The Western nations reject this suggestion, terming it a 'Trojan horse' and an attempt to undermine NATO.

12 APRIL 1954

USA The Atomic Energy Commission reports the withdrawal of Dr J Robert Oppenheimer's security clearance on 22 December 1953 on orders from the President. Oppenheimer's Communist associations and his opposition to the hydrogen bomb are seen as 'proof of fundamental defects in his character.' However, Oppenheimer is not found to be disloyal.

13 APRIL 1954

Australia The government announces that Soviet embassy secretary Vladimir Petrov has been granted political asylum, after disclosing a Russian spy ring

---

COLD WAR

Within a few months of World War II, a worldwide confrontation between communism and the free world had begun in earnest. The origins of what would develop into a massive arms race and its nuclear-weapons balance of terror lay in two key postwar dilemmas. One resulted from conflicting views on the future of Eastern Europe. The United States interpreted the overthrow of noncommunist regimes and replacement by communist dictatorships as glaring evidence of Soviet expansionism. The Soviets saw it in their national interest to maintain this buffer of sympathetic nations between itself and the West. Postwar Germany quickly solidified into communist and noncommunist areas, creating the second dispute. In response to unification of Germany's Western zones, the Soviets blockaded West Berlin, demanding that Western nations leave. Instead, they flew over the blockade, unwilling to risk war by shooting their way to Berlin. Meanwhile, between 1945 and 1950, Iran, China, Vietnam, and Korea became arenas of confrontation between the two ideologies. The hope that had greeted the end of World War II in 1945 had been dashed, replaced by the forebodings of a cold war.

---

in Australia that implicated Australian citizens as well as Russian agents. On 23 April Russia severs diplomatic relations with Australia.

15 APRIL 1954

Japan Birth-control advocate Margaret Sanger, previously barred from Japan by Allied occupation forces, becomes the first American woman to testify before the Diet. She says that birth control would eventually solve the problem of overpopulation in Japan. Legislation is passed providing for government clinics and the free circulation of birth-control information.

2 MAY 1954

International In Colombo, Ceylon, an Asian conference of leaders from India, Ceylon, Pakistan, Burma, and Indonesia ends. Participants support a compromise plan for peace in Indochina, agree to resist external intervention in their countries, support the admission of Communist China to the UN to ease world tension, call colonialism a violation of fundamental human rights, and ask that further hydrogen bomb tests be banned. On 29 April India and Communist China had concluded a pact for 'peaceful coexistence,' in which India recognized Tibet as part of China.

7 MAY 1954

Vietnam Shortly after a conference has begun (26 April) at Geneva to negotiate a peace between France and the Vietnamese revolutionaries, the French suffer a devastating defeat at Viet Minh hands with the fall of their fortress at Dien Bien Phu following a 55-day siege. Of the 16,000-man garrison, 10,000 are captured and 6000 are killed or wounded.

2 DECEMBER 1954

US President Eisenhower sends the French the message that Dien Bien Phu 'will forever stand as a symbol of the free world's determination to resist dictatorial aggression.' Shortly after taking office, Eisenhower had rejected French pleas for US ground troops and massive US air intervention in Indochina, stating, 'I can conceive of no greater tragedy than for the US to become involved in an all-out war in Indochina.' But on 11 May US Secretary of State Dulles declares that the US hopes to prevent a 'falling domino' reaction—the loss of all Southeast Asia if Indochina falls. (In fact, it was Eisenhower who first publicly referred to the 'falling domino principle' on 7 April 1954.)

13 MAY 1954
Canada-USA The US receives authorization to join Canada in constructing the St Lawrence Seaway—an operation involving dredging and the building of canals and locks so that ocean-going ships may travel to Great Lakes ports.

17 MAY 1954
USA In a landmark ruling, the Supreme Court, in *Brown v Board of Education*, unanimously finds racial segregation in American public schools unconstitutional, rejecting the principle of 'separate but equal' established in an 1896 ruling. Desegregation of public schools is ordered with 'all deliberate speed'; beyond that, this ruling will open the way for black Americans to demand access to all areas of society.

18 JUNE 1954
France Radical Pierre Mendès-France is chosen premier, 419 to 47. He rejects the support of the 95 Communist members of the National Assembly who voted for him. Mendès-France's majority is attributed to his pledge to negotiate a cease-fire in Indochina by 20 July.

21 JULY 1954
Vietnam Geneva agreements mark the end of the French struggle for Indochina. The conferees agree to a provisional division along the 17th parallel, with a communist regime in the north and a nationalist government in the south. An internationally supervised election is to be held in two years, with the ultimate aim of reuniting the country. Thus the Communists win 77,000 square miles and a population of 12 million. The accords are signed neither by the US nor the South Vietnamese delegation, and some Communist troops will remain in the South, working in support of their cause.

28 JULY 1954
Cyprus Agitation by Greek residents for union (Enosis) with Greece is met by a determined British refusal, since 'sovereignty over the island will enable the United Kingdom to carry out its strategic obligations to Europe, the Mediterranean and the Middle East.' Britain has plans to make Cyprus a major base to offset the loss of Suez.

24 AUGUST 1954
USA The Communist Party is outlawed on the ground that it is 'an instrumentality of a conspiracy to overthrow the Government of the US.' Membership in the party is not defined as a crime.

8 SEPTEMBER 1954
International. In Manila, the Southeast Asia Treaty Organization (SEATO) is formed by a collective defense pact signed by the US, Britain, France, Australia, New Zealand, the Philippines, Pakistan, and Thailand.

27 SEPTEMBER 1954
Canada-USA As a means of improving radar stations protecting the US and Canada from surprise attack, the two nations agree on a Distant Early Warning (DEW) line, the third string of radar stations north of their common border, reaching from Arctic Canada to Greenland.

19 OCTOBER 1954
Egypt Egypt and Britain conclude a pact on the Suez Canal, ending 72 years of British military occupation. Britain agrees to withdraw its 80,000-man force from the Canal Zone within 20 months, while Egypt guarantees freedom of canal navigation.

22 OCTOBER 1954
Vietnam As a result of the Geneva accords granting Communist control over North Vietnam, US President Eisenhower authorizes a crash program to train the South Vietnamese Army.

23 OCTOBER 1954
West Germany In Paris an agreement is signed providing for West German sovereignty and permitting West Germany to rearm and enter NATO and the Western European Union (formed 11 October). The Saar agreement provides for an internationalized zone, but gives France economic and political privileges until the final peace treaty.

2 NOVEMBER 1954
USA In the biggest voter turnout in an off-year election, Democrats win control of both the Senate and the House.

6 NOVEMBER 1954
Algeria Terrorist bands from the French protectorates of Tunisia and Morocco raid Algeria, killing nine persons and wounding 30. French paratroopers are sent to curb attacks by nationalists, and police raid the offices of the Algerian nationalist movement in Paris and other French cities. This marks the beginning of the war for independence, though France will try to maintain control until 1962 in the face of Front de Libération National (FLN) agitation and violence.

2 DECEMBER 1954
USA The Senate censures Senator Joseph Mc-

IN SEARCH OF STABILITY 1946-1962

Roy Cohn, Senator Joseph McCarthy and Don Surine confer at the Army-McCarthy hearings.

Carthy, the relentless investigator of Communist subversion, for his insults to Senate members and for his accusations of treason against army officials. McCarthy's tactics included accusations without proof and the designation of guilt through association. With this Senate action, McCarthy is stripped of his powers.

23 DECEMBER 1954
International Visiting India, Yugoslavia's Tito issues a joint declaration with Prime Minister Nehru that the peaceful coexistence of rival ideolo-

gies is imperative. But the two leaders reject proposals for a neutralist bloc of third world nations on the grounds that it would further complicate the cold war.

OTHER EVENTS OF 1954
Medicine/Health Continued testing of atomic devices is producing widespread concern about threats to health and life. Surgeons in Boston make the first successful organ transplant (of a kidney) from one identical twin to another. It will be 1959 before doctors can transplant a kidney between non-identical twins.

25 JANUARY 1955

Technology The USSR opens its first atomic power station at Obninsk (about 55 miles from Moscow), producing some 5000 kilowatts of electrical energy for industry and agriculture. The US launches the first nuclear-powered submarine, the *Nautilus*; designed by a team headed by Admiral Hyman Rickover, it will begin sea trials in January 1955 and journey some 69,000 miles before refuelling. Two US laboratories—Bell Telephone and Air Research and Development Command—develop two of the earliest practical solar batteries. Britain demonstrates the first practical vertical take-off aircraft, or VTOL.

Environment The Yangtze River in China unleashes a flood even more destructive than that of 1931 (previously China's worst on record).

Social Sciences Egyptian archaeologists find an extraordinary solar boat in Cheops' Tomb, near the Great Pyramids. German archaeologists begin to excavate Warka in Iraq, and British archaeologists find a Roman-era temple of Mithra in London.

Literature William Golding's *Lord of the Flies*; Max Frisch's *I'm Not Stiller*; Mann's *Confessions of Felix Krull, Confidence Man*; Ilya Ehrenburg's *The Thaw*; Kingsley Amis's *Lucky Jim*; C P Snow's *The New Men*.

Drama/Entertainment Williams's *Cat on a Hot Tin Roof*; Fellini's *La Strada*; Kazan's *On the Waterfront*.

The Arts Picasso's *Sylvette*; Stuart Davis's *Colonial Cubism*; Graham Sutherland completes another of his controversial portraits, that of Winston Churchill (which Lady Churchill will later destroy).

Music Britten's *Turn of the Screw*; Walton's *Troilus and Cressida*; Copland's *The Tender Land*; Menotti's *The Saint of Bleecker Street*; Prokofiev's *Stone Flower*; Roy Harris's *Fantasy for Piano and Orchestra*; Rolf Lieberman's *Concerto for Jazz Band and Symphony Orchestra*.

Miscellaneous Billy Graham holds mass evangelical meetings in New York City, London, Berlin, and other cities. In Japan, a ferryboat, the *Toya Maru*, sinks with the loss of 1000.

4 JANUARY 1955

Japan-USA The US agrees to pay Japan $2 million for damages resulting from atomic tests in the Marshall Islands in March 1954. The 22 Japanese fishermen injured and the family of one who died from contact with radioactive ash are to share in the award. Fishing interests that suffered losses from contaminated fish will also be compensated.

12 JANUARY 1955

USA Secretary of State John Foster Dulles states that US defense is now 'to depend primarily upon a great capacity to retaliate instantly by means and at places of our choosing.' This policy becomes known as 'massive retaliation' and incurs criticism for alarming America's allies. On 15 March Dulles modifies the statement, saying that smaller nuclear weapons, rather than hydrogen bombs, will be used on military targets, not entire cities.

17 JANUARY 1955

USSR The Soviet Union reports it will shares its nuclear materials and scientific knowledge with Communist China, Czechoslovakia, Poland, East Germany, and Rumania.

25 JANUARY 1955

Panama Panama and the US sign a new treaty on

CHIANG KAI-SHEK, 1887–1975

Chiang Kai-shek began as a revolutionary compatriot of Sun Yat-sen and Mao Tse-tung, but ended as an exile from the China he had helped to build. With a professional military education, Chiang was a trusted member of Sun Yat-sen's revolutionary organization, and upon Sun's death Chiang became head of the Nationalist Army. He soon built the Nationalists into the strongest group in China: by 1928 he was the effective ruler. But by then Mao Tse-tung and his communists were mounting their own revolution, and although Chiang had to cooperate with them when Japan attacked China in 1937, the rivalry between the two leaders was no secret. Chiang kept up China's resistance during World War II: the noncommunist world recognized him as the nation's leader, although he was a prickly ally. Elected president of China in 1948, Chiang and his Nationalist supporters fled the following year to Taiwan, off the coast of China, from Mao Tse-tung's successful communist revolution. As Mao killed those compatriots who might obstruct his new China, Chiang eliminated those Taiwanese who opposed his Nationalist Chinese government. He remained in control of Taiwan for a quarter of a century, constantly threatening to retake the Chinese mainland, but never returned.

IN SEARCH OF STABILITY 1946-1962

the Canal Zone, increasing the yearly payment to Panama from $430,000 to $1,930,000, and returning to Panama certain land areas valued at over $20 million.

28 JANUARY 1955

Taiwan (Formosa) The US Congress approves President Eisenhower's request for emergency powers to permit US forces to protect Formosa and the nearby Pescadores Islands, to assist in consolidating Nationalist Chinese forces, and to take action if Communist China invades. The President says that American forces are needed for defense only. Communist forces are massed on the islands off the Chinese mainland, apparently for an invasion of Formosa. Communist China rebuffs UN truce efforts with a demand for the ouster of Nationalist China from the UN, and its replacement by Communist China.

31 JANUARY 1955

South Africa About 60,000 black Africans begin a peaceful 13-day protest against government plans to move them from Johannesburg to a new town outside the city. The forced removal of the blacks from their homes begins on 9 February. On 9 November South Africa will quit the UN over apartheid.

8 FEBRUARY 1955

USSR Georgi Malenkov steps down as head of the Soviet Government after reading an admission of incompetency and requesting to be relieved. He is succeeded by Marshal Nikolai Bulganin.

23 FEBRUARY 1955

International The first meeting of the SEATO Council begins at its new headquarters in Bangkok, Thailand. The nations agree to help one another combat subversive forms of international communism.

27 MARCH 1955

International France ratifies the Paris agreements to create the Western European Union, to authorize a West German army of 12 divisions, to grant West Germany sovereignty and end occupation, to Europeanize the Saar, and to admit West Germany to NATO. (Residents of the Saar will reject this principle by a referendum in October 1955. The Saar will join the Federal Republic of Germany in 1957.)

5 APRIL 1955

Great Britain Sir Winston Churchill, 80, resigns as prime minister because of his age. He declines a peerage offered by Queen Elizabeth, preferring to remain an elder statesman in the House of Commons, where he has served almost 50 years. Foreign Secretary Sir Anthony Eden succeeds him on 6 April and on 21 April is unanimously elected leader of the Conservative Party. Harold Macmillan, defense minister, becomes foreign secretary.

18–27 APRIL 1955

International At Bandung, Indonesia, delegates from 29 African and Asian countries call for an end to colonialism, and endorse independence, self-determination, and UN membership for all. Chinese Premier Chou En-lai announces China's willingness to negotiate with the US on tensions in Formosa and the Far East. Indian Prime Minister Nehru condemns NATO as a protector of colonialism.

29 APRIL 1955

South Vietnam Civil war begins as the Binh Xuyen rebel forces fire mortar shells into the grounds of Premier Ngo Dinh Diem's palace. About 100 people are killed in the battle that rages in the Saigon streets. The rebels, who strongly oppose the US-backed premier, controlled the police force until 26 April, when Diem appointed his own police chief.

3 MAY 1955

Turkey-USA The two nations sign the first atoms-for-peace pact, calling for the lease of up to 6 kilograms of enriched uranium to begin work on a research reactor in Turkey. The pact also provides for the exchange of unclassified information and for the use of radioactive isotopes in medicine, industry, and agriculture.

5 MAY 1955

West Germany The Federal Republic of West Germany becomes a sovereign state as ratifications are deposited in Bonn. President Eisenhower signs an order ending US occupation, but American troops remain on a contractual basis.

6 MAY 1955

Falkland Islands Britain asks the International Court of Justice at The Hague to order recognition of British sovereignty over these islands off the east coast of South America, and reject the claims of Argentina and Chile. Argentina announces the two nations will not accept arbitration by the Court.

14 MAY 1955

International The USSR, Albania, Bulgaria, Czechoslovakia, Hungary, Poland, Rumania, and East Germany sign the Warsaw Pact—a 20-year treaty of mutual defense to offset the 'remilitarization' of West Germany.

15 MAY 1955

Austria Foreign ministers of the US, Britain, France, and the USSR sign the Austrian State Treaty returning sovereignty to the Republic of Austria—17 years after Hitler destroyed the nation's independence by the *Anschluss* and 10 years after the end of the war. The delay was caused by the obstructive tactics of the Soviet Union, which exploited Austria's industrial resources in the interim. The pact restores Austria's pre-1938 borders, prohibits economic union with Germany, and provides for withdrawal of occupation forces.

26 MAY 1955

Yugoslavia Six high Soviet officials, led by Premier Bulganin and First Secretary Khrushchev, fly to Belgrade to make amends with Marshal Tito for the seven years of abuse and estrangement initiated by Stalin. During the six-day meeting, Soviet officials recognize peaceful coexistence of different forms of socialistic development and noninterference in internal affairs. This is seen as a major victory for Yugoslavian independence.

18 JULY 1955

International The Geneva summit begins, the first conference of the Big Four—the US, USSR, Britain, and France—since 1945. One of the summit's most important results is the atmosphere of accommodation and cooperation achieved by the participants—hailed by some as the 'spirit of Geneva.'

21 AUGUST 1955

Morocco In response to widespread violence in Algeria and Morocco, French Premier Faure meets with Moroccan leaders to seek peace. The compromise plan worked out provides for the resignation of the pro-French sultan and the resident general. The sultan's refusal to resign prolongs the conflict until his 30 October abdication.

29 AUGUST 1955

Cyprus A London conference of British, Turkish, and Greek representatives opens to deal with Cyprus's problems. On 7 September the talks become deadlocked.

19 SEPTEMBER 1955

Argentina Dictator and President Juan Perón is deposed by a military revolt. He flees to exile in Paraguay and then Spain until his return in 1971.

11 OCTOBER 1955

USA-USSR President Eisenhower, recovering from a heart attack, writes to Soviet Premier Bulganin about armaments control. Proposals for inspection are seen as a prelude to arms limitation.

14 OCTOBER 1955

International In New Delhi, India, the Colombo Plan conference reports that one of Asia's greatest needs is for technical assistance and commends the US for its contribution in this area.

6 NOVEMBER 1955

USSR On the 38th anniversary of the Bolshevik Revolution, Deputy Premier Lazar Kaganovich cites Soviet efforts to relieve international tension: Communist disarmament proposals, recent acceleration of diplomatic exchanges with the West, withdrawal of Russian troops from Port Arthur (Communist China) and Porkhala (Finland), the Austrian State Treaty, establishment of relations with West Germany, and prisoner releases. He sees these actions as conducive to 'cessation of the cold war.'

21 NOVEMBER 1955

International In its first meeting, the five-nation defense alliance of Turkey, Iraq, Iran, Pakistan, and Britain opens with an Iraqi pledge to aid any Arab state threatened by Israel. This defense chain along the USSR's Asian frontier links up with NATO through Turkey and Britain, with SEATO through Pakistan and Britain. Later it will be renamed METO (Middle East Treaty Organization).

1 DECEMBER 1955

USA In Montgomery, Alabama, Rosa Parks defies a city segregation ordinance by refusing to give up her bus seat to a white man. The ensuing boycott led by Martin Luther King and others will lead to a Supreme Court decision that declares the ordinance unconstitutional.

14 DECEMBER 1955

Great Britain Hugh Gaitskill, an economist, succeeds Clement Attlee as leader of the Labour Party and of Her Majesty's Opposition in the House of Commons.

International The United Nations General Assembly admits 16 additional nations, bringing total membership to 76. Admission of four communist nations—Albania, Bulgaria, Hungary, and Rumania—boosts communist-bloc votes to 9. Noncommunist nations admitted are Austria, Cambodia, Ceylon, Finland, Iceland, Italy, Jordan, Laos, Libya, Nepal, Portugal, and Spain. This is a compromise effected after a plan to admit 18 nations failed because Nationalist China vetoed Outer Mongolia, and the USSR vetoed all 13 noncommunist nations included in the plan. The USSR vetoed a move by the US to admit Japan after Outer Mongolia was dropped.

OTHER EVENTS OF 1955

Science Seymour Benzer, American molecular biologist working with viral genes, discovers that recombinations can occur not only between, but within genes, opening the way for recombinant work.

DAG HAMMARSKJÖLD, 1905–1961

The 'quiet diplomacy' of Dag Hammarskjöld was to make him the visible embodiment of the aims of the organization he so ably led, the United Nations. The son of a prime minister of Sweden, Hammarskjöld pursued a civil service career that took him to the United Nations as a Swedish representative in 1952. Elected the UN's second secretary general in 1953, he brought to the office a persuasive personal style and a firm commitment to the ideal of nations united. His quiet man-to-man diplomacy was dramatically successful—he helped defuse international problems on the Suez Canal and in the Congo, smoothing for a time the rocky path of decolonization. Hammarskjöld died in a plane crash in the Congo, en route to effect a peace settlement, and was posthumously awarded the Nobel Peace Prize in 1961.

IN SEARCH OF STABILITY 1946-1962

Frederick Sanger establishes the structure of the molecule of insulin. Owen Chamberlain and Emilio Segre, American physicists, discover the antiproton, a negatively charged proton, reinforcing the theory that every elementary particle has an opposite counterpart.

Medicine/Health Dorothy Hodgkin discovers the composition of Vitamin B_{12}, useful in treating pernicious anemia.

Technology A basic text, *A History of Technology*, is published by Charles Singer, E J Holmyard, and A R Hall.

Social Sciences Yigael Yadin begins to excavate at Hazor; Anati finds prehistoric rock engravings at Val Camonica, Italy; Stillwell and Sjoquist begin to excavate at Morgantina, Sicily.

Ideas/Beliefs James Baldwin's *Notes of a Native Son*; Walter Lippmann's *The Public Philosophy*.

Literature J R R Tolkien completes his trilogy *Lord of the Rings*; Jorge Luis Borges's *Extraordinary Tales*; Patrick White's *The Tree of Man*; Gabriel Garcia Marquez's *Leaf Storm and Other Stories*: Graham Greene's *The Quiet American*; Dylan Thomas's *Quite Early One Morning*; Alain Robbe-Grillet's *The Voyeur*; the first definitive edition of Emily Dickinson's poetry is issued in three volumes edited by T H Johnson.

Drama/Entertainment Miller's *A View from the Bridge*; Ray Lawler's *The Summer of the Seventeenth Doll*; Nicholas Ray's *Rebel Without a Cause*.

The Arts Dali's *Lord's Supper*; Edwin Dickinson's *Window and Oar*.

Architecture Le Corbusier completes a revolutionary structure: the church of Notre-Dame-du-Haut at Ronchamp, France. Eero Saarinen's General Motors Technical Center opens in Michigan.

Music Carlisle Floyd's *Susannah*; Michael Tippett's *The Midsummer Marriage*. Bill Haley's 'Rock Around the Clock' starts a revolution in pop music.

Lift/Customs 'Flying saucers' are being reported by many in various lands.

1 JANUARY 1956
Sudan The nation attains independence as the Anglo-Egyptian condominium of 1898 ends. A five-man council of state rules until the 2 February appointment of a cabinet. On 19 January Sudan enters the Arab League. On 5 July the leader of the Nationalist (Umma) Party, Abdullah Khalib, is elected premier.

11 JANUARY 1956
USA Secretary of State Dulles issues a policy statement on the cold war struggle against communism, saying: 'We are in a contest in the field of economic development of underdeveloped countries which is bitterly competitive. Defeat in this contest could be as disastrous as defeat in an armaments race.'

13 JANUARY 1956
Middle East Syria and Lebanon sign a mutual

defense pact providing for joint retaliation if either is attacked by Israel. This is in response to the 11 December 1955 Israeli attack on Syrian positions along the Sea of Galilee. On 19 January the UN Security Council votes unanimously to censure Israel for the attack as a 'flagrant violation' of the Palestine armistice.

1 FEBRUARY 1956
International Ending a three-day Washington conference, President Eisenhower and British Prime Minister Eden issue the Declaration of Washington—a joint statement warning the peoples of Asia and Africa against looking to the Soviet Union for political or economic aid.

South Africa The government orders the Soviet Union to close all its consulates by 1 March, charging that they had been used to spread communist propaganda among the black and Indian populations.

6 FEBRUARY 1956
Algeria French Premier Guy Mollet is greeted in Algiers by a tomato-throwing mob that shouts 'Catroux to the gallows!' and 'Mollet to the gallows!' (General Georges Catroux, newly named Resident Minister for Algerian Affairs, has not yet left Paris for his new post: he will resign a few hours later.)

14–25 FEBRUARY 1956
USSR In Moscow, at the 20th congress of the Soviet Communist Party, party chief Khrushchev and others proclaim a new party line featuring the destruction of Josef Stalin as a national idol, repudiation of Stalinism, and a presentation of the Soviet Union in a more peaceful guise. Stalin portraits are removed from the Tretyakov Art Gallery.

2 MARCH 1956
Jordan King Hussein dismisses Lt Gen John Bagot Glubb, commander of the British-subsidized Arab Legion since 1939. Glubb is cited for defying a royal decree to reorganize the Legion to meet the danger of an Israeli attack. The dismissal is viewed as a fresh blow to British prestige in the Middle East.

Morocco The 44-year old French protectorate ends. On 14 March nationalist leaders report they have ordered mountain guerrillas to cease fighting now that the nation is independent.

9 MARCH 1956
Cyprus Archbishop Makarios is arrested by the British as a terrorist and deported with several aides to the Seychelles Islands in the Indian Ocean. On 18 March British Governor Sir John Harding declares there will be no move to reopen negotiations on self-government until Greek-Cypriot terrorism is crushed. Over the next months, the British execute a number of terrorists.

20 MARCH 1956
Tunisia A protocol ends the 75-year-old French protectorate with national independence. In the 25

March election, the pro-Western National Front led by Habib Bourguiba wins all 98 seats in the constituent assembly.

23 MARCH 1956
Pakistan The nation becomes the world's first Islamic Republic, but remains in the British Commonwealth. Its president must be a Moslem.

17 APRIL 1956
USSR Cominform, the Soviet-led coalition of Communist Parties, is dissolved, as announced in the Communist press. This is seen as a victory for Yugoslavia's Tito, whose Communist Party was ousted from the alliance in 1948 for resisting Kremlin dictation.

10 MAY 1956
Middle East UN Secretary General Dag Hammarskjöld announces that unconditional cease-fire agreements have been signed by Israel, Egypt, Jordan, Syria, and Lebanon.

31 MAY 1956
South Korea The UN Command announces expulsion of neutral inspection teams from South Korea because of armistice violations by North Korean Communists. It accuses Czech and Polish inspection-team members of non-neutral conduct. On 1 June the UN Command rejects communist proposals for new talks on peaceful unification of Korea.

13 JUNE 1956
Egypt Britain's 74-year military occupation of the Suez Canal Zone ends as the last British soldier leaves Port Said, in accordance with the 1954 British-Egyptian treaty.

28 JUNE 1956
Poland In Poznan, workers riot against communist rule in a demand for bread and freedom. The biggest anticommunist demonstration in the Soviet sphere since the 17 June 1953 East German uprising is witnessed by many Westerners attending the Poznan industrial fair. More than 100 are killed and hundreds more wounded.

21–22 JULY 1956
International In a conference of presidents of 19 Western Hemisphere republics, the Panama Declaration is drafted, calling for 'Inter-American co-operative efforts to seek the solution of economic problems and to raise the living standards of the continent.' US President Eisenhower also proposes shared peaceful uses of nuclear energy.

26 JULY 1956
Egypt Under a nationalization decree, President Nasser seizes the Suez Canal after denouncing the Western withdrawal of financial support for the proposed Aswan Dam project. Nasser intends to use Canal revenues to build the dam.

1–2 AUGUST 1956
Egypt In reaction to the Suez Canal crisis, Britain, France, and the US hold high-level talks in London. At the same time a war scare is touched off by British and French deployment of forces in the Mediterranean. Tensions ease by 16 August, when representatives of 22 nations open Suez discussions in London; only Egypt and Greece refuse participation.

4 SEPTEMBER 1956
USSR-Afghanistan Reports reveal that the Soviet Union has agreed to provide guns, ammunition, and planes for the 40,000-man Afghan Army. In the first delivery under the pact, 11 MiG jet fighters are delivered on 26 October.

27 SEPTEMBER 1956
Poland The first of a series of trials from the June riots in Poznan begins. Those accused are permitted to testify freely. Three youths accused of slaying a secret-police corporal are convicted of murder, but receive lenient sentences of 4 to $4\frac{1}{2}$ years. On 24 October Warsaw Radio announces that the new Polish Government has freed the other 151 persons indicted in connection with the riots.

19–21 OCTOBER 1956
Poland Polish Communist leaders defy Kremlin leadership and elect Wladyslaw Gomulka to head a more independent government. Gomulka was recently released from four years in prison as a Titoist.

23 OCTOBER 1956
Hungary A revolt begins against the Soviet-dominated regime, and spreads rapidly throughout the country, despite concessions offered by the Hungarian Communist Party. Soviet troops first withdraw and then return to crush the rebellion and to install Janos Kadar as premier.

29 OCTOBER 1956
Middle East Israel invades Egypt's Sinai Peninsula. After Egypt rejects the cease-fire demands made by Britain and France, the two nations bomb Egypt by air beginning on 31 October, and land forces on 5–6 November. The US condemns the Anglo-French attack, supporting a cease-fire demand by the UN. Egypt and Israel accept the cease-fire, and Britain and France follow. Fighting ends on 7 November. The truce is supervised by a UN international police force. The British and French captured the upper quarter of the Suez Canal, and Israel gained control of the Sinai and the Gaza Strip. The Canal itself was blocked by scuttled and sunken ships and destroyed bridges. Egypt emerges from the war with the US and USSR as virtual allies, at least on this issue.

6 NOVEMBER 1956
USA In the election the Eisenhower-Nixon ticket wins by a landslide, again defeating Adlai Stevenson —a testimony to Eisenhower's personal popularity. But the Democrats win a majority in both Houses.

IN SEARCH OF STABILITY 1946-1962

11 NOVEMBER 1956
Yugoslavia-USSR In a party speech, Tito says there is a sharp split in the Kremlin high command, that a 'Stalinist' group with erroneous attitudes toward Eastern European countries has prevailed. On 25 November the Polish Communist Central Committee supports Tito's viewpoint.

12 NOVEMBER 1956
International Three Arab nations—the Sudan, Morocco, and Tunisia—are elected unanimously to UN membership. This increases the Asian-African bloc to 26 members, enough to exercise a veto over General Assembly resolutions by combining with the Soviet bloc of 9 (such resolutions require a two-thirds majority).

18 NOVEMBER 1956
Poland-USSR Poland's Gomulka signs an agreement with the Soviets that grants Poland concessions including greater independence, territorial integrity, noninterference in internal affairs, a limitation of Soviet troop movements on Polish soil, and a cancellation of past debts to the USSR.

29 NOVEMBER 1956
France The oil shortage resulting from the Suez crisis worsens, as France establishes stringent gasoline rationing.

2 DECEMBER 1956
Cuba With an invading force of 82 Cuban exiles trained in Mexico, Fidel Castro lands on Cuban soil. After most of his band is captured or killed, Castro initiates a guerrilla campaign against President Fulgencio Batista from the Sierra Maestra. He calls it the '26th of July Movement,' after his 1953 attack.

29 DECEMBER 1956
Middle East UN salvage crews begin clearing the Suez Canal of sunken vessels and other obstacles. The Suez Canal will reopen to maritime traffic on 7 March 1957.

OTHER EVENTS OF 1956
Science Chen Ning-yang and Tsung Dao-lee, Chinese-born American physicists, describe an experiment that will disprove the principle of parity, or right-left symmetry for weak interactions in the atom, which has been a cornerstone of modern physics. At Los Alamos, the neutrino—postulated by Wolfgang Pauli in the early 1930s—is detected. It is announced that the bristlecone pine, which grows in California (some trees being over 4000 years old) is being used to establish dates as far back as 7400 years ago, because even dead trees retain their rings. This new dating method will serve as a corrective of the dendrochronology derived from the work of Douglass (who used the giant sequoia) and also on radioactive carbon dating.
Medicine/Health The first large-scale testing of the oral contraceptive developed by Doctors Gregory

Pincus and John Rock is initiated in Puerto Rico, with 1308 women participating. The first clinical test was in 1954; as a result of this successful Puerto Rican test, 'The Pill' will be sold commercially in 1960.
Technology The first large-scale atomic power station in the world, Calder Hall, in England, begins generating electricity; at its peak it can generate 90,000 kilowatts. The Bell X-2, a rocket-powered research plane, sets a new speed record of 2100 mph. F W Müller develops the ion microscope. Transat-

GAMAL ABDEL NASSER, 1918–1970

A significant leader of Arab unity, Gamal Abdel Nasser began his activism as a child in demonstrations against British control of Egypt. In 1952 he led a coup that deposed King Farouk; thereafter, as prime minister and later president of Egypt, he developed the nation's military strength and economy, began the Aswan Dam, and nationalized the Suez Canal (which led to an abortive invasion by Britain, France, and Israel). The respect he commanded among Arabs helped Nasser promote pan-Arab movements including the United Arab Republic, formed with Syria in 1958 with Nasser as president (Syria withdrew in 1961). A fervent anti-Zionist, Nasser attacked Israel in 1967; after the resulting quick defeat he resigned, but was immediately returned to office by popular acclaim. His last years were spent rebuilding his military forces with Soviet support, and seeking inroads to negotiations with Israel. He died in 1970, having brought increased respect and dignity to the Arab world.

lantic telephone service via cable begins.

Environment Jacques Cousteau anchors his research ship *Calypso* over the 24,500-foot-deep Romanche Trench in the Atlantic; he uses specially designed equipment to obtain spectacular photographs of the ocean depths down to some $4\frac{1}{2}$ miles.

Social Sciences Prehistoric frescoes painted on rocks at Tassili in Algiers are discovered.

Ideas/Beliefs Colin Wilson's *The Outsider*; A J Ayer's *The Revolution in Philosophy*; William H Whyte's *The Organization Man*.

Literature Vladimir Dudintsev's *Not by Bread Alone*; Yukio Mishima's *The Temple of the Golden Pavilion*; Allen Ginsberg's *Howl*; John Berryman's *Homage to Mistress Bradstreet*; João Gimares Rosa's *The Devil to Pay in the Backlands*; Angus Wilson's *Anglo-Saxon Attitudes*.

Drama/Entertainment John Osborne's *Look Back in Anger* revolutionizes contemporary British theater; O'Neill's *Long Day's Journey into Night*; Friedrich Dürenmatt's *The Visit*; Jean Genet's *The Balcony*; Bergman's *The Seventh Seal*.

The Arts Jean Dubuffet's *Extremus Amibolis*; Barbara Hepworth's *Orpheus*.

Architecture Construction begins on Brazil's new capital, Brasilia, on barren ground in east-central Brazil; one of the world's major examples of large-scale city planning, it will be dedicated as the capital in 1960. The Opera House designed by Jorn Utzon is begun in Sydney, Australia, to open in 1973.

Music Hans-Werner Henze's *King Stag*; Douglas Moore's *The Ballad of Baby Doe*; Leonard Bernstein's *Candide*. Rock 'n roll begins to take over pop music.

Life/Customs The first large march by nuclear radiation protesters occurs in England, as hundreds set out from Aldermaston.

Miscellaneous The Italian liner *Andrea Doria*, new and supposedly unsinkable, collides with a ship off Nantucket Island, Massachusetts; it sinks quickly, but only 51 people are lost. Two American airliners crash over the Grand Canyon, Arizona, and leave 128 dead—the first airplane disaster involving more than 100 deaths.

1 JANUARY 1957

West Germany In accordance with a treaty signed with France on 27 October 1956, the Saar becomes the tenth state of West Germany.

5 JANUARY 1957

Middle East-USA President Eisenhower asks Congress for the right to use military force to resist communist aggression in the Middle East. With the offer of US aid to Middle East nations to resist communism, this policy becomes known as the Eisenhower Doctrine, and is signed into law on 9 March.

6 JANUARY 1957

Ireland After a series of raids across the Northern Ireland border by the Irish Republican Army, Irish Prime Minister John A Costello condemns all efforts to unite the six counties of Northern Ireland with the Republic of Ireland by force.

9 JANUARY 1957

Great Britain Citing ill health, Prime Minister Eden resigns. After consulting with Sir Winston Churchill, Queen Elizabeth chooses Harold Macmillan on 10 January as Eden's successor.

15 FEBRUARY 1957..

USSR The appointment of Andrei A Gromyko as Soviet Foreign Minister, replacing Dmitri Shepilov, is announced. A career diplomat and protégé of Molotov, Gromyko is regarded as a 'hard liner' toward the West.

6 MARCH 1957

Ghana Ghana is proclaimed an independent nation, merging the former British colonies of the Gold Coast and Togoland. It takes its name from an independent African empire that flourished in West Africa 1000 years ago. Dignitaries from over 50 nations are welcomed to the celebration by Premier Kwame Nkrumah.

Middle East Israeli forces complete their withdrawal from Egyptian territory as UN Emergency Forces take control of the Gaza Strip and Sharm el Sheikh.

13 MARCH 1957

Jordan-Great Britain Termination of the 1948 Anglo-Jordanian treaty of alliance severs economic and military ties between the countries. All British forces are to withdraw within six months. Jordan will pay $11.9 million over six years for British military installations and supplies left behind, and the British will end their annual $35 million subsidy to Jordan.

20 MARCH 1957

Great Britain-USA A Bermuda Conference begins between President Eisenhower and Prime Minister Macmillan. The object is to repair the damage done to the Anglo-US alliance by the Suez crisis.

25 MARCH 1957

International In Rome, treaties creating the European Economic Community (Common Market) and the European Community of Atomic Energy (Euratom) are signed by representatives of France, West Germany, Italy, Belgium, the Netherlands, and Luxembourg.

28 MARCH 1957

Cyprus Archbishop Makarios is released by the British from exile in the Seychelles Islands after he agrees to issue a call for an end to violence in Cyprus. He is forbidden to return to the island.

4 APRIL 1957

Great Britain A government white paper announces

IN SEARCH OF STABILITY 1946-1962

a new defense policy, including a five-year plan to reshape Britain's armed forces to atomic and missile needs rather than massive conventional forces. The plan involves a progressive reduction of the colonial garrison wherever practicable.

14 APRIL 1957
Jordan King Hussein quells a revolt led by pro-Egyptian elements in his army. To affirm support for Hussein, the US moves its Sixth Fleet to the eastern Mediterranean. King Hussein announces that the crisis is over on 5 May.

7 MAY 1957
USSR Khrushchev proposes a program to decentralize the Soviet economy, eliminating and reorganizing much of the old economic bureaucracy. He denies any crisis in the Soviet economy, despite the 10 April announcement of a freeze on the Soviet debt in the form of compulsory bond purchases.

8 MAY 1957
South Vietnam-USA Vietnamese President Diem begins a state visit and tour of the US. In an 11 May statement, he and President Eisenhower proclaim the communists 'a continuing threat to the safety of all free nations in Asia.'

3 JUNE 1957
International The US joins the Baghdad Pact (METO) at a Karachi conference and reaffirms its determination to aid the member nations—Turkey, Iraq, Iran, Pakistan, and Britain—in countering communist aggression.

7 JUNE 1957
Poland-USA The two nations sign a $95-million loan agreement by which Poland is to receive a $30 million loan for mining machinery and raw materials with the balance in the form of surplus goods.

10 JUNE 1957
Canada In a major political upset, the Liberal Party that has ruled Canada for 22 years loses its 170-seat majority in the House of Commons elections to the Conservatives, led by John Diefenbaker who stressed 'time for a change.' Louis St Laurent, prime minister since 1948, resigns on 17 June.

3 JULY 1957
USSR It becomes known that Khrushchev has deposed his rivals in a major shakeup of Soviet leadership. Known for their Stalinist sympathies, the three are Georgi Malenkov (named manager of a hydroelectric plant in East Kazakhastan), Vyacheslav Molotov (dispatched as ambassador to Outer Mongolia), and Lazar Kaganovich (made manager of a cement plant east of the Urals).

17 JULY 1957
Sultanate of Muscat and Oman Civil war erupts in the sultanate on the southeastern edge of the Arabian

President Dwight D Eisenhower salutes the flag on the White House lawn.

Peninsula. Sultan Said bin Taimur calls for British help. Combined British ground forces and tribal forces loyal to the Sultan recapture rebel strongholds by 14 August.

26 AUGUST 1957
USSR The Soviets announce that they have successfully tested an intercontinental ballistic missile (ICBM) a few days before. On 17 December the US will follow suit.

31 AUGUST 1957
Malaya British rule ends. Two days earlier rulers of the nine Malay states elected Sir Abdul Rahman to a five-year term as constitutional monarch. Independent Malaya becomes the tenth member of the British Commonwealth.

4 SEPTEMBER 1957
USA A controversy over school desegregation climaxes as Arkansas Governor Orval Faubus orders National Guardsmen to bar nine black students from entering all-white Central High School in Little Rock. Following a federal court order, the students enter the school on 23 September but are ordered to withdraw by local authorities because of fear of mob violence. Next day President Eisenhower orders federal troops to Little Rock to enforce desegregation.

5 SEPTEMBER 1957
Cuba Members of the Cuban armed forces first join the uprising led by Fidel Castro in heavy fighting 150 miles southeast of Havana. Batista's army crushes the revolt and the commander of the mutinous navy force is dismissed.

6 SEPTEMBER 1957
International London disarmament talks end in a deadlock.

22 SEPTEMBER 1957
Haiti François Duvalier, a physician, is elected president according to returns announced by the military junta that has ruled Haiti since it ousted President Daniel Fignole three months ago.

4 OCTOBER 1957
USSR The Soviets successfully launch *Sputnik I*,

the first man-made satellite. The US will launch its first satellite, *Explorer I*, on 31 January 1958.

10 OCTOBER 1957
USA President Eisenhower apologizes to Ghana's Finance Minister Komla Agbeli Gbdemah, who was refused service in a Delaware restaurant.

12–22 OCTOBER 1957
Great Britain Queen Elizabeth and Prince Philip conduct a popular goodwill tour through Canada and the US. In Ottawa, wearing her coronation gown and tiara, the Queen becomes the first reigning sovereign to open Parliament. From there the royal couple travel to Jamestown, Virginia, to observe the 350th anniversary of the first permanent English settlement in the New World. Other visits and an address to the UN General Assembly highlight their US stay, which restores Anglo-American ties damaged by the Suez crisis.

26 OCTOBER 1957
USSR The government announces that Marshal Georgi Zhukov, the nation's most prominent military hero, has been relieved of his duties as Minister of Defense. Accused of promoting his own 'cult of personality,' Zhukov was seen as threatening Khrushchev's popularity.

5 NOVEMBER 1957
Great Britain Prime Minister Macmillan announces

Members of the US 101st Airborne Division on duty in Little Rock, 24 September 1957.

he will introduce legislation permitting women to sit and vote in the House of Lords for the first time.

16–19 DECEMBER 1957
International In Paris, the first NATO heads-of-government conference is held. All 15 member nations except Portugal are represented by their heads of state, who reach agreement on establishment of a NATO nuclear missile force and on closer political co-ordination of member states. They also agree to try to seek a disarmament pact with the Soviet Union.

26 DECEMBER 1957
International In Cairo, delegates from 40 African and Asian states and colonies open the Afro-Asian Peoples Solidarity Conference, which adopts resolutions backing Soviet appeals for peaceful coexistence, condemning Western imperialist and colonialist policies, and attacking the Eisenhower Doctrine. A Soviet spokesman offers economic and technical aid to all Asian and African peoples 'as brother helps brother.'

OTHER EVENTS OF 1957
Science The activity of interferon is described by the research team of Alick Isaacs and Jean Lindenmann; interferon is a natural substance produced when cells are invaded by a virus, which protects against other viruses; it will be regarded as holding great promise in treating many diseases, including some types of cancer. On 1 July the International Geophysical Year begins: thousands of scientists worldwide will co-operate in investigations involving oceanography, meteorology, Antarctic exploration, and space satellites.
Environment The HMCS *Labrador* discovers a new northwest passage across the far reaches of Arctic Canada.
Social Sciences Archaeologists discover the great tomb at Gordian, Turkey, and make the first finds at the site of Pella, in Macedonia.
Ideas/Beliefs Noam Chomsky's *Syntactic Structures* introduces his revolutionary ideas on transformational, or generative, grammar.
Literature Boris Pasternak's *Doctor Zhivago*, denied publication in the USSR, is published in Italy; Jack Kerouac's *On the Road*; Camus's *The Fall*; Max Frisch's *Homo Faber*; I B Singer's *Gimpel the Fool*; Patrick White's *Voss*; Nabokov's *Pnin*; John Braine's *Room at the Top*.
Drama/Entertainment Beckett's *Endgame*; John Osborne's *The Entertainer*; Harold Pinter's *The Dumb Waiter*; Bernstein's *West Side Story*; Lerner and Lowe's *My Fair Lady*; Bergman's *Wild Strawberries*; Fellini's *Nights of Cabiria*.
The Arts Francis Bacon's *Screaming Nurse*; Victor Vasareley's *Vega*; Mark Rothko's *Violet Bar*; Epstein's *Christ in Majesty*.
Architecture Pier Luigi Nervi and others complete the UNESCO Conference Hall in Paris.
Music The first complete performance of Proko-

Lester Pearson, the Canadian Nobel Prize winner.

fiev's *War and Peace* (produced only in part since 1944); Samuel Barber's *Vanessa*; Stravinsky's *Agon*; Poulenc's *Dialogue des Carmelites*; Elliott Carter's *Variations for Orchestra*.
Miscellaneous The International Atomic Energy Agency is founded, with headquarters in Vienna, to control proliferation of atomic devices.

3 JANUARY 1958
West Indies The West Indies Federation comes into being with the swearing-in of Lord Hailes as its first governor general at Port-of-Spain, Trinidad. The British Caribbean islands, now part of the Commonwealth, include Trinidad-Tobago, Jamaica, Barbados, St Lucia, St Vincent, Grenada, Montserrat, St Kitts-Nevis-Anguilla, Dominica, and Antigua.

13 JANUARY 1958
International A petition signed by more than 9000 scientists from 43 countries, urging an immediate international agreement to halt tests of nuclear bombs, is presented to UN Secretary General Hammarskjöld by 1954 Nobel Prize winner Dr Linus Pauling. Japan and India had urged similar bans the previous year.

21 JANUARY 1958
International The USSR warns the Baghdad Pact nations against any Western attempt to introduce nuclear weapons and missile bases into their territories.

Elvis Presley.

IN SEARCH OF STABILITY 1946-1962

1 FEBRUARY 1958
Middle East   Egypt and Syria merge as the United Arab Republic, with Nasser as president per results of a 21 February election. Yemen joins the union on 8 March. On 14 February Jordan and Iraq counter this move by merging as the Arab Union.

3 FEBRUARY 1958
International   Belgium, the Netherlands and Luxembourg sign a 50-year treaty establishing the Benelux Economic Union, already in partial operation through prior agreements. The pact provides for free movement of persons, goods, services, and capital among the three countries; a co-ordination of national economic and social policies; and unification of trade policies.

8 FEBRUARY 1958
Tunisia-France   Twenty-five French planes bomb and strafe a Tunisian village on the Algerian border, killing 68 and wounding 100, in reprisal for the alleged Tunisian destruction of a French plane earlier in the day. Tunisia denies the charge and blockades French military bases within Tunisia, demanding withdrawal of all 15,000 French troops based there under the 1956 independence agreement. Another French bombing incident on 25 May brings the two nations to the brink of war. A 17 June pact calls for withdrawal of French forces from Tunisia, excepting Bizerte.

15 FEBRUARY 1958
Indonesia   In central Sumatra, a rebel group proclaims a revolutionary government. President Sukarno orders bombing raids on rebel centers.

27 MARCH 1958
USSR   Khrushchev assumes full control of the Soviet Union by succeeding Bulganin as premier, abandoning the pretense of collective leadership and returning the Soviet Government to one-man rule for the first time since Stalin's death in 1953.

31 MARCH 1958
USSR   The USSR scores a propaganda coup by announcing an end to atomic tests and calling on the US and Britain to follow its example. If they do not, the USSR will feel free to resume testing. The Soviet announcement follows completion of Soviet tests and precedes a planned US series for a 'cleaner' bomb.

5 APRIL 1958
Cuba   Fidel Castro proclaims 'total war' against the Batista regime. On 26 June his rebel forces kidnap 47 Americans, including servicemen, and three Canadians from the Guantanamo Bay area to draw world attention to his cause. Following negotiations, all are freed by 18 July.

14 APRIL 1958
Poland   Party leader Gomulka announces that Polish workers' councils must give way to larger groups more susceptible to Communist Party control and discipline, that strikes are illegal, and that trade unions will be subject to the Communist Party.

23 APRIL 1958
Algeria   The French have lost 6000 men since the Algerian rebellion began (1954); 62,000 rebels have died.

27–30 APRIL 1958
Algeria   In Tangier, Morocco, representatives from Tunisia, Morocco, and the Algerian nationalists recommend formation of an Algerian government-in-exile and a permanent organization to work toward establishment of a North African federation.

1 MAY 1958
Egypt-USSR   On an 18-day state visit to the USSR, Egyptian President Nasser has the place of honor at the Lenin tomb for the traditional May Day parade in Moscow. The USSR and Egypt sign a joint statement committing Nasser to support Soviet foreign policy and the Soviets to promote liberation of all Asian and African peoples.

13 MAY 1958
USA   On a seven-nation Latin American goodwill tour, Vice-President Nixon encounters a hostile mob in Caracas, Venezuela, that pelts his car with rocks and attempts to attack him and his wife. Other countries have also shown ill will: he cuts his tour short.

19 MAY 1958
Canada-USA   The joint North American Air Defense Command (NORAD) is established by the US and Canada. With headquarters at Colorado Springs, NORAD has already functioned for over 8 months on the basis of a verbal agreement.

1 JUNE 1958
France   The National Assembly approves Charles de Gaulle as premier, after he has demanded six months of full-decree power, renewal of special powers in Algeria granted previous governments, and power to revise the constitution. De Gaulle's accession averts the threat of civil war in France. During a month-long cabinet crisis, a committee of public safety, headed by Brig Gen Jacques Massu and Commander-in-Chief Raoul Salan, had seized control in Algeria. The revised constitution for a Fifth French Republic is approved by referendum on 28 September, and de Gaulle is named president for a seven-year term, beginning 8 January 1959.

17 JUNE 1958
Hungary   The executions of former premier Imre Nagy, Maj Gen Pal Maleter and two other leaders of the 1956 revolt are announced by the Hungarian Justice Ministry. At the news, a wave of revulsion and anticommunist demonstrations sweeps the West.

6 OCTOBER 1958

14 JULY 1958

Iraq The pro-Western monarchy of King Faisal II is overthrown by an Arab nationalist group of Iraqi army officers led by Brig Gen Abdul Karim el-Kassem. The king, the crown prince and Premier Nuri as-Said are assassinated, and rebels proclaim a republican cabinet with Gen Kassem as premier. On 19 July Iraq and the UAR agree to unite against aggression. Britain recognizes the new Iraqi Government on 1 August, followed by the US a day later.

15 JULY 1958

Lebanon US President Eisenhower announces he has ordered US Marines into Lebanon at the request of Lebanese President Camille Chamoun, who fears that Lebanon will be unable to survive against Moslem rebels, allegedly supported by the UAR and the USSR. Withdrawal of US troops will begin on 12 August after calm is restored.

17 JULY 1958

Jordan British Prime Minister Macmillan announces that 2000 British troops are being flown to Jordan at the request of King Hussein, who fears that Jordan is faced with an imminent attempt by the UAR to create internal dissension and to overthrow his monarchy on the pattern of the Iraqi revolt. British forces begin to withdraw on 20 October.

4 AUGUST 1958

Cyprus The Greek-Cypriot underground declares a truce with Turkish Cypriots and British security forces, permitting progress toward an eventual solution of the Cyprus issue.

9 AUGUST 1958

USA-China The US reaffirms its decision not to recognize Communist China, holding that 'Communism's rule in China is not permanent and that one day it will pass.' By withholding recognition, the US 'seeks to hasten that passing.'

24 AUGUST 1958

Great Britain Racial tensions erupt in violence when hundreds of whites and blacks battle in Nottingham. The following day nine youths are arrested in London for assaulting blacks.

30 SEPTEMBER 1958

USSR The Atomic Energy Commission announces that the USSR has resumed testing nuclear devices with two detonations north of the Arctic Circle. This ends the Soviet test ban, announced six months earlier.

6 OCTOBER 1958

China The communists order a one-week cessation of the shelling (since 23 August) of Quemoy and other Nationalist-Chinese offshore islands. After Taiwan talks between Chiang Kai-shek and US Secretary of State Dulles, the Nationalists announce on 23 October that they will not use force to return to the mainland. Two days later Communist China announces that the offshore islands will not be bombarded on even-numbered days of the month.

CHARLES DE GAULLE, 1890–1970

Charles de Gaulle had the confidence to match his impressive height of six feet, four inches. Fellow Frenchmen were confident in turn of his leadership in time of crisis. Having served in World War I, he tried unsuccessfully to convert the French military and government to his ideas about defending France in 1939. When the nation signed an armistice with Germany in 1940, he fled to England to organize the Free French. With little more than his stirring rhetoric—'Soldiers of France, wherever you may be, arise!'—he led his forces beside the Allies and entered Paris in triumph in August 1944. His postwar government lasted only two months because he felt his views on a strong executive were ignored. When France was close to a civil war over the Algerian crisis in 1958, de Gaulle came out of retirement and was granted virtually dictatorial powers to govern and revise the Constitution. He survived numerous attempts on his life, alternately antagonized and amused the world with his imperious and idiosyncratic ways, and undoubtedly held France together during the next ten years. Typically, he resigned in 1969 because he felt the French people had not accepted one of his constitutional reforms. But he managed to convince many (besides himself) that where he lived, France lived.

IN SEARCH OF STABILITY 1946-1962

9 OCTOBER 1958
Vatican Pope Pius XII dies. He is succeeded by Angelo Giuseppe Cardinal Roncalli, who is elected Pope on 28 October and takes the name of John XXIII.

13 OCTOBER 1958
Cuba Rebel leader Fidel Castro warns in a broadcast that participants in the general elections sched-

NIKITA S KHRUSHCHEV, 1894–1971

A man of great energy and ambition who never lost the rough edges of his peasant origins, Nikita Khrushchev fought with the Bolsheviks in the Civil War, joined the Communist Party in 1918, and rose to supreme power in Russia within a few years of Stalin's death in 1953. Banging his shoe on his desk at the UN, peppering his speeches with a seemingly endless stream of anecdotes and proverbs, his moods alternated between good-natured humor and unpredictable rages and threats. Before his fall from power in 1964 he modified Lenin's position that war between communism and capitalism was inescapable. By placing emphasis on economic competition and keeping peace with the Western powers, he alienated the Chinese, while at home his policy of increased consumer production accompanied by agricultural failures precipitated the criticism that eventually proved fatal to his career.

> **THE COMMON MARKET EVOLVES**
>
> Establishment of the Common Market in 1958 symbolized a move toward the reunification of European countries while stimulating their individual economies. Formally known as the European Economic Community, this coalition initially included Belgium, the Netherlands, Luxembourg, Germany, Italy, and France. Its primary aims were to eliminate tariffs among member nations and to devise a standard tariff for other countries. This integrated economic community began in 1948 when the United States set up the Organization for European Economic Coordination. An offshoot of this organization, also formed in 1948, was a customs union comprising Belgium, the Netherlands, and Luxembourg, called Benelux. The success of these groups led French Foreign Minister Robert Schuman and economist Jean Monnet to develop the French-German Coal and Steel Authority in 1950. By 1952 the promise of economic renewal led to the creation of the European Coal and Steel Community, an organization that joined the Benelux countries with France, Germany, and Italy. The Common Market went on to become one of the largest traders in the world. But it wasn't until nearly two decades after it was founded that Great Britain and several other European nations decided to join the economic community. Still showing some growing pains in the 1980s, the Common Market nevertheless continues to thrive.

uled for 3 November will be guilty of treason, and that all candidates face execution unless they withdraw by 30 October.

20 OCTOBER 1958
Thailand Field Marshal Sarit Thanarat, commander of the nation's armed forces, seizes control of the country in a bloodless coup. Next day, he abolishes political parties and begins to arrest those involved in communist activity.

23 OCTOBER 1958
Egypt-USSR The USSR offers to lend Egypt $100 million toward the construction of the Aswan High Dam on the Nile River. Included in the offer are Soviet technicians, machinery, and materials. The proposal generates strong pro-Soviet sentiment in the Middle East.

27 OCTOBER 1958
Pakistan President Iskander Mirza is forced to resign in favor of Gen Mohammed Ayub Khan.

17 NOVEMBER 1958
Sudan Lt Gen Ibrahim Abboud seizes control of the government in an orderly coup. He makes himself premier, dissolves the coalition parliamentary government, suspends the constitution, and abolishes all political parties. Abboud will be deposed in 1964.

27 NOVEMBER 1958
International Soviet Premier Khrushchev threatens

to give East Germany control of all communications lines to West Berlin unless the Western powers agree within six months to make West Berlin a demilitarized free city.

23 DECEMBER 1958

Egypt United Arab Republic President Nasser accuses Syrian Communists of working against Egyptian-Syrian unity and Arab nationalism. Many Syrian Communists are reported arrested; on 1 January more than 200 Egyptian Communists are arrested.

OTHER EVENTS OF 1958

Science The steady-state theory of the universe—that it is eternally unchanging and ever-expanding—is fully formulated by Hermann Bondi, Thomas Gold, and Fred Hoyle (elements of this cosmology have been discussed for at least 20 years). Gordon Gould invents the optically pumped laser amplifier while Russian physicists Basov and Prokhorov are proposing it. This year, Arthur Schawlow and Charles Townes of the Bell Laboratories apply for a patent on a laser; in 1960 the first (ruby) laser will be operated by Theodore H Maiman, to be followed by the first continuous laser in 1961.

Technology *Explorer I*, the first US satellite, is sent into orbit on 31 January; it will discover the Van Allen radiation belts.

Environment Eric de Bisschop, trying to disprove Heyerdahl's claim that Polynesia was settled from South America, sets out from Tahiti on his own raft, but drowns when it hits a reef off South America. The submarine *USS Nautilus* makes an undersea passage of the North Pole in a journey lasting 96 hours.

Social Sciences Levi-Strauss's *Structural Anthropology*; John Kenneth Galbraith's *The Affluent Society*.

Literature William Carlos Williams completes his poem *Paterson* (begun in 1956); Nabokov's *Lolita*; Giuseppe di Lampedusa's *The Leopard*; Carlos Fuentes's *Where the Air is Clear*; T H White's *The Sword in the Stone*; Chinua Achebe's *Things Fall Apart*; Lawrence Durrell's *Justine* (the first of his Alexandria Quartet).

Drama/Entertainment Genet's *The Blacks*; Pinter's *The Birthday Party*; Andrzej Wajda's *Ashes and Diamonds*.

The Arts Sidney Nolan's *Gallipoli* series; Jasper Johns' *Three Flags*.

Architecture The Seagram Building is completed in New York City, primarily the work of Mies van der Rohe, with assistance from Philip Johnson. In Brasilia, Oscar Niemeyer's President's Palace is completed; and Eero Saarinen's Hockey Rink opens at Yale University.

Music Stravinsky's *Threni* (his first full-scale work in the serial style); Britten's *Noye's Fludde*; Vaughan Williams's *9th Symphony*. A young American pianist, Van Cliburn, creates a sensation when he wins the international piano competition in Moscow.

Life/Customs American churches begin to admit women as ministers. The 'Beatnik' movement spreads among young Americans: its adherents reject social conventions and embrace rootlessness, unconventional clothing, earthy language, drugs and alcohol, and Eastern religion and philosophy.

Miscellaneous Commercial jet passenger service between London and New York begins. The Geneva Conference on the Law of the Sea launches international efforts to end spoilation of the world's oceans. Linus Pauling, a US chemist who received the 1954 Nobel Prize for his work on atoms in large molecules, presents a petition to the Secretary General of the UN for a ban on nuclear testing. (Pauling will receive the Nobel Peace Prize for such efforts in 1962.)

1 JANUARY 1959

International The European Economic Community, or Common Market, becomes effective. The goal of its six members—France, West Germany, Belgium, Luxembourg, the Netherlands, and Italy—is gradual elimination of tariffs and other trade barriers. Members have already pooled coal, steel, and atomic energy through the European Coal and Steel Community and Euratom.

Cuba Batista's dictatorial regime collapses. Abandoning his guerrilla tactics, Fidel Castro leads his rebel army across the island nation and takes control. On 2 January he proclaims a provisional government headed by Dr Manuel Urrutia, with himself as commander-in-chief of the armed forces. On 7 January the US recognizes the new government, following recognition by Britain and other countries. Castro, who insists that he is neither a socialist nor a communist, becomes premier on 16 February. In the first $3\frac{1}{2}$ months of his regime, 500 Batista supporters are executed.

FIDEL CASTRO, 1927–

Fidel Castro has been a controversial figure on the world scene since he became prime minister—and effectively dictator—of Cuba in 1959. The son of a prosperous sugar planter and a lawyer by profession, Castro became so opposed to the corrupt and oppressive Batista regime that he led a revolution to improve the lot of the masses. Initially hailed as a daring and dedicated revolutionary, Castro's increasingly Marxist-Communist rhetoric and policies began to lose him many supporters, not only in the United States but among Cubans. Although many continued to admire his numerous social and economic reforms, others were disturbed by his willingness to tie the Cuban economy to the Soviet Union. His image as a vigorous revolutionary willing to take to the fields to help harvest sugar cane still leads many to idolize him, while his critics point to his control over all aspects of Cuban life and his dispatch of forces to fight in other lands. To paraphrase Castro's own words about himself, history will be his judge.

IN SEARCH OF STABILITY 1946-1962

3 JANUARY 1959
USA Alaska is admitted as the nation's 49th state; Hawaii brings the total to 50 on 21 August.

7 FEBRUARY 1959
Iraq-USSR Plans are announced for Soviet participation on a 'vast scale' in Iraq's economic development: a preliminary agreement on technical and economic co-operation provides for training of Iraqi students in Soviet institutions and factories.

11 FEBRUARY 1959
Iran-USSR Talks break off between Iran and the USSR, after two weeks of negotiation on a new non-aggression pact and economic aid. The Shah of Iran has been persuaded to reject the Soviet offer in favor of a US economic and defense proposal. On 2 March Iran renounces the 1921 treaty with the Soviets that allowed them to send their troops into Iran.

19 FEBRUARY 1959
Cyprus The long quarrel between Turkey and Greece over the British Crown Colony ends with an agreement establishing a free Cyprus republic, beginning a year from today, governed by a Greek president and a Turkish vice-president. Britain will be permitted to maintain two military bases on the island. On 24 February Britain revokes the order exiling Archbishop Makarios from Cyprus for alleged encouragement of terrorist activities there; he returns on 1 March to a welcome by 150,000 Greek Cypriots.

21 FEBRUARY 1959
Great Britain-USSR British Prime Minister Macmillan begins an eleven-day visit in the Soviet Union, the first such visit since World War II. He rejects Khrushchev's offer of a nonaggression pact and declares Britain's commitment to its alliances.

13 MARCH 1959
France France notifies the NATO Council that one-third of the French Mediterranean Fleet, earmarked for NATO command in wartime, will remain under French control. This shift is linked by observers to de Gaulle's demand for a greater French voice in NATO. On 4 June France will call for Allied support of its Algerian policy in return for full NATO participation by France.

13–27 MARCH 1959
Tibet A revolt breaks out against Chinese Communist rule. Following open fighting in Lhasa, the Tibetan Kashag (Cabinet) unanimously denounces the 1951 treaty under which China took control of Tibet's foreign and military affairs, but guaranteed Tibetan autonomy and recognized the Dalai Lama's role. The rebellion is crushed, and the Dalai Lama flees to India, where he is granted asylum.

24 MARCH 1959
Iraq Premier Kassem announces his country's withdrawal from the Baghdad Pact (METO), signed in 1955 to prevent the spread of communism in the Middle East.

The St Lawrence Seaway.

10 APRIL 1959
Japan Heir-apparent Akihito becomes the first crown prince to marry a commoner in the 2619-year history of the Japanese Throne.

15 APRIL 1959
Cuba-USA Castro begins an unofficial 11-day goodwill tour of the eastern US and Canada. In Washington, he lunches with Secretary of State Christian Herter, visits Vice-President Nixon at his home, speaks informally with members of Congress, is interviewed on nationwide television, and confers with UN Secretary General Hammarskjöld. Welcomed by the public throughout his tour, Castro professes friendship for the US.

18 APRIL 1959
China Premier Chou En-lai reports to the Second National People's Congress on gains of some 65 percent in industrial and farm output during 1958—an 'unprecedented leap forward' in the first year of China's second five-year plan. But the Great Leap Forward will prove unsuccessful in its attempt to force the pace of development by substituting labor for investment.

25 APRIL 1959
Canada-USA The St Lawrence Seaway opens: the $500-million, 400-mile waterway is the largest since the Panama Canal and took five years to build. On 26 June Queen Elizabeth II and President Eisenhower join in dedicating the Seaway.

11 MAY 1959
International In Geneva, foreign ministers of the USA, Britain, France, and the USSR meet to tackle problems of German reunification, the future of West Berlin, and European security. They fail to reach accord, and the conference recesses indefinitely on 5 August.

28 MAY 1959
China In Munich, the International Olympic Committee votes to withdraw recognition from Nationalist China (Taiwan) on the ground that it 'no longer represents sports in the entire country of China.' IOC President Avery Brundage says that Communist China will be recognized by the IOC if it applies for membership. The US condemns the action and the House of Representatives votes to withdraw $400,000 support of the 1960 Squaw Valley Winter Games.

3 JUNE 1959
Singapore The British Crown Colony becomes a self-governing state within the Commonwealth as its new constitution goes into effect. British Governor William Goode serves as interim ceremonial chief of state, and Lee Kuan Yew becomes the first prime minister on 5 June.

6 JULY 1959
USA New York Governor Nelson Rockefeller

proposes a system of compulsory fallout shelters for homes and other buildings to save millions from death or injury by radioactive fallout in the event of a nuclear attack.

23 JULY 1959
USA-USSR Vice-President Nixon flies to Moscow to open the American National Exhibition there. This ceremonial visit becomes a major diplomatic effort in which Nixon spends more time with Khrushchev than any other American statesman to date. As they visit a model American kitchen, they carry on a running public debate on the merits of capitalism vs communism—recorded on videotape, this argument becomes known as the 'Kitchen Debate.'

30–31 JULY 1959
Laos The government reports that Communist-led Pathet Lao guerrillas, armed by bordering North Vietnam, have attacked Laotian army posts in the north. On 4 August Laos declares a state of emergency. On 26 August the US promises to send it additional funds and equipment.

12 AUGUST 1959
International In Santiago, Chile, foreign ministers of the 21 member nations of the OAS meet in emergency session and adopt measures designed to ease tensions in the Caribbean area. During the past six months, at least six Caribbean nations—Nicaragua, Haiti, Panama, Honduras, Cuba, and the Dominican Republic—had complained of invasion or infiltration by 'foreign elements.' The ministers issue the Declaration of Santiago, denouncing the 'existence of anti-democratic regimes.'

29 AUGUST 1959
India Before Parliament, Prime Minister Nehru charges that Communist Chinese troops have crossed the northern frontier twice in recent weeks and that Longju is in Chinese hands. Nehru rejects governmental demands for immediate military retaliation, but dispatches Indian troops to man the Indian-Tibetan border.

15–27 SEPTEMBER 1959
USA-USSR Soviet Premier Khrushchev pays an unprecedented visit to the US. He confers with President Eisenhower at Camp David, following a tour of the country in which he visits Eleanor Roosevelt at Hyde Park, views a dance from the film *Can-Can* performed in his honor in Hollywood, accuses Walter Reuther and six other AFL-CIO officers of being 'agents for capitalists' in San Francisco, and visits a cornfield in Iowa.

7–9 OCTOBER 1959
International In Washington, the Council of Ministers of the Baghdad Pact (METO) meets for the first time under its new name, Central Treaty Organization (CENTO)—signifying location between the NATO and SEATO regions. Member nations—

IN SEARCH OF STABILITY 1946-1962

The 'kitchen debate' between Khrushchev and Nixon.

Britain, Turkey, Pakistan, and Iran—reaffirm their pledge of mutual defense and economic development, in the face of growing communist propaganda against Iran.

8 OCTOBER 1959
Great Britain Prime Minister Macmillan's Conservative Party triumphs in the general elections, almost doubling its majority in Commons. This is the first time since 1910 that any British party has won a third consecutive election.

13 NOVEMBER 1959
International The 21-nation Colombo Plan, founded in 1950 and scheduled to end in 1961, is extended for five years. The loosely knit organization was conceived by British Commonwealth countries to spur the economic growth of noncommunist South and Southeast Asia. The plan's six 'donor' nations are Australia, Britain, Canada, Japan, New Zealand, and the US. So far they have provided more than $6 billion in aid to the 15 recipient states—Burma, Cambodia, Ceylon, Malaya, India, Indonesia, Laos, Nepal, North Borneo, Pakistan, the Philippines, Sarawak, Singapore, Thailand, and South Vietnam. Of this amount, about $5.66 billion was US aid.

OTHER EVENTS OF 1959
Science Mary Leakey—who with her husband Louis Leakey will discover several of the earliest

President Eisenhower tees off for a round of golf.

IN SEARCH OF STABILITY 1946-1962

fossils crucial to understanding human evolution—finds in the Olduvai Gorge in northern Tanzania a humanlike skull that she identifies as a new species of *Homo zinjanthropus* (other anthropologists classify it as *australopithecus*).

Technology The Russian *Luna II* is the first spacecraft to land on the moon (although it crashes and is not retrieved). The first full-size Hovercraft—invented by Briton Christopher Cockerell—makes a Channel crossing. The first transatlantic TV broadcast is sent from London to Montreal (then relayed to New York); it shows Queen Elizabeth and Prince Philip departing for Canada to open the St Lawrence Seaway. In Stockholm, a 17th-century ship, the *Vasa*, is raised from the harbor where it sunk to be restored and exhibited.

Social Sciences I and P Opie's *The Lore and Language of Schoolchildren*.

Ideas/Beliefs Pierre Teilnard de Chardin's *The Phenomenon of Man*. Pope John XXIII calls for a Vatican Council.

Literature Günter Grass's *The Tin Drum*; Bellow's *Henderson the Rain-King*; Lowell's *Life Studies*; Heinrich Böll's *Billiards at Half-Past Nine*; Uwe Johnson's *Speculations About Jacob*; Hugh Mac-Lennan's *The Watch that Ends the Night*; Mordecai Richler's *The Apprenticeship of Duddy Kravitz*.

Drama/Entertainment Ionesco's *Rhinoceros*; Brendan Behan's *The Hostage*; Arnold Wesker's *Roots*; Sartre's *The Condemned of Altona*; Edward Albee's *Zoo Story*; Alain Resnais' *Hiroshima, Mon Amour*; Antonioni's *L'Aventura*; Fellini's *La Dolce Vita*.

The Arts Miro's murals for the UNESCO building in Paris; Franz Kline's *Black, White and Gray*; Dali's *Discovery of America by Christopher Columbus*; Robert Frank's collection of photographs, *The Americans*.

Architecture Frank Lloyd Wright's Guggenheim Museum in New York City is completed.

Music Karl-Heinz Stockhausen's *Gruppen* and *Kontakte*; Boulez's *Livre du Quattuor*; Poulenc's *La Voix Humaine*.

Miscellaneous C P Snow, the British scientist-author, gives the Rede Lecture on 'The Two Cultures' in which he deplores a growing gap between the humanistic-artistic culture and the scientific-technological world. The American Post Office Court rules that D H Lawrence's *Lady Chatterley's Lover* is not objectionable, which will allow this and many other books once excluded to be imported or published in America.

4 JANUARY 1960
International In Stockholm, the treaty establishing the European Free Trade Association, or the Outer Seven, is signed. It is composed of Austria, Britain, Denmark, Norway, Portugal, Sweden, and Switzerland—those nations not party to the European Common Market.

24 JANUARY 1960
Algeria Several thousand European ultranation-alists, rightists, and sympathetic home guardsmen, opposing de Gaulle's liberal Algerian policies, stage an abortive insurrection in Algiers. With the fate of the French Fifth Republic in the balance, President de Gaulle dons his general's uniform and delivers a radio-TV address on 29 January on self-determination for Algeria. Loyal French troops finally force the collapse of the barricaded rebels on 1 February. The principal leader of the revolt, Pierre Lagaillarde, is arrested and flown to Paris. De Gaulle then receives the right to rule by decree for one year.

1 FEBRUARY 1960
USA In Greensboro, North Carolina, a wave of sit-in protests begins when four black college students refuse to leave a Woolworth lunch counter when they are denied service. By September 1961 more than 70,000 students, both black and white, have participated in sit-ins.

4 FEBRUARY 1960
Cuba-USSR Soviet First Deputy Premier Anastas Mikoyan arrives for a ten-day visit, during which he and Castro sign a commercial pact by which the USSR agrees to buy a million tons of sugar a year for the next five years at world market prices and extends Cuba a credit of $100 million repayable over 12 years at 2.5 percent interest. The USSR also expresses willingness to sell military planes to Cuba. On 23 July Cuba signs a similar pact with Communist China.

13 FEBRUARY 1960
France France becomes the world's fourth nuclear power when it successfully detonates a plutonium device in the Sahara Desert.

18 FEBRUARY 1960
USA In a move to stop illegal arms shipments from the US to Cuba or other Latin American countries, President Eisenhower issues an executive order authorizing seizure and detention of ships and planes carrying munitions and weapons intended for such shipment, as well as the arms themselves.

19 FEBRUARY 1960
Great Britain Queen Elizbeth gives birth to a son—the first child born to a reigning British sovereign since 1857. Prince Andrew becomes second in line of succession to the throne.

22 FEBRUARY 1960
USA President Eisenhower leaves on a two-week goodwill tour of Latin America, on which he reaffirms US pledges of cooperation and help.

9 APRIL 1960
South Africa Prime Minister Hendrik Verwoerd is shot twice in the face and seriously wounded by a white farmer opposing apartheid. This assassination attempt caps a series of antiapartheid demonstrations in which 89 blacks were shot by the police.

27 APRIL 1960

South Korea Syngman Rhee resigns the presidency. On 15 March, running for his fourth term unopposed, Rhee was re-elected president, but on 19 April over 100,000 student demonstrators marched on government buildings in Seoul to protest alleged rigging of the elections. Rhee declared martial law but was rebuked by the US for using repressive measures unsuited to a democracy. The National Assembly revoked the March elections and called for new elections, leading to Rhee's resignation. On 29 May Rhee flees to Hawaii.

1 MAY 1960

USA-USSR A US reconnaissance plane, a U-2 piloted by Francis Gary Powers, is shot down in the Soviet Union. Premier Khrushchev refuses to participate in the Paris summit conference scheduled for 16 May unless President Eisenhower apologizes for U-2 flights over the USSR. The Big Four leaders go to Paris, but the conference does not take place. Powers is convicted of espionage in Moscow on 19 August and is sentenced to a ten-year term. He will be freed in February 1962 in exchange for a Soviet spy.

23 MAY 1960

Israel Premier David Ben-Gurion announces that Israeli agents have captured Adolf Eichmann, the former Nazi SS general accused of complicity in the deaths of 6 million European Jews. Eichmann has been brought from Argentina to Israel to stand trial.

27 MAY 1960

Turkey A military junta, headed by Lt Gen Jemal Gursel, ousts the government of Premier Adnan Menderes in a bloodless coup.

A detachment of the French Foreign Legion leaves the training barracks at Sidi-bel-Abbes, Algeria.

IN SEARCH OF STABILITY 1946-1962

French Prime Minister de Gaulle at a ceremony at the war memorial in Mostaganem in Northern Algeria.

13 NOVEMBER 1960

12 JUNE 1960
USA President Eisenhower leaves on a two-week tour of the Far East. He is warmly greeted in the Philippines and Taiwan, but encounters a hostile demonstration in Okinawa. A tumultuous welcome greets him in South Korea, but he cancels his Japanese visit because of leftist riots.

30 JUNE 1960
Congo The Belgian Congo becomes the Republic of the Congo in ceremonies at Leopoldville. President Joseph Kasavubu expresses goodwill toward Belgium, but Premier Patrice Lumumba, leader of the Congolese National Movement, makes a militant speech attacking colonialism.

6 JULY 1960
USA-Cuba In response to Cuban anti-US policies, President Eisenhower orders a 95 percent cut in Cuban sugar imports. On 14 July Eisenhower warns the USSR that the principles of the 1823 Monroe Doctrine are still valid and support the US policy of preventing establishment in the Western Hemisphere of any despotic political system contrary to the independent status of the American states, a view also supported by the OAS.

11 JULY 1960
Congo Premier Moise Tshombe of Katanga, the nation's richest province, proclaims Katanga independent and asks for Belgian military aid. The Lumumba Government appeals to the UN for military assistance. Meanwhile, Lumumba seeks to suppress a Congolese Army mutiny that began on 6 July.

21 JULY 1960
Ceylon Sirimavo Bandaranaike is sworn in as prime minister. She is the first woman elected to head the government of a modern state.

16 AUGUST 1960
Cyprus After 82 years of British rule, the former Crown Colony becomes the independent republic of Cyprus. Archbishop Makarios is the nation's first president.

20 SEPTEMBER 1960
International Following Khrushchev's lead, heads of many governments attend the opening of the UN General Assembly's 15th session in New York. Leaders present include British Prime Minister Macmillan, Indian Prime Minister Nehru, Cuban Premier Castro, Yugoslav President Tito, Egyptian President Nasser, Canadian Prime Minister Diefenbaker, Jordan's King Hussein, Australian Prime Minister Menzies, Indonesian President Sukarno and Ghana's President Nkrumah. The most disorderly meeting in UN history occurs on 12 October when Khrushchev becomes enraged at a Philippine delegate, calls him names, then takes off his shoe and pounds it on his desk.

26 SEPTEMBER 1960
USA The first of four hour-long nationally televised debates between presidential candidates John F Kennedy and Richard M Nixon takes place in Chicago. Viewers' complaints that Nixon looks haggard and drawn make television image an issue in the campaign. Many observers feel that the debates help Kennedy's cause by giving him a wider audience and demolishing Republican arguments on his immaturity. Others feel that Nixon's participation is the biggest single factor in his defeat.

1 OCTOBER 1960
Nigeria The former British colony and protectorate in West Africa is proclaimed an independent nation within the British Commonwealth.

5 OCTOBER 1960
South Africa An all-white referendum approves the plan to make South Africa a republic rather than a constitutional monarchy owing allegiance to the British Crown. Most rural Afrikaaners support the proposal; most urban English-speaking citizens oppose it. The nonwhite majority of over 11 million is barred from the polls.

19 OCTOBER 1960
Canada-USA The two nations agree to undertake a joint Columbia River project to provide hydroelectric power and flood control. On 24 October the US and Mexico agree to co-construction of a dam on the Rio Grande.

28 OCTOBER 1960
Cuba In a note to the OAS, the US charges that Cuba has 'been receiving substantial quantities of arms and numbers of military technicians' from the Soviet bloc. Requesting an inter-American committee to investigate the shipments, the note warns that 'Cuba is expanding rapidly its capacity to give armed support to the spread of its revolution in other parts of the Americas.'

8 NOVEMBER 1960
USA John F Kennedy is chosen the nation's 35th president, the first Catholic and the youngest man (43) ever elected. He defeats Nixon by a margin of little more than 100,000 votes.

11 NOVEMBER 1960
South Vietnam A brigade of South Vietnamese paratroopers attempts to oust the government of President Diem—accusing him of corruption and suppression of liberties. Troops loyal to the president put down the revolt some 24 hours later.

13 NOVEMBER 1960
Guatemala-Nicaragua Rebel Guatemalan troops revolt against the government of President Miguel Fuentes but are soon overcome. On 11 November a rebel force of more than 200 invaded Nicaragua from Costa Rica. Guatemala and Nicaragua allege that

IN SEARCH OF STABILITY 1946-1962

President-elect John F Kennedy (right) confers with President Eisenhower at the White House.

Fidel Castro is behind the uprising and ask the US to patrol their Caribbean coasts to prevent an invasion from Cuba. President Eisenhower orders US naval units to the region.

1 DECEMBER 1960
Congo Deposed Premier Patrice Lumumba is arrested by the troops of Col Joseph D Mobutu, who seized control of the Congo on 14 September. Mobutu plans to try Lumumba for inciting the army to rebellion and other crimes.

6 DECEMBER 1960
USSR-China Following a three-week world congress of Communist leaders in Moscow, a new communist manifesto that represents a Soviet-Chinese compromise over ideological differences is issued.

9 DECEMBER 1960
Laos The neutralist government of Premier Souvanna Phouma collapses, and Souvanna and his family flee to Cambodia in the face of advances on the capital by Pathet Lao guerrillas and pro-Western insurgents led by Gen Phoumi Nosavan. A short-lived pro-Communist government collapses as Phoumi's forces occupy Vientiane; on 18 December a rightist regime under Prince Boun Oum is installed. The US resumes arms shipments to Laos, which had been stopped by request of the neutralist Souvanna regime.

OTHER EVENTS OF 1960
Science The first quasars are reported by three observatories—Jodrell Bank in England, the California Institute of Technology, and Mt Wilson-Palomar, California: quasars are compact galaxies that radiate enormous amounts of light and radio waves. Initial reports are unable to identify their sources, which will be done in 1963. Niko Tinbergen publishes another of his seminal works on animal behavior, *The Herring Gull's World*. Kendrew elucidates the three-dimensional structure of protein myoglobin.

Medicine/Health Dr Albert Sabin, Russian-American microbiologist, reveals that he has developed a live-virus vaccine against poliomyelitis that can be taken orally; more effective than the Salk vaccine in several ways, it will be adopted in many countries soon after successful tests in 1961. Surgeons in Birmingham, England, develop a 'pacemaker' to control the rhythmical beating of a human heart.

Technology The US bathyscaphe *Trieste*, developed by the Swiss Auguste Piccard, dives 35,800 feet to the bottom of the Challenger Deep. There are now 20 satellites in orbit assuming specialized tasks; the US, for instance, launches a radio-reflector satellite this year, while the USSR recovers dogs that have made 17 orbits. The first submerged circumnavigation of the globe is made by the US nuclear submarine *Triton*.

Environment An eathquake at Agadir, Morocco, kills some 12,000.

Social Sciences Paleolithic fossils are found at Petralona Cave, in northern Greece, among the earliest indications of human habitation of Europe. Off Cape Gelidonya, Turkey, a well-preserved Bronze Age shipwreck is found by two pioneer underwater archaeologists. More scrolls of the pre-Christian and early-Christian era are found in the Dead Sea region.

Literature Lawrence Durrell, with *Clea*, completes his Alexandria tetrology (which began in 1957 with *Justine*, and includes *Balthazar* and *Mountolive*, both in 1958). I B Singer's *The Magician of Lublin*; Morley Callaghan's *The Many-Colored Coat*; Mazo de la Roche, with *Morning at Jalna*, completes her 16-volume saga of the Whiteoaks, a Canadian family, in progress since 1927.

Drama/Entertainment Pinter's *The Caretaker*; Hellman's *Toys in the Attic*; Antonioni's *La Notte*; Hitchcock's *Psycho*; Visconti's *Rocco and his Brothers*.

The Arts Picasso's *Corrida* series; Sidney Nolan's *Leda and the Swan* series; Jasper Johns' *Painted Bronze*; Jean Tinguely's *Homage to New York*, a self-destructing sculpture, is displayed in the garden of the Museum of Modern Art. Mark Rothko finishes the last of 14 large canvases he has been working on since 1958; this suite of somber, intense paintings will be placed in a special interdenominational chapel in Houston, Texas.

Music Boulez's *Pli selon pli*; Britten's *Midsummer Night's Dream*; Copland's *Nonet for Strings*; Hans Werner Henze's *The Prince of Homburg*.

Miscellaneous Archaeologists and other concerned groups from many nations begin work to save ancient temples, statues, and other treasures in Nubia before they are flooded by waters backed up from the new Aswan Dam in Egypt.

3 JANUARY 1961
Cuba/USA The US severs diplomatic and consular relations with Cuba, following a Castro request that the US reduce its Havana diplomatic personnel to 11. On 16 January the State Department announces restrictions on travel to Cuba.

5 JANUARY 1961
Dominican Republic In Washington, the Council of the Organization of American States (OAS) recommends sanctions against the government of Dominican leader Hector Trujillo Molina for his 'aggression' against Venezuela.

6–8 JANUARY 1961
Algeria/France De Gaulle's Algerian reform program is approved in a referendum in France, Algeria, and French overseas territories. This will permit the Algerians to choose independence, autonomy, or French provincial status, and is an important step toward ending the six-year rebellion.

7 JANUARY 1961
Africa Following a four-day Casablanca con-

IN SEARCH OF STABILITY 1946-1962

ference, five African chiefs of state announce plans for a NATO-type organization to ensure common defense and co-ordinate policies. Leaders are King Mohamed V of Morocco, President Nasser of the United Arab Republic, Ghana's President Nkrumah, Guinea's President Touré, and Mali's President Keita.

17 JANUARY 1961
Congo Patrice Lumumba, the ousted Congo premier, is murdered in the secessionist province of Katanga.
USA In a farewell TV-radio address to the nation, President Eisenhower warns, 'We must guard against the acquisition of unwarranted influence . . . by the military-industrial complex.'

18 JANUARY 1961
USSR The Communist Party central committee adopts Khrushchev's proposals for a sweeping reorganization of agriculture. Khrushchev charged that Soviet farm administrators had lied to make it appear that farm goals set by the Seven Year Plan were reached.

20 JANUARY 1961
USA John F Kennedy is inaugurated as the nation's 35th president. In his brief address, Kennedy advises 'Ask not what your country can do for you—ask what you can do for your country.'

1 MARCH 1961
USA By executive order, Kennedy creates the Peace Corps 'to help foreign countries meet their urgent needs for skilled manpower.' Its first project, announced 21 April, will be to help local technicians plan and build roads in Tanganyika. On 15 October the Peace Corps is embarrassed by publication of a postcard written by a volunteer decrying the 'squalor' in Nigeria. During the Vietnam War the corps will become a sought-after alternative to military service.

13 MARCH 1961
USA Kennedy proposes the Alliance for Progress—a ten-year program of helping Latin American nations raise living standards, provide basic education, end hunger, and become self-sustaining. After ten years of massive US aid, few of these goals are attained.

17 APRIL 1961
Cuba/USA An anti-Castro Cuban exile force of 1400, organized and equipped by the CIA and trained in Guatemala, lands at the Bay of Pigs with air support. The invasion is crushed by Castro's forces, a blow to US prestige that strengthens the Castro regime. Anti-American demonstrations occur throughout Latin America and in Europe. The 17 May Castro plan to exchange the Bay of Pigs prisoners for 500 US tractors fails, but on 10 October 1962 the US agrees to help pay the $60 million ransom set by Castro for the release of 1113 prisoners.

22–26 APRIL 1961
Algeria/France A right-wing rebellion in Algeria led by four French generals collapses in the face of determined opposition by de Gaulle and Premier Michel Debre's warning that an invasion of France by the insurgents is imminent. French civilians rally behind the government, and loyal forces move into Algiers to little opposition.

1 MAY 1961
Cuba In a $3\frac{1}{2}$-hour May Day speech, Castro proclaims Cuba a socialist nation and abolishes elections. In earlier celebrations, President Kennedy was

JOMO KENYATTA, 1893?–1978

Born into Kenya's Kikuyu tribe, Jomo Kenyatta was campaigning for African political rights in his twenties as a member of his tribe's Central Association. In the thirties he studied in England, taking a postgraduate degree at Oxford and cofounding the Pan-African Federation. After his return home he led the Kenya African Union and was imprisoned by the British in 1952 for allegedly supporting the Mau Mau uprising. Released after seven years and then exiled, Kenyatta became a *cause célèbre* to his countrymen. In 1961 Kenyatta was one of the negotiators with Britain on Kenyan independence. He was elected president of the new republic in 1964 and remained in office until his death. Perhaps the most visible, skilled, and brilliant of the early African nationalist leaders, he made Kenya one of the strongest and most stable of the postcolonial African nations.

Drs L S B and Mary Leakey on their archaeological dig at Olduvai Gorge, Tanganyika.

burned in effigy and huge portraits of Karl Marx were displayed. In a 2 December speech Castro will announce plans to make Cuba a communist nation, declaring 'I am a Marxist-Leninist and will be one until the day I die.'

2 MAY 1961
Canada/China Canada announces a pact to sell 6 million tons of wheat, barley, and flour to Communist China for $362 million, one of the biggest grain sales in Canadian history.

3 MAY 1961
Laos Following a joint British-Soviet appeal, a cease-fire between the Laotian Government and procommunist rebels goes into effect. On 22 June the three rival princes—leftist Souphanouvong, neutralist Souvanna Phouma, and rightist Boun Oum—announce agreement on a coalition government, but their negotiations deadlock 27 December.

4 MAY 1961
USA A series of Freedom Rides—bus trips to challenge Southern segregationist practices—begins. Attacks by Alabama whites cause the Kennedy Administration to send 600 armed US marshals to Montgomery to protect the riders. After two busloads of Freedom Riders are escorted safely by National Guardsmen and police to Jackson, Mississippi, 27 riders are arrested there on 24 May for trying to use segregated washrooms.

16 MAY 1961
South Korea An anticommunist military junta under the leadership of Lt General Do Young Chang deposes the government and arrests President Posun Yun. On 3 July Major General Chung Hee Park becomes chairman of the junta. Elections in October 1963 give Park the presidency.

30 MAY 1961
Dominican Republic Generalissimo Rafael Leonidas Trujillo, in power since 1930, is shot to death by assassins who ambush him in his car. His family leaves the country in November, fearing a military coup. US warships patrol the nation's coast.

31 MAY 1961
South Africa South Africa becomes a republic, severing affiliation with the British Commonwealth. British Prime Minister Harold Macmillan had tried to work out a compromise by which South Africa could remain in the commonwealth, despite its 'abhorrent' apartheid policy. The nation's first president, Charles R Swart, endorses the policy, and on 11 October the UN General Assembly censures South Africa.

3–4 JUNE 1961
International President Kennedy and Soviet Premier Khrushchev confer in Vienna. No substantive agreement is reached on such issues as nuclear testing, disarmament, and Germany; the leaders reaffirm their support for a neutral Laos and see the talks as opening channels of communication. On his week-long European trip, Kennedy also visits de Gaulle in Paris and Macmillan in London.

IN SEARCH OF STABILITY 1946-1962

19 JUNE 1961
Kuwait Britain relinquishes its 62-year-old protectorate over the oil-rich sheikdom. On 25 June Iraq threatens to annex Kuwait. Determined to maintain the nation's independence, Sheik Abdullah appeals to Britain, which lands troops and fighter planes in Kuwait on 1 July. British forces begin withdrawal on 19 September, replaced by Arab League troops.

19 JULY 1961
Tunisia/France Tunisian forces begin a blockade of the French military base at Bizerte. The French parachute 800 Foreign Legionnaires into the base: after fierce fighting that leaves 700 Tunisians dead, the French break the siege on 21 July, and take most of Bizerte and environs. On 18 September France and Tunisia reach agreement on French troop withdrawal from the city.

1 AUGUST 1961
Congo President Joseph Kasavubu names socialist labor leader Cyrille Adoula premier; on 14 August Dag Hammarskjöld extends UN recognition to the Adoula government.

12–13 AUGUST 1961
East Germany The Communist regime closes the border between East and West Berlin to stop the exodus of East Germans. East Germans erect a five-foot-high concrete block wall along most of their border with West Berlin, to remain in place until it becomes 'a demilitarized neutral free city.' On 10 October it is revealed that Soviet troops near the West German border, ostensibly taking part in Warsaw Pact maneuvers, have increased to 300,000.

24 AUGUST 1961
Cuba/USA At the UN Cuba challenges the treaty under which the US retains its naval base at Guantanamo Bay, charging that its purpose is aggression against Latin American nations.

1 SEPTEMBER 1961
USSR The USSR resumes atmospheric nuclear testing, and within the next five days detonates three more bombs over Siberia. These tests are not disclosed by the Soviets, but are detected by US long-range equipment. On 5 September the US announces resumption of underground testing.

9 SEPTEMBER 1961
France In the first of four unsuccessful assassination attempts against de Gaulle, a plastic bomb fails to detonate properly as his car drives through a sheet of flame. The second and third attempts, in May and June 1962, also misfire, but in August de Gaulle's car is machine-gunned and a shot passes within inches of his head. The terrorist campaign in Algeria and France by the mutinous Secret Army Organization (OAS) fails to halt the decolonization of Algeria.

13 SEPTEMBER 1961
Congo Declaring an end to the secession of the Katanga regime headed by Moise Tshombe, UN forces attack Elisabethville, capital of the rebel province. Strong resistance throughout Katanga ends in a cease-fire on 21 September. The Katangans claim victory, with 63 UN soldiers dead and 186 captured, and the UN suffers a considerable loss of prestige.

17 SEPTEMBER 1961
Turkey Former Premier Adnan Menderes, whose government was overthrown in May 1960, is hanged in Istanbul for crimes against the nation's constitution. Menderes and 600 members of his regime had been arraigned in a mass trial before a revolutionary court. Protests by Britain, the US, and other NATO members go unheeded.

18 SEPTEMBER 1961
Congo En route to confer with Tshombe, UN Secretary General Hammarskjöld is killed in a plane crash near Ndola, Northern Rhodesia. His death creates a UN crisis, intensified by a Soviet campaign to abolish the secretary general's office and replace it by a three-member executive board of Soviet, Western, and neutralist blocs. Burma's U Thant succeeds him and is elected to a full term on 30 November 1962.

28 SEPTEMBER 1961
Syria A revolt by army officers against Egyptian domination of the Syrian region of the United Arab Republic (UAR) begins in Damascus; next day Syria proclaims independence and installs Dr Mahmoun al-Kuzbari as premier, ending the Egyptian-Syrian merger proclaimed by Nasser on 1 February 1958. On 30 September the new government orders deportation of most of the 27,000 Egyptians in Syria.

14 NOVEMBER 1961
South Vietnam/USA President Kennedy decides to increase US advisers in South Vietnam from 1000 to 16,000 over two years. On 11 December two US Army helicopter companies, the first direct military support for South Vietnam, will arrive in Saigon. The 33 twin-rotor helicopters are accompanied by 400 US troops to fly and maintain them.

7 DECEMBER 1961
International Common Market nations agree to admit 18 African countries as 'associates.'

15 DECEMBER 1961
Israel Adolf Eichmann, the former German Gestapo official accused of a major role in the Nazi murder of 6 million Jews, is sentenced by a Jerusalem court to be hanged. The execution is carried out 31 May 1962.

18–19 DECEMBER 1961
India Indian troops invade Goa, Damao, and Diu,

Portuguese territories for over 400 years on India's west coast. Indian Defense Minister Krishna Menon says the military action was due to breakdown of the civilian colonial administration in the three enclaves and repeated provocations against the Indian border.

22 DECEMBER 1961
Vietnam War Specialist 4 James Davis of Livingston, Tennessee, is killed by the Viet Cong. Later he is cited by President Johnson as 'the first American to fall in defense of our freedom in Vietnam.'

31 DECEMBER 1961
Lebanon The nation's troops crush a right-wing army coup trying to overthrow President Fuad Chehab's regime. The Popular Syrian Party, which favors a merger of Syria, Lebanon, Iraq, and Jordan to form 'Greater Syria,' supports the insurgency; its leader Abdullah Saadeh is among those arrested.

OTHER EVENTS OF 1961
Science Researchers at New York University and the National Institutes of Health in Washington decipher the genetic code for an amino acid. Murray Gell-Mann, American theoretical physicist, proposes classifying the elementary particles 'the eightfold way,' (grouped into families according to similarities of mass, electric charge, and other properties). Gell-Mann uses his system to predict other undiscovered particles, which later researchers confirm. Harry Hess, American geologist, offers a theory to explain how the continents have moved: by 'sea-floor spreading,' convection currents carry molten rock from deep within the earth's mantle to oceanic ridges, forcing large cracks and displacing the ocean floor and the continents.

Medicine/Health External cardiac massage is introduced by J R Jude, an American cardiologist, and his associates. It will be taught to many, including laymen, to save lives in cardiac-arrest emergencies.

Technology On 12 April the Russians report sending the first human being into orbit—27-year-old Yuri Gagarin, in *Vostok I*, a five-ton satellite. After completing one orbit, he lands safely. (It will later be alleged that the Russians lost up to four men in previous attempts at space flights. Gagarin himself will die in a plane crash on 27 March 1968.) On 5 May the first American astronaut, Alan Shepard, makes a suborbital flight in a Mercury capsule. In Freeport, Texas, the first practical seawater conversion plant goes into operation.

Environment An international conference is held in Tanganyika, Africa, to consider ways of preserving African wildlife threatened with extinction.

Social Studies James Mellaart, British archaeologist, begins excavating Catal Huyuk, a neolithic town in Turkey; wall paintings and other finds reveal an unexpectedly advanced community of 6000 BC. Arnold Toynbee publishes the twelfth and final volume of *A Study in History*. B F Skinner, American psychologist, publishes *Walden Two*, a utopian work that will gain a wide readership.

JOHN F KENNEDY, 1917–1963

The 35th president of the United States, John Fitzgerald Kennedy was born in Brookline, Massachusetts, to a prominent Irish-American family and studied at Harvard University and in London. As a torpedo-boat commander in World War II, he was decorated for bravery and returned to make a career in Democratic politics. Elected representative (1946) and senator for Massachusetts (1952), he was the youngest person and the first Roman Catholic to be elected president of the United States (1960)—by the smallest majority of the popular vote ever. Kennedy called for a 'new frontier' in social legislation and worked toward implementing federal desegregation policies and extending opportunities for the disadvantaged. He was criticized for his role in the abortive CIA-sponsored invasion of Cuba in 1961, but won praise the following year for his handling of the Cuban missile crisis, in which the Soviet Union backed down. On 22 November 1963, he was assassinated by rifle fire while riding in an open car through Dallas, Texas. A stunned nation followed the tragedy and its aftermath on television —including the fatal shooting of accused assassin Lee Harvey Oswald during a jail transfer two days later. Kennedy was buried in Arlington National Cemetery with full military honors.

IN SEARCH OF STABILITY 1946-1962

Ideas/Beliefs *The New English Bible*, a contemporary translation of the New Testament, appears on the 350th anniversary of the King James Authorized Version.

Literature Günter Grass's *Cat and Mouse*; Garcia-Marquez's *No One Writes to the Colonel*; Joseph Heller's *Catch-22*; Yevtuskenko's *Babi Yar*; John Updike's *Rabbit, Run*; I B Singer's *The Spinoza of Market Street*; Iris Murdoch's *A Severed Head*.

Drama/Entertainment Tennessee Williams's *The Night of the Iguana*; Osborne's *Luther*; Max Frisch's *Andorra*; Beckett's *Happy Days*; Athol Fugard's *The Blood Knot*; Truffaut's *Jules and Jim*. The British revue *Beyond the Fringe* introduces refreshing new talents and humor.

The Arts Motherwell's *Elegy to the Spanish Republic*. The Metropolitan Museum of Art pays $2,300,000 for Rembrandt's *Aristotle Contemplating the Bust of Homer*, a record at this time for a single painting.

Music Hans Werner Henze's *Elegy for Young Lovers*; Luigi Nono's *Intoleranza*.

Sport Roger Maris of the New York Yankees breaks Babe Ruth's record of 60 homeruns in one season by hitting 61.

Life/Customs Henry Miller's *Tropic of Cancer* and *Tropic of Capricorn* are first legally published in the USA; previously published in Paris in 1934 and 1939 and smuggled in, the legalization of Miller's work is a sign of emerging sexual revolution. The first live TV coverage of a presidential news conference is of President Kennedy on 25 January; on 29 May the first member of the British royal family, Prince Philip, is interviewed on TV.

Miscellaneous The last scheduled trip is made by the famed Orient Express from Paris to Bucharest (the name will be revived later for another train). On a National Airlines flight from Miami to Key West, Florida, a Cuban using the name of 'The Pirate Cofresi' threatens crew and passengers with a pistol and knife and forces the plane to take him to Havana in the first successful 'skyjack,' soon to be punishable by strict laws.

3 JANUARY 1962
Cuba/USA The US State Department makes public a report to the Organization of American States stating that Cuba 'represents a bridgehead of Sino-Soviet Imperialism and a base for Communist agitation and subversion within the inner defense of the Western Hemisphere.' The document reports that Cuba has received Soviet-bloc weapons valued up to $100 million, including many MiG fighters and other aircraft and Cuba's ground forces are estimated at 250,000 to 400,000—a larger force than any American republic except that of the US. In a 22 January meeting in Punta del Este, Uruguay, the OAS ostracizes Cuba. On 3 February President Kennedy declares an embargo on all trade.

4 JANUARY 1962
Algeria The outlawed Secret Army Organization (OAS) issues an open call for insurrection in Algeria and intensifies its terrorist campaign, killing some 555 persons and wounding nearly 1000 in the next four weeks. Their methods include bombings, strikes, bank robberies, and the murder of European and Moslem 'traitors.' OAS bombings also become commonplace in Paris.

29 JANUARY 1962
International After 39 months of fruitless Geneva meetings, US/British/USSR talks on a treaty to end nuclear-weapons tests are suspended indefinitely, following the 353rd session. US and British representatives charge that the USSR has repudiated proposals for international controls.

8 FEBRUARY 1962
South Vietnam/USA The Defense Department announces creation of a new US military command in South Vietnam, to be known as the Military Assistance Command (MAC) under General Paul Harkins. On 14 February President Kennedy states that US troops in training missions in South Vietnam have been instructed to fire to protect themselves if fired upon, but are 'not combat troops in the generally understood sense of the word.'

10 FEBRUARY 1962
USA/USSR The US releases convicted Soviet spy Col Rudolf Abel in exchange for captured U-2 pilot Gary Powers. On 6 March the CIA announces that Powers has been absolved of any dereliction of duty.

26 FEBRUARY 1962
South Vietnam The Saigon palace of President Diem is bombed and partially burned by two dissident pilots of the South Vietnamese Air Force (American-trained, and flying American-built planes) who drop napalm bombs and strafe the area. The president is unharmed.

9 MARCH 1962
Guatemala A long period of civil strife begins with a student strike protesting results of the 1961 elections and demanding dissolution of President Miguel Ydigoras Fuente's regime. Ydigoras claims Cuban instigation, and on 19 March the army imposes a 30-day siege on Guatemala City. On 25 November loyal troops crush a revolt by elements of the Guatemalan Air Force.

14 MARCH 1962
International In Geneva, the 17-nation disarmament conference begins deliberations on general and complete disarmament under joint US/USSR chairmanship. France has refused to participate. The USSR again rejects US-proposed international inspection in any nuclear test ban.

18 MARCH 1962
Argentina Perónist parties gain widespread election victories, including 10 governorships. The military, opposed to the Perónists, calls for resignation of

Fidel Castro addresses a crowd in Havana and announces a Communist victory: 4 February 1962.

IN SEARCH OF STABILITY 1946-1962

President Arturo Frondizi, who had lifted the government ban against Perónist candidates. When Frondizi refuses to accede, a military coup seizes control on 28 March. New President José Maria Guido establishes rule by decree in May.

7 APRIL 1962
Yugoslavia Milovan Djilas, formerly number-two man in the Tito regime, is rearrested after 15 months of freedom (he had served a four-year term for anti-communist writings). Convicted 14 May of having divulged official secrets in his new book *Conversations With Stalin*, he is sentenced to five years in prison.

20 APRIL 1962
USA In apparent response to the Freedom Rides challenging Southern discrimination in public-transport facilities, a New Orleans segregationist group begins providing free one-way transportation and travel expenses for blacks to Northern cities.

25 APRIL 1962
USA The US resumes atmospheric nuclear testing, with a detonation near Christmas Island in the Pacific. The Geneva nuclear test-ban talks reconvened on 15 March.

12 MAY 1962
Laos After a series of attacks on Royal Laotian government posts, the procommunist Pathet Lao drives government forces from northern Laos, in violation of the 1961 cease-fire. In response, on 15 May President Kennedy orders 4000 more US troops to neighboring Thailand, by invitation of the Thai Government; 1000 US troops are already stationed there. By 29 May a squadron of British jet fighters, and small air and ground forces from Australia and New Zealand, have also arrived in Thailand.

17 MAY 1962
Hong Kong/China The Hong Kong Government begins a barbed-wire fence on the colony's Chinese border to deter illegal immigration. This month 50,000 refugees have entered Hong Kong without interference by communist border guards. On 21 May Nationalist China offers to accept all who want to come to Taiwan. By the end of May the flow of refugees ends. Of the estimated 70,000 who crossed the border, all but 12,000 were sent back to Communist China.

11 JUNE 1962
Laos The three feuding princes agree on formation of a coalition government, with neutralist Prince Souvanna Phouma as premier. On 22 June Souvanna declares that Laos no longer recognizes SEATO protection. On 17 September the US begins withdrawing its military contingent, per the 23 July Geneva agreement on Laotian neutrality.

16 JUNE 1962
Africa The Casablanca bloc nations (Morocco, Ghana, Guinea, Mali, and the UAR) agree to form a high military command with headquarters in Ghana under leadership of an Egyptian general. On 17 June they establish an African common market, to become effective 1 January 1963.

18 JUNE 1962
Canada With growing economic problems, national elections result in defeat of the Conservative Party led by Prime Minister John Diefenbaker. Diefenbaker forms a minority government and on 24 June announces an austerity program, including a $250-million reduction in government expenditures and arrangement of international loans and credits totaling over $1 billion.

25 JUNE 1962
USA In a 6-to-1 decision based on the First Amendment, the Supreme Court rules that the reciting of an official prayer in New York State public schools is unconstitutional.

1 JULY 1962
Algeria In a national referendum, Algerians cast an overwhelming vote for independence, with most Europeans favoring the move. On 3 July de Gaulle proclaims the independence of Algeria.

1 AUGUST 1962
Ghana President Kwame Nkrumah is unhurt in an assassination attempt in northern Ghana by a bomb that kills four and injures 56. This is the first reported attempt on his life, although 10 months earlier 50 persons charged with plotting his assassination had been arrested.

6 AUGUST 1962
Jamaica After 307 years as a British possession, the Caribbean island becomes independent, with dominion status within the British Commonwealth. On 31 August Trinidad and Tobago become independent within the Commonwealth.

15 AUGUST 1962
Indonesia The Netherlands and Indonesia sign an agreement transferring administration of West New Guinea to the UN on 1 October, then to Indonesia on 1 May 1963. A cease-fire between Dutch troops and Indonesian paratroopers and guerillas in West New Guinea goes into effect 17 August.

10–19 SEPTEMBER 1962
Great Britain In London, leaders of the 15 Commonwealth nations and 9 British colonial territories confer on the issue of Britain's admission to the Common Market. Prime Minister Macmillan predicts the Common Market could become a third-world power rivalling the US and USSR in population, wealth, and skills. Commonwealth leaders express doubt about the protection of their exports, but allow that the decision on joining is Britain's alone.

6 NOVEMBER 1962

13 SEPTEMBER 1962
USA President Kennedy denounces burning of churches in Georgia to discourage black voter-registration drives and assures government protection.

26 SEPTEMBER 1962
Algeria Following a postindependence power struggle and a threat of civil war, Mohammed Ben Bella is designated premier after the 20 September national election. Ben Bella pledges to build a socialist state which would be 'neutralist and nonengaged' in the East-West conflict.

30 SEPTEMBER 1962
USA Riots occur at the University of Mississippi in Oxford after several hundred US marshals escort James Meredith to the campus to take up residence and register as the school's first black student. Rioting is quelled with the aid of some 3000 US soldiers and federalized National Guardsmen.

9 OCTOBER 1962
Uganda Uganda becomes an independent nation within the British Commonwealth. Milton Obote becomes prime minister, and a federal government is established to overcome objections by Buganda ruler Sir Edward Mutesa II.

11 OCTOBER 1962
Vatican Pope John XXIII opens the 21st Ecumeni-

cal Council, or Vatican II, with a call for Christian unity. This is the largest gathering of the Roman Catholic hierarchy in history; among delegate-observers are representatives of major Protestant denominations, in itself a sign of sweeping change.

20 OCTOBER 1962
India/China Chinese Communist troops invade India along the common border. On 29 October Prime Minister Nehru requests US and British military aid; on 31 October he dismisses Krishna Menon as Defense Minister and assumes the post himself. As Indian forces continue to retreat before the massive Chinese advance, Nehru requests further US aid on 19 November. Two days later the Chinese unexpectedly announce a unilateral cease-fire and withdrawal of forces from the northeast frontier.

22–28 OCTOBER 1962
Cuba/US/USSR A Soviet offensive buildup in Cuba is revealed to the American people by President Kennedy, who orders a naval and air blockade on further shipment of military equipment to the island nation. Following a confrontation that threatens nuclear war, Kennedy and Khrushchev agree 28 October on a formula to end the crisis. On 2 November Kennedy reports that Soviet missile bases in Cuba are being dismantled.

6 NOVEMBER 1962
USA In the largest election turnout to date in a

KASIMOV WITH IL–28 FUSELAGE CRATES ENROUTE TO CUBA
28 SEPTEMBER 1962

The Russian ship Kasimov *carrying IL-28 airplane fuselages to Cuba, 28 September 1962.*

IN SEARCH OF STABILITY 1946-1962

nonpresidential year, the Democrats retain Congressional strength. Results are viewed as a substantial endorsement of President Kennedy's programs. In gubernatorial races, former Vice-President Richard M Nixon is defeated for the California governorship. Bitter in conceding defeat, Nixon denounces the press as biased against him.

8 DECEMBER 1962

Borneo A revolt begins against British control of Brunei, a protectorate on the island of Borneo, and spreads to the neighboring British Crown Colonies of Sarawak and North Borneo. Rebels oppose British plans to merge the three territories with Singapore and Malaysia in the proposed Federation of Malaysia. Thousands of British troops are rushed in from Singapore, and by 13 December the main strength of the revolt has been crushed.

9 DECEMBER 1962

Tanganyika The British-mandated territory becomes a republic within the commonwealth, with Julius K Nyerere as its first president.

14 DECEMBER 1962

International Following a three-day Panama City meeting, foreign ministers of five Central American countries sign the San Salvador Charter to establish the Organization of Central American States, patterned after the Organization of American States. Parties to the pact are Costa Rica, Nicaragua, Honduras, El Salvador, and Guatemala. Permanent headquarters will be in San Salvador.

20 DECEMBER 1962

Dominican Republic In its first free election in 38 years, the nation chooses leftist Juan Bosch Gaviño as president.

23–24 DECEMBER 1962

Cuba/USA The 1113 prisoners of the 1961 Cuban invasion are released and flown to Miami following an agreement providing for delivery to Cuba of $53 million worth of medicine, medical equipment, and baby food, donated by drug, medical, and food companies. A last-minute obstacle was removed when $2.9 million ransom in cash was raised from private sources.

29 DECEMBER 1962

Congo In an apparent attempt to end Katanga's secession, United Nations troops attack Elisabethville and other points.

OTHER EVENTS OF 1962

Science The first evidence for 'restriction enzymes' (which could serve as 'scalpels' to cut out genes in chromosomes and allow for gene splicing) is found.

Medicine/Health The Thalidomide scandal breaks out in the US, although phocomelia ('seal limbs') a congenital deformity, had begun to appear in West Germany as early as 1955. European physicians began to realize that the high incidence of deformity was resulting from ingestion of the tranquilizer Thalidomide by pregnant women. Some 7000 children will be affected (80 percent of them in West Germany). The US was spared primarily because Dr Frances Kelsey, a Canadian-born medical officer with the Food and Drug Administration, denied the drug clearance on the grounds of inadequate testing. Britain's Royal College of Physicians issues a report linking smoking to health problems.

Technology On 20 February John Glenn becomes the first American to orbit the earth. The US completes the first interplanetary mission when *Mariner II* passes within 22,000 miles of Venus. The US launches the first nuclear-powered merchant vessel, the *Savannah*, and Britain inaugurates passenger service with a Hovercraft.

Environment An earthquake in Iran leaves 10,000 dead, and an avalanche in Peru kills 3500. Rachel Carson, American biologist, publishes *Silent Spring*, one of the first works to alert the public to the growing ecological danger of using chemicals as pesticides.

Social Studies Claude Levi-Strauss's *The Savage Mind*; Thomas Kuhn's *The Structure of Scientific Revolutions*; Marshall McLuhan's *The Gutenberg Galaxy*.

Literature Solzhenitsyn's *One Day in the Life of Ivan Denisovich*; Faulkner's *The Reivers*; Katherine Ann Porter's *Ship of Fools*; Doris Lessing's *The Golden Notebook*; Mario Vargas Llosa's *The City and the Dogs*; James Baldwin's *Another Country*; Vladimir Nabokov's *Pale Fire*; Ken Kesey's *One Flew Over the Cuckoo's Nest*.

Drama/Entertainment Edward Albee's *Who's Afraid of Virginia Wolff?*; David Lean's *Lawrence of Arabia*.

The Arts Pop Art breaks onto the New York art scene with works by Andy Warhol, Roy Lichtenstein, James Rosenquist, Jasper Johns, and Robert Indiana. Sidney Nolan, the Australian artist, does his *Ned Kelly Series*.

Architecture Eero Saarinen's Trans World Flight Center at Kennedy Airport. The new Coventry Cathedral is consecrated; Basil Spence has been the primary architect and major British artists are represented throughout the edifice.

Music Britten's *War Requiem*; Shostakovich's 13th Symphony (*Babi Yar*).

Miscellaneous Tokyo becomes the first-known city to have a population over 10 million. World population is now about 3,100,000,000; 44 percent of all adults are still illiterate.

Pope John XXIII reads his Easter message to the world, 2 April 1961.

The Pentagon, Washington, DC.

1963-1973:
A TURBULENT DECADE

An A-7 Corsair II is launched from the USS Ranger *to conduct an air strike in North Vietnam.*

1 JANUARY 1963
Taiwan/China Taiwan reveals that the Nationalist Chinese have sent many specialists to the Chinese mainland to train anticommunist guerrillas and reports anticommunist uprisings in Kwangtung Province six months earlier. In his New Year's message, Chiang Kai-shek predicts the downfall of the Chinese Communists.

2 JANUARY 1963
South Vietnam/USA The number of Americans killed in action since the US began aiding South Vietnam rises to 30 when five US helicopters are shot down by Communist guerrillas in the Mekong Delta.

14 JANUARY 1963
France/Great Britain President de Gaulle vetoes Britain's 17-month effort to enter the Common Market. At a news conference, de Gaulle recalls that Britain refused to participate when it was formed and had then tried to impede its progress by setting up the Outer Seven. The French position is attacked by the other five Common Market nations, and on 30 January British Prime Minister Macmillan accuses de Gaulle of 'trying to dominate Europe.' At the

same press conference, de Gaulle rejects the US-British agreement for a multilateral NATO nuclear force armed with Polaris missile submarines, forged by Macmillan and Kennedy in their December Nassau conference. De Gaulle reiterates determination to build an independent French nuclear force.

15 JANUARY 1963
Congo Following a successful UN campaign, Katanga President Moise Tshombe announces willingness to accede to UN demands that he end his province's 30-month secession from the Congo.

15–21 JANUARY 1963
USSR At the East German Communist Party congress in East Berlin attended by delegates from 70 Communist Parties, the Sino-Soviet political rift widens as East Germany's Walter Ulbricht attacks China for invading India; Khrushchev defends his line of peaceful coexistence with the West and rejects Chinese criticism of his withdrawal of Soviet missiles from Cuba.

22 JANUARY 1963
France/West Germany France's de Gaulle and

A TURBULENT DECADE 1963-1973

A member of the Vietnam Junk Force searches a native fishing vessel for Viet Cong shipments.

West German Chancellor Konrad Adenauer sign a treaty pledging co-operation in foreign policy, defense, and cultural affairs.

5 FEBRUARY 1963
Canada The minority Conservative Government of Prime Minister Diefenbaker is overthrown when the Liberal Party, led by Lester Pearson, is joined by the Social Credit Party and the New Democrats in a vote of no confidence. Diefenbaker dissolves Parliament and calls for new elections on 8 April. Following a Liberal victory, Diefenbaker resigns 17 April; Pearson is sworn in as prime minister on 22 April.

8 FEBRUARY 1963
Iraq A coup headed by the air force and supported by anticommunist army leaders overthrows the government and kills Premier Kassem and several

followers. A pro-Nasser government with absolute powers proceeds to round up communists.

15 FEBRUARY 1963
Ghana/Bulgaria A group of 17 Ghanian students, accompanied by Ghana's ambassador to Bulgaria, arrives in Vienna from Sofia to complain of racial discrimination and harsh treatment by Bulgarian authorities. Students from African nations are studying in Bulgaria, Poland, East Germany, and the USSR on scholarships provided by communist governments.

7 MARCH 1963
Yemen The US warns UAR President Nasser that bombing of Saudi Arabian towns (an outgrowth of the civil war in Yemen) endangers US-UAR relations. The UAR has provided 20,000 troops to the republi-

can government of Yemen; Saudi Arabia has helped royalist forces trying to regain control there.

8 MARCH 1963

Syria The government of Premier Khaled el Azm is overthrown by a coup of pro-Nasser army officers and Baath Party followers. During the next five months a power struggle ensues.

19 MARCH 1963

International In Costa Rica, the presidents of the US and six Central American nations sign the Declaration of San José calling for a Central American Common Market, advance of social and national development plans, and measures to alleviate the problem of exports. Pledging $6 million, President Kennedy asserts that 'economic prosperity is the handmaiden of political liberty.'

2 APRIL 1963

USA A major black civil-rights campaign against segregation, led by Martin Luther King, begins in Birmingham, Alabama. Within three weeks, over 400 protestors have been arrested. On 2–7 May police use dogs and firemen high-pressure firehoses to break up parades; 2500 demonstrators are arrested, including many children. The 11 May bombings of a black leader's home and of a desegregated motel cause President Kennedy to reassign federal troops to bases near Birmingham.

27 APRIL 1963

Cuba/USSR Castro leaves on a month-long visit to the Soviet Union. He is honored at the traditional May Day celebration in Red Square, and at a 23 May Kremlin reception is awarded the USSR's highest decoration, Hero of the Soviet Union.

28 APRIL 1963

Haiti/Dominican Republic The Dominican Republic warns of possible armed reprisals against Haiti over a conflict on violation of diplomatic immunity. Twenty-two political foes of the Duvalier regime have taken refuge in the Dominican embassy, leading Haiti to surround the Port-au-Prince embassy with armed soldiers. After an OAS emergency meeting, Duvalier backs down.

9 MAY 1963

South Vietnam South Vietnam agrees to pay the total $17 million cost of establishing 'strategic hamlets.' In a controversial attempt to isolate rural peasants from Vietcong guerrillas, President Diem institutes the unpopular program of uprooting villagers to resettle them in barbed-wire compounds.

11 MAY 1963

Canada/USA The issue of Canadian nuclear armament, which brought down the Diefenbaker government, is resolved as Prime Minister Pearson reaches an agreement to accept US nuclear warheads for Canadian missiles. The final pact is signed on 16

THE CIVIL RIGHTS STRUGGLE

Slavery as a legal institution had been banished in the United States in 1865 by the Thirteenth Amendment. Yet nearly a century later black Americans were still denied full citizenship rights. Blacks successfully challenged this latter-day 'peculiar institution' with the Civil Rights Movement and won equality under the law. The centuries-old struggle for racial equality first gained momentum after December 1955, when Rosa Parks was arrested in Montgomery, Alabama, for violating a public transportation segregation ordinance. Throughout the late 1950s and 1960s blacks and their white supporters battled racism with sit-ins, voter registration drives, and protest marches. The greatest display ever of racial solidarity in America came on 28 August 1963, when 250,000 Civil Rights activists participated in the March on Washington. It was here that Dr Martin Luther King Jr, the strongest voice in the struggle, gave his famous 'I Have a Dream' speech, exhorting the United States and other nations to work for universal peace and justice. It was by no means the end of the struggle, but that event moved it into an arena where no one could deny its existence—or outcome.

August, with the stipulation that the nuclear warheads would remain under US control on Canadian soil, but could not be used without Canadian authorization.

18 MAY 1963

Indonesia The 600-member Congress, whose delegates were appointed by President Sukarno, votes unanimously to make Sukarno president for life.

22 MAY 1963

International The USSR announces that it will not pay its share of United Nations expenses, initiating a lengthy dispute about the UN peace-keeping forces, to which a number of members object.

22–25 MAY 1963

Africa Representatives of 30 independent African states, including 29 heads of state, meet in Addis Ababa, Ethiopia, to form the Organization for African Unity for co-operation in politics, economics, education, and defense.

3 JUNE 1963

Vatican Pope John XXIII dies at 81 after a brief $4\frac{1}{2}$-year reign that had worldwide effects. He is hailed for his advocacy of world peace, initiative toward Christian unity, and efforts toward modernizing the Roman Catholic Church. On 21 June Giovanni Battista Cardinal Montini, Archbishop of Milan, is elected to succeed him (crowned Pope Paul VI on 30 June).

5 JUNE 1963

Cuba An Organization of American States report reveals that Communist subversion in Latin America,

A TURBULENT DECADE 1963-1973

A scene from the Birmingham riots.

with Cuba as its base, 'has increased considerably during the past year' and that Castro 'has begun a new phase of promoting and encouraging violent subversion.'

10 JUNE 1963

South Vietnam Buddhist priest Ngo Quang Duc commits suicide by self-immolation to dramatize the Buddhist protest against persecution by the Diem Government. In the following months Buddhists organize a series of mass demonstrations, and other monks and nuns burn themselves to death—marshaling world opinion against Diem.

11 JUNE 1963

USA Alabama Governor George Wallace defies a presidential order to allow registration of two black students at the University of Alabama. Kennedy federalizes the Alabama National Guard and Wallace steps aside from his position in front of the registration room. On 2 September Wallace blocks desegregation of Tuskegee High School and various elementary schools until Kennedy again federalizes the National Guard.

12 JUNE 1963

USA Medgar Evers, NAACP field secretary and civil-rights leader, is murdered by a white sniper in Jackson, Mississippi.

1 JULY 1963

Great Britain Former British diplomat and newspaper correspondent Kim Philby is revealed as the third man in the 1951 Guy Burgess-Donald Maclean spy case. On 30 July *Izvestia* reports that Philby has been granted Soviet asylum and citizenship.

31 JULY 1963

Great Britain The lurid scandal involving former Secretary of State for War John Profumo that rocked the Macmillan Government concludes with the conviction of osteopath Stephen Ward for living off the earnings of prostitutes Christine Keeler and Marilyn Rice-Davies. Ward commits suicide.

5 AUGUST 1963

International In a Kremlin ceremony, the nuclear test-ban treaty is signed by foreign ministers of Britain, the US, and the USSR. Its duration unlimited, the pact bans nuclear tests in the atmosphere, outer space, and underwater, and provides for ongoing negotiations on underground tests. The treaty becomes effective 10 October.

7 AUGUST 1963

West Germany The government reports that 16,456 East Germans have escaped to the West in the two years since the Berlin Wall went up.

28 AUGUST 1963

USA In the largest demonstration to date in Washington, over 200,000 persons—mostly black,

---

MARTIN LUTHER KING, JR, 1929–1968

American minister and civil-rights leader Martin Luther King, Jr came from a respected family of Baptist ministers in Atlanta, Georgia. As a student at Crozier Theological Seminary and Boston University, he joined his Christian beliefs with a deep desire for racial harmony through nonviolent resistance to discriminatory laws. In 1955 he led the Montgomery, Alabama, boycott of city buses protesting Rosa Parks's arrest for violation of segregation laws. He and his family were subjected to harassment, his home was bombed, and he was jailed on conspiracy charges. In 1957 he helped form the Southern Christian Leadership Conference and became a national symbol of the aspirations of black Americans. His 'I have a dream' address to the civil rights march on Washington in 1963 moved the conscience of the nation. In 1964 he received an honorary doctorate from Yale, the Kennedy peace prize, and the Nobel Peace Prize. Like his hero Gandhi, the nonviolent King was destined to die by violence: he was assassinated by James Earl Ray during a civil-rights mission to Memphis, Tennessee, in 1968. Riots erupted in 63 cities as the black community expressed its outrage and grief; 150,000 mourners attended his funeral in Atlanta. The tragedy of King's death ultimately served to advance the cause of civil rights still further, and its leader was honored in 1983 by the creation of a national holiday in his name.

---

but including thousands of whites—demand full civil rights for blacks. The peaceful demonstration climaxes in Martin Luther King's Lincoln Memorial speech in which he proclaims 'I have a dream. . . .'

30 AUGUST 1963

USA/USSR The 'hot line,' or direct communications link between Moscow and Washington, becomes operational. It is designed to reduce the risk of accidental war by allowing heads of the US and Soviet Governments to exchange messages immediately rather than through diplomatic channels.

15 SEPTEMBER 1963

USA In Birmingham, Alabama, a bomb explodes in a black church during Sunday services, killing four girls and injuring 20 others. The church had been used as a rallying point for civil-rights demonstrations. The explosion leads to racial rioting that is quelled by the National Guard and state troopers.

16 SEPTEMBER 1963

Malaysia Malaysia comes into being as a new nation federated from Malaya, Singapore, Sarawak, and North Borneo (renamed Sabah). Kuala Lumpur is to be the capital.

1 OCTOBER 1963

Nigeria Nigeria is declared a republic, with Nnamdi Azikiwe as its first president.

A TURBULENT DECADE 1963-1973

10 OCTOBER 1963
Great Britain Citing ill health, Prime Minister Macmillan announces his decision to retire after nearly seven years in office. His resignation is effective 18 October, and the Queen calls on Foreign Secretary Lord Home to form a government. Home renounces all his titles as a peer, becoming Sir Alec Douglas-Home, and runs for a Commons seat in a by-election, meeting the traditional qualifications for prime minister.

15 OCTOBER 1963
West Germany Chancellor Konrad Adenauer, 87, submits his resignation after a 14-year tenure during the nation's recovery from World War II. On 16 October the Bundestag elects his successor, Ludwig Erhard, the Vice-Chancellor and Economics Minister.

1–2 NOVEMBER 1963
South Vietnam A group of South Vietnamese generals, with Kennedy Administration complicity, overthrows the government of President Ngo Dinh Diem. Diem and his brother, secret police chief Ngo Dinh Nhu, are seized and killed.

22 NOVEMBER 1963
USA President Kennedy is fatally wounded by an assassin as he rides in a motorcade through Dallas, Texas. Vice-President Lyndon B Johnson is sworn in as president shortly afterward. Lee Harvey Oswald is arrested and charged with Kennedy's murder, but he is shot to death on 24 November by Dallas nightclub owner Jack Ruby during a jail transfer.

12 DECEMBER 1963
Kenya Kenya becomes an independent nation within the British Commonwealth, with Jomo Kenyatta as prime minister. A year later Kenya becomes a republic and a one-party state, when the opposition Kenya African Democratic Union led by Tom Mboya merges with Kenyatta's African National Union Party.

18 DECEMBER 1963
USSR Some 500 African students stage a demonstration in Moscow's Red Square, protesting racial discrimination and the death of a Ghanian student under suspicious circumstances. Among the placards displayed is one proclaiming, 'Moscow, a second Alabama.'

21 DECEMBER 1963
Cyprus Fighting breaks out between Turkish and Greek Cypriots, when the Turks oppose Archbishop Makarios's efforts to amend the Cypriot Constitution to the detriment of the Turkish minority.

OTHER EVENTS OF 1963
Science 'Quasistellar radio sources' have been reported for several years. At an historic international symposium in Dallas, Texas, astrophysicists begin to define 'quasars.'

Medicine/Health The first live measles-virus vaccine is made available for immunization of the public. Dr Michael De Bakey first uses an artificial heart device to take over the circulation of a patient's blood during heart surgery.
Technology Space research is producing new data on Mars and Venus. Gerald Hawkins, a British astronomer teaching in the US, proposes that Stonehenge was used as an astronomical observatory.
Environment In the North Atlantic, an underwater eruption begins forming an island; named Surtsey, it will cover a square mile by 1967. In Indonesia, volcanic Mount Agung erupts, killing 2000 people and producing red sunsets around the world through the dust and ashes it sends into the atmosphere. Hurricane Flora leaves 6000 dead in Cuba and Haiti.
Social Sciences Yigael Yadin, Israeli archaeologist, begins excavations at Masada, the ancient fortress where in AD 73 the Romans, after a two-year siege, overwhelmed the Jews. Konrad Lorenz, the ethologist, publishes his controversial On Aggression.
Ideas/Beliefs Pope John XXIII issues the encyclical Pacem in terris, advocating peaceful settlement of disputes between Catholics and non-Catholics, particularly Communists. James Baldwin, black American author, publishes The Fire Next Time, warning that unless white America resolves its problems with blacks great violence will ensue. Betty Friedan publishes The Feminine Mystique, a book that will help trigger off what soon becomes known as the 'women's liberation movement.'
Literature Günter Grass's Dog Years; Thomas Pynchon's V; Julio Cortazar's Hopscotch; Yukio Mishima's The Sailor Who Fell from Grace with the Sea; John Le Carre's The Spy Who Came in from the Cold.
Drama/Entertainment Rolf Hochhuth's The Deputy; Kobo Abe's film The Woman in the Dunes; Fellini's $8\frac{1}{2}$; Wole Soyinka's Nigerian drama A Dance of the Forest.
The Arts Robert Indiana's The Demuth Five; Larry Rivers's Dutch Masters; Roy Lichtenstein's Girl at Piano; Rauschenberg's Windward; George Segal's Woman Sitting on a Bed. A major exhibit at the Guggenheim Museum accepts Pop Art—soup cans, comic strip-style silk screens, inflatable sculpture, and all—into the Establishment.
Architecture Le Corbusier's Carpenter Center for Visual Arts at Harvard University; Gordon Bunshaft's Beinecke Library at Yale University.
Music Shostakovich's Katerina Ismaylova (a revised version of his Lady Macbeth of Mtensk); Bernstein's Kaddish Symphony. Singers like Bob Dylan and Joan Baez lead a US revival of folk music.
Life/Customs The Second Vatican Council approves use of vernacular languages in the Roman Catholic liturgy. The Italian tourist island of Capri bans transistor radios. Four young Englishmen— John Lennon, Paul McCartney, George Harrison, Ringo Starr—named the Beatles for their insistent 4–4 beat, score a tremendous hit in a concert at the London Palladium. This will become 'Beatlemania.'

The assassination of President John F Kennedy.

A TURBULENT DECADE 1963-1973

enhanced by their appearance on America's *Ed Sullivan Show* on 9 February 1964.

Miscellaneous The Soviets send the first woman into space on 16 June: Valentina Tereshkova makes a three-day flight. The Vaiont Dam in northern Italy collapses, the resultant flood killing 1800 people. The USS *Thresher*, an American submarine, sinks in the North Atlantic with its crew of 129. The Glasgow-to-London mail train is robbed of £2,500,000.

6 JANUARY 1964

East Germany A 17-day Christmas agreement by which 1.25 million crossed the Berlin Wall from West Berlin into the Communist East for one-day visits with relatives expires.

9–10 JANUARY 1964

Panama Armed clashes between US troops and Panamanian mobs in the Canal Zone lead to a major international crisis and the deaths of 21 Panamanians and four US soldiers. Violence stems from continuing disputes over the flying of US and Panamanian flags in the Canal Zone. When the US refuses to enter formal negotiations to revise the Panama Canal treaties, Panama temporarily severs relations.

12 JANUARY 1964

Zanzibar The predominantly Arab government of the East African island, which had become independent of Britain only a month earlier, is overthrown by African nationalist rebels who proclaim a people's republic, with labor leader Abeid Karume as president and Kassim Hanga as prime minister. The US asserts that some of the rebels had been trained in Communist China and Cuba. On 26 April Zanzibar accepts the invitation to merge with Tanganyika.

13–17 JANUARY 1964

Middle East Leaders of 13 Arab League nations meet in Cairo and agree to set up a joint military command for possible use against Israel. The Arabs also take 'necessary practical resolutions' against the Israeli plan for diverting the waters of the Jordan.

25 JANUARY 1964

Africa/Great Britain Mutinies by African troops demanding higher wages and dismissal of British officers in the former British East African colonies of Tanganyika, Kenya, and Uganda are put down by British troops by request of the heads of government—Tanganyika's Julius Nyerere, Kenya's Jomo Kenyatta, and Uganda's Milton Obote.

27 JANUARY 1964

China/France The two nations announce their decision to establish diplomatic relations. The US is opposed, and on 10 February Taiwan breaks relations with France.

30 JANUARY 1964

South Vietnam The junta that has ruled the nation since Diem's overthrow is toppled from power in a bloodless coup led by Major General Nguyen Khanh, who proclaims himself chief of state and pledges victory over the communists. Three more changes of government will occur in a year's time.

6 FEBRUARY 1964

Cuba/USA Cuba cuts off the water supply to the US naval base at Guantanamo in reprisal for US seizure of four Cuban fishing boats off Florida. The US counters with a water shuttle from Jamaica and plans to build a $5 million permanent salt-water conversion plant at the base.

18 FEBRUARY 1964

USA/Cuba To penalize them for trading with Cuba, the US curtails military aid to five nations. Aid to Britain, France and Yugoslavia is ended at once, and aid to Spain and Morocco is delayed until they comply with US demands.

18 FEBRUARY 1964

Gabon/France Several hundred French soldiers are flown into Gabon's capital of Libreville to restore the government of President Leon Mba after a bloodless army coup the day before. France asserts that it is acting under a 1961 French-Gabonese defense treaty, and that the action had been requested through diplomatic channels.

8 MARCH 1964

USA Malcolm X, suspended Black Muslim leader, announces in New York City that he is forming a black nationalist party that will try to persuade blacks to shift from nonviolence to active self-defense against white supremacists.

16 MARCH 1964

USA . President Johnson submits to Congress his 'war on poverty' program, which would cost $962.5 million the first year and be administered by an Office of Economic Opportunity. Its goal is to help young people break the cycle of poverty through job training.

25 MARCH 1964

USA In a Senate speech, Chairman of the Foreign Relations Committee J W Fulbright warns that the US is 'clinging to old myths in the face of new realities,' because there are great diversities among the Communist nations, and it is time to relax the cold war. He also suggests that Panama has valid grievances against the Canal Zone treaty, and that the optimum course with Cuba may be 'acceptance of the continued existence of the Castro regime.' President Johnson publicly disagrees with Fulbright's views on Panama and Cuba.

13 APRIL 1964

Rhodesia After a right-wing faction of the white supremacist Rhodesian Front Party forces resignation of Prime Minister Winston Field, former

Treasury Minister Ian Smith is appointed. Smith vows to press for independence from Britain of Southern Rhodesia, on terms preserving the status quo—a nation of nearly four million blacks ruled by a white minority of 221,000. On 16 April Smith's Government banishes four African leaders without trial, including nationalist Joshua Nkomo.

25 MAY 1964

Egypt/USSR Khrushchev ends a 16-day trip to the UAR that includes opening the first stage of the Aswan Dam project and promising to lend $227 million to help finance the UAR's second five-year plan, scheduled to begin in 1965.

27 MAY 1964

India Prime minister of India for almost 17 years of independence, Jawaharlal Nehru dies at 74. The foremost exponent of nonalignment in the conflict between the West and the communists, he is survived by a daughter, Mrs Indira Gandhi. On 2 June Lal Bahadur Shastri is elected leader of the Indian Congress Party, automatically becoming Prime Minister-elect. Shastri, who has already served as acting prime minister for the past four months, pledges to continue Nehru's policies of domestic reform and foreign nonalignment.

28–29 MAY 1964

Middle East In the Jordanian section of Jerusalem, in its first meeting since the 1948 Arab-Israeli war, the Palestine National Congress establishes the Palestine Liberation Organization to mobilize Palestinians for recovery of their usurped homes.

3 JUNE 1964

South Korea President Park declares martial law in Seoul after 10,000 student demonstrators overpower the police in clashes around the presidential palace and other government buildings. Charging corruption and abuse of power, the students have demanded a government apology for Park's alleged misrule. Several ministers resign to placate the protesters. Martial law is lifted on 28 July.

22 JUNE 1964

USA Three civil-rights workers are reported missing in Mississippi. On 4 August the bodies of Michael Schwerner, Andrew Goodman and James E Chaney are found buried near Philadelphia, Mississippi. Twenty-one white men, including the sheriff and deputy sheriff of Neshoba County, are arrested, but charges against 19 of them are dismissed by a US Commissioner on 10 December, and the federal government drops charges against the other two.

26 JUNE 1964

Congo After a year in European exile, Moise Tshombe returns by invitation of the central Congolese Government to help form a government of reconciliation in the revolt-torn nation. On 30 June Premier Adoula resigns; 10 July Tshombe becomes premier. Insurrections continue, especially in the eastern provinces, with Communist Chinese support.

29 JUNE 1964

Cuba Castro's sister, Juana Castro Ruz, announces on Mexican television that she has defected from Cuba and is seeking political asylum in Mexico. She charges Castro with betraying Cuba to 'Russian imperialism,' inhuman treatment of thousands of political prisoners, and directing subversive infiltration in Latin America. On 2 July it is announced that she has provided information to the CIA for the past four years.

2 JULY 1964

USA President Johnson signs the Civil Rights Act of 1964, banning racial and religious discrimination in many spheres, including public accommodations.

18 JULY 1964

USA Racial tensions erupt in riots and looting in Northern urban black ghettos, beginning with New York City's Harlem. Over the next month and a half, riots break out in Brooklyn's Bedford-Stuyvesant section, several New Jersey cities, Chicago, and Philadelphia.

2–5 AUGUST 1964

Vietnam War Two US destroyers patroling in the Gulf of Tonkin off North Vietnam are attacked by North Vietnamese PT boats and sink two of them before bombing their nearby bases (5 August). On 7

TELEVISION

The cultural and communications critic Marshall McLuhan called it a 'cool' medium for the burgeoning 'electronic village,' but even those who did not look upon the phenomenon so dispassionately saw that television was having a great effect on society in the second half of the 20th century. Other countries would soon catch up, as new viewers around the world found themselves gaping at the fleeting pictures on 'the boob tube' by the hour. While its potential for enriching lives was accepted, the reality of its contents was soon subject to suspicion or outright condemnation. In 1961, for instance, Newton Minow, a member of the United States Federal Communications Commission, described American TV as 'a vast wasteland,' for its vapid offerings. By 1963 Great Britain's government was establishing a special committee to inquire into the 'moral impact' of TV on the young, and in the years to come many US groups would study the effects of violence on the young. But if McLuhan was right, none of these well-intentioned criticisms or investigations is truly pertinent. 'The medium is the message,' he declared, meaning that the content of any single program is not as significant as the fact that people are looking at television. Put another way, it did not matter whether television gained access to your living room in blue jeans or a tuxedo: it was going to make a change.

A TURBULENT DECADE 1963-1973

British Marines carry their water supplies to positions on Capbadge Peak in South Arabia.

August the US Congress passes the Gulf of Tonkin Resolution, giving President Johnson the power 'to take all necessary measures to repel any armed attack against the forces of the United States and to prevent further aggression.' Johnson will use this measure to commit massive forces in Vietnam.

7–9 AUGUST 1964
Cyprus Turkish Air Force fighter jets attack Greek Cypriot positions in a 'police action' designed to stop attacks on Turkish Cypriot villages on the northwest coast. The danger of a full-scale war in the Mediterranean abates as Turkey and Cyprus accept a UN cease-fire on 10 August.

27 SEPTEMBER 1964
USA The 888-page Warren Commission report on the assassination of President Kennedy is released. It finds that Lee Harvey Oswald acted alone. In subsequent years, based on new evidence, proponents of a conspiracy theory will posit the CIA, a group of Texas millionaires, the Mafia, the Soviet Union, and Cuba as possible instigators or agents of the assassination.

14–15 OCTOBER 1964
USSR After ten years as premier and Soviet Communist Party chief, Khrushchev is ousted, Aleksei N Kosygin replaces him as premier and Leonid I Brezhnev assumes party leadership.

15 OCTOBER 1964
Great Britain The Labour Party ends 13 years of Conservative rule, as Harold Wilson becomes prime minister, succeeding Sir Alec Douglas-Home. Labour's program includes nationalization of the steel industry, income-tax and gasoline price increases, and new welfare and national health benefits.

16 OCTOBER 1964
China The government announces that it has conducted its first successful nuclear test in the western province of Sinkiang, and demands a world summit to outlaw atomic weapons and destroy existing nuclear stockpiles.

24 OCTOBER 1964
Zambia The former British protectorate of Northern Rhodesia becomes the republic of Zambia, ending 73 years of British rule. Sworn in as president of the new state is Dr Kenneth D Kuanda, leader of the United National Independence Party.

1 NOVEMBER 1964
Vietnam War Communist guerrilla mortar fire rakes the US air base at Bien Hoa, killing four Americans and wounding 72, with two Vietnamese fatalities and five injuries. The attack destroys five US B-57 jet bombers and damages 15 others, plus four US helicopters and three Vietnamese A1H Skyraider bombers. This is the worst military setback sustained by the US to date.

LYNDON BAINES JOHNSON, 1908–1973

The 36th president of the United States, Lyndon B Johnson was born in Stonewall, Texas, and worked his way through college to become a teacher. Gaining political acumen as a congressman's secretary, he was elected as a Democratic representative in 1936 and served in the US Navy after Pearl Harbor. 'LBJ' became a senator in 1948 and vice-president under John F Kennedy in 1961, after a long tenure as Senate majority leader. He succeeded to the presidency upon Kennedy's assassination in November 1963 and was elected to a full term in 1964. During his administration the Civil Rights Act (1964) and the Voting Rights Act (1965) were passed under the aegis of his 'Great Society' program for civil-rights and social-welfare legislation. His pursuit and escalation of the Vietnam War eroded the popular support that had won him a huge majority in 1964. In 1968 he announced his decision not to seek reelection and retired from politics.

---

2 NOVEMBER 1964
Saudi Arabia Prince Faisal becomes king of Saudi Arabia after his incompetent brother Saud is deposed.

3 NOVEMBER 1964
USA Lyndon B Johnson scores a landslide victory over Barry Goldwater to win a full term as president.

10 NOVEMBER 1964
Australia The government institutes compulsory military training in view of impending troop commitments in Southeast Asia. Australia had allocated troops to the Korean War, and in September it dispatched forces and equipment to southern Malaysia for the campaign against Indonesian guerrillas.

25 NOVEMBER 1964
Congo A 600-man Belgian paratroop battalion is flown to Stanleyville, the Congolese rebel capital, in US Air Force planes to rescue white hostages. Withdrawal of Belgian troops and American planes begins on 27 November, after rescue of 1650 persons of 17 nationalities, including 55 Americans. More than 80 others had been slain by the rebels.

2 DECEMBER 1964
Argentina Former dictator Juan Perón flies to Brazil from Spain in an effort to return to his native land; detained in Rio de Janeiro by Brazilian authorities for 16 hours, he is returned to Madrid.

OTHER EVENTS OF 1964
Science Physicists at Brookhaven on Long Island, New York, discover a fundamental particle, the omega-minus, whose properties provide a link between other particles in the atom's nucleus.

Medicine/Health The US Surgeon General issues the report *Smoking and Health*, which strongly links cancer with cigarette smoking.

Technology First photographs of the lunar surface

A TURBULENT DECADE 1963-1973

DAILY NEWS
NEW YORK'S PICTURE NEWSPAPER ®

Vol. 46, No. 113 Copt. 1964 News Syndicate Co. Inc. New York, N.Y. 10017, Wednesday, November 4, 1964*   WEATHER: Sunny and pleasant.

ELECTION FINAL

7¢
10¢ OUTSIDE L I AND SUBURBS

LBJ WINS BIG

Kennedy Senator, Swamps Keating

Lyndon Johnson smiles after his election.

and close-ups of Mars are transmitted by satellites. Jack Kilby, an American, receives the first patent for miniaturized electronic circuits.

Environment One of the worst recorded earthquakes (8.4 on the Richter scale), centered near Anchorage, Alaska, causes much damage in Alaska and on the northwestern US coast, with 110 lives lost.

Social Studies Ioannis and Eti Sakellarakis, Greek archaeologists, begin excavations at Arkhanes, Crete, that will yield an extensive necropolis. Marshall McLuhan's *Understanding Media* will become influential.

Literature Solzhenitsyn's *The First Circle*; Bellow's *Herzog*; William Golding's *The Spire*; John Berryman's *77 Dream Songs*; Donald Barthelme's *Come Back, Dr Caligari*.

Drama/Entertainment Arthur Miller's *After the Fall*; John Osborne's *Inadmissible Evidence*; Kubrick's *Dr Strangelove, Or How I Learned to Stop Worrying and Love the Bomb*; Antonioni's *Red Desert*; the Beatles' *A Hard Day's Night*.

The Arts Op Art begins to attract admirers with such works as Bridget Riley's *Current*. David Smith's *Cubi* sculpture adds to his reputation.

Music Ginastera's *Bomarzo*; Stockhausen's *Plus/Minus*; Mahler's *10th Symphony* (as completed by Deryck Cooke); Roger Sessions's opera *Montezuma* (completed in 1947).

Life/Customs The Twist and its variations (Frug, Monkey, Watusi) become the rage on the dance floor.

Miscellaneous The first US pilot is shot down and captured in Vietnam, and the first US Congressional Medal of Honor of the Vietnam War is awarded.

4 JANUARY 1965

USA In his State of the Union address, President Johnson describes his goals for the Great Society, calling for federal support of education, health care, and the arts, and projects to improve the cities, break down regional pockets of poverty, and reduce water pollution. He also appeals to Congress to eliminate all obstacles to the right to vote. Before the end of the month the president calls on Congress to provide health care for the elderly and disabled (Medicare), grants for public schools, and appropriations for a new submarine missile—the Poseidon.

20 JANUARY 1965

Israel/West Germany West Germany has begun shipping $80 million worth of military equipment, including helicopters, antiaircraft guns, tanks, and submarines, to Israel. Chancellor Erhard has authorized the shipments on the ground that West Germany has a moral obligation to help the Jewish state attain security. After a United Arab Republic warning, shipments stop on 12 February. After the 24 February visit of Walter Ulbricht to Cairo, West Germany ends economic aid to the UAR.

1 FEBRUARY 1965

USA Martin Luther King and 770 other civil-rights workers are arrested in Selma, Alabama, during a demonstration to end discrimination in voter-registration procedures. King spends four days in jail, then confers with President Johnson, who promises prompt action on voter-rights legislation.

6 FEBRUARY 1965

Vietnam War Viet Cong guerrillas attack the US military base at Pleiku killing eight Americans and wounding 126. Next day President Johnson orders bombing of North Vietnamese positions, including the Don Hoi base. On 10 February the Vietcong blow up a US barracks at Quinhon, killing 23 Americans. In reprisal 160 US and South Vietnamese planes bomb and strafe barracks and staging areas in North Vietnam in the biggest air strike of the war thus far.

15 FEBRUARY 1965

Canada The nation's new maple leaf flag, symbolizing desired unity between French- and Anglo-Canadians, is raised for the first time in an Ottawa ceremony.

21 FEBRUARY 1965

USA Malcolm X, former Black Muslim leader and founder of his own extremist Black Nationalist movement, is shot to death as he is about to address a rally in New York City. The three men arrested for the slaying are connected to the Black Muslims.

24 FEBRUARY 1965

West Germany In view of the many cases still pending, the Cabinet votes unanimously to extend the statute of limitations for the prosecution of Nazi war criminals. The old statute is due to expire 8 May.

2 MARCH 1965

International Cabinet ministers of West Germany, France, Italy, Belgium, the Netherlands, and Luxembourg agree to merge executive bodies of the European Community's three groups—The European Common Market (EEC), European Atomic Energy Community (Euratom), and European Coal and Steel Community (ECSC)—effective 1 January 1966. The merger is seen as proof of the economic integration of the six nations.

Vietnam War With the first raid in a massive bombing campaign (Rolling Thunder) US forces openly cross the line between military advisors and combatants. Continuous US bombing raids over North Vietnam are meant to force the communists to the conference table, but Hanoi says there will be no negotiations until US forces withdraw. A 13–19 May halt in the raids engenders no response from the North.

4 MARCH 1965

Syria The government orders nationalization of nine oil companies, including affiliates of two American firms and a British-Dutch owned company.

A TURBULENT DECADE 1963-1973

8–9 MARCH 1965
Vietnam War Over 3500 Marines, the first official US combat troops in Vietnam, arrive to protect the air force base at Danang. They join 23,500 US personnel already in Vietnam as military advisers.

19 MARCH 1965
Indonesia The government seizes three American oil companies, a Dutch-British oil firm, and Goodyear Tire and Rubber Company. All other foreign-owned properties are taken over on 24 April.

20 MARCH 1965
USA President Johnson federalizes the Alabama National Guard and orders regular forces to Alabama to protect the Selma-to-Montgomery voting rights march led by Martin Luther King. The five-day, 54-mile trek begins 21 March with 3200 protestors, but a court order limits the number of participants to 300 each day. On 25 March 25,000 demonstrators mass before the state capitol to deliver a civil-rights petition to Governor Wallace.

19 APRIL 1965
Turkey/Greece The Turkish Government announces that 3000 Greek citizens will be expelled from Turkey. Over the past year 9000 Greeks have left voluntarily or have been deported as a result of hostilities over the Cyprus situation.

28–29 APRIL 1965
Dominican Republic/USA President Johnson sends 405 Marines and airborne units to the Dominican Republic, in the throes of a military power struggle, to protect US citizens in the Caribbean nation and 'to see that no Communist government is established.' Fighting continues despite a 5 May truce, by which date the US has 12,439 soldiers and 6924 Marines in the strife-torn nation. At the end of May, OAS troops will replace US forces, which reach a maximum of 20,000.

29 APRIL 1965
Australia Prime Minister Menzies announces the unpopular decision to send an 800-man battalion to South Vietnam to fight the Vietcong. This is at the request of the South Vietnamese Government and in consultation with the US Department of Defense. Despite popular opposition, New Zealand also sends a small contingent to South Vietnam.

12 MAY 1965
Israel/West Germany In a joint communique, the two nations announce the establishment of diplomatic relations. This move prompts the Arab nations of Jordan, Iraq, Syria, Lebanon, Yemen, Saudi Arabia, Algeria, Kuwait, Sudan, and the UAR to sever relations with West Germany.

8 JUNE 1965
Vietnam War The State Department reports that General William Westmoreland, Commander of US forces in South Vietnam, has been authorized by President Johnson to commit his ground troops to direct combat against the Vietcong, if requested to do so by the South Vietnamese Army.

19 JUNE 1965
Algeria President Ahmed Ben Bella, in power for three years, is arrested and deposed in a bloodless, army-backed coup led by his long-time supporter Colonel Houari Boumedienne, vice-president and defense minister. Boumedienne, a socialist and nationalist, becomes president on 5 July.
South Vietnam Air Vice-Marshal Nguyen Cao Ky, 34, becomes the nation's youngest premier, forming its eighth government since the November 1963 overthrow of the Diem regime.

15 JULY 1965
Greece Premier George Papandreou is forced to resign following a dispute over his plan to assume the post of defense minister and purge the army of right-wing elements. Student rioting follows on 21 June in Athens, and a general strike on 27 July.

28 JULY 1965
Vietnam War President Johnson announces that US forces in Vietnam will be increased from 75,000 to 125,000 men, and that the draft will be doubled from 17,000 to 35,000 a month to support the war in Indochina. At the press conference, Johnson proclaims, 'We will not surrender, and we will not retreat.' By year's end America has 184,000 men in Vietnam.

5 AUGUST 1965
India/Pakistan A new Kashmir crisis begins as India charges that Pakistani infiltrators from across the cease-fire line have fired on Indian patrols. Other incidents follow, and on 16 August India announces that its troops have begun a major drive across the cease-fire line in the direction of Lahore. On 24 August India reports that it has trapped 3000 Pakistani troops and guerrillas. On 22 September both sides accept a UN truce, but sporadic cease-fire violations continue.

7 AUGUST 1965
Singapore Prime ministers of Singapore and Malaysia sign a pact separating Singapore from the new Federation of Malaysia, which has been repeatedly attacked by Indonesian guerrillas and suffers from internal tension between the ethnic Chinese (who make up 75 percent of the Singapore population) and the Malayans, who control the central government. The pact provides for a joint defense council and commercial ties, as well as for continued British military bases in Singapore.

11–16 AUGUST 1965
USA A major race riot breaks out in the Watts area of Los Angeles. Urban blacks, protesting police brutality, loot and burn stores and other buildings,

Rhodesian Prime Minister Ian Smith casts his ballot—Election Day 1977.

A TURBULENT DECADE 1963-1973

resulting in the deaths of 35 persons and property damage estimated at $200 million. A later commission report will suggest that high unemployment played a major role in the violence.

2 SEPTEMBER 1965
China A global strategy article by Defense Minister Lin Piao calls for a 'people's war' in Africa, Asia, and Latin America to win final victory over the US and Western Europe. This marks the beginning of the cultural revolution, to last through 1968, as China tries to spread revolution abroad and impose internal progress in the midst of an often violent political struggle.

28 SEPTEMBER 1965
Cuba Castro announces that all Cubans who wish to may leave for the US in small boats; in the same speech he cites Cuba's severe housing shortage. The exodus begins on 7 October; on 1 December a US airlift of refugees begins. Over the next five years, several hundred thousand Cubans, many from the educated classes, will leave their homeland.

30 SEPTEMBER 1965
Indonesia The army crushes a communist attempt to seize power after kidnapping its chief of staff and five generals. President Sukarno appoints General Suharto as temporary army chief. On 8 October a general rout of the communists begins—tens of thousands of them are massacred throughout the country.

4 OCTOBER 1965
Vatican Pope Paul VI visits New York primarily to deliver a peace appeal before the UN General Assembly.

15–16 OCTOBER 1965
Vietnam War A series of nationwide antiwar demonstrations begins in California with a 10,000-person march from Berkeley to the Oakland army base. A like number march down New York's Fifth Avenue, and similar demonstrations occur in Philadelphia, Boston, and Ann Arbor, Michigan. Draft cards are burned and in coming months two Quakers and a member of the Catholic Worker movement burn themselves to death in symbolic protest.

11 NOVEMBER 1965
Rhodesia The minority white government led by Ian Smith declares the country independent of Britain; Britain declares this illegal and treasonable, announcing a series of economic sanctions. The next day the UN Security Council calls on all nations to refrain from rendering aid or recognition to 'this illegal racist minority regime.' On 17 December Britain imposes an oil embargo on Rhodesia, which counters by barring oil shipments to neighboring Zambia, a leading copper producer. Britain and the US begin an oil airlift to Zambia. Meanwhile, nine member states of the Organization of African Unity

sever relations with Britain because of its failure to crush the Rhodesian regime.

25 NOVEMBER 1965
Congo In a bloodless coup, General Joseph Mobutu, the Congolese Army commander, deposes President Kasavubu to end the stalemated struggle between Kasavubu and Moise Tshombe, whom Kasavubu ousted as premier on 13 October. Mobutu makes himself president, names Colonel Leonard Mulamba premier, and cancels the presidential elections scheduled for spring 1966.

5 DECEMBER 1965
China/North Vietnam A Peking pact is signed between the two nations whereby China is to provide large amounts of material aid for the war against South Vietnam. Chinese troops are already in North Vietnam helping to repair bridges destroyed by US air raids. In February the USSR completed a defensive pact with North Vietnam for military supplies. Soviet defensive missile sites have been in place around Hanoi since April.

15 DECEMBER 1965
Vietnam War In the first attack on a major North Vietnamese industrial target, US planes drop 12 tons' of bombs on a power plant near Haiphong, the nation's chief port. So far Haiphong has been spared because of the large amount of Soviet shipping there.

17 DECEMBER 1965
Philippines Ending an election campaign marked by extreme bitterness and violence, Ferdinand Marcos is declared president, succeeding Diosado Macapagal. Marcos will continue the programs of land and other reforms.

24 DECEMBER 1965
Vietnam War In a Christmas truce, the US suspends bombing of North Vietnam to try to initiate peace talks. But Ho Chi Minh reiterates his conditions for peace—cessation of US bombing and removal of US troops and armaments.

OTHER EVENTS OF 1965
Science Arno Penzias and Robert Wilson, researchers at Bell Telephone Laboratories in New Jersey, aim an antenna to study emissions from the Milky Way and detect a 'universal glow' or 'noise' identified as radio waves given off by the alleged 'Big Bang' of creation. These faint radio waves exist throughout the universe and enforce the theory that it is expanding. R G Woodward and R Hoffmann publish a seminal paper, 'The Conservation of Orbital Symmetry.'
Medicine/Health Two American surgeons, Drs Michael De Bakey and Adrian Kantrowitz, implant 'assisting hearts,' mechanical devices that augment a diseased or overworked left ventricle.
Technology A Soviet cosmonaut makes the first 'space walk' when he leaves the *Voskhod II* on 18

March; on 3 June an American astronaut walks in space. The American satellites *Gemini VI* and *VII* rendezvous, but do not dock, in space. The *Early Bird*, the first commercial satellite, is placed into orbit to be used for TV transmissions.

Environment In East Pakistan, two cyclones and accompanying tidal waves leave an estimated 45,000 dead. Hurricane Betsy strikes Florida, Louisiana, and Mississippi, causing an estimated $715,000,000 in damage.

Ideas/Beliefs Pope Paul VI declares that the Jewish people were not responsible for the death of Christ and have been persecuted unjustly for 2000 years.

Literature Auden's *About the House*; Norman Mailer's *An American Dream*; Henry Miller's trilogy *The Rosy Crucifixion*.

Drama/Entertainment Miller's *Incident at Vichy*; Pinter's *Homecoming*; Fellini's *Juliet of the Spirits*.

The Arts Michelangelo's *Pieta* is exhibited in New York as part of the celebration of Pope Paul VI's visit to address the UN General Assembly.

Music Henze's *The Young Lord*; Bernstein's *Chichester Psalms*.

Life/Customs The first 'teach-ins' are held at universities in the US and Britain to protest events in Vietnam and Southern Rhodesia, and violations of civil rights. Britain bans cigarette advertising on commercial TV. The first miniskirt is sighted in London near the end of the year; by 1966 it will have caught on in many lands.

Miscellaneous Women and blacks are becoming increasingly visible in the US and Great Britain: the American Stock Exchange admits its first female members; Britain has its first woman coroner and member of the London Stock Exchange; the US has its first woman chief justice of a supreme court (in Arizona). The first black woman, Patricia Harris, becomes an American ambassador and the first black American Roman Catholic Bishop is named. Great Britain observes the 900th anniversary of Westminster Abbey, the 750th of the Magna Carta, and the 700th of Parliament. India adopts Hindi as its official language. The Beatles are awarded the MBE in the Queen's Birthday Honors (some previous recipients return their honors in protest.) Northeastern US and southeastern Canada are plunged into darkness for several hours by a power failure (an increase in the birth rate is reported nine months later).

17 JANUARY 1966

USA/Spain During a refueling operation over Spain's Mediterranean coast, two US planes collide, dropping four hydrogen bombs near Palomares. One is recovered intact, two rupture, scattering radioactive particles, and the fourth is lost in the Mediterranean. The 20-megaton bomb is recovered after an exhaustive search. More than 1000 tons of topsoil and vegetation are removed for disposal in the US.

19 JANUARY 1966

India Mrs Indira Gandhi, only child of the late Prime Minister Nehru, is elected leader of the ruling Congress Party which makes her prime minister. Prime Minister Shastri died on 11 January after concluding a Tashkent pact with Pakistani President Ayub Khan; in the agreement on Kashmir, both nations would withdraw forces to pre-1965 positions. Prime Minister Gandhi pledges to support the Tashkent agreement.

31 JANUARY 1966

Vietnam War After a 37-day hiatus, the US resumes bombing raids on North Vietnam, citing its failure to respond to the US peace 'offensive.'

5 FEBRUARY 1966

Israel/USA The US announces it will sell 200 tanks to Israel, taking over West Germany's 1965 obligation to do so. On 20 May the US announces a sale of tactical military aircraft to Israel. Both sales are intended to maintain arms 'stabilization' in the Mideast, in view of sales by the US and Soviet Union to Israel's Arab adversaries.

6 FEBRUARY 1966

Cuba/China Castro accuses Communist China of interfering in Cuban internal politics by spreading

---

YOUTH CULTURE

Among the more 'interesting' 1960s phenomena (as in the Chinese curse, 'May you live in interesting times!') was the eruption of youth as a presence and force in advanced industrialized societies. Some commentators would attribute this to demographics —the 'population curve' that brought the postwar baby boom into its adolescent years with an explosion of energy. Equally contributory may have been such historical factors as the pressure building up from the repressive 1950s, the models provided by the civil-rights and women's-liberation movements, and the crisis psychology induced by the Vietnam War. Whatever the causes, youth in many countries suddenly seemed driven to challenge the Establishment in its broadest sense. The 'Hippies' appeared, international nomads, unkempt in hair and clothing, who dropped out of the work world and mainstream culture and 'turned on' with drugs and meditation, shocking their elders with nudity and obscenities. Much of this had been pioneered by the Beatniks of the 1950s, but the Hippies were a distinctive, if temporary, phenomenon. Music became a powerful mode of expression, whether the folk music of Bob Dylan, the soft-rock of the Beatles, or the harder rock of the Rolling Stones: even a small sampling of popular music from the 1960s reveals its creative energy. Still another arena was politics. In France, young people virtually brought down the government; cities like London and Amsterdam had to bend their rules to accommodate youthful protest; in the US, such groups as Students for a Democratic Society and the violent Weathermen challenged the system. By the early 1970s, the movement had receded, but in ways yet difficult to measure, the youth culture had changed the world.

The Beatles: Left to right, *John Lennon, Paul McCartney, George Harrison, Ringo Starr.*

A TURBULENT DECADE 1963-1973

propaganda, and of betraying the Cuban Revolution by reneging on a rice-exporting deal.

6–8 FEBRUARY 1966
Vietnam War In Honolulu President Johnson and South Vietnamese Premier Ky confer on the war. Ky later says he will not participate in negotiations with the Vietcong and that he would refuse to let them join a coalition government. Ky also calls for heavier bombing of North Vietnam and urges destruction of the port of Haiphong.

21 FEBRUARY 1966
Yemen Saudi Arabian King Faisal says his country has ended aid to the Yemeni royalists and calls for Nasser to withdraw his troops. The next day Nasser responds that the 60,000 UAR troops helping Yemeni republican forces will remain in Yemen for five years if necessary until a plebiscite. Meanwhile, the first fighting between royalist and republican forces since the August 1965 truce breaks out.

24 FEBRUARY 1966
Ghana President Nkrumah's 15-year rule ends with a military coup led by General Joseph Ankrah, while Nkrumah is en route to China on a Vietnam peace mission. Ankrah becomes chief of state, purging the government of Nkrumah's appointees and suspending the constitution. Nkrumah seeks asylum in Guinea, where President Sékou Touré names him copresident.

10 MARCH 1966
South Vietnam Dismissal of Buddhist General Thi leads to a series of widespread, often violent anti-government demonstrations by Buddhists. On 16 March 10,000 Buddhists protest in Saigon, charging the US-supported Ky government with corruption. On 14 April the government promises early elections for a constituent assembly, temporarily ending the unrest. But on 31 May Buddhist rebels protest intervention in Danang with the burning of the US consulate in Hue.

12 MARCH 1966
Indonesia President Sukarno surrenders power to Lieutenant General Suharto following an ultimatum on behalf of the armed forces. Suharto immediately bans the Indonesian Communist Party and orders arrest of leftist politicians. Sukarno is permitted to remain for the interim as a figurehead president.

25–27 MARCH 1966
Vietnam War Over the weekend, parades and rallies are held in seven US and seven foreign cities to protest the war. The biggest demonstrations are in New York (25,000) and Rome (15,000). On 15 May over 10,000 picket the White House, and at a Washington Monument rally 63,000 'voter's pledges' are displayed—promising that signers will vote only for antiwar candidates. Antiwar sentiment has spread from the campuses of the US to the world.

29 MARCH 1966
USSR The 23rd Soviet Union Communist Party congress, with observers from 86 foreign parties, begins in Moscow. The Chinese delegation is conspicuous by its absence. Discussions center on maintaining the status quo, eliminating irritating dissidents, and maintaining peace. This is the first congress headed by First Secretary Leonid Brezhnev, who together with Premier Aleksei Kosygin, deposed Khrushchev in 1964.

INDIRA PRIYADARSHINI GANDHI, 1917–

This forceful woman's charisma as the daughter of India's first prime minister, Jawaharlal Nehru, her concern for the poor, her secular ideology, and her image as a strong leader gave her the popular support to become India's first woman prime minister in 1966. Educated in India and abroad, Gandhi was imprisoned with her husband Feroze Gandhi (not related to Mohandas K Gandhi) for their part in India's struggle for independence. Devoted to national unity and progress, she was willing to use coercive measures to achieve her economic and social programs in the face of resistance. But measures which instituted forced sterilization and imprisonment of those who opposed her goals and methods resulted in the end of her prime ministership in 1977. Reorganizing her party, she returned to office in 1980, and has maintained better-balanced relations both at home and abroad in the years that followed.

Vietnamese farmers harvest their rice guarded by a member of the 101st Abn Division.

A TURBULENT DECADE 1963-1973

31 MARCH 1966
Great Britain Prime Minister Harold Wilson's Labour Party wins a landslide victory, increasing its majority from 3 to 97 seats. Wilson sees this as approving the Labour plan to nationalize the steel industry.

1 MAY 1966
Vietnam War Artillery of the US First Infantry Division shells targets in Cambodia after US troops operating on the South Vietnam side of the Caibac River come under fire from the Cambodian shore. This is the first time the US has intentionally fired on Cambodian soil.

5 MAY 1966
Vietnam War The Vietnam debate continues, as Senator Fulbright declares the US is 'succumbing to the arrogance of power' by confusing 'its power with virtue and its major responsibilities with a universal mission.' Quick to defend his Vietnam policy, President Johnson responds on 11 May that 'The exercise of power in this century has meant for all of us in the United States not arrogance but agony.' Fulbright is urged to step down as chairman of the influential Senate Foreign Relations Committee by ex-Senator Barry Goldwater, who accuses Fulbright of 'giving aid and comfort to the enemy.'

5 JUNE 1966
USA In Mississippi, on a 220-mile pilgrimage to encourage unregistered blacks, James Meredith is shot three times as he walks along the highway. Superficially wounded, Meredith reveals that he had sought federal protection and been refused. Meredith's march is finished by a coalition of black groups that reveal tensions between nonviolent and black-power factions of the civil-rights movement.

29 JUNE 1966
Vietnam War For the first time, the North Vietnamese capital of Hanoi is bombed in a major escalation. US jets from Thailand and Navy aircraft carriers in the Gulf of Tonkin knock out an estimated two-thirds of North Vietnam's oil supplies and destroy facilities for off-loading oil from tankers at Haiphong. US officials claim that only militarily useful targets have been hit and that the bombings were executed carefully to avoid loss of civilian life.

1 JULY 1966
France France withdraws its armed forces from NATO, which transfers its headquarters to Casteau, Belgium. On 7 September France announces that it will cease paying its share of NATO military expenses, with certain exceptions, at year's end.

12 JULY 1966
USA Another summer of urban race riots begins with gunfire, looting of stores, and fire-bombing on Chicago's West Side. The hot weather, lack of recreational facilities, unemployment, degraded liv-ing conditions, and racial tensions are seen as factors in the disturbances, which spread to Cleveland, Brooklyn, Omaha, Baltimore, San Francisco, and Jacksonville.

Vietnam War North Vietnamese threaten to try captured US pilots as war criminals. Urgent international appeals from the UN's U Thant, Pope Paul VI, and others, forestall the plan.

11 AUGUST 1966
Indonesia/Malaysia The two nations sign a treaty ending their three-year undeclared war. The pact calls for a referendum in the Malaysian states of Sabah and Sarawak, which Indonesian President Sukarno had claimed for Indonesia.

6 SEPTEMBER 1966
South Africa Prime Minister Verwoerd, architect of the nation's apartheid plan of strict racial segregation, is stabbed to death during a session of Parliament in Capetown. The assassin is a drifter who claimed that the government was doing too much for the nonwhites and not enough for the 'poor whites.' On 13 September Balthazar Vorster, another apartheid advocate, becomes prime minister.

27 SEPTEMBER 1966
South Africa The UN General Assembly votes to end the South African mandate in Namibia, or Southwest Africa. Over objections from the South African Government, the mandate ends on 27 October with the UN taking over administration of the region.

24-25 OCTOBER 1966
Vietnam War In the Manila Conference called by Philippine President Marcos, President Johnson meets with the leaders of the six other nations involved in the war (Australia, New Zealand, the Philippines, Thailand, South Korea, and South Vietnam). The allies pledge political self-determination, as well as economic, social, and cultural co-operation to break 'the bonds of poverty, illiteracy and disease.' On the military front, they pledge to withdraw troops six months after North Vietnam ceases its aggression. On 26 October President Johnson pays an unscheduled visit to the US base at Camranh Bay, where he awards medals for heroism to wounded soldiers.

13 NOVEMBER 1966
Middle East In continuing guerrilla warfare on its Syrian and Jordanian frontiers, Israel takes severe reprisals against the Hebron area of Jordan. On 25 November the UN Security Council censures Israel. On 10 December the Arab League decides to send Iraqi and Saudi Arabian troops to help Jordan, which prohibits entry of Syrian and Palestine liberation fighters who might undermine King Hussein's position.

30 NOVEMBER 1966
West Germany Ludwig Erhard resigns as chan-

cellor and is succeeded the next day by Kurt Kiesinger, a one-time Nazi Party member, now a Christian Democrat. Kiesinger forms a 'grand coalition' government with Franz Josef Strauss as minister of finance and Willy Brandt as minister of foreign affairs.

26 DECEMBER 1966

Vietnam War The US Defense Department concedes that while US pilots have tried to bomb only military targets in North Vietnam, some civilian areas have 'accidentally' been hit. American troop strength in South Vietnam now totals 389,000.

OTHER EVENTS OF 1966

Science The chemical make-up of DNA—the sequence of amino acids that serve as the genetic instruction code—is revealed. The oceanographic research vessel *Eltanin* takes a core sample from the South Pacific ocean floor that provides strong evidence for a spreading sea floor and continental drift.

Technology The first soft landing on the moon is achieved when the Soviets' *Luna IX* lands on 3 February; the Russian *Venus III* makes the first landing on another planet, Venus, on 1 March. The first X-ray 3-dimensional (stereo) fluoroscope system is exhibited by its developer, Joseph Quinn, in San Francisco.

Environment A flood in Florence, Italy, damages many works of art, books, and museum collections: an international effort is launched to restore these works.

Social Studies Truman Capote's *In Cold Blood* launches a new genre—sociology-as-fiction.

Literature Mario Vargas Llosa's *The Green House*;

Astronaut John Glenn.

A TURBULENT DECADE 1963-1973

Malamud's *The Fixer*; Martin Walser's *The Unicorn*; Graham Greene's *The Comedians*; John Barth's *Giles Goat-Boy*.

Drama/Entertainment   Fernando Arrabal's *The Architect and the Emperor of Assyria*; Albee's *A Delicate Balance*; Antonioni's *Blow-Up*; Warhol's *Chelsea Girls*.

The Arts   Victor Vasareley's *Arcturus II*; Chagall's mural *The Triumph of Music* is dedicated at the Metropolitan Opera in New York.

Music   Samuel Barber's *Antony and Cleopatra* (commissioned to open the new Metropolitan Opera House); Stravinsky's *Requiem Canticles*; Henze's *The Bassarids*; Penderecki's *Passion According to St Luke*.

Sports   The British sailor Francis Chichester sails from Plymouth, England, to· Sydney, Australia, 13,750 miles, in 107 days—the longest nonstop solo sea voyage on record.

Life/Customs   Timothy Leary, a former Harvard professor who has espoused the cause of marijuana and other drugs, founds the League of Spiritual Discovery (LSD) based on the 'sacramental' use of LSD, peyote, and marijuana. US Roman Catholic bishops decree that American Catholics need no longer abstain from meat on Fridays except in Lent.

Miscellaneous   The National Organization of Women (NOW) is founded. The Salvation Army observes its centenary. The first black senator elected by popular vote is Edward Brooke of Massachusetts. At Aberfan, Wales, a coal tip collapses, killing 144. A Greek ship sinks in the night en route to Crete with a loss of 264.

8 JANUARY 1967
Vietnam War   The largest offensive of the war thus far (16,000 US and 14,000 South Vietnamese troops) begins against the Iron Triangle, 25 miles northwest of Saigon. 'Operation Cedar Falls' ends after 19 days with 711 Vietcong reported dead and removal of 6000 of 10,000 civilian residents to refugee centers after their homes are destroyed by bulldozers or fire.

18–26 JANUARY 1967
Vietnam War   South Vietnamese Premier Ky tours Australia and New Zealand to thank them for their help in the war, a visit disturbed by antiwar demonstrations. Australian Labour Party leader Arthur Caldwell calls Ky 'a murderer.'

21 JANUARY 1967
China   The cultural revolution continues as fighting breaks out in Kiangsi Province between a worker-peasant militia and Red Guards. On 23 January Mao Tse-tung calls on Defense Minister Lin Piao to mobilize the People's Liberation Army to support the 'left revolutionary masses.' Lin Piao had reportedly called for a purge of 'bourgeois reactionary elements in the army's Cultural Revolution Committee.'

27 JANUARY 1967
International   A treaty limiting use of outer space

for military purposes is signed by representatives of 62 nations in ceremonies in London, Washington, and Moscow. It limits orbiting of nuclear weapons and forbids claims of national sovereignty on celestial bodies.

13 FEBRUARY 1967
USA   The National Student Organization discloses that it has secretly and indirectly received over $3 million from the CIA between 1952 and 1966 for use in its overseas programs. The following day the State Department admits that the CIA supported such projects to counter communist student group activities.

13 MARCH 1967
Congo   Former Premier Moise Tshombe is tried in absentia for treason, found guilty, and sentenced to death by a military court. He is convicted of recruiting mercenaries to fight the Congolese Government and organizing rebellion in the 1960–1963 Katanga secession and the 1966 Kisangani mutiny. Tshombe has been living in exile since his 1965 overthrow in a bloodless coup.

21 MARCH 1967
Vietnam War   It is disclosed that Ho Chi Minh has turned down President Johnson's bid for direct US-North Vietnamese peace talks. The US had offered to halt bombing and buildup of forces if infiltration into South Vietnam was stopped. Ho reiterates his demand that the bombing stop and US troops be withdrawn unconditionally from South Vietnam before talks take place.

22 MARCH 1967
Vietnam War   Washington reports that Thailand has agreed to allow US B-52 bombers to use bases in its country for raids on communist targets in Vietnam. The shift from Guam, the current base for the B-52s, would shorten the flight distance to enemy targets from 2500 to several hundred miles.

28 MARCH 1967
Vatican   In an encyclical outlining social, political, diplomatic, and economic means for resolving the problems of the world's poor, Pope Paul VI approves land expropriation when required by the 'common good.'

4 APRIL 1967
Vietnam War   Claiming that twice as many blacks as whites are in combat in Vietnam, Martin Luther King urges all draft-age Americans, black and white, to boycott the war by declaring themselves conscientious objectors. Dr King calls the US 'the greatest purveyor of violence in the world' and compares testing of new weapons in Vietnam to World War II Nazi concentration-camp experiments.

12–14 APRIL 1967
International   A summit conference of 19 chiefs of

state from Western Hemisphere countries meets in Punta del Este, Uruguay, on an economic program for the Americas. President Johnson pledges continued US assistance.

21 APRIL 1967
Greece A group of rightist army officers, led by Colonel George Papadopoulos and Brigadier General Styliano Patakos, stages a bloodless preelection coup by ousting the interim government of Premier Panayotis Kanellopoulos. Claiming support of King Constantine, the junta rounds up communists and antimonarchists, suspends constitutional guarantees, and imposes censorship of the press. Among leftists arrested are former Premier George Papandreou and his son, Andreas.

USSR In a spectacular defection, Svetlana Aliluyeva, only daughter and last surviving child of the late Soviet dictator Joseph Stalin, arrives in New York after seeking political asylum in the US embassy in New Delhi. In a press conference, the 42-year old widow insists that responsibility for Stalinist purges should be shared by communist officials still in power.

2 MAY 1967
Vietnam War Called by British philosopher Lord Bertrand Russell, 18 members of an 'International Tribunal on War Crimes' convene in Stockholm to hear charges of US atrocities in Vietnam. After eight days of reviewing evidence, the tribunal finds the US guilty of crimes of aggression, including 'widespread, systematic and deliberate' bombing of civilians. Australia, New Zealand, and South Korea are named as accomplices.

13 MAY 1967
Vietnam War An eight-hour parade 'supporting our men in Vietnam' is held on New York's Fifth Avenue to counter the massive Peace Mobilization marches of 15 April. The 70,000 marchers include members of veterans groups, labor unions, and fraternal and religious organizations.

30 MAY 1967
Nigeria The nation's eastern region secedes as the independent republic of Biafra. This culminates a bloody struggle between the predominantly Moslem north and Christians in Nigeria's eastern region, which is an exporter of crude oil with extensive US and British investments. On 6 July civil war breaks out as federal troops clash with secessionist forces. The struggle will last for $2\frac{1}{2}$ years.

5 JUNE 1967
Middle East The Six-Day War begins as the Israeli air force conducts surprise raids on 25 Arab airports, destroying almost all Egyptian, Jordanian, Syrian, and Iraqi planes, most of them still on the ground. Concurrently, Israeli armored forces sweep across the Sinai, reaching the Suez Canal on 8 June. By the 10 June UN cease-fire, Israel is in control of

territory four times its own size—including the Sharm el Sheikh base, all of Jordan's West Bank, and Syria's Golan Heights. Egyptian losses total 10,000 dead and 15,000 captured. Another 900,000 refugees join the ranks of the million displaced by the 1948–49 war.

8 JUNE 1967
Israel/USA Thirty-four US seamen are killed and 75 wounded when Israeli torpedo boats and planes attack and heavily damage the USS *Liberty* in international waters 15 miles north of the Sinai Peninsula. Israel apologizes and offers compensation, but some US officials believe the attack was intentional, designed to prevent the vessel from intercepting messages proving that Israel started the war with the Arabs.

23–25 JUNE 1967
USSR/USA President Johnson and Premier Kosygin meet for ten hours of talks at Glassboro State College, New Jersey. No accord is reached on the major issues of the Six-Day War, Vietnam, or nuclear controls, but President Johnson cites 'great progress in reducing misunderstanding.'

30 JUNE 1967
International In Geneva, 46 nations sign the new General Agreement on Tariffs and Trade, following four years of negotiations among 53 nations. Dramatic cuts in tariff duties are to stimulate world trade, and there is a 35-percent reduction on industrial products, 50 percent on chemical goods, and substantial cuts on agricultural products. The accord pledges support for a worldwide food program, to supply some 4.5 million tons of grain a year to developing countries.

12 JULY 1967
USA Race riots erupt in Newark, New Jersey, leaving 26 dead, 1500 injured, and over 1000 arrested. The 23–30 July Detroit riots leave at least 40 dead, 2000 injured, and 5000 homeless through burning and looting. On 24 July President Johnson calls in 4700 federal paratroopers aided by 8000 National Guardsmen. This is the first time in 24 years that federal forces have been used to quell civil disorders. Detroit property damage is estimated at between $250 and $400 million.

23 JULY 1967
Puerto Rico Puerto Ricans vote to remain a commonwealth associated with the US, rather than becoming the 51st state or an independent country.

24 JULY 1967
Canada On a state visit, French President de Gaulle endorses the French separatist movement by shouting in a Montreal speech *'Vive le Québec Libre!'*—Long Live Free Quebec. He is sharply rebuked by the Canadian Government.

A TURBULENT DECADE 1963-1973

Ariel Sharon with his field commanders during the Six Day War, 1967.

12 AUGUST 1967
China/USSR Relations between the two nations deteriorate as Soviet Premier Kosygin sends a telegram to Chinese Premier Chou En-lai protesting detention of a Russian freighter in the port of Talien. The ship and its men are released the following day.

3 SEPTEMBER 1967
South Vietnam Chief of state Nguyen Van Thieu is elected to a four-year term as president, with Nguyen Cao Ky as vice-president, on the military slate. They receive nearly 35 percent of the vote in defeating ten other candidates. On 4–5 September seven of the defeated candidates charge fraud, accusing the winners of using government troops to jam voting places and use up ballots, among other practices.

11–14 SEPTEMBER 1967
India/China Chinese and Indian troops exchange rifle and artillery fire at the border of Tibet and the Indian protectorate of Sikkim. Each side accuses the other of border intrusions. On 15 September the communists halt shelling at Natu La, despite no response to an Indian cease-fire proposal.

20 SEPTEMBER 1967
Hong Kong The death toll from communist-inspired rioting and terrorism in the British Crown Colony rises to 13, as the Chinese press their anti-British campaign. More than 100 have been injured and 1200 arrested since 10 July.

2 OCTOBER 1967
USA Thurgood Marshall is sworn in as the first black US Supreme Court Justice. On 7 November Carl B Stokes (Cleveland) and Richard G Hatcher (Gary) become the first black mayors of major cities.

4 OCTOBER 1967
Vietnam War American military leaders report that

the month-long communist siege of the Marine base at Conthien, just south of the demilitarized zone, has been broken. It is estimated that 3000 North Vietnamese troops were killed or wounded in the daily artillery exchange that began on 1 September.

8 OCTOBER 1967
Bolivia Cuban revolutionary Ernesto Che Guevara falls in a battle between Bolivian troops and guerrilla forces near Higueras. Bolivian officials claim Guevara died of his wounds, but a post-mortem indicates that he had been shot to death after capture.

14 OCTOBER 1967
Vietnam War The US charges that American prisoners of war in North Vietnamese hands are being mistreated and that films of allegedly well-treated POWs are being sold to the media for 'hard cash.' US Deputy Defense Secretary Paul Nitze accuses Hanoi of violating the 1949 Geneva Convention by parading prisoners for filming, denying International Red Cross access to the prisoners, failing to supply a list of all prisoners, and restricting or denying mail privileges.

21 OCTOBER 1967
Vietnam War Two days of antiwar demonstrations begin in Washington. Of 35,000 protestors, 647 are arrested while trying to enter the Pentagon. In a 31 October speech President Johnson reaffirms America's commitment in Vietnam.

2 NOVEMBER 1967
Aden Calling it 'the end of the imperial era,' Foreign Secretary George Brown announces that Britain will withdraw all military forces from Aden and South Arabia later in the month, an operation involving 5000 British troops and 500 civilians.

7 NOVEMBER 1967
USA Selective Service head Lewis Hershey directs local draft boards to crack down on deferred college students who interfere with recruitment on campus by putting them on top of the draft list.

8 DECEMBER 1967
Cyprus The Greek Government begins removing troops from Cyprus in accordance with a pact signed by Greece, Turkey, and Cyprus that averted a Greco-Turkish war in mid-November.

13 DECEMBER 1967
Greece To oust the military junta that seized control in April, King Constantine broadcasts an appeal to the Greek people to support him in re-establishing democratic government. It is soon apparent that he has failed to rally the necessary support, and next day Constantine flies to exile in Rome with his family and close advisers. The junta names a cabinet with Colonel George Papadapoulos as premier and appoints a 'regent' in place of the king.

HO CHI MINH, 1890–1969

'Uncle Ho' to his admirers, virtually the Devil Ho to his enemies, Ho Chi Minh commanded respect for dedicating his life to his nation's independence. Born Nguyen That Thanh, he left Vietnam in 1911 to work on a French liner, and by World War I was working in the United States. After the war he appeared at the Paris Peace Conference to demand independence for Vietnam from the French. He stayed in Paris and became a founder of the French Communist Party, then went to Moscow to study, having become a committed communist revolutionary. In the late 1920s and throughout the 1930s, he moved back and forth between Russia and China, organizing the Vietnam Communist Party and promoting revolution. When World War II began, he returned to Vietnam (known now as Ho Chi Minh, 'Ho the Enlightener') where he organized a resistance movement against the Japanese—with considerable support from Americans in China. When the war ended, he proclaimed an independent Republic of Vietnam, but the French resisted and by 1946 Ho Chi Minh had begun a guerrilla war that culminated in 1954 in the defeat of the French and the division of his country by a Geneva Conference. As President of the Republic of North Vietnam, Ho Chi Minh organized the guerrilla movement in the south known as the Viet Cong, and by 1964 was conducting open warfare against the combined armies of South Vietnam and the US. He did not live to see the final victory, but when the two Vietnams were united in 1975, Saigon was renamed Ho Chi Minh City.

A TURBULENT DECADE 1963-1973

17 DECEMBER 1967
Australia Prime Minister Harold Holt drowns while swimming off Portsea, Victoria. He is succeeded by Liberal Party leader John G Gorton.

OTHER EVENTS OF 1967
Science The pulsar—a celestial object that emits radio waves in brief, sharp pulses—is discovered by Jocelyn Bell and Antony Hewish at Cambridge University. At Stanford University, a research team headed by biochemist Arthur Kornberg synthesizes biologically active DNA. Several laboratories discover the ligating enzyme that joins fragments of DNA. Elwyn Simonds, a paleontologist from Yale, finds the fossil skull of an ape in Egypt that he dates to 28 million years and claims as the earliest known ancestor of the anthropoid line.

Medicine/Health On 2 December Dr Christiaan Barnard and his surgical team in Cape Town, South Africa, perform the first heart transplant: the recipient is Louis Washkansky, who will die 18 days later from a lung infection. Dr Irving Cooper develops cyrosurgery to treat Parkinson's Disease.

Technology China explodes its first hydrogen bomb. *Surveyors 5* and *6* land on the moon, gather data, and transmit photos to the earth. Three American astronauts (Grissom, Chaffee, and White) are trapped in the capsule of their Saturn rocket while still on the launching pad and killed by a fire.

Social Studies After preliminary surveys in 1962–64, Spyridon Marinatos, Greek archaeologist, begins excavating the Akrotiri site on Santorini (Thera), where he will uncover a vast town buried under volcanic pumice and ash about 1475 BC. It had ties with the Minoan civilization of Crete (65 miles due south), and some people will also correlate it with the ancient tale of a 'lost Atlantis.' Desmond Morris's *The Naked Ape* becomes an international best-seller.

Literature William Styron's *The Confessions of Nat Turner*; Mikhail Bulgakov's *The Master and Margarita* (the first uncensored version, in an English translation); Gabriel Garcia Marquez's *One Hundred Years of Solitude*; Carlos Fuentes's *A Change of Skin*; Borges's *The Book of Imaginary Beings*; Miguel Asturias's *Mulata*; I B Singer's *The Manor*; Robert Stone's *A Hall of Mirrors*.

Drama/Entertainment Tom Stoppard's *Rosenkrantz and Guildenstern Are Dead*; Hochhuth's *Soldiers*.

The Arts Picasso's gift to Chicago, a 50-foot high, 163-ton steel sculpture, creates controversy. Washington's National Gallery acquires a Leonardo Da Vinci portrait, *Ginevra de Benci*, from the Prince of Liechtenstein for $6 million. The Metropolitan Museum of Art in New York admits that three large sculptures it has been exhibiting as ancient Etruscan works are modern forgeries.

Architecture At Montreal's Expo '67, The Habitat, an apartment complex comprised of a series of prefabricated boxes, is the work of Moshe Safdie, a young Israeli architect. Another interesting Expo structure is the geodesic dome, designed by Buckminster Fuller to house the US pavilion.

Music Marvin Levy's *Mourning Becomes Electra*; the Beatles release their most innovative album, *Sgt Pepper's Lonely Hearts Club Band*.

Sports/Leisure Francis Chichester finishes his solo voyage around the world, 30,000 miles in 226 days, in *Gypsy Moth IV*.

Life/Customs Twiggy, a slat-thin British fashion model, becomes the rage.

Miscellaneous A fire on the US aircraft carrier *Forrestal* kills 134.

5 JANUARY 1968
USA A Boston federal grand jury indicts Dr Benjamin Spock, Yale Chaplain William Sloan Coffin, and several others for conspiracy to abet, aid, and counsel violations of the draft law. They are found guilty on 14 June, but are exonerated in a 1969 appeal.

9 JANUARY 1968
Sweden/USA Four US sailors who deserted in Japan in 1967 because of their objections to the Vietnam War are given asylum by Sweden on 'humanitarian grounds.' Other US servicemen, reportedly deserters from West German bases, also seek political asylum in Sweden. Many others will go into exile in Canada and other countries.

23 JANUARY 1968
North Korea/USA During a routine electronic intelligence mission, the US Navy ship *Pueblo* and its 83-man crew are seized by North Koreans who insist the ship has intruded within their 12-mile limit. Despite diplomatic and military pressure, the North Koreans insist on an apology. They finally receive it on 22 December, and the crew is released. The US continues to deny charges of intrusion.

30 JANUARY 1968
Vietnam War On the first day of what is supposed to be a mutually-agreed-upon Tet or Lunar New Year truce, Communist forces unexpectedly launch a large offensive against 30 South Vietnamese provincial capitals. In the early stages of the Tet Offensive, communists reach key targets in Saigon, including the grounds of the US embassy and General Westmoreland's headquarters. They also capture the city of Hue and hold it for 25 days. Because the North Vietnamese fail to create a popular uprising against the government and must retreat with heavy losses, the US sees it as a military defeat for the communists. But it is a psychological victory for them in that it broadens the US peace movement and discourages many Johnson Administration war supporters. On 22 March President Johnson names Westmoreland Army Chief of Staff, a reassignment that returns him to the US by July.

5-7 FEBRUARY 1968
Canada In Ottawa, the Federal Constitutional Convention convenes to revise the nation's constitution. With Prime Minister Pearson and the ten

The site of Expo '67 in Montreal.

provincial premiers participating, it is agreed that both French and English should be official Canadian languages.

29 FEBRUARY 1968
USA The Kerner Commission report on civil disorders cites white racism as the chief cause of black violence and riots. Contributing factors include unemployment, inadequate housing, and discriminatory police practices. Among recommendations are creation of 2 million new jobs, decentralization of city governments, a national system of income supplements based on need, and new low- and moderate-income housing.

1 MARCH 1968
Great Britain A bill restricting the immigration of Asian British citizens to Britain becomes law, to curb immigration of 200,000 Asians from Kenya, where noncitizens are being deprived of jobs.

8–9 MARCH 1968
Poland Apparently inspired by the liberalizing trend in Czechoslovakia, Warsaw university students clash with police, shouting 'Down with censorship' and 'Long live Czechoslovakia.' On 11 March office and factory workers fight police and militia in downtown Warsaw. The Communist Party blames the

riots on Zionists—anti-Semitism has reportedly been on the rise since the 1967 Israeli-Arab war.

16 MARCH 1968
Vietnam War US soldiers sweep through the South Vietnamese hamlet of My Lai, gunning down at least 300 civilian men, women, and children. The massacre is revealed to the world in November 1969. On 29 March 1971 Army Lieutenant William Calley is found guilty of the murders by a court-martial and sentenced to hard labor for life. His sentence is reduced to 20 years, then to 10 years, and he is finally released. A 1970 Army Peers panel finds the entire command structure of the American Division guilty of misconduct in its first investigation of the slaughter.

31 MARCH 1968
USA In a nationally televised speech, a discouraged President Johnson announces unilateral cessation of US bombing of North Vietnam north of the 20th parallel and calls on Hanoi to agree to peace talks. He concludes with the surprising announcement that he will not run for re-election later that year. Three days later Hanoi agrees to preliminary talks.

4 APRIL 1968
USA Nobel Prize-winner and nonviolent civil-rights leader Martin Luther King is killed by sniper

A TURBULENT DECADE 1963-1973

Dr Martin Luther King Jr, flanked by Jesse Jackson (left) and Ralph Abernathy—April 1968.

James Earl Ray in Memphis, Tennessee. Fear and violence mount as the shock of the assassination spreads across the nation and sets off a wave of black rioting and looting.

5 APRIL 1968

Vietnam War In Operation Pegasus, a 30,000-man US and South Vietnamese force lifts the 76-day siege of the 6000-man US Marine garrison at Khe Sanh. The controversial outpost near the demilitarized zone had been turned eight months ago into a test of US prestige—the 'crucial anchor' in the defense of the sector. On 5 July the US abandons Khe Sanh.

20 APRIL 1968

Canada Justice Minister Pierre Elliott Trudeau, a French-Canadian who opposes the Quebec separatist movement, succeeds retiring Lester Pearson as prime minister. A decisive 25 June victory in House of Commons elections gives Trudeau's Liberal Party Canada's first majority government since 1962 and ensures his mandate.

23 APRIL 1968

USA A left-wing student protest led by Mark Rudd at New York's Columbia University becomes a major upheaval marked by clashes with police and a two-week paralysis of the prestigious institution. Student turmoil spreads to other colleges throughout the nation.

2 MAY 1968

France A protest led by leftist student militant Daniel Cohn-Bendit at the University of Nanterre mushrooms into a month-long movement of civil and economic disobedience by 10 million French that threatens to end the 10-year regime of President de Gaulle's Fifth Republic. On 24 May de Gaulle announces he will submit a broad reform program to the people through a referendum.

2 MAY–24 JUNE 1968

USA In a poor people's march planned by the late Martin Luther King, caravans from all parts of the nation converge on Washington and set up camp on a 16-acre site named Resurrection City. Participants, led by Ralph Abernathy, include Southern blacks, Indians, Mexican Americans, and Appalachian whites.

8 MAY 1968

Nigeria Ten months of fighting between Nigeria and the secessionist government of Biafra end in agreement when the civil war reaches an impasse. Fearing genocide at the hands of other tribes, Biafra's Ibos have fought on desperately, even though Nigeria's well-equipped 85,000-man army has captured all but one of Biafra's major cities.

10 MAY 1968

Vietnam War Preliminary peace talks begin in

PIERRE ELLIOTT TRUDEAU, 1919–

When he first appeared in the public eye as prime minister of Canada in 1968, Trudeau was perceived by some as Canada's answer to John Fitzgerald Kennedy. As the years went by, Trudeau retained his power as prime minister, but his popularity waxed and waned with many of his constituents. Son of a wealthy Montreal businessman—old French family on his father's side, old English family on his mother's side—Trudeau attended the University of Montreal and pursued graduate studies at Harvard, the School of Political Sciences in Paris, and the London School of Economics. He spent several years traveling to increase his awareness of international conditions. Returning to Montreal to practice law, he worked on behalf of French-Canadian laborers. He was first elected to the House of Commons in 1965, and by 1968 succeeded Lester Pearson as prime minister. Trudeau undeniably provided a new and stirring image for Canadians, particularly for young people, and he worked hard to unify the country's French- and English-speaking elements. He also spoke out against the US and its policies when he disagreed. The recession of the early 1980s restricted Trudeau's choices, but despite the problems that have beset his nation, he has proved to be one of Canada's major political figures of this century.

Paris, with Averell Harriman and Cyrus Vance heading the US and Xuan Thuy and Ha Van Lau the North Vietnamese delegations. Talks soon stall out.

5 JUNE 1968

USA Senator Robert F Kennedy is shot and fatally wounded after celebrating victories in the California and South Dakota presidential primaries. Jordanian immigrant Sirhan B Sirhan is convicted of his murder.

23–30 JUNE 1968

France In national elections, Gaullists win decisively, reflecting French fear of a communist takeover.

A TURBULENT DECADE 1963-1973

Members of Company B, 2nd Battalion, 9th Infantry Division take cover south of the 'Y' Bridge.

17 JULY 1968
Iraq Army officers sympathetic with the right wing of the Baath Socialist Party topple the government of President Abdel Rahman Arif, calling his leftist regime 'opportunists, thieves . . . Zionist spies.' The Revolutionary Command Council, headed by Major General Ahmed Hassan al-Bakr, urges immediate liberation of Palestine.

15 AUGUST 1968
Nigeria The government rejects an International Red Cross plan to continue emergency airlifts of food to starving Biafrans via a neutral airstrip. Since July some 6000 Ibos a day have been dying from malnutrition.

20–21 AUGUST 1968
Czechoslovakia More than 200,000 Soviet troops, supplemented by token forces from other Warsaw Pact nations, invade with tanks and paratroops. The USSR demands reversal of the Alexander Dubcek regime's liberalization of communism. As street demonstrations by Czechs threaten to lead to violence, Soviet troops increase to 650,000. In meetings with the Soviets, Czech leaders are forced to promise (3–4 October) abandonment of democratizing reforms and to accept an indefinite Soviet military

occupation. During 1969 Alexander Dubcek is removed from all positions of influence.

26–29 AUGUST 1968
USA In the Chicago Democratic National Convention, one of the most turbulent in the nation's history, delegates split sharply over the issue of Vietnam. Violence erupts outside the convention hall as police and troops clash with 10 to 15,000 antiwar demonstrators.

11–14 OCTOBER 1968
Canada Two Quebec separatist groups merge into the *Parti Quebécois (PQ)*, dedicated to independence by peaceful, democratic means for a republican Québec linked in an economic union with Canada. René Levesque is its president.

5 NOVEMBER 1968
USA Richard M Nixon is elected president by a narrow margin over Democratic candidate Hubert Humphrey. Democrats retain control of both Houses of Congress.

6 DECEMBER 1968
France The French Communist Party, second largest in Western Europe, issues a manifesto that

Quebec separatists demonstrating in Montreal, October 1969.

A TURBULENT DECADE 1963-1973

asserts it is developing a socialist program taking into account 'French particularities' to be implemented by means other 'than those used in Russia and other countries.'

13 DECEMBER 1968
Mexico/USA As agreed in 1963, President Johnson and Mexico's President Gustavo Diaz Ordaz meet on a bridge at El Paso, Texas, between the two countries, to officiate at ceremonies returning the long-disputed El Chamizal area to the Mexican side of the border.

28 DECEMBER 1968
Lebanon/Israel In a commando raid on Beirut Airport, Israelis destroy 13 Arab airliners in reprisal for a terrorist attack on an Israeli plane in Athens and other such attacks on Israel from Lebanese territory. The Lebanese Government of Premier Abdullah Yaffi resigns, and a French embargo on the sale of arms to Israel ensues. Sporadic fighting between the neighboring nations will continue through 1969.

OTHER EVENTS OF 1968
Science The *Glomar Challenger*, a US oceanographic research vessel, begins the Deep Sea Drilling Project to learn more about formation of the ocean floor and the forces that formed the continents; the cores it brings up via drilling pipes generally confirm the theory of plate tectonics.

Medicine/Health Dr Norman Shumway performs the first heart transplant in America in California. The USSR bans the operation. A vaccine against the mumps, developed in 1966, is approved for use. Geneticists reveal that certain male criminals have an extra Y chromosome (XYY instead of the normal XY) that seems to be linked with their appearance and behavior.

Technology *Intelsat 3A*, the first of a new breed of communications satellites, is put into orbit.

Environment An earthquake in Iran kills 12,000.

Social Studies In China, archaeologists discover a major prehistoric tomb at An Yang.

Ideas/Beliefs James Watson, a discoverer of the structure of DNA, publishes *The Double Helix*, providing inside views on contemporary scientific research. Norman Mailer publishes *The Armies of the Night*, a provocative account of protest against the war in Vietnam.

Literature Solzhenitsyn's *First Circle* and *Cancer Ward*, circulating in the USSR via the underground *samizat*, are published in the West. John Updike's *Couples*; Vonnegut's *Welcome to the Monkey House.*

Drama/Entertainment Miller's *The Price*; Arthur Kopit's *Indians*; Howard Sackler's *The Great White Hope*; Kubrick's *2001: A Space Odyssey*; *The Graduate*; the Beatles' *Yellow Submarine.*

The Arts The Museum of Modern Art in New York exhibits 'Dada, Surrealism and Their Heritage'; Shoji Hamada, a master Japanese ceramicist, is awarded his nation's prestigious Order of Culture Medal for reviving the art.

Architecture Eero Saarinen's Gateway Arch is dedicated at St Louis, Missouri.

Music Stockhausen's *Spiral*; Orff's *Prometheus*; Dallipiccola's *Odysseus.*

Life/Customs 'Student unrest,' as it is now labeled, leaves many US campuses in turmoil or inoperable. At the Olympics, several black American athletes give the black power salute (a raised fist) from the winners' stand. Pope Paul VI reiterates the Roman Catholic Church's ban on artificial birth control in his encyclical *Humanae vitae.*

Miscellaneous An American B-52 bomber crashes in Thule, Greenland, and scatters radioactive fragments from the hydrogen bombs it carried.

7 JANUARY 1969
USA As student riots continue to close college campuses nationwide, opposition mounts. Governor Ronald Reagan asks the California legislature to 'drive criminal anarchists and latter-day Fascists off the campuses,' asserting that 'higher education in our state college and universities is not a right, it is a privilege.' The protests, often led by a handful, are often by black and minority-group students demanding black studies programs and open admission policies, with support from white students and faculty members. White radical students, led by Students for a Democratic Society (SDS), join them but are more concerned with ending ROTC, opposing Dow Chemical recruiting on campus, and seeking a voice in curriculum faculty choices. All oppose the Vietnam War.

27 JANUARY 1969
Iraq Defying worldwide criticism and spurring a new Mideast crisis, the government hangs 14 alleged Iraqi spies for Israel, including nine Jews. Executions continue on 20 February when seven more Iraqis, all Moslems, are killed. On 13 April four Moslems charged as US Central Intelligence Agency spies are hanged. Baghdad Radio terms the executions 'a victory for the Palestinian cause and Vietnam.'

Northern Ireland The Reverend Ian Paisley, leader of the Protestant extremists, is sentenced to three months' imprisonment for actions against Catholics. A 73-mile civil rights march from Belfast to Londonderry, beginning 1 January, in which Catholic students protested discrimination in housing, voting, and employment, had been harassed and attacked by Protestant counterdemonstrators.

2 MARCH 1969
China/USSR Thirty-one Soviet soldiers are reported killed in the first of two clashes between thousands of Russian and Chinese soldiers on the Manchurian border 250 miles north of Vladivostok. Each country blames the other for starting the fighting. On 21 March a Hong Kong newspaper quotes Mao Tse-tung as saying that China is prepared to use nuclear weapons in the event of a Soviet nuclear attack. The Soviet Defense Ministry's *Red Star* depicts Mao as a 'traitor to communism.'

17 MARCH 1969
Israel Golda Meir is sworn in as the nation's fourth premier, succeeding the late Levi Eshkol. Meir pledges direct talks with the Arabs to attain peace.

19 MARCH 1969
Anguilla A 100-man task force of British paratroopers, marines, and policemen lands on the tiny Caribbean island in a dispute dating back to May 1967 when the island pulled out of the Associated State of St Kitts-Nevis-Anguilla, made up of former British colonial territories. Hundreds of the 6000 inhabitants shout protests, but there is no resistance. Britain justifies the invasion on grounds that the island (whose chief natural resource is a small salt pond) could not go it alone.

25 MARCH 1969
Pakistan After ten years as the nation's military strong man, President Mohammad Ayub Khan resigns after several months of antigovernment demonstrations by students and workers. Commander-in-Chief of the Army General Agha Mohammad Yahya Khan takes over and proclaims martial law.

3 APRIL 1969
Canada Prime Minister Trudeau announces plans for a phased cut in Canada's NATO forces, which will be reduced from 9800 to 5000 men by year's end; Canada will end its nuclear role in NATO by 1972.
Vietnam War The US command reports that total American combat deaths since 1 January 1961 have reached 33,641, topping casualties in the Korean War (33,629).

19–21 APRIL 1969
Northern Ireland A new wave of civil-rights strife between Protestants and Catholics hits Londonderry and Belfast, bringing more than 1000 British soldiers to protect reservoirs, telephone exchanges, and power stations. In the thick of street fighting in Bogside by the Catholic Party of Londonderry is Bernadette Devlin, a 21-year-old student protester who had won a seat in the British House of Commons on 18 April. She leaves the melee to make a pugnacious maiden speech in Parliament, promising to 'knock sense into Harold Wilson.'

28 APRIL 1969
France Following an expected narrow defeat in a referendum on constitutional change and political decentralization, President de Gaulle resigns. He is succeeded on 20 June by Georges Pompidou.

14 MAY 1969
Canada Prime Minister Trudeau's controversial omnibus Criminal Code Amendments Bill is passed by the House of Commons, 149 to 55, after a two-week filibuster by opponents of sections that allow for abortion and legalize private homosexual acts.

GOLDA MEIR, 1898–1978

The first woman to become foreign minister and prime minister of Israel, Golda Meir established herself as an able political leader. Her sincere efforts at shaping Israeli policy and furthering Middle Eastern peace gained her worldwide recognition. Born Golda Mabovitz in Russia, she emigrated to the United States with her family, where she worked as a teacher and a librarian until emigrating to what was then Palestine with her husband in 1921. Soon becoming active on the woman's labor council, she was appointed labor minister, and after service as defense minister and ambassador to Moscow she was appointed foreign minister by David Ben-Gurion, taking the Hebrew name Meir (to light u as a member of his cabinet. Succeeding Levi Eshkol as prime minister, she remained in office for five years, rounding out fifty years of politics. She resigned in 1974 under the cloud of her government's near-defeat during the Arab-Israeli war.

8 JUNE 1969
Vietnam War President Nixon meets with South Vietnamese President Thieu on Midway, then announces phased withdrawal of US forces from Vietnam, beginning with a 25,000-man contingent. The administration plans to de-escalate American involvement by gradually turning over the combat role to the South Vietnamese, a program known as Vietnamization.

24 JUNE 1969
El Salvador/Honduras Sparked by rioting over a series of soccer games, a long-smoldering animosity over economic and territorial disputes flares into an undeclared war between the two Central American

A TURBULENT DECADE 1963-1973

Members of the 25th Infantry Division patrol along the 'Iron Triangle' during Operation 'Cedar Falls.'

nations. Resentment had been high over enforcement of an agrarian law permitting only native-born Hondurans to own land and dislodging Salvadorans from land they had farmed. The law affects some 300,000 Salvadorans who had left their land-poor country to farm in sparsely populated Honduras. Sporadic fighting continues through July.

8 JULY 1969
Vietnam War The American 25,000-man troop withdrawal begins as 814 men return to the US. In April US forces in Vietnam had peaked at 543,400.

9 JULY 1969
Canada Prime Minister Trudeau's language bill, giving Canadians the right to use either French or English, is signed by the governor general. A keystone of Trudeau's election campaign, the law is due to go into effect 7 September.

18 JULY 1969
USA A car driven by Senator Edward M Kennedy plunges off a bridge at Chappaquiddick, Martha's Vineyard, Massachusetts. Kennedy escapes, but his companion, Mary Jo Kopechne, is found dead in the car when Kennedy inexplicably fails to report the accident until 10 hours later. Although Kennedy will maintain his Senate seat in the 1970 election, the incident continues to shadow his political career for years to come.

20 JULY 1969
USA Astronaut Neil Armstrong, commander of the Apollo II mission, becomes the first man to set foot on the moon, declaring it 'One small step for a man, one giant leap for mankind.' On 19 November the US makes a second lunar landing.

22 JULY 1969
Spain Generalissimo Francisco Franco designates Prince Juan Carlos his successor and heir to the Spanish Throne, a position for which he has been groomed by Franco since 1948. Juan Carlos is formally invested Prince of Spain on 23 July.

2–4 AUGUST 1969
Northern Ireland In the country's worst sectarian rioting in over 30 years, Protestants and Catholics wage gunfights, gasoline-bomb, and fire attacks in Belfast, Londonderry and other Ulster cities. Sending troops to quell the violence, Britain (15 August) rejects Ireland's peace-force bid and gives its army control of Ulster security.

3 AUGUST 1969
USA Ending a 12-day global tour, President Nixon spells out a new foreign policy stressing self-help for Asian nations and willingness to negotiate with communist countries in 'mutual respect.'

1 SEPTEMBER 1969
Libya A military coup led by Captain Muammar el-Qaddafi topples the regime of King Idris. A revolutionary council replaces Parliament, and the socialist Libyan Arab Republic is proclaimed.

3 SEPTEMBER 1969
North Vietnam Ho Chi Minh, 79, one of the most effective revolutionaries of modern times, dies. He is succeeded by a collective leadership that reiterates determination to press the war until 'there is not a single aggressor in our country.'

15 OCTOBER 1969
USA Hundreds of thousands of Americans participate in Moratorium Day events across the nation to demonstrate opposition to the Vietnam War. On 15 November more than 250,000 gather in Washington for the largest antiwar demonstration to date; another large demonstration is held in San Francisco.

21 OCTOBER 1969
West Germany In a run-off chancellor's election, Social Democrat Willy Brandt wins the required majority over incumbent Kurt Kiesinger to head the first postwar socialist regime in Bonn.

17 NOVEMBER 1969
International The US and the USSR begin preliminary Strategic Arms Limitation Talks (SALT) in Helsinki, Finland. On 24 November a breakthrough is achieved when the two superpowers sign the UN-sponsored Nuclear Nonproliferation Treaty, pledging signatories not to spread nuclear weapons, know-how, or material to countries lacking that technology.

20 NOVEMBER 1969
USA A group of 89 American Indians occupies Alcatraz in San Francisco Bay, claiming the bleak former prison island 'by right of discovery.' During the 18-month occupation, the group demands that the government return the island to the Indians and provide money for an Indian cultural center.

25 NOVEMBER 1969
Lebanon Ending a seven-month crisis that had ended in the fall of the caretaker government created by fighting between Lebanese troops and Palestinian commandos, premier-designate Rashid Karami forms a cabinet. On 3 November the government had concluded a secret pact with Palestinian commandos allowing them to take control of Palestinian refugee camps in Lebanon and conduct raids against Israel from specific bases.

18 DECEMBER 1969
Great Britain The House of Lords approves the end of capital punishment, reaffirming a vote by the House of Commons on 16 December.

OTHER EVENTS OF 1969
Science Joseph Weber of the US conducts an

A TURBULENT DECADE 1963-1973

Rockets fired by gunships hit VC positions in Western Cholon.

The launch of Apollo 11 *space vehicle, 16 July 1969.*

A TURBULENT DECADE 1963-1973

President Richard Nixon waves to US GIs in the base camp of the 1st Infantry at Di An.

experiment that seems to identify the gravitational waves postulated by Einstein in 1915. At Uppsala, Sweden, at the Twelfth Nobel Symposium, scientists present evidence of fluctuations in the rate of production of carbon 14 over the millennia. This requires modification of dates arrived at by carbon-14 calculations, especially those before 1500 BC. An early result will be backdating of some European finds that changes traditional concepts of relations between prehistoric Europe and the Middle East.

Medicine/Health   At Cambridge University, researchers achieve the first *in vitro* fertilization of human egg cells. The US government removes the artificial sweetener cyclamate from the market, citing experiments with mice that link it to cancer.

Technology   Space research is dominated by the US moon landing but the Russians take a notable step when two space vehicles rendezvous and exchange cosmonauts.

Environment   Representatives of 39 nations meet in Rome to discuss growing dangers of pollution in the world's seas. Sweden and Denmark ban use of DDT as a pesticide; the US Government studies the reported dangers, but will not ban DDT till 1972. There is a massive oil spill off Santa Barbara, California.

Social Studies   Stuart Struever begins digging at the Koster site in Illinois, where he will discover one of the most important prehistoric Indian settlements in North America. Thor Heyerdahl sails a balsam raft *Ra II* from North Africa to Barbados in 57 days, claiming to prove that Egyptians could have crossed the Atlantic in ancient times.

Ideas/Beliefs   Erik Erikson's *Gandhi's Truth* brings the insights of psychoanalysis to bear on biography and history.

Literature   Grass's *Local Anaesthetic*; Doris Lessing's *The Four-Gated City*; I B Singer's *The Estate*; James Dickey's *Deliverance*; Philip Roth's *Portnoy's Complaint*; Nabokov's *Ada*; John Fowles' *The French Lieutenant's Woman*; Vonnegut's *Slaughterhouse-Five*.

Drama/Entertainment   Agatha Christie's *Mousetrap* has its 5000th performance in a continuous 18-year run. *Oh, Calcutta!*, a revue featuring frontal nudity, causes controversy.

The Arts   Oldenberg's *Lipstick* is a monumental sculpture at Yale.

Architecture   The Oakland Museum, by Kevin Roche and John Dinkeloo; Boston's new City Hall, by Kallmann, McKinnell, and Knowles.

Music   Shostakovich's *Symphony No 14*; Henze's *Symphony No 6*; Stockhausen's *Stimmung*; Berio's *Sinfonia*; Messiaen's *The Transfiguration*.

Sports/Leisure   The New York Mets cap an incredible saga in modern sports by coming from far behind in the closing weeks of the baseball season to win the World Series.

President Richard M Nixon greets members of the US 1st Infantry Division during his Vietnam tour.

A TURBULENT DECADE 1963-1973

Life/Customs After a homosexual bar in New York's Greenwich Village, the Stonewall, is attacked, homosexuals stage a protest march and initiate what becomes the Gay Rights movement. A Gallup Poll shows that 70 percent of Americans feel the influence of religion is declining in their society.

Miscellaneous In August a three-day rock concert is held at Bethel, New York, which becomes known as Woodstock (its originally intended site). It attracts 300,000 young people and problems are minimal. The prevailing spirit is one of celebration, and Woodstock becomes a symbol of what is best in the youthful counterculture. Among the worst excesses of this period are the brutal murders committed by followers of cult leader Charles Manson in California. The US government-sponsored *Scientific Study of UFOs*, directed by American physicist Edward Condon, concludes that UFOs reported are not from other planets; as a result the US Air Force discontinues its Project Blue Book, which has been monitoring the reports. Pope Paul VI eliminates over 200 saints from the Roman Catholic Church's calendar, including the popular St Christopher, patron of travelers.

7 JANUARY 1970

Middle East Israel launches a jet barrage against military targets inside Egypt, in response to a war of attrition against Israeli positions on the east bank of the Suez Canal. 'Moshe's Marauders,' as Israel's better-trained pilots are known, hit close to Cairo in subsequent strikes on 13, 18, 23, and 28 January. Egypt steps up commando and air raids on Israel's Sinai positions. In early February ships are sunk by both sides.

12 JANUARY 1970

Nigeria The 31-month civil war, with 2 million dead, including nearly a generation of Ibo tribe children, ends with the surrender of secessionist Biafra after its leader, General Odumegwu Ojukwu, flees the country. The Red Cross estimates that there are 5 million starving Biafran refugees behind federal lines, and a massive international relief effort is mounted.

26 JANUARY 1970

Philippines The worst riots in the nation's peacetime history erupt as demonstrators protest corrupt government practices after President Marcos's State of the Nation address. On 30 January 2000 demonstrators try to storm the grounds of the presidential palace, leaving 5 dead and 157 wounded. Sporadic civil, religious, and political unrest will continue over the year.

10–12 FEBRUARY 1970

Jordan A government directive barring Palestinian commandos from carrying arms precipitates a clash between King Hussein's troops and guerrillas around Amman, with 30 killed or wounded. The directive also bans demonstrations, unauthorized publications, political party activity, and possession of weapons and explosives; it is attacked by Al Fatah, largest of the ten Palestinian commando groups operating in Jordan, as a US-supported move to disarm the guerrillas.

11 FEBRUARY 1970

Thailand Withdrawal of 4200 US troops, leaving a total of 43,800 agreed upon by President Nixon and Prime Minister Thanon Kittikachorn during Nixon's 1969 Asian tour, is disclosed.

18 FEBRUARY 1970

USA A federal grand jury finds the defendants in the turbulent 21-week trial of the Chicago Seven innocent of conspiring to incite riots during the 1968 Democratic National Convention. Five of them (Tom Hayden, Abbie Hoffman, Rennie Davis, Jerry Rubin, and David Dellinger) are convicted of crossing state lines with intent to incite riots. This decision is later overturned on appeal, citing Judge Hoffman's prejudicial courtroom behavior.

21 FEBRUARY 1970

Laos After an 11-day drive, the pro-Communist Pathet Lao and North Vietnamese troops sweep across the strategic Plaine des Jarres with Soviet-built tanks and take control. Laotian troops, with US air support, had taken the plain the previous fall after the Communists had held it for five years.

6 MARCH 1970

USA The leveling of a four-story townhouse in New York City is the first of six explosions in a week. The townhouse was a bomb factory for the violent Weather Underground, and the explosion marks a nationwide rise in terrorist bombings.

11 MARCH 1970

Iraq The government agrees to grant the Kurds autonomy, ending an $8\frac{1}{2}$-year war. Terms of settlement include the acceptance of two nationalities (Kurds and Arabs), a Kurdish vice-president, and proportional Kurdish representation in a new Parliament. The Kurds eventually refuse these terms.

18 MARCH 1970

Cambodia While visiting Moscow, Prince Sihanouk is deposed by General Lon Nol, his premier, who had nearly succeeded in a similar attempt two years earlier over presence of North Vietnamese and Viet Cong troops in Cambodia. On 23 March Sihanouk announces from Peking establishment of a national liberation army, with North Vietnamese support; on 5 May he forms a government in exile in Peking. On 9 October Cambodia becomes the Khmer Republic with Lon Nol as president.

8 APRIL 1970

Middle East An Israeli air strike on the Nile delta town of Bahr El-Bakr kills 30 schoolchildren and

Moshe Dayan.

injures 70 other civilians, including 40 more children. On 20 May a band of Palestinian guerrillas slips over the Lebanese border and ambushes an Israeli school bus, killing eight children and four adults, and wounding 20 children.

14 APRIL 1970

Yemen The civil war between republicans and royalist rebels ends as Saudi Arabia agrees to recognize the republican regime and to stop supplying arms to the royalists.

22 APRIL 1970

USA The environmentalist movement gains momentum as millions across the nation mark Earth Day with antipollution demonstrations that include urban clean-ups and mock funerals of car engines.

29 APRIL 1970

Canada In the first Quebec election with separatism as a key campaign issue, French Canadian voters reject the call to independence by René Levesque.

30 APRIL 1970

Cambodia/USA President Nixon tells the nation that he has ordered US troops into action against Communist sanctuaries inside Cambodia to destroy enemy bases and supplies, in support of the Lon Nol regime. US involvement of more than 30,000 soldiers (until 29 June) generates criticism.

4 MAY 1970

USA Student reaction to US operations in Cambodia results in a confrontation between 100 National Guardsmen and 500 to 600 students at Kent State University in Ohio. Four students die after the guardsmen fire into the demonstrators.

14 MAY 1970

Vietnam War Paris peace talks enter their third year, 66th session: hopes for a Vietnam settlement remain faint.

4 JUNE 1970

El Salvador/Honduras The nations agree to establishment of a demilitarized zone along their common border, in an attempt to end the continuing clashes since their June 1969 war. An OAS advisory force is to supervise and police the security zone.

18 JUNE 1970

Great Britain In the national election, the opposition Conservative Party, attacking the state of the economy, upsets the incumbent Labour Party by gaining a 30-seat majority in the House of Commons. Conservative leader Edward Heath replaces Prime Minister Harold Wilson.

29 JULY 1970

USA After five years of strikes and a nationwide boycott, Cesar Chavez, head of the AFL-CIO's United Farm Workers Organizing Committee, signs contracts with 26 major grape growers (representing three-quarters of California's grape production). A challenge by the Teamsters leads to a 2 August 'peace pact' under which Chavez' United Farm Workers have the right to organize agricultural field workers, while the Teamsters retain jurisdiction over organizing cannery workers.

7 AUGUST 1970

Middle East A 90-day cease-fire begins within a 32-mile-deep zone on each side of the Suez Canal. There is no change in the status quo of Israeli and Egyptian positions. Despite numerous charged violations, the cease-fire is extended for three months on 5 November.

12 AUGUST 1970

West Germany/USSR Chancellor Willy Brandt and Premier Aleksei Kosygin sign a nonaggression treaty in Moscow. In a separate letter, Bonn adds that this should not interfere with German efforts to attain 'unity again' in self-determination. Bonn also assures Western powers that the pact does not affect their 'rights and responsibilities' in reference to Berlin.

6 SEPTEMBER 1970

Middle East Palestinian commandos hijack three Western airliners bound for New York in the skies over Europe, precipitating a crisis that endangers the 90-day Middle East cease-fire and sparks civil war in Jordan.

17 SEPTEMBER 1970

Jordan A ten-day civil war erupts between King Hussein's army and Palestinian guerrillas the day after Hussein turns his government over to the military. An East-West confrontation looms as US army units in Europe are alerted and the 6th Fleet hovers in the Mediterranean, while Russia's ally Syria attacks Jordan to help the commandos. Meanwhile, Israeli forces man the border, ready to hit the Syrians in Jordan. On 22 September Hussein's air force turns the tide after intense fighting. On 24 September four guerrilla leaders agree to peace terms and Al Fatah's Yasir Arafat, the top rebel leader, joins in ordering a nationwide cease-fire. By mid-1971, Hussein will have crushed Palestinian strength in Jordan.

28 SEPTEMBER 1970

Egypt The Arab world's most powerful leader, Egyptian President Nasser, dies of a heart attack. He is succeeded on 7 October by Vice-President Anwar Sadat, who pledges 'to continue the struggle for the liberation of Arab lands.'

16 OCTOBER 1970

Canada Prime Minister Trudeau mobilizes troops and imposes the War Measures Act, giving the police emergency powers and suspending many civil liberties in response to two terrorist kidnappings by the Front for the Liberation of Quebec. When one of the kidnapped officials is discovered murdered, the House of Commons supports Trudeau's emergency measures by a vote of 190 to 16. To head off the threat of insurrection, police round up suspected terrorists in the greatest manhunt in Canada's history.

3 NOVEMBER 1970
Chile Salvador Allende Gossens, the first Marxist to be democratically elected head of a government in the Western world, is sworn in as president. Leader of the Socialist Party, Allende reiterates his campaign promise to nationalize much of the economy and form diplomatic ties with several Communist countries. A week later Chile recognizes Cuba.

1 DECEMBER 1970
Spain Basque nationalists kidnap a West German businessman and diplomat to protest the arrest and court-martial of 16 fellow Basques. The trial spurs massive demonstrations, leading Franco to decree a state of emergency on 14 December, in the gravest crisis of his 31-year regime. On 30 December he commutes six death sentences to 30 years in prison. The West German is released unharmed on 25 December.

7 DECEMBER 1970
Poland/West Germany The two nations sign a pact renouncing use of force to settle disputes, recognizing the Oder-Neisse River as Poland's western frontier, and acknowledging transfer to Poland of 40,000 square miles of former German territory.

15 DECEMBER 1970
Poland Sharp hikes in food prices and labor unrest in Gdansk's Lenin Shipyards result in a protest that spreads to other cities. Troops suppress rioting and looting by demonstrators, 300 of whom are reportedly killed before disturbances end on 19 December. On 20 December Communist Party leader Wladyslaw Gomulka is replaced after 14 years in power by party first secretary Edward Gierek.
USSR In Leningrad, a secret trial begins of 11 persons—9 of them Jews—charged with plotting to hijack a plane to escape to Israel. Found guilty of treason for conspiracy to flee abroad, two of the Jews are condemned to death; the other nine receive stiff prison sentences. The Communist regime is deflating Russian Jewish hopes of emigrating to Israel. Following a worldwide outcry, the two death sentences are reduced to 15 years in a labor camp.

OTHER EVENTS OF 1970
Science Discoveries at three laboratories support Howard Termin's 1964 hypothesis that under special circumstances viruses, whose genetic material is ribonucleic acid, not DNA, can dictate production of DNA; this could explain the induction of cancer by viruses. At the University of Cambridge, scientists using X-ray crystallography discover the 3-dimensional structure of ATP, the substance that provides energy for cell metabolism; at Oxford, other scientists discover the 3-dimensional structure of the insulin molecule. A team of researchers at the University of Wisconsin synthesize the first complete gene; at the State University of New York, Buffalo, researchers achieve the synthesis of a living and reproducing cell. Observations reveal that the center of the Milky Way emits much infrared radiation.
Medicine/Health Linus Pauling suggests that massive doses of Vitamin C can help prevent the common cold and flu. L-dopa is approved in the US as a prescription drug to control Parkinson's disease.
Technology The USSR's *Venera 7* is the first satellite to transmit data from the surface of Venus.
Environment The US Government establishes the Environmental Protection Agency (EPA). Tsunamis (tidal waves) and cyclones sweep across the coast of East Pakistan (Bangladesh) in one of the worst natural disasters on record, leaving 300,000 dead and 7 million homeless. In Peru, the worst earthquake in the Western Hemisphere leaves 67,000 dead.
Social Sciences Richard MacNeish finds a succession of stone tools in a cave at Ayacucho, Peru, of which the earliest dates to 20,000 BC, confirming the early settlement of South America.
Literature Bellow's *Mr Sammler's Planet*; Hemingway's (posth) *Islands in the Stream*; Ted Hughes's *Crow*; Borges's *Doctor Brodie's Report*; Eudora Welty's *Losing Battles*; Donald Barthelme's *City Life*; C P Snow's *Last Things* (the 11th and last volume of his Strangers and Brothers series).
Drama/Entertainment David Storey's *Home*; Christopher Hampton's *The Philanthropist*; Bergman's *The Passion of Anna*.
The Arts The Metropolitan Museum of Art pays $5,540,000 for Velasquez's *Portrait of Juan de Paraja*; Jean Dubuffet's *L'hourloupe* sculptures catch the attention of critics and public; Nam Jun Paik, a Korean-American, is among innovators using TV as an art form; Robert Smithson, a leading environmental artist, creates the 'Spiral Jelly' at Great Salt Lakes, Utah.
Architecture Minoru Takeyama's Ichi-Ban-Kan department store in Tokyo; Kevin Roche's Knights of Columbus Building in New Haven, Connecticut.
Music Berio's *Opera*; Carlisle Floyd's *Of Mice and Men*; Michael Tippett's *The Knot Garden*.
Life/Customs The Beatles disband. Beethoven's 200th birthday is widely celebrated. The US outlaws cigarette commercials on TV.
Miscellaneous Expo '70 is held at Osaka, Japan.

22 JANUARY 1971
Cambodia Red commandos shell central Pnom-Penh for the first time, penetrate Cambodia's major airport, and destroy much of its fleet. Meanwhile, Cambodian troops, supported by the South Vietnamese, attack two Communist-held mountain passes along Highway 4, ending the North Vietnamese blockade of the strategic road.

A TURBULENT DECADE 1963-1973

Salvador Allende, the Marxist president of Chile.

25 JANUARY 1971

Uganda President Milton Obote is deposed in a bloody 12-hour military coup while he is attending a Commonwealth conference in Singapore. Army officers headed by Major General Idi Amin take control of the eight-year-old East African republic.

3–9 FEBRUARY 1971

Northern Ireland Eleven die in new Ulster riots as Irish Republican Army (IRA) factions fight each other and Protestants and Catholics clash again. An arms search in a Catholic district by British troops started the riots. The district was a refuge for leaders of the IRA 'provisionals' faction, which had split with IRA 'leftist officials' to seek forceful unification of Ulster and Eire. On 10 March three British soldiers are killed execution-style. Prime Minister Chichester-Clark resigns on 20 March, succeeded by Brian Faulkner, who pledges a vigorous law-and-order drive. Terrorist bombings and shootouts between the IRA and British troops continue to take a toll on the civilian population.

8 FEBRUARY 1971

Laos/South Vietnam South Vietnamese troops, supported by heavy US airpower and artillery fire, cross into Laos for a 44-day assault on the Ho Chi Minh Trail, the Communists' 300-mile infiltration network from Hanoi south into Cambodia and South Vietnam. The drive on Hanoi's supply routes and depots, code-named Operation Lam Son 719, is described as the bloodiest fighting of the Indochina war.

11 FEBRUARY 1971

International In ceremonies in Washington, Moscow, and London, 63 nations sign a treaty prohibiting installation of nuclear weapons on the seabed beyond any nation's 12-mile coastal zone.

25 FEBRUARY 1971

USSR Six hundred delegates from international Jewish groups meeting in Brussels to 'affirm solidarity with our Jewish brothers in the Soviet Union' call on the USSR to allow Jewish citizens to leave for Israel, or to let them practice their religion freely. On 2 March Soviet officials inform 30 Jews, many of whom had staged a sit-in at the Supreme Soviet Praesidium during the three-day Brussels conference, that they may emigrate. In the months that follow, other Soviet Jews receive similar permission. In May the USSR tries Soviet Zionist Jews for anti-Soviet activity and transmitting anti-Soviet propaganda to Israel, finds them guilty, and sentences them to prison camp terms.

12 MARCH 1971

Turkey In a bloodless coup the armed forces compel Premier Suleyman Demirel to resign or face a military takeover under an ultimatum demanding a government strong enough to stop 'anarchy.' This army move comes after months of unrest and violence. After the four major party leaders agree to a coalition government, Nihat Erim, a moderate, is named premier.

25 MARCH 1971

Pakistan Civil war erupts as President Yahya Khan orders troops, planes, and tanks to crush the East Pakistani movement for home rule. Close to one million East Pakistanis, or Bengalis, are killed in the fighting or are massacred later; 10 million refugees seek safety in India.

10 APRIL 1971

China/USA The US table tennis team arrives in China by invitation, marking the movement toward reconciliation between the two nations. On 26 April a Nixon study group urges that Red China be admitted to the UN, concurrently with the Nationalist Chinese. These diplomatic initiatives are climaxed by the dramatic announcement on 15 July that President Nixon will visit China before May 1972 in a 'journey for peace.'

20 APRIL 1971

USA In a unanimous decision, the Supreme Court upholds busing as the primary way of achieving school integration. When the new school year opens in the fall, busing is countered by demonstrations and violence in both North and South.

21 APRIL 1971

Haiti François (Papa Doc) Duvalier, who has ruled the impoverished Caribbean island nation as dictator since 1964, dies and is succeeded on 22 April by his 19-year-old son, Claude.

24 APRIL 1971

USA In a massive but orderly demonstration, 200,000 antiwar protestors conduct a 'march for peace' in Washington, echoed by 156,000 in San Francisco. During a second march on 3–5 May, Washington police arrest 12,614 protestors, at least 7000 of them on the first day—a record for arrests in a civil disturbance—for attempting to 'stop the government' by blocking traffic. Most are released after 24 hours.

13 MAY 1971

Egypt The nation's new President Anwar Sadat consolidates his position by ousting or jailing his foremost opponents and purging prowar politicians and pro-Russian elements. He signs a 15-year friendship and co-operation treaty with Soviet President Podgorny in Cairo on 28 May.

20 MAY 1971

USA/USSR In a breakthrough in the strategic arms limitation talks (SALT), President Nixon and the USSR announce agreement in the current Vienna session 'to concentrate this year on working out . . . limitation of the deployment of antiballistic missile systems—ABMs.'

A TURBULENT DECADE 1963-1973

21 MAY 1971
France/Great Britain After 12 hours of Paris talks, French President Pompidou and British Prime Minister Heath reach agreement allowing Britain's entry into the European Common Market. On 28 October the British House of Commons approves the negotiated entry terms.

8 JUNE 1971
Chile Allende imposes a state of emergency after three men with machine guns kill an outspoken anti-left politician in the nation's second political assassination since Allende won the election. The emergency allows arrests without warrant, press censorship, and suspension of some individual rights. It is accompanied by an alert to the nation's military units.

13 JUNE 1971
USA *The New York Times* begins publication of the *Pentagon Papers*, a top-secret study of US involvement in Vietnam from 1945 to 1967. The 47-volume Pentagon analysis is leaked to the press by military strategist Daniel Ellsberg. On 30 December he is charged with theft, conspiracy, and espionage, but the case will be dismissed.

17 JUNE 1971
Japan/USA The two nations sign a treaty returning Okinawa, a major US military base since World War II, to Japanese rule effective 15 May 1972.

1 JULY 1971
Argentina/Great Britain The two nations reach agreement on opening the Falkland Islands to sea and air links; Britain announces that it will build an airport at Port Stanley. The long-smoldering question of sovereignty over the islands, known as the Malvinas to the Argentines, is deferred.

9 JULY 1971
Vietnam War Five hundred US forces at Fire Base Charlie 2, four miles below the demilitarized zone, turn the stronghold over to South Vietnamese troops, completing the transfer of defense responsibilities for the border area that began in 1969.

13–19 JULY 1971
Jordan In a drive to crush the Palestinian guerrilla movement on Jordanian soil, King Hussein's troops capture over 2000 commandos in northern villages, despite protests from other Arab nations. Many guerrillas flee to Lebanon, which becomes the new base for their operations against Israel.

18 JULY 1971
Middle East Meeting in Dubai, emirs of six Persian Gulf states—Abu Dhabi, Sharja, Ajman, Umm al Quiwan, Fujaira, and Dubai—announce a pact for federation before the planned withdrawal of British military forces by year's end. Ras al Khamina, a seventh emirate, does not join them.

18 AUGUST 1971
Vietnam War Australia and New Zealand announce that their combat forces will be withdrawn from Vietnam by the end of the year.

21 AUGUST 1971
Philippines In Manila, terrorist bomb explosions kill 10 and wound 74, including all eight senatorial candidates due to oppose those supported by Marcos in the upcoming local elections.

23 AUGUST 1971
West/East Germany Envoys of Britain, France, the US, the USSR, and both Germanys reach the first Berlin accord since the end of the war. Signed 3 September, it pledges 'unhindered' passage of traffic between West Berlin and West Germany across East German territory. The Berlin Wall is to remain, and East Germans are still not free to go West.

1 SEPTEMBER 1971
Middle East A constitution creating a federal union of the three Arab countries of Egypt, Syria, and Libya goes into effect with overwhelming popular approval in national referendums.

12 SEPTEMBER 1971
China Former Defense Minister Lin Piao, once designated Mao's successor, mysteriously dies in a Mongolian plane crash. The Chinese later reveal that Lin Piao had tried to seize power and assassinate Mao. When discovered, he tried to flee to the USSR by air.

13 SEPTEMBER 1971
USA Over 1000 New York state troopers and police storm Attica State Prison, ending a four-day revolt by 1200 inmates holding 38 guards hostage and demanding better food and medical care, and more political and religious freedom. In the assault 9 hostages and 29 prisoners are shot to death.

24 SEPTEMBER 1971
Great Britain In the biggest single strike ever made against Soviet spies, the government announces expulsion of 105 Russian officials, based on information received from a defecting senior Soviet intelligence agent.

26 SEPTEMBER 1971
Japan/USA In a historic visit, Emperor Hirohito meets with President Nixon in Anchorage, Alaska, before continuing on a 17-day tour of Europe.

28 SEPTEMBER 1971
Chile The nation expropriates copper mines owned by two US firms as Allende subtracts $774 million from the proposed compensation for 'excess profits' over the past 16 years.
Hungary Cardinal Mindszenty ends 15 years of exile in Budapest's US embassy after an agreement with the government permits him to leave for Rome.

25 OCTOBER 1971
China The UN General Assembly adopts an Albanian resolution to seat Communist China and to oust Taiwan's Chinese Nationalists. In his 15 November debut speech, the Chinese representative blasts US global aggression and vows to liberate Taiwan.

10–20 NOVEMBER 1971
Ecuador/USA With the capture of 16 more US tuna-fishing boats, Ecuador has seized 42 US ships along the Pacific coast. The seizures are based on the nation's claim of a 200-mile territorial water limit, whereas the US recognizes only the 12-mile limit. A total of more than $500,000 in fines is paid by the boats.

3 DECEMBER 1971
Pakistan/India Following increased rebel activity aided by Indian troops in East Pakistan, war erupts. In the 14-day conflict India's superior air power and naval blockade easily cut off Pakistan's vulnerable supply and reinforcement lines. On 6 December India recognizes the rebel government of Bangladesh, to be headed on 12 January 1972 by the charismatic Sheik Mujibur Rahman. On 20 December Foreign Minister Zulfikar Ali Bhutto takes over the Pakistani presidency.

26 DECEMBER 1971
Vietnam War In the sharpest escalation since the end of saturation bombing in November 1968, US fighter bombers begin a five-day assault on North Vietnamese airfields, missile sites, antiaircraft emplacements, and supply facilities in retaliation for increased Communist activity and DMZ violations. By year's end US forces in Vietnam are down to 140,000.

OTHER EVENTS OF 1971
Science American researchers announce revision of the previous structure of the human growth hormone (HGH). Chemical analysis of the Murchison meteorite (found in Australia in 1969) reveals 18 different amino acids—indications that these exist in space and might have provided basis for organic life. Astronomers discover a new galaxy (Maffei 1) close to the Milky Way.

Medicine/Health The British Royal College of Surgeons reports that cigarette smoking kills some 27,500 people a year in Britain.

Technology The first microprocessor is introduced, an essential component in electronic computers. *Uhuru* is the first satellite launched exclusively for investigation of cosmic X-ray sources. US *Apollo 14* and *15* crews are the third and fourth to explore the moon's surface. The USSR softlands a capsule on Mars; three Russian cosmonauts die as another capsule develops an air leak on re-entry. The supersonic *Concorde* makes its first commercial flight.

Social Science Alexander Marshack, a researcher at Harvard University, publishes the results of years of study on bone tools from the Paleolithic Age (ca 10,000–32,000 BC) and claims that their markings are not random but indicate calendar calculations. Norman Mailer publishes two provocative books on contemporary topics: *Of A Fire on the Moon*—about America's space program—and *The Prisoner of Sex*, on the women's liberation movement.

Ideas/Beliefs The Church of England and the Roman Catholic Church end a 400-year estrangement with agreement on the 'essential meaning' of the Eucharist.

Literature Solzhenitsyn's *August 1914* is published in the West after circulating underground in the USSR; Jerzy Kosinski's *Being There*; E M Forster's (posth) *Maurice*; Sylvia Plath's (posth) *The Bell Jar*; V S Naipaul's *In a Free State*; Mordecai Richler's *St Urbain's Horseman*; Updike's *Rabbit Redux*; George Garrett's *Death of the Fox*; Wallace Stegner's *Angle of Repose*.

Drama/Entertainment Tennessee Williams's *Out Cry*; David Williamson's *The Removalist*; David Rabe's *Sticks and Bones*; Pasolini's *The Decameron*; film of *A Clockwork Orange*; Warhol's film *Trash*; the musical *Jesus Christ Superstar*. The Dance Theater of Harlem is established, the first all-black classical ballet company.

The Arts 'Conceptual art' becomes the fad in the US. 'Embarcadero Plaza Fountain, by Armand Vaillancourt, is dedicated in San Francisco.

Architecture Two major public buildings—the Kennedy Center for the Performing Arts in Washington, DC, and the Lyndon Baines Johnson Library at the University of Texas, Austin—come in for harsh criticism from architectural experts.

Music Bernstein's *Mass*; Ginastera's *Beatrix Cenci*; Stockhausen's *Hymnen*; Penderecki's *Utrenja Symphony*.

Sports Billie Jean King becomes the first woman athlete to win $100,000 in a single year.

Miscellaneous Roman Catholic bishops, meeting in Rome, reaffirm the tradition of celibacy for the clergy. It is revealed that in 1970 a tribe of natives known as the Tasaday were discovered in a remote Philippine rain forest living at a Stone-Age level, without agriculture or metals. They had been cut off for hundreds of years, and plans are made to help the Tasaday go on living unmolested.

1 JANUARY 1972
International Austrian diplomat Kurt Waldheim begins his first five-year term as Secretary General of the UN, succeeding U Thant.

25 JANUARY 1972
Vietnam War The Nixon Administration reveals an eight-point peace proposal calling for a cease-fire and release of US prisoners of war, in return for a complete US withdrawal, after which South Vietnam is to hold new elections in which the US will remain neutral. It is also disclosed that secret negotiations

A TURBULENT DECADE 1963-1973

between Henry Kissinger and the communists have been going on since last June.

30 JANUARY 1972
Northern Ireland On 'Bloody Sunday' in Belfast, 13 unarmed civilians are shot as British troops clash with Catholic demonstrators. These deaths touch off retaliatory attacks against British forces by guerrillas and demonstrations in the Irish Republic. In Dublin, an outraged mob storms the British embassy, razing it with fire bombs. In the British Parliament, militant Ulster member Bernadette Devlin strikes Home Secretary Reginald Maudlin as he addresses the House of Commons on the issue.

21 FEBRUARY 1972
China/USA President Nixon arrives in Peking for a historic eight-day visit which ends with a joint communique pledging that both powers will work for 'a normalization of relations.'

27 MARCH 1972
Sudan A treaty ending the civil war between the predominantly Arab Moslem north and the Black Christian and pagan south is signed, ending the 17-year state of emergency.

28 MARCH 1972
Middle East Defying demands by Jordan's King Hussein and the Palestinian commandos for a boycott of balloting, 84 percent of the 16,000 eligible Arab voters turn out in municipal council elections in ten towns on the Israeli-occupied West Bank. Those opposing Hussein and favoring an independent Palestinian state win in five towns; those committed to union with Jordan are re-elected in the other five.

30 MARCH 1972
Northern Ireland Britain ends 51 years of semi-autonomous rule by the Ulster Government and imposes direct rule for at least a year. Prime Minister Heath appoints William Whitelaw, leader of the House of Commons, to the new post of secretary of state for Northern Ireland. This move is hailed by Catholic moderates and opposed by Protestant extremists.
Vietnam War In the biggest communist offensive since 1968, North Vietnamese troops attack South Vietnam through the demilitarized zone. On 16 April US planes begin retaliatory bombing of fuel and supply facilities near Hanoi and Haiphong, the first raids in those areas in more than three years.

6 APRIL 1972
Middle East Egyptian President Sadat announces severance of diplomatic relations with Jordan to protest King Hussein's proposal for federation with Israeli-occupied territory on the West Bank.

9 APRIL 1972
Iraq/USSR During a Baghdad visit, Soviet Premier

Kosygin signs a 15-year friendship pact with Iraq, pledging their 'determined struggle against Zionism and for the total elimination of colonialism.' Russia indicates willingness to supply more arms to Iraq.

15 APRIL 1972
Canada/USA Ending three days of talks, President Nixon and Prime Minister Trudeau sign a pact in Ottawa to clean up the Great Lakes and remove sources of pollution. US-Canadian relations on this matter are balanced by Canadian moves, during the year, to establish limited controls over foreign (mostly American) investments in Canadian resources and industry.

1 MAY 1972
Vietnam War North Vietnamese troops capture Quang Tri, the capital of South Vietnam's northern-most province, after five days of intensive artillery shelling. Saigon forces will recapture the city on 15 September.

8 MAY 1972
Vietnam War In an effort to stem the flow of communist military supplies, President Nixon orders mining of Haiphong and North Vietnam's other ports.

12 MAY 1972
East/West Germany In their first treaty, the two nations agree on all traffic but air transport.

15 MAY 1972
USA While campaigning for the presidency at a Maryland shopping center, Alabama Governor George Wallace is shot in an assassination attempt that leaves him partially paralyzed.

22 MAY 1972
Sri Lanka Ceylon becomes an independent republic after 24 years as a British Dominion. The nation adopts a new Constitution and the traditional name of Sri Lanka (resplendent island). Governor General William Gopallawa becomes president; Mrs Sirimavo Bandaranaike continues as prime minister.
USA/USSR In the first visit of a US president to Moscow, Nixon arrives for a week of summit talks with Kremlin leaders, culminating in a landmark arms pact designed to balance missile forces and halt the nuclear arms race.

30 MAY 1972
Israel/Japan Three Japanese terrorists disembark from a plane and turn machine guns and hand grenades against a crowd of 300 in Tel Aviv's Lod Airport, killing 28 and wounding 76: they had been recruited by a Palestine guerrilla group.

17 JUNE 1972
USA Five men are arrested for breaking into the Watergate offices of the Democratic National Committee in Washington. All are employed by the

5 SEPTEMBER 1972

An A-7E Corsair II is ready for launching from the USS Constellation.

Committee to Reelect the President—the attempted burglary is to obtain political material. Investigation of the break-in will lead to Nixon's resignation.

18 JULY 1972
Egypt/USSR President Sadat announces that he will 'terminate the mission of the Soviet military advisers and experts' in Egypt and orders their immediate withdrawal: the USSR had failed to give Egypt advanced arms to use against Israel.

28 JULY 1972
India/Pakistan In the Simla pact, the two nations agree to withdraw some troops along their 800-mile border, return most of the land captured in the December war, reduce tension over disputed Kashmir, and renounce force in their relations.

9 AUGUST 1972
Uganda President Idi Amin orders 60,000 Asians out of the country within 90 days; ten days later he expels 23,000 Asians holding Ugandan citizenship because they control the economy to the detriment of Africans. Britain says it will accept all its passport holders who cannot find homes elsewhere.

11 AUGUST 1972
Vietnam War The US ends its Vietnam ground combat role in withdrawal of its last unit, the 92-man 3rd Battalion of the 21st Infantry.

22 AUGUST 1972
South Vietnam The Thieu Government abolishes democratic elections in the nation's 10,775 hamlets. Henceforth all village and hamlet posts are to be appointive.

5 SEPTEMBER 1972
International Eight members of the Arab Black September terrorist group invade the Israeli dormitory of the Olympics village in Munich, killing two members of the Israeli squad. After tense negotia-

A TURBULENT DECADE 1963-1973

tions 23 hours later, the terrorists and nine hostages are flown by helicopter to an airport where five terrorists and all hostages are killed. On 29 October two Arab terrorists armed with grenades hijack a Lufthansa jetliner over Turkey and force the Bavarian Government to release the three guerrillas involved in the Olympics killings.

23 SEPTEMBER 1972
Philippines President Marcos proclaims martial law as a 'last desperate step' to save the islands from communist insurgency and attack their deep-rooted social and economic problems. On 29 November the constitutional convention adopts parliamentary democracy in place of the US-style Constitution signed in 1935.

29 SEPTEMBER 1972
Japan/China Japan's Prime Minister Kakuei Tanaka and China's Premier Chou En-lai sign an accord to end the technical state of war existing since 1937 and renew diplomatic relations. Tanaka accepts China's position that 'Taiwan is an inalienable part' of the People's Republic of China. On the same day, Japan severs relations with Taiwan.

3 OCTOBER 1972
USSR/USA In White House ceremonies, President Nixon and Soviet Foreign Minister Andrei Gromyko sign final documents implementing the SALT accords limiting land-based and submarine-borne missile forces. The second phase of the strategic arms control negotiations, covering offensive weapons systems, is to begin on 21 November in Geneva.

11 OCTOBER 1972
Chile Strikes and shutouts begin against Marxist President Allende's economic and political policies. Allende declares a state of emergency in 20 of the nation's 25 provinces by 20 October, as strikers and mounting civil disturbances shut down the country. A government ultimatum ends disorder on 5 November.

26 OCTOBER 1972
Vietnam War Returning from South Vietnam, Secretary of State Henry Kissinger informs the nation that peace is 'within reach in a matter of weeks or less,' two weeks before the US presidential election. Peace talks break down, and on 16 December Kissinger charges that Hanoi has ceased to bargain in 'good faith.'

7 NOVEMBER 1972
USA In the presidential election, Nixon wins an overwhelming victory over his Democratic antiwar challenger, Senator George McGovern. The Democrats maintain majorities in both House and Senate.

1 DECEMBER 1972
Ireland The Irish Parliament votes for a bill to crush the outlawed Irish Republican Army.

2 DECEMBER 1972
Australia In the nation's first Labour Party win in 23 years, Gough Whitlam becomes prime minister. Whitlam will call for a large increase in social welfare appropriations, including funds for a national health service and for urban development.

7 DECEMBER 1972
India/Pakistan With accord reached on a Kashmir truce line, Indian and Pakistani troops begin mutual withdrawal from territories captured in the December 1971 war.

23 DECEMBER 1972
South Korea President Park Chung Hee is re-elected to a six-year term by a National Conference for Unification. Just before the election, a new constitution gave Park the power to extend his term indefinitely and to dissolve Parliament and curb civil rights: he had dissolved the National Assembly and imposed martial law on 17 October.

OTHER EVENTS OF 1972
Science US researchers propose a structure-model for the ribosome cell, site of protein synthesis. British scientists clarify the role of Vitamin D. Early in September, the faint radio star Cygnus X-3 flares up with a great gain in its radio-wave energy output, a phenomenon that cannot be fully explained. Richard Leakey discovers fragments of a humanlike skull near Lake Rudolf in Kenya; it is 2,500,000 years old, pushing back the onset of human evolution.

RICHARD MILHOUS NIXON, 1913–

The 37th president of the United States, Richard M Nixon was born in Yorba Linda, California, and studied at Whittier College and Duke University School of Law. He served in the US Navy during World War II and was elected to Congress in 1946. He became a senator in 1950 and vice-president in 1952 under Dwight D Eisenhower, achieving political prominence mainly through his work on the Alger Hiss case with the House Un-American Activities Committee. As vice-president, Nixon's reputation increased as a result of his outspoken exchanges with Nikita Khrushchev at a Moscow trade fair (1959). He lost the 1960 presidential election to John F Kennedy by a narrow margin and suffered another reverse two years later in an unsuccessful bid for the governorship of California. In 1968 he resurfaced politically to win the Republican nomination (with Spiro T Agnew) and the presidency. His foreign-policy successes, including detente with the USSR and diplomatic contact with the People's Republic of China, were offset by the disclosure (after his 1972 re-election) of complicity in illegal harassment of his political opponents. The June 1972 Watergate burglary precipitated a two-year investigation by the Senate Watergate Committee and Special Prosecutors Archibald Cox and Leon Jaworski that embittered the nation and culminated in Nixon's resignation from the presidency in August 1974.

American draft resisters in Toronto.

A TURBULENT DECADE 1963-1973

Medicine/Health Boston University researchers develop a new surgical technique using carbon dioxide lasers to remove tumors from vocal cords. San Francisco surgeons report success in transplanting leg veins from one person to another. A study affirms the therapeutic value of lithium in treating manic-depressive psychosis. DES (diethylstilbesterol), a synthetic hormone that had been widely administered to pregnant women, is linked to cancer in their daughters.

Technology US *Apollo* crews spend time on the moon, setting a record of almost 75 hours there. The Russians' *Venera 8* softlands on Venus and transmits data for 50 minutes; the Russian *Luna 20* softlands on the moon, obtains samples, and returns to earth.

Environment An earthquake in Nicaragua leaves 10,000 dead and the capital, Managua, destroyed. Hurricane Agnes causes great damage in the Northeast US. Ninety-one nations, including the US, agree to stop dumping pollutants into the world's oceans. The US bans DDT as an insecticide and general use of hexachlorophene as a germ killer.

Literature Robertson Davies's *The Manticore*; Margaret Atwood's *Surfacing*; Richard Adams' *Watership Down*; Eudora Welty's *The Optimist's Daughter*; Yukio Mishima's (posth) *Spring Snow*; Nabokov's *Transparent Things*; John Gardner's *The Sunlight Dialogues*; John Barth's *Chimera*.

Drama/Entertainment Miller's *The Creation of the World*; Tom Stoppard's *Jumpers*; David Williamson's *Jugglers Three*; *The Godfather*; Bergman's *Cries and Whispers. Fiddler on the Roof* (3242 performances) becomes the longest running show on Broadway.

The Arts Michelangelo's *Pieta* in St Peter's is damaged by a hammer-wielding madman.

Architecture The unusual suspended tentlike structures designed by Frei Otto for the Munich Olympics are widely admired. New York City's World Trade Center twin towers are topped off at 1350 feet, making them the world's tallest buildings. Robert Venturi's *Learning from Las Vegas* causes controversy with its thesis that American popular structures like billboards have more contemporary significance than the cathedrals of Europe.

Music Shostakovich's *Symphony No 15*. Robert Moog patents his Moog Synthesizer, an electronic instrument that duplicates sounds of various instruments with some accuracy.

Life/Customs Acupuncture, the ancient Chinese pain-killing technique, attracts adherents in the US. The US military draft ends. Four US Episcopal bishops defy their church's law to ordain 11 women as priests; the first woman rabbi in the US is ordained. As a sign of changing times and tastes, *LIFE* magazine (since 1936) ceases publication in December; in January *Ms* magazine offers a new vehicle for the spirit of women's liberation.

Miscellaneous Athenagoras I, Patriarch of the Eastern Orthodox Church, dies and is succeeded by Dimitrios I. The largest known diamond (969.8 carats) is discovered in Sierra Leone, Africa.

1 JANUARY 1973
International Great Britain, Ireland and Denmark enter the European Common Market. Britain's mood is skeptical, with public fears of higher food costs and the influx of cheap labor.

17 JANUARY 1973
Philippines President Marcos proclaims a new constitution extending his rule indefinitely; other decrees extend martial law and suspend an interim assembly which would have served as a legislature under the new constitution.

27 JANUARY 1973
Vietnam War In Paris ceremonies, the USA, North Vietnam, South Vietnam, and the Viet Cong sign the four-party Agreement on Ending the War and Restoring Peace in Vietnam. Due to South Vietnam's unwillingness to recognize the Viet Cong's Provisional Revolutionary Government, all references to it are confined to a two-party version of the document signed later by North Vietnam and the US. A formal cease-fire begins 28 January; the US is to withdraw all troops within 60 days.

12 FEBRUARY 1973
Uruguay Following a military-civilian confrontation, agreement gives the military control of the government through a National Security Council. Severe inflation will persist, and urban guerrillas known as Tupamaros continue their assassinations, kidnappings, bombings, and bank robberies, leading to still greater government repression.

Vietnam War The prisoner-of-war release begins as the first 142 Americans are turned over at Hanoi's Gia Lam airport; on 14 February the first group of 20 POWs arrives on US soil at California's Travis Air Force Base. The release program will continue after a delay on 27 February, when North Vietnam accuses the US of 'encouraging' the Saigon Government to create obstacles for the Four-Party Joint Military Commission and claims that Saigon has conducted 20,000 military operations since the beginning of the cease-fire.

15 FEBRUARY 1973
Cuba/USA The two nations sign a five-year 'memorandum of understanding' to curb hijacking of aircraft and ships, agreeing either to try hijackers for the offense or to extradite them. US officials state that the pact does not foreshadow any improvement in relations with Cuba.

21 FEBRUARY 1973
Israel/Libya Israeli fighter planes shoot down a Libyan civilian jetliner which had strayed over Israeli-occupied Egyptian territory in the Sinai Desert. The final death toll in the crash is 108. On 24 February Israel concedes an 'error of judgment,' emphasizing the shared responsibility of the French pilot. The following day Israel announces it will pay

compensation to families of the victims.

Laos Ending 20 years of war, the government and communist-led Pathet Lao announce a cease-fire that provides for withdrawal of foreign forces, division of government ministry posts between the Pathet Lao and Vientiane Government, nationwide elections, and exchange of prisoners.

27 FEBRUARY 1973

USA Close to 300 members of the militant American Indian Movement take over Wounded Knee, the site of an 1890 Indian massacre, on the Oglala Sioux Reservation in South Dakota, demanding a government investigation of its treatment of Indians. Prolonged negotiations will lead to the 8 May evacuation of the post by the insurgent Indians.

1 MARCH 1973

International Less than two weeks after the US devalued its dollar by 10 percent, a new monetary crisis sweeps Europe. Over $3 billion is absorbed by at least nine countries to maintain the present value of their currencies. All Japanese and Western European banks are ordered closed the following day; major foreign exchange markets will remain closed for nearly two weeks.

8 MARCH 1973

Northern Ireland A heavy Protestant vote and a Catholic boycott result in a 'yes' in the referendum on whether Ulster should remain part of the United Kingdom. On 20 March the long-awaited British White Paper on constitutional proposals for Northern Ireland, including a more just representation for Catholics in government and measures for reducing anti-Catholic discrimination, is released. Moderate Catholics support it, but extremists in the IRA and among Protestants oppose it.

29 MARCH 1973

Vietnam War The last US troops leave South Vietnam, ending nearly ten years of American military presence. Some 8500 US civilians remain, most of them technicians helping the South Vietnamese armed forces.

8 APRIL 1973

India/Sikkim Following two weeks of antigovernment violence in the Indian protectorate, the Indian Government takes administrative control of Sikkim at the request of its ruler, the Chogyal, Palden Thondup Namgyal. In September 1974 Sikkim will become an associate Indian state, and an April 1975 referendum will abolish the monarchy.

27 APRIL 1973

USSR A major reorganization of the ruling Politburo confirms the prevailing trend toward both easing tensions with the West and stricter defense and security measures at home. Foreign Minister Gromyko, armed forces leader Andrei Grechko, and secret police head Yuri Andropov achieve full membership in the Politburo, while two conservatives are retired early. The 'Old Guard' of Soviet leadership is giving place to a new generation.

30 APRIL 1973

USA In a television address on the Watergate crisis, President Nixon, as 'top man in the organization,' accepts full responsibility for those 'people whose zeal exceeded their judgment,' but denies any personal role in the cover-up. He accepts the resignations of his three top aides, H R Haldeman, John D Erlichman, and John W Dean, and that of Attorney General Richard Kleindienst. On 17 May the Senate committee begins hearings on the Watergate scandal.

19 MAY 1973

West Germany/USSR In Bonn, Soviet leader Brezhnev and West German Chancellor Brandt sign a ten-year pact for economic, industrial, and technical co-operation.

1 JUNE 1973

Greece Premier George Papadopoulos announces that the military-led government has abolished the monarchy and proclaimed a republic.

16–25 JUNE 1973

USA/USSR On Soviet leader Brezhnev's visit to the US, he and President Nixon sign nine agreements, including a pact to avoid military confrontations that might lead to a nuclear war with each other or with a third power. The two nations agree to enter into immediate consultation if relations between

---

THE MEANING OF VIETNAM

During America's direct involvement (1961–73) in Vietnam's long war (which really began during World War II and still may be underway), the United States employed massive forces (including the largest concentration of explosive force used against a single nation), only to witness this war against guerrilla units and a lightly equipped army end in military stalemate and eventual political victory for the enemy. Little wonder that Americans would continue to ponder what it all meant. Some found the meaning in the casualty figures: if the US were willing to fulfill its mission of defending 'the free world,' then it must accept the heavy sacrifice of lives. Many others draw the opposite conclusion from the casualties: the sacrifice of Americans in such a remote and hopeless struggle simply wasn't justifiable. On another level, the meaning of the conflict was debated in traditional geopolitical terms. Here Vietnam was linked to the 'domino theory'—the notion that once one land is conceded to the enemy, others adjacent are inexorably doomed to fall. At this point, too, another notion is often invoked—that of 'appeasement.' It is no coincidence that the name most often associated with appeasement in our century—that of Munich—cropped up repeatedly in the disputes surrounding America's obligations in Vietnam. The debate goes on.

Infantrymen of the US 9th Marines and artillerymen of the 12th Marines attend services in Vietnam.

A TURBULENT DECADE 1963-1973

them, or between one of them and some other country, 'appear to involve risk of nuclear conflict.'

25 JUNE 1973
USA In a sensational disclosure before the Senate Watergate committee, former presidential counsel John Dean reveals Nixon's complicity in the Watergate cover-up. On 16 July another witness reveals that all conversations in the president's office were routinely tape-recorded. On 23 July Nixon defies a legal order to hand over the tapes, claiming they contain 'privileged' executive information.

17 JULY 1973
Afghanistan The nation is proclaimed a republic following a coup d'etat of junior army officers led by Lt Mohammad Daud Khan, King Mohammad Zahir Shah's brother-in-law and cousin. The takeover ends a ten-year experiment in democracy that failed to alleviate the famine brought on by a three-year drought.

14 AUGUST 1973
Cambodia The US ceases bombing in Cambodia around midnight, in accord with a June Congressional ruling. The bombing halt is preceded by several days of intensive bombing around Pnom-Penh. The US will continue unarmed reconnaissance flights and military aid to Cambodia and Laos.

24–28 AUGUST 1973
China The Chinese Communist Party holds its tenth congress, adopting a revised constitution, selecting a new Central Committee, and endorsing a political report by Premier Chou En-lai that labels the USSR the major threat to China.

28 AUGUST 1973
USSR An open letter from the Soviet Academy of Sciences is published, condemning physicist Andrei Sakharov for his public criticism of the Kremlin's domestic and foreign policies. A press campaign against the dissident begins, evoking protests from Western leaders.

1 SEPTEMBER 1973
Libya Following a breakdown in negotiations, Libya proclaims nationalization of foreign oil companies operating in the country, declaring that it will pay them an as-yet-undetermined compensation.

11 SEPTEMBER 1973
Chile A four-man military junta overthrows President Allende in a violent coup, ending 46 years of civilian rule. Allende and 2700 others die. Army chief of staff General Augusto Pinochet Ugarte becomes president and maintains a state of siege until March 1978. The right-wing dictatorship vows to 'exterminate Marxism.' (It will be revealed in 1974

The USS Ohio *takes its place in the nuclear navy.*

that the US Central Intelligence Agency had tried to 'destabilize' Allende's Government.)

23 SEPTEMBER 1973

Argentina After 18 years out of power, Juan Perón is elected president, with his third wife, Isabel, as vice-president. Perón returned to Argentina on 20 June. He will die in office nine months later.

6 OCTOBER 1973

Middle East The fourth and largest Arab-Israeli war in 25 years begins on Yom Kippur, the Jewish holy day of atonement, as Egyptian forces cross the Suez Canal at five points and Syrian forces attack at two positions on the Golan Heights. After losing ground on both fronts, Israel counter-attacks. By the time a UN cease-fire takes effect on 24 October, Israel has reversed most Arab gains, but with high casualties.

10 OCTOBER 1973

USA Vice-President Spiro Agnew resigns and pleads nolo contendere to tax-evasion charges. He is sentenced to three years probation and fined $10,000. On 6 December he is succeeded by Gerald R Ford.

19–21 OCTOBER 1973

Middle East The Arab oil-producing nations impose a total ban on oil exports to the US and declare a 10 percent cut in production to put pressure on the US and its Western European allies to force Israeli withdrawal from Arab lands. On 15 October the US had announced it was resupplying Israel with military equipment to counter support given by the USSR to Arab forces. The ban on oil exports is lifted 18 March 1974. The oil embargo will trigger an energy crisis in the industrialized nations, as huge oil price increases result in a severe recession in the US and Europe during the next two years.

20 OCTOBER 1973

USA The Watergate drama continues with the

THE OIL CRISIS

Economists predict sluggish growth and above-normal unemployment for developed nations in the 1980s. This is the second decade in a long cycle of 'bad times' (referred to as a 'Kondratieff contraction,' after the economist who claimed to discover fifty-year business cycles, twenty-five good, followed by twenty-five bad). The good years began with the discovery of the vast and cheap oil fields in the Middle East in 1938. After World War II, the world's energy system quickly transformed itself into one based on petroleum and natural gas rather than coal. But the era of cheap energy ended abruptly in 1973, and though it is clearly not the single cause of the contraction, it played a dramatic role in the timing. That year, oil prices took a quantum leap (another in 1979) and since oil is produced largely outside the developed world, as money flowed to the oil-exporting nations, growth in income levels and employment in the developed nations dropped. There is simply less money available to buy other goods and services. Government efforts to artificially stimulate the economy have not cured the stagnation, and recovery from the recession will dramatically raise the price of oil again. The developed world, in response to the basic problem of rising energy cost, needs to find ways to economize on scarce energy. That, however, will entail a virtual redesigning of its production, living, and transportation methods. Eventually, it is promised, there must be a future free from dependence on oil, but for the present the crisis continues to exact its toll.

'Saturday Night Massacre,' as Attorney General Elliot Richardson and his deputy William D Ruckelshaus resign. Watergate Special Prosecutor Archibald Cox is fired when he rejects Nixon's compromise offer on the disputed Watergate tapes. On 1 November Leon Jaworski is named special prosecutor. Public outrage forces Nixon to agree to turn over the nine tapes on 23 October. Of these tapes, the administration claims that two never existed; an 18-minute gap, caused by multiple erasures, appears on a third. Serious talk of impeachment begins on 23 October.

25 OCTOBER 1973

International The US places its military forces on a worldwide alert based on 'ambiguous' signs that the USSR might intervene militarily in the Middle East. The crisis ends when the USSR and US join in a UN Security Council vote barring either from participation in a 7000-man Middle East peacekeeping force.

7 NOVEMBER 1973

Egypt/USA The two nations announce resumption of diplomatic relations following a break that extended back to the 1967 Arab-Israeli war.

11 NOVEMBER 1973

Middle East A US-sponsored agreement worked out by Secretary of State Henry Kissinger is signed by

---

JUAN PERÓN, 1895–1974

Juan Perón rose to power in Argentina during World War II as a leader of a militant pro-Fascist group that envisioned Argentinian hegemony in South America. As vice-president in 1944, he began to court labor, which would give him most of his future support. He became president in 1946 and inaugurated a strongly nationalistic reform program which came to be called *Peronisimo*. Perón was a colorful and dynamic leader with a strong hold on his people; his charismatic wife Eva was as popular as he. In spite of his initial wide public support, the increasing totalitarian nature of his regime, plus his conflicts with the Church and the death of his wife, led to his ouster by the military in 1955. After 18 years of exile Perón was welcomed back to become president of Argentina in 1973; in the midst of violent factional disputes he died nine months later and was succeeded by his second wife.

A TURBULENT DECADE 1963-1973

Israel and Egypt, solidifying the cease-fire, allowing a prisoner exchange, and ending Israeli sieges of Suez City and the Egyptian Third Army. On 21 December Middle East peace talks begin in Geneva.

21 NOVEMBER 1973

Northern Ireland Seven weeks of stormy negotiations between Britain's Secretary of State for Ulster, William Whitelaw, and Northern Ireland's political leaders, culminate in a compromise plan for a coalition government in which Protestants and Catholics would share power. This executive body will control all of Northern Ireland's affairs except security, justice, foreign relations, and some financial matters.

25 NOVEMBER 1973

Greece Following weeks of student-worker riots, President Papadopoulos is deposed and placed under house arrest in a bloodless coup by military leaders who oppose a too-hasty return to democracy.

20 DECEMBER 1973

Spain Premier Louis Carrero Blanco, heir apparent to Generalissimo Franco, is assassinated in Madrid by an outlawed Basque terrorist group in retaliation for the killing of nine Basque militants by the government.

OTHER EVENTS OF 1973

Science A California team headed by Drs Herbert Boyer and Stanley Cohen develops procedures to produce recombinant DNA molecules, achieved by splicing a human gene into the molecules of bacteria's DNA; the bacterium then produces the human substance. Belgian geneticists determine the sequence of molecules in genes. Researchers synthesize the parathyroid hormone regulating the level of calcium in blood plasma. Robert Woodward and others announce synthesis of Vitamin B_{12}: 99 workers from 19 countries have worked on this for at least 11 years. Lubos Kahoutek, of the Hamburg (Germany) Observatory, discovers a new comet heading toward Earth in March; by November Comet Kahoutek has created speculations of disaster, but it passes harmlessly behind the sun by early 1974.

Medicine/Health A vaccine to prevent rabies is developed. Marijuana is used to treat glaucoma.

Technology *Skylab 1* is launched to perform astronomy experiments; its solar panels fail to extend properly, but *Skylabs 2* and *3* are launched successfully.

Environment The US passes the Endangered Species Act, prohibiting the Federal Government from supporting projects that might jeopardize designated animals. The Mississippi/Missouri River system floods to the highest point in a century; a vast area is inundated, but relatively few lives are lost.

Social Science A bone tool found in the Yukon, Alaska, is dated to about 27,000 BC, one of the earliest dates for human beings in the New World. (In California some claim to find tools dating to

500,000 years ago.) Cotton cultivation in the New World is traced to 3500 BC in Mexico.

Literature Pynchon's *Gravity's Rainbow;* Grass's *From the Diary of a Snail*; Patrick White's *The Eye of the Storm*; Graham Greene's *The Honorary Consul*; Alice Munroe's *Lives of Girls and Women*; Heinrich Böll's *Group Portrait with Lady*; Anthony Powell's *Temporary Kings* (the 11th in his series A Dance to the Music of Time).

Drama/Entertainment Peter Shaffer's *Equus*; David Storey's *Changing Room*; Lanford Wilson's *Hot L Baltimore*; Woody Allen's *Sleeper*; *Last Tango in Paris*; *Day for Night.*

The Arts The Metropolitan Museum of Art in New York 'reattributes' 300 of its works, downgrading them from such masters as El Greco, Goya, and Rembrandt, to 'pupils' or 'followers'.

Architecture Australia's Sydney Opera House, begun in 1957, opens. I M Pei's Herbert Johnson Museum of Art at Cornell University is a notable structure.

Music Britten's *Death in Venice*; Piston's *Fantasy for Violin and Orchestra*; Conrad Susa's *Transformations.*

Miscellaneous Solzhenitsyn's *Gulag Archipelago*—a carefully researched exposé of the Soviet prison camp network—begins publication in Paris; it will soon appear in many Western languages. In Chicago, the Sears Tower is completed at 1454 feet (443 m), making it the tallest building in the world. (In 1974 the Canadian National Tower in Toronto will reach 1805 feet but it is regarded as a freestanding structure, not a true building.)

Sigmund Freud on his estate near Vienna.

A TURBULENT DECADE 1963-1973

The Middle East flares up again: Syrian oil fields ignited by Israeli bombs.

1974- :
AN ERA OF ANXIETY

The end of HMS Sheffield *during the Falkland Islands crisis of 1982.*

8 JANUARY 1974
South Korea In response to mounting opposition to his new constitution, President Park issues two decrees. The first prohibits any attempt to oppose, deny, or repeal the constitution; the second establishes emergency courts to deal with violations of the first. Even after 26 opposition leaders are placed under police guard, civic and religious leaders continue their campaign to collect a million signatures for a petition demanding a 'democratic' constitution.

17 JANUARY 1974
Middle East A disengagement agreement is reached by Israel and Egypt with US mediation. Egyptian forces occupy a narrow strip on the east side of the Suez Canal, with a UN-patrolled buffer zone separating them from the Israeli forces farther east. The Israelis withdraw from west of the canal, and troops and equipment of both sides are limited. Following more intensive shuttle diplomacy by US Secretary of State Kissinger, Israel and Syria sign a 31 May agreement disengaging forces on the Golan Heights, the first armistice between the two nations since the 1948 war.

19–20 JANUARY 1974
China/South Vietnam The long-standing dispute over the remote Paracel Islands flares into warfare as 600 Chinese troops, with MiG support, seize the archipelago from the South Vietnamese.

23 JANUARY 1974
USA Beginning with Exxon, the major oil companies announce sharp rises (50 to 70 percent) in fourth-quarter 1973 earnings. Prices remain high and continue to rise even after the end of the Arab oil embargo on 18 March. Widespread shortages stimulate a government program aimed at energy self-sufficiency.

10 FEBRUARY 1974
Iran/Iraq On their mutual border near Badra, Iraqi and Irani forces backed by armor and artillery clash, leaving 70 dead. Iraq claims the Iranians are massing more troops near the border and are flying jet fighters deep into Iraqi air space.

13 FEBRUARY 1974
USSR Russian Nobel Prize-winning author Alex-

AN ERA OF ANXIETY 1974–

ander Solzhenitsyn is deported to West Germany. An outspoken critic of the Soviet Government, Solzhenitsyn had recently published in Paris *The Gulag Archipelago*, exposing the Soviet prison-camp system. He will eventually make his home in the United States.

4 MARCH 1974

Great Britain Failing to form a coalition with Jeremy Thorpe's Liberal Party, Prime Minister Edward Heath resigns, leaving Labour Party leader Harold Wilson to form the nation's first minority cabinet in 45 years. Prime Minister Wilson will fail to solve the major problems of unemployment and a poor economy.

2 APRIL 1974

France President Georges Pompidou dies after nearly five years in office. On 19 May conservative Valery Giscard D'Estaing wins narrowly over his socialist opponent François Mitterand in a run-off election for the presidency. Giscard names a cabinet characterized by nonpolitical specialists and pledges to develop France 'as a country of political and intellectual asylum.'

9 APRIL 1974

India/Pakistan India, Pakistan, and Bangladesh settle a three-year dispute on Pakistani prisoners of war taken in 1971. The pact restores normal relations; India and Pakistan agree to reinstitute communication and travel links, as well as trade, economic, and cultural ties.

10 APRIL 1974

Israel Premier Golda Meir resigns in a dispute over blame for the nation's unpreparedness in the 1973 Yom Kippur War. Itzhak Rabin becomes premier and forms a coalition government.

WILLY BRANDT, 1913–

After gaining fame and popularity through his anticommunist policies as mayor of West Berlin, Willy Brandt emerged as one of the most dynamic politicians in postwar Germany. Born Herbert Frahm, the illegitimate son of a poor salesgirl in Lübeck, Brandt openly opposed the Nazis. Changing his name to escape arrest when Hitler came to power, he fled to Norway, where he remained active in the resistance. On his return to Germany after the war, Brandt was elected to the Bundestag as a representative in West Germany's first government. He was a committed Social Democrat, but when a coalition government was formed in 1966 by the Christian Democrats and Social Democrats, Brandt became vice-chancellor and foreign minister. In 1969 he became chancellor, West Germany's highest official. He resigned in 1974 when it was revealed that an aide was an East German spy. Brandt has remained a prominent spokesman for the ideas of social democracy long past the time when he wielded power in his government.

---

11 APRIL 1974

Middle East Three Arab guerrillas conduct a raid on the Israeli border town of Qiryat Shemona, killing 18 persons, mostly women and children. Claiming responsibility, the Lebanese-based Marxist Popular Front for the Liberation of Palestine announces the raid was aimed at sabotaging upcoming Geneva Middle East peace talks. In retaliation Israeli forces raid several Lebanese border towns; Israel warns of additional punitive raids if Lebanon fails to police guerrillas. The incidents continue.

18 APRIL 1974

Egypt/USSR Charging the Soviet Union with attempts to influence Egypt by deferring requests for arms, President Sadat announces that Egypt will end its reliance on Soviet arms aid.

25 APRIL 1974

Portugal Premier Marcello Caetano is ousted by a military group pledging democracy and peace for Portugal's African territories. General Antonio de Spinola emerges as leader of the new government.

6 MAY 1974

West Germany Chancellor Willy Brandt resigns, taking responsibility for the 'negligence' that allowed an East German spy to become a member of his staff. The Social Democrats choose moderate Finance Minister Helmut Schmidt to succeed Brandt; on 16 May he is sworn in as the nation's fifth postwar chancellor.

9 MAY 1974

USA The House Judiciary Committee opens impeachment hearings against President Nixon. On 27–30 July, following six months of investigation, the committee votes three articles of impeachment, charging obstruction of justice, abuse of power, and contempt of Congress.

18 MAY 1974

India India conducts a successful test of a powerful nuclear device in 'a peaceful nuclear explosive experiment,' becoming the sixth nation with a nuclear bomb.

29 MAY 1974

Northern Ireland Following collapse of the five-month-old Protestant-Catholic coalition government, the British Government resumes direct rule. Despite assignment of more British forces to Ulster, violence is unabated.

27 JUNE 1974

Iran/France The two nations sign a $4 billion ten-year development pact, including the sale to Iran of five nuclear reactors.

1 JULY 1974

Argentina President Juan Perón dies at 78, succeeded by his vice-president and wife, Isabel Martinez de Perón, the Western Hemisphere's first woman head of state. The nation's severe economic and political problems continue.

Turkey Defying US threats to cut off aid, Turkey announces it will allow the growth and sale of opium again, under strict control. In 1971 Turkey had promised the US to outlaw the trade in exchange for $35.7 million over four years.

15 JULY 1974

Cyprus In a violent coup led by 650 Greek officers, the Cypriot National Guard overthrows the government of Archbishop Makarios, who flees the country. International negotiations falter, and Turkey invades Cyprus on 20 July, ostensibly to protect the Turkish minority (18 percent) there. An uneasy UN-sponsored cease-fire is reached 22 July.

23 JULY 1974

Greece The Cyprus crisis forces resignation of the seven-year-old military junta; former Premier Constantine Karamanlis returns from exile to become chief of state. On 1 August his civilian government restores the 1952 constitution, postponing a controversial decision on the role of exiled King Constantine. A wide-ranging purge of military figures associated with the junta follows. On Cyprus fighting continues until Turkey controls the northeast third of the island, then declares a unilateral cease-fire on 16 August.

9 AUGUST 1974

USA President Nixon resigns, and Vice-President Gerald R Ford is sworn in as president. Nixon's support in the Watergate struggle began eroding on 5 August, when he released three tapes admitting he originated plans to have the FBI halt its probe of the Watergate break-in for political as well as national security reasons. His supporters in both Houses of Congress then said they would vote for his impeachment. One month later, on 8 September, President Ford will issue Nixon an unconditional pardon, arousing a storm of criticism.

23 AUGUST 1974

South Korea President Park partially rescinds the emergency status in effect since January, but not the decrees permitting secret courts-martial and arrests without warrant. In a 15 August assassination attempt on Park, his wife was killed; investigators charge North Korean complicity.

26 AUGUST 1974

Portugal Ending over eleven years of fighting, the government begins dissolution of its African empire by signing an agreement to free Portuguese Guinea. On 10 September the new nation becomes Guinea-Bissau.

4 SEPTEMBER 1974

East Germany/USA The two nations establish diplomatic relations, the US becoming the last major

---

WATERGATE

What began as a 'third-rate burglary' on the night of 17 June 1972 ended some 26 months later with the first resignation of an American President. It was what happened in the interim that provided a lesson for history. The break-in at the National Democratic Headquarters was serious enough, but it would almost certainly have been forgotten had those close to President Nixon assumed responsibility. In the months that ensued, all involved had several more chances to stop the snowball; as late as October 1973 President Nixon could probably have dissipated the scandal by simply admitting that, in trying to protect his subordinates and, yes, his own position as President, he had foolishly authorized a cover-up. Governments, after all, have often tried to dissemble their errors. But Nixon now made the crucial mistake—trying to cover up the cover-up. He fired Special Prosecutor Archibald Cox, turned over tapes with an 18-minute gap, submitted edited transcripts, and issued increasingly evasive statements. Meanwhile, Congressional hearings and the media revealed widening circles of break-ins, wiretaps, secret funds, and other deceptions and illegalities. So it was that 'Watergate' entered our national vocabulary as a synonym for wrongdoing in high places that threatens the very institutions of government. The American people might have accepted that the White House had used some 'bricks of straw'; what they could not accept was 'stonewalling.'

Western power to recognize East Germany since it emerged from international isolation three years ago. This was facilitated by East Germany's agreement to hold future discussions on possible compensation for Jewish victims of Nazism.

12 SEPTEMBER 1974

Ethiopia Emperor Haile Selassie is deposed after 58 years by armed forces leaders who have planned the bloodless coup since February. The provisional military government dissolves Parliament and suspends the constitution. On 20 December they declare Ethiopia a socialist state, leading to widespread nationalization of financial institutions and rural land in 1975.

16 SEPTEMBER 1974

USA President Ford proposes conditional amnesty for Vietnam-era draft evaders and deserters in exchange for up to two years' public service work: the program is condemned by both Vietnam War veterans and organized exile groups.

30 SEPTEMBER 1974

Portugal Provisional President General de Spinola resigns with several associates accused of a right-wing plot against the government. Leftist military officers and civilians take power.

28 OCTOBER 1974

Middle East Meeting in Rabat, Morocco, heads of

AN ERA OF ANXIETY 1974–

20 Arab nations, including Jordan's Hussein, unanimously call for creation of an independent Palestinian state 'on any Palestinian land that is liberated' from Israeli occupation. The Arab leaders recognize Palestine Liberation Organization leader Yasir Arafat as the 'sole legitimate representative of the Palestinian people.' On 13 November Arafat addresses the UN, as the PLO is granted observer status; on 22 November the UN votes 89–9, with 37 abstentions, in support of the Palestinian cause.

5–10 NOVEMBER 1974
Angola Rioting in and around Luanda leaves 100 dead and 200 injured. Much of the violence, centered in the city's African slum suburbs, is believed to be sparked by a faction of the Popular Movement for the Liberation of Angola (MPLA). On 12 November Portuguese negotiators announce they have temporarily shelved a plan for an interim coalition government that would include the former guerrillas.

29 NOVEMBER 1974
Northern Ireland The British House of Commons approves emergency legislation to outlaw the IRA and to give police sweeping powers of arrest and detention, and stricter controls over travel between England and Ireland, following two Birmingham bar bombings.

7 DECEMBER 1974
Cyprus Archbishop Makarios returns to reassume the presidency, offering self-government to the Turkish minority, but rejecting partition of the island.

8 DECEMBER 1974
Greece By a more than 2-to-1 margin, the people reject the nation's 142-year-old monarchy and choose to remain a parliamentary republic. On 9 December Parliament meets for the first time in seven years.

11 DECEMBER 1974
Rhodesia Prime Minister Ian Smith announces that the white minority government and black nationalists have agreed on an immediate cease-fire on the nation's northern border. All nationalist prisoners will be released immediately, and a conference will be held to fix a role for the black majority in the government.

28 DECEMBER 1974
Nicaragua Sandanista guerrillas seize about 30 hostages, including three leading Nicaraguan diplomats. The government-negotiated release of the hostages includes a $1-million ransom, free passage to Cuba for the guerrillas, release of 14 political prisoners to Cuba, and the publication/broadcast of an anti-Somoza-regime statement that the Sandanistas are gaining strength in their battle against dictatorship.

OTHER EVENTS OF 1974
Science American researchers Burton Richter and Samuel C C Ting find a new elementary particle, the psi. Swedish researchers find a new amino acid. An expedition in Ethiopia, led by Donald Johanson and Maurice Taieb, finds fossilized remains of humanlike beings 3–4 million years old (1,500,000 years older than comparable finds). Skulls found in California are 45,000 years old, indicating humans in the New World much earlier than formerly proposed.

Medicine/Health Dr Christiaan Barnard, the South African surgeon who performed the first heart transplant in 1967, implants a donor heart without removing the patient's own—providing a back-up pump. A smallpox epidemic sweeps through India, Bangladesh, Nepal, Pakistan, and Ethiopia, killing 26,000 Indians alone. Reports show that males who smoke large amounts of marijuana have lower levels of testosterone; heavy alcohol drinkers have higher rates of mouth, throat, and liver cancer; and vinyl chloride, used in various plastics, causes cancer.

Technology The USA launches *SMS-1*, a weather satellite placed in synchronous orbit (staying in the same spot above the earth). West Germany launches *Helios 1*, a space probe to study the sun. A computerized X-ray scanner for examining cross-sections of the human body is announced.

Environment Floods, followed by cholera, smallpox, and crop failures, leave 100,000 dead in Bangladesh. Hurricane Fifi kills 8000 in Honduras, and an earthquake in Pakistan kills 5200. The US passes the Safe Drinking Water Act to set standards for water pollution. Freon, a fluorocarbon propellant in many aerosol sprays, is said to endanger the earth's ozone layer. The US National Academy of Science urges a ban on genetic experiments with bacteria, especially those involving *E coli*, because of the potential threat to human lives should a deadly form escape.

Social Sciences Near Sian, China, one of the most extraordinary archaeological discoveries of all time is made: the burial mound of an emperor who died in 206 BC houses 6000 life-size ceramic figures (plus at least 10,000 other valuable artifacts). Each figure is sculptured to depict an individual, including details of the clothing; they were substitutes for the practice of burying royal retainers. A provocative book, *Time on the Cross*, by Robert Fogel and Stanley Engerman, analyzes statistically the economics of the US slave system: because it takes a nonjudgmental analytical approach—slavery as a mode of production—it offends many.

Literature Joseph Heller's *Something Happened*; Muriel Spark's *The Abbess of Crewe*; Yukio Mishima's (posth) *The Decay of the Angel*, completing his tetralogy The Sea of Fertility.

Drama/Entertainment Tom Stoppard's *Travesties*; Bergman's *Scenes from a Marriage*.

The Arts Britain's Royal Academy of London celebrates the 100th anniversary of the first Impressionist exhibit with a retrospective.

Architecture The Joseph Hirshhorn Musum and Sculpture Garden, designed by Gordon Bunshaft, is dedicated in Washington, DC.

Music Henze's *La Cubana*; William Schuman's

16 APRIL 1975

Concerto on Old English Rounds; Bruno Maderna's *Quadrivium*; Thea Musgrave's *The Voice of Ariadne*; Charles Wuorinin's *Concerto for Piano*.

Sports Henry Aaron betters Babe Ruth's lifetime record of 714 home runs in American baseball when he hits his 715th on 8 April; when he retires in 1976, Aaron will have hit 755.

Life/Customs 'Streaking'—running naked through public gatherings—spreads from college campuses to public events, then to televised occasions. The game of backgammon, played for centuries in many parts of the world, becomes fashionable in the West. American women score a series of firsts: elected governor in her own right (Ella Grasso of Connecticut); mayor of a major city (San Jose, California); navy chaplain; grandmother elected to Congress (Millicent Fenwick of New Jersey); chairperson of a national party (Republican); avowed lesbian elected to state office (Elaine Nobel, Massachusetts legislature); woman police officer killed in line of duty.

Miscellaneous A Turkish airliner crashes in Paris with loss of 346; a Russian destroyer explodes in the Black Sea with loss of 275. The American Telephone & Telegraph Corporation, the largest private employer in the US, bars discrimination against homosexuals.

2 JANUARY 1975
Middle East/USA In a magazine interview, US Secretary of State Kissinger hints that the US might use military force in the Middle East 'to prevent the strangulation of the industrialized world' by Arab oil producers.

13–17 JANUARY 1975
China For the first time in a decade, the National People's Congress, China's highest legislative body, meets secretly in Peking and endorses the leadership of Premier Chou En-lai. Chairman Mao Tse-tung does not appear at the congress. The ailing Chou delivers a report predicting complete modernization of a stable, orderly China by the end of the century and offering a vision of inevitable world war.

31 JANUARY 1975
Ethiopia The 12-year war for Eritrean independence intensifies as insurgents launch a mortar and bazooka attack on three military installations in Asmara, capital of the beleaguered province. By 6 February the casualties are reported at 1200 dead; on 15 February the government imposes a state of emergency.

9 FEBRUARY 1975
Northern Ireland The IRA announces a new, open-ended cease-fire to begin the next day, following agreement with British officials. To monitor the truce, Britain is to set up a network of centers in 24-hour contact with IRA units in Northern Ireland. The British military presence there is to become 'progressively less obtrusive.'

13 FEBRUARY 1975
Cyprus Turkish Cypriots proclaim the Turkish-occupied northern section of Cyprus a separate state, offering to join in a bi-regional federal state with Greek Cypriots. Three-quarters of the ethnic Turks in the Greek zone cross over into the Turkish region, and 200,000 Greek Cypriots ask to return to their homes in the Turkish zone.

15 FEBRUARY 1975
South Korea President Park announces liberation of almost all the nation's 203 political prisoners. This conciliatory move follows a 12 February referendum supporting Park's rule and the 1972 constitution giving him unlimited powers. Government critics charge that the referendum has been rigged.

21 FEBRUARY 1975
Israel The UN Human Rights Commission censures Israel for actions in its occupied Arab territories, citing civilian war victims, desecration of Moslem and Christian shrines, and imprisonment of the Greek Catholic Archbishop of East Jerusalem.

6 MARCH 1975
Iran/Iraq In a joint communique, Iran promises to end support of Kurdish rebels in Iraq. After an offensive against Kurdish insurgents, Iraq announces a two-week cease-fire on 13 March to allow Kurdish rebels and civilians to cross into Iran. By 2 April, meeting little resistance, Iraqi forces reoccupy rebel-held border areas.

17 MARCH 1975
Thailand Newly installed Premier Kukrit Pramoj announces that his government will seek withdrawal of 25,000 US troops and 350 aircraft within a year, but only if 'the political and military situation in this region permits.' Kukrit says he will try to establish relations with China and open talks with North Vietnam.

25 MARCH 1975
Saudi Arabia At a Riyadh palace reception, King Faisal is assassinated by a deranged nephew, who will be beheaded on 18 June. Faisal is succeeded by his brother Crown Prince Khalid, but his half-brother Prince Fahd will exercise power. Saudi Arabia's close relations with the US remain unchanged.

13 APRIL 1975
Lebanon Warfare breaks out between Moslems and Christians. Three days of fighting in Beirut between Palestinian guerrillas and the right-wing Christian Phalangist Party militia leave 120 dead and 200 wounded. Sporadic hostilities will continue for more than a year.

16 APRIL 1975
Cambodia Under insurgent military pressure from all sides, the Lon Nol Government surrenders to the

435

AN ERA OF ANXIETY 1974–

Khmer Rouge, ending the five-year war. Lon Nol had already fled by air on 1 April. Prince Sihanouk will return from his Peking exile, but a new constitution in December establishes a 250-member People's Assembly headed by Pol Pot, whose brutal regime causes two to four million deaths over the next three years.

24 APRIL 1975

West Germany Terrorists seize West Germany's Stockholm embassy, demanding release of 26 members of the Baader-Meinhof anarchist group from West German prisons. Refused, the terrorists blow up part of the embassy. Four persons, including one terrorist, die during the siege.

30 APRIL 1975

South Vietnam Hours after the emergency helicopter evacuation of all Americans remaining in Saigon, and thousands of South Vietnamese who fear for their lives, South Vietnamese President Duong Van Minh announces unconditional surrender to the communists.

14 MAY 1975

Cambodia/USA President Ford orders a ground, air, and sea operation to rescue the US cargo ship *Mayaguez*, seized by Cambodia's Khmer Rouge Government two days earlier. The mission is successful, but 38 US servicemen are killed. Ford's forceful handling of the incident is hailed by many Americans who view the seizure as piracy: the Cambodian Government charges that the US ship was part of a spy operation.

16 MAY 1975

USA/South Vietnam Congress votes $405 million for South Vietnamese refugees, of whom 130,000 are resettled in the US.

5 JUNE 1975

Egypt The Suez Canal is reopened to all but Israeli ships, exactly eight years after its closing by Egypt during the 1967 Arab-Israeli war.

10 JUNE 1975

USA A commission headed by Vice-President Nelson Rockefeller issues findings on illegal domestic CIA operations—including record-keeping on 300,000 persons and groups; infiltration of agents into black, antiwar, and political movements; monitoring of overseas phone calls; mail surveillance; and drug-testing.

25 JUNE 1975

Mozambique After 470 years of colonial rule, Mozambique gains independence from Portugal. The most militant Marxist black government in Africa, led by President Samora Machel, takes over.

26 JUNE 1975

India In a massive crackdown on government

critics, the Gandhi Government declares a state of emergency, arrests 676 persons, including leaders of all opposition parties, and institutes press censorship. The crisis was sparked by a 12 June High Court decision that Gandhi must relinquish her seat in Parliament because she had won it illegally. On 23 July the Parliament extends the emergency indefinitely, ignoring demands for Gandhi's resignation.

1 AUGUST 1975

International A nonbinding security and co-operation pact is signed by 33 European nations, Canada, and the US in Helsinki. It freezes postwar European borders, broadens detente, renounces force and aid to terrorists, and pledges to respect human freedoms.

14 AUGUST 1975

Philippines The government announces that the Moro Liberation Front, the leading rebel group in Moslem Mindanao, has accepted a cease-fire. The group has challenged government forces in the southern Philippines for the past five years. Earlier, about 20 other rebel groups accepted government concessions and ended the warfare that claimed many lives.

15 AUGUST 1975

Bangladesh President Mujibur Rahman, who led the nation to independence four years earlier, is killed in a predawn army coup led by his commerce minister, Khondar Kar Mushtaque Ahmed. Mushtaque is sworn in as president.

23 AUGUST 1975

Laos The Communist takeover is complete as the Pathet Lao assumes control of the province of Vientiane, promising to 'respect and uphold the throne' and support the coalition government of the Pathet Lao and the right-wing Vientiane faction..

21 DECEMBER 1975

4 SEPTEMBER 1975

Egypt/Israel The two nations sign a second-stage Sinai agreement, providing for new Israeli withdrawals from oil wells and strategic passes in the Sinai, permission for nonmilitary shipments to and from Israel through the Suez Canal, and a team of 200 US civilians to operate an early warning system at the passes.

26 OCTOBER 1975

Egypt/USA As the first Egyptian president to make an official visit to the US, Sadat arrives on a ten-day goodwill trip during which he seeks arms and economic aid and explains his policies to Americans.

11 NOVEMBER 1975

Angola As the Portuguese withdraw from their first and last African colony, two rival governments are proclaimed in newly independent Angola. The Soviet and Cuban-aided Luanda regime of Dr Agostinho Neto will eventually gain ascendancy over the Western- and Chinese-supported Democratic People's Republic at Huambo.

Australia In a move unprecedented in the nation's history, Governor-General Sir John Kerr removes Laborite Prime Minister Gough Whitlam from office, after Whitlam fails to move the budget through the opposition-controlled Senate, leading to a 28-day monetary crisis. Kerr asks opposition leader Malcolm Fraser to form a caretaker government. In the 13 December election, Fraser's conservative-oriented Liberal-National Country Party coalition wins the biggest coalition majority in the nation's history. The swing to the right is interpreted as a reaction to recession and unemployment.

15 NOVEMBER 1975

France/Italy Western Europe's two largest communist parties, French and Italian, issue a joint statement asserting that the road to power is through their democratic systems and declaring opposition to 'all foreign interference,' specifically by 'American imperialism' and, by implication, the Soviet Union.

20 NOVEMBER 1975

Spain After 36 years as dictator, Franco dies at 82. On 22 November Juan Carlos takes an oath of office and is proclaimed king in a short Parliamentary ceremony.

2–4 DECEMBER 1975

Indonesia/Netherlands Two bands of South Moluccan terrorists, seeking independence from Indonesia for their homeland, stage attacks in the Netherlands, seizing a train on 2 December and the Indonesian consulate two days later. The Dutch Government refuses to make concessions, but through mediation efforts the hostages are released; the terrorists surrender by 19 December.

5 DECEMBER 1975

USA President Ford concludes a five-day visit to the Far East that included stops in China, Indonesia, and the Philippines. In Peking, Ford talked with Mao Tse-tung and was warned of the danger of trying to 'appease' the Soviet Union—China has become alarmed by US detente with Moscow.

21 DECEMBER 1975

Middle East Six Palestinian terrorists raid the Vienna meeting of the Organization of Oil Exporting Countries (OPEC), killing three and wounding six others. They seize 81 hostages, including Saudi Arabian oil minister Sheik Ahmed Zaki Yamani and ten other OPEC ministers. Austria provides the terrorists with a jetliner to fly the hostages to Algeria. Two days later all the hostages have been freed and the terrorists surrender to Algerian authorities.

OTHER EVENTS OF 1975

Science John Hughes and associates at the University of Aberdeen report that enkaphalin, a substance found in pig and beef brain tissues in 1975, is formed of two peptides (chains of amino acids); with this knowledge, researchers will be able to isolate and synthesize enkaphalins, to prove useful in controlling forms of mental illness, drug addiction, and pain. Georges Kohler and Cesar Milstein in England first synthesize a monoclonal antibody. University of California astronomers discover a new galaxy, 3C-123, at least ten times stronger than the Milky Way and the most distant yet found.

Medicine/Health Heart valves from pigs are used to replace defective valves in human hearts.

Technology Russian cosmonauts now routinely spend weeks in their space vehicles. The *Soyuz 19*

THE CUBAN REVOLUTION

When Fidel Castro rode in triumph into Havana in January 1959, virtually everyone cheered; not only did the Batista regime have few defenders, but Castro himself had the aura of a romantic revolutionary hero. But as the years passed, not only did the aura vanish from Castro himself—at least in the eyes of many Americans—some of the glow left his revolution. Cuban economic growth was modest and the economy became dependent on Soviet subsidies. There were qualitative improvements in health, housing, literacy, and education, and a general economic redistribution, but there were also repression and conformity. Castro perhaps maintained the support of the majority, but many Cubans chose exile, not all of whom can be dismissed as malcontents or wealthy proprietors. Some see this as an internal problem, but others point out that Castro has extended aid to revolutionaries in Latin America, Angola, Ethiopia, and Grenada. Cuban officials defend this as 'principled international defense of revolutionary nations,' or help and protection for poor countries beginning the process of social revolution and economic development. One point all sides agree upon: Castro's Cuban revolution has given this relatively small land a major role in world politics since 1959.

docks with *Apollo 18*; astronauts from the US and cosmonauts from the USSR visit in space.

Environment Iceland establishes a 200-mile fishing zone off its coast, as do other nations. At Asilomar Conference Center in California, scientists from 16 countries agree on voluntary guidelines to control experiments in which genes are transmitted from one organism to another; this meeting has been prompted by a call for action before a dangerous organism is released.

Social Sciences Italian archaeologists digging at the northern Syria site of Ebla, a city-state that flourished around 2500–2200 BC, find 15,000 clay tablets that will yield a wealth of information on the economy, politics, law, and religion of ancient Middle East civilizations. E O Wilson publishes *Sociobiology*, a provocative text that makes pressing claims for the influence of biology on human behavior.

Literature Bellow's *Humboldt's Gift*; Naipaul's *Guerrillas*; Gaddis's *JR*; E L Doctorow's *Ragtime*; Heinrich Böll's *The Lost Honor of Katharina Blum*; Doris Lessing's *The Memoirs of a Survivor*; Kawabata's *Beauty and Sadness*; Morley Callaghan's *A Fine and Private Place*; Anthony Powell's *Hearing Secret Harmonies* completes his 12-volume series A Dance to the Music of Time (begun in 1951).

Drama/Entertainment *A Chorus Line*, conceived by Michael Bennett, is an innovative musical that will go on to break all records in its run. Ballet is dominated by the performances of four defectors from the USSR—Rudolf Nureyev, Mikhail Baryshnikov, and Valery and Galina Panov. Lina Wertmuller's *Seven Beauties* becomes an international film success.

The Arts Theft and damage of art is becoming an international problem: three Renaissance masterpieces are stolen from the Ducal Palace in Urbino, Italy, other major works disappear from museums in Milan and Hanover; in Amsterdam, Rembrandt's *Nightwatch* is slashed by a vandal.

Music Luigi Nono's *To the Great Sun Charged with Love*; George Rochberg's *Concerto for Violin and Orchestra*; Gunther Biala's *Puss in Boots*.

Life/Customs The year is observed worldwide as International Women's Year. For the first time there are over 1 million divorces in the US.

Miscellaneous Elizabeth Ann Seton is canonized the first American-born saint for Roman Catholics. The 'Elderhostel' program begins, a network of colleges that provide special courses for older people during the summer months. World population passes 4 billion.

6 JANUARY 1976

Italy/USA Anti-Communist Italian politicians deny reports that the US Central Intelligence Agency secretly paid them $6 million in cash to prevent further gains by the Communist Party in national elections. The resulting crisis leads to the 7 January resignation of Prime Minister Aldo Moro and his coalition cabinet when the Socialists withdraw from Moro's government.

8 JANUARY 1976

China Following a long illness, Prime Minister Chou En-lai dies at 78, to be succeeded (7 April) by Hua Kuo-feng, a relatively unknown deputy prime minister and public security official. In October, Hua, a compromise choice between radicals and moderates, will succeed Mao Tse-tung (died 9 September) as chairman of the Communist Party.

22 JANUARY 1976

Lebanon President Suleiman Franjieh announces the 24th cease-fire of the civil war after the worst week of disorder and conflict since April 1975. The Syrian-mediated truce is to grant some Moslem demands for greater participation while preserving the Christian community's position. The newly formed Higher Military Committee, composed of Lebanese, Palestinian, and Syrian officers, is to enforce the cease-fire, which collapses in March as Lebanese Moslem soldiers revolt.

27 JANUARY 1976

Spain As strikes spread throughout the nation, King Juan Carlos issues a decree postponing new parliamentary elections for at least one year, to allow time for the government to draw up a new electoral law and institute other reforms for legislative election by free universal suffrage.

4 FEBRUARY 1976

USA A Senate subcommittee discloses that Lockheed Aircraft Corporation has paid $22 million in bribes abroad to sell its airplanes. Recipients include officials in Japan, Turkey, Italy, and the Netherlands. On 16 August former Japanese Prime Minister Kakuei Tanaka is indicted on charges of accepting $1.6 million; on 26 August Dutch Prince Bernhard, consort to Queen Juliana, resigns his military and business positions in the face of official criticism of his involvement with Lockheed.

24 FEBRUARY 1976

USA/Mariana Islands The Senate votes to grant commonwealth status to the northern Mariana Islands, leading toward the first US territorial expansion since 1924. The 21 Pacific islands are located over 3500 miles west of Hawaii.

24 FEBRUARY–5 MARCH 1976

International The growing independence of Western Communist Parties—particularly those of France, Italy, and Yugoslavia—highlights the 25th Soviet Communist Party Congress in Moscow. The Italian party leader stresses support for individual liberties in religion and the arts, while the French reject the key Marxist doctrine of the dictatorship of the proletariat.

15 MARCH 1976

Egypt At the request of President Sadat, the assembly approves legislation ending the 1971 treaty of friendship and co-operation with the Soviet

Union. On 3 March US President Ford had disclosed his intention to encourage Egypt on a moderate path by lifting the long-standing embargo on military sales. On 21 April Egypt and China sign a military protocol.

16 MARCH 1976
Great Britain In an expected move, Labourite Prime Minister Harold Wilson resigns while Parliament is still in session. On 5 April Foreign Secretary James Callaghan becomes prime minister: his budget focuses on revival of the nation's ailing industries rather than on the traditional Labour areas of public services and social welfare.

24 MARCH 1976
Argentina The armed forces overthrow Isabel Martinez de Perón as president, placing her under house arrest (until July 1981). On 29 March General Jorge Rafael Videla becomes president, suspending the Perónist and all other political parties and instituting censorship and new security laws.

12 APRIL 1976
Israel In local elections on the Israeli-occupied West Bank, Palestinian nationalists and Arab radicals make large gains toward an independent Palestinian state there. Israeli Defense Minister Shimon Peres views these results as 'a national challenge.' On 17–21 April, anti-Israeli rioting breaks out against a march by 30,000 nationalists dramatizing their claim to the West Bank territory and demanding the right to settle there.

8 MAY 1976
Lebanon In a crushing defeat for the leftist-Moslem alliance and its leader Kamal Jumblat, Parliament elects conservative Christian Elias Sarkis to the presidency. President Franjieh refuses to step down, so Sarkis is not inaugurated until 23 September.

10 MAY 1976
Great Britain Pressured by allegations of homosexuality, Jeremy Thorpe resigns as leader of the Liberal Party.

28 MAY 1976
USA/USSR The two nations sign a five-year treaty limiting the size of underground nuclear explosions for testing purposes: it provides for US on-site inspection of Soviet tests.

9 JUNE 1976
Spain Parliament votes to legalize political parties, banned since 1939. On 1 July Prime Minister Carlos Arias Navarro and his cabinet resign unexpectedly because of tensions over proposals for democratic change in Spain.

16 JUNE 1976
South Africa The worst racial violence in the nation's history breaks out when a 10,000-strong student protest turns into a riot in Soweto. Students had gathered to protest a government requirement that Afrikaans, the language of the ruling Nationalist Party, be used for instruction in some subjects in the black township's schools. Riots spread to seven other black townships around Johannesburg: by 21 June the police report 128 dead, 1112 injured, and $34.5 million in property damage.

25 JUNE 1976
Poland Workers' riots force the government to cancel a plan—announced the day before—to raise food prices drastically. Striking workers tear up railroad tracks outside Warsaw; others plunder factories and shops.

2 JULY 1976
Vietnam After almost 20 years of continuous warfare, North and South Vietnam are officially reunited as one nation, with Hanoi as its capital. North Vietnamese Prime Minister Pham Van Dong becomes prime minister in the new government.

3 JULY 1976
Israel After flying 2500 miles from Tel Aviv, Israeli commandos rescue 103 hostages held in the Entebbe, Uganda, airport by pro-Palestinian terrorists under protection of Idi Amin's troops.

21 JULY 1976
Ireland/Great Britain Newly appointed British ambassador to Ireland, Christopher Ewart-Biggs, and his secretary are killed when a land mine explodes beneath their car on the outskirts of Dublin.

23 JULY 1976
Portugal Socialist Party leader Mario Soares is sworn in as prime minister of the nation's first constitutional government since the 1974 overthrow of the rightist dictatorship. Soares stresses a more active role in the Atlantic alliance and the integration of Portugal into 'all European institutions.'

26 JULY 1976
Italy For the first time in the republic's history, the Communist Party wins chairmanships of four Parliamentary committees. But the new cabinet, led by Giulio Andreotti, is formed entirely of Christian Democratic Party members. Earlier in the month, the US, West Germany, France, and Britain had announced an informal understanding to bar further loans to Italy if the Communists received cabinet posts.

4–5 AUGUST 1976
Sudan The government of President Gaafar al-Nimeiri executes 98 persons convicted of plotting an unsuccessful 2 July coup that left 1000 rebels and troops dead after a Khartoum battle. Nimeiri, citing Libyan and Soviet instigation, breaks relations with Libya and in 1977 expels 90 Soviet advisers.

AN ERA OF ANXIETY 1974–

7 AUGUST 1976
Iran/USA The two nations announce that Iran will spend $10 billion for military purchases in the US, despite a recent US Senate committee study charging that the $10 billion in arms already sold to Iran was excessive, ill-used, and required undue employment of Americans to operate the systems. Shah Mohammed Reza Pahlavi denied the charges, arguing that the US must continue arms sales to Iran or risk instability and war in his area.

20 AUGUST 1976
International Ending their fifth formal Colombo conference since 1961, representatives of 85 non-aligned nations warn that the acute problems in international relations are economic, and that nothing short of a complete rearrangement of economic relations would enable developing countries to reach an acceptable level. The Colombo communique also calls for an oil embargo against France and Israel in reprisal for arms deals with South Africa, deplores US 'imperialist aggression' in Korea, welcomes Soviet-US detente, calls for independence for Puerto Rico, and hails the people of Vietnam for victory in 'their struggle against aggressive US imperialism.'

20 SEPTEMBER 1976
Sweden Ending over four decades of socialist rule, the electorate gives a narrow victory to a coalition of three nonsocialist parties. Prime Minister Olof Palme resigns and is succeeded by Thorbjorn Falldin, who had promised to close the nation's five nuclear power plants and to abandon plans to build eight more by 1985.

24 SEPTEMBER 1976
Rhodesia Prime Minister Ian Smith announces that Rhodesia has accepted a proposal by US Secretary of State Henry Kissinger for immediate biracial government and for black majority rule within two years. On 26 November black nationalist leaders Robert Mugabe and Joshua Nkomo accept a British plan setting 1 March 1978 as the latest independence date for Rhodesia under black rule.

18 OCTOBER 1976
Lebanon Through mediation by Saudi Arabia, Christians and Moslems agree on a plan to end the nation's long civil war. On 16 June unidentified gunmen had killed US Ambassador Francis E Meloy Jr, aide Robert O Waring, and their Lebanese chauffeur. On 20 June the US Navy evacuated about 140 Americans from Beirut; another 308 left 27 July. On 29 September Syrian peace-keeping forces dislodged Palestinian Liberation Organization troops from mountainous areas near Beirut after PLO leader Yasir Arafat refused to withdraw them.
South Africa In a Pretoria interview, Prime Minister John Vorster states that he cannot 'foresee such a day' when his nation's 4.2 million ruling whites would cede power to the 18 million blacks. Vorster

pledges that all discriminatory measures 'that serve no purpose' will be scrapped.

2 NOVEMBER 1976
USA Promising to make the federal government more efficient and responsive, outsider James Earl Carter, former Governor of Georgia, defeats incumbent President Ford by a narrow margin. In December 'Jimmy' Carter announces top members of his cabinet, including two women and two blacks.

15 NOVEMBER 1976
Lebanon Syrian peace-keeping forces take control of Beirut, meeting a cautious welcome by most Christian and Moslem residents.

OTHER EVENTS OF 1976
Science Khorana and his associates at MIT report synthesis of the first functioning gene; not only can it survive within a living cell, it supplies new confirmation of the theoretical structure of DNA. The first precise measurements of a pulsar's mass give a value of 1.3 times that of the sun's mass. Two Viking spacecraft land on Mars, transmit photos back to Earth, and take soil samples: data analysis reveals that 2–3 percent of the Martian atmosphere is nitrogen; there is no conclusive evidence of life forms on Mars.
Medicine/Health Members of the American Legion attending a convention in Philadelphia are stricken with a mysterious disease that will kill 29 and leave 150 hospitalized; 'Legionnaires' disease' will be traced to a bacterium that thrives in stagnant water (accumulated in the convention hotel's air-conditioning system).
Technology The Russians begin observations with the world's largest optical telescope (237 inches) on Mount Pastukhov. The British-French supersonic transport *Concorde* begins commercial service from Europe to Washington, DC, reducing the 7-hour flight time by half.
Environment Earthquakes take an estimated 690,000 lives this year, 650,000 of them in Hopeh Province, China; it is one of the costliest natural disasters in recorded history, surpassed only by another Chinese earthquake of 1556. An accident at a Swiss-owned chemical plant in Seveso, Italy, releases toxic fumes of TCDD that force townspeople to evacuate. The US Government bans PCBs (polychlorinated biphenyls) starting in two years.
Social Studies Archaeologists report that finds in Thailand include bronze artifacts from 3600 BC— 600 years before the formerly oldest-known bronze work in the Middle East.
Literature Gabriel Garcia Marquez's *The Autumn of the Patriarch*; Carlos Fuentes's *Terra Nostra*; Robertson Davies' *World of Wonders*; Margaret Atwood's *Lady Oracle*; Nadine Gordimer's *Selected Stories*; Heinrich Böll's *The Bread of Those Early Years*.
Drama/Entertainment Martha Graham celebrates the 50th anniversary of her modern-dance company.

US President James Earl Carter.

AN ERA OF ANXIETY 1974–

The Arts Exhibits in the US and abroad celebrate the American Bicentennial. Several large wall-drawings, thought to be Michelangelo's, are discovered in a room under the Medici Chapel, in Florence. Photo-realism in painting is ascendant.

Architecture The velodrome and stadium designed by Roger Taillibert for the Montreal Olympics are admired as 'concrete sculptures.'

Music Works commissioned for the American Bicentennial include David Del Tredici's *The Final Alice*; Otto Luening's *A Wisconsin Symphony*; Lukas Foss's *Folk Song for Orchestra*; Carlisle Floyd's *Bilby's Doll*; William Schuman's *The Mighty Casey*.

Sports The sensation of the Montreal Olympics is 14-year-old Nadia Comaneci, a gymnast from Rumania who is the first to score a perfect 10 in her events.

Life/Customs The first women are admitted to the US service academies (West Point, Annapolis, the Air Force Academy). Video games like hockey, tennis, and handball played on TV screens are a new fad.

Miscellaneous Amsterdam hosts the posthumous premiere of *Emperor of Atlantis*, an opera by Viktor Ullmann and Peter Klein, based on their experiences in the early 1940s at Terezin, a Nazi concentration camp where both died. Americans celebrate their bicentennial throughout the year, the focal point coming on 4 July with 'Operation Sail': over 50 vessels—16 of them square-riggers—from all over the world sail up New York's Hudson River to the George Washington Bridge; 6 million people line the shores, 30,000 spectator craft stand by, and millions more watch on television.

21 JANUARY 1977
USA In his first major presidential act, James Carter pardons almost all draft evaders of the Vietnam War era (10,000) but makes no decision on the status of deserters. The announcement brings protests from veterans' groups as 'more divisive than healing.'

23–24 JANUARY 1977
Spain Political violence takes seven lives in Madrid and spreads fear throughout the nation. On 25 January thousands of workers in Madrid and Barcelona strike to protest the violence, attributed to a terrorist campaign by the so-called Fascist International to undermine progress toward representative government. Following the shooting deaths of three policemen, Prime Minister Adolfo Suarez (29 January) issues a royal decree suspending constitutional rights for 30 days.

24 JANUARY 1977
Rhodesia Prime Minister Ian Smith rejects British proposals for a transition government leading to black rule in 14 months because they allow for immediate control of the country by a 'Marxist-indoctrinated minority.'

27 JANUARY 1977
USA/USSR The US State Department warns the USSR that attempts to silence political dissident Andrei Sakharov would be in conflict 'with accepted international standards of human rights.' Sakharov had been warned of criminal charges unless he stopped his 'hostile and slanderous' activities. Reportedly, he had sent President Carter a letter asking him to 'raise your voice' on behalf of persecuted political and religious activists in the Soviet sphere.

6 FEBRUARY 1977
Rhodesia At a mission station northeast of Salisbury, a dozen black guerrillas kill seven white Catholic missionaries. According to a black nun, unharmed, like other blacks, the guerrillas had said, 'We want our country.'

16 FEBRUARY 1977
Uganda The mysterious deaths of Anglican Archbishop Janari Luwum and two cabinet ministers focus world attention on the brutal regime of Idi Amin. On 21 February a Tanzanian Government newspaper reports that Amin himself killed the archbishop during a torture session. Refugees from Uganda report widespread killings, predominantly among the Christian Lango and Acholi tribes. Amnesty International reports that 300,000 may have died under Amin's rule. On 25 February Amin bars US citizens (200 people, mostly missionaries) from leaving the country before he meets with them. On 1 March he cancels the travel ban.

18 FEBRUARY 1977
International It is disclosed that the CIA made secret payments totaling millions of dollars to Jordan's King Hussein over 20 years; reports suggest similar payments to other world leaders, including Taiwan's Chiang Kai-shek, South Korea's Syngman Rhee, South Vietnam's Ngo Dinh Diem, and Zaire's Sese Seko Mobuto.

24 FEBRUARY 1977
USA The Carter Administration announces reduction of US aid to specified foreign nations because of human rights violations—included are Argentina, Uruguay, and Ethiopia. Aid to South Korea and other strategically placed allies will continue for security purposes. Secretary of State Cyrus Vance admits that the US is vulnerable to charges of hypocrisy for this policy.

8 MARCH 1977
Zaire Katanga secessionists calling themselves the Congolese National Liberation Front invade Zaire from Angola. They overrun Shaba Province, formerly Katanga, and occupy three mining and communications centers. Answering President Mobutu's pleas for help, the US, France, and Belgium provide military supplies. In April France flies in 1500 Moroccan troops.

9 MARCH 1977
USA President Carter ends restrictions on travel by US citizens to Cuba, Vietnam, North Korea, and Cambodia, effective 18 March. Carter ties this to his desire to improve US support for human rights per the 1975 Helsinki accords. To ease relations with Cuba, the Carter Administration lifts (26 March) a ban on the spending of dollars by US visitors there.

21 MARCH 1977
India In what is hailed as a victory for democracy, Prime Minister Gandhi and the ruling Congress Party are soundly defeated in national elections. In a surprise acknowledgment of its defeat, the government revokes the 20-month-old emergency rule. Gandhi, who has held office for 11 years, resigns the next day, saying 'The collective judgment of the people must be respected.' On 24 March the leader of the Janata or People's Party, Morarji Desai, is sworn in as prime minister.

7 APRIL 1977
West Germany The nation's chief prosecutor, Siegfried Buback, who has conducted the government case in the trial of three left-wing terrorist leaders of the Baader Meinhof gang, is assassinated. The two-year trial has been the longest in the nation's history. Of the original five defendants, two died in prison and the other three are sentenced on 28 April to life imprisonment for the murder of four US servicemen in a series of 1972 bombings. The defendants admit responsibility but claim the anti-Vietnam War bombings qualify them for prisoner-of-war status.

9 APRIL 1977
Spain In ruling that the Communist Party is not 'subject to international discipline' or 'totalitarian' in its aims, the government recognizes the party and allows it to participate in upcoming Parliamentary elections. (For the four decades of Franco's rule, the Communist Party was portrayed as Spain's chief enemy.)

28 APRIL 1977
Cuba/USA The two nations announce they have approved a pact governing fishing rights in the waters between Cuba and Florida, necessitated by the mutual extension of territorial waters to 200 miles out effective 1 March. The agreement climaxes the first formal negotiations between the two nations since 1961.

1–2 MAY 1977
USA In Seabrook, New Hampshire, 1414 protestors, known as the Clamshell Alliance, are arrested in the nation's first massive show of civil disobedience against nuclear plant construction.

7–8 MAY 1977
International In London, leaders of the world's seven major noncommunist industrialized nations hold an economic summit conference to co-ordinate policies on global inflation and recession. They agree not to resort to higher tariffs and protectionism and to create a multibillion-dollar cushion through the International Monetary Fund against trade deficits caused by rising oil prices.

3 JUNE 1977
Cuba/USA The two nations agree to post diplomats to their respective capitals for the first time in over 16 years. This does not constitute a full resumption of relations, as the US will operate under the Swiss flag and Cuba under the Czech flag; both staffs are to be considered 'interest sections' rather than formal missions. Bars to full diplomatic relations include US claims on over $2 billion in property seized in Cuba, Cuba's refusal to allow imprisoned Americans and Cubans with US relatives to leave the island, and Cuba's demands for an end to the US economic boycott and control of the Guantanamo naval base.

15 JUNE 1977
Spain In the nation's first free election in 41 years, Prime Minister Adolfo Suarez leads the Union of the Democratic Center—a coalition of a dozen centrist and rightist parties—to victory.

16 JUNE 1977
USSR Communist Party general secretary Leonid Brezhnev is named president of the Soviet Union by the Supreme Soviet. This is the first time in history that the party chief has also held the post of chief of state. The 70-year-old Brezhnev replaces former President Nikolai Podgorny who had resigned under pressure on 24 May.

21 JUNE 1977
Israel Menachem Begin, conservative coalition leader, is elected prime minister, ending 30 years of Labor rule; the party of David Ben-Gurion and Golda Meir was beset by scandal and faltering leadership. The new government takes a hard line on relations with the Arabs.

5 JULY 1977
Pakistan The army seizes power from Prime Minister Bhutto in a bloodless coup d'etat. Army chief of staff General Mohammed Zia ul-Haq takes over as chief martial-law administrator. On 3 September Bhutto is arrested on charges of conspiring to murder a political opponent in 1974. Convicted, he is executed on 4 April 1979, despite worldwide protests.

21 JULY 1977
Sri Lanka In national elections, Prime Minister Bandaranaike is defeated, after governing the nation under emergency rule since a 1971 communist-inspired student rebellion. She first came to power in 1960. Junius Jayawardene, head of the small United National Party, becomes prime minister.

AN ERA OF ANXIETY 1974–

22 JULY 1977

China The government announces that Deng Xiaoping, toppled in a 1976 power struggle, has been 'rehabilitated,' and that his radical opponents, the so-called Gang of Four, have been expelled from the Communist Party. Deng is to resume his posts as deputy party chairman and deputy prime minister.

6 AUGUST 1977

International The US, five other industrial nations, and five oil-exporting nations agree to provide $10 billion in loans to a special International Monetary Fund account to help poor nations hurt by the global economic slowdown and oil price rises.

21 AUGUST 1977

China Announcement of a 26-member Communist Party Politburo concludes the Communist Party's 11th congress. Its members and those of the new 333-member Central Committee include many military men, technocrats, and former officials purged during the 1960s. Party chairman Hua Kuo-feng announces that the cultural revolution, symbol of Mao Tse-tung's radical revolution, has been completed with the arrest of Mao's widow, Chiang Ching. A new party constitution, published 23 August, sets economic growth as a major national goal.

23 AUGUST 1977

South Korea/USA Korean businessman Tongsun Park is indicted by a US federal grand jury on criminal charges related to alleged bribery of US Congressmen. Hearings have disclosed that several million dollars in cash, possibly from US aid funds, were given by South Korean agents to more than 150 US politicians to secure favorable votes.

7 SEPTEMBER 1977

Panama/USA Ending 13 years of negotiations under three US Administrations, the two nations sign two new Panama Canal treaties: the first will turn the canal over to full Panamanian control at the end of 1999; the second guarantees the canal's perpetual neutrality.

20 SEPTEMBER 1977

Canada/USA The two nations sign an agreement to construct a 2700-mile pipeline to carry Alaskan natural gas across Canada to the continental US. The $10-billion pipeline is designed to save US consumers $5 billion over the next 20 years and to supply the gas-short Middle West.

21 SEPTEMBER 1977

International The USA, USSR, and 13 other nations sign a nuclear nonproliferation pact aimed at limiting spread of nuclear weapons.

24 SEPTEMBER 1977

Rhodesia Representatives of Angola, Botswana, Mozambique, Tanzania, and Zambia give qualified support to the latest British-US plan for black

---

TERRORISM

The first image of a terrorist is that of a masked figure gunning down innocent bystanders or telephoning to take credit for the bombing of some building. Individual and organized terrorists—dedicated to one cause or another—have undeniably turned to random acts of violence in an effort to win by sheer overkill. Many of these causes may even be worthwhile in themselves, but most people are repulsed by the means adopted. Terrorism has also been defined as 'a mode of governing or opposing governments by intimidation,' and as such has been employed by rulers throughout history. Stalin's torture and 'disappearance' against dissidents, as well as 'death squads' operating under government sanction. Aside from what it does to its immediate victims, terrorism breeds more terrorism. Yet where is the line to be drawn? Many leaders of regime in the USSR owed much to institutionalized terrorism, as has Pol Pot's regime in Cambodia. The governments of both North and South Korea have practiced terrorism against their own people, while several Latin American nations have used systematic former colonial and occupied lands began their struggles for independence with acts of terrorism and went on to be held in high esteem. Ultimately, most people would agree that terrorism—whatever its goals—is reprehensible, in human behavior, never to be condoned.

---

majority rule in Rhodesia. It is expected that the five African governments will encourage Rhodesian guerrilla groups to accept the plan, but Rhodesian Prime Minister Ian Smith objects to it, especially where it calls for a new national army composed of guerrilla forces.

19 OCTOBER 1977

South Africa In the severest crackdown in nearly 20 years, the government bans black protest groups, closes the principal black newspaper and arrests its editor and others, and bans many from political activities. On 4 November the UN Security Council unanimously votes a mandatory embargo on arms and military material to South Africa to protest repressive racial policies.

3 NOVEMBER 1977

France/Canada In an unusual move, French President Giscard D'Estaing makes Quebec Premier René Levesque a grand officer of the Legion of Honor. Giscard's support for Quebec's right to self-determination angers Prime Minister Trudeau and his government.

13 NOVEMBER 1977

Somalia/USSR In a dramatic reversal, Somalia expels all Soviet advisers effective within seven days and breaks diplomatic relations with Cuba. Somalia has been Moscow's prime ally in East Africa for eight years, providing strategic naval facilities on the Indian Ocean. This move is spurred by Somalia's anger over Soviet support for Ethiopia in the four-

A BBC soundman leaps to safety from the Iranian embassy in London during the siege.

month-old war in Ethiopia's Ogaden district, where Cuban advisers are also present.

19 NOVEMBER 1977

Egypt/Israel In a historic journey to promote Middle East peace, Egyptian President Sadat travels to Jerusalem at the invitation of Israeli Prime Minister Begin. This is the first time since the creation of Israel in 1948 that an Egyptian leader has met with an Israeli leader on Israeli soil. In the Knesset, Sadat delivers an eloquent plea for peace, contingent on Israeli withdrawal from occupied Arab lands, including East Jerusalem, and recognition of the rights of Palestinians. The Arab states condemn Sadat's initiative; on 5 December he breaks diplomatic ties with Syria, Iraq, Libya, Algeria, and South Yemen.

24 NOVEMBER 1977

Rhodesia Following breakdown of the latest British-US peace effort, Prime Minister Ian Smith states that he is prepared to accept majority rule based on universal suffrage as a starting point for negotiations with black nationalist leaders in Rhodesia. Smith indicates he has abandoned his long-held opposition to majority rule because the black nationalists have agreed to safeguard the confidence of white Rhodesians in a black government via an independent judicial system and special representation for minorities. On 25 November the African National Council and the Zimbabwe United People's Organization state they are prepared to begin negotiations.

4 DECEMBER 1977

Bermuda After 250 British soldiers are flown to the island, Bermuda police restore order after three nights of rioting by angry blacks protesting the 2 December hanging of two criminals convicted of several murders, including that of Bermuda's Governor Sir Richard Sharples in 1972. The riots result in an estimated $5 million in damage.

10 DECEMBER 1977

USSR On UN Human Rights Day, the government places 20 prominent dissidents under house arrest, cutting off telephones and threatening to break up a planned silent demonstration in Moscow's Pushkin Square. Soviet newspapers decry human rights violations elsewhere in the world.

OTHER EVENTS OF 1977

Science In California, researchers report they have

AN ERA OF ANXIETY 1974–

used bacteria to make somatostatin, an animal hormone—a major breakthrough for work in recombinant DNA and artificial gene synthesis, showing that bacteria can be used to manufacture useful biological substances. Scientists searching the ocean floor of the Pacific west of Ecuador find the first undersea hot springs predicted by plate tectonics theory; what is more startling, previously unknown communities of creatures are living there in total darkness, forming a complete food chain that depends primarily on heat from the earth; this heat transforms the sulfate in seawater to hydrogen sulfide, feeding bacteria that support larger and larger forms up to clams. This will lead scientists to propose a 'third life form,' even simpler than bacteria, that lives on carbon dioxide and hydrogen; in ensuing years more members of this 'third form' will be found in hot springs. The rings of Uranus are discovered. Infrared observations of the star MWC 349 indicate it is giving birth to its own solar system. Fossil finds in South and East Africa, northern Greece, and China begin to fill out the human family tree.

Medicine/Health The last known natural cases of smallpox appear in Somaliland in October 1977; in 1978 smallpox is declared eradicated. Malaria continues to take its toll—120 million cases reported this year—and a cholera epidemic spreads throughout the Middle East.

Technology The Trans-Alaska pipeline goes into operation between Prudhoe Bay in northern Alaska and Valdez. It is the most expensive privately financed construction project in history.

Environment A cyclone and tidal waves in South India kill 15,000.

Social Studies A Greek archaeologist, Manolis

Andronikos, digging at Vergina in northern Greece, discovers a treasure-filled tomb that he identifies as that of King Philip II, father of Alexander the Great. Denise Schmandt-Besserat reports that symbols on clay tokens used in Mesopotamia as early as 10,000 BC are a rudimentary form of writing (thought to have begun about 5200 BC). Michael Harner, an anthropologist, proposes that the Aztecs practiced human sacrifice as a means of adding protein to their diet.

Literature Toni Morrison's *Song of Solomon*; John Cheever's *Falconer*; Walker Percy's *Lancelot*; Yannis Ritsos's *The Fourth Dimension*; Morley Callaghan's *Close to the Sun Again*; Italo Calvino's *The Castle of Crossed Destinies*.

Drama/Entertainment David Mamet's *American Buffalo*; Michael Cristofer's *The Shadow Box*; revival of Brecht-Weill's *Happy End*; Woody Allen's *Annie Hall*; *Star Wars*; *Close Encounters of the Third Kind*.

The Arts Public sculpture gains attention, including Carl Andre's *Stone Field*, 36 boulders in a triangle in Hartford, Connecticut, and Oldenberg's *Batcolumn* in Chicago.

Architecture Louis Kahn's Yale Center for British Art; the Georges Pompidou National Center for Art and Culture in Paris. Vigorous attacks are mounted against the modern international style of strictly functional architecture.

Music Michael Tippett's *The Ice Break*; Hohvannes' *Euphonium Concerto*; Stockhausen's *Sirius*; Thea Musgrave's *Mary, Queen of Scots*; George Crumb's *Star Child*; Elliott Carter's *Symphony for Three Orchestras*.

Sports A 17-year-old apprentice jockey, Steve Cauthen, wins 524 races and purses totaling $4,300,000 by June, the end of his apprenticeship; by December 31 he has broken all records with purses totaling $6,151,750. The first woman to compete in the Indianapolis 500 is Janet Guthrie.

Life/Customs Alex Haley's account of his African ancestry, *Roots*, becomes a major hit as a television miniseries. The skateboard fad spreads—as do injuries caused by skateboards. Punk rock emerges from England. Gary Gilmore, a condemned murderer, refuses to appeal his death sentence and is executed by a firing squad in Utah, the first American to undergo capital punishment since 1967.

Miscellaneous Two jetliners crash while still on the ground at the Canary Islands and 528 people die—the highest total for any single airplane disaster.

13 JANUARY 1978

Japan/USA The two nations announce agreement on economic measures aimed at balancing their trade relationship. Japan will reduce some protectionist import duties and liberalize some agricultural import quotas to counter the 'rising tide of protectionism' in the US Congress.

24 JANUARY 1978

Canada/USSR A Soviet spy satellite powered by a

nuclear reactor breaks up over northwestern Canada. By 4 February Canadian and US scientists retrieve fragments, some radioactive, at seven sites along a 200-mile track. US President Carter calls on the Soviet Union to sign a pact banning use of nuclear reactors in earth satellites.

28 JANUARY 1978
Nicaragua President Anastasio Somoza Debayle imposes emergency rule to end a nationwide strike aimed at forcing him to resign. The crisis arose when the editor of the nation's only opposition newspaper was shot to death on 10 January. After Somoza announces concessions to the protestors and calls for an inquiry into the death, the US restores $12 million in military aid on 16 May.

6 FEBRUARY 1978
Chad/Libya Chad breaks diplomatic relations with Libya because of Libyan aid to the Moslem guerrillas conducting a civil war since 1965 against the Chad Government. As the rebels make inroads, the French rush in 1700 troops by 10 May. A 24 May newspaper report discloses that France has 12,000 troops in Africa, helping the governments of Chad, Zaire, and Mauritania against guerrillas. French forces in Africa are second only to Cuban among foreigners.

16 FEBRUARY 1978
China/Japan After a year of negotiation, the two nations sign an eight-year, $20-billion trade pact, the single most important link since the 1972 resumption of diplomatic relations. China is to purchase $7 to $8 billion worth of Japanese plants and technology, Japan over 56 million tons of Chinese coal and oil.

26 FEBRUARY 1978
Israel Despite US opposition, the Israeli cabinet decides to continue its limited policy of establishing settlements in the Sinai and on the West Bank.

3 MARCH 1978
Rhodesia Prime Minister Ian Smith and three black nationalist leaders sign an agreement to transfer power to Rhodesia's black majority by the year's end. A transitional government will supervise election of a new Parliament and enactment of a constitution for the nation, to be renamed Zimbabwe. Patriotic Front guerrillas and African nations denounce the action. On 21 March the signers of the pact—Bishop Abel Muzowera, the Reverend Ndabaningi Sithole, and Chief Jeremiah Chirau—are sworn in as leaders of the provisional government, along with Ian Smith. Blacks named to each cabinet post serve as coministers with whites already in these positions. The release of political prisoners begins on 13 April but guerrilla violence continues.

14 MARCH 1978
Lebanon/Israel Up to 22,000 Israeli ground troops supported by air and naval forces invade southern Lebanon to 'root out terrorist bases' used by Pales-

---

MUAMMAR AL-QADDAFI, 1942–

Libya's controversial Muammar al-Qaddafi is the highly visible strongman of a very small country. In 1969 he emerged from obscurity as leader of a coup that deposed King Idris. In various capacities, Qaddafi led Libya thereafter, his regime an odd mixture of personal messianic fervor, puritanical Islam, nationalism, and a kind of socialistic populism. Meanwhile he consolidated his nation's great oil resources and, with Soviet arms, built a military establishment. Qaddafi was an impassioned leader of Arab opposition to Israel and to Sadat's Egypt-Israeli peace pact, yet he has quarreled regularly with Arab neighbors. His hostility to the United States led to the accusation, never proved, that Qaddafi planned an assassination of President Reagan in 1981. A hero to his own people and a sabre-rattling dictator of dubious sanity to much of the rest of the world, Qaddafi showed in the late 1970s that he could mend fences with Arab countries when his oil exports were threatened.

---

tinian guerrillas for attacks into Israel. Three months later Israel withdraws, handing over its positions to the Lebanese Christian militia in preference to a UN peacekeeping force.

16 MARCH 1978
Italy Former Prime Minister Aldo Moro is kidnapped by Red Brigade urban terrorists who demand release of compatriots on trial in Turin. When the government refuses to negotiate, Moro is 'executed' by the terrorists; his body will be found in a car in Rome on 9 May. Despite the capture of some of those responsible, shootings, bombings, and kidnappings continue.

12 APRIL 1978
India Former Prime Minister Indira Gandhi's new political party—the Congress Party-I (for Indira)—is recognized by Parliament as the official opposition, after winning several state elections.

20 APRIL 1978
South Korea/USSR A Soviet jet fighter fires on a Korean Air Lines passenger plane, forcing it to crash-land on a frozen lake after straying over Soviet territory near the Arctic Circle: two are killed and 13 injured.

27 APRIL 1978
Afghanistan A military junta overthrows the government of President Mohammed Daud Khan, who is killed resisting the coup. Thousands of Daud's supporters and government officials are also reportedly killed. Afghan Communist Party leader Noor Mohammed Taraki assumes power; his attempt to create a Marxist state with Soviet aid results in armed resistance by conservative Moslems.

1 MAY 1978
Vietnam Hundreds of ethnic Chinese are reported

AN ERA OF ANXIETY 1974–

to be fleeing after nationalization of their businesses and alleged mistreatment by Vietnamese authorities. At the end of the month, 133,000 ethnic Chinese have escaped; a year later the total has reached 500,000. After half of them have reached China by land or sea, the rest are turned away. Of the 'boat people' an estimated 100,000 die; thousands of others reach Malaysia, Indonesia, Thailand, and Hong Kong.

4 MAY 1978
South Africa/Angola Up to 700 South African troops raid SWAPO (South-West African People's Organization) bases in Angola in response to recent guerrilla attacks into Namibia (South-West Africa). SWAPO headquarters and two smaller bases are destroyed. On 6 May the UN Security Council condemns the raid as a violation of Angolan sovereignty.

8–11 MAY 1978
Iran Moslem antigovernment riots sweep the nation as religious leaders oppose modernization plans and demand return of mosque lands confiscated under the Shah's land reform program.

16 MAY 1978
Ethiopia Following the March ouster of Somali forces, the Ethiopian army—with Soviet aid and reportedly with Cuban troops—begins a major offensive against secessionist guerrillas in the coastal province of Eritrea. In July the government forces claim victory in cutting off guerrillas from their sources of supply in the Sudan. The guerrillas maintain control over many parts of the region.

19–20 MAY 1978
Zaire A thousand French paratroopers and 1750 Belgian soldiers are dropped from 18 US Air Force transport planes into the coppermining town of Kolwezi in Shaba (formerly Katanga) Province to rescue over 2500 Europeans trapped there in fighting between government troops and secessionist rebels who had launched a second invasion from Angola on 15 May. President Mobutu claims Cuban-Soviet participation in the rebel assault. Most African leaders endorse the rescue.

21 MAY 1978
Egypt A nationwide referendum gives overwhelming support to President Sadat's plan to curb political opposition from both left and right. It is disclosed on 26 May that Sadat has called home 30 Egyptian journalists living abroad to face charges of working 'against the national objectives of the Egyptian people.'

24 JUNE 1978
Yemen/South Yemen Yemen's President Ahmed Hussein Ghashmi is assassinated; two days later South Yemen's President Salem Robaye Ali is desposed and executed by a pro-Soviet group implicated in Ghashmi's death.

28 JUNE 1978
USA The Supreme Court rules in the Bakke case that rigid quota systems are not permissible means of redressing racial imbalances. While upholding affirmative action procedures in general, the Court holds that the University of California Medical School system, which had rejected Bakke, unfairly discriminated against qualified nonminority candidates.

3 JULY 1978
China/Vietnam China announces the end of all aid to Vietnam, citing Vietnam's reported mistreatment of ethnic Chinese. (Since 1958 China has given Vietnam $10 billion in aid.) On 13 July China announces the end of all technical and economic aid to Albania because of strained relations over Albania's support for Vietnam in its dispute with China and Chinese-supported Cambodia. Chinese aid to Albania, once its closest ally, totals $5 billion since 1954.

14 JULY 1978
USSR Anatoly Scharansky, a leader in the Jewish emigration movement, is sentenced to 13 years in prison and labor camps for spying for the US. The day before, leading dissident Aleksandr Ginzburg was sentenced to eight years at forced labor for 'anti-Soviet agitation and propaganda'—he had managed a fund for families of political prisoners. Conviction of these leaders is seen as a strong rebuke to President Carter's human rights campaign and marks deterioration of US-Soviet relations.

22 JULY 1978
India Former Prime Minister Gandhi is formally charged with conspiracy and criminal misconduct during her 1977 election campaign. Earlier she had been charged with abuses committed during her emergency rule. On 19 December Parliament expels her and she is imprisoned until the session ends.

6 AUGUST 1978
Vatican Pope Paul VI dies. His successor John Paul I, elected 26 August, dies in his sleep 28 September.

22 AUGUST 1978
Kenya President Jomo Kenyatta, a leader among Africa's fighters for independence, dies. On 10 October Vice-President Daniel Arap Moi is elected to succeed him.
Nicaragua Sandinista guerrillas seize the National Palace and hold 1500 hostage. President Somoza meets their demands of a $500,000 ransom and release of 59 political prisoners, and the hostages are freed on 24 August. On 27 August the nation's businessmen vote to support a general strike aimed at forcing Somoza to resign. On 9 September the Sandinistas launch an offensive against the Somoza regime, and on 22 September, the US Senate votes to cut off most military aid to Somoza, who still refuses to step down and permit a peaceful transition to a new government.

8 SEPTEMBER 1978

Iran Martial law is imposed after a demonstration by 100,000 demanding the return of exiled Moslem leader Ayatollah Ruholla Khomeini and establishment of an 'Islamic government' to replace the Shah's monarchy. As violence continues, the Shah sets up a military government (November), then a civilian government headed by Shahpur Bakhtiar (29 December).

17 SEPTEMBER 1978

Middle East Private talks mediated by US President Carter culminate in the Camp David Accords between Egyptian President Sadat and Israeli Prime Minister Begin, establishing a timetable for peace negotiations. Arab nations and the PLO denounce the pact.

20 SEPTEMBER 1978

South Africa Prime Minister Vorster resigns and is succeeded on 28 September by Defense Minister Pieter Willem Botha, who adopts a more liberal racial policy, including easing of job restrictions for blacks and increased union rights. Botha names a multiracial advisory council to work on a proposed constitutional revision. The council, which includes Asians and people of mixed blood but no blacks, meets for the first time on 3 February 1981.

5 OCTOBER 1978

Sweden Prime Minister Falldin resigns when conservative members of his coalition government call for fewer restrictions on nuclear power. He is succeeded by Ola Ullsten.

16 OCTOBER 1978

Vatican The college of cardinals elects 58-year-old Karol Cardinal Wojtyla, a Pole, the first non-Italian Pope since 1523. His installation as John Paul II is attended by top officials of Poland's Communist Government, as well as by thousands of Poles who have been issued special passports to make the pilgrimage.

3 NOVEMBER 1978

Vietnam/USSR The two nations sign a 25-year pact of friendship and mutual aid, an agreement seen as a warning to China, with whom Vietnam's relations have deteriorated.

5 NOVEMBER 1978

Middle East A four-day Baghdad summit of 20 Arab League nations ends with a communique calling on Egypt to cease peace negotiations with Israel and denouncing the Camp David Accords as infringing on the rights of Palestinians and other Arab peoples.

OTHER EVENTS OF 1978

Science An experiment supports a 1960s theory by Steven Weinberg, Sheldon Glashow, and Abdul Salaam that attempted to explain the relationship between the weak nuclear force and that of electromagnetism by predicting a small violation of parity. Experiments at Cornell support the theory of superfluid density (the Kosterlitz-Thouless theory). Jane van Lawick-Goodall, an ethologist, reports observing a band of gorillas that repeatedly attacked and eventually killed all gorillas in another band that had split off; this is one of the few reported examples of other mammals 'making war' (van Lawick-Goodall attributes it to 'too many males and too much tension').

Medicine/Health The first 'test-tube baby,' Louise Joy Brown, is born to a couple in England on 25 July; the mother's egg was fertilized by her husband's sperm in a culture dish before placement in the uterus. India announces the world's second test-tube baby in October. Clinical testing of interferon begins; this is an antivirus substance that some researchers see as potentially valuable against cancer. Although naturally occurring smallpox has been eliminated, two English researchers contract it from escaped laboratory viruses; the man in charge commits suicide.

Environment An earthquake in Iran kills 26,000. Severe storms and gales batter Europe during the winter, one of the worst on record. Monsoon rains in Southeast Asia cause serious flooding and crop loss.

Social Sciences Researchers at the Yerkes Primate Center in Atlanta report success in teaching chimpanzees to communicate by manipulating geometric symbols. In Mexico City, repairmen digging up a street uncover a huge 15th-century Aztec bas-relief.

Literature Grass's *The Flounder*; John Irving's *The World According to Garp*; Mario Vargas Llosa's *Captain Pantoja and the Special Service*; George Konrad's *The City Builder*; James Webb's *Fields of Fire*.

Drama/Entertainment The televised miniseries *Holocaust*, a fictionalized account of the slaughter of the Jews by Nazi Germany, draws a large audience and will also be shown to Israelis and Germans. *Superman* and *Saturday Night Fever* are the big US movie hits.

The Arts The 2000-year-old Egyptian Temple of Dendur, presented to the US by Egypt in recognition of America's aid in saving the temples threatened by the Aswan Dam, opens to the public at the Metropolitan Museum. Photography is increasingly being exhibited and treated as a major art form.

Architecture I M Pei's East Building, a new wing of the National Gallery in Washington, DC, is hailed as a major work. Philip C Johnson confounds the architectural world with his design for the New York headquarters of the American Telephone & Telegraph Company; it calls for classical elements and is compared to a piece of 'Chippendale furniture.'

Music Shostakovich's *The Gambler*; Gyorgy Ligeti's *The Ballad of the Grand Macabre*; Samuel Barber's *Third Essay*; Penderecki's *Paradise Lost*; Aribert Reimann's *Lear*; Easley Blackwood's *Symphony No 4*; Donizetti's 150-year-old *Gabriella di Vergy*, discovered only recently.

AN ERA OF ANXIETY 1974–

Life/Customs The last Volkswagen Beetle rolls off the German manufacturer's assembly line (although foreign subsidiaries will continue to make them). The US Senate allows live radio coverage of its sessions in February; the British House of Commons follows in April, the US House of Representatives in June.

Miscellaneous At Jonestown, Guyana, named for an American cult leader, Jim Jones, 911 people (including Jones) die by poison or gunfire when their leader convinces them their lives on earth are threatened: the mass suicide shocks the world and enforces popular sentiment against religious cults and their leaders.

1 JANUARY 1979

China/USA The two nations establish diplomatic relations while US-Taiwan relations break off. In a step toward normalizing relations, China promises to pay (1 March) about 41 cents on the dollar in settlement of $196.6 million in claims for US property seized when the Communists gained control in 1949.

7 JANUARY 1979

Cambodia Phnom-Penh and the Chinese-supported government of Pol Pot fall to forces led by dissident Khmer Rouge leader Heng Samrin aided by Vietnamese forces. Although the defeated Pol Pot/Sihanouk Kampuchea regime retains Cambodia's United Nations seat with the support of China and other Asian nations, Vietnamese troops in Cambodia increase from 60,000 to 200,000 by 1982 to suppress remnants of Pol Pot's Khmer Rouge army.

16 JANUARY 1979

Iran Ending 37 years of rule and a year of demonstrations and crippling strikes, Shah Mohammed Reza Pahlavi leaves the country with his family. Demonstrations continue against the civilian government of Prime Minister Shahpur Bakhtiar, which authorizes the return of Ayatollah Khomeini at the end of the month. After 15 years of exile, Khomeini returns on 1 February; more demonstrations follow, and Bakhtiar resigns 11 February when the army declares its neutrality. The Khomeini Government, with Mehdi Bazargan as premier, imposes conservative Islamic laws—prohibiting alcohol, music broadcasts, and mixed bathing and urging women to return to the veil—and executes 'enemies of God.' Financial institutions and industry are nationalized.

28 JANUARY 1979

China/USA The first official visit to the US by a top Communist Chinese leader begins with arrival of senior Deputy Chairman Deng Xiaoping in Washington. Deng and President Carter sign agreements on cultural and scientific exchanges—including US assistance for building a nuclear particle accelerator in China and launching a civilian communications satellite. In diplomatic meetings, Deng criticizes the USSR for its militarism, warns Vietnam to curb its aggression, and expresses hope of uniting Taiwan with the mainland.

EINSTEIN AND 20TH-CENTURY SCIENCE

The words 'scientific revolution' usually refer to discoveries between the lifetimes of Copernicus and Newton—say, 1543 and 1687. But a second scientific revolution occurred in the first decades of the 20th century: revelation of the innermost structure and behavior of the atom; a new view of the universe in both breadth and detail: the discoveries of molecular biology that unlock and manipulate the code of life; mathematical calculations and theorems that underlie everything from the computer to the cosmos—these are only the major components. Others include the new view of geology indicated by plate tectonics and the discovery of fossils that have pushed human ancestry back millions of years. Although it would be simplistic to attribute all this to an individual and a single year, the fact is that in 1905 an obscure young German scientist in the Zurich patent office published five articles containing enough ideas to generate scientific thought and work for decades to come. That man, of course, was Albert Einstein, and although some of his theories were so abstruse that they defy ordinary intelligence, others gave birth to such tangibles as the photoelectric cell, the laser—and the atomic bomb. Personally, Einstein was the least revolutionary of men: as a Jew, he had to flee from Nazi Germany; he eventually decried the uses to which his atomic discoveries might be put. But if ever there has been a scientific revolution, 1905 was its year and Albert Einstein was its leader.

---

14 FEBRUARY 1979

Afghanistan/USA The US ambassador to Afghanistan, Adolph Dubs, is kidnapped and murdered by Moslem terrorists in Kabul. President Carter will reduce US aid to the country and the State Department will lodge a formal protest against the Soviet Union for its role in supplying guns to the assassins.

14–16 FEBRUARY 1979

Mexico/USA President Carter visits Mexico for talks with President José Lopez Portillo, who criticizes the US for lack of respect toward Mexico and for its sudden interest when vast new oil reserves were discovered there. Agreements are signed on scientific and technological co-operation, but little progress is made on trade matters or the touchy subject of illegal immigration.

17 FEBRUARY 1979

China/Vietnam Some 200,000 to 300,000 Chinese troops supported by aircraft and artillery invade Vietnam along the 480-mile border. Over 700 Vietnamese border incidents and Vietnam's 'aggression' against Cambodia are given as reasons: the action comes six weeks after Vietnam's invasion of Cambodia and 15 weeks after Vietnam signed a treaty of peace and co-operation with the USSR. China withdraws all troops from Vietnam by 15 March.

7 MARCH 1979

North Yemen/USA The US speeds arms and military advisors to North Yemen for its border war with

Albert Einstein (1879–1955).

AN ERA OF ANXIETY 1974–

South Yemen, which broke out 24 February. The arms shipment, worth $390 million, is part of a US effort to replace Iran as a defender of Western interests in more moderate Arab nations. It is reported on 8 March that some 3000 Cuban and Soviet military personnel have been sent to South Yemen. On 17 March a cease-fire goes into effect under supervision of an Arab League border patrol.

26 MARCH 1979
Egypt/Israel Egyptian President Sadat and Israeli Premier Begin sign a peace treaty ending nearly 31 years of war. Points include withdrawal of Israeli military forces and civilian settlements from the Sinai in phases over a three-year period; establishment of normal relations and exchange of diplomats after nine months; a right of passage for Israel through the Suez Canal; the end of Egypt's economic boycott of Israel; Israeli right to purchase oil from the Sinai; and the start of negotiations on Palestinian self-rule on the West Bank and the Gaza Strip. The other Arab nations and the PLO denounce the pact, impose an economic boycott of Egypt, and sever diplomatic ties with Cairo.

28 MARCH 1979
USA The nation's first major nuclear reactor accident occurs at Three Mile Island near Harrisburg, Pennsylvania. Human and design error produce the threat of a meltdown or an explosion of a hydrogen bubble trapped in the reactor. Catastrophe is averted, but deep public fears, demand for stricter safety standards, and the threat of similar accidents cast doubt on the future of the nuclear-power industry.

11 APRIL 1979
Uganda After six months of fighting, a force of Ugandan exiles and Tanzanian soldiers occupies the nation's capital of Kampala, ending the brutal eight-year rule of Idi Amin, who flees to Libya.

3 MAY 1979
Great Britain In the largest win by any party since 1966, the Conservatives sweep Parliamentary elections. Their leader, Margaret Thatcher, becomes the nation's first woman prime minister the next day. In her campaign, Thatcher had pledged to cut income taxes, scale down social services, and reduce the role of the state in daily life.

22 MAY 1979
Canada Ending 11 years in power, Prime Minister Trudeau's Liberals lose Parliamentary seats in national elections to the Progressive Conservatives led by Joseph Clark, making him the new prime minister in the nation's fifth minority government since the late 1950s. Trudeau's defeat is attributed to his proposed changes in the nation's constitution, high inflation, opposition to his energy policies, and public ire over a sensational autobiography written by his estranged wife.

18 JUNE 1979
USA/USSR Ending six years of negotiation, US President Carter and Soviet President Brezhnev sign a new strategic arms limitation treaty (SALT II). After the December Soviet invasion of Afghanistan, US Senate consent to the treaty is delayed indefinitely.

27 JUNE 1979
Israel/Syria In the first air combat since 1974, Israeli and Syrian jets clash over southern Lebanon as Israeli jets bomb Palestinian targets. Washington expresses serious concern over Israeli use of the advanced US-supplied F-15s, which had been sold to Israel on condition that they be used only for defensive purposes.

17 JULY 1979
International The first European Parliament elected by citizens of the member states meets in Strasbourg, France.
Nicaragua Sandinista rebels take over the nation's capital of Managua after defeating the National Guard in a seven-week civil war. President Somoza resigns and flees the country, and a five-member junta takes power.

21 JULY 1979
International An international conference on Indochinese refugees ends with UN Secretary General Kurt Waldheim's announcement that Vietnam has promised to stem the flow of its refugees. The Indochina refugee problem has been growing dramatically worse over preceding months, with 300,000 jammed into makeshift camps in other countries of Southeast Asia and new arrivals being turned away. On 28 June the US announced it would double its admission quota for Indochinese refugees.

3 AUGUST 1979
Cambodia Red Cross and UN officials report that 2.25 million Cambodians are facing starvation and that international relief efforts are being hindered by the nation's rival governments. No assurances can be given that the food and medicine are going to any besides military forces.

27 AUGUST 1979
Northern Ireland/Great Britain The IRA claims its most prominent victim so far in a bomb explosion in a fishing boat off the Irish coast—the 79-year-old Earl Mountbatten of Burma, a World War II hero, former head of British defense, last Viceroy of India, and the cousin of Queen Elizabeth. Three others, including Mountbatten's grandson, die from the blast. Mountbatten's 5 September military funeral is the most magnificent since that of the Duke of Wellington in 1852.

1 OCTOBER 1979
Panama The American Canal Zone in Panama ceases to exist, as Panama takes control of the terri-

Soviet President Leonid Brezhnev. Behind him is Foreign Minister Andrei Gromyko.

tory. The canal itself will revert to Panamanian control on the last day of the century.

6 OCTOBER 1979

East Germany/USSR President Brezhnev announces that the USSR will withdraw up to 20,000 troops and 1000 tanks from East Germany in 1980, but warns that deployment of new US nuclear missiles in Western Europe 'would radically alter the strategic situation on the Continent.'

26 OCTOBER 1979

South Korea Park Chung Hee, ruler for over 18 years, is assassinated by the director of the Korean Central Intelligence Agency. Martial law is imposed, but the new president, Choi Kyu Hah, begins to free political prisoners.

4 NOVEMBER 1979

Iran/USA An international crisis begins when about 500 Iranian militants seize the US embassy in Teheran, taking about 90 hostages, including 65 Americans. The students vow to occupy the embassy and hold the captives until the Shah, who is undergoing medical treatment in New York, is returned to Iran by the US to stand trial for alleged torture, murder, and robbery. When negotiations fail, President Carter (10 November) orders deportation of Iranian students illegally in the US; on 12 November he suspends Iranian oil imports, and on 14 November freezes Iranian assets in US banks. The Iranians release 13 women and black hostages on 19 November, ten more the next day, and the last five non-American hostages 22 November. The remainder—except for one released in July 1980 for medical reasons—remain captive until 1981.

21 NOVEMBER 1979

Pakistan/USA Believing erroneously that the US is involved in the takeover of an Islamic mosque in Mecca, thousands of Moslem Pakistanis overrun the US embassy, burning it and killing two Americans. The Pakistani Government comes to the aid of 90 others trapped on the building's roof, rescuing them by helicopter. On 26 November the US State Department calls for voluntary evacuation of all non-essential personnel from the embassies of ten Islamic countries.

24 NOVEMBER 1979

USA The government General Accounting Office reports that thousands of US troops were exposed to the herbicide Agent Orange in the Vietnam War, a fact previously denied by the Defense Department. Nearly 5000 veterans had reported serious health problems related to the toxic defoliant.

12 DECEMBER 1979

International NATO members, except France and Greece, agree to install 572 medium-range nuclear missiles in Europe by 1983. The Netherlands and Belgium say they will not accept their quotas of 48

missiles each until negotiations for arms control are tried again. The missiles would be the first nuclear weapons in Europe capable of hitting targets within the Soviet Union.

21 DECEMBER 1979

Rhodesia Following difficult negotiations mediated by British Prime Minister Thatcher, all factions sign peace pacts in London to end the seven-year civil war. The signatories, including guerrilla leaders Robert Mugabe and Joshua Nkomo, agree to a cease-fire, a new draft constitution, and a period of British Administration before general elections leading to black majority rule.

25–26 DECEMBER 1979

Afghanistan/USSR Following a coup by Babrak Karmal, the USSR airlifts 5000 troops to Kabul to shore up Karmal's Marxist Government against Islamic resistance. On 28 December the USSR augments its first use of ground troops outside Eastern Europe by 15,000 men in several mechanized divisions. The Soviets ignore almost universal calls for withdrawal; by June 1980 their invasion forces total 85,000. Afghan guerrilla groups continue effective resistance.

OTHER EVENTS OF 1979

Science Two research teams in California report they have produced the human growth hormone in the laboratory using recombinant DNA techniques with bacteria cells; this is the first success with a medically useful substance unavailable from other

---

THE WOMEN'S MOVEMENT

After women had won the vote in such countries as the US and Great Britain—followed soon by most others—the drive seemed to go out of the women's movement. There were, of course, exceptions, but from about 1930 to 1960 women seemed to be making little headway in the quest for recognition and rights. Two books were to signal the movement's revival. *The Second Sex*, Simone de Beauvoir's profound analysis of the female condition, appeared in French in 1949; it won the respect of intellectuals, but did not provide the focal point for a mass movement. That came with *The Feminine Mystique*, Betty Friedan's 1963 attack on the circumscribed, gender-based role-playing that women had been forced to accept by society. Although lacking the depth of de Beauvoir's book, *The Feminine Mystique* reignited the movement. Prompted by the emerging civil rights movement—which in turn had been inspired by the courage of Rosa Parks in demanding a seat in a segregated bus—American women were soon in the vanguard of what became a worldwide resurgence. Setbacks and diversions would occur, even from within the movement—as when some factions chose to stress lesbianism and antifamily positions—but there could be no turning back. Throughout the world, the drive for women's rights had become irresistible.

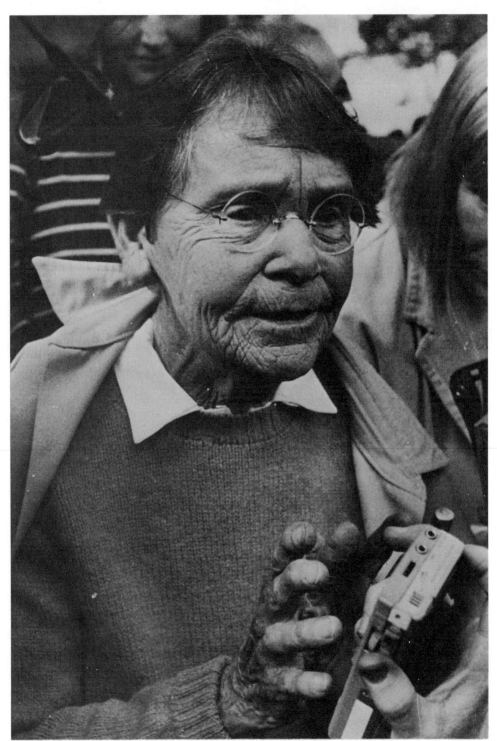

Dr Barbara McClintock, winner of the 1983 Nobel Prize for medicine.

AN ERA OF ANXIETY 1974–

A view of Saturn from Voyager II.

sources. In Switzerland, researchers report successful transplant of a cell nucleus to create an embryo; this is cloning, or duplication of an organism by asexual means. US space vehicle, *Voyager II*, on its mission to Jupiter, sends back photographs revealing details of the planet's atmosphere and larger moons, including a volcano in Io. Scientists discover in Burma remains of two primates that lived 40 million years ago, far earlier than any other known primates. Johanson and White, Americans, propose a new hominid species, *Australopithecus afarensis*, based on fossil finds from Ethiopia; their new 'family tree' for humans will not be accepted by all authorities. Finds of what appears to be cultivated barley in the Aswan area of Egypt push cultivated crops back to 18,300 years ago—10,000 years earlier than previously known.

Medicine/Health A genetic 'flaw' is linked to kidney cancer. A pain control chemical in the brain, dynorphin, is found. Two new contraceptives are announced: a nasal type is demonstrated in Britain, and the Chinese claim that a substance extracted from cottonseed oil is used successfully by men. In the US, government researchers call for changes in Americans' diets to help cut down on cancer and other diseases.

Technology New production methods make smaller electronic circuits that will allow computers to become smaller and faster.

Environment In June, an oil well in the Gulf of Mexico blows out and begins to leak oil; before it is capped in March 1980, it will be the world's worst oil spill. Industrialized nations are beginning to discuss the threat posed by acid rain, which is killing vegetation and freshwater life.

Social Studies The first translations of the 15,000 tablets found at Ebla, Syria, in 1976, yield a variety of texts—everything from basic inventories and expense accounts to political documents and dictionaries of up to 3000 words.

Ideas/Beliefs Elaine Pagel's *Gnostic Gospels* provide a revealing glimpse of early Christianity. The Reverend Hans Küng, a liberal Swiss Roman Catholic theologian, is censured by the Vatican and barred from teaching.

Literature Styron's *Sophie's Choice*; V S Naipaul's *A Bend in the River*; Stanlislaw Lem's *A Perfect Vacuum*; Heller's *Good as Gold*; Brian Moore's *The Mangan Inheritance*; Margaret Atwood's *Life Before Man*; Wallace Stegner's *Recapitulation*; Malamud's *Dubin's Lives*.

Drama/Entertainment Shaffer's *Amadeus*. Cop-

Rebel Moslem fighters in Barikot, Afghanistan, along the Afghanistan-Soviet border.

Afghan guerrillas, 1981.

AN ERA OF ANXIETY 1974–

pola's *Apocalypse Now*; *The Deerhunter*; Olmi's *The Tree of the Wooden Clogs*; Fassbinder's *The Marriage of Maria Braun*.

The Arts 'Performance' and 'conceptual' art are in vogue. In Paris 800 Picassos, a fraction of those donated to the French Government by his heirs in lieu of taxes, go on temporary display until a permanent museum is built.

Architecture The John F Kennedy Library in Boston, designed by I M Pei, is dedicated.

Music Malcolm Arnold's *Eighth Symphony*; Dominick Argento's *Miss Havisham's Fire*; Hans Henkeman's *Winter Cruise*; Siegfried Matthus's *Omphale*; Menotti's *La Loca*; Leon Kirchner's *Metamorphoses*.

Life/Customs Roller skating revives as a popular sport, and electronic games played on home TV screens remain popular. A US Navy ship has its first woman commander on a regular patrol, and the first woman dies in a coal mine disaster.

Miscellaneous The Chinese Government rules that as of January 1979 all information originating in China in Western alphabets will use a new Pinyin system of transcription: this replaces the Wade-Giles system (devised by two Englishmen in the 1800s).

2 JANUARY 1980
USA/USSR In response to the Soviet invasion of Afghanistan, President Carter recalls the US ambassador to the USSR and announces that he will ask the Senate to delay consent to the SALT II treaty. Two days later Carter orders an embargo on wheat exports, fishing privileges, and export of high-technology equipment to the USSR. On 22 April the US Olympic Committee will vote to boycott the Summer Olympics in Moscow.

6 JANUARY 1980
India In a dramatic political comeback, Indira Gandhi and her party win an overwhelming victory in parliamentary elections. Her campaign called for reducing inflation, restoring law and order, and recognizing the new Vietnamese-backed Heng Samrin Government in Cambodia. Gandhi is sworn in as prime minister on 14 January; next day a New Delhi court dismisses two cases against her dating from her rule in 1975.

22 JANUARY 1980
USSR Human rights activist and physicist Andrei Sakharov is arrested and sent into internal exile in Gorky for speaking out against Soviet actions in Afghanistan. His wife continues to transmit messages from Sakharov to foreign reporters, and he is threatened with a harsher exile or commitment to a psychiatric hospital.

28 JANUARY 1980
Canada/Iran Six US embassy employees who had been in hiding for three months are flown out of Iran with the help of Canadian diplomats. As a precautionary measure, the small Canadian embassy staff remaining in Teheran also leaves the country. Meanwhile, UN and US strategies to release the hostages remain unsuccessful.

3 FEBRUARY 1980
USA In the most sweeping inquiry into suspected political corruption ever undertaken by the FBI, the press reveals that 31 public officials, including a US Senator and seven Representatives, have been subjects of a two-year undercover operation. By the end of June, five Congressmen will have been indicted in the so-called Abscam investigation.

18 FEBRUARY 1980
Canada Former Prime Minister Trudeau and his Liberal Party capture a clear majority in the House of Commons. In his campaign he had promised to hold down energy costs—the Conservative plan to increase the excise tax on gasoline by 18 cents contributed to their defeat—and to renew his attempts to reform federal-provincial relations.

24 MARCH 1980
El Salvador Roman Catholic Archbishop Oscar Romero, one of the nation's most respected leaders, is assassinated by a sniper's bullet as he celebrates Mass. No group claims responsibility for the killing of the outspoken prelate, who had supported the

---

THE ATOMIC AGE

The paradox inherent in the harnessing of atomic power was quickly apparent to one of those most responsible for devising the atomic bomb. J Robert Oppenheimer, upon witnessing the first successful test in New Mexico, quoted: 'I am become Siva, the destroyer.' But once people had recovered from the initial shock of its destructive power at Hiroshima and Nagasaki, they began to accept that atomic power would become a helpful and productive force. Perhaps the commonest image in the early years was that of a glass of water, which people were constantly told held enough energy to power great ships and achieve other marvels. As the decades passed, however, the peaceful applications of the atom took second place to more threatening uses. Even the promised ships turned out to be primarily submarines or aircraft carriers, while nuclear power-generating plants presented a host of side-effects that cast serious doubts on their safety and economics. Although the uncontrolled testing of nuclear weapons eventually came under sanctions, a new problem arose with the disposal of nuclear wastes. Meanwhile, the US and the USSR (and other nations as well) had built up a stockpile of nuclear weapons that dwarfed anything suggested by the first few atomic bombs. Defenders of these weapons argue that their net effect has been to deter a major conflict since 1945; those who protest such weapons argue that a balance of terror exists, a state far too unsettling and fragile to be called peace. All would agree that 'the atomic age' has turned out to be something other than even an Oppenheimer could have imagined.

poor and called for peace in the strife-torn country. In the past two years, at least six priests have been killed by right-wing terrorists.

5–6 APRIL 1980
Cuba As Cuban guards leave the Peruvian embassy, 10,000 Cubans seeking exit visas crowd into the compound. An airlift takes them to Costa Rica for reassignment to other countries. Castro insists they go directly to their final destination and opens the port of Mariel to a flotilla of small boats from the US. Before Castro closes Mariel on 26 September, over 125,000 Cubans leave.

17 APRIL 1980
Zimbabwe Rhodesia becomes the independent nation of Zimbabwe, ending 90 years of white rule. Britain's Prince Charles presides over the ceremonies as Robert Mugabe, the black leader who had been elected in March by a landslide, is sworn in as prime minister. Mugabe reiterates the theme of reconciliation and, himself a Marxist, pledges his support for the existing free-market economy.

24 APRIL 1980
Iran/USA After failure of diplomatic initiatives, the US attempts to rescue the Americans held hostage in the US embassy in Teheran, but the commando mission is called off due to equipment failure. Eight soldiers are killed and five injured during the pull-out in a collision between a helicopter and a transport plane. On 28 April Secretary of State Cyrus Vance resigns over President Carter's decision to undertake the military rescue mission.

4 MAY 1980
Yugoslavia After a four-month illness, Josip Broz Tito, president since World War II, dies. He is succeeded by a collective rotating presidency.

20 MAY 1980
Canada In one of the heaviest voter turnouts in Quebec's history, a separatist referendum ends in overwhelming defeat for the Quebec independence movement.

1 JUNE 1980
South Africa In one of the most successful guerrilla actions to date against the white minority government, two petroleum plants and one of the nation's largest oil refineries are bombed. The London-based African National Congress, a black nationalist group banned in South Africa, claims responsibility for the bombings.

Members of Britain's Special Air Service storm the Iranian embassy in London.

Ash and steam erupting from Mount St Helens.

AN ERA OF ANXIETY 1974–

The Iranian hostages arrive in West Germany after their release.

23 JUNE 1980
Thailand/Vietnam Vietnamese forces invade Thailand from Cambodia, apparently in search of Pol Pot sympathizers among Cambodian refugees in camps there. A Thai appeal for help brings military supplies from the US and promises of more aid if needed.

27 JULY 1980
Iran The Shah dies in Egypt, the sixth nation in which he had sought refuge since fleeing his homeland. An Iranian Government spokesman says that the Shah's death will have no effect on the 52 US hostages held in Teheran.

5 AUGUST 1980
USA President Carter announces a major policy shift in the nation's nuclear-weapons strategy, giving top priority to knocking out the Soviet missile system rather than using nuclear weapons to conduct a massive assault against civilian targets.

30 AUGUST 1980
Poland After two months of labor turmoil cripple the nation, the government grants striking workers at the Gdansk Lenin Shipyard the right to form independent trade unions, an unprecedented political development in the Soviet bloc. Polish Communist Party leader Edward Gierek is replaced on 6 September by Stanislaw Kania.

7 SEPTEMBER 1980
China In the most sweeping peaceful change of leadership since 1949, Premier Hua Guofeng resigns, as do five vice-premiers and a number of ministerial appointees. Zhao Ziyang takes over as premier. The change is part of a campaign to end the practice of granting lifelong posts to leading officials. The National People's Congress also launches a new economic policy emphasizing profits and local control. These changes are seen as victories for the nation's leader, Deng Xiaoping, a pragmatist and proponent of modernization.

22 SEPTEMBER 1980
Iraq/Iran After skirmishing for ten months over the disputed Shatt al-Arab waterway dividing their nations, Iraq and Iran go to war when Iraqi fighter-bombers attack ten Iranian airfields including the Teheran Airport; Iranian planes retaliate with strikes on two Iraqi bases.

3 OCTOBER 1980
France A terrorist bomb explodes in front of a Jewish synagogue in Paris, killing four people and injuring 12. On 7 October 100,000 march in protest of the incident, which arouses fears of a resurgent anti-Semitism in the country.

4 NOVEMBER 1980
USA Republican Ronald Reagan wins a landslide

US President and Mrs Ronald Reagan.

victory over President Jimmy Carter (the first time since 1932 that an elected incumbent has not been retained in office). Most analysts see the Democratic defeat as reflecting voter dissatisfaction with Carter's handling of both domestic and international affairs.

5 DECEMBER 1980

El Salvador Following the killings of four US women—three nuns and a lay worker—in El Salvador, the US suspends $25 million in new military and economic aid pending reorganization of the government. On 13 December José Napoleon Duarte is named the first civilian president in 49 years and the leader of a four-member junta. On 17 December the US announces resumption of $20 million in economic aid, but no money for military aid.

OTHER EVENTS OF 1980

Science Scientists have begun to find uses for monoclonal antibodies—reagents that react with a specific antigen like a particular virus. This year researchers in Zurich produce interferon from bacteria by transplanting human genes; the hope is that interferon can be mass produced and prove helpful in fighting cancer viruses. The oldest known biological cells are found in fossils 3,500,000 years old, pushing back the date for the origin of life.

Voyager I continues its space flight and sends back dramatic pictures of Saturn's rings.

Medicine/Health Some reports question the link between cholesterol intake and heart ailments, but lung cancer is on the rise in American women, traced to the rise in smoking. A vaccine for hepatitis B is developed.

Technology A new microscope that uses very short sound waves is developed for use in acoustic scanning. The US Department of Transportation announces that most automobiles sold in the US fail to pass the test for protection in crashes at 35 mph.

Environment Mt St Helens, a long-dormant volcano in Washington, erupts several times, killing at least 26 people and devastating the countryside as far as 120 miles away. Earthquakes kill 3000 in Algeria and 4000 in Italy.

Social Studies The Japanese report finding wreckage of the invasion fleet dispatched to Japan by Kublai Khan 700 years ago.

Literature William Golding's *Rites of Passage*; Anthony Burgess's *Earthly Powers*; Russell Hoban's *Riddley Walker*; Shirley Hazzard's *The Transit of Venus*; Patrick White's *The Twyborn Affair*.

Drama/Entertainment David Edgar's adaptation of *Nicholas Nickleby*; Barton and Cavander's *The Greeks*; Pinter's *The Hothouse*; Athol Fugard's *A*

The inauguration of President Ronald Reagan.

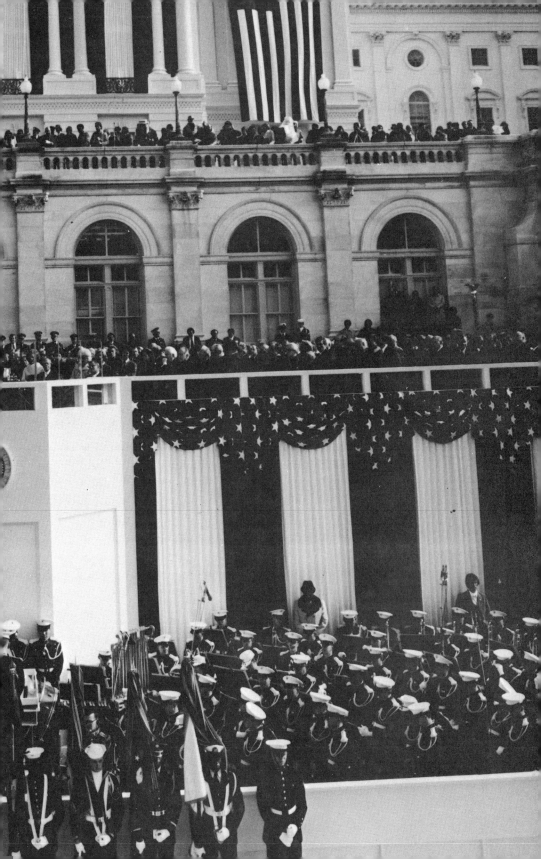

AN ERA OF ANXIETY 1974–

Lesson from Aloes; Lanford Wilson's *Talley's Folly*; David Williamson's *Travelling North*; Truffaut's *The Green Room*; *My Brilliant Career*.

The Arts The talk of the New York art world is the Picasso retrospective at the Museum of Modern Art, 1000 works viewed by over 1 million people. A crack in the church wall on which da Vinci's *Last Supper* is painted demands immediate restoration efforts. Jasper Johns' *Three Flags* is auctioned for $1 million (a new record for a living American painter).

Music Michael Tippett's *Triple Concerto*; Stockhausen's *Michaels Heimkreis*; Philip Glass's *Satyagraha*; Peter Maxwell-Davies' *The Lighthouse*.

Miscellaneous The US Supreme Court rules (in *Diamond vs Chakrabarty*) that new forms of life resulting from research can be patented.' John Lennon of the Beatles is shot and killed by a disturbed youth, marking for many the end of an era.

17 JANUARY 1981

Philippines President Marcos ends the state of martial law under which he has ruled the nation for eight years and four months. He frees 341 prisoners and transfers his legislative powers to the national assembly. These moves are apparently taken to improve relations with the US and to mark the coming visit of Pope John Paul II.

20 JANUARY 1981

Iran/USA Minutes after Ronald Reagan is inaugurated president, the 52 Americans held hostage by Iran are released after 444 days of captivity. Negotiations centered around Iran's demand for return of the late Shah's wealth and release of Iranian assets frozen in US banks since 1979. On 25 January the hostages arrive in the US to a tumultuous national welcome.

25 JANUARY 1981

China Sentences are handed down in the trial of the Gang of Four, leaders of the Cultural Revolution who were charged with plotting to seize power and with persecuting political enemies. Chairman Mao Tse-tung's widow Jiang Qing receives a death sentence suspended for two years during which she would be 'helped to reform through labor.'

31 JANUARY 1981

Poland Ending a month of labor strikes, the government and Solidarity, the independent trade union led by Lech Walesa, announce an agreement making three of every four Saturdays nonworking days and allowing trade union leaders a weekly hourlong television program. On 9 February Prime Minister Jozef Pinkowski is replaced by the Minister of Defense, General Wojciech Jaruzelski, in a move to increase the power of the military in the face of continuing labor unrest.

23 FEBRUARY 1981

Spain A group of Civil Guards seizes the lower house of Parliament and takes most of the nation's

THE THIRD WORLD EMERGES

By 1980, the United Nations had swelled to 140-odd members, over a hundred more than at its founding in 1945. The majority of these countries were former colonial possessions of the great powers, emerging during the years following World War II. They carry the umbrella title of Third World, suggesting a unity that is misleading. Many, not all, are politically nonaligned, wary of and uncommitted to either the United States or the Soviet bloc. Rich oil-exporting nations, nations with abundant resources and those with few, nations with capitalist and socialist economies—all share the label 'Third World.' What these nations do have in common is serious economic underdevelopment. Rates of economic growth are insufficient, with standards of living unacceptably low. Countries in the Third World, believing that the world system of trade, investment, and finance entraps them in a state of limited development, seek to promote a New International Economic Order—a demand for global reorganization. Politically, Third-World countries, faithful to their own histories, have pressed for complete colonial liberation. Most of the world's population resides in the Third World, and men's ability to make life truly human, rather than something to be endured, will be tested there.

350 legislators hostage. The uprising collapses 18 hours later following firm action by King Juan Carlos, who appears on television to denounce the seizure and pledge his faith in democracy.

2 MARCH 1981

Great Britain Twelve members of Parliament resign from the Labour Party to form a new party—the Social Democrats—in the belief that Labour has become too left-wing.

30 MARCH 1981

USA President Reagan is shot in the chest by would-be assassin John W Hinckley, Jr; three others are seriously wounded in the attack. After a remarkable recovery, Reagan leaves the hospital 12 days later. In a controversial decision, Hinckley is later acquitted on grounds of mental incompetency and confined to a mental hospital.

11–12 APRIL 1981

Great Britain Race riots flare in the Brixton section of London, spreading to other cities. In early July violence recurs as racist and unemployed youths riot in London, Liverpool, Manchester, Birmingham, Nottingham, and over 30 other cities. Thousands of arrests crowd the jails, and the traditionally unarmed police are equipped with armored vehicles, plastic bullets, and water cannon.

5 MAY 1981

Northern Ireland In Belfast's Maze Prison, IRA gunman and member of Parliament Bobby Sands dies on the 66th day of a hunger strike aimed at

General Alexander M Haig Jr—President Reagan's first Secretary of State.

gaining political-prisoner status for inmates. Nine other fasters die before the hunger strikes end in November.

10 MAY 1981
France In an upset victory, Socialist party leader François Mitterand defeats incumbent President Giscard D'Estaing. Next day turmoil hits the nation's financial markets, and extra customs officials are posted to prevent smuggling of money and other valuables. In the 14 and 20 June national assembly elections, the socialists win by a landslide, assuring Mitterand full power. He appoints four Communist members to his cabinet, begins nationalization of financial institutions and industry, ends nuclear tests and raises taxes for the rich.

13 MAY 1981
Vatican Pope John Paul II is shot and seriously wounded, as he is driven through a crowd of 10,000 in St Peter's Square. Following lengthy intestinal surgery and a painful three-week recovery, he walks out of the hospital on 3 June. A militant Turkish terrorist, Mehmet Ali Agca, is found guilty of the attempted assassination and sentenced to life in prison on 22 July.

7 JUNE 1981
Iraq/Israel Israeli warplanes bomb and destroy a nearly completed $275-million atomic reactor near Baghdad, killing a French technician. The Israeli Government claims the reactor would have enabled the Iraqis to manufacture nuclear weapons that could have been used against Israel.

10 JUNE 1981
Iran President Abolhassan Bani-Sadr is relieved of his position as commander in chief of the army by the Ayatollah Khomeini because of suspected pro-Western sympathies. Bani-Sadr goes into hiding three days later, and arrives in France on 29 July aboard a hijacked Iranian military plane. He is granted political asylum. Back in Iran at least 23 of his supporters have been executed by firing squads.

28 JUNE 1981
Iran A bomb explosion in the Islamic Republican Party's Teheran headquarters kills 72, including Chief Justice Ayatollah Mohammed Beheshti, cabinet officials, and members of Parliament.

29 JUNE 1981
China Hua Guofeng, the hand-picked successor of Mao Tse-tung, is replaced as head of the Communist Party by Hu Yaobang, a protegé of Deng Xiaoping. Next day the party announces that Mao had made mistakes in leadership, including emphasis on class struggle and quick results instead of slow modernization and party-building.

6 AUGUST 1981
USA President Reagan decides to go forward with production of neutron weapons, which produce more radiation and less blast than other nuclear weapons and are thus able to kill people without damaging their surroundings. On 2 October Reagan calls for 100 new MX missiles.

19 AUGUST 1981
Libya/USA Two US Navy F-14s shoot down two Soviet-built Libyan jets over the Gulf of Sidra in the Mediterranean Sea. The Libyans, who fired on the American planes first, claim they were flying through Libyan air space; the US insists the area is over international waters.

26 AUGUST 1981
El Salvador Deaths in the nation's civil strife since October 1979 total 26,000, many of them civilians: 305,000 reportedly fled the country last year to escape violence and hunger. On 12 August it was disclosed that in its campaign against the guerrillas, the army was using toxic gases, white phosphorus, and bacteriological weapons that had caused the deaths of thousands of children and elderly people.

29 AUGUST 1981
Angola/South Africa South Africa claims to have killed 240 Angolans and destroyed radar and anti-aircraft installations in what it describes as a 'limited' operation aimed at Angola-based guerrillas fighting for Namibian independence. Five days earlier two South African armored columns had invaded southern Angola to attack SWAPO guerrilla bases.

5 SEPTEMBER 1981
Egypt Fearing the rise of religious factionalism, President Sadat deposes the nation's Coptic Pope. Sadat also criticizes certain Islamic organizations for increasing religious tension in Egypt. On 7 September the government announces that it will gradually take over the supervision of 40,000 mosques. To date, 1536 people have been arrested as dissidents—Moslem clerics, Coptic Christian priests, journalists, politicians, lawyers, and professors. On 17 September 1000 Russians are expelled.

20 SEPTEMBER 1981
Belize Independence comes to Britain's last colony on the American mainland, the former British Honduras. A contingent of British troops remains to protect Belize against possible attack from neighboring Guatemala, which had refused to recognize its independence and claims it as a part of Guatemalan territory.

6 OCTOBER 1981
Egypt President Sadat is shot and killed by extremist Moslem soldiers as he reviews a military parade near Cairo. On 13 October Vice-President Hosni Mubarak is elected and orders a crackdown on Moslem fundamentalists, of whom thousands are arrested.

17 DECEMBER 1981

Soviet President Leonid I Brezhnev (lower right) and other members of the Politburo.

18 OCTOBER 1981

Greece The first Socialist Government in the nation's history comes to power as Andreas Papandreou is elected president. Papandreou initially calls for the removal of US military bases from Greece and threatens to leave NATO, but subsequently moderates his stance.

Poland Communist Party leader Kania is dismissed and replaced by Prime Minister Jaruzelski. Along with the dismissal comes a demand for stronger action in the nation's economic crisis and against 'antisocialists' in Solidarity.

24 OCTOBER 1981

Great Britain A series of mass demonstrations for nuclear disarmament begins in Europe with a London march of 150,000 and comparable marches the next day in Paris, Brussels, and Potsdam, East Germany. On 21 November 300,000 to 400,000 march in Amsterdam.

26 OCTOBER 1981

Sweden/USSR A Soviet submarine runs aground near a Swedish naval base, in violation of the restricted zone. Its captain blames a faulty compass and bad weather. On 6 November the submarine is released to rejoin a Soviet Navy flotilla.

13 DECEMBER 1981

Poland The nation's military leaders decree martial law, restricting civil rights and suspending operation of the independent trade union Solidarity. General Jaruzelski, prime minister and Communist Party leader, announces that a strict regime is necessary to save Poland from catastrophe and civil war. Public gatherings and demonstrations are banned, and internment is threatened for those of dubious loyalty. Solidarity leader Lech Walesa is arrested, but labor unrest continues.

14 DECEMBER 1981

Israel Prime Minister Begin pushes a measure through the Knesset to annex the Golan Heights, the strategic area along the Syrian border from which the Syrians have been harassing the Israelis. In response to US threats to suspend military aid, Begin accuses the US of treating Israel as a vassal state and refers to its sale of AWACs planes to Saudi Arabia as anti-Semitic.

17 DECEMBER 1981

Italy/USA Red Brigade terrorists kidnap Brigadier General James Dozier, the highest-ranking US NATO officer in Italy, from his Verona apartment: 42 days later Italian antiterrorist forces rescue Dozier in Padua and seize five of his captors.

OTHER EVENTS OF 1981

Science Experimenters in Switzerland announce the first successful cloning of a mammal when three mice are born. The first substance to be available commercially from gene splicing is a vaccine against foot-and-mouth disease. At CERN, in Switzerland, the first collision of matter and antimatter releases up to 100 times as much energy as ever released before in particle accelerators. Astronomers discover four of the most distant galaxies—some 10 billion light years away—and find a vast area of the universe that

AN ERA OF ANXIETY 1974–

A Polish Army armored personnel carrier on the streets of downtown Warsaw enforces martial law.

appears to be totally empty. *Voyager II* comes within 63,000 miles of Saturn and sends back dramatic photos of its rings.

Medicine/Health An artificial skin for burn victims is developed.

Technology The first successful flight of the US space shuttle *Columbia* occurs in April, the second in October. The joint European space rocket *Ariane* also makes two flights this year. The US National Ocean Survey announces discovery of ore deposits (copper, iron, silver, etc, valued at $2 billion) on the floor of the Pacific west of Ecuador. The USSR announces it has drilled the deepest hole ever—to some 35,371 feet—and found microscopic life in extremely hot conditions at 22,000 feet.

Environment The Yangtze River floods in China, leaving some 1100 dead or missing. An epidemic of the Mediterranean fruit fly threatens California's fruit crop and requires drastic steps to curtail it. Scientists warn again of the 'greenhouse effect'—a dangerous warming of the earth's atmosphere due to too much carbon dioxide.

Literature Salman Rushdie's *Midnight's Children*; D M Thomas's *The White Hotel*; Nadine Gordimer's *July's People*; Alan Paton's *Ah! But Your Land is Beautiful*; Brian Moore's *The Temptation of Eileen Hughes*; John K Toole's *A Confederacy of Dunces* (posthumous).

Drama/Entertainment Brian Friel's *Translations*; Beth Henley's *Crimes of the Heart*; Peter Nichols' *Passion Play*; C P Taylor's *Good*; film version of *The French Lieutenant's Woman*; *Chariots of Fire*; *Mephisto*.

The Arts During the centenary of Picasso's birth, his *Guernica*—which has been in the Museum of Modern Art in New York since 1939—is returned to Spain under the provisions of his will (when his native land had restored liberty).

Music Stockhausen's *Donnerstag aus Licht*; Michael Tippett's *The Mark of Time*; Carlisle Floyd's *Willie Stark*; Friedrich Cerha's *Baal* and *Netzwerk*; John Tavaner's *Akhmatova Requiem*; a Mozart symphony written in 1765 when the composer was nine years old, is found in Bavaria.

Sports The longest strike by professional athletes occurs in the US when major league baseball players go out for 49 days.

Miscellaneous On 29 July Charles, Prince of Wales, marries Lady Diana Spencer in a televised ceremony viewed by at least 700 million. Sandra Day O'Connor becomes the first woman to sit on the US Supreme Court.

The US space shuttle Columbia.

AN ERA OF ANXIETY 1974–

Baryshnikov and Tcherkassky dance 'The Nutcracker' with the American Ballet Theater.

8 JANUARY 1982
USA In one of the largest antitrust cases in history, the Justice Department orders the American Telephone & Telegraph Company (AT&T), one of the world's largest corporations, to divest itself of the 22 Bell System companies that provide most local service in the US.

11 JANUARY 1982
Poland NATO nations condemn the Soviet Union for supporting the military government running Poland under martial law; they warn that Western Europe might join the US in imposing economic and other sanctions against the USSR.

25 JANUARY 1982
Poland General Jaruzelski—under fire from all sides in Poland because of martial law and the austere economic situation—attacks the US for its sanctions and calls for hard work and sacrifice from the Polish people.

26 JANUARY 1982
USA In his state of the union speech, President Reagan proposes a new partnership between federal and state governments—what he calls 'the new federalism'—under which the states would assume responsibility for many programs including food stamps, aid to dependent children, and highway construction. It is generally attacked by Democrats, and few Republicans seem willing to get behind the program.

FEBRUARY 1982
Central America Violence continues in both El Salvador and Guatemala, where leftists guerrillas clash with government forces. On 9 February the Salvadoran Government arrested two more suspects in the 1980 deaths of four American churchwomen in 1980, bringing the total arrested to six, one of whom has allegedly confessed. On 14 February an American missionary is shot to death in Guatemala.

14 FEBRUARY 1982
France Mitterand and his Socialist Government begin to assume ownership of companies with combined work forces of 650,000, including five of France's largest industrial groups, 18 commercial banks, and two leading investment banks. The government will pay $8 billion for them.

17 FEBRUARY 1982
Zimbabwe Robert Mugabe, prime minister of the coalition government since black Africans took over, dismisses Joshua Nkomo, his chief rival, and charges that Nkomo was plotting to take over the government by force.

18 FEBRUARY 1982
Mexico As Mexico's economy slides drastically and its debts rise, the government announces it will devalue the peso by 30 percent against the US dollar.

23 FEBRUARY 1982
Greenland In a referendum, the people of Greenland vote to leave the European Economic Community, or Common Market, which they had joined when affiliated with Denmark.

25 FEBRUARY 1982
Social Change The European Court of Human Rights rules that British parents may refuse to allow corporal punishment of their children in public schools.

27 FEBRUARY 1982
Poland The nation's Roman Catholic bishops call for an end to martial law, freedom for those imprisoned under this law (including Lech Walesa), and a national covenant in which Solidarity is represented.
South Africa Prime Minister Botha rebuffs a challenge to his relatively moderate policies from the far-right wing of his National Party.

8 MARCH 1982
Afghanistan A US State Department official tells the Senate Foreign Relations Committee that the Soviets have killed at least 3000 people in Afghanistan with poison gas and other chemical weapons; he claims that the Soviets are using torture and summary execution and that 3 million Afghans have fled recently, most to neighboring Pakistan.

9 MARCH 1982
Ireland After elections of 18 February which ousted Garret Fitzgerald as prime minister but failed to produce a clear majority, a wealthy businessman, Charles Haughey, is elected prime minister by a coalition of independents and the Fianna Fail Party. Haughey will be defeated on 4 November, and Fitzgerald will return to office on 14 December 1982.

12 MARCH 1982
Central America/USA Backing up Reagan Administration claims that Salvadoran guerrillas are supported by Nicaraguans and Cubans, the US State Department holds a press conference to introduce a young Nicaraguan captured in El Salvador who was reportedly trained in Cuba and Ethiopia. At the press conference he denies this and claims he has never seen another Nicaraguan or Cuban in El Salvador. The next day he is handed over to the Nicaraguan embassy.

18 MARCH 1982
El Salvador Four Dutch television correspondents are killed in a remote area where they had gone to film a guerrilla group; the government claims they were accidentally shot in the clash between guerrillas and government troops, but witnesses claim they were deliberately shot by government soldiers.

23 MARCH 1982
Guatemala A military coup ousts the regime headed by President Lucas Garcia, denounces the elections

The US Supreme Court poses with President Reagan.

AN ERA OF ANXIETY 1974–

held earlier in March as fraudulent, and installs a junta led by Brigadier General Efrain Rios Montt.

24 MARCH 1982
Bangladesh A military coup ousts President Abdus Sattar, and Lieutenant General Mohammad Hossain Ershad assumes power; the new junta suspends the constitution and declares martial law, promising to restore democracy in early elections.

28 MARCH 1982
El Salvador In the first free elections in fifty years, Salvadorans elect a constituent assembly; it will be several days before the ballots can be counted— under the eyes of international monitors—to reveal that the centrist Christian Democrat Party, led by junta chief José Napoleon Duarte, has a 40.5 percent plurality. Five right-wing parties comprising the other 60 percent agree to form a government of national unity.

2–3 APRIL 1982
Falklands War Argentine Army, Navy, and Air Force units invade the Falklands Islands, 250 miles off the southeastern coast of Argentina, claimed by the British as a colony for 150 years. The force of 84 British Marines on the main island resists at first but is soon forced to surrender. The UN Security Council votes to demand removal of Argentine forces, President Reagan telephones Argentine President Galtieri to ask him to call off the invasion, and Prime Minister Thatcher announces that several Royal Navy ships have already sailed for the Falklands; a major naval task force will depart 5 April.

8–19 APRIL 1982
Falklands War US Secretary of State Alexander Haig meets in London with British officials to negotiate an end to the conflict. The British have threatened to sink any Argentine ship that comes within 200 miles of the Falklands after 11 April. Haig begins his shuttle diplomacy, flying back and forth between London and Buenos Aires without firm results. The European Economic Community has voted to ban imports from Argentina.

15 APRIL 1982
Egypt President Mubarak rejects all pleas for clemency and the five militant Moslems condemned for assassinating Sadat are executed.

17 APRIL 1982
Canada In Ottawa, Queen Elizabeth II transfers constitutional power from Britain to Canada, terminating the British North America Act of 1867 that has served as the nation's constitution. Premier René Levesque of the Province of Quebec boycotts the ceremony, claiming that the new constitution infringes on Quebec's powers.

25 APRIL 1982
Falklands War British troops, carried by helicopter

MARGARET HILDA THATCHER, 1925–

One of the leading British politicians of her time, Prime Minister Margaret Thatcher has played a key role in the economic recovery of the United Kingdom in the early 1980s. Prior to becoming prime minister in 1979, Thatcher served as secretary of the state for education and science, and as a leader of the Conservative Party. Holding firmly to her economic policies despite constant criticism, she has been able to maintain projected levels of government spending as well as proposed tax increases, and has been successful in keeping US and British relations open and active. Looking to the people as the ultimate basis of government, Thatcher told the press in 1981, 'Government . . . can make the law, police and courts can uphold the law, but a free society will only surive if we, its citizens obey the law and teach our children to do so.'

---

from the task force still sailing toward the Falklands, capture South Georgia, a nearby island, after a two-hour battle with Argentine troops.
Middle East The last Israeli soldiers leave the Sinai Peninsula per the treaty with Egypt. President Mubarak and Prime Minister Begin pledge their determination to maintain peace.

30 APRIL 1982
Falklands War US President Reagan, having determined that Argentina and Britain cannot resolve their differences through negotiations, announces that the US will support Britain; he offers some materiel support, and imposes limited economic sanctions against Argentina.

1 MAY 1982
Poland On May Day an estimated 50,000 Poles march through Warsaw to express support for Solidarity and protest military rule. No incidents or arrests are reported, but on 3 May protesters clash with police in Warsaw and other cities; on 3 May the military government reintroduces the curfew and imposes other restrictions, including suspension of sports and cultural events and banning of private cars from the streets.

2–4 MAY 1982
Falklands War A British submarine torpedoes the Argentine cruiser *General Belgrano* (36 miles outside the blockade zone, the Argentines will claim) with the loss of 368 lives. On the 4th an Argentine jet fighter hits the British destroyer *Sheffled* with a missile, sinking it with a loss of 20 lives.

9 MAY 1982
Disarmament President Reagan proposes a new plan for reduction of US and USSR nuclear weapons by one-third, with an eventual ceiling on total warheads. On the 18th President Brezhnev will respond that Russia is ready to begin talks, although Reagan's plan favors the US; on 31 May it is announced that

British Prime Minister Thatcher joins US President Reagan in the Oval Office of the White House.

the USA and USSR will open negotiations in Geneva 29 June on strategic nuclear weapons.

11 MAY 1982
Great Britain The House of Commons rejects a bill that would restore the death penalty.

21 MAY 1982
Falklands War British troops make their first landings on the main Falkland island, gaining a beachhead at San Carlos Bay; five British ships are damaged, one British plane downed, and there are 20 casualties; the Argentines lose 17 planes and by the 22nd 5000 British marines and paratroopers are ashore.

24 MAY 1982
Iran-Iraq War Iran claims to have recaptured its port city of Khurramshahr and taken 30,000 Iraqi prisoners; the Iranians are now being supplied with many Soviet arms funnelled through Syria.

27–28 MAY 1982
Falklands War British troops move out from their beachhead at San Carlos Bay; by the 28th they have captured Darwin and Goose Green, the only sizable settlements besides Port Stanley.

30 MAY 1982
NATO Spain is accepted into NATO as its 16th member state.

2 JUNE 1982
Falklands War British troops have advanced to within sight of Port Stanley and control all the high ground around that city, now defended by some 7000 Argentine troops.

3 JUNE 1982
Middle East The Israeli ambassador to Britain, Shlomo Argov, is shot and seriously wounded in London by Palestinian terrorists. On the 4th Israeli planes take reprisal by raiding Palestinian targets near Beirut.

6 JUNE 1982
Lebanon Israeli land, sea, and air forces invade southern Lebanon to little resistance; thousands of troops soon take all territory up to a line from Tyre on the coast to the foothills of Mount Hermon. The Israeli Government justifies its actions as retaliation for the assassination attempt on its ambassador in London on 3 June.

7 JUNE 1982
Chad It is reported that the capital, Ndjamena, has fallen to rebel forces led by Hissen Habre, who has been fighting to seize power from President Ouedda for two years.

8 JUNE 1982
Great Britain/USA President Reagan, on his official visit to Britain, becomes the first American President to address a combined meeting of both Houses of Parliament. Reagan asks Britain to join the US in a crusade to encourage freedom and democracy in communist countries.

9 JUNE 1982
Lebanon Israeli troops are within four miles of Beirut. They claim their air force has shot down 61 Syrian MiGs since the invasion and destroyed surface-to-air missile systems in the Bekka Valley—Soviet hardware operated by Syrians. It is clear that the Israelis are determined to stamp out the PLO in Lebanon.

14 JUNE 1982
Falklands War The commanding general of the Argentine troops in Port Stanley surrenders to the British. Air attacks from the mainland continue for awhile, but the conflict is over. The British now find themselves with 15,000 Argentine prisoners, many suffering from the severe cold and damp, hunger, and diseases. The Argentines will soon send ships to remove their troops, but refuse to declare a formal end to hostilities.
Lebanon West Beirut, dominated by Moslems, is cut off by Israeli troops; the PLO's lesdership and most of its fighters are trapped there. The Israelis continue to bombard Palestinian enclaves, including refugee camps.

15 JUNE 1982
Disarmament Foreign Minister Andrei Gromyko speaks at the UN and conveys a pledge from Brezhnev that the USSR will never be first to use nuclear weapons in any conflict. President Reagan dismisses this announcement as a gesture and says he prefers to negotiate a reduction of nuclear arms.

17 JUNE 1982
Argentina President Leopoldo Galtieri, who led the Argentines into the disastrous war in the Falklands, resigns as president, commander in chief of the army, and a member of the ruling junta. On 22 June Major General Reynaldo Bignone is appointed president. Argentina still refuses to declare an end to hostilities, demanding that Britain withdraw its troops first.

21 JUNE 1982
USA After an eight-week trial, John Hinckley is found not guilty by reason of insanity on charges of shooting President Reagan and three others on 30 March 1981. There is a public outcry. Hinckley is sent to St Elizabeth's Hospital, Washington, DC, for additional testing before commitment.

25 JUNE 1982
USA Secretary of State Alexander Haig resigns over differences with the administration on foreign policy. Reagan nominates George Shultz, former secretary of the treasury, to replace him. Shultz will be confirmed by the Senate on 15 July.

Israeli General Ariel Sharon.

Night fighting during the Israeli-Lebanese conflict in 1982.

27 JUNE 1982

Lebanon The Israeli Government issues a peace proposal that calls on all PLO members to turn over their weapons and leave the country. It is rejected by the PLO, and on 4 July the Israelis prevent food, water, and fuel from entering the section of Beirut controlled by the PLO. In addition to the 6000 Palestinian guerrillas living there, 500,000 Lebanese civilians are affected.

30 JUNE 1982

USA The Equal Rights Amendment (ERA), which would specifically ban discrimination based on sex in the US Constitution, is defeated by failure to gain ratification from 38 states in the ten years since Congress passed it (only 35 states ratified).

1 JULY 1982

Argentina General Bignone is sworn in as president; he lifts the ban on political activity and promises national elections by March 1984. In response, President Reagan lifts economic sanctions on 12 July.

4 JULY 1982

Dominican Republic President Antonio Guzmàn dies of a gunshot wound to the head, apparently self-inflicted. The Vice-President is sworn in until elections make Salvador Jorge Bianco president on 16 August.

Mexico Miguel de la Madrid is elected president; he will be sworn on 1 December 1982.

6 JULY 1982

Lebanon President Reagan announces that he has agreed in principle to contribute a small contingent of US troops to a multinational force for peace-keeping in Beirut if some settlement can be reached among Israelis, the PLO, and Syrians. On 10 July France agrees to do the same.

25 JULY 1982
Lebanon   PLO leader Yasir Arafat signs a document accepting the UN resolutions on Israel's right to exist in the presence of six visiting US Congressmen acting on their own initiative. On 26 July the Reagan Administration rejects this document as a basis for recognizing the PLO.

1 AUGUST 1982
Lebanon   Israelis step up their shelling of West Beirut before Philip C Habib, the US special envoy, can arrange a cease-fire.

12 AUGUST 1982
International   Representatives of the European Economic Community in Washington deliver a formal protest to the US for the latter's imposition of a ban on supplying technology to the USSR for constructing its gas pipeline to Europe. The Reagan Administration goes ahead and imposes sanctions on French

and British firms that were defying the ban. By 31 August members of Reagan's cabinet try to persuade him to soften his stand.

19–30 AUGUST 1982
Lebanon   The Israeli cabinet agrees to an evacuation plan for the PLO calling for a multinational force of troops from the US, France, and Italy to move into Beirut as the PLO, Syrians, and Israelis withdraw. The first Palestinians begin to leave by ship for Cyprus on 21 August when the first French troops arrive; US Marines land on the 25th; Yasir Arafat leaves on the 30th. By 1 September all PLO fighters are out of Beirut, as are Syrian troops. Italian, French, and US troops will gradually be removed in the next two weeks.

20 AUGUST 1982
Mexico/USA   The US Government outlines its plan for financial aid to keep Mexico from defaulting on

AN ERA OF ANXIETY 1974–

Street fighting in South Beirut, Lebanon, 10 August 1982.

28 OCTOBER 1982

its massive debts; the US plan includes loans from foreign central banks and US prepayments for crude oil. The devaluation of Mexico's peso has hurt US investors there and disrupted the economies of Mexican and American border residents.

23 AUGUST 1982
Lebanon Bashir Gemayel, leader of the Lebanon Christian Phalangist Party, is elected president by the Parliament. As Gemayel is identified with a military and anti-Moslem group, this does not promise well for uniting Lebanon.

31 AUGUST 1982
Poland Pro-Solidarity Poles have been demonstrating in various cities; riot police have restricted themselves mainly to water-cannon. Today, Solidarity leaders call out large demonstrations in many cities; the one in Warsaw is dispersed by tear-gas grenades.

1–2 SEPTEMBER 1982
Middle East President Reagan proposes a new plan for settling problems between Israel and the PLO; it calls for full autonomy for Palestinians living on the West Bank, and Israel promptly rejects it.

1–6 SEPTEMBER 1982
Mexico President Lopez Portillo announces that all banks are closed until 6 September, when they will reopen as nationalized banks under the central Bank of Mexico. Mexican businessmen protest, but many American bankers favor this move as showing that the Mexican Government will stand behind the debts of private banks.

12–13 SEPTEMBER 1982
China In a major shakeup in Chinese leadership, Hua Guofeng, the chosen successor of Mao Tse-tung, loses his high position. Deng Xiaoping is elected chairman of the newly formed Central Advisory Commission to the Communist Party, consolidating his power in both party and government.

13 SEPTEMBER 1982
Great Britain A report issued some ten years ago by Lord Shackleton on the Falkland Islands is now revived by the government and its recommendations —including £100 million for economic development—are considered.

14 SEPTEMBER 1982
Lebanon Bashir Gemayel, recently chosen president of Lebanon, is killed (along with eight others) in a bomb explosion at his Christian Phalangist Party headquarters in east Beirut. Palestinians or Druse Moslems are suspected. His brother, Amin Gemayel, is chosen to succeed him and becomes president 23 September.

15 SEPTEMBER 1982
Middle East Brezhnev attacks American proposals

for a settlement of the Palestinian-Israeli problems and offers his own plan. This same day, Yasir Arafat has an audience with Pope John Paul II, part of Arafat's campaign to gain support as a responsible leader. It will turn more militant members of the PLO against him.

16 SEPTEMBER 1982
Iran Former Foreign Minister Gotzbadeh, familiar to Americans from the hostage crisis when he presented the position of the Ayatollah Khomeni, is executed under orders from the Ayatollah for his treasonous actions.

17–18 SEPTEMBER 1982
Lebanon Christian Phalangist militiamen are allowed by the Israeli Army to enter Palestinian refugee camps in West Beirut, where they massacre 800 men, women and children. The Phalangists see this as reprisal for the murder of Bashir Gemayel, but the world condemns it as an atrocity. The Israeli army is blamed for its failure to prevent the slaughter.

20 SEPTEMBER 1982
Lebanon President Reagan agrees to Italy's proposal that US, French, and Italian troops return to Beirut to keep the peace, in view of the latest violence; on 29 September US Marines return to Beirut.

1 OCTOBER 1982
West Germany Helmut Schmidt, the Social Democrat chancellor, fails to get a vote of confidence in the Bundestag and is replaced by opposition party leader, Helmut Kohl.

1–13 OCTOBER 1982
Sweden Swedish antisubmarine helicopters and ships search along the Baltic seacoast for a suspected foreign submarine—assumed to be Russian; by 5 October the Swedes claim they have trapped it and are dropping depth charges. They finally abandon the search without having located any vessel.

8 OCTOBER 1982
Poland Parliament approves a law banning Solidarity, the independent labor union. President Reagan suspends the 'most favored nation' trade status that Poland had enjoyed with the US for 22 years. Workers at the Lenin Shipyard in Gdansk strike in protest on 11 October but return two days later when the government subjects them to military orders.

26 OCTOBER 1982
Poland The funeral of a young Polish worker slain by the police turns into a pro-Solidarity rally.

28 OCTOBER 1982
Spain In national elections, the Socialist Party wins a majority in Parliament and their leader Felipe Gonzalez, 40, becomes the youngest prime minister in Europe. He will be sworn in on 2 December.

485

AN ERA OF ANXIETY 1974–

30 OCTOBER 1982
Portugal The new constitution goes into effect, ending eight years of military domination.

2 NOVEMBER 1982
USA In midterm elections, Democrats take control of the House of Representatives, but Republicans retain control of the Senate.

4 NOVEMBER 1982
International The UN General Assembly votes a resolution calling for Britain and Argentina to resolve their differences over the Falkland Islands by negotiation; neither country is prepared to do so.

10–12 NOVEMBER 1982
USSR President Leonid Brezhnev, 75, dies. President Reagan sends condolences but does not attend the 15 November funeral. Brezhnev's successor is Yuri Andropov, head of the KGB since 1967; he is elected general secretary of the Communist Party's Central Committee on 12 November.

11 NOVEMBER 1982
Lebanon A bomb explosion at Israeli military headquarters in Tyre kills 100.

13 NOVEMBER 1982
Poland The military government releases Solidarity leader Lech Walesa from the place of detention where he has been held since 13 December 1981.

Authorities state that Walesa is 'no longer a threat to internal security,' and it appears he has had to give assurances, however ambiguous, that he will not take an active role in stirring up protest.

International President Reagan announces that the US is lifting sanctions against domestic and foreign companies that sell US-developed technology for use in the Soviet gas pipeline to Western Europe. Reagan puts his reversal in the context of broad agreements with European allies over trade policies with Russia (although President Mitterand of France denies there has been any such agreement).

24 NOVEMBER 1982
Japan Yasuhiro Nakasone succeeds Zenko Suzuki as Prime Minister; Suzuki's economic policies had come under fire from his Liberal Democratic Party.

10 DECEMBER 1982
Environment The Law of the Sea Convention, under negotiation for over ten years, comes into effect with signature by 119 nations. (The US, Britain, and other industrialized nations refuse to sign it.) The treaty covers such matters as free passage of ships through specified bodies of water and arrangements for exploiting oil, gas, fish, and minerals in the world's oceans. Underdeveloped and Third World nations are the biggest supporters of the law, which favors a co-operative approach and sharing of profits.

21 DECEMBER 1982
Disarmament Soviet leader Andropov proposes to reduce Russian intermediate-range missiles in Europe if the US will abandon plans to deploy Pershing II and cruise missiles in Western Europe. The US, Britain, and France immediately reject this proposal, primarily on ground that British and French nuclear arsenals are independent of NATO.

31 DECEMBER 1982
Poland General Jaruzelski suspends martial law, but retains governmental restrictions including the right to reimpose it.

OTHER EVENTS OF 1982
Science The first fossil bones of a mammal—a small ratlike marsupial—are found in Antarctica; also found there is an eight-pound rock identified as originating on Mars. Four and possibly six new moons of Saturn are revealed by analysis of photos sent back by *Voyager 2*.

Medicine/Health The first transplant of an artificial heart—known as the Jarvik heart for its principal developer, Dr Robert Jarvik—is made at the University of Utah Medical Center where 61-year-old Barney Clark receives the polyurethane device on 2 December. He will live until 23 March 1983, when he dies of secondary complications. Twenty-two year old Nan Davis, paralyzed from the waist down by an automobile accident, begins to walk with the aid of a computer that controls electrical stimulation of her

Major Haddad in a vehicle surrounded by Israeli and Lebanese troops, 1982.

leg muscles. The American public becomes aware of an apparently new disease, acquired immune deficiency syndrome (AIDS), that tends to afflict male homosexuals and other specific groups including drug addicts; its high incidence and mortality rate cause concern. A US Government-sponsored study reports no therapeutic benefit from Laetrile in cancer therapy. The US Surgeon General intensifies the government's long-standing warning against the dangers of smoking tobacco.

Technology The US space shuttle *Columbia* completes its third and fourth flights, releasing a satellite on the latter (the first commercial 'payload.') Two Russian cosmonauts set a record of 211 days in space.

Environment One of the worst oil spills ever occurs off the coast of Lithuania, when a British tanker breaks up in a storm and releases 4,800,000 gallons. At the 10th anniversary of the UN Conference on the Human Environment, representatives from 70 nations discuss gains and losses since their first meeting in Stockholm.

Literature Gabriel Garcia Marquez' *Chronicle of a Death Foretold*; Bellow's *The Dean's December*; Böll's *The Safety Net*.

Drama/Entertainment Athol Fugard's *Master Harold . . . and the Boys*; Pinter's *A Kind of Alaska*; Tom Stoppard's *The Real Thing*; Edward Bond's *Summer*; Caryl Churchill's *Top Girls*; *Cats*, a musical derived from T S Eliot's poems; most-admired films are *Gandhi* and *ET*.

The Arts European artists experiment with neo-expressionism, producing large showy canvases. Melina Mercouri, Greek Minister of Culture, renews the issue of Britain's returning the Elgin, or Parthenon, marbles to Greece.

Music The centenary of Stravinsky's birth is celebrated. Berio's *La vera storia*; Udo Zimmermann's *The Miraculous Shoemaker's Wife*; William Mathias's *Lux Aeterna*.

Sports/Leisure The World Cup football (soccer) final—in which Italy defeats West Germany 3–1—is viewed by an estimated half the world's population, the largest audience in history.

Life/Customs In Little Rock, Arkansas, after a long trial, a Federal Judge rules unconstitutional a state law requiring Arkansas schools to teach 'creationism' in tandem with the theory of evolution, as advocated by the fundamentalist-Christian movement.

Ideas/Beliefs Pope John Paul II becomes the first pope to visit Britain, whence he proceeds to Argentina to show impartiality in the on-going hostilities over the Falkland Islands. Billy Graham, the American evangelist, is allowed to preach in Russia and arouses criticism for claiming that he finds general freedom of worship there.

5 JANUARY 1983

International The USSR and Warsaw Pact allies make a series of proposals on disarmament and non-aggression to NATO; they suggest that Warsaw Pact and NATO nations sign a nonaggression treaty. NATO nations respond cautiously.

6 JANUARY 1983

Australia Senator Neville Bonner, the only Aborigine member of the Federal Parliament, calls for creation of a separate Aborigine nation.

16–18 JANUARY 1983

International USSR Foreign Minister Andrei Gromyko visits Bonn and warns West Germany not to accept the intermediate-range nuclear missiles— the Pershing II—scheduled for deployment in the fall. He offers USSR reduction of its arsenal of such missiles in Europe if NATO agrees not to install any more; NATO nations regard this as neither a new nor an equitable offer.

21 JANUARY 1983

USA-Central America The Reagan Administration certifies to Congress that the government of El Salvador has made progress in curbing violations of human rights, making it eligible for continued US aid. Many Americans protest that the killings and other violations continue.

25 JANUARY 1983

WW II: Aftermath Klaus Barbie—a Nazi convicted years before for crimes committed as chief of the German Gestapo in occupied Lyons, France—is arrested in Bolivia on the charge of dealing in cocaine. On the 27th France announces it is seeking extradition of 'the butcher of Lyons.'

27 JANUARY 1983

International The US and USSR resume negotiations in Geneva on reducing intermediate-range nuclear missiles in Europe. The USA's opening position is Reagan's 'zero option': the USSR will dismantle all its intermediate-range nuclear missiles in Europe if NATO doesn't deploy any new Pershing IIs and cruise missiles. The Soviets reject this proposal and insist on including missile counts for Britain and France in any settlement with NATO and the US.

31 JANUARY 1983

International President Reagan offers to meet the USSR's Andropov 'wherever and whenever he wants' to sign an agreement banning US and USSR intermediate-range land-based missiles world wide. Andropov rejects this as 'nothing new.'

8 FEBRUARY 1983

Israel After weeks of investigation, the state board of inquiry into the massacre of Palestinian refugees in West Beirut (16–18 September 1982), denies allegations of direct complicity by Israelis but finds Defense Minister Ariel Sharon and three Israeli generals guilty of neglect of duty. On 11 February Sharon will be forced to resign; he remains in Begin's cabinet as minister without portfolio.

11 FEBRUARY 1983
International The International Monetary Fund agrees to a 47-percent increase in its lending resources to meet the demand for emergency loans from debt-ridden developing nations. The IMF urges steps to save the threatened structure of the international economy from recession and inflation.

24 FEBRUARY 1983
India The Indian Government confirms reports that at least 1300 have died during three weeks of violence in the northeastern state of Assam. Victims are mostly Bengali-speaking Moslem immigrants who have entered Assam since Bangladesh was formed in 1971; they are resented by native Hindus, who turn against them because of coming elections in which immigrants are to have the vote.

2–9 MARCH 1983
The Papacy Pope John Paul II travels through eight Central American and Caribbean nations, where his words inevitably take on political overtones. This is most true in Nicaragua, where he openly rebukes Catholic priests serving in the leftist Sandinista Government; at an outdoor assembly he is all but drowned out by those in the crowd shouting revolutionary slogans.

5 MARCH 1983
Australia The Labour Party, led by Robert Hawke, defeats the Liberal-National Party coalition led by Prime Minister Malcolm Fraser that has governed Australia for eight years. Hawke, former president of the Australian Council of Trade Unions and a member of Parliament since 1980, will pursue an independent course.

6 MARCH 1983
West Germany Chancellor Helmut Kohl's ruling center-right coalition gains a majority in national elections to the Bundestag; the Greens, a growing environmentalist-antinuclear movement, gets 5.6 percent of the vote (27 of 498 seats in the Bundestag).

8 MARCH 1983
Zimbabwe Joshua Nkomo, fearing he is marked for death because of his opposition to President Mugabe, flees to Botswana and then to England. On 16 August he returns to Zimbabwe and takes his seat in Parliament on assurances of his safety.

14 MARCH 1983
International OPEC nations agree—for the first time in their 23 years—to cut the benchmark price of oil (from $34 to $29 a barrel) and to maintain national quotas, in an attempt to deal with the mounting oil glut on the world market.

25 MARCH 1983
USA Congress passes the bill that reforms the Social Security system, which had been approaching bankruptcy; a bipartisan commission had made the recommendations that were largely incorporated into the bill, which calls for concessions from all involved. President Reagan announces that a 'dark cloud' has been lifted from the system.

5 MAY 1983
France-USSR France expels 47 Soviet diplomats, journalists, and UN officials on charges of conducting espionage. This is an unprecedented move in French-Soviet relations.

10 APRIL 1983
Middle East King Hussein of Jordan announces he will no longer support Reagan's Middle East peace plan—which includes assurances that the US will work to halt Israeli settlement on occupied territory of the West Bank; Hussein also charges that PLO leader Yasir Arafat has broken agreements with Jordan.

12 APRIL 1983
USA After a bitterly contested campaign, Harold Washington becomes the first black mayor of Chicago.
Southeast Asia In the ongoing conflict, Vietnam claims victory in Cambodia after a two-week offensive against the Pol Pot 'clique'; on the 22nd Vietnam charges China with shelling its border positions; Thailand has charged Vietnam with threatening its territory.

18 APRIL 1983
Lebanon The US Embassy in Beirut is almost demolished by a car-bomb that kills over 50 people and injures over 100; it is believed this action was sponsored by radical Iranian Moslems.

22 APRIL 1983
Life/Customs The German newsweekly *Stern* claims it has acquired 60 volumes of diaries kept by Hitler; a few reputable experts are duped, but the diaries are proved forgeries, the work of Konrad Fischer, a Stuttgart dealer in Nazi memorabilia.

28 APRIL 1983
Argentina The Argentine Government declares that the thousands of Argentinians who disappeared in the 1970s—when the military was stamping out opposition suspected of being leftist—are 'for administrative and juridical purposes, considered dead.' The resultant outcry embarrasses the government.

3 MAY 1983
International The USSR's Andropov offers a new proposal to reduce the number of nuclear warheads it deploys in Europe to the level of the combined warheads of Britain and France, so long as NATO does not deploy the 572 intermediate-range nuclear missiles planned for the fall.

4–17 MAY 1983
Lebanon After months of talks the Lebanese

AN ERA OF ANXIETY 1974–

Government accepts a US proposal for withdrawal of all foreign troops. Israel accepts it on 6 May, and Lebanon and Israel sign the agreement on the 17th, with approval by both Parliaments. Syria rejects it on the 13th. Although Israel will withdraw into an agreed-upon security zone in southern Lebanon, Syria will leave its forces in place and continue to support Druse Moslems and Palestinians opposed to negotiating settlements with the Lebanese Government and Israel.

20–23 MAY 1983
South Africa   A car-bomb explodes outside headquarters of the nation's air force in Pretoria, the capital, killing 18 and injuring 200; it is the most serious single terrorist attack by blacks opposed to the government. Credit is taken by the African National Congress (AFN) on the 23rd, and South African fighter planes attack a camp in Mozambique said to be a center of the exiled AFN movement.

28–30 MAY 1983
International   Leaders of the seven major industrial democracies (the US, Great Britain, Canada, France, West Germany, Italy, Japan) meet at Williamsburg, Virginia, to discuss economic issues: they call for strategies to halt protectionism, encourage new technologies, and improve the international monetary system.

6 JUNE 1983
Nicaragua-USA   Nicaragua expels three US diplomats, charging them with plotting to poison the defense minister; the US denies it and orders Nicaragua to close its six consulates in the US; 21 Nicaraguan consular officials are expelled.

9 JUNE 1983
Great Britain   Prime Minister Thatcher and her Conservative Party sweep Parliamentary elections, gaining 397 of 650 seats, an endorsement of her hard-line approach to foreign and domestic issues.

16 JUNE 1983
USSR   Yuri Andropov, who has held the titles of general secretary of the Communist Party and minister of defense, is elected president of the Presidium of the USSR.

16–23 JUNE 1983
Poland   Pope John Paul II visits his native Poland in what is viewed as an attempt by General Jaruzelski, its leader, to signal some relaxation of controls if the Polish people restrain their support for such movements as Solidarity. The pope's previous visit (1979) was seen as fomenting public unrest and the emergence of Solidarity; this time the pontiff tries to avoid outright confrontations with the regime, although he speaks openly on behalf of human freedoms and rights and grants Lech Walesa a private audience.

26–27 JUNE 1983
Italy   In national elections for Parliament, the Christian Democrats retain their place as the largest party, but the gap between them and the Communists narrows (32.9 vs 29.9 percent) and both parties lose to the socialists and others.

8 JULY 1983
USA   The National Bureau of Economic Research announces that the recession (which began in July 1981) 'bottomed out' in November 1982. The Labor Department reports today that unemployment fell to a seasonally adjusted 9.8 percent in June (the lowest since August 1982).

21 JULY 1983
Poland   The government announces an end to martial law but effectively retains tight controls into 1985.

26 JULY 1983
USA-Central America   President Reagan denies that his administration is planning any war in Central America; he rejects comparisons between the US role there and in Vietnam. US military maneuvers scheduled to begin in August are 'a shield for democracy and development.' This same day the US Government releases a letter from Reagan to the presidents of the four Contadora Group nations (Mexico, Colombia, Venezuela, and Panama) expressing support for their proposals to bring about a peaceful resolution of problems in Central America.

3–4 AUGUST 1983
Chad   As the government comes under increasing pressure from Libyan-backed insurgents, the US approves a $15-million increase over the current $10-million aid for Chad and announces that it is sending two AWACs to Egypt in advance of their scheduled arrival for military exercises (a further warning to Libya). The US is also sending antiaircraft weapons and three military advisers to Chad to back up increasing aid from France.

4 AUGUST 1983
Italy   Bettino Craxi, leader of Italy's Socialist Party, is elected premier of a five-party coalition government; of the 44 governments since World War II, this is the first not led by a Christian Democrat.

8 AUGUST 1983
Guatemala   A military coup overthrows President Efrain Rios Mott and installs the defense minister as chief of state; the new government restores civil liberties and ends special tribunals to suppress opposition.

10 AUGUST 1983
Chad   Libyan-backed insurgents overrun Faya-Largeau, a strategic outpost in northern Chad; President Habre appeals for foreign help.

18 AUGUST 1983

Chad France sends 450 paratroopers to Chad, while Qaddafi of Libya rejects an offer from President Habre to negotiate, claiming it is an internal problem. A French newspaper article reveals that President Mitterand is annoyed by President Reagan's attempts to pressure France to take more action in Chad.

21 AUGUST 1983

Philippines Benigno Aquino, the opposition leader who had been living in the USA for three years, is shot to death within three minutes of arriving at the airport in Manila, where he has come to lead opposition to President Marcos. Marcos condemns the killer—an otherwise unknown and unaffiliated criminal—and denies involvement, but the killing triggers off a series of riots and protests that challenge the government.

28–30 AUGUST 1983

Lebanon Druse Moslem militia launch attacks on the Lebanese Army in Beirut; that escalate into a full-scale civil war; four US Marines and four French soldiers in the international peacekeeping force are killed in the shellings.

1 SEPTEMBER 1983

International A Korean Air Line Flight 007 Boeing 747 is shot down by a heat-seeking missile from a Soviet jet fighter as the plane crosses Soviet territory en route between Alaska and Korea: all 240 passengers and 29 crew members die as the plane plunges into the sea. It will be 6 September before the Soviets admit to 'stopping' the plane, and there is an international outcry over Russian handling of the situation. Questions remain as to why the Korean plane was over Soviet territory, since all its guidance systems appear to have been functioning correctly.

12 SEPTEMBER 1983

Israel Menachem Begin, who had announced his intention of resigning as prime minister on 28 August, does so. This is attributed to chronic illness, the recent death of his wife, and his depression over events in Lebanon. Yitzhak Shamir wins out in the contest to head Begin's Herut Party and succeeds Begin as Prime Minister.

29 SEPTEMBER 1983

USA President Reagan cancels plans to visit the Philippines during his forthcoming trip to several Far Eastern nations.

This same day Congress authorizes the president to keep US Marines in Lebanon for another 18 months; this is the first time it has invoked the War Powers Resolution passed in 1973 after the Vietnam War. The resolution states that the president must get Congressional support for committing US troops to foreign actions of over 60 days. Reagan believes he did not need such authorization for this 'multinational force' in Lebanon, but hails the passage as a 'great victory' for a 'responsible, bipartisan foreign policy.'

5 OCTOBER 1983

International Lech Walesa, the Polish labor leader, is awarded the Nobel Peace Prize for his efforts to gain rights for Poles through nonviolent means.

9 OCTOBER 1983

Korea The President of South Korea, Chun Doo Hwan, with his cabinet and other top officials, has just begun a tour of Southeast Asia. They are scheduled to lay a wreath on a monument in Rangoon, Burma, when a bomb explodes; President Chun Doo Hwan, not yet arrived, is uninjured, but 17 Koreans—including the deputy prime minister, the foreign minister, and two other cabinet ministers —and two Burmese are killed. North Korea is blamed despite official denials.

13–19 OCTOBER 1983

Grenada On this small (133-square-mile) island in the Caribbean, Maurice Bishop, the premier—who had seized power in a coup in 1979—is placed under house arrest by more militant Marxists; on the 19th he is freed by supporters. He is soon captured by those supporting the new insurgents—who are led by General Hudson Austin—and Bishop is shot.

23 OCTOBER 1983

Lebanon A truck filled with explosives, driven by a suicidal Moslem, crashes through the flimsy defenses around the US Marine barracks in Beirut; in the explosion that ensues, 237 US Marines will die, another 80 are wounded. Almost simultaneously, a similar incident occurs at French military quarters, where 58 die and 15 are injured. The Islamic Holy War, a pro-Iranian Shiite Moslem group, seems responsible. Questions are raised as to why US authorities did not take more precautions against such an attack, especially since they had been warned of its possibility by the CIA.

25 OCTOBER 1983

Grenada Early in the morning, 1800 US troops and 300 Caribbean troops land on Grenada, meeting more resistance than expected—much of it apparently from some of the 600 or more Cubans ostensibly there to construct a large airfield. Most resistance is put down within the first day, but pockets hold out for several days, by which time 18 Americans have been killed. The Reagan Administration cites the need to protect some 600 Americans studying at a medical school on Grenada; the next stated reason is that six of Grenada's neighboring Caribbean island states requested US intervention because they feared a possible Communist Grenada. US forces soon turn up evidence of a strong Cuban and Soviet presence—large stores of arms, documents suggesting close links to Cuba. On 27 October the

491

Rescue workers searching for victims of the bombing of the Marine Command Center near Beirut.

AN ERA OF ANXIETY 1974–

US troops moving through Greenville, Grenada, 25 October 1983.

UN Security Council votes a resolution to 'deplore' the US action, which the US delegate vetoes.

30 OCTOBER 1983
Argentina Raul Alfonsin and his center-left Radical Civic Union Party decisively outpoll the Perónist candidate, Italo Luder, and his party (52 percent to 40 percent), for the first time in an open election. This is interpreted as a rejection of the military government that has killed many in recent years.

31 OCTOBER 1983
International Britain's House of Commons votes to deploy the new missiles provided by the US as part of NATO's defense plan; this same day, the US Senate rejects, 58–40, a resolution calling for a unilateral freeze on nuclear weapons.

4 NOVEMBER 1983
Lebanon A truck-bomb of the type that killed American and French soldiers in Beirut crashes into the Israeli military post in Tyre, killing 29 Israeli soldiers and 32 Palestinian and Lebanese prisoners. The same pro-Iranian Shiite Moslem group is held responsible.

Open fighting begins again between PLO members who oppose Yasir Arafat's command and those who remain loyal to him; Arafat and his supporters have been pushed back into one section of the Lebanese city of Tripoli; shelling of their positions will continue for three weeks and claim many Lebanese lives.

8–13 NOVEMBER 1983
International President Reagan visits Japan and South Korea to affirm ties with these nations despite any differences; in the case of Japan, these center around America's displeasure with trading policies; in the case of South Korea, around government denial of civil rights to those opposed to its leadership.

14 NOVEMBER 1983
Great Britain Despite months of protests and demonstrations by Britons opposed to nuclear weapons, the first intermediate-range cruise missiles arrive at Greenham, 50 miles west of London.

15 NOVEMBER 1983
Cyprus The Turks on Cyprus—divided since the war in 1974 between the Turkish community in the north and the Greek in the south—declare an independent Turkish Republic of Northern Cyprus. Few countries besides Turkey are willing to recognize it.

US troops near Greenville, Grenada after securing the town, 25 October 1983.

AN ERA OF ANXIETY 1974–

20 NOVEMBER 1983
USA A special two-hour film, *The Day After*, is seen on American TV by an estimated half of US adults; the film depicts graphically the effects of a nuclear attack on a typical American community; pro- and anti-nuclear weapons proponents agree that it stimulates public discussion of a kind long avoided.

22–23 NOVEMBER 1983
International On the 22nd the West German Bundestag votes to accept deployment of Pershing II and cruise missiles as part of the NATO defense plan; hours later it is announced that the first components are being flown into West Germany from the US. On the 23rd the Soviet delegation walks out of the US-USSR arms-reduction talks in Geneva—as threatened. On the 24th the USSR announces its intention to increase its nuclear force.

24 NOVEMBER 1983
Lebanon In Damascus, intermediaries announce that PLO Arafat loyalists and insurgents have agreed to a truce calling for a cease-fire, negotiations on internal differences, and departure of all Palestinian fighters from Tripoli and environs.

THE COMPUTER REVOLUTION

The origins of the computer can be traced back many years—thousands, in fact, to the abacus—but in the strict sense it was not until 1947, with the invention of the transistor, that digital computers could become so much smaller, faster, and cheaper that they were revolutionized. Advances since then have been phenomenal. Silicon wafers, for instance, used for integrated circuits, can now hold 500,000 logic circuits on a minuscule area. In the US alone some 724,000 personal computers were sold in 1980, 2,800,000 in 1982. But even these statistics on the 'hardware' do not explain the 'computer revolution.' That is the result of the 'software,' the programs that allow people to put computers to so many uses. The space program, assembly lines, financial transactions, warehousing and distribution, military logistics and weaponry, bookkeeping and personnel records, printing and communications—these and many other jobs are being performed by computers. In short, they are changing the ways people work, learn, think, communicate, and relate to the world at large. The computer revolution shares at least one trait with the other thresholds in human history signified by tools, fire, language, agriculture, printing, and industry—the potential for both good and evil uses.

A front view of the Automatic Sequence Controlled Calculator—the highest-technology calculating machine.

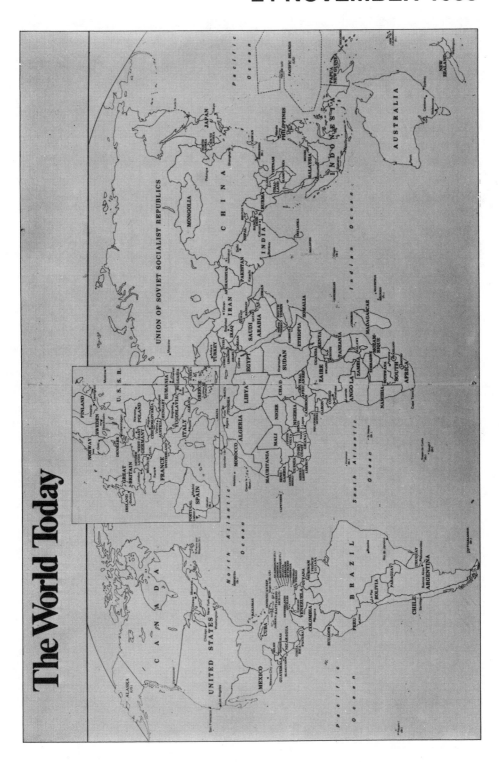

The World Today

AN ERA OF ANXIETY 1974—

The global village.

PHOTO CREDITS

Associated Press Photo: 162, 196, 213, 326, 332, 341, 345, 346, 351, 353, 354, 378, 431, 464
Bettmann Archive: 144 (center), 154
Bison Library: 49, 247, 268, 458–9
Black Star: 372
Browne Collection: 109
Bundesarchiv: 180, 200, 210, 223, 231
Canadian Consulate General: 348, 397, 399
Culver Service: 65
Edison National Historic Site: 61
Editions Stock: 205
Franklin D Roosevelt Library: 174, 192, 320
George Eastman House: 20–21
Imperial War Museum: 119, 120 (top), 122 (bottom), 123 (bottom), 149, 219, 220, 227, 255, 257
Israeli Government Press Office: 394, 482–3, 484, 487
John F Kennedy Library: 361
Landesbildstelle: 454
Library of Congress: 4–5, 6–7, 18–19, 34, 52, 60, 71, 76, 77, 80, 84, 100, 129 (bottom), 141, 143, 144 (top), 146 (right), 148 (top), 157, 158, 159 (bottom), 193, 309, 350
Martha Swope: 474
Museum of Modern Art: 208
NASA: 407, 456, 473, 498
National Archives: 10–11, 89, 120 (bottom), 122 (top), 123 (top), 124, 129 (top), 230, 261, 323
New York Daily News: 380
New York Public Library: 17, 44, 64, 70, 75, 95, 144 (center), 155, 199
Newark Public Library: 94
Novosti Press Agency: 24, 50, 86, 90, 137, 256, 259, 284–5, 286
Public Archives of Canada: 43, 83, 140

Radio Times Hulton Collection: 327
René DAZY: 191, 197
Robert Hunt Library: cover, 55, 91, 97, 103, 195, 204, 206, 216, 222, 228–9, 239, 244, 253, 262, 395, 408
St Louis *Globe Democrat*: 303
Smithsonian Institution: 307, 329 (bottom)
US Air Force: 2, 148 (bottom), 274, 288–9
US Army: 265, 271, 277, 291, 293, 314, 317, 318, 322, 340, 356, 370, 389, 400, 404, 406, 409, 469
US Defense Department: 29
US Information Services: 127
US Marine Corps: 278–9, 281, 314, 424–5
US Navy: 185, 215, 237, 242–3, 250, 272, 328, 369, 419
US Steel Corporation: 37
Western Pennsylvania Conservancy: 214
Westport (Conn) Public Library: 85, 358, 403
The White House: 465, 466–7, 476–7
Wide World Photos: 47, 87, 96, 101, 102, 107, 128, 144 (bottom), 146 (left), 152, 159 (top), 170, 175, 254, 296, 299, 310, 313, 329 (top), 342, 359, 363, 367, 375, 383, 386–7, 388, 398, 401, 414, 421, 429, 430–31, 441, 445, 453, 455, 457, 461, 471, 472, 479, 492–3, 496

ACKNOWLEDGMENTS

The publisher would like to thank the following people who have helped in the preparation of this book: Eva Weber and Jane Eliot, who wrote sections of the chronology; Dorothy Clark, Ann Meeropol, Jan Swafford, and Joel Zoss, who wrote biographies and topic essays; Robin L. Sommer, who edited it; A. Christopher Simon and Lester Kaplan, who designed it; John K. Crowley, who did the picture research; Cynthia Klein, who prepared the index.

INDEX

500

INDEX

INDEX

INDEX

INDEX

INDEX

INDEX

INDEX

INDEX

INDEX

Yasunari, Kawabata 304, 320
Yeats, William 52, 135, 159
Yemen 344, 370, 388, 412, 448
Yevtushenko, Yevgeny 361
youth culture 410; profile 385;
Yuan Shih-k'ai 74, 75, 79, 83,
   92, 102
Yugoslavia 45, 159, 128, 132,
   134, 136, 160, 178, 181, 193,
282, 291, 294, 325, 364, 461;
USSR 301, 335, 337; in World
War II (invasion 233, 235)
(occupation 236) (resistance
238)

Z

Zaire 442, 448

Zambia 379, 442
Zamora, Niceto 165-6, 187
Zanzibar, merger with
   Tanganyika 376
Zapata, Emiliano 91, *101,* 131
Zelaya, José 61, 70
Zeppelin, Ferdinand von 35
Zhukov, Gregory 208, *286*, 341
Zimbabwe 445, 461, 475, 489

See also Rhodesia
Zinoviev, Grigori 153
Zionism 287, 296
Zog, King of Albania 207
Zogu, Ahmed Beg 148
Zola, Emile 35

HB 7 P